MARGARET MITCHELL'S

Gone With the Wind

LETTERS, 1936–1949

BOOKS BY RICHARD HARWELL

Confederate Belles-Lettres (1941), *Confederate Music* (1950), *Songs of the Confederacy* (1951), *The Confederate Reader* (1957), *The Union Reader* (1958), *The Confederate Hundred* (1964), *Brief Candle: The Confederate Theatre* (1972), *The Mint Julep* (1975)

BOOKS EDITED BY RICHARD HARWELL

Destruction and Reconstruction, by Richard Taylor (1955), *Cities and Camps of the Confederate States,* by FitzGerald Ross (1958), *Kate: The Journal of a Confederate Nurse,* by Kate Cumming (1959), *Lee,* by Douglas S. Freeman (1961; one-volume abridgment), *Washington,* by Douglas S. Freeman (1968; one-volume abridgment), *Tiger-Lilies,* by Sidney Lanier (1969), *Georgia Scenes,* by A. B. Longstreet (1975)

MARGARET MITCHELL'S

GONE WITH THE WIND

LETTERS 1936-1949

Edited by Richard Harwell

MACMILLAN PUBLISHING CO., INC.

New York

COLLIER MACMILLAN PUBLISHERS

London

Macmillan Publishing Co., Inc.
866 Third Avenue, New York, N.Y. 10022
Collier Macmillan Canada, Ltd.

Library of Congress Cataloging in Publication Data
Mitchell, Margaret, 1900–1949.
    Margaret Mitchell's Gone with the wind letters, 1936–1949.
    Includes index.
    1. Mitchell, Margaret, 1900–1949—Correspondence. I. Harwell,
Richard Barksdale. II. Title. III. Title: Gone with the wind letters,
1936–1949.
PS3525.1972Z53   1976   813'.5'2   [B]   76–13190
ISBN 0–02–548650–0

First Printing 1976

Designed by Jack Meserole

PRINTED IN THE UNITED STATES OF AMERICA

TO
Stephens Mitchell
AND
Ernie Harwell

CONTENTS

1936

1937

1938

1939

1940

1941

1942

1943

1944

1945

1946

1947

1948

1949

ILLUSTRATIONS

The following illustrations appear between page 202 and page 203:

Photographic portrait by Leonid Skvirsky

Margaret Mitchell as a student at Smith College, a jazz age flapper, and a reporter for The Atlanta Journal

Page from Macmillan's spring 1936 catalog describing Gone With the Wind

Two pages from Margaret Mitchell's original Gone With the Wind *manuscript*

Letter to Duncan Burnet of Athens, Georgia, July 3, 1936

Margaret Mitchell and her father leafing through one of the first copies of the novel

Margaret Mitchell with Edwin Granberry and Herschel Brickell at Blowing Rock, North Carolina, 1936

Rea Irvin's cartoon on the casting of the movie, which appeared in The New Yorker, *February 20, 1937*

Margaret Mitchell at a Macmillan press conference

Telegram to Margaret Mitchell from David O. Selznick, concerning the casting of the movie, January 13, 1939

Clark Gable as Rhett Butler; Olivia De Havilland as Melanie Wilkes; Vivien Leigh as Scarlett O'Hara; Leslie Howard as Ashley Wilkes

Hattie McDaniel as Mammy; Eddie Anderson as Uncle Peter; Everett Brown as Sam; Butterfly McQueen as Prissy

Jane Darwell as Mrs. Merriwether; Laura Hope Crews as Aunt Pittypat; Leona Roberts as Mrs. Meade

Snapshots of Susan Myrick on the movie set with Clark Gable, Leslie Howard, and Ona Munson

Snapshots taken on the movie set by Wilbur G. Kurtz

The split-rail fence at Tara; the double staircase at Twelve Oaks

Scarlett and Melanie tending the wounded

xxi

PREFACE

Flames blazed in the personality of Margaret Mitchell, flames from fires of energy. She was a remarkable woman. As everyone sees different dreams and visions in the flames of a hearth fire, each friend and acquaintance has a different vision of the same person. The visible flames of Margaret Mitchell's inner fires produced a multitude of impressions because she had a multitude of friends, and because her *Gone With the Wind* had an even greater multitude of readers.

Margaret Mitchell wrote fiction—and repeatedly denied that her fictional characters were based on any real people because it is only a created character whom an author can fully know and whose actions she can fully control. She was a very private person, and she vigorously opposed the publication of any of her letters during her lifetime. Dr. William Lyon Phelps wrote her in 1938 asking permission to include the letter she had written him September 23, 1936 in his *Autobiography with Letters*. In declining his request she said: "My reason is that I have a passionate desire for personal privacy. I want to stand before the world, for good or bad, on the book I wrote, not on what I say in letters to friends, not on my husband and my home life, the way I dress, my likes and dislikes, et cetera. My book belongs to anyone who has the price, but nothing of me belongs to the public."

In an interview with Lamar Q. Ball of the Atlanta *Constitution* in the fall of 1936 she said: "I know that the public's interest in my book is inextricably tied up with its interest in me. There is no separating them I suppose. I do believe, though, that my private life is my own. After all, I am not trying to sell my personality like a moving picture actress or some candidate for public office. I am merely selling a book I have written."

Margaret Mitchell's brother Stephens inherited her literary rights after the death of her husband John R. Marsh in 1952. These rights include, of course, the publication of any letters she wrote, and he has steadfastly opposed any invasion of them. He has now, generously but reluctantly, given permission for this compilation of his sister's correspondence. However, he admonishes: "It would be wise to warn the reader that she thought a false view of people was reached, when the

evidence on which the view was based, was from private letters. I am
sure that this is true in this case."

Because of her well-realized fear that her letters would find their
way into print shortly after her correspondents received them, many of
them are more restrained than she might have wished. Of necessity there
was created in her letters, her interviews, and her other public contacts
a Margaret Mitchell who was very different from the ebullient, effer-
vescent Peggy Marsh her friends knew.

A quarter of a century after her death her letters become a last link
with her, for the friends who knew her well are a diminishing few. One
trait they remember most positively is her conversational ability, her
ability to tell an anecdote, her agility with delightfully outrageous exag-
geration and embellishment. Though she fled a besieging public of
strangers, Margaret Mitchell loved people and liked to entertain them,
liked to make them her friends. Her charm was best reflected in her
ability to tell a story. One is especially conscious of this if he attempts to
put her conversational stories on paper. There the charm is likely to slip
away, and he realizes that it was essentially Margaret Mitchell, not the
anecdote, that was so entertaining.

Before I began work on this book I remarked to a cousin who had
known Margaret Mitchell when they were both young girls that I was
going to put together a volume of Miss Mitchell's letters. She responded:
"If she wrote letters half as entertainingly as she talked, it will be a
wonderful book." She did not know it, but she was echoing what Miss
Mitchell's friend Lois Dwight Cole (Mrs. Allan Taylor) at The Macmillan Company said when she told Macmillan's Harold Latham to check
on Peggy Marsh's book when he was getting ready to go to Atlanta on an
editorial scouting trip in 1935: "that if she wrote as she talked it would
be a honey." She did write as she talked, almost.

Her letters have been a delight to work with. They are a delight to
read. Each reader must judge for himself whether or not they create a
real Margaret Mitchell.

The letters in this book have been selected from the magnificent
collection of the papers of Margaret Mitchell Marsh in the University
of Georgia Libraries. This collection totals well over fifty thousand items:
file copies of letters from Mrs. Marsh, letters to her, clippings, pictures,
and a variety of miscellaneous items. (The carbon copies of letters from
Mrs. Marsh alone number more than ten thousand.) The letters published
here have been selected from the Margaret Mitchell Marsh Papers with
slight exceptions—the little holograph letter of July 3, 1936, to Mr. Duncan Burnet, at that time Librarian of the University, and the letters of
February 10 and April 17, 1939, to Susan Myrick.

For permission to use and to edit these letters for publication I am deeply indebted to Mr. Stephens Mitchell, who gave these letters to his alma mater in 1970. I think my gratitude to Mr. Mitchell even exceeds his reluctance to have these letters of his sister appear in print.

The selection was the most difficult part of putting together this book. Even so, it was a happy part; for I was privileged to range as widely as I wished in choosing which letters would most thoroughly and most truly record Margaret Mitchell in what comes as close as anything ever will to being her autobiography. Choice was often difficult. As delightful as these letters are, another volume of equal size and including equally delightful letters could probably be put together.

The editorial mechanics have been as light as possible. A few omissions of private material (usually private about someone else) are noted by the customary marks of ellipsis. Most often, however, the marks of ellipsis indicate repeated information or merely conventional sentences of polite letter writing. Miss Mitchell wrote better than she spelled (or better than her several typists spelled); a few spelling errors have been silently corrected.

The lion's share of my thanks is certainly due Mr. Mitchell, but I am indebted to many others too: among Mrs. Marsh's correspondents, to James C. Bonner, Mrs. Norma Brickell, Katharine Brown, Dr. Robert W. Burns, Erskine Caldwell, Henry Steele Commager, Virginius Dabney, Olivia de Havilland, Jackson P. Dick, Jr., Clifford Dowdey, Thomas H. English, Mrs. Willie Snow Ethridge, Berry Fleming, Daniel Whitehead Hicky, Archibald MacLeish, Olin Miller, Susan Myrick, James S. Pope, and Mrs. Allan Taylor; among my colleagues at the University of Georgia Libraries, to Mrs. Susan Aldrich, Warren Boes, John Bonner, Mrs. Ruth Bunker, Mrs. Joyce Colquitt, Mrs. Faye Dean, Anthony R. Dees, Mrs. Linda Kahn, W. Porter Kellam, Royce McCrary, Buck Pennington, William E. Pope, Mrs. Susan Provost, Mrs. Geneva Rice, Marvin Sexton, Mrs. Dorothy Shackelford, Mrs. Susan Tate, Mrs. Eileen Vetter, and John Via; among a great many others, Rucker Agee, Paul H. Anderson, Mrs. Margaret L. Branson, Herb Bridges, Mrs. Timmy Brown, Mrs. Mary Tyler Freeman Cheek, Mrs. Anne Springs Close, Leodel Coleman, Julie Compton, Marshall Doswell, Jr., Roland Flamini, Orion Harrison, Norman Kotker, Mrs. Annie P. Kurtz, Mrs. Donna Lee, Bessie M. Lewis, Elaine P. Massey, Roger E. Michener, Ralph G. Newman, John Pilkington, James I. Robertson, Jr., Mrs. Dorothy Rozier, John W. Rozier, Elizabeth H. Schumann, Sen. Herman Talmadge, Robert C. Vose, Jr., Robert M. Willingham, Jr., and Mrs. Ella Gaines Yates. And very special thanks are due my editor at Macmillan, William Griffin.

INTRODUCTION

In response to a telegram from *Time* magazine questioning a statement in *Gone With the Wind*, Margaret Mitchell's husband, John R. Marsh, wired on August 3, 1936: "MRS MARSH SICK IN BED AS RESULT OF STRAIN OF BECOMING TOO FAMOUS SUDDENLY."

This was a condition from which the Atlanta author never fully recovered. Thirteen years later—less than three weeks before her death—she wrote James M. Cox steadfastly reaffirming her policy of no autographs, not even for her old paper, the Atlanta *Journal*, which Cox then owned: "I hope you will forgive my unpardonably long delay in replying to your request . . . for an autographed copy of 'Gone With the Wind' to be placed in the Library of the Atlanta Journal. [It] came at the busiest time of our lives and it is only now, weeks later, that I have come up for air. I had a breach of contract in Japan at that time and was on the cables cancelling the contract, there was a copyright infringement in France that took a great deal of trouble to settle. . . . I hired another secretary and John and I and the two young ladies have been working as if we were shoveling coal."

Gone With the Wind burst upon the world on its publication date, June 30, 1936, a literary and publishing phenomenon. Already it was a Book-of-the-Month Club selection, and advance orders assured it bestseller classification. Acclaim by critics in newspapers and the popular reviewing magazines was matched by public enthusiasm and by sales that burgeoned to as many as fifty thousand in a single day. In scarcely three months it sold more than half a million copies. Sales passed the million mark before Christmas and for the book's first year averaged more than 3,700 copies a day. Almost overnight, its author became a person of international fame.

GWTW (as it soon came to be called) is one of the most widely read books in the world. Total sales are well over twenty million copies. Every year it sells more copies than most current bestsellers. It has been printed in twenty-seven languages and in editions in thirty-seven countries. Its appeal has been almost as strong in Germany, Scandinavia, and Japan as in the Old South. It is the literature of the reader, not of the critic, and, as such, has passed into that mass of popular culture that forms a national folk heritage. Scarlett O'Hara, Rhett Butler, Ashley and Melanie

Wilkes, and Belle Watling have transcended the novel and become characters in the American mind. As Stephen Vincent Benét wrote to Miss Mitchell shortly after *GWTW* was published: "... the story moves and has fire in it, and the reader sits up, wanting to know what happens next. There are lots of books like that when you're young—'The Three Musketeers' and 'The Cloister and the Hearth' and all the good ones. There aren't so many, now. I admire and respect the serious, high-minded, case histories—the technical jobs in the novel that are like a series of finely-stained slides under the microscope. But fiction is still fiction—and when a book keeps going on in your mind, even when you're not reading it, you don't need anybody to tell you it's good. It was that way with 'Gone With the Wind.' "

The novel was quickly sold to the movies—at a record price for a first novel, which turned out to be a bargain price for David O. Selznick. A highly publicized search for new screen talent with which to cast the film did nothing to slow continuing sales of the book, or to diminish the incredible demands on Miss Mitchell's time. Finally cast by January 1939, the film's camera work was completed that summer, and it opened in Atlanta in December with a premiere that outshone the gaudiest Hollywood gala. Though the story was severely trimmed for the film version, *GWTW* was the longest commercially successful motion picture made to that time and preserved the essentials as well as the spirit of Miss Mitchell's work with remarkable fidelity. The film's initial runs were record-breaking, first in Atlanta and New York, later in London and Berlin. After a dozen times around the world's circuits of cinema houses, *GWTW* is still a fabulously valuable property, the most popular motion picture of all time.

"I was born in Atlanta," Miss Mitchell wrote in a brief autobiographical sketch that appeared in *The Wilson Bulletin* of September 1936, "and have lived here all my life. My parents were born in Atlanta. My grandparents had cotton plantations in the vicinity of Atlanta before the town was built." She was even more Atlantan than Scarlett, the character who was the very personification of the city. "I was educated in the Atlanta Public Schools," she continued, "and at Washington Seminary, an Atlanta Preparatory School. I hoped to study medicine but while I was at Smith College my mother died and I had to come home to keep house. A year or so later I got a job on the *Atlanta Journal* and wrote run-of-the-mine reporting stuff for about six years."

Margaret Mitchell was born November 8, 1900, at 296 Cain Street, and lived her early years in the Jackson Hill neighborhood just east of downtown Atlanta. Her parents were Eugene Muse Mitchell and Maybelle Stephens Mitchell. She had one brother, Stephens Mitchell. She was graduated from Washington Seminary in 1918 and entered Smith in the fall of that year. Her mother died in the flu epidemic of 1919. Margaret came home, of course, for her mother's funeral, but she returned to Northampton, Massachusetts, and completed her freshman year at Smith. That fall she remained in Atlanta to keep house for her father and brother in the home at 1401 Peachtree Street to which the family had removed in 1912. Near the end of 1922 Margaret got herself a job as a staff reporter for *The Atlanta Journal Sunday Magazine* at $25 a week. Winning a job as a reporter was no small task for a girl in those days. William S. Howland, a fellow *Journal* reporter, quotes another veteran of the paper as saying: "That was a hard team to make in those days—but Peggy made the team and then some." Grantland Rice, Don Marquis, Laurence Stallings, and Jacques Futrelle all served apprenticeships on the *Journal.* Peggy's editor there, Angus Perkerson ("a very canny Scot and a very able judge of reportorial ability and feature news writing," says Howland), wrote Walter Winchell in 1940 protesting a disparaging remark about her career as a reporter:

> . . . I was Margaret Mitchell's only newspaper "boss." She worked on the staff of the Atlanta Journal from 1922 to 1926 as a member of the staff of The Journal's Sunday Magazine, a section that I edited then and still edit.
>
> Even from the first she was one of the best reporters I've ever seen. She turned out good copy and did it in a hurry. She was accurate and she was thorough. She had a keen news sense and she didn't mind hard work.
>
> You know Ward Greene. Well, he and W. B. Seabrook and Ward More-house all worked on The Journal just before Margaret Mitchell did. They couldn't cover a story—any story—a bit better than she could. And they were good.

On July 4, 1926, Margaret Mitchell married John Robert Marsh, a former newspaperman who had joined the Georgia Power Company as an advertising man. This was a marriage of warmth and love and understanding. They were a devoted couple until her death. The Marshes set up housekeeping in a small apartment. She continued to work on the *Journal* for a little over a year, finally leaving because a badly sprained ankle refused to heal without special care.

Howland writes of the Marshes' life in those days:

> They moved into a physically dark but intellectually bright small apartment at 979 Crescent Avenue, just back of the Tenth Street shopping center, which they accurately referred to as "The Dump." They had no car and they had no money for entertainment, but they did have books, friends, and intellectual stimulation and imagination. So "The Dump" became the gathering place of many of Atlanta's brightest minds and some

of its prettiest faces. Life was never dull in "The Dump," even in the days when Peggy had to spend weeks in bed because of her injured ankle.

It was here that *Gone With the Wind* was begun. As she told a reader in June 1936:

> It is very difficult for me to say how long I spent in writing my book. To save explanations, I usually say, "Oh, ten years." But that's really not true. I began it in 1926 and except for three chapters it was completed by 1929. And I wrote the three missing chapters after the book was bought. I labored under considerable difficulties in my writing. For one thing I have a large number of friends and kin to whom I am devoted and for five years there wasn't a day that some one of them wasn't in the hospital with babies, gall stones, automobile accidents etc. . . . Then I was crippled for four years with arthritis with no expectation of ever walking again—but I walk very nicely now, thank you. And for months my hands were too stiff and swollen to touch a typewriter. So there were months between the writing of one chapter and another—years between the writing of some of them. It's hard to explain all of this to a casual questioner so I usually say, "Oh, ten years," and let it go at that. I suppose if I could have squared off and had days without hospitals calling me that my friends were dying, I could have done the book in a year.

The usual story of how the novel began, the one that has passed into folklore, runs that while she was confined to their apartment John Marsh brought his wife books from the Carnegie Library of Atlanta until he had exhausted its resources. He then brought her a stack of newspaper copy paper and said: "Write a book. I can't find anything at the Carnegie that you haven't read, except books on the exact sciences."

She told that story on herself, but in a more serious vein she wrote out some notes for Norman Berg, Macmillan's representative in Atlanta, when he was preparing a story about her for the Atlanta *Constitution* in the fall of 1936 in which she said:

> I did not think about "Gone With the Wind" for years before it was written. If I did any thinking about writing, it was about a novel which I never wrote and never will write. A day came when I thought to myself "Oh, my God, now I've got to write a novel, and what is it going to be about," and that day I started "Gone With the Wind." It is true that I had thought for years of the historical background but not in connection with putting it into a book. It was not so much that I thought of this background as that I was raised up on it. I knew, of course, the history of old Atlanta, how it was born (part of the old South; part of the new South, different from any other Southern city). And of course I had always thought the campaign between Johnston and Sherman the most dramatic of the war. So that day

when I sat down to write I did not have to bother about my background for it had been with me all my life. The plot, characters, etc., had not been with me. That day I thought I would write a story of a girl who was somewhat like Atlanta—part of the old South; part of the new South; [how] she rose with Atlanta and fell with it, and how she rose again. What Atlanta did to her; what she did to Atlanta—and the man who was more than a match for her. It didn't take me any time to get my plot and characters. They were there and I took them and set them against the background which I knew as well as I did my own background.

It is singular that in all the writing about *Gone With the Wind* the parallel of Scarlett to Atlanta has been largely neglected. Of the major reviewers only Herschel Brickell of the New York *Post* commented on it:

"Gone With the Wind" has a deftly handled double theme, the life of Scarlett O'Hara . . . and the life of Atlanta as a city.

Miss Mitchell does not labor the relationship, nor does it matter materially, except that it is so well done. Scarlett did not belong to the gentle tradition of the Old South any more than the young Georgia metropolis, which first became a city during the Civil War and was regarded as an upstart by Charleston, Savannah, Montgomery and the other older towns.

Miss Mitchell established the parallel very explicitly in the novel:

Atlanta was of [Scarlett's] own generation, crude with the crudities of youth and as headstrong and impetuous as herself. . . . In a space of time but little longer than Scarlett's seventeen years, Atlanta had grown from a single stake driven in the ground into a thriving small city of ten thousand that was the center of attention for the whole state. The older, quieter cities were wont to look upon the bustling new town with the sensations of a hen which has hatched a duckling. Why was the place so different from the other Georgia towns? Why did it grow so fast? After all, they thought, it had nothing whatever to recommend it—only its railroads and a bunch of mighty pushy people. . . . Scarlett always liked Atlanta for the very same reasons that made Savannah, Augusta, and Macon condemn it. Like herself, the town was a mixture of the old and new in Georgia, in which the old often came off second best in its conflicts with the self-willed and vigorous new. Moreover, there was something personal, exciting about a town that was born—or at least christened—the same year she was born.

Brickell (who later became a good friend of Miss Mitchell's but who did not know her when he reviewed *GWTW*) noted that Scarlett "liked the newness and brashness and the young vigor of Atlanta because it answered some need in her." The post–World War I Atlanta was not too different in spirit from the post–Civil War Atlanta. And, however differ-

ent in her way of life, Margaret Mitchell was not very different in spirit
from Scarlett O'Hara. She was of an age with the twentieth-century Atlanta
as Scarlett was with the city of the 1860s. In memoranda written in 1962
Berg comments:

> To me she was part and parcel of the Southern Scott Fitzgerald era . . . of
> the aftermath of Camp Gordon in Atlanta in 1917 and what troops do to
> any city . . . of Frances Newman and The Hardboiled Virgin . . . of the re-
> bellion of young southern women against the mores and patterns and restric-
> tions of the past . . . and yet an unreconstructed southerner. She was the
> flaming flapper of the 20's . . . of the bootleg era in the south.

As a member of that Lost Generation produced by World War I,
Margaret Mitchell flaunted her independence and freedom in ways that
shocked her elders, both during her season as a debutante and later as
a reporter. In a letter to a reviewer in Chattanooga shortly after *GWTW*
was released she wrote:

> Melanie has been fitted to a number of people, last of all to me. Harry
> Stillwell Edwards announced that in the Journal and that was one of the
> reasons I left town so abruptly. It was dear and sweet of him but I shall
> never live it down, especially with my own generation. Being a product of
> the Jazz Age, being one of those short-haired, short-skirted, hard-boiled
> young women who preachers said would go to hell or be hanged before
> they were thirty, I am naturally a little embarrassed at finding myself the
> incarnate spirit of the old South!

Her fellow reporter Howland comments: "They say any novel is
largely biographical; so perhaps the best way to sum up Peggy's personality—and this is a summary which would make her angry because
she never liked the Scarlett she created—is to say that she was a living
combination of the fictional Scarlett and Melanie, with Scarlett's fire and
toughness, with Melanie's understanding and compassion and integrity."
He also says: "Those who knew her always will regard her as a romantic
realist—an intensely human person who knew and loved and was a part
of humanity, an intensely realistic person who understood the failings as
well as the triumphs of humankind." And: "She didn't look like a famous
author. At times she looked like a very good little girl—which she was. At
other times she looked like a very bad little girl; which she could be. But
never a dull little girl. Or a mean little girl."

Though The Dump was a gathering pace for Atlanta's white-collar
Bohemians, only a few of Peggy Marsh's friends knew she was writing
a novel. To those it was, jokingly, "The Great American Novel." A very
few accompanied her on occasional Sunday afternoon jaunts into Clayton

County to see again the land she would make the site of Tara and its neighbors. One or two true confidants heard her describe the principal characters of her story. But only her husband had read any of the manuscript when Harold Latham called on her in Atlanta in the spring of 1935 on an editorial scouting trip for The Macmillan Company.

How Mr. Latham was at first refused, then given Peggy's manuscript, and how he had to buy an extra suitcase to carry it is another story that has passed into folklore. Like most folklore it has been variously embellished. (Three of Margaret Mitchell's good friends, for example, in telling this story give as Mr. Latham's next destination after Atlanta three different cities: Charleston, Greenville, and New Orleans. It was New Orleans.) Mrs. Marsh's longtime friend Lois Cole, who was an editor working for Mr. Latham, related Peggy's own version of the story for the first time in 1961. Miss Cole wrote:

> I had revealed to a mutual friend, who was being catty about Peggy's never-finished novel, that she had been given a contract. This I had confessed to Peggy, since she wished no one to know until the revision was finished. She wrote that she understood, adding that friends and acquaintances had kept her from finishing the book long ago. . . .

Peggy went on:

> I've gone through deaths and handled funerals and the very people who call on me for these things are the very ones who say, in all affection, "Isn't it a shame that somebody with a mind like Peggy's hasn't any ambition?" It never made me especially mad—till the last straw came. After all, when you give your friends something, be it money, love, time, encouragement, work, you either give it as a free gift, with no after remarks, or you don't give it at all. And, having given, I had no particular regrets. But this very same situation was what really made me turn over the manuscript to Mr. Latham. He'd asked for it, and I'd felt very flattered that he even considered me. But I'd refused, knowing in what poor shape the thing was. And that day he was here, I'd called up various and sundry hopeful young authors and would-be authors and jackassed them (that is a friend's phrase) about in the car and gotten them to the tea where they could actually meet a live publisher in the flesh.
>
> One of them was a child who had nearly driven me crazy about her book. I'd no more than get settled at my own work than here she was, bellowing that she had gone stale or that she couldn't write love scenes and couldn't I write them for her? Or she was on the phone picking my brains for historical facts that had taken me weeks to run down. As twilight eve was drawing on and I was riding her and some of her adoring girl friends home from the tea, somebody asked me when I expected to get my book finished and why hadn't I given it to Mr. Latham.

Then this child cried, "Why, are you writing a book, Peggy. How strange you've never said anything about it. Why didn't you give it to Mr. Latham?" I said I hadn't because it was so lousy I was ashamed of it. To which she remarked—and did not mean it cattily—"Well, I daresay. Really, I wouldn't take you for the type who would write a successful book. You know you don't take life seriously enough to be a novelist. And you've never even had it refused by a publisher? How strange! *I've* been refused by the very best publishers. But my book is grand. Everybody says it will win the Pulitzer Prize. But, Peggy, I think you are wasting your time trying. You really aren't the type."

Well, suddenly, I got so mad that I began to laugh, and I had to stop the car because I laughed so hard. And that confirmed their opinion of my lack of seriousness. And when I got home I was so mad still that I grabbed up what manuscript I could lay hands on, forgetting entirely that I hadn't included the envelopes that were under the bed or the ones in the pot-and-pan closet, and I posted down to the hotel and caught Mr. Latham just as he was about to catch the train. My idea was that at least I could brag that I had been refused by the very best publisher. And no sooner had I done this and Mr. L. was out of town than I was appalled both by my temper and by my acting on impulse and by my giving him the stuff when it was in such sloppy shape and minus so many chapters.

Miss Cole and Mr. Latham read the manuscript and, poor shape or not, were enthusiastic about it. Their opinion was confirmed by Professor Charles Everitt of Columbia. A contract was offered Mrs. Marsh and soon signed. She hoped earnestly that the book would sell enough copies to pay the publishers for their trouble in publishing it; Macmillan had been so nice to be interested in her work. Revisions were made, and the author put in eight months of hard work checking the facts she had written largely from an amazingly accurate memory. Still, neither she nor the publisher was satisfied with the working title, *Tomorrow Is Another Day*. There were other suggestions—*Another Day, Tote the Weary Load, Not in Our Stars, Bugles Sang True*. None hit the mark. Then in Ernest Dowson's poems she read the phrase that did: gone with the wind. Author and publisher liked this title. They soon learned the public liked it too.

The letters in this volume take up Margaret Mitchell's story on the eve of her book's publication. These are the *Gone With the Wind* letters, letters relating to the book and the film, and letters that grew out of friendships made through, or because of, *GWTW*. Though her private letters were destroyed after her death, these letters do tell her story from the time of *GWTW's* publication to her tragic death on August 16, 1949. She wrote full and charming letters, personalizing them while seldom revealing her private self.

The extent to which *GWTW* changed Margaret Mitchell's life is hard

to believe—till one reads her letters. It changed her life, but it did not change her. "Alas," she wrote Sidney Howard in January 1937, "where has my quiet peaceful life gone?"

Gone With the Wind had a unique effect on its readers. She noted in October 1936: "This section has taken the book to its heart and that is something which makes me prouder than anything else. But each and every reader feels that he has a part ownership in it."

In the spring of 1939 George Brett, Jr., president of The Macmillan Company, wrote asking that the Company be permitted to sponsor a party for Miss Mitchell at the time of the premiere of *Gone With the Wind* in Atlanta. She replied:

> In your letter you referred to the premiere as "Selznick's show." I don't believe Atlanta people feel that way about it at all. Mr. Selznick will put on the show, of course, but the premiere will be *Atlanta's* night, not Selznick's. Long ago I gave up thinking of "Gone With the Wind" as my book; it's Atlanta's, in the view of Atlantians; the movie is Atlanta's film; and the premiere will be an Atlanta event, not merely the showing of a motion picture.

When a rumor hit the city that Selznick had decided not to have the premiere in Atlanta, protesting ladies, Miss Mitchell reported to Lois Cole, "descended on Mayor Hartsfield's office like a pack of well dressed Eumenides. His Honor, a passionate Confederate and a stout defender of Atlanta's civic rights and honors, leapt eight feet into the air when the ladies told him the rumor. Jimmy [Pope, city editor of the Atlanta *Journal*] said the reporter at City Hall phoned in excitedly that it sounded like a WPA riot and he, for one, wanted a police reserve called out. Mayor Hartsfield announced to the press that this was the worst outrage since Sherman burned the town. Of course Atlanta was going to have the premiere. 'Why,' said the Mayor, 'in a large way the book belongs to all of us.' "

Gone With the Wind belonged to Atlanta. Margaret Mitchell belonged to Atlanta too. Alas for her quiet and peaceful life. "When you have published a book, you have given a hostage to fortune," she wrote Evelyn Hanna in 1938, and none knew better. As she had told a New York *World-Telegram* reporter two months before, the two years since the publication had been "months of torment, mixed with joy beyond comprehension." This echoed what she had said to Lamar Q. Ball in November 1936: "The nice things outweigh the bad. The best discovery I have made since I have written the book is the kindness of many utter strangers. A lot of them go out of their way to do me a good turn." And she wrote Herschel Brickell May 25, 1938: "It has been my lot to meet a number of skunks during the last two years, but, as I balance my books,

I find I've met with far more understanding and kind people than skunks."

Success did not tarnish the charm of Margaret Mitchell. The years have not slowed the racing narrative of *Gone With the Wind* nor dimmed the recollection of its characters. Forty years after its publication, Margaret Mitchell and her book are indelible parts of America. She furnished our past with a Scarlett O'Hara, a Melanie Wilkes, a Rhett Butler, and an Ashley Wilkes. They are as American as Jefferson Davis and Robert E. Lee, Abraham Lincoln and Ulysses S. Grant, Tom Sawyer and Huckleberry Finn.

Why, in a large way they—book and author—belong to all of us.

MARGARET MITCHELL'S

Gone With the Wind

LETTERS, 1936–1949

1936

Mr. Julian Harris
The Chattanooga Times
Chattanooga, Tennessee

Atlanta, Ga.
April 21, 1936

Dear Julian:

John told me of your interest in my book and of your request for information and photograph and I do thank you for both. I am sorry about the delay. I've been trying to get a picture out of Asasno,[1] the Japanese photographer, ever since John came home and today I have succeeded. He made me up a complete set of proofs instead of newsprints and then made the wrong picture and finally when I was frenzied, called me and said he had the one I wanted. And I will send it to you this afternoon.

When John was talking to you he did not know that the publication of the book was to be delayed due to the choice of the Book of the Month Club. The publishers are not sure just when it will come out as the B.M.C. picks books several months in advance. But they think it will be in July. I am enclosing the Journal[2] clipping.

As I am not sure just what information you want, I'll tell you something about the book and if you want anything else please let me know. I've interviewed a thousand and more people but never been interviewed myself and I'm as green as can be and hardly know what to put in. I wrote this book about eight years ago, I think. It was after I left the Journal and after I married John in 1925 but I can't quite place the date. It was while I had a bad ankle and was on crutches. I couldn't walk for a couple of years so I put in my time writing this book. When my foot got well, I stopped writing because walking seemed far more interesting. I didn't finish the book and it just lay around the house. I never sent it to any publishers because, to be quite frank, I didn't think much of it. Written as it was at the height of the Jazz Age, I didn't think it would sell as it was a "Victorian" type novel, almost as long as "Anthony Adverse"[3] and about war and hard times in Georgia. And, also there was

[1] George Asasno.
[2] The Atlanta *Journal*.
[3] Hervey Allen, *Anthony Adverse* (New York, 1933).

1

precious little obscenity in it, no adultery and not a single degenerate and I couldn't imagine a publisher being silly enough to buy it.

Then, some months back Mr. Latham, of Macmillan, was in town. He was referred to me by Lois Cole (who you may remember was here at Macmillan's for several years) and Lois asked me to dig up all the manuscripts among my friends for him. I dug up some for him and he, being the kind of man who can charm birds out of trees, dug up mine and took it off with him and bought it before I could catch my breath. Since that time, I've been rechecking my historical facts. However lousy the book may be as far as style, subject, plot, characters, it's as accurate historically as I can get it. I didn't want to get caught out on anything that any Confederate Vet could nail me on, or any historian either.

I can't think of anything else about it except the publishers say this is the first novel to cover both war and reconstruction. I don't know how true that is.

John so enjoyed seeing you and he says you've done wonders since arriving there. I was very sorry I couldn't make the trip with him as I want to go to Chattanooga for pleasure. My other trip wasn't pleasure for I was trailing the way the campaign from Tennessee to Atlanta was fought and wondering mournfully how I was ever going to compress such an epic and heart-breaking affair into a few lines instead of giving it a whole book as it deserved. I wonder why the military historians concentrate so much on the Virginia and Mississippi River campaigns and slight Johnston's retreat which has, to me, at least, far more drama than anything else in the whole war.

Give my regards to Hunt Clements and please remember me to Mrs. Harris. She probably won't remember me but I had a grand time one afternoon at the Studio Club, sitting beside her and talking about "Our Movie Minded Children."

Mrs. Julia Collier Harris   Atlanta, Ga
The Chattanooga Times   April 28, 1936
Chattanooga, Tennessee

My dear Mrs. Harris:

I did appreciate your letter so much, especially when I learned that you had been ill and were forbidden the typewriter. A letter in long hand is an awful ordeal to me and I become tongue-tied when I have to use a pen. And, knowing that you do your work with a machine, I doubly appreciated your letter. I was sorry to learn of your illness and hope you are better now. Several times when you were here in Atlanta I made plans with Elaine Minick to come to see you but invariably learned that you were not feeling so well—arthritis, I think it was, wasn't it? So I didn't call for I've had arthritis for many years and know that one can do without company at such times.

Thank you for your and Mr. Harris' interest in the book. I would be more than flattered if you used me in your column. I've been clawing my brain trying to think of something interesting or exciting to write you in connection with it and can think of nothing so I'll just have to give you plain facts.

First, the story does not include anything about the campaigns around Chattanooga. The action never gets outside of Georgia, except, of course, incidents such as the news of the fall of Vicksburg and the defeat at Gettysburg. Chickamauga, of course, is mentioned but the part of the book devoted to actual fighting begins when the Yankees under Sherman were above Dalton at Rocky Face and it carries the two armies through the fighting from May until the city fell in September. I was trying to give a picture of how it felt to be in a city a hundred miles away from the war, with the war coming closer every day as General Johnston fell back toward Atlanta. If I'd had my way the whole book would have been about that running fight but I realize that the reading public does not care for military campaigns as much as my family do, so I cut prodigiously and rewrote that part about fifty times in an effort to keep it from being too heavy.

And about me—I'm Eugene M. Mitchell's and Maybelle Stephens' daughter. Yes, she was one of the numerous Stephens girls who lived on Jackson Hill between Highland Avenue and Cain Street. Mother was one of the three oldest girls and Edythe, Eugenia and Ruth were the younger ones whom you probably knew. Mother was tiny and red haired and the least pretty . . . of all the girls in that family. As to how I got started on Civil War material, I suppose I started in my cradle. Father is an authority on Atlanta and Georgia history of that period and Mother knew about as much as he did. I heard so much when I was little about the fighting and the hard times after the war that I firmly believed Mother and Father had been through it all instead of being born long afterward. In fact I was about ten years old before I learned the war hadn't ended shortly before I was born. Mother used to sing me to sleep with those doleful tunes of the Sixties, "Jacket of Grey"[1] and "Somebody's Darling,"[2]

---

[1] *GWTW*, p. 297. "The Jacket of Gray" was published in Mrs. Caroline A. Rutledge Ball's *The Jacket of Gray and Other Fugitive Poems* (Charleston, 1866). It was later set to music by Stratford Benjamin Woodberry. (This page number and later citations of *GWTW* page numbers are to the original 1936 edition, and are accurate for all printings with 1037 pages.)

[2] *GWTW*, p. 297.

varying them with "If you want to have a good time, jine the cavalry"[3] and "Bonnie Blue Flag."[4] She was completely tone deaf and couldn't carry a tune in a bucket but she made up for these lacks with enthusiasm and I attribute the insomnia that has plagued me for years to the fact that she knew so many grand and harrowing songs that I refused to go to sleep for fear I'd miss some verse.

When I went to school and learned to "recite" on Friday afternoons, my pieces, picked by Father and Mother, were Henry Grady's "The New South," "Little Giffen"[5] and "The Conquered Banner."[6] On Sunday afternoons when we went calling on the older generation of relatives, those who had been active in the Sixties, I sat on the bony knees of veterans and the fat slippery laps of great aunts and heard them talk about the times when Little Alex[7] was visiting them and how much fried chicken Father Ryan could put away and how nice thick wrapping paper felt when put between the skin and the corset in the cold days during the blockade when woolen goods were so scarce. And how Grandpa Mitchell[8] walked nearly fifty miles after the battle of Sharpsburg with his skull cracked in two places from a bullet. They didn't talk of these happenings as history nor as remarkable events but just as part of their lives and not especially epic parts. And they gradually became a part of my life.

So it's not remarkable that I had an early interest in that period. I'd have lost my mind from boredom if I hadn't been interested. Even now, when John and I go to call on Father we usually find him and my brother and friends hotly arguing about what would have happened if Longstreet had only brought up his corps sooner and why Jeff Davis didn't put Hood in command at Dalton instead of waiting till the last ditches of Atlanta. Occasionally, when we take some Northern friend to call on the family, they sit bewildered, hearing the merits of Pelham extolled and the gallantries of General Gordon discussed as though they were happenings of only yesterday.

I went to the Atlanta public schools and to Washington Seminary and then to Smith College. While I had always written stuff and always liked to write, I wanted to be a doctor and had intentions of taking a medical degree. But Mother died when I was in my Freshman year and there was no one to keep house for Father and Stephens so I came home. I made my debut and then went onto the Magazine Section of the Journal, somewhat to the consternation of my father. I had had no newspaper ex-

[3] *GWTW*, p. 161.
[4] *GWTW*, p. 170.
[5] Poem by Francis Orrery Ticknor.
[6] Poem by Father Abram Ryan.
[7] Alexander Hamilton Stephens, Vice President of the Confederate States.
[8] Russell Crawford Mitchell.

perience and had never had my hands on a typewriter but by telling poor Angus Perkerson outrageous lies about how I had worked on the Springfield Republican (How could I? And all my people good Democrats?) and swearing I was a speed demon on a Remington, I got the job.

I was on the Journal five or six years and did run-of-the-mine feature stories. Eventually they let me do historical stories which I enjoyed immensely. Best of all I liked interviewing the Oldest Inhabitants. Most of the things I asked them had nothing to do with the story I wrote eventually. I was interested in how people felt during the siege of Atlanta, where casualty lists were posted, what they ate during the blockade, did boys kiss girls before they married them and did nice ladies nurse in the hospitals. I had no intention, at that time, of ever writing a book. I just wanted to know those things. And they came in very handy when the actual writing began.

Then I broke my ankle and arthritis set in and I was on crutches for about three years with no prospect of ever walking again. I read swiftly and enormously and can and will and do read anything, murder stories, love stories, history, medicine, archaeology. Poor John wore himself out lugging home arm loads of books every night. You can read an awful lot in three years and get pretty sick of reading but John had to keep me occupied for it wasn't very pleasant, lying there thinking I'd never walk again.

Finally he brought home a pound or so of copy paper and said "write a book. I can't find anything at the Carnegie that you haven't read, except books on the exact sciences."

So I started on this book. I don't recall exactly why I picked this subject, probably because it was the subject that I knew best and, not being the modern scene, it was an escape.

I began it in 1926, I think. Perhaps you will remember that this was during the high tide of the "Realistic" era, or the Jazz Age. I had gotten pretty tired of Jazz Age fiction, after reading steadily for years. I had gotten so tired of finding "son of a bitch" on the first page of every novel I opened that I'd about quit reading fiction. I don't mean that to sound prissy because it wasn't that I was shocked but I just got good and tired of it. So I thought I'd try to write a book that didn't use that phrase a single time. And write a book in which no one was seduced and there wouldn't be a single sadist or degenerate in my book. Of course I knew it would never sell but I didn't intend to sell it. I was just writing to keep from worrying about never walking again.

I don't mean that I wrote a sweet, sentimental novel of the Thomas Nelson Page type. My central woman character does practically every thing that a lady of the old school should not do. And so do many of the characters. But whatever their shortcomings they are the shortcomings of strength and exuberant health and tough mental fibres. For when I look back on the survivors of those hard days of war and reconstruction they all impressed me as a remarkably tough bunch of people. I don't mean tough in the modern slang meaning of the word. But tough in its older meaning, hard, resistant, strong. The old ladies were certainly not lavender and old lace ladies. They had more drive at eighty than their children and grandchildren and when they had nothing better to do they went to meetings of patriotic societies and rended the societies apart. And while they scorned votes for women, they could go to the Mayor and City Council and reduce them to jelly by a few well chosen words concerning male shilly-shallying and inefficiency—and they got civic improvements in a way that voting women never did.

So I thought I'd write about the young days of these old ladies and the things that had happened to them that made them tough and fearless and outspoken—and very gentle.

It took so long writing the book. There was a year when my hands were too stiff to type at all and months when fever ran too high for me to work. And when I got well there were illnesses in the family that kept me from finishing. Finally I just put the thing away unfinished and I suppose it would never have been finished if Mr. Latham hadn't bought it "as is."

I think I've answered all your questions except one and probably answered them at far greater length than you wanted. You asked what I liked to do best. I like best to listen to people talk about something that they know about. I don't care whether it's dog catching if they know it thoroughly and are interested in it.

Speaking of reading, I used to ride the car to town with your husband quite frequently. And I always had about ten books in my arms. I was dreadfully anxious to impress him with my erudition but it never failed that when he sat down beside me and took a peek at my arm load the titles of my books were "The Corpse in Cold Storage," "A Scream in the Night," "The Clutching Claw." Sometimes I ardently wished I could have swallowed them. Not that I am ashamed of my passion for low murder stories but I did so want to impress him! On the days when I was lugging "Excavations in Ur in the Chaldes" did he get on the car? Never. When I was laden down with "Records of the War of the Rebellion" (each book weighed three pounds) did he come and sit by me? Never. But just let me have a cargo of mystery murder stories and up he popped and grinned and said "Aha! Ruining your mind again with cheap mysteries!" . . .

I have written a long letter for a convalescent to have to read but you are to blame for writing me such a flattering and encouraging letter.

Mr. Paul Jordan-Smith　　　　　　　　　　　　　Atlanta, Georgia
Los Angeles Times　　　　　　　　　　　　　　　May 27, 1936
Los Angeles, California

My dear Mr. Jordan-Smith:

　I am Margaret Mitchell, the author of "Gone With the Wind" which
the Macmillan Company is bringing out at the end of June. Mr. Latham
and the Atlanta branch of Macmillan's told me of the kind things you had
said about my book and I took the liberty of autographing a copy for you,
which I hope you have now received.

　I could not let the book alone tell you how grateful I am to you for
your praise and I had to write you this letter. When Mr. Latham was in
Atlanta a while back I was talking with him about the probable reception my book would have in the South and at the hands of Southerners. I
told him that I was a little frightened because, while I had written nothing that was not true, nothing that I could not prove and much that I had
heard, as a child, from eye witnesses of that era, I feared some of it might
not set well upon Southerners. I suppose Southerners have been lam-
basted so often and so hard, in print, that they have become unduly
sensitive. With some types of Southerners, nothing pleases them about the
South, no matter how laudatory or how well intentioned. Critics in the
North had been most kind—the few who had read advance copies—and
I was very grateful to them but what would people of Southern birth
say? I didn't intend to retreat one step on anything I had written but
still—I had the feeling that "Uncle Peter" summed up, "Miss Scarlett,
tain' gwine do you no good to stan' high wid de Yankees ef yo' own folks
doan' 'prove of you."[1]

　Then Mr. Latham spoke of you and said that you were from Tennessee and that you had not denounced me as a traitor to my section and that
you had liked the book. I was happy enough to stop the car and embrace
him violently, right in the shadow of Stone Mountain. Then, sometime
later, Mr. Berg[2] at the Macmillan office here told me of other exciting
things you had said and when he came to the part about you comparing
me with Mary Johnston, I had to go home and take a luminal and lie
down with a cold towel on my head.

　Mary Johnston was a schoolmate of my mother's and before I could
read, I had her books read to me. Mother was strong minded but she
never failed to weep over "The Long Roll" and "Cease Firing,"[3] and I

---

[1] *GWTW*, p. 675.
[2] Norman Berg.
[3] *The Long Roll* (Boston and New York, 1911); *Cease Firing* (Boston, New York,
1912).

always bellowed too, but insisted on her not skipping sad parts. While in the process of checking the part of my book about the campaign from the Tennessee line to Atlanta, I was very bothered about the weather during the fighting. Veterans of that campaign had told me how it rained for twenty-five days at Kennesaw Mountain—"Up to the seat of my pants," as one expressed it. But I didn't want to trust my memory on such matters so I began trying to find out about the weather for, like as not, if I didn't get it right, seven hundred old vets would rise up out of Soldiers' Homes and denounce me.

So I reread Generals Hood, Johnston and Sherman[4] and several other reference books but got little satisfaction. Then I remembered "Cease Firing," which I had not read in many years. I knew it to be the best documented novel ever written so I consulted it to see about the weather. And unfortunately I became so engrossed in the story that I read on through till the tragic end. And when I had finished, I found that I couldn't possibly write anything on my own book. I felt so childish and presumptuous for even trying to write about that period when she had done it so beautifully, so powerfully—better than anyone can ever do it, no matter how hard they try. It was weeks and weeks before I could go back to work and then I went back pretty humble. Her book was so marvelous. So, you can see why your comparison pleased me to the point of putting me to bed!

Mr. Berg said that you had said my characters were real and how happy I was to hear that from a born Tennessean! For I know they are different from the usual Civil War characters. They aren't lavender-and-lace-moonlight-on-the-magnolias people. But, as I recall from childhood, the survivors of that era were remarkably tough. I mean tough in the old sense of the word not the slang meaning. I figured out they had to be tough or they'd never have survived. I'm sure if you are Southern born you must have seen many old ladies who had lived through that era who could scare the liver and lights out of you with one word and blast your vitals with a look. They owned their negroes, still, and their children and their contemporaries' children, too. And they were the bossiest, hard boiledest bunch of old ladies I ever saw. And they could be so plain spoken upon occasion that they made the brashest flapper blush. But they never got too old to be attractive to the gentlemen. I felt certain that people who were like that in old age couldn't have been completely Thomas Nelson Page in their youths. And I am very glad that you liked them.

[4] John Bell Hood, *Advance and Retreat* (New Orleans, 1880); Joseph Eggleston Johnston, *Narrative of Military Operations* (New York, 1874); William Tecumseh Sherman, *Memoirs* (New York, 1875; 2 vols.).

I have inflicted an awful long letter on you when I could have merely said "thank you." But your words made me far too happy to let it go at that.

Mr. Harold Latham   Atlanta, Georgia
The Macmillan Company   June 1, 1936
New York, New York

Dear Mr. Latham:

When Lois Cole's letter arrived, telling me of the revision upward of the royalties, I wired her immediately—well, not exactly immediately for I had to wait to get my breath—and asked her to thank everyone concerned in the matter. And now I want to thank you personally because I know you were very much concerned in it.

Your letter of May 27 has just arrived and at the end of it you speak of this rearrangement of royalties as being one more evidence of your desire to deal fairly with me. I really do not need further evidence of that now! I am firmly convinced that even Jurgen[1] himself never dealt more fairly with a woman than Macmillan has with me! You have been more than kind, more than generous in this matter, as in others. Really, I had put the whole matter of the cut in royalties out of my mind, for so much had happened since then. Besides, at the time when the matter first came up, when you were in Europe, I thought, "They are putting a lot of money behind my book for advertising purposes. A lot more money than they usually put up for a new and unknown author. And the advertising probably more than makes up for the cut in royalties." So, you see, I wasn't sucking my thumb and pouting all this time and when the good news arrived it was just as exciting and delightful as when the Easter Rabbit used to pay his annual visit when I was a child. (I always liked the Easter Rabbit far better than other magical folks, Santa Claus, birthday-gift, being-brave-about-pulling-a-tooth boss, as the Easter Rabbit never extracted any advance promises of good behavior on my part, never harped on my past delinquencies. He just hopped along and laid the eggs gratis in the most generous manner possible with no strings attached.)

In the matter of my coming to New York: Your suggestion about putting the trip off until the Fall made me very happy. I'm quite sure, short of Acts of God, that such a trip could be arranged then. I have felt guilty of rudeness ever since you first mentioned the trip, rudeness

[1] The protagonist of James Branch Cabell's *Jurgen: A Comedy of Justice* (New York, 1919).

because I did not clap my hands and leap upon your neck. The truth is that while I was very thrilled about the prospect of going to N.Y. the prospect of going in the summer gave me to think. I know that you, being a New Yorker, will think this foolish and think me an awful liar, but the truth is, I can't stand the heat of N.Y. I love hot weather and never feel more than half alive until the thermometer gets above 95 but here in Atlanta we are about 1400 feet high[2] and the heat never fags me. In fact when I was a child, spending my summers on relatives' cotton plantations, I've picked cotton for my pocket money when the heat stood near 100 and never hardly sweated. I've never had sun stroke or even heat prostration. But every time I go to N.Y. in the summer I spend most of the trip under a fan packed in ice. And twice the N.Y. doctors ruined my trips by sending me home because I had heat prostration. I didn't want to accept your grand invitation, come to N.Y., get sick and be no comfort whatever to myself or to you all.

Another draw back is that I'm pretty tired at present, due to my own foolishness, for I've been going out too much recently, far more than I should and far more than I've gone out in years, but everyone I've ever known has flung me a party and I didn't see any way out of it. And I'd have hated to land in N.Y. looking like a hag and with my eyes hanging out so far you could wipe them off with a broom stick. And the Annual Georgia Editors convention comes off soon and I would either have had to miss it entirely or cut corners so sharply that I'd have arrived in N.Y. with my tongue hanging out. And it wouldn't have done me much good to cut it (regardless of my own desire to be there) for they're nice enough to give me a banquet and expect me to stumble frightenedly through a few words. So you can see that the prospect of coming in the Autumn appeals to me greatly.

Speaking of a "few words"—I believe I wrote you that I was to make a talk to the Atlanta Librarians. I did and it is, thank God, my swan song as a speaker. No one, except the Atlanta Historical Society, of which my father is president, is going to get me to rise swaying to my feet, grasping at the table edge for support. And they've showed a laudable desire not to hear a few words from me. "Our Miss Baugh"[3] of the Atlanta Macmillan branch is a member of the Librarians Club and it was she who bullied me into making the speech. I thought I'd show her and the Library Ladies just how dull the job of writing was so I elected to talk on reference books pertaining to the Sixties. I put in anguished days going

[2] The altitude of Atlanta is 1,050 feet.
[3] Margaret E. Baugh. Miss Baugh became Miss Mitchell's secretary in January 1937. After Miss Mitchell's death she continued her work with the enormous correspondence growing out of *GWTW* for John Marsh until his death in 1952, and then for Stephens Mitchell until her own death in 1967.

through my bibliography and if I do say it myself, Carlyle's Essay on Burns couldn't have been duller. Then the woman who introduced me[4] spoke briefly, saying she was presenting an author whose book had been variously compared to "Vanity Fair," "War and Peace," and "Gentlemen Prefer Blondes."

This so upset me that I forgot even the titles of the reference books I had in mind and I drew a blank and when I came to myself I was telling indelicate stories. Did I tell you about my experience with the backwoods farmer? It was when I was madly scouring the back country of Clayton County hunting for the planting time of late maturing, long staple, pre–boll weevil cotton (a date which I could find in no book). And I found one old boy spreading manure on his granddaughter's vegetable garden. He answered my questions and then, curious about writers, asked a plenty. I told him with deep feeling that writing was a dreary dull job. You sweated and groaned and itched and broke out in rashes and then felt like you smelled bad. And he said with sympathy, "When you come right down to it, writing a book ain't so very different from spreading manure, is it?"—When I came to myself I was telling the librarians this instead of what a help the Records of the War of the Rebellion had been to me. I shall never forget Miss Jessie Hopkins'[5] face. I think I am perfectly safe from having to address librarians in the future.

How nice that you are getting your vacation. I remember a picture of the interior of your house that you sent me on a card last winter and it looked the perfect place to get away from authors. I don't see how you keep your good disposition, being in the publishing business. I'd as soon try to drive tandem two strange wild cats and a rattler with ten buttons as have to do with authors! I'll bet you need your vacation when it comes. . . .

Mr. Latham, I am imposing on you to the extent of enclosing a letter which I hope you will address and forward for me. I admit my ignorance of New York, New York critics, etc., and to be perfectly frank have never heard of this kind gentleman. And I'll further admit my ignorance and say that I don't know if it's good form for an author to write to a critic. But I am fairly bursting at what Joseph Henry Jackson wrote about me, three days running, in the San Francisco Chronicle.[6] The date line on his column is New York but I do not know his New York address so I'm sending the letter to you. I practically went from one swoon into another at his remarks, especially those about the "simplicity" of my literary style. "Simple," good Heavens! Thank God, some simplicity did remain. But

---

[4] She was introduced by Alma Hill Jamison, head of the Reference Department of the Carnegie Library of Atlanta.

[5] Librarian of the Carnegie Library of Atlanta.

[6] Jackson's columns appeared in the San Francisco *Chronicle* May 11, 13, and 14 and were dated, respectively, May 8, 9, and 10.

when I think of rewriting some chapters fifty times I wonder how any simplicity did survive. It reads more like hash to me.

Now, as usual, I've written you a novelette. Perhaps you'd better put this letter up and take it away to read on your vacation.

Mr. Joseph Henry Jackson   Atlanta, Georgia
San Francisco Chronicle   June 1, 1936
San Francisco, California

My dear Mr. Jackson:

I am Margaret Mitchell, author of the book "Gone With the Wind," of which you wrote so kindly in the "Chronicle" on May 13 and 14. It is my first book and I am so new and green at the business of authoring that I do not even know if it is good form for an author to write to a critic. But your columns gave me so much pleasure and happiness that I have to write you and say thank you.

I suppose you would call my reactions "pleasure and happiness" even if I did have to go to bed with a cold pack on my head and an aspirin after I read your words. God knows I'm not like my characters, given to vapors and swooning and "states," but I was certainly in a "state." I have always been able to bear up nobly under bad news but your good news floored me. I suppose it was because it was so unexpected.

I wrote the book nearly ten years ago, beginning it some time between 1925 and 1926 and laying it aside, minus a few chapters, sometime around 1927 or 1928. It seemed, to be quite frank, pretty lousy and I never even submitted it to any agent or publisher. In fact, I had about forgotten it when Mr. Latham of the Macmillan Company came here on a visit and exhumed it and bought it. Since then, I've been in a twitter ducking at every sound and expecting brickbats—and prepared for brickbats. So when I read what you had to say—and you were the first critic who had written anything about it—I was overcome. Like the old lady in the nursery rhyme I feel like, "Lawk and a mercy on me! This is none of I!"

I was very interested in what you wrote in the Chronicle of May 14 (New York date line May 10) about the new novelists turning their attention to "destruction and rebirth" and the "upheavals." I was interested because, as I stated above, I wrote this book when the Great American Boom was at its height and the high tide of the Jazz Age was with us. Everyone I knew had a car, a radio, an electric ice box and a baby that they were buying on time (everybody except me!). Everyone had money, or thought they had, and everyone thought that life was going to continue just as it was. Heaven knows I didn't foresee the Depression and try to write a novel paralleling it, in another day. I was writing about an upheaval I'd heard about when I was a small child. For I spent the Sunday afternoons of my childhood sitting on the bony knees of Confederate Veterans and the fat slick laps of old ladies who survived the war and reconstruction. And I heard them talk about friends who came through it all and friends who went under. They were a pretty outspoken, forthright, tough bunch of old timers and the things they said stuck in my mind much longer than the things the people of my parents' generation told me.

And all during my childhood I'd been told to be prepared for the next time the world turned over. My family live to incredible ages and have incredible memories and I was brought up on stories of the hard times after the Revolution and what happened to kinfolks after the Seminole Wars and who went under in the panic during Andy Jackson's regime and what happened to people after 1865 and how bad things were in the panics of 1873 and 1893 and 1907. So I suppose that explains why I wrote a book about hard times when the country was enjoying its biggest boom.

I do thank you, too, for your kind remarks about my style—if you could call it a "style."[1] I haven't any literary style and I know it but have never been able to do anything about it. I am very conscious of my lack in this particular and I was expecting more brickbats about it than any other thing. I wish I could tell you how very happy you have made me! Just saying thank you seems so inadequate!

Mr. Harry Stillwell Edwards   Atlanta, Georgia
Macon, Georgia   June 18, 1936

My dear Mr. Edwards:

Only a very small remnant of decorum prevents me from addressing you as "my *very* dear Mr. Edwards," or "you utterly darling person," or "you kind, kind man." But I will try to remember my raising and merely address you as—

My dear Mr. Edwards:

I did not see any newspapers while on the trip to Savannah with

---

[1] In his column of May 13 Jackson declared: "Like most simply written novels that carry their own utter sincerity for all to see, this is one of those books that you will hate to finish. . . . And you won't be far along in the book before you realize that this frank, honest story-telling is impressing you far more than all the fine writing that the more consciously artistic novelists sometimes attempt."

the Georgia Editors.[1] I came home slowly, stopping along the way to see friends throughout the state, and only arrived in Atlanta yesterday. And I was met by my proud father with a copy of your Sunday review of "Gone With the Wind" in his hand.[2] May I thank you first for the happiness you brought to my father? You see, he was especially anxious that Southerners and Georgians should like my book and especially afraid that they wouldn't, although the book is as true as documentation and years of research could make it. He didn't like the notion of my offending the people of my state nor did I. And when he read your perfectly marvelous review his mind was set at ease. "If Mr. Edwards likes it— etc."

Thank you for the length of your review and thank you for the detail of it. Shall I tell you what made me happiest and proudest? It was your remark about the "minutiae of the story is incredibly vast. The author must have had access to every war time diary from the mountains to the sea, to old letters and records, to the mental pictures of the very old." Mr. Edwards, you are one of the very few people who are clever enough to see my source material, one of the few who realize how the back ground of my book developed. Yes, I have read most of the old memoirs I could lay my hands on. Not recently, perhaps but from my childhood. I was raised on "Surry of Eagle's Nest"[3] and the "War Time Diary of a Georgia Girl"[4] and other books of that type when most children were reading "Peter Rabbit" and the "Rover Boys." And throughout the years I have run down every book of that kind I could find, every old diary (unpublished) that I heard about, old letters, too. Long before I even thought of writing a book of this period, I was searching out this material. And you spoke so truly about the "mental pictures of the very old." I have always loved the "very old," always felt more at home with them than with people of my own age or those younger and I have loved to listen to them talk. In fact, my "best beau" until his lamented death last September was an elderly cousin, made dearer to me by the fact that he was my dead mother's god-father, Mr. John Marion Graham, the Supreme Court Reporter. He had been Alexander H. Stephens' secretary many years ago and he was a man of great erudition and wonderful memory and his conversations about life in the Seventies was fascinating.

And may I thank you, too, for your kind words about "Melanie." No other reviewer or commentator has seen fit to mention her which bothers

[1] The Georgia Press Association held its annual meeting in Milledgeville June 10–12 and in Savannah June 12 and 13. Atlanta *Journal*, June 7.

[2] Edwards devoted his column, "Coming Down My Creek," in the Atlanta *Journal* of June 14 to a review of *GWTW*.

[3] John Esten Cooke, *Surry of Eagle's-Nest* (New York, 1866).

[4] Eliza Frances Andrews, *The War-Time Journal of a Georgia Girl, 1864–1865* (New York, 1908).

me a little, for, Mr. Edwards, she is really my heroine, not "Scarlett." I wanted to picture in "Melanie" as in "Ellen" the true ladies of the old South, gentle and dear, frail of body perhaps, but never of courage, never swerving from what they believed the right path, and, no matter what they were called upon to do, by rude circumstance, always remaining ladies. But few commentators have seen fit to notice my ladies and it takes a "gentleman of the old school" like yourself to appreciate the timid creatures for I imagine that you, like myself, have known and loved gentle ladies who could fight wild cats, if the necessity arose.

As for your statement about the book being the "greatest historical novel written by an American"—Well, I can only say that that left me breathless and I still find it hard to believe that it was actually written and published! I have to take out the clipping and look at it fondly again and again to reassure myself that you actually wrote such words. I shall treasure this clipping and those words as long as I live and if I keep on rereading them so often the paper will be worn out in a week. I hope you did not mind but I sent another clipping to my publishers, the Macmillan Company, by air mail, so happy and pleased and proud was I that a Georgian had written so wonderful an article about me. And how glad I am that you wrote that "much of the book was contemporaneous with my own life." You see, those words give me a firm rock to stand upon when ignorant people who do not know the sad history of the South shout against me that I have overdrawn my picture, that such things could never happen, had never happened. But they did happen and had I pictured some of the more dreadful things I uncovered in my research, my book could never have been published. I am sure that my publishers will be as glad and proud as I to have such authentic backing as yours as to the truthfulness of the period. . . .

Mr. Clark Howell   Atlanta, Georgia
The Atlanta Constitution   June 28, 1936
Atlanta, Georgia

Dear Mr. Howell:

I never dreamed you were going to do so much for me! A review would have been adequate and made me most happy, or the roto pictures, or a "personality" story. But I wasn't expecting all three. I thought, as the resume of the novel ran so long, you would just tack a couple of paragraphs on and let it ride. But such a long story! And on "page opposite editorial page!" Yes, I'm still newspaperman enough to know what an honor that position is and still newspaperman enough to be flattered to death by it.

I thought Yolande[1] did a grand interview even if I will have a tough time living up to all the nice things she said. But then Yolande always does good stuff. And she was so clever about her style that for the life of me I couldn't tell where the resume began and her story left off! I think that's genius!

You said you'd "make me famous" and if the Constitution's spread yesterday doesn't do just that, then nothing will. I can't get over your kindness and generosity and wish I had a dozen different ways to say "thank you," each one sounding more happy than the last. I especially was touched by the fact that you thought of me and took so much trouble to see about my stuff at a time when you must have been so busy and rushed with Convention[2] affairs, with national matters of great importance beside which my book is very small potatoes indeed. . . .

The Atlanta Historical Association had a reception for me yesterday and I believe that every pioneer family in town was represented. John said it was interesting just to stand and watch the faces of the guests and see the difference between them and the average Atlanta face, said there was a quiet strength about them that was startling—and that they all looked a trifle alike! I wish you had been there. I started to call you and then I thought either you wouldn't have arrived home yet or, if you had returned, you would have been fatigued from the Convention and had no desire to stand about, drinking punch and talking early Atlanta history. But I wanted you, just the same.

Mrs. Julia Collier Harris   Atlanta, Georgia
Chattanooga, Tennessee   June 29, 1936

My dear Mrs. Harris:

Thank you so much for the clipping. And at the risk of sounding both gushing and hysterical, let me say thank you so much for the last part of your letter, which had to do with not being gobbled up by clubs and exploited by this and that person. It was a great comfort to me, coming from a person like you. Except for my husband, I have found no one who takes this attitude. The result is that between the desire of well meaning friends to "do something" for me and my ardent desire not to be "done

---

[1] Yolande Gwin.
[2] The Democratic National Convention. Mr. Howell was Georgia's Democratic National Committeeman.

for" this period of my life has been my unhappiest one. And I resent this as I think it should be happy and exciting.

I did not realize that being an author meant this sort of thing, autographing in book stores, being invited here and there about the country to speak, to attend summer schools, to address this and that group at luncheon. It all came as a shock to me and not a pleasant shock. I have led, by choice, so quiet and cloistered a life for many years. John likes that sort of life and so do I. Being in the public eye is something neither of us care about but what good does it do to say it? No one believes a word of it or if they do believe it they get indignant. I have been caught between two equally distasteful positions, that of the girlishly shy creature who keeps protesting her lack of desire for the limelight but who only wants to be urged. And that of a graceless, ungracious, blunt spoken ingrate who refuses to let people do her honor. It has all been very distressing to me. I was brought up to consider it better to commit murder than be rude and it is hard to depart from Mother's teachings. Yet, I find no other way, short of rudeness, in meeting the situation.

When I try to explain to those I know well, try to explain that while I speak only for myself, and not for other authors, that I think such exploitation cheapens a person—they look at me and say "Why be dumb? Here's your chance to cash in!" It is useless to say that I do not want to cash in. Then friends would probably have me committed for insanity.

Some while back the Macmillan Company wanted me to come to New York for publication date and when I asked if I'd have to make speeches or autograph in book stores they were stunned. But of course! So I didn't go to New York. That very kind and understanding man, Mr. Harold Latham, then came south for a day and I talked it over with him and he, thank Heaven, did understand. I was so happy to hear him say that he did not really think such "literary circuses" sold books. I'm sure he wouldn't want to be quoted on that but he did say it. And he seemed to understand when I said I'd rather never sell a book than autograph in department stores, other than those of Atlanta. I see no way of escaping those. This is my home town. Everyone has been so kind and helpful that I can never repay them enough. And I *would* seem an eccentric and ungracious person if I refused, here in Atlanta. But it has made me very unhappy.

It is not that I think myself such a wonderful and precious vessel of genius that I do not wish to expose myself to the public gaze. It is only that I don't especially like the public gaze and would like to continue my life, which has been a happy one, in its old tenor. And I intend to do it, if there is any way possible, until this present limelight subsides (and experience on newspapers has showed me that literary limelight subsides in from six weeks to two months).

But what to do with ladies' organizations who want me to speak? And what to do when called upon to address the young and give them an inspiring word? As if the young, of all people, needed inspiration! And what to do with clubs who want a few words on the aims of my book when I had no aims at all?

Mrs. Harris, I did not intend to inflict all this incoherence upon you. But your letter with its common sense attitude tapped the spring. How comforting it was to read your words—how pleasant to know that some one like you felt like John and I, upon this subject. I feel that I had a strong rock on which to stand for if someone of your stature refuses, then I, too, can refuse.

Mr. Duncan Burnet   Atlanta, Georgia
Athens, Georgia   July 3, 1936

Dear Mr. Burnet:

You said in your nice letter that "this requires no reply." But I must reply to thank you for it and to tell you that I *haven't* sold the movie rights for three to ten million dollars, as rumor has it. In fact, I haven't even had an offer from the movies. I don't know where this rumor started but it's about run me crazy. Of course, I'd *like* to sell it but don't see how the book could be made into a movie. You can help me a lot by denying the story. As you can imagine, every one in Georgia on the Relief Rolls is after me to give them a thousand dollars and they get mad when I say I've never had the thousand, much less three million!

Father J. M. Lelen   Atlanta, Georgia
Falmouth, Kentucky   June 6, 1936[1]

My dear Dr. Lelen:

The Atlanta Journal forwarded to me your card and I thank you so much for your kindness in writing me and for your commendations. I never realized before how much it means to a writer to hear from a reader. This is my first book and I am realizing now that it's like shooting an arrow in the air and having it fall to earth you know not where. People may like your book or detest it but except for scattered newspaper criti-.cisms you'll never know how it was received. So I do appreciate your card so much.

[1] Misdated. Should be July 6, 1936.

I was so interested in your remark about "Scarlett" and "Becky Sharp" —interested for this reason. I never read "Vanity Fair" till last year when I was making a long convalescence from an automobile accident. And I wrote "Gone With the Wind" about eight years ago. I know it sounds illiterate of me not to have read about Becky years ago but I didn't. All my "classical" reading, if you could call it that, was done before I was twelve years old. Mother used to give me a nickel for each of Shakespear's plays, a dime for Bulwer-Lytton (And was I under paid!), a dime for Dickens, fifteen cents for Nietzsche and Kant and Darwin. "Vanity Fair" was in the fifteen cent class but I couldn't or wouldn't read it. Even when the price was raised to a quarter, I wouldn't read it. I never could get past the place where Becky threw away the book. Even after being spanked I made no progress with the book. But last year, in desperation I took up Thackeray because I had read everything else the library had to offer and I was so charmed with Becky that I read my eyes out. I must have been a singularly stupid child not to have liked it. Perhaps if I'd ever gotten as far as Waterloo I would have liked it. Last week, the book reviewer for the Atlanta Journal also remarked about "Becky" and I was very thrilled that my first effort should get such a grand comparison.[2]

Mr. Herschel Brickell   Gainesville, Georgia
The New York Evening Post   July 7, 1936
New York, New York

My dear Mr. Brickell:

I am Margaret Mitchell, of Atlanta, author of "Gone With the Wind" and I want to thank you so very much for the marvelous review you gave me on June 30. It was my intention to write you the kind of letter that would show you just how much I did appreciate all your kind words. But I'm afraid I can't write that kind of letter tonight.

As you may observe from the postmark, I'm not at home in Atlanta. I'm on the run. I'm sure Scarlett O'Hara never struggled harder to get out of Atlanta or suffered more during her siege of Atlanta than I have suffered during the siege that has been on since publication day. If I had known being an author was like this I'd have thought several times before I let Harold Latham go off with my dog-eared manuscript. I've lost

[2] Sam Tupper, Jr., reviewed *GWTW* in the Atlanta *Journal*, June 28. He noted: "Miss Mitchell has told a story of Atlanta immeasurably above the usual story of local interest, a kind of Southern 'Vanity Fair' with lovely high-bred Melanie and unscrupulous, fascinating Scarlett instead of Amelia and Becky."

ten pounds in a week, leap when phones ring and scurry like a rabbit at the sight of a familiar face on the street. The phone has screamed every three minutes for a week and utter strangers collar me in public and ask the most remarkable questions and photographers pop up out of drains, always in the hope, poor things, that they can get a picture of me that doesn't look like Margot Asquith.

This morning three boys from the A.P. gave me a brisk work out that lasted three hours and when they left I got in the car and left town, without a change of underwear or a tooth brush. And I got as far as here. Being anti social by nature and accustomed to a very quiet life, it has all been too much for me.

The point of this letter is this. I just long distanced Atlanta and talked to my husband and he said that he had talked to Lois Cole at the New York Macmillan Company this morning. And she said that you were coming South within the next two weeks—and that you said you'd like to meet me. That was the first good news I've heard since the day I went on sale. Will you really come to see me? I can't tell you how happy it would make me. It was marvelous enough that you said such things about my book but it will be more marvelous if I could meet you, because—and I must fall back on a trite statement—"I have long been an admirer of yours." I cannot tell you how flattered I am at the very idea.

When I left town this morning I intended to hide out in the mountains where there are no telephones and no newspapers and no one reads anything but the Bible—and to stay there till my money ran out. Or till my local fame ran out. And from my experiences as a reporter, I recall that local literary celebrities usually last three weeks. However, I won't ever be more than twelve hours or so from Atlanta and my family knows how to locate me. So should you decide to come, please communicate with my husband, John R. Marsh. During the day you can get him at the Georgia Power Company. Nights and Sundays at home, 4 East 17th St. N.E. apt. 9, Atlanta. And I'll come home with the greatest pleasure. If there is even a chance of seeing you, I won't write you ten pages to tell you how nice I thought you were about "Gone With the Wind." I'd have a lot better time telling you and thanking you, in person. But still, I've got to say a few things.

Thank you for picking up the parallel between Scarlett and Atlanta. No one else (as far as I know) caught it. Thank you for going on record that while my story "bordered on the melodramatic" at times, the times of which I wrote *were* melodramatic. Well, they were but it takes a person with a Southern background to appreciate just how melodramatic they really were. I had to tone down so much, that I had taken from actual incidents, just to make them sound barely credible. And thanks for your defense of Captain Butler and his credibility. I never thought, when I wrote him, that there'd be so much argument about whether he was true to life or not. His type was such an ordinary one in those days that I picked him because he was typical of his times. Even his looks. I went through hundreds of old ambro-types and daguerreotypes looking at faces and that type of face leaped out at you. Just as surely as the faces of the pale, shy looking boys with a lock of hair hanging on their foreheads were always referred to with a sigh as "dear cousin Willy. He was killed at Shiloh." (I've often wondered why the boys who looked like that were *always* killed at Shiloh.)

In the matter of Captain Butler I am caught between cross fires. Some of the Northern critics I've read (and I've been too rushed to read many reviews yet) have said he wasn't true to life. Down here, folks find him so true to life that I may yet have a lawsuit on my hands despite my protests that I didn't model him after any human being I'd ever heard of.

And how did you know I had a "memory for what older people had told me"? Because you have that type of memory and had the same things told you? Good Heavens, I am running on. And I was only going to say "thank you"! But if you only knew how strange it felt to read your words about that book. . . . And to finish up with your reference to Freeman's "R. E. Lee"[1] which is, to me, the most wonderful thing of its kind ever turned out—well, perhaps you contributed to a practical nervous collapse and are really the cause of me being on the run! I just can't take it.

Come to see me. I'll give you a party if you want a party or I'll feed you at home and sit and listen to you talk. My cook's a good old fashioned kind, strong on turnip greens and real fried chicken and rolls that melt in your mouth. Personally, I'd rather listen to you talk—and thank you—than give you a party.

Mr. George Brett   Gainesville, Georgia
The Macmillan Company   July 8, 1936
New York, New York

My dear Mr. Brett:

Thank you for the check and please excuse my long delay in acknowledging it. Life has been so much like a nightmare recently that it was all I could do to stay on my feet, much less write letters. I finally ran

---

[1] Douglas Southall Freeman, *R. E. Lee* (New York, London, 1934–35; 4 vols.). Brickell wrote of *GWTW*: "I can only compare it for its definitiveness, its truthfulness and its completeness with Douglas Southall Freeman's 'R. E. Lee,' and I know of no higher praise that can reasonably be bestowed upon it than this."

away from town yesterday. A brisk three hour work out with three Associated Press boys and a couple of photographers finally finished me and I left town with practically no clothes and no money. I do think it's awful when you've sent me a check for five thousand dollars that I haven't had time to buy me a new dress, or have my car overhauled! I didn't know an author's life was like this.

I've started for the back of beyond in the mountains and stopped here because I was going to sleep at the wheel and was afraid I'd kill myself in a ditch. When I reach a place where there aren't any telephones and no newspapers for my picture to be in, I'll stop and write you a letter to tell you just how much I do appreciate the check and all you and Macmillan have done for me. Good Heavens! The advertising you've put behind me! With all those ads and the grand publicity the newspapers have given me, Macmillan could have sold Karl Marx up here in these hills!

Mr. Gilbert Govan   Gainesville, Georgia
University of Chattanooga   July 8, 1936
Chattanooga, Tennessee

Dear Mr. Govan:

I have made my escape from my own private siege of Atlanta and with far more difficulty, I'm sure, than my heroine made hers and I'm off to the mountains where there are no telephones. And I only wish I had a "Tara" to run to.

I stopped here to get some sleep and a chance to read the reviews on my book. Yes, life has been whizzing by so fast that I didn't even have time for that and that has been maddening. I left town so abruptly that I haven't a change of underwear or a tooth brush. My baggage consists of a typewriter, newspaper clippings and four murder stories.

I did like your review so much. I do thank you for it so much—the way you handled it, the things you said, the atmosphere of it all and the very grand lead.[1] It was a grand lead and when I say it was an obvious lead I do not mean that it was trite or ordinary or that anyone else has used it. No one has and I wonder why not? Because it is so true. As I read it there came to mind the hundreds of time I've heard Northerners say those same words. And I remembered how I looked at them always in a blank confusion, faced with the fact that I couldn't explain why the

---

[1] Govan reviewed *GWTW* in the Chattanooga *Times* July 5. His review begins: "One of the things which most northerners say that they cannot understand about southerners is what they call an obsession with the Civil war. 'We've forgotten about it,' they say, 'why can't you?' "

war is an "obsession" with us. I couldn't explain without taking all night —or writing a book as long as the one I wrote. And I remembered especially one night when I was having supper with Lois Cole and Allan Taylor[2] and I asked him what prison his kin folks had been in during the war. And he asked me what prison mine had been in. And I asked what the death rate had been in the prison of his kin. And he wanted to know whether pneumonia or small pox accounted for most of the deaths in the jail where my folks were imprisoned. It seemed an ordinary enough conversation to us and we spoke of it all as though we'd been there. But we came out of it suddenly when Lois looked at us curiously and made the same remark you made in your lead, asked the same question.

I am so glad you gave your own personal background. It lent such an authenticity to my own story. And while I'm on the subject of your background, are you of the Govan family who had a store down on Whitehall, next to where High's store used to be? If so, man and boy, we traded with that firm for many years.

Thank you for your remark about Gerald who "recognizes that security can never be found apart from the land." No one else picked that up; no one seemed to think of it or to notice it. And that depressed me for while I didn't hammer on it I meant it for an undercurrent. And I felt, as I suppose all authors are prone to feel, nine tenths of the time, that I had utterly failed in getting my ideas over.

. . . I appreciate so much your statement in your review that the characters were not taken from real life.[3] I'm appreciating it more now even than I would have a week ago. For, God knows, I didn't expect the book to sell like this. I didn't expect it to cause any talk. In my wildest imaginings I didn't believe that that old mess of copy paper which hung around the house so many years, which I didn't think even worth retyping and sending off, would ever make the best seller lists. And I'm flabbergasted. I appreciate your remarks, as I wrote above, for already people are doing the usual thing of trying to fit the characters to real people.

And I am caught embarrassingly between cross fires. On the one hand, some of the Northern critics say that Rhett Butler, for instance, is not credible nor is Melanie. And on the other hand, people are picking out Rhett Butlers to such an extent that I may have a law suit on my hands yet for using the grandfather of certain people who must be nameless.

---

[2] An Atlanta newspaperman who married Miss Cole. Later he became editor of the New York *Times Magazine* and she an editor for Macmillan.

[3] Govan mentioned in his column, "Roaming the Book World," in the Chattanooga *Times* June 21, that Miss Mitchell had "used material out of her own family." She wrote him on June 23: "But I didn't. I wouldn't even think of writing about my own family. Besides, none of them were in Atlanta during the fighting or the fall of the city. . . . True, I did get my background out of what the old timers told me. . . . But all the characters and all the incidents came out of my own head."

And I never heard of their darned grandfather. And Melanie has been fitted to a number of people, last of all to me. Harry Stillwell Edwards anounced that in the Journal and that was one of the reasons I left town so abruptly.[4] It was dear and sweet of him but I shall never live it down, especially with my own generation. Being a product of the Jazz Age, being one of those short-haired, short-skirted, hard-boiled young women who preachers said would go to hell or be hanged before they were thirty, I am naturally a little embarrassed at finding myself the incarnate spirit of the old South! So I thank you for saying the characters weren't real. Honestly, they weren't. But all of us have seen types like foolish Miss Pittypat and Melanie—that is, all of us who were brought up in this section. My characters were just composites.

Thanks for everything. Can I come to see you if I ever get to Chattanooga? Lois told me so much about you that I always wanted to meet you.

Mr. Hunt Clement　　　　　　　　　　　　　　　Gainesville, Georgia
The Chattanooga Times　　　　　　　　　　　　　July 8, 1936
Chattanooga, Tennessee

Dear Hunt:

What a grand telegram and how sweet of you to send it! It arrived just when flash lights were going off and the A.P. boys were giving me a brisk three hour work out on what aims I had in the book (no aims) What did I wish to prove? (I didn't want to prove anything) Is it a propaganda novel? (Oh, God, no!) Did you write it because you felt the whole story had never been told before? (No, it's been told so often everybody's sick and tired of it) Are you writing another book? (Do I look like that kind of a fool?)—And then along came your wire, which gave me a chance to get away for a minute and collect my addled brains and order some coffee for the gang and also pleased me so much and touched me so much that I sat in the dark by the telephone and wept.

I *do* thank you so much. You are every bit as nice and kind today as you were the first day I ever laid eyes on you, when harassed by interviews with debutantes who thought the League of Nations "cute," I unburdened my soul to you over a weak cup of coffee in the Journal "Roachery."

---

[4] In the Atlanta *Journal* of July 7 Edwards wrote: "Inevitably, the true novelist writes herself into her story; a bit here and a bit there, in the characters assembled. And sometime, one of them may reveal her as a whole. In 'GONE WITH THE WIND' . . . the real heroine is Melanie. . . . And Peggy Mitchell is the reincarnation of Melanie."

Mrs. Julia Collier Harris   Gainesville, Georgia
Chattanooga, Tennessee   July 8, 1936

My dear Mrs. Harris:

As you will note from the above heading I'm no longer at home but on the run. If I had known being an author was going to be like this I'd have thought several times before becoming one! I'm on my way to the mountains to find a place where telephones don't ring and photographers don't materialize with the first cup of coffee of the morning. I have always felt that that first cup was a rite and one to be practised in complete privacy. Furthermore my soul refuses to return to my body until the cup has been drunk. So I've been minus a soul for a week or more.

I stopped off here to get a night's sleep and to write to you and Mr. Govan and Hunt Clement. I wanted to write and thank you immediately for the copy of your column[1] which you so kindly sent but things were moving too fast for me to get to the typewriter. So now I'm thanking you, not only for the copy but the newspaper clipping as well—yours and the one of the New York "Times," too. You *were* nice to pencil that margin note about Ralph Thompson being shallow and spiteful![2] However, what ever he wrote couldn't be as bad as what I expected for Heaven knows I never expected the book to get such good reviews or people to be so kind. The book will never seem like a book to me but just that old dog-eared and dirty bunch of copy paper which took up so much space in our small apartment and seemed with each rewriting to get worse.

I didn't mind Mr. Thompson not liking the book for that's a critic's privilege but I do object to his calling attention to inaccuracies which do not happen to be inaccurate. And it annoys me to think that anyone would think me such a fool as to get myself out on a limb about such matters as the "Gotterdammerung" where I could be sawed off so easily. I only put in three weeks checking up on that small statement. Of course, the opera itself was produced several years after the war but the poems were written in the late Forties or early Fifties, I believe. (I haven't my

---

[1] On July 5 Mrs. Harris devoted all of a long column, "From My Balcony," to Miss Mitchell and her book. The column is based on Miss Mitchell's letter of April 28 to Mrs. Harris.

[2] Thompson's review was not wholly unfavorable. He wrote, for example: "The historical background is the chief virtue of the book, and it is the story of the times rather than the unconvincing and somewhat absurd plot that gives Miss Mitchell's work whatever importance may be attached to it. How accurate this history is is for the expert to tell, but no reader can come away without a sense of the tragedy that overcame the planting families in 1865 and without a better understanding of the background of present-day Southern life." New York *Times*, June 30.

notes with me and my brain is too addled at present to be absolutely sure.) And after going through all the books in the Library on German folklore and the Wagnerian cycle I found that the phrase "dusk of the Gods" was an ancient one and, Heaven knows, the legend was an ancient one. And old time Southerners did travel and practically all of them made the Grand Tour which included Germany. And a few of them in this section did read books, odd though that may seem, and did know music!

And where he rode me about the word "sissy"—saying that I put it into mouths a whole generation too early—I picked up that word and the line in which it was used from a letter, dated in 1861, from a boy to his father, explaining why he had run away and joined an outfit in another section. "I just didn't want to join any Zouaves. I'd have felt like a sissy in those red pants etc.—" Well, I suppose I should be happy that he, at least, gave me credit for a good historical background and I am happy because I wasn't even expecting that from reviewers.[3]

But how to thank you for your column! And my family was so pleased and happy. Though they would die before admitting it, I'm sure they all feel in the old fashioned Southern way—that a lady's name appears in print only when she's born and buried. And I know they had well concealed qualms about seeing my name in print. However, after I took the plunge and was published they rallied to me to a fifth cousin, ready to stand by even if I was referred to in print as the world's worst novelist. And they were so pleased at your column, not only the nice things you said but the way you said them. So I am saying "thank you" for the clan as well as myself.

Your closing remarks were heartening, especially in view of the almost universal objections to my style—or rather, to my lack of style. So I appreciated the "even poetic"! I'm not a stylist, Heaven knows, never could be one, don't want to be one and don't like to read stylists, except James Branch Cabell. And I sweat blood to make my style simple and stripped and bare. I know I'm wrong and out of date but I always felt that a style shouldn't obtrude, always felt that if story and characters wouldn't stand up against a bare style, then that particular story and those characters ought to be abandoned. And how could I have any other style, coming of a legal family who have gained fame from writing wills

---

[3] Thompson noted: "There are a good many questionable touches in the dialogue —the word 'sissy' (implying an effeminate man) is put into the mouths of characters a whole generation too early, and such expressions as 'on the make,' 'like a bat out of hell,' 'Götterdämmerung' and 'survival of the fittest' sound very strange upon the tongues of Civil War Southerners." In A Supplement to the Oxford English Dictionary (Oxford, 1972), the earliest citation of "Götterdämmerung" (GWTW, p. 527) is 1909. "Sissy" (GWTW, p. 16), meaning effeminate, is cited by M. M. Mathews, A Dictionary of Americanisms on Historical Principles (Chicago [c. 1951]), as having been used as early as 1846.

and abstracts that are so simple and clear and easy to read that a child can understand them—and the Supreme Court can't overturn them? I'm sure if I had evidenced any style in early childhood, it would have been smacked out of me with a hair brush!

How nice you've been to me from the beginning of all this. You've given me of your time and your work and your advice and I hope some day to be able to tell you adequately how much I appreciate it all.

Mr. Edwin Granberry   Gainesville, Georgia
New York, New York   July 8, 1936

My dear Mr. Granberry:

I am Margaret Mitchell of Atlanta, author of "Gone with the Wind." Your review of my book was the first review I read,[1] and it made me so happy that I tried to write you immediately. I have been trying to write you for over a week, but you can see just how far my good intentions have gotten me!

As soon as I read what you said, I had what I thought was a perfectly marvelous letter to write you, a letter which would tell you just exactly how much I appreciated your kindness. But that letter has gone, disappearing somewhere along the road of this last nightmare week and I find myself tonight here in a hotel in Gainesville, incoherent from exhaustion and from gratitude to you. So forgive this letter its inadequacies.

I didn't know that being an author was like this, or I don't think I'd have been an author. I've led so quiet a life for so many years, quiet by choice because I'm not a social animal, quiet because I wanted to work and quiet because I'm not the strongest person in the world and need plenty of rest. And all my quiet world has blown up recently. The phone has rung every three minutes, the door bell rings and perfect strangers bounce in asking the most extraordinary and personal questions, photographers arrive with the morning coffee. Reporters arrive too, but I don't mind them for I used to report myself and I can't help realizing what a tough go-round they're having with me. For I'm perfectly normal, not eccentric, had no romantic experiences with the writing of my book. So they can't find anything hot to write about me! And then teas and parties, the first I've been to in years, have about ruined me. Yesterday it got too much and I climbed in the car and set out with no baggage to speak of: a typewriter, four murder novels, and five dollars. When I reached here I was too tired to go on. So I'm staying here till tomorrow and then I'm

---

[1] Granberry reviewed *GWTW* in the New York *Evening Sun* June 30.

going back into the mountains where there aren't any telephones and no one will recognize me from my pictures and ask me if it's hard to write a book.

I did not mean to fling all my troubles upon you, a stranger, who has been so kind to me. But I'm trying to explain my seeming discourtesy in not writing to you sooner; explain, too, why this letter is such a hash.

I don't believe I can make plain to you how much your review meant to me unless I tell you something about the background of the writing of my book. I wrote it so long ago. It must have been nearly ten years ago, and I'd finished most of it by 1929. That is, I'd about stopped writing on it both because pressure of illness among friends and family never seemed to let up, and because the thing didn't seem worth finishing. I know it sounds silly for me to write that I thought the book too lousy to bother with retyping and trying to sell, but I didn't think it humanly possible that any one would buy it. It seems silly to write that when I see by this evening's paper that the fifth printing sold out the day after the publication date, but I know good writing and mine didn't seem good. So I never tried to sell it.

After Mr. Latham came along and pried it out of me last year and got me to sign the contract, I was utterly miserable. I thought I'd been an awful fool to let a job like that go out where people could see how bad it was, where people could remark on its badness at the top of their lungs and in the public prints. My only comfort was that there wasn't much criticism they could give me that I hadn't already given myself. Criticism wouldn't hurt me (and it hasn't!) but it would upset my family, especially my father. So you can see what my frame of mind was when I got an advance clipping of your review.

How much space you gave me! Good heavens, I can never thank you enough for that! And when I read along to the breath-taking remark about being bracketed with Tolstoy, Hardy, Dickens, and Undset—well, I gave out. I have strong nerves but after all, I hadn't had much sleep for a week and little food because of callers at meal time, and God knows I wasn't expecting anything like that. I lay down and called for an ice pack and my husband read the rest to me. (When I woke up the next morning I told him that I had had the queerest dream the night before. A man named Edwin Granberry had written the most remarkable things about the book!)

I must confess right now that I've never read Tolstoy. I just couldn't. I've tried and tried. I can't read any of the Russians. And I've never been able to read Hardy, either. I did read Dickens because Mother gave me fifteen cents per copy for the reading of them. But even when she raised the ante to twenty-five cents with a licking thrown in, I coudn't read Tolstoy, or Hardy or Thackeray either, for that matter. Yes, I know that sounds illiterate but it's true. Last year, while recovering from an automobile accident, I read "Vanity Fair" and adored it and wondered why I was so dumb in early youth as not to have appreciated it. And last year at the same time, I read Galsworthy and Undset. I became so impassioned about Undset that I read eight long books one after another, and was blind for weeks thereafter. Isn't she the most wonderful writer!

For you to mention me in the same breath with her is quite the most exciting thing that ever happened to me!

And thank you for saying that my book was primarily a novel, a tale. Not Joycean, not Proustian, not Wolfish. You are so very right, not only in your summation of the type of book, but the type of mind behind the book. I can't read stream-of-consciousness books. And, as I started out to be a neurologist or a psychiatrist, I know too much on the practical side, have seen too much of the back waters and jungles of the human mind to want to put them on paper.

Thank you for your kind words about poor Scarlett, for saying that she still keeps your sympathy and explaining why. It never occurred to me while writing her that such a storm of hard words would descend upon the poor creature's head. She just seemed to me to be a normal person thrown into abnormal circumstances and doing the best she could, doing what seemed to her the practical thing. The normal human being in a jam thinks, primarily, of saving his own hide, and she valued her hide in a thoroughly normal way.

And I look at you with awe and respect for your remarks about my handling of Rhett Butler, that "we are never . . . let directly into his mind; the author is always able to find an action or speech which reveals the havoc." I didn't know anybody would catch up with me in that! I could live in his mind so thoroughly that I neglected to write about his mind. And I positively got goose bumps when you referred to the incident of Wade Hampton and the scar on Rhett's belly.[2] It was one of my favorites and, to me, the turning point of the book, or at least of Rhett's character, when he realized that no man who has taken a wife and a child can ever live utterly as he pleases. And to say he is one of the great lovers of fiction—well, good heavens! If I hadn't been so completely certain my book was rotten, hadn't thought it rotten for so many years, I would be so conceited about that line that I'd be unbearable!

You have been so kind, have made me so happy and my family so happy. (My reserved and unenthusiastic father simply purred when he read your review—and why not?) I wish there was some way I could tell you how much I appreciated everything you said. I wish I could see you because I talk better than I write and perhaps I could make you

[2] *GWTW*, p. 900.

understand what your review meant to me. And I hope I do see you sometime.

Mr. Donald Adams   Atlanta, Georgia
New York, New York   July 9, 1936

My dear Mr. Adams:

I am Margaret Mitchell, author of "Gone With the Wind" and I am yet so new an author that I do not know whether it is good form for an author to write a critic and say "thank you"! For all I know of literary etiquette an author should keep haughtily silent, thus intimating that marvelous reviews were only what she expected. Or only address a critic to ask why in Hell the review wasn't better and point out sad lacks in the critic's critical abilities.

But, as stated above, I am a brand new author and your review pleased me so much and made me so happy that I only wish I knew a dozen ways to say "thank you."[1] I suppose I was even more pleased than the average author would have been at the fine things you said because most authors I met in my newspaper days seemed to expect *something* nice and, honestly, I wasn't expecting anything. In the first place, I never expected to sell my book and didn't write it to sell but only to amuse and occupy myself while on crutches. I suppose an author shouldn't say she thought her work not especially good but I didn't think so much of my book. In fact, I thought so little of it that I never bothered to try to sell it. I know good work and I know good writing and I didn't think mine good. And I didn't think anyone except my history minded family would be interested in a book about the Civil War. And, in the second place, after Harold Latham pried the manuscript out of me, I was utterly miserable thinking just how the critics would ride me. I thought I'd been several kinds of an ass to get myself into so vulnerable a position and if it hadn't been that I feared the Macmillan Company would have me certified as a lunatic, I'd have tried to get the manuscript back.

So, with all that in the background, perhaps you can understand why I ran a temperature after reading your kind review. I've been trying to write to you ever since I got an advance copy of the "Times" but have had no luck, until today. I didn't realize all that being an author meant, telephones, reporters, photographers and requests to speak at luncheons. Everyone has been so very kind and the town and state papers so grand to me and friends and kin so shamelessly proud and loving that I got frightened for the first time in my life and last week I bolted out of town,

---

[1] Adams reviewed GWTW in the New York Times Book Review July 5.

minus baggage, reading matter and any remnant of brain. And since then I've been riding about the countryside looking for a place where I didn't know anybody or where I wasn't kin to anybody so I could settle down and read reviews and get some rest and write some letters.

I never found the place so I doubled back and came home.

I should start at the beginning of your review and go on to the end, telling you what I liked, but I must start in the middle and tell you that I so appreciated the way you played up the Atlanta angle. As you said, Atlanta in that period has never been done before (except some of the middle chapters of Josephine Herbst's novel[2]—I can't remember the name but it wasn't "The Executioner Waits.") which dealt with carpetbagging from the Carpetbagger's angle. Mary Johnston did have a chapter about the fighting at Kennesaw and Pumpkin Vine in "Cease Firing." But outside of those two I never ran across any other mention, in fiction, of Atlanta in those days.

And the more I dug into the back history of the town the more I realized how important it was in those days. But for all that's known about it, the war might have been waged exclusively in Virginia. And I got pretty sick and tired reading about the fighting in Virginia when for sheer drama the campaign from the Tennessee line to Atlanta has no equal. I cut my teeth on that Johnston-Sherman running fight, dug bullets out of the old breastworks when I was little, climbed the steep side of Kennesaw mountain where the guns were pulled up by hand (and it's hard climbing even when you aren't dragging cannon!). And went out at low water to see in the shallows of the river the Federal cannon lost in a brave attempt to cross the ford in the face of the Confederate rifles. And while Reconstruction wasn't as bad in Georgia as in South Carolina or Louisiana, Atlanta had its own peculiar, wild kind of Reconstruction because it was a town in the process of rebuilding, money was being invested here and I think we attracted more people on the make than any other town in the South.

And all of the above is to say how I appreciated your phrase about "the anxious and bedeviled city." How I wish I'd thought of just that phrase! I tried not to hammer on the theme of Atlanta and its growth and its railroads and its differences from other Southern cities of the time but I wanted it there in the background of Scarlett and I appreciate your noting it and calling attention to it.

And good heavens, all the fine things you said in your lead about narrative sense and characterization! And putting my name up with folks like Mary Johnston and Ellen Glasgow and Stark Young and Tolstoy and Thackeray! Just saying "thank you" is too inadequate but I don't know

[2] *Pity Is Not Enough* (New York [c. 1933]).

what else to say. And while I'm on the subject, it looks to me as though I'm going to *have* to read "War and Peace." You and other critics have been kind enough to mention "Gone With the Wind" in the same breath as "War and Peace" and it is shameful for me to have to admit that I never read it, never could read it or anything by any Russian no matter how hard I tried. Most of my "classical" reading was done before I was twelve, aided by five, ten and fifteen cents a copy bribe from my father and abetted by the hair brush or mother's number three slipper. She just about beat the hide off me for not reading Tolstoy or Thackeray or Jane Austen but I preferred to be beaten. Since growing up, I've tried again to read "War and Peace" and couldn't. One of my Russian friends has upbraided me frequently, saying that the life in old Russia was more akin to that in the old South than any he had ever known—that the old Russian type of mind was more peculiarly Georgian than a Georgian could realize. But the Russian mind, in fiction, at least, still defies me. But I'm going to read "War and Peace" now if it takes a month.

Yes, I know Rhett Butler is the "stock figure of melodrama." Thank you for saying I made him credible. I knew when I picked him just what he was. But he was what I wanted, what I needed and he belonged. He belonged because he was pretty typical of a certain mind and viewpoint of the sixties. Even his looks were typical. I went through so many daguerreotypes, hundreds of them, cagily questioned old ladies about the beaux of their youth, the men they remembered the longest. And that face and that type kept recurring, not as a north Georgia face and type but as a coastal, deep South face and type. Well, I needed him and I used him. Just as I needed and used all my Victorian background. And when you come right down to it, if you go back to original sources for background you have to go back to original sources for characters. And I thought that no matter how blurred with usage, how hackneyed, how "stock" those characters were it was better to use them against the background in which they once lived than throw in a set of characters who were out of time and out of key. This isn't an apology for Rhett Butler or an excuse. It's an explanation in which I thought you might be interested because you had been so understanding about him.

And about the dialect which you didn't think Uncle Remus would have liked. No, I don't guess he would. And I sweat blood to keep it from being like Uncle Remus. Uncle Remus is tough reading as I know from having had to read it to many children. It sounds grand but it's tough reading. So is most dialect and I, a Southerner, usually refuse to read any dialect stuff that's like Uncle Remus. And so do most Southerners. I wanted it easily readable, accurate and phonetic. And I scoured the back country of this section routing out aged darkies who were born in slavery days. I don't know about Uncle Remus liking it but his son, Lucien

Harris, took the trouble to go to my father and give me a good rave. And his daughter-in-law, Mrs. Julia Collier Harris (Mrs. Julian Harris of Chattanooga), has been most kind in her letters to me. And his granddaughter, Mary Harris, on the Georgian here has gone to bat for me in her column so frequently and so kindly that I've been embarrassed. And a grandson of Uncle Remus[3] has been one of my kindest press agents. Dialect is tough going, even when you've been raised on it, and I take oath I'll never try it again. The different sections of the state have different dialects. The coast darkies speaking Geechee might just as well be speaking Sanscrit for all they mean to me. The middle Georgia darkies (around Macon) have different constructions from the North Georgia ones. And those from the older sections of the state around Washington, Ga., have some pronunciations and constructions that are practically Elizabethan. When you get into such tangles as the word "if" which in some localities is "ef" in others is "effen" and in still others is "did" (for instance, "Did I picked up a snake I'd be a fool") it is enough to drive one mad. No, I'm not a dialectitian (if there is such a word!) Latin is far easier: But I'm running on and maybe you aren't interested in dialect anyway. But if you ever get down to Charleston I wish you'd go out to Magnolia Gardens where they give you a negro guide to show you through and listen to *their* combination of English accent and Gullah. "Get" for "gate," "race" for "rice" etc. I can never understand half they say.

Your closing lines about my second book charmed me as you hoped that I'd not set about a second book too soon. I not only do not intend to set about a book too soon but, thank God, never intend to write another one if I keep my sanity. I have heard other writers make that same remark and then observed that they were stricken suddenly with a novel while in their bath or woke up in the night with a violent attack of short story. I hope Fate will be kinder to me. I wouldn't go through this again for anything. When I look back on these last years of struggling to find time to write between deaths in the family, illness in the family and among friends which lasted months and even years, childbirths (not my own!), divorces and neuroses among friends, my own ill health and four fine auto accidents which did everything from fracturing my skull to splintering my vertebrae—it all seems like a nightmare. I wouldn't tackle it again for anything. Just as soon as I sat down to write somebody I loved would decide to have their gall bladder removed or would venture into the office of a psychiatrist and for months thereafter wonder, at the top of their lungs, if they were really realizing their fullest potentialities.

I didn't mean to go on at such length. I really meant just to say

---

[3] Lucien Harris, Jr.

"thank you." But your review was so kind and so fair and so understanding that, to use a good old cliche, I felt as though I knew you. I hope I
do meet you some time, I may be in New York some time this Winter,
provided always that I gain back the seventeen pounds I've lost getting
this book proof read and off to the press. And I hope to meet you.

Mr. Stephen Vincent Benét   Gainesville, Georgia
New York, New York   July 9, 1936

My dear Mr. Benét:

I am Margaret Mitchell, author of "Gone With the Wind" which you
reviewed in the July 4th Saturday Review. I think you'd better put this
letter away till you have plenty of time to read for I feel it coming over
me that it will be a long letter!

I am not in the best condition to write you the kind of letter I'd like
to write you, the kind of letter that would adequately tell you how much
I appreciated your review, how happy it made me. I have just made my
escape from Atlanta after losing ten pounds since my publication day,
after having photographers with the morning coffee, and strangers col-
laring me at the bank and ladies' societies at me on the phone all day
wanting me to make a "little talk." My life has been quiet, here-to-fore,
quiet by choice and I find all this goings-on very upsetting. So I bolted
until things should quiet down. And now, some fifty miles up the road
toward the mountains, I find myself even tireder and more flabbergasted
than ever. For I never dreamed the book which I didn't think worth
retyping and trying to sell would ever sell, or having sold, would ever
get a kind word from a reviewer.

But I want to write you now and thank you for when I do get to
the mountains I know I'll go to bed and not get up for a week.

I must admit that when I heard that you were to review me my heart
sank. I suppose that needs some explanation and the explanation is this.
Your "John Brown's Body"[1] is my favorite poem, my favorite book. I know
more of it by heart than I do any other poetry. It means more to me, is
realer than anything I've ever read by any poet, bar none, and I've read
an awful lot of poetry. When your book was published, I was almost
finished with my book (it was in 1928 or 1929, wasn't it?). I do not write
with ease and I was toiling miserably through part of the first chapters,
rewriting and rewriting and finding each rewriting worse than the one
before. And an enthusiastic young man arrived one afternoon with your
book, fresh off the press, and demanded that I stop work and listen to it.

---

[1] *John Brown's Body* (Garden City, N.Y., 1928).

I refused because I was busy and he sat down and began at that point "This was his Georgia—" and my heart sank and I said "Don't read me any more of that." The reason was that you had caught so clearly, so vividly and so simply everything in the world that I was sweating to catch, done it in a way I could never hope to do it and with a heart-breaking beauty. And, just listening to it made me realize my own inadequacies so much that I knew if I heard more I wouldn't be able to write because I'd get the same attack of the humbles I got when I was foolish enough to reread Mary Johnston's "Cease Firing." I was looking through her book to find out whether or not it rained during the retreat from Kennesaw Mountain and lacked the strength of character to stop reading after finding what I wanted. And I couldn't write for weeks because I knew she'd done what I'd wanted to do and done it so much better that there seemed little use of me trying.

But the young man disregarded me and flipped the pages over to the "This is the last" part and read on. I never had anything in the world take hold of me more swiftly, more absolutely. He read all afternoon and when he went home that night he went without the book for I bought it from him and sent him home protesting. And I sat up all night to finish it. And then it was months before I could bear to try to write again. After reading what you'd done nothing I wrote sounded above the level of the "Rover Boys" or perhaps, to be kinder, "The Little Colonel."

And the original glow never died from the book. A month ago while driving home from Savannah through the cotton section, through the old plantation section where the Greek Revival houses still stand (and we have very few in our newer North Georgia section) it was brought home again to me how true and how lovely your poem was and I rode for miles quoting it aloud to the crowd. Not that they needed my quoting. They know "John Brown" but I can remember poetry and they can't.

I know this sounds like a rave and I don't care if it does for I mean it all and more. And I've long since forgiven you for keeping me away from my work for so long and for making me conscious of my own inadequacies. Because "John Brown's Body" was worth it.

And perhaps you'll understand now why I say my heart sank when I heard you were to review my book. You were my favorite poet; you had written my most loved book. You knew so much and appreciated good writing so much that I fully expected you to blast me at the top of your lungs. I suppose I should have realized that anyone who can write something great can be generous, too. But I was in such a dither about it that I didn't stop to think of that.

So when I read the kind things you had to say about "Gone With the Wind," I could hardly believe them. I can hardly believe them now! There's no one I'd rather have say them than you.

I'm glad now and proud that you did it. Glad because with your background and your own research you could travel along the reference paths I'd travelled. Do you know, you're the only reviewer who has picked up the diaries and memoirs out of my background? Of course, I used everybody from Myrta Lockett Avary to Eliza Andrews and Mary Gay and Mrs. Clement Clay and Miss Fearn and Eliza Ripley and the Lord knows how many unpublished letters and diaries.[2]

And I'm glad, with your Southern background, that you noticed and mentioned that Tara wasn't a movie set but a working plantation. It's hard to make people understand that North Georgia wasn't all white columns and singing darkies and magnolias, that it was so new, so raw. Even people in other sections of the state, older sections, still don't get the distinction and ask me why I didn't make Tara a Greek Revival house. I had to ride Clayton County pretty thoroughly before I found even one white columned house in which to put the Wilkes family. And I found that its life had been brief, built in the mid-fifties, burning in 1864.

I could go on for pages, thanking you for this and that until I had quoted all your review back to you. But I won't inflict that on you.

Yes, I think everybody thinks I picked up my girls from "Vanity Fair." It is useless for me to say that I never read Thackeray until a year ago. Anyway, I'm all too flattered at being mentioned in the same breath to care. And I yelled with delight at your mentioning St. Elmo.[3] I had a bet up that either St. Elmo or Mr. Rochester[4] would be Rhett's comparison. As for Lord Steyne[5]—I'm afraid I don't know him and must say, like Scarlett, "Oh, a foreigner!" But I knew that if I was going back to original sources for my background, I'd have to go back to original sources for my characters or else they wouldn't fit. And once the masterful Mr. St. Elmos and Mr. Rochesters were shining new, as new as Joyce Kilmer's "Trees" was before the radio foully murdered it. They are pretty hackneyed now but, as far as I could see, there was nothing for me to do but take Victorian types and put them into my Victorian background.

How kind you were and how much I thank you![6]

[2] Myrta Lockett Avary, *Dixie After the War* (New York, 1906); Eliza Frances Andrews, *The War-Time Journal of a Georgia Girl, 1864–1865* (New York, 1908); Mary Ann Harris Gay, *Life in Dixie During the War* (Atlanta, 1892); Virginia Tunstall Clay-Clopton, *A Belle of the Fifties* (New York, 1904); Frances Hewitt Fearn, editor, *Diary of a Refugee* (New York, 1910); Eliza Moore Chinn McHatton Ripley, *From Flag to Flag* (New York, 1889).

[3] A character in Augusta Evans Wilson's *St. Elmo* (New York, 1867).

[4] Hero of Charlotte Bronte's *Jane Eyre*.

[5] A character in *Vanity Fair*.

[6] Benét's answer to this letter appears in *Selected Letters of Stephen St. Vincent Benét* (New Haven, 1960), pp. 286–89.

Mr. Henry Steele Commager   Atlanta, Georgia
New York, New York   July 10, 1936

My dear Mr. Commager:

If this letter arrives on one of your busy days, just put it away till you have spare time, for it is coming over me that this will be a long letter. When I think of all the exciting things you said in your review of "Gone With the Wind,"[1] and when I think of your grasp of the underlying thought and your sympathy, I feel that I could write you 1037 pages about it. But, take heart! I won't.

I've been trying to write to you ever since Constance Skinner sent me an air mail advance copy of your review. (And her kindness in doing so made our wedding anniversary an even better affair than it already was!) But my normal quiet life has been upset recently, everyone has been so kind and so enthusiastic and so nice to me that it's about killed me. For the last week I've been touring the blistered countryside of North Georgia trying to find a wide place in the road where no one knew me and where none of my kin lived, so that I could get some sleep. I didn't find that place so I waited till dark yesterday and came home. But as I rode the red clay back roads, I thought an awful lot about you and your review. I thought of a number of nicely worded phrases in which I would thank you—And I lost them all somewhere along the way.

How to begin to thank you! As I read your review I kept saying "Dear God! I *do* believe some of the stuff got over after all!" And to an author there can be no more wonderful feeling. It's fine to be told that you've written a nice book or a book that will sell etc. But it's a sight finer to realize that the thoughts you put down on paper convey to the reader the exact thoughts you had in your own head. When in the earlier part of your review you wrote the "real victory is to such as keep the covenant and remember his precepts to do them," I rose from my chair and pranced. For a number of critics and readers had laid it on me that I'd written of the triumph of materialism. (As a matter of fact I didn't write the book to prove any point, to show any moral, to either low-rate or praise my section. I tried to write a simple story of what happened with few if any comments.)

For those who kept the covenant, they won. For those who didn't— well, they won, too. At least they won what they thought they wanted. How pleased I was that you picked up this idea!

And how happy I was that you were impressed enough by Rhett's

---

[1] Commager reviewed *GWTW* in the New York *Herald Tribune Books* July 5.

remarks about the upside-down world to quote them in full.[2] For in that paragraph lies the genesis of my book and that genesis lies years back when I was six years old and those words minus the reference to Ashley Wilkes were said to me. They were said to me not by a materialist but by one of the most idealistic people I ever knew but an idealist with a very wide streak of common sense, my mother. I didn't want to go to school. I couldn't work arithmetic (I still can't) and I saw no value at all in an education. And Mother took me out on the hottest September day I ever saw and drove me down the road toward Jonesboro—"the road to Tara" and showed me the old ruins of houses where fine and wealthy people had once lived. Some of the ruins dated from Sherman's visit, some had fallen to pieces when the families in them fell to pieces. And she showed me plenty of houses still standing staunchly.

And she talked about the world those people had lived in, such a secure world, and how it had exploded beneath them. And she told me that my own world was going to explode under me, some day, and God help me if I didn't have some weapon to meet the new world. She was talking about the necessity of having an education, both classical and practical. For she said that all that would be left after a world ended would be what you could do with your hands and what you had in your head. "So for God's sake, go to school and learn something that will stay with you. The strength of women's hands isn't worth anything but what they've got in their heads will carry them as far as they need to go." Well, I never could learn the multiplication table above the sevens but I was frightened and impressed enough by her words to learn enough rhetoric to land a job on a newspaper some years later!

You were good to Scarlett, understanding her so well and crediting her with what she had instead of what she didn't have. I think your paragraph of summation beginning that she wanted to be her mother's child but wasn't is perfectly marvelous and I look at it and wonder why I couldn't have thought of writing it myself! I thanked God as I read along that you accepted characters for what they were and not what they should be. And I wondered if you accepted people, too, in so realistic a manner. I have been so set upon by readers who wanted to know

[2] GWTW, p. 772: "Ashley Wilkes—bah! His breed is of no use or value in an upside-down world like ours. Whenever the world up-ends, his kind is the first to perish. And why not? They don't deserve to survive because they won't fight—don't know how to fight. This isn't the first time the world's been upside down and it won't be the last. It's happened before and it'll happen again. And when it does happen, everyone loses everything and everyone is equal. And then they all start again at taw, with nothing at all. That is, nothing except the cunning of their brains and the strength of their hands. But some people, like Ashley, have neither cunning nor strength or, having them, scruple to use them. And so they go under, and they should go under."

why I didn't make Scarlett do this or that or think this or that and why
I ended it the way I did and wouldn't a happy ending have been both
pleasanter and more logical? that it was so pleasant to read your summing up of her.

What in the world am I going to say to you about the lead of your
review,[3] about my philosophy and my ability to create character and
narrative vigor and all the other fine things you attribute to me? I can
think of nothing to say as I have a very strong notion that they can't be
true or that I'm dreaming it all. I expect momentarily to wake up and
find myself back on the Atlanta Journal, tugging wildly at my hair and
listening to my editor's oft repeated statements that I wouldn't be sitting
in that seat if it wasn't that men reporters always got drunk and didn't
show up for work and always had women no better than they should be
phoning them at all hours. . . .

You speak of my book not "ruffling your historical feather." Thanks
for that. I positively cringed when I heard that you a historian were
going to review me. I cringed even though I knew the history in my tale
was as water proof and air tight as ten years of study and a lifetime of
listening to participants would make it. Historians, like those who deal
in the exact sciences, are prone to be tough!

I should have ended this letter long ago but I cannot close without
telling you how much I liked "Theodore Parker."[4] I liked him, I mean it,
first because it held me through a bad spell of insomnia not long ago.
I have long since stopped traffic with notions of getting to sleep when a
four-day spell sets in. I think only of ways to divert myself until the spell
passes. And diversion is hard because I can't read fiction at such times
for it won't hold me and I'm so tough about biographies that they can't
hold me either. But "Theodore" was marvelous, both as a diversion and
as swell reading. The parts about the fugitive slaves I liked best and
reread. I was interested in the parts about Parker knowing all the theory
of slavery and little of the real side of it. I was interested in what went
into the background of an abolitionist. And I smiled as always at the
mention of the Grimké sisters.[5] For here in Atlanta there is a family who
are about my best friends. They are most unreconstructedest of Rebels
imaginable. And contrary to Northern belief Southerners can get pretty
tired of their own unreconstructed's goings-on.

Unfortunately this poor family numbers among their collateral kin the
Grimké girls and when ever they get too unreconstructed and talk about

[3] His review begins: "This novel is the prose to 'John Brown's Body,' and the
theme is the same."

[4] Commager, *Theodore Parker* (Boston, 1936).

[5] Angelina Emily and Sarah Moore Grimké, originally of Charleston, Quaker
converts who were antislavery crusaders and advocates of women's rights.

how grandpa did this and great uncle did that, we slyly introduce the
Grimké girls into the conversation. It always has the same effect of a
bastard at a family reunion and for hours we hear about how they were
not really close kin but steenth cousins, how they had always been considered mentally unbalanced!

Miss Virginia Morris   Atlanta, Georgia
New York, New York   July 11, 1936

Dear Ginnie:
    The hell you say, I use to borrow your tooth brush! Everybody at
Smith College was under the impression that you never owned a tooth
brush.
    I don't know where the rumor started that I turned down 40,000
smackers from the movies. It seems a very widespread rumor, but there
is no truth in it. Now I ask you, can you imagine poor folks like me turning down $40—much less $40,000?
    Weren't the New York reviewers wonderful to me? I am still so breath-
less that my tongue is dry—and I thank you so much for saying that you
like my book.
    I will write you more later when life settles down—if it ever does.
For two weeks I have been running like a rabbit.

Dr. Thomas H. English   Atlanta, Georgia
Emory University, Georgia   July 11, 1936

Dear Doctor English:
    I was certainly set up at the very notion of you wanting my manu-
script for the Emory collection. I never thought I would be invited into
such distinguished company.
    Unfortunately, I still do not have my manuscript as the publishers
have not returned it, and unfortunately, too, I want to keep the manuscript; and if I did not want it, John and my father and my brother would
skin me alive if I parted with it. I do thank you for the honor of being
invited, for it is indeed an honor, but I just cannot part with the first
"baby."

Miss Fanny Butcher   Atlanta, Georgia
Chicago, Illinois   July 11, 1936

My dear Miss Butcher:

There are so many things in your review of my book "Gone With the Wind"[1] that I want to say "thank you" about. But I'm going to content myself with saying "thank you" for the observation that pleased me most.

In your lead you spoke of the "spirit" of the period and how it was recorded "not from the point of view of a historian looking back but from that of a contemporary participating." How very fine of you to say that and how happy it made me! For that's exactly what I set out to do whether or not I achieved my purpose. And a lot of the brickbats I've received since the day I went on sale have been because reviewers seemed to miss that very point. So they point out a number of things I didn't do, a number of obvious lacks in the book. Some of them want more propaganda (don't ask me for what!), some think I missed the great sociological and economic feeling of the day, some say—oh, never mind! But I ask you, when you are trying to see an era, day by day, incident by incident through the eyes of a woman who was not an analyst, when you try to record what she saw and thought and felt, not what you would see and think and feel—then how are you going to work in propaganda and sociology and "mass movements"? Poor Scarlett's lil ole brain would sure have busted had she tried to think of "mass movements"!

So thank you for bringing out that point. Yes, it was tough going writing it from the participant point of view, rather than the omniscient looking-backward point of view.

Dr. Mark Allen Patton   Atlanta, Georgia
Virden, Illinois   July 11, 1936

My dear Dr. Patton:

Your letter was such a joy to me for so many reasons and I will go into the reasons later. Your letter wasn't the kind of letter which I could answer with a "dear sir, thank you so much etc." So I waited until today when I had cleared out a lot of work and had some time to answer you. For it is a pleasure to write to you, even as it was a pleasure to get your letter. How can you speak of yourself as being a "pest"?

[1] Miss Butcher reviewed *GWTW* in the Chicago *Tribune* July 4.

I gave a yelp of delight and leaped up and pranced at your remarks about "War and Peace." And behind that statement lies a small story. So many critics have been kind enough, flattering enough to bracket "Gone With the Wind" with "War and Peace," saying of course that it didn't approach it but was the nearest thing to it they could think of. I've read review after review saying the same thing and have realized with a sense of growing horror that eventually I'm going to *have* to read "War and Peace."

You say you read it twice to figure what it meant. I'm in a worse state than that. I've never read it. Once, in adolescence, I'd have died before I'd have admitted that. In fact I recall that during adolescence I used to talk learnedly and at great length about Tolstoy and the other Russian writers, when I hadn't read a one of them. But one of the great joys of growing up, of getting older is being able and unafraid to speak your own mind. And maturity descended upon me in the very moment when I frankly said that I thought Tolstoy and most of the Russian writers were the damned dullest, most muddled headed, confused thinking bunch I'd ever tried to read. Well do I recall the horror in our "little group of serious thinkers" at this admission!

I did try to read "War and Peace." I tried time and again but there's something about the Russian mind, as it shines through their literature, at least, that defies me. In so many of them, I sense a confusion of mind back of their words, an uncertainty of thought, a groping after God-knows-what and a violent, youthful delight in the hopeless and the sordid. Well, I started out to be a doctor, either a neurologist or a psychiatrist, and I never got there because I had to leave college and keep house for the family when my mother died. But I've read all I could, tried to keep up and have, unofficially and without a license, practiced on my friends. (I mean that as a joke of course but I mean it seriously, too.)

And in the course of growing up in the Jazz Age and living through the depression, I've seen so much of confused thinking, been so impatient with minds that couldn't start at the beginning of things and work them through logically to the end etc., that when I sit down to read I don't want to have to read about muddled minds even if the muddled minds *are* muddling along in lovely prose!

The foregoing seems as muddled minded as can be as I reread it but perhaps it will give you some notion as to why I can't read the Russians.

And I did like what you said about style being like music, that the reader should be as unaware of it as a listener is to the notes of a well played musical composition. Such has been my humble belief for many years but it is a belief I share largely with myself. Just as I don't like the Russians, I'm not very fond of stylists either, James Branch Cabell and a few others excepted. Perhaps it's a hangover from my newspaper days but I always felt that if your story and characters weren't strong enough to stand up against stripped and bare prose, then those characters and that story had better be abandoned. I'm not a stylist, God knows, and couldn't be, if I tried. Moreover, I sweat blood to keep my style as bare as a law report, as uncolored as the newspaper versions of a hit-and-run accident.

I know I was going to be hammered on for my lack of style and I was and it didn't hurt a bit. As a matter of fact, I was so grateful for all the fine things the critics said about me that I hardly noticed that they said my "style was undistinguished" until my father blew up. He is a lawyer of the careful, cautious old fashioned kind. He's a Phi Beta Kappa, a great reader and the most brilliant man I'll ever know. And he shouted, "What do they mean, 'undistinguished style'? Good heavens, I can actually understand every word you write without having to read it twice! In this day and time that amounts to sheer genius!"

I wrote above that I was so grateful to the critics. You see, I wasn't expecting them to say *anything* good. I had written the book nearly ten years ago and had had it put away and thought it too rotten to try to sell. And after an editor came down here last year and pried it out of me, I nearly perished with misery as I realized in what a vulnerable spot I had put myself. Why good heavens! Every reviewer in the U.S. would shoot me full of holes! So when so many of them said such nice things, who was I to quibble about my undistinguished style? But I think you were very kind to take up for my style and to disagree with Miss Butcher's review. And I feel very close to you because you voice the same notions about easy reading that my family, all great readers, voice.

You said so many nice things about the book and the characters and the way the narrative held up that I hardly know how to thank you adequately. But I must say thank you for wanting to put me next to the Forsyte Saga. That's the best compliment I've had so far!

You asked if Tara and the characters really existed. No, they all came out of my head with the exception of the little black maid, "Prissy." But I picked them all because they were pretty representative of the type of people I've heard about who lived in Atlanta in the Sixties. Practically all the incidents in the book are true. Of course, they didn't all happen to the same person and a few of them didn't happen in Atlanta. The shooting of the Yankee bummer, for instance, did not take place on Sherman's March but on General Wilson's Raid, over in Alabama. But it could as easily have happened in Georgia and in Clayton county. Of course I had to tone down numbers of the incidents to make them barely credible, so I get a loud laugh when reviewers speak of the book being too melodramatic. For any one who cares to study that period, there lies the discovery that melodrama is too mild a word to use! ...

Mr. and Mrs. Stephen Vincent Benét　　　　　　　Atlanta, Georgia
New York, New York　　　　　　　　　　　　　July 23, 1936

Dear Mr. and Mrs. Benét:

Your letters were waiting here for me when I came home from the mountains yesterday and they gave me great pleasure—just about as much pleasure as the review did, and that's saying a lot.

Thanks for all the kind words about the book moving and being "like the books one reads when one is young." When I read that my mind went back a great number of years to the books that I used to smuggle into bed and read, under the covers, by a flash light and they were "The Three Musketeers" and all those marvelous novels of Lever, "Harry Lorriker," "Charles O'Malley" and the improving works of Mr. Bulwer-Lytton which did not seem at all improving then, and Jules Verne and "With Fire and Sword" and "Pan Michael." Thanks for putting me in such good company. I'd feel mighty happy if I knew that some small girl was ruining her eyes reading my book under cover by flash light!

You asked if I ever came to New York—and if I came, would I come to see you. Would I? Oh, most foolish of questions! I can think of nothing that would make me happier. The only draw back is that I do not know when I will come to New York. I had intended to go North this Autumn to see some shows and call on old friends but now I do not think I'll make the trip. Not until I'm off the best seller list, at any rate. I asked the man at the local Macmillan Company if he didn't think I'd be off the list by September and he said I might stay on until Christmas but then publishers are always optimistic.

Of course I know New York would not be as bad as Atlanta for after all this is my home town and everyone has been kind enough to put the big pot in the little one for me. But recent events have made me timid of crowds and strangers who ask peculiar and very personal questions and reporters who persist in describing me as a brunette when I have red hair and blue eyes. So I thought I'd wait till after I'd stopped being a best seller and then make my trip so that I could see the few people I really wanted to see.

And I very much want to see you two. Please don't forget me. I'll let you know when I do come to New York.

Miss Kate Duncan Smith   Atlanta, Georgia
The Birmingham News   July 24, 1936
Birmingham, Alabama

My dear Miss Smith:

What a lovely letter yours was and how happy it made me, especially the part about my book seeming an authentic picture of the South and of Southerners. I take lots more satisfaction in reading such words than I would in reading that some N.Y. critic had cried aloud that I had indeed written the Great American Novel. (And may I add hastily that none of them have cried just these words although they have been most kind.) But I did want Southerners to like the book and I would have curled up like a salted slug if they hadn't. And so, thank you for that statement and for all the other nice things you wrote me.

And now about the radio review. I must cast myself upon your mercy and do some explaining which I hope you will understand. I was not cut out to make speeches or public appearances. I get the jitters just being in crowds and as for opening my mouth for public words—So far, I have made three public appearances and it made me so ill that I was sick in bed. I lost ten pounds, which I could ill afford to lose and had to go away to the mountains to try to recuperate. One speech was to the Librarians Club here. How kind all the librarians were to me! I would never have dared send away my book without checking a million facts and the ladies worked with me like they were paid only to work with me. I spoke to them and even though they were all my friends, all so loving and kind, I was in bed for a week afterward.

And then my old managing editor on the Journal put me on the air with my old boss, Mrs. Perkerson, interviewing me.[1] For a week before the interview life was a Hell indeed and for the week afterward I was in bed. Finally the doctor sent me away and said if I had good sense I'd never speak again. It is not that I do not appreciate their kindness—or yours—in wanting me to speak. It is that I just can't do it. I have so much work to do that I can't afford to be laid out for days.

And another thing—there's really nothing much of interest to be gotten out of me. I realize that when I see poor reporters sweating as they try to get some colorful story from me. My life has been so quiet and so uneventful. There was no romance about my writing my novel. I just sat down and wrote it. I didn't have any exciting experiences in the writing of it nor did I have the usual romantic and distressing experiences

[1] The text of this interview was printed in *The Atlanta Journal Sunday Magazine* July 5, 1936, and reprinted in its "Margaret Mitchell Memorial Issue" December 18, 1949.

of having it rejected by this and that publisher before it was finally accepted. And I had no aim or purpose in writing the book, didn't want to prove a point, point a moral, give a lesson to the world etc. Nor did I have any overwhelming urge to write. As a matter of fact, I hate writing worse than anything in the world and would far rather scrub floors or pick cotton than write.

As an ex-reporter I realize what poor material I am for interview purposes.

I do not think I will be in Birmingham any time in the very near future. I do not think I will go anywhere, except to the mountains, until I am off the best seller list and can be Mrs. John Marsh again instead of Margaret Mitchell. I do hope to visit in Birmingham sometime, however. . . .

Mr. George A. Cornwall　　　　　　　　　Atlanta, Georgia
White Plains, New York　　　　　　　　　July 25, 1936

Dear Mr. Cornwall:

Thank you for your letter and all the fine things you said about the book.

I was most interested in the movie cast you selected—especially because you did not pick Clark Gable as "Rhett." All of my friends are determined that he should play this part, as tho what anyone thought could influence casting directors! Yes, I, too, think Miriam Hopkins would be fine as "Scarlett." She has the looks and, best of all, the voice.

Thank you for saying you will reread the book. Considering the length, that's the finest compliment you could give me.

Mrs. Julia Peterkin　　　　　　　　　Atlanta, Georgia
Fort Motte, South Carolina　　　　　　　　　July 25, 1936

My dear Mrs. Peterkin:

A review such as you gave my book in the July 12 issue of the Washington "Post" surely called for an immediate letter of sincere thanks. And that letter would have been sent to you long ago except that the review only came to my eyes yesterday.

I left town three days after I was published. I'd lost about ten pounds in an alarmingly short time; I felt dreadfully; wept when the phone rang (and it rang every five minutes from can't see till can't see); I was unable to think of even half-way plausible excuses not to address ladies' clubs— in short, I couldn't stand lime light. I had not expected the book to be a best seller. In my wildest imaginings I never thought that anyone except my friends and my relatives would read it. And I thanked the Lord that with the exception of the descendants of T. R. R. Cobb,[1] I had more relatives than anyone in the state. So when the book went over, my surprise and alarm and confusion completed what standing in line at interminable receptions had done.

So I went away to Blowing Rock. I went for three reasons—Mr. and Mrs. Edwin Granberry (he reviewed the book for the N.Y. "Sun") promised me sanctuary, Herschel Brickell of the N.Y. "Post" would be there and, most important, I had heard that you would be in Blowing Rock, too.

I very much wanted to meet you, not only because I had always admired your work and liked you so much when you spoke here in Atlanta[2] but because Mr. Brickell had an advance copy of a Macmillan ad in which you said some mighty fine things about "Gone With the Wind." I didn't know at the time that you had reviewed the book. I thought you'd just contributed that statement out of the kindness of your heart.[3]

Well, you didn't come to Blowing Rock and we were all sorry. And I came home and found laid carefully on the top of my pile of letters and clippings your [review]. My husband knew that would be the most exciting thing that could happen and it was.

It was a marvelous review! I don't know how to say "thank you enough." I so wanted Southerners to like the book. I would have curled up like a salted slug if they hadn't, I suppose, whereas the slings and arrows of an outrageous Yankee critic would have glanced off. I suppose that proves me a provincial lady, indeed, but I can't help it. And I was made so happy by the way you wrote of the background of the book.

---

[1] Thomas Reed Rootes Cobb, Confederate general.

[2] In a letter of June 17 Miss Mitchell wrote Mrs. Peterkin: "I admired you so much that, some years ago when you were present here in Atlanta at a Writers Club dinner, I insisted on being invited. I am not a member of the Writers Club and everyone in town felt just like me and wanted to go and there were not enough tables to go round. But I acted in what is known in these parts as 'plain ugly,' said I'd make my reporter friends who were covering the affair refer to it as a fiasco, a shambles and a holocaust (all those being pet words of my reporter friends) and further more stated that I'd act drunk and crash the party and mortify everyone. So they let my husband and me come. I enjoyed it all so much and you looked just as I had hoped and your voice was so lovely so I acted ugly after the meeting and got to meet you (and I'm sure you won't remember me, of course, but I remember you!)."

[3] Mrs. Peterkin was quoted in Macmillan's advertisements. In her review she said: "It seems to me that 'Gone With the Wind' by Margaret Mitchell is the best novel that has ever come out of the South. In fact, I believe it is unsurpassed in the whole of American writing."

It would take a Southerner to pick that up—such things as "how many types of Southerner there are," and how the gentlemen of the old South disdained the commercialism and industrialism of the North and thereby cut their own throats. No other reviewer—and I have a stack of reviews *that* high here by me—seemed to grasp that. And yet it was, as you said, their way of living that brought about their downfall. It not only took a Southerner to pick that up but someone who knows Southerners and the South as you do.

And no other reviewer seemed to grasp the difference between the old coast sections and the new up-country and I wondered, forlornly, as all writers must wonder occasionally, I suppose, if the fault was altogether mine in not being able to write my thoughts so clearly that they got across. And if they got across to you, then I'm satisfied!

Thank you for saying I was "clear eyed—and without sentimentality." I wasn't aware that I was but I should be, I suppose, now that I think about it. I come of a singularly hardheaded bunch of people. Legal people have a way of being that way. But, to date, I've been the addle-brain of the clan. Now that I think further on the matter, I never recall hearing, from my own people, anything sentimental or nostalgic about the old South. I read that sort of thing in books and poems and memoirs. I never heard it from the survivors of that era. Something had given them a tough way of looking at things.

And when you say the book is a "great book . . . !" Well, words fail me. And when you say there wasn't "a dull page," then all the sweating and rewriting and re-rewriting and cutting and misery I went through seem very much worth while. You've made me awfully happy and I cannot thank you enough.

Mr. Kenneth A. Fowler   Atlanta, Georgia
Yonkers, New York   July 26, 1936

My dear Mr. Fowler:
    . . . When you write me that your review is "inadequate" I feel like taking an oath from Gerald and shouting "God's nightgown!" For if your review[1] is inadequate then I will never get a good review, this side of paradise. I thought it perfectly marvelous and I've about read it to pieces. How can I say "thank you" in enough different ways to show you my real appreciation? How can I make plain to you my pleasure at the fact that you caught so many of the underlying thoughts of the book which I

---

[1] Fowler reviewed *GWTW* in the Mount Vernon, N.Y., *Argus* July 11.

feared I had not written clearly enough? I expected so few kind words about "Gone With the Wind." If I had expected them I suppose I'd have tried to sell it years ago instead of making a fool of myself and practically fighting off Mr. Latham of the Macmillan Company when he first asked to see it. And expecting so little and getting so much is both an exciting and humbling experience.

I won't go down the line, thanking you item-by-item for all the fine things you said or else I'd be practically quoting your review back to you. But I must thank you for what you said about my style. I know it's bare and plain and stripped. It was purposely so, for many reasons, one of which was that I don't like books where the author's personality intrudes. Another reason is that I was brought up to write English simply—so simply, as my Mother said, "that it could be easily read from a galloping horse." And another (perhaps a newspaper heritage!)—I felt that if a story and characters won't hold up under a bare style, then it's just as well to junk the story. So thank you for saying that it held up.

You were nice to pick up that bit about the long visits in the South.[2] Lots of people from out of this section think I was exaggerating or trying to be funny. But those visits were true.

I am sending you the autograph with the greatest pleasure and I'm sending you payment for your review, too. I realize that it's unethical for an author to pay a reviewer before hand but perhaps it's not unethical to pay one after the review is written. And I'm paying you in the coin you deserve, in Confederate money.[3]

How grand of you to say the book might probably become a "classic of American literature"! I wish I could honestly believe that. I'd become unendurable.

Miss Harriet Ross Colquitt   Atlanta, Georgia
Bluffton, South Carolina   August 7, 1936

Dear Miss Colquitt:
    So fine a letter as yours certainly deserved a speedy answer. I apologize for the long delay. To be quite frank, I took to the mountains as soon as my book was published, and have been hiding out there practically ever since. I had no mail forwarded to me as I was not very well, and in need of a rest. Now that I have returned home, my eyes are in such poor

---

[2] *GWTW*, p. 153.
[3] Miss Mitchell had two stanzas of Major S. A. Jonas's "Lines on the Back of a Confederate Note" printed so that they could be pasted on the back of Confederate bills. It was one of these that she sent to Fowler.

condition that I am still not able to read or to write. That is the reason why I have delayed so long in answering your letter. I had hoped to write you personally, instead of being forced to dictate a letter.

Of course, I was very set-up when you said my book should be "compulsory reading for every Yankee." What amazes me is that the Yankees seem to be reading it in large numbers. I certainly never expected that— the most I hoped for was that a few Southerners would like it.

When you ask how I gathered my material, I am at a loss for an answer. I can only say that I grew up with most of it. I have always loved old people, and from childhood listened eagerly to their stories—tucking away in my mind details of rickrack braid, shoes made of carpet, and bonnets trimmed with roosters' tails. I have always liked Southern literature and Southern history, and since I could first read I have read everything I could find on the subject of the Civil war. In later years, I have hunted down private letters and diaries of that period. Somehow, the period of the Sixties always seemed much more real to me than my own era, which Scott Fitzgerald called "The Jazz Age."

Mr. Harold Latham   Atlanta, Georgia
Tannersville, New York   August 13, 1936

Dear Harold:
(Have I called you Harold since you invited me to do so?)

I have been on such a dead run since publication date that I can not recall whether or not I have written you during the past month. At any rate, I call you Harold even though I feel exactly as though I had referred to God Almighty familiarly as "G.A."

I wish I could use the typewriter now, for there are so many thousands of things I want to write you, so many thousands of things I want to thank you for, but unfortunately, the strain of answering hundreds of letters has finished what reading proof did to my eyes. For ten days I have been in a dark room with a black bandage over my eyes, forbidden by the doctor to even think of any kind of work or writing, so this letter will be brief as I have not yet caught the trick of dictating.

But I wanted to ask one question. How did you know six months ago that "Gone With the Wind" would be a success? You remember when you were last in Atlanta you told me that just this thing would happen and I laughed, of course, thinking you were just being very kind. I do not see how you anticipated the enormous sales which have been so unexpected and so bewildering to me. I suppose that is why everyone writes and tells me that you are a genius at publishing, for you have a positively uncanny ability to see what will go over with the public. God knows I never expected to go over at all. A sale of five thousand was the height of my expectations. I know whom to thank for my good fortune, and I do thank you from the bottom of my heart.

Yes, the moving picture deal was closed up about two weeks ago. However, I was ill at the time, and as my eyes were going bad on me I made a quick two-day trip to New York with my brother, who is a lawyer. I went off in lather of rage about the contract, all ready to throw it in the movie company's face. It was the stupidest contract I ever saw, a contract that no rational person could sign, regardless of the amount of money involved. The contract held me liable for so many things, such as damage suits, that I could not sign it. Also, the contract was worded idiotically. In many items it referred to me as the holder of the copyright.

The Selznick lawyers were mighty nice. So were the pretty young ladies in the Selznick office.[1] They smoothed me down. They made concessions and I made concessions and the contract was rearranged so that it was possible for me to sign it. I know, too, whom I have to thank for making this contract possible, and I am thanking you again.

The reviews have been marvelous. What has especially warmed my heart has been the reviews in the small Southern papers. I know nothing more heartening than to have your own people rally around you. This has not always been the case, unfortunately, with Southern writers.

At some indefinite period in the future the doctor will let me use my eyes, and then I will write to you.

Dr. W. T. Oppenhimer   Atlanta, Georgia
Richmond, Virginia   August 14, 1936

Dear Doctor Oppenhimer:

I appreciate so much your letter of praise about "Gone With the Wind." Nothing could please an author more than to know that her book actually made a reader sit up late at night to finish it. . . .

I am simply consumed with curiosity about your remark that Belle Watling should have had a parrot. Should she have had a parrot? Why should she have had a parrot? I have racked my brains. In all my researches into life in the sixties I find nothing about parrots.

---

[1] Dorothy Modisett, Katharine Brown and Harriett Flagg.

Mrs. Julia Peterkin   Atlanta, Georgia
Fort Motte, South Carolina   August 14, 1936

Dear Mrs. Peterkin:
Thank you for your letter and the sound common sense advice it contained. I had no idea I would become a best seller, so of course was completely unprepared for the deluge of ladies' clubs who wished me to speak. However, from the very first invitation, I was determined that no one could or would make me speak, and I have held to that determination. I cannot understand the great American passion for being spoken to. I continue to marvel as the mail mounts up with requests. It is a side of the American nature I had never seen before. People seem to think that because an author can get a book published she can hop up on a minute's notice and make a forty-minute address, but, alas, this is not true in my case.
My husband and I had established a pattern of living that pleased us very much. It was a very quiet pattern, perhaps, but we liked it and we are determined to keep it. Perhaps when I am no longer a best seller we will find it easier to adhere to this pattern. I was glad to have your letter warning me off of the ladies' clubs and lion hunters, for while I personally felt that way, I was very glad to know that someone with a reputation as great as yours felt similarly. It gives me a great deal of comfort.
Forgive me for dictating this letter instead of writing to you. My eyes have finally given out on me and the doctor has ordered a long rest for them.

Mr. Thomas Dixon   Atlanta, Georgia
Raleigh, North Carolina   August 15, 1936

Dear Mr. Dixon:
Your letter of praise about "Gone With The Wind" was very exciting, and the news that you want to write a study of the book was even more exciting. . . .
I was practically raised on your books, and love them very much. For many years I have had you on my conscience, and I suppose I might as well confess it now. When I was eleven years old I decided that I would dramatize your book "The Traitor"[1]—and dramatize it I did in six acts. I played the part of Steve because none of the little boys in the neighborhood would lower themselves to play a part where they had to "kiss any

---

[1] *The Traitor: a Story of the Fall of the Invisible Empire* (New York, 1907).

little ol' girl." The clansmen were recruited from the small-fry of the neighborhood, their ages ranging from five to eight. They were dressed in shirts of their fathers, with the shirt tails bobbed off. I had my troubles with the clansmen as, after Act 2, they went on strike, demanding a ten cent wage instead of a five cent one. Then, too, just as I was about to be hanged, two of the clansmen had to go to the bathroom, necessitating a dreadful stage wait which made the audience scream with delight, but which mortified me intensely. My mother was out of town at the time. On her return, she and my father, a lawyer, gave me a long lecture on infringement of copy-rights. They gave me such a lecture that for years afterward I expected Mr. Thomas Dixon to sue me for a million dollars, and I have had a great respect for copy-rights ever since then.

Mr. Robert C. Taylor   Atlanta, Georgia
New York, New York   August 15, 1936

Dear Mr. Taylor:
    I appreciated your letter about "Gone With The Wind" very much, and was very interested in your remarks about the troop movement before the battle of Chickamauga. I would like to write you at length upon this subject after reconsulting all my authorities. Unfortunately, at present, due to eye strain, I can neither read nor write, so I must pass that up.
    However, I want to give this word of explanation. The whole book was written from the viewpoint of a person living at that time. There was no looking back from the present day—nor was there any historical perspective—and from the viewpoint of a person of that day Longstreet's troops really were "rushed."[1] I know this for I have talked to so many survivors of that era—both the soldiers who came down from Virginia and the civilians who stood in the depot in Atlanta watching the endless troop trains roll past. Invariably the words "rushed" or "hurried" or "raced" were used. Time and again, old ladies have told me, "I stood in the depot in my brightest dress so my husband would recognize me. I held up our baby, who he had never seen, but the trains went by so fast I never saw him, and he told me afterward he did not see me."
    I am very glad to hear from anyone on the historic angle of this book, for I labored a long time over my background, and my bibliography runs into the thousands of volumes. I only wish, as I said before, that I was able at present to consult some of my authorities and cross sabers with you in this matter.

    [1] *GWTW*, p. 278.

Mrs. E. L. Sullivan   Atlanta, Georgia
Metamora, Illinois   August 18, 1936

Dear Mrs. Sullivan:

Your letter wanting to know what happened to Rhett and Scarlett made me very happy indeed for it made me feel that you thought of them as real people and not fictional characters. I wish I could tell you what happened to them both after the end of the book but I cannot, for I know no more about them than you do. I wrote my book from back to front. That is, the last chapter first and the first chapter last and as I sat down to write it that seemed the logical ending. I do not have a notion of what happened to them and I left them to their ultimate fate. With two such determined characters, it would be hard to predict what would happen to them.

You said so many fine things about "Gone With the Wind" that you made me very happy and I want to say thank you for them all.

Mrs. Eleanor Hoyt Witte   Atlanta, Georgia
Little Deer Isle, Maine   August 19, 1936

Dear Mrs. Witte:

That was a very delightful letter you wrote me about "Gone With the Wind" and I appreciated it very much. When you tell me that you have six children and still read that long book, then my appreciation is even greater.

Many people have kidded me about hiding the wallet in Beau's diaper.[1] I have no children of my own but I ask you, as woman to woman, what more logical hiding place could Scarlett have thought of? It would take a brave invader indeed to rifle a baby's diaper!

Dr. Charles E. Mayos   Atlanta, Georgia
East Moline, Illinois   August 22, 1936

Dear Doctor Mayos:

Since my book "Gone With the Wind" was published I have received a number of letters, but none quite as penetrating as yours. I had thought,

[1] *GWTW*, p. 462.

and frequently said with all sincerity, that I had written a purely objective novel—a novel that had nothing of myself or my own experiences in it—then your letter comes and sets me to wondering.

Nothing could have pleased me more than to have a psychiatrist praise the pattern of Scarlett O'Hara's emotional life. I am one of those people who are disliked by all real psychiatrists. I am a layman who knows just a little about abnormal psychology. I started out to be a psychiatrist, but, unfortunately, was forced to leave college when my mother died as I was the only daughter in the family, and was needed at home to keep house. I hoped for years to go back to medical school, and with that idea in view kept up my studies. I realize that I know all the tops of abnormal psychology—and have none of the basic and rudimentary knowledge. It's like knowing geometry and never having known the multiplication tables. Perhaps you can understand, after this explanation, why your words of praise about "The accurate description of human emotions" pleased me so much.

Mr. K. T. Lowe   Atlanta, Georgia
Time Magazine   August 29, 1936
New York, New York

Dear Mr. Lowe:

I regret very much my long delay in answering your wire of August 3 about the desecration of the Atlanta City Cemetery by Federal troops, referred to in my novel "Gone With The Wind."

As my husband wired you, I was ill at the time your telegram arrived. I was, and still am, suffering from severe eye strain due to overwork in finishing my book. Even now, I am unable to read or write. This condition has severely hampered me in checking back through my reference works and assembling the authorities for the statement in question. As you can imagine, in writing a book as long as "Gone With The Wind" my bibliography ran into thousands of volumes. However, with the help of friends, I have been able to get together the data, so that my reply will not be further delayed.

It never occurred to me that the matter of Federal desecration of Southern cemeteries would ever be questioned. In childhood I heard vivid stories from so many different people who had seen the desecrated cemeteries in Atlanta and other cities. However, I am now citing a few authorities.

In the book "Georgia Land and People" by Frances Letcher Mitchell (no relative of mine), published by the Franklin Publishing Company, Atlanta, Georgia, 1893, the following appears on page 348:

"The city (Atlanta) was a desolate ruin. Its cemetery had before this been desecrated in every way—horses were turned loose to graze upon the grass and shrubbery, monuments were broken and scattered around, coffins were taken from the vaults, the silver name-plates and tippings stolen, and Federal dead were deposited there. Similar acts of vandalism had marked the progress of Sherman's army at Rome, which had been partly burned, and at Kingston, Acworth and Marietta."

In "The History of the State of Georgia from 1850 to 1881" by I. W. Avery, published by Brown & Derby, New York City, 1881, the following statement appears on page 307 in the description of the destruction of Atlanta by General Sherman's troops:

"The very dead were taken from their vaults, and the coffins stripped of silver tippings."

Colonel Avery's history is a standard work of great merit, and is considered an authority on this period.

I also want to cite a passage in "The History of Atlanta and Its Pioneers," published Atlanta, Georgia, Byrd Printing Company, 1902, page 96. In this passage, mention is made of the appropriation of funds by the Atlanta City Council in 1865 for the purpose of rebuilding the City Cemetery destroyed by the Federal troops.

As further evidence of the looting of the Atlanta City Cemetery, now known as Oakland Cemetery, I wish to quote from the official report of the Confederate General W. P. Howard, made on December 7, 1864. At this time Sherman's army had marched on to Savannah, and the Confederate forces were reoccupying Atlanta. Governor Joseph E. Brown, of Georgia, ordered General Howard to give him a detailed report of the condition of Atlanta—how many houses burned; how many left standing; the condition of the people, black and white; whether any materials, such as brick and iron, were worth salvaging, etc. General Howard rendered a lengthy and detailed report on all these things. At the end of his report he speaks of the condition of the City Cemetery as follows:

"Horses were turned loose in the cemetery to graze upon the grass and shrubbery. The ornaments of graves, such as marble lambs, miniature statuary, souvenirs of departed little ones, are broken and scattered abroad.

"The crowning act of all their wickedness and villainy was committed by our ungodly foe in removing the dead from the vaults in the cemetery, and robbing the coffins of the silver name plates and tippings, and depositing their own dead in the vaults."

I will not take up your time by listing more books and documents which contain similar statements, but there are very many of them. I hope that this information covers the question.

I hope that my letter does not stir up any sectional bitterness or controversy. I did not write "Gone With the Wind" in any spirit of bitterness. I have been made very happy by the numerous reviews in Northern papers and letters from Northern readers commending the book's freedom from animus and its attitude of fairness. Many people have written me that the book should help to allay sectional feeling by creating a better understanding of what the South endured in the days of the Civil war and Reconstruction. So, I am asking that you make clear to your readers that this letter was written at your request. The evidence cited in it is offered, not as proof of the wickedness of Yankees, but to authenticate a statement in my book.

May I take this opportunity to thank you for the excellent review you gave my book in your issue of July 6? I do not know who wrote it, so I cannot thank him personally, but I would like him to know that I enjoyed it very much. I especially appreciated the fact that the reviewer brought out the differences between the new city of Atlanta and the older cities of the coast.[1]

Miss Ellen Glasgow   Atlanta, Georgia
Harcourt Brace Publishing Co.   September 1, 1936
New York, N.Y.

Dear Miss Glasgow:

I do not believe you can realize how happy your complimentary words about "Gone With the Wind" made me.[1] I have been wanting to write and thank you ever since my husband read them to me. Unfortunately, my eyes have been troubling me greatly for months and I cannot read or write. I have delayed writing you for this cause but will delay no longer to tell you of my appreciation. Your words, coming from a Southerner and from a Southerner whose books I have loved, were very exciting and flattering. I thank you for your kindness.

---

[1] This letter (without the first two and last paragraphs) was published in *Letters,* II, No. 19 (September 14, 1936), p. 2.

---

[1] A Macmillan advertisement in the New York *Times* June 30 quotes Miss Glasgow: "The book is absorbing. It is a fearless portrayal, romantic yet not sentimental, of a lost tradition and a way of life."

Mr. George Ward   Atlanta, Georgia
Birmingham, Alabama   September 1, 1936

Dear Mr. Ward:

I am Margaret Mitchell, daughter of Eugene Mitchell, to whom you sent the wonderful copy of your mother's testimony.[1] Due to trouble with my eyes, I have been unable to read all of it, as I must wait until my husband has time to read it to me. But how I have enjoyed it! And how wonderfully interesting I have found it!

I hope you will not think me foolishly enthusiastic when I write you that I think your mother's testimony is undoubtedly the most perfect and valuable and complete picture of a long gone day that I have come across in ten years of research into the period of the Sixties. If I had had that book, I am sure I would not have had to read hundreds of memoirs, letters and diaries to get the background of "Gone With the Wind" in accurately. Moreover, the character of your mother, her wit, her common sense, her charm simply leap from the pages. How I wish I could have known her!

I am going to make a request of you and I hope that you will be completely frank in refusing if you do not feel agreeable to the request. I should like so much to have two copies of this wonderful document, one to keep in my own library, the other to place in the Reference Department of our Carnegie Library. I feel that so valuable a book should be where the children of the South could have access to it. If you would give me the name and address of the Washington, D.C., firm who have the photostatic negatives, I would write to them and have them make me two copies.

If, for any reason, you do not wish your mother's testimony to go out of your hands and into those of strangers, please tell me so and I will understand.

May I keep the little book a while longer? I hope my husband will find time to finish it for me this week. . . .

---

[1] The testimony is that of Mrs. Margaret Ketcham Ward before a committee of the Senate taken at Relay House, Birmingham, November 15, 1883. It appears in U.S. Congress, Senate, Committee upon Relations Between Labor and Capital, *Report . . . and Testimony Taken Before the Committee . . .* (Washington, 1885), IV, 311–47. Mrs. Ward's testimony has twice been reprinted in small editions, as *War Memories* (Birmingham, 1936) and as *Testimony of Mrs. George R. Ward* (Birmingham, 1965).

Mr. Stark Young   Atlanta, Georgia
Ridgefield, Connecticut   September 1, 1936

My dear Mr. Young:

Thank you so much for your letter. The thought that prompted it was both kind and considerate. However, I must tell you that it never occurred to me that you had anything to do with the review of "Gone With the Wind" which was published in The New Republic.[1] From reading all your books and hearing the Herschel Brickells talk of you, I feel that I know a little, at least, about what kind of a person you are. Your letter proves how correct my opinion was!

I would not have taken offense even if I had thought you did have something to do with Mr. Bishop's review, because I thought it a very good one. Of course, he thought it was necessary, before he finished, to chide me for not concerning myself with social significances, mass movements and economic problems, but I suppose that was to be expected in The New Republic, which apparently believes that "if it isn't propaganda, it isn't art." My book was not interested in propaganda, but attempted only to be a story. In view of the fact that The New Republic and I have such different viewpoints, my opinion, when I read Mr. Bishop's review, was that the magazine had done rather well by me. . . .

I did not read "So Red the Rose" when it came out.[2] I was afraid to read it. I had been foolish enough to read "John Brown's Body" while I was working on my own book and it gave me such an attack of the humbles that it was months before I could write again. I felt that if I read "So Red the Rose" I would never even try to finish my book. Now I am so glad I waited, for when I did read your book later I saw that my idea was right. You do so beautifully all the things I wanted to do and do them with such ease, that I am sure my inferiority complex would have swamped me and "Gone With the Wind" would never have gone to press. I won't try to tell you on paper how marvelous I thought "So Red

---

[1] John Peale Bishop reviewed *GWTW* in the *New Republic* July 15. His review is "mixed," balancing favorable and unfavorable comments. *GWTW*, he says in summary, is "neither very good nor very sound. The historical background is handled well and with an extraordinary sense of detail. The moral problem is less sure in its treatment. It is this: In a society falling apart, upon what terms can the individual afford to survive? Scarlett wants only to last and takes any terms life offers. Miss Mitchell seems to approve of her persistence. But she also implies that civilization consists precisely in an unwillingness to survive on any terms save those of one's own determining." Bishop declares that Miss Mitchell used Scarlett and Rhett "to assert indirectly the virtues of the society whose destruction they witness. By this device, she has clearly hoped to avoid sentimentality in treating a subject she fears as sentimental."

[2] Stark Young, *So Red the Rose* (New York, 1934).

the Rose" was. I hope I will get the chance some day to tell you personally.

Dr. Mark Millikin   Atlanta, Georgia
Hamilton, Ohio   September 3, 1936

Dear Dr. Millikin:

Your letter about "Gone With the Wind" gave me so much pleasure. I appreciated it especially as it came from one who has obviously given much thought to the history of the period of which I wrote. You were very kind to suggest that I go on with a saga but, just at present, I feel that I will never write anything again. Certainly, I don't want to.

No, I did not see "Tobacco Road" but I read the book.[1] When I read it I thought it was intended for a grand parody on the gloomy Russian novelists and I laughed almost as much as I did over "Gentlemen Prefer Blondes."[2] Shortly afterwards, I learned it was supposed to be stark realism and must admit I was somewhat bewildered!

If you only knew how much it means to an author to know that her book struck a responsive chord! Thank you for your letter.

Miss Katharine Brown, Story Editor   Atlanta, Georgia
Selznick International Pictures, Inc.   September 3, 1936
New York, New York

Dear Miss Brown:

You and Miss Modisett must have thought me several kinds of a varmint for not writing you sooner to thank you for what you did in the matter of the sale of "Gone With the Wind" and also for your many courtesies to me. I have delayed writing you in the hope that I could write you personally but can delay no longer and so must struggle through a dictated letter. Dictation is new and strange and fearsome to me.

My eyes were so bad when I was in New York that I could barely see. That was the reason for my unmannerly desire to get the contract closed up immediately. I had overstrained my eyes badly on the proof reading of the book and had about finished them on the heavy correspondence

---

[1] Erskine Caldwell, *Tobacco Road* (New York, 1932). It was made into a play by Jack Kirkland in 1933 and had a Broadway run of 3,182 performances.
[2] Anita Loos, *Gentlemen Prefer Blondes* (New York, 1925).

that followed the publication of the book. At the time I went to New York I was supposed to be in bed in a dark room, giving them a complete rest. Since I saw you last that's what I have been doing and it has been a wearisome and boring period of time.

Thank you both so much for your enthusiasm about the book, your cordiality to me—and the cocktails! Being a "Provincial Lady" and coming from a state that has been bone dry for about fifty years, that cocktail was about the first legal cocktail I ever drank!

Miss Dorothy W. Brown　　　　　　　　　　　　Atlanta, Georgia
Beverly Hills, California　　　　　　　　　　　September 5, 1936

Dear Miss Brown:

Thank you so much for your letter about "Gone With the Wind." For an author to get a letter from a book reviewer is high praise indeed. I appreciated so much all the fine things you said about the book, and only wish I were in a position to write you a more detailed letter but, having strained my eyes badly in the final proof reading of the book, I am having to dictate letters, and this cramps my style somewhat.

However, I would like to briefly answer some of the questions you brought up in your letter. No, I am not writing a sequel. I have no intention of writing a sequel. At present, if I keep my sanity, I have no intention of ever writing anything again.

No, the title did not come from the Bible. Frankly, it came from sheer desperation and the second verse of Ernest Dowson's poem "Cynara."[1] The title, of course, has no connection with the poem. I had submitted dozens of titles to the publishers, and they would have none of them. They had submitted titles to me which brought screams of anguish from me. Just as we were going to press titleless, I picked "Gone With the Wind." They accepted it.

With the exception of feature articles written while I was a reporter on the Atlanta Journal, I have never written anything else. I had never even submitted "Gone With The Wind" to any publisher. I know the rumor is abroad that I took an enormously long time writing this book. The truth is that I could have written it in a fairly short while, had I had uninterrupted time, but during the years when I was trying to finish it,

---

[1] The title phrase appears in the first line of the third stanza of Ernest Dowson's "*Non sum qualis eram bonae sub regno Cynarae*": "I have forgotten much, Cynara! gone with the wind." The poem was first printed in the *Century Guild Hobby Horse* for April 1891 and has been reprinted widely. It may be found in Dowson's *Cynara: A Little Book of Verse* (Portland, Me., 1907), pp. 3-4.

there was so much illness in my family and all my friends had babies or divorces, and there would be months when I would not have a minute to call my own. . . .

Mrs. Herschel Brickell   Atlanta, Georgia
Ridgefield, Connecticut   September 18, 1936

Dear Norma:

For some time I have been wanting to thank you all over again for the fan you gave me the night I arrived at Acorn Cottage. The weeks when I was laid up with bandages were very hot weeks. To make the heat even more oppressive, all the shades were down. I did not dare use the electric fan, for fear it would make me sneeze and I was forbidden both sneezing and coughing. So your fan was a Godsend. I practiced fanning myself in the most elegant manner. I also learned how to close it with the most terrific clacking noise. I found this noise most gratifying.

I never told you how much I appreciated you taking me in and being so nice when I was in a state. I know you and Herschel must think me both a Grade A neurotic and a complete invalid, for he met me when I had had no sleep for a week and you met me when my eyes were so bad it hurt to look at anything. I only hope I get to see both of you when I am normal. Alas, I am the most normal of creatures. Sometimes when I reflect upon this, I realize I can never become truly great, not being abnormal and having no temperament.

I had a letter from Stark Young this morning. Such a grand letter that, of course, I fell in love with him immediately. I suppose all the literary ladies do the same thing but I do not feel depressed about it. You told me that he "did not like well people." Then what will I do if I ever meet him when my eyes are well? However, if he is as charming as he sounds, I will have a nervous breakdown if it will endear me to him. . . .

Well, life goes merrily on. The mail mounts and mounts. Special deliveries wake us at dawn, demanding to know if Scarlett ever got him back, registered letters get us from the supper table demanding the same information. The phone goes on and on, people boldly asking me my age, my royalties, can I get their cook in the movies in "my" film, am I a Catholic? And why haven't I any children? Am I kin to them? They had a cousin named Margaret Mitchell. How can they find the road to Tara? They went to Jonesboro last week end and nobody could tell them how to get there. But so *many* people had told them positively that two of the wings of Tara were still standing. (When I say I made it up, they refuse to believe because they've seen so many people who've seen Tara and they think I'm pretty ungracious not to direct them there.) And is it true that I was born the last year of the Civil War? Then is that picture they publish a picture of my Granddaughter? Most of the time Bessie[1] answers the phone. I'd as soon pick up a snake as the receiver. But Bessie is [not] here lots of the time and so I get caught, thinking it's John on the wire or Western Union. It is appalling the barefaced questions people will ask. I thought I had learned most of the peculiarities of mankind while I was a reporter but this is an education. After all, when I was a reporter I only saw criminals, prize fighters, politicians, debutantes and fatigued celebrities. It was seldom that I met the sturdy middle classes. If I could just gain about fifteen pounds I could stand meeting them a bit better. . . .

Miss Katharine Brown　　　　　　　　　　　　　Atlanta, Georgia
New York, New York　　　　　　　　　　　　　September 23, 1936

Some days ago I received a letter from Miss Annie Laurie Williams in which she said that Mr. Selznick wanted me to come to Hollywood about the script of "Gone With the Wind." I regret very much my delay in answering this letter but I have been ill. I was also having so much trouble with my eyes that I could neither read nor write. The truth of the matter is, I did not even see the letter until a day or so ago.

It will be impossible for me to go to Hollywood, for many reasons. The main ones are the two stated above, my health and my eyes. If I go anywhere at all during the coming six months, it will be a brief trip of two or three days, to New York. The Macmillan Company wish to give me a tea. Until my eyes are better and I can gain ten or more pounds, I won't even get to New York. Another reason for not going to Hollywood is that I simply hate traveling and hate to leave Atlanta even for a day or two.

You said, at the time of the signing of the contract, that someone from your organization might come to Atlanta. If they do, please don't forget that I'd be glad to do all in my power to assist them in any way. Should you wish to communicate with me about this or any other matter, will you please write me directly, instead of through Miss Williams? She is not my agent. The Macmillan Company was my agent for the sale of the motion picture rights in my novel, and I understand that they employed Miss Williams to assist them in the transaction.

---

[1] Bessie Berry, later Jordan.

Dr. William Lyon Phelps   Atlanta, Georgia
New Haven, Connecticut   September 23, 1936

My dear Dr. Phelps;

I am Margaret Mitchell of Atlanta, author of "Gone With the Wind." Some days ago when I was lying in a dark room with a black bandage over my eyes, regretting very much that I had ever written that book and strained my eyes, I turned on the radio. I had never had a radio until I was forced to stop reading and writing and I was so tired of hill-billy songs that I hesitated to spin the dial. But I did and to my intense excitement heard a newspaper commentator call my name. Of course, I practically laid my ear on the radio and was never so thrilled as to hear him say that you had judged "Gone With the Wind" the best novel of the year.[1] In that minute I recovered from my regret at having written it, even if it did put my eyes out of commission for several months.

You were so kind to do this and I haven't the words to thank you. As one newspaper columnist said, Dr. Phelps' ranking of the novels of the year really means more than the award of the Pulitzer prize. You made my stay in the dark very happy and I just wanted you to know how much your words were appreciated.

I am out in the light now and can see perfectly but cannot read or write for some weeks to come. But I could not delay any longer my thanks to you, so I am dictating this letter and I hope that you do not find it too awkwardly expressed. Dictating is a new experience for me and I doubt if I will ever master the art of making such letters say what I really feel.

Mr. Paul Jordan-Smith   Atlanta, Georgia
Los Angeles, California   September 23, 1936

Dear Mr. Smith:

My clipping bureau, late as usual, sent me today a brief item from the Los Angeles Times of August 23rd. When it was read to me, I nearly fainted from excitement and pleasure, as it said that the writer of the item nominated "Gone With the Wind" for both Pulitzer and Nobel

---

[1] In his annual lecture at Pointe Aux Barques, Mich., Dr. Phelps selected seventy-seven books for favorable comment. *GWTW* was selected as the best novel, and George Santayana's *The Last Puritan* named as second best. H. L. Mencken's *The American Language* headed his list of general books and Stephen Vincent Benét's *Burning City* his list of poetry. New York *Evening Post*, August 31.

prizes! There was no by-line on this item and I am wondering if you were the author of it. If you were, and something tells me you were, I thank you from the bottom of my heart and only wish I thought such grand things possible. . . .

Mr. Stark Young Atlanta, Georgia
The New Republic September 29, 1936
New York, N.Y.

My dear Mr. Young:

Your letter was both a comfort—and a disillusionment. I am referring to the part of the letter where you disclaimed the "ease in writing" which I attributed to you. You see, I had believed that established writers, writers who really knew how to write, had no difficulty at all in writing. I had thought that only luckless beginners like myself had to rewrite endlessly, tear up and throw away whole chapters, start afresh, rewrite and throw away again.

I knew nothing about other writers and their working habits and I thought I was the only writer in the world who went through such goings-on. After I had rewritten a chapter ten or twelve times and had what I thought was a workable "first draft," I'd put it away for a month. When I dug it out again I'd beat on my breast and snatch out my hair, because it was so lousy. Then the chapter would be thrown away, because the content of it had not been reduced to the complete simplicity I wanted. Simplicity of ideas, of construction, of words. Then there would be another awful month of substituting Anglo-Saxon derivatives for Latin ones, simple sentence constructions for the more cumbersome Latin constructions.

Then before I went to press I snatched out double hands full of copy, whole chapters. Snatched them out under such pressure that I didn't have time to tie up the severed arteries. In my eyes the book will bleed endlessly and reproachfully.

But I had thought that people who knew how to write just breezed along. Now your letter arrives and disillusions me. Doesn't ease ever come?—However, there is comfort in the knowledge that the author of so many grand books as you didn't just sit down and bang them out. I know that's an Unchristian kind of comfort—the misery loves company kind of comfort—and I should feel guilty about feeling that way but I cannot prod my emotions into a sense of guilt.

You wrote that you didn't usually write about "authors' secrets, etc." Well, neither do I. I never spoke of them to anyone but my husband and

Herschel Brickell. I never thought my book was very good and felt that everybody else would agree enthusiastically with my opinion if I confessed the years of sweating, groaning and rewriting that went into it. So thank you for your friendly remarks. They are a comfort really.

About the review in the September 16th New Republic—I sent out and bought it as soon as I got your letter. It was a joy, wasn't it? I had had a cheerless day and that review brought cries of joy from me. A number of friends called during the day and each one read it aloud with joy equal to mine. When they'd read the part about the legend of the old South being "false in part and silly in part and vicious in its general effect on Southern life today" they'd throw themselves on the sofa and laugh till they cried.[1]

I suppose I must lack the exquisite sensitivity an author should have. Otherwise, I should be upset by such criticism. But the truth of the matter is that I would be upset and mortified if the Left Wingers liked the book. I'd have to do so much explaining to family and friends if the aesthetes and radicals of literature liked it. Why should they like it or like the type of mind behind the writing of it? Everything about the book and the mind are abhorrent to all they believe in. One and all they have savaged me and given me great pleasure. However, I wish some of them would actually read the book and review the book I wrote—not the book they imagine I've written or the book they think I should have written.

---

[1] Malcolm Cowley wrote in this review: " 'Gone With the Wind' is an encyclopedia of the plantation legend. Other novelists by the hundreds have helped to shape this legend but each of them has presented only a part of it. Miss Mitchell repeats it as a whole, with all its episodes and all its characters and all its stage settings—the big white-columned house sleeping under its trees among the cotton fields; the band of faithful retainers, including two who faintly resemble Aunt Jemima and Old Black Joe; the white-haired massa bathing in mint juleps . . . it is all here, every last bale of cotton and bushel of moonlight, every last full measure of Southern female devotion working its lilywhite fingers uncomplainingly to the lilywhite bone.

"But even though the legend is false in part and silly in part and vicious in its general effect on Southern life today, still it retains its appeal to the fundamental emotions. Miss Mitchell lends new strength to the legend by telling it as if it had never been told before, and also by mixing a good share of realism with the romance. She writes with a splendid recklessness . . . I would never, never say that she has written a great novel, but in the midst of triteness and sentimentality her book has a simple-minded courage that suggests the great novelists of the past. No wonder it is going like the wind."

Of this Young wrote Miss Mitchell on September 14: "And now by the way I see in the last New Republic they are at it again. And Malcolm has it all finally wrong about the book's including the entire plantation legend etc.—the house with columns, of massa, magnolias etc.; when as a matter of fact *a part of the freshness of your choice* lay in your choosing the upstate region . . . I'll take this up with Malcolm sooner or later (and perhaps in the January Virginia Quarterly, but it's no use saying anything at present. The *New Republic,* along with other knowledges, knows more about the South than you or I do.)"

From Mr. Broun, who calls it "sweetly Southern,"[2] to (I can't remember the reviewer's name) who announced that I had missed all the sociological implications and mass movements, they have reviewed ideas in their own heads—not ideas I wrote.

By the way, isn't Malcolm Cowley the man Ernest Boyd and Burton Rascoe wrote about in Boyd's "Portraits: Real and Imaginary"?[3] I have a vague memory of a delightful passage about a young man named Cowley, recognizing his "portrait" and throwing stink bombs on Mr. Boyd.

You were sweet to think of offering your Viennese doctor to me. The offering of one's own doctor is the ultimate in friendliness, I think. But I didn't—and do not—need any doctor except an eye specialist. When the proof reading ordeal was on, I fell far behind my dead line, due to illnesses and deaths in my family. To catch up I had to work twenty hours a day for weeks. My eyes were never much good and this treatment did not help them. After the book was published, there was never a chance to rest them, never a chance for me to rest and regain my lost weight. The New York trip was a last straw and I came home with my eyes looking like two fried eggs. They are better now, after many weeks in bed. That is, I can see all right but cannot read or write and I do not know when I will be able to. This is a bore, as I habitually read not less than three books a day.

I cannot tell you how much your letter meant to me. If I did, I would sound like the gushing Southern Lady Authoress. I can only say that your two letters proved again something I learned when I was a reporter— people who've reached the top in any line are the simplest, kindest, most unassuming and approachable of all humans. But Godalmighty, the second-raters!

Miss Katharine Brown   Atlanta, Georgia
New York, N.Y.   October 1, 1936

Dear Miss Brown:
    I had not forgotten about the copy of "Gone With the Wind" for Mr. Selznick. But I delayed sending it for two reasons, first because I haven't been well enough to stir about much and, second because I wanted to find a first edition for him. The only first editions I can locate are in the hands of my family and my close friends. They become incensed and show their teeth when I suggest they give them up. I haven't even one

² Heywood Broun in the New York *World Telegram*, September 19.
³ Ernest A. Boyd, *Portraits Real and Imaginary* (New York [c. 1924]).

first edition of my own. I never thought the book would sell one-half of one edition, so I didn't lay in a supply. I am mailing an autographed copy to Mr. Selznick today in your care.[1]

Will you please thank Mr. Selznick for me for his renewed invitation for me to go to California. I just do not think that it will be possible. But I am appreciative of the invitation just the same. . . .

Mr. Louis Sobol   Atlanta, Georgia
The New York Evening Journal   October 1, 1936
New York, N.Y.

Dear Mr. Sobol;
I have just received a clipping of your column of Thursday, September 24th, in which you made mention of my book, "Gone With the Wind." I wanted to write you and correct an error in it. I am confident that the error was no fault of yours but it does an injustice to a charming young lady and I feel that it should be corrected.

You state that "Scarlett O'Hara" in the book is modeled after Miss Betty Timmons, of Atlanta. Certainly that is no compliment to any girl, for "Scarlett" was not a very nice person. I am not personally acquainted with Miss Timmons (she is not my niece nor is she a relative of mine) but I know many of her friends and know she is a girl of charm and beauty and character. "Scarlett" was not the same type of person as Miss Timmons and I am distressed that so fine a girl as Miss Timmons should be compared with her. I did not take the character of "Scarlett" from anyone, living or dead.

Mr. Harry Slattery   Atlanta, Georgia
Washington, D.C.   October 3, 1936

My dear Mr. Slattery;
. . . I was very sorry about taking the Slattery name in vain and I think I will explain about it, even at the risk of boring you. As you perhaps know, there are many, many characters in "Gone With the Wind" and just as many names as there are characters. The "checking" of these names was as great a job as the checking of all the historical facts put together.

---

[1] This copy was sold at auction by Christie's, London, in 1971 for £ 225.

For this reason I did not want to use the actual names of anyone living in Clayton County, Fayette County, Savannah, Charleston or Atlanta during the period between 1840 and 1873—the time covered by the story. I did not wish to embarrass anyone now living or make it appear as though I were writing about their kindred, long dead. Not even if the character [bearing] their name was an utterly admirable character, such as "Melanie Wilkes," for instance. I never knew another writer who bothered about this. Most writers just grab a name out of their heads and use it regardless. But I went to infinite pains, first to choose names that while Southern were not peculiar to Atlanta and its surrounding rural territory. Second, I spent weeks and weeks in county court houses checking the names of my characters against tax books, from 1840 to 1873, against deed books, against militia muster rolls, against Confederate muster rolls, against lists of jurymen, against wills and titles. Wherever I found a duplication of names, even if it were only the surname of one of my characters, I changed the character's name, chose another name and started checking all over again. It was, as you can imagine, a wearisome job. In one instance, the name of "Hilton" was changed about a dozen times, necessitating trip after trip to the Jonesboro court house until I was absolutely certain as far as written legal papers could prove it, that no one by the name of Hilton had lived in Clayton County in the period covered by "Gone With the Wind."

So you see why I am so sorry that the matter embarrassed you. Alas, I went to such infinite pains not to embarrass anyone. I was very relieved when Mr. Collier[1] said that your family came from South Carolina instead of Georgia! . . .

P.S.

My letter to you was mislaid under some mail and not posted and I am adding to it. This morning news arrived which upset me so much that I hardly know how to write to you about it. Several letters came to me from strangers, confusing letters, which said that after reading the article in the Washington Post they understood much about "Gone With the Wind" which they had not understood before. They said they had felt that no woman could have written such a book and, after reading in the paper that my husband had collaborated with me in the writing of it, they understood.[2]

[1] Charles Collier, an official of the Georgia Power Company.
[2] A long story in the Washington *Post* of September 29 explained that Slattery had intended to sue Miss Mitchell because of the way in which she had used his family name. "But," declares the *Post*'s story, "an exchange of letters and conversation with the young Atlanta author [have] convinced him . . . that no malice was intended." The story continues: "He told how her tremendous success on her first book has not

I was completely bewildered at this news—bewildered by the very idea that my husband had written any part of "Gone With the Wind"— bewildered about what *had* appeared in the Washington paper. Then a clipping arrived, sent by a friend who knew all about how the book was written and that I alone had written it and then I understood.

I am so upset about this error that I have been unable to do anything but cry ever since I read the clipping. I have given so many years of my life to the writing of this book, injured my eyes, endangered my health and this is my payment—that I didn't write it! And I did write it, every word of it. My husband had nothing whatever to do with it. In the first place he is not a Georgian (he was born in Kentucky) and no one but a Georgian with generations of Georgian ancestors could have written it. In the second place, he has a very responsible position and works very hard and he seldom gets time to play golf much less write books.

In fact, he never even read the whole of my manuscript until after the Macmillan Company had bought it. It was not that I didn't want him to read it. It was because the book was not written with the second chapter following the first, and the third following the second. It was written last chapter first and so on until the first chapter was written last—written, in fact several months after the book was sold. My husband could not be expected to catch the continuity of the story when I could only give him scattered chapters to read, which, to him, did not connect up.

Not all the financial rewards I may receive can make up to me for this. Moreover it puts me in such a dreadful light before the world—that I had concealed my husband's work on this book. And he actually had no part in it except helping me with the proof reading when my eyes gave out and my deadline was upon me.

Mr. Slattery, can you not ask the paper for a retraction of the statement that my husband collaborated with me in the writing of "Gone With the Wind"? Of course, the story has already gone out into the world, to rise up and plague me all of my life but a retraction would help some. You see, it is my whole professional reputation which is at stake—my reputation which has been ruined through no fault of my own. I am so distressed about all this that I do not know what to do. Will you please write me as soon as you can about it? I would appreciate it.

---

altered her balance. 'She still cooks breakfast in her little flat in Atlanta and he keeps on working at his job, in spite of the fact that they suddenly came into a fortune. Atlantans have tried to fete and exploit them—they wrote the book in collaboration over a period of seven years—but they keep their heads and decline all the invitations.' " Additional gross inaccuracies in the *Post's* interview with Slattery, Under Secretary of Interior, are ignored in this letter by Miss Mitchell.

Miss Katharine Brown   Atlanta, Georgia
New York, N.Y.   October 6, 1936

Dear Miss Brown:
    I hope you will let me know as far ahead as possible when and if Mr.
Cukor[1] is coming to Atlanta. As I told you, I am very anxious to be here
then. However, I have ahead of me a trip to New York for the Macmillan's tea, just as soon as my eyes are in good condition again. When this
will be, I do not know, so my plans are somewhat uncertain.
    I want to render any aid possible to Mr. Cukor. For that reason, I am
writing you this information. Mr. Wilbur Kurtz of Atlanta is a well known
architect and painter. More than that, he is our greatest authority on the
Civil War in this section. He has studied every campaign, been over every
battlefield, mapped out the positions of troops. He has also a fine collection of early Atlanta pictures. He would be the proper man to show Mr.
Cukor around. Of course, I would go too but Mr. Kurtz is the real authority. I am sending to you the Red Barrel,[2] which has a story about me
in it. Most of the facts in the story are errors but I am sending it to you
so you can see some of the drawings of Mr. Kurtz. I want to call your
attention especially to the picture on Page 18. It shows a typical house in
before-the-war Atlanta. Atlanta was not a city of white columned houses
and it would be pretty terrible if it was pictured that way. The picture on
Page 16, showing Five Points, is probably a scene in the 1840's. I believe
that the Cyclorama, a portion of which is shown on Page 14, would be
a great help to anyone staging battle scenes. This Cyclorama is enormous
and the only thing of this kind in the world. It shows the complete Battle
of Atlanta.[3]
    Life has been awful since I sold the movie rights! I am deluged with
letters demanding that I do not put Clark Gable in as Rhett. Strangers
telephone me or grab me on the street, insisting that Katharine Hepburn
will never do. It does me no good to point out sarcastically that it is Mr.
Selznick and not I who is producing this picture. I suppose you know that
casting this picture is the favorite drawing room game these days and

[1] George Cukor had been selected to direct *GWTW*.
[2] "Gone With the Wind, the 'Story Behind the Story' of Peggy Mitchell's Famous
Novel . . ." by Ralph McGill, *The Red Barrel*, XV, No. 9 (September 1936), pp.
14–20.
[3] The Cyclorama of the Battle of Atlanta and a similar painting of the Battle of
Gettysburg are the last survivors of an art form popular in the nineteenth century. The
Cyclorama of the Battle of Atlanta records the fighting of July 22, 1864, on a canvas
fifty feet high and four hundred feet in circumference. It was first exhibited in
Detroit in 1887 and has been in Atlanta since 1893. As a WPA project, the painting
was restored under the direction of Wilbur G. Kurtz.

every newspaper has been after me to say just who I want to play the parts. It has been difficult but so far I have kept my mouth shut. I wish to goodness you all would announce the cast and relieve me of this burden!

P.S.

I have not talked to Mr. Kurtz and so do not know if he will be available as he is pretty busy. If you like I will get in touch with him.

I forgot to say that not only do strangers assault me about not having Gable and Hepburn and Bankhead in the picture but they assault me with demands that Lamar Trotti do the scenario. When I wearily reiterate that after all Mr. Selznick is producing the picture, they say "But there's no one *but* Mr. Trotti who can do it. I shall never speak to you again if he doesn't do the scenario."

Lamar Trotti is an Atlantan, you see, knows the section and has made a deep study of this period. Everyone feels that he wouldn't let a character say "you all" while addressing one person. (This one thing, I may add, so incenses Southerners that they want to secede from the Union again every time they hear it in a movie.) Is there any chance that Mr. Trotti will do the scenario?

You mentioned that someone would come down with Mr. Cukor to see me about "changes in the continuity." Of course, I would love to help out in any way I can but I have no ideas at all about any changes and could be of no help whatsoever in such a matter. Besides, if the news got out that I was in even the slightest way responsible for any deviations from the book, then my life wouldn't be worth living. You see, this section has taken the book to its heart and that is something which makes me prouder than anything else. But each and every reader feels that he has part ownership in it and they are determined that nothing shall be changed. I am dogged by people who say they'll never speak to me again if "I let the movie people change one line." So I would not be of any assistance in the continuity.[4]

[4] In response to one of Susan Myrick's letters from Hollywood detailing the difficulties Selznick International Pictures was having in developing a satisfactory screenplay Miss Mitchell wrote Miss Myrick February 28, 1939: "I hate to say 'I told you so' but there is no one but you to whom I can say it. When movie agents were hounding me in 1936 to let them unload GWTW on the movies, I refused, saying it wasn't possible to make a movie out of it. This remark drove them to hysteria. Finally, I let The Macmillan Company sell it. Before I signed the contract I told Katharine Brown and the other Selznickers assembled in the room they were making a great mistake, for a picture could not be made from that book. They all laughed pityingly and patted me, saying 'there, there.' They said it was a natural and just look at all that dialogue! Why they would not have to write another line. I said yes indeed and thank you, but I knew how that book was written. It had taken me ten years to weave it as tight as a silk pocket handkerchief. If one thread were broken

It will be a pleasure to me to meet Mr. Cukor and your scenarist and I will be so glad to do anything I can to make their visit to Atlanta pleasant and interesting and to help them meet anyone they would like to talk to, but I don't believe that I personally could be very helpful in the business of turning a novel into a movie. I hope things will work out so that you can come to Atlanta with them. As you may have gathered from "Gone With the Wind" I think a lot of this town and I would enjoy showing it to you.

Mr. Herschel Brickell   Atlanta, Georgia
Ridgefield, Connecticut   October 9, 1936

My dear Herschel;

Steve[1] will arrive in New York on Tuesday Morning and he will stay at the same hotel we stayed at before—the Grosvenor which is down in the neighborhood of the Macmillan Company. I do not imagine he will be at the hotel for long after his arrival for he is having a conference with Mr. George Brett and the Macmillan Company's lawyers that day. I do not know, of course, whether the conference will be held in the offices of the Macmillan Company or the lawyers' offices....

This present business and legal tangle in which we are now involved has about exhausted us all. It has ruined what ever disposition I had, taken all John's time after his working hours and most of Steve's after-office time too. I think if it can just be settled perhaps I will begin to get well. As it is I can't seem to gain a pound ... I hope Steve can settle it all by a trip North. Of course, I should go with him as there will be papers to be signed but I would as soon stick my head in a lion's mouth as leave this house. You haven't any idea how *peculiarly* people can act around a new celebrity. Really, we've been living behind a barricade for weeks. If the pressure doesn't let up soon, I do not know what will happen to John and me as we are very tired and harassed. John needs a vacation badly and I am mad to get out of town but business holds us here and moreover, things would probably be worse away from Atlanta than they are here....

---

or pulled an ugly ravel would show clear through to the other side of the material. Yet they would have to cut for a script, and when they began cutting they would discover they had technical problems they never dreamed about. They all said I was overwrought and were very sympathetic and sent Miss Flagg and Miss Brown out with me to buy me a cup of tea. Now they have run into exactly the problem I foresaw. And may God have mercy on their souls."

 [1] Stephens Mitchell.

When you say the book will go to 600,000 I am appalled. That will mean that this present misery will keep up till after Christmas, at least. Things have gotten so bad that I never say anything but "yes" and "no," knowing I'll be quoted and quoted wrongly. You must realize what a burden it is for me to keep my mouth shut and only open it to make completely innocuous remarks. I wasn't cut out to be a celebrity and, as you have probably gathered, I don't like it worth a damn. It's not that I do not appreciate the kindness of many people or their enthusiasm but it's wearing me down.

Herschel, sometimes, when I have a minute I ponder soberly upon this book. And I can not make heads or tails of the whole matter. You know the way I felt toward it—and still feel toward it. I can not figure what makes the thing sell so enormously. I ponder soberly in the light of letters, newspaper articles and what people tell me. At first I thought the book might sell a few thousands to people who were interested in the history of that period. A few hundreds to college libraries for use in collateral readings in American History. But I've had to give up that idea because—well, my small nephew,[2] aged nearly five, has had the book read to him several times and he has announced that it doesn't bore him with repetition as do other books. Here in Atlanta, the fifth and sixth grade students are reading it—obstetrical details and all—and with their parents' permission. I get scads of letters from school girls ages ranging from thirteen to sixteen who like it.

As for the old people—God bless them! There are scores of grandchildren whose voices are rasping and hoarse from reading aloud to them and Heaven knows how many indignant grandchildren have told me that they had to sit up all night reading because the old folks wouldn't let them quit till after Scarlett was safe at Tara again.

And in the ages between—this is what stumps me. The bench and bar like it, judges write me letters about it. The medical profession must like it—most of my letters from men and my phone calls from men are from doctors. The psychiatrists especially like it, but don't ask me why. And now, the most confusing thing of all. File clerks, elevator operators, sales girls in department stores, telephone operators, stenographers, garage mechanics, clerks in Helpsy-Selfy stores, school teachers—oh, Heavens, I could go on and on!—like it. What is more puzzling, they buy copies. The U.D.C.s have endorsed it, the Sons of Confederate Veterans crashed through with a grand endorsement, too. The debutantes and dowagers read it. Catholic nuns like it.

Now, how to explain all of this. I sit down and pull the story apart in my mind and try to figure it all out. Despite its length and many details

2 Eugene Mitchell.

it is basically just a simple yarn of fairly simple people. There's no fine writing, there are no grandiose thoughts, there are no hidden meanings, no symbolism, nothing sensational—nothing, nothing at all that have made other best sellers best sellers. Then how to explain its appeal from the five year old to the ninety five year old? I can't figure it out. Every time I think I've hit on the answer something comes up to throw out my conclusion.

Reviews and articles come out commending me on having written such a "powerful document against war . . . for pacificism." Lord! I think. I never intended that! Reviews speak of the symbolism of the characters, placing Melanie as the Old South and Scarlett the New. Lord! I never intended that either. Psychiatrists speak of the "carefully done emotional patterns" and disregard all the history part. "Emotional patterns?" Good Heavens! Can this be I? People talk and write of the "high moral lesson." *I* don't see anything very moral in it. I murmur feebly that "it's just a story" and my words are swallowed up while the storm goes over my head about "intangible values," "right and wrong" etc. Well, I still say feebly that it's just a simple story of some people who went up and some who went down, those who could take it and those who couldn't. And when people come along and say that I've done more for the South than anyone since Henry Grady I feel very proud and very humble and wish to God I could take cover like a rabbit. . . .

P.S.

Small things do make me happy. The marked clipping, for instance. I sweated blood to try to make the voices sound differently and never dreamed anyone would catch it. The problem, for instance, of Archie and Will. Both Georgians, both practically illiterate, but one with a mountain voice and one with a wire grass voice. And Rhett and Ashley, both gentlemen, both educated, but with different intonations. It meant completely different sentence constructions, vocabularies not only in their words but in their thoughts and when I, as author, wrote about them.

Mr. Dudley Glass
The Atlanta Georgian
Atlanta, Georgia

Atlanta, Georgia
October 11, 1936

My dear Dudley:

Naturally I consider it a compliment that Cosmopolitan still wants me to do any article for them, even though I had to turn down their first request, but my answer must be the same as it was before.

I'm sorry but I just cannot write anything at present. The first reason why—as you know my eyes have given me much trouble since I finished proofreading "Gone With the Wind." Only during the last three weeks have I been able to abandon the bandage I wore for two months about my eyes. I do not know when I will be able to read or write. I certainly do not intend to push my eyes and strain them again.

The second reason—who could possibly do any writing in the middle of a hurricane? As you know the phone starts ringing at six in the morning and never lets up one minute until long after midnight. The mail is swamping me and my secretary and we are always four days behind. Strangers burst into the house at all hours and take up my time.

The third reason is that I do not want to write anything for anybody on any subject. I do not like to write. Moreover, I think I have earned a rest and I intend to take it. My health and my eyes depend on my getting a complete rest and I see no reason why I should jeopardize health and eyes by writing, especially when I haven't the slightest desire in the world to write anything.

The fourth reason is this—even if my eyes were perfectly well and I had a passionate desire to write something, I would not write anything in a hurry. I do not work that way. I write slowly, rewrite twenty or thirty times, throw away what I've rewritten and start over again. Then when, after many rewrites, I have what I call a "rough first draft" (usually the fiftieth version) I put it away for five months or more. Then I take it out, re-read it, throw it away and start all over again. I have no intention of rushing into print with some sloppy, hastily written article or story, just because I happen to be a "best seller" at present and because my name will command a good market. In the future I may turn out rotten stuff but it will never be stuff that I have not honestly labored over, thought over and rewritten fifty times.

I do not know where Cosmopolitan got the idea that I have some special objection to writing for magazines. Nothing could be further from the real facts. The real facts are that I am tired and sick and harassed with many things and honestly I do not want to write anything for anybody.

Please thank them for their offer and tell them that I am sorry that I cannot accept.

Miss Betty Timmons	Atlanta, Georgia
New York, New York	October 13, 1936

Dear Miss Timmons:

It was a mix-up, wasn't it? I hope it hasn't bothered you. I know it wasn't your fault and I have long since become hardened to newspaper errors. I am enclosing some Atlanta clippings, which may interest you. Even after I explained that we were no blood kin, the reporter insisted on quoting me as saying that we were kin!

I hope you have all the luck in the world in the movies. I'd be mighty proud if you were my niece!

Mr. Douglas S. Freeman   Atlanta, Georgia
Richmond, Virginia   October 13, 1936

My dear Mr. Freeman:

I cannot tell you how thrilled (yes, I know that is a school girl adjective but I really mean it) I was at having a letter from you! But any Southerner would be thrilled and any Southerner, who had done a little research into the period with which you dealt, would naturally have palpitations.

Your "Lee" was the very first thing I purchased with my very first royalty check. I had refused to read it until I could have it for my own and it is impossible for me to tell you of the pleasure it gave me and of the great admiration I conceived for you. Your "Lee" is something that will make anyone who writes about the South of that period feel very humble. And also very proud that such a truly great book came out of our section. I wanted to write to you at the time but I knew you must be getting thousands of letters from people who were certainly better historians, research workers, military strategists and critics than I. And so I did not. And now I welcome the chance to thank you for the book and the excitement and pleasure it gave me and will continue to give me throughout the years.

You were more than kind to add your invitation to the other invitations from the good people of Richmond. I have never been so pleased and so flattered. I only wish I could accept, for it has always been my dream to see Richmond and Virginia. (I have only been through the state on the train.) Having had a grandfather who fought up and down that state and many great uncles and cousins, too, the state is as familiar to me, in my imagination, as Georgia is. And, of course, I've read so much about it that I feel that I would recognize landmarks as soon as I reached the Virginia line.

But I cannot come. I have been ill almost since "Gone With the Wind" was published around the first of July. I did my proof reading under great pressure of time, working sometimes twenty hours a day. And it about finished my eyes. They were already strained by the agate type in old time newspapers, which I read by the hundreds in checking the historical accuracy of my book. I have only recently been able to abandon the black bandages which I wore for weeks. But even now I cannot read or write and find lights very painful to my eyes.

A rather bad automobile accident last year left me in a condition where I easily become fatigued, cannot stand long, etc. So you see why I am forced to refuse your invitation, much as I would love to come to Richmond. I should hate to promise to come and then not be able to come. I should hate, too, to come and then have to go back to bed for several months.

But some day when I am strong and completely recovered, I am coming to Richmond. Could I meet you then?

Mrs. Frances Scarlett Beach   Atlanta, Georgia
Brunswick, Georgia   October 19, 1936

Dear Mrs. Beach:
Thank you so much for your letter and the many kind things you said about "Gone With the Wind."

As to why I chose the name of Scarlett—first, because I came across the name of Katie Scarlett so often in Irish literature and so I made it Gerald's Mother's maiden name. Second, while I of course knew of the Scarlett family on our Georgia Coast, I could find no record of any family named Scarlett in Clayton County between the years 1859 and 1873. I was very anxious not to use the names of any family actually living in the County during that period, lest I embarrass people now living and bearing the same names. Of course it would have been impossible for me to find any names that someone in Georgia has not borne at some time. My efforts, therefore, were confined to choose names that did not appear in records in the counties where my characters lived.

The name Scarlett was chosen six months after my book was sold. My heroine had an entirely different name for nearly ten years.[1] I submitted nearly a hundred names to my publishers and they chose Scarlett,—I may add it was my choice too. . . .

Mr. David O. Selznick   Atlanta, Georgia
Culver City, California   October 19, 1936

Dear Mr. Selznick:
I was so happy to have your letter and delighted to know that there is a possibility that you may come to Atlanta with Mr. Cukor and Mr.

---

[1] Scarlett's original name was Pansy. The name was changed in September 1935. Finis Farr, *Margaret Mitchell of Atlanta* (New York, 1965), p. 105.

Howard. I hope you will not think me very selfish if I ask you to please let us—my husband and I—have you out to our apartment for supper on at least one night. I know very well that everyone in Georgia will descend upon you as soon as you arrive, but we do want to see you and hope you will save us at least one evening.

Yes, Miss Brown wrote me that Mr. Howard was to do the adaptation and I was very pleased. I have long admired Mr. Howard's work in the theatre and of course I know of his screen adaptations. I saw "Dodsworth"[1] just this week and thought it a real and moving affair.

I would like to take this opportunity to tell you how very happy I am that my book has fallen into your hands. I have seen the care and the patience which you have lavished on your other productions and so I know that my book will enjoy the same happy fate.

Mr. James Montgomery Flagg   Atlanta, Georgia
New York, New York   October 22, 1936

Dear Mr. Flagg:

Thank you very much for coming to my rescue so gallantly in the matter of Scarlett O'Hara's pointed chin and square jaw.[1] A word from you certainly settled the matter and everyone who has been twitting me about the remark in the New Yorker has apologized handsomely.[2]

For my part, I don't understand quite what the item meant because, according to my observation, most women who have jaws that are square in the angle have pointed chins. This seems especially true in girls of Irish descent.

---

[1] Miss Brown wrote October 13: "Although the actual contracts have not been signed, Sidney Howard will adapt 'Gone With the Wind' for the screen. We are enormously pleased about this and hope you will be, as we feel Howard is a dramatist of the very first rank. He did, as you recall, a superb job on both the play and the picture version of 'Dodsworth.' "

The film *Dodsworth* was based on the novel by Sinclair Lewis (New York, 1929). It had been dramatized for the stage by Sidney Howard in 1934, and Howard wrote the script for the 1936 motion picture.

---

[1] *GWTW*, p. 3.

[2] "A week or so ago [September 26] there was a small item concealed in these pages, twitting Margaret Mitchell for describing a character as 'pointed of chin, square of jaw.' It was our notion that a person couldn't have a pointed chin and a square jaw. Our readers say different. Several of them, including James Montgomery Flagg, who has looked closely at many a pretty chin, have written in to protest that Miss Mitchell was quite within the bounds of anatomy and propriety. We bow to superior observations. Our apologies to Miss Mitchell, and also to Carole Lombard and Dolores Costello, to name, thanks to Mr. Flagg, two." *The New Yorker*, October 17, 1936, pp. 13–14.

Mr. Herschel Brickell   Atlanta, Georgia
Ridgefield, Connecticut   October 22, 1936

Dear Herschel:

No, I will not bet you on any figures for "Gone With the Wind." You got me licked on it. However, I will bet you $50.00 (Confederate) with the poem "Lines on the Back of a Confederate Note" upon it that I do not win the Pulitzer prize. I think I am very safe in making this bet. I do not think I am safe in making any bets on sales. I am completely floored by what has happened. . . .[1]

The column was grand and as I told you before, if I do not win the Pulitzer prize it certainly won't be your fault. No one has ever done as much for me as you have and when I think how you started your kindness long before you knew me, I am doubly grateful. While we are on the subject of your column—I would appreciate it so much if you would clip and send me some of your stuff ever so often. You know how interested I am.

What did you think of "Steps Going Down"?[2] I know you don't like prize novels but I'd like to know about this one. As I can't read it, I might as well have your opinion on it.

About the article by Jimmy Street—John says I am improving. He brought the article and I was all prepared to sit on my head while he read it to me. It was a stupid affair, wasn't it? But I managed to laugh even though I was irritated. What irritated me the most was his bland assumption of an intimacy that never existed. You can gather just how intimate we were when he said I had black eyes and black hair. Of course his reference to my family as "the proud old hill clan of the Mitchells" was enough to make the proud Mitchells buckle on their six-shooters. I only saw Mr. Street three times in my life and the conversation he wrote never existed, except in his own mind. He never even knew I was writing a book. He was too busy telling me about the book he was going to write. . . .[3]

[1] Brickell wrote in the New York *Evening Post* for October 22: "A week after this novel appeared I made the prophecy that it would sell 400,000 copies by January 1, 1937, and 600,000 by June 30 of the same year, a twelvemonth after its appearance. There is every chance that it will have touched the 600,000 mark by November 1, 1936, with the big rush of the Christmas season still to come.

"I should not be at all surprised now to see it sell a million copies in this country alone, since it is rapidly approaching the mathematical point where almost anything may happen. . . . It will go on and on, because there is nothing factitious about its success; people are reading it and recommending it because they enjoy it."

[2] John Thomas McIntyre, *Steps Going Down* (New York, Toronto [c. 1936]).

[3] James H. Street, "'Gone With the Wind,' a Woman's Way of Telling the South's True Story," New York *World-Telegram Week-End Magazine Section*, October

October 26

I am sorry to have delayed so long in getting this letter off. Everything in the world happened—out of town people descending who just must see dear little Peggy, painters and upholsterers going through the apartment like Attila and his Huns, swarms of autograph seekers, people who just want to look at me, people who want me to make speeches, people who want me to get them in the movies. ("If you can get your niece Betty Timmons in the movies you can certainly get my granddaughter, grandmam, colored cook etc. in the movies." I could kill the person who launched that story about me picking my niece Miss Timmons for Scarlett.[4] She is no kin to me and I've never even laid eyes on her and, as you know, have stubbornly refused to have anything to do with the movies. But all creation is on my neck to get them in the movies. Can it be possible that I am the only woman in the world who doesn't want to be in the movies?) And me trying to wade through a heavy mail, on top of everything else. What makes me mad is that I wear myself out writing to people I don't give a hoot about and then am too tired to write to people I want to write to—you, for instance.

Well, I've made one interesting discovery. I thought when a person reached exhaustion that was as far as they could go but I've made the discovery that there is a country on the other side of exhaustion. At the risk of sounding dramatic, I'll say that it's a mighty queer and twilit country.

Today there arrived the dummy of the pamphlet the MacM. Company is getting out about *GWTW*.[5] I was so happy to see that they had included your interview. I keep telling you it's the best thing that's been written about me—not only the kindest, Heaven knows, but the most accurate. I was so glad they included it. I haven't told you before (and I hope you don't mind) but I had your article mimeographed and whenever club ladies deviled me for information I sent it to them. . . .

Did you write anything about "The Long Night?"[6] And do you know

---

3, 1936, pp. 8, 9, 12. "The book he was going to write" is probably Street's *Look Away! A Dixie Notebook* (New York, 1936), or possibly, his *By Valour and Arms* (New York, 1944).

[4] Louis Sobol wrote in his column in the New York *Journal* October 6: "The charming Miss Timmons, who insists she is a niece of Miss Mitchell, must have been misled, too—for it was she who furnished me with the information." An Associated Press dispatch of October 9 from New York quoted Miss Timmons: "We are cousins by marriage, which makes us no relation at all." (Atlanta *Journal*, October 9.) In a long story in the Atlanta *Constitution* for October 10 it was noted: "She [Miss Timmons] is a daughter of the late Colonel Bob Timmons. . . . Her father's brother, Willis Timmons, married Miss Allene [Aline] Mitchell, a sister of Eugene Mitchell, who is Margaret Mitchell's father."

[5] *Margaret Mitchell and Her Novel* Gone With the Wind (New York, 1936).

[6] Andrew Lytle, *The Long Night* (Indianapolis, New York [c. 1936]).

anything about Caroline Gordon's forthcoming book (I do not know the title but Scribner's is bringing it out) about Nathan Bedford Forrest?[7] By the way, speaking of Forrest, John and I are thinking seriously of having one of Forrest's statements printed up and using it. So many people want me to make speeches and I refuse as nicely as I know how. Undeterred they write back and insist that I make speeches or "just come and let us look at you." (Oh, nauseous thought! Have I become a freak like the quintuplets or Jo-Jo, the Dogfaced Boy?) An officer had applied twice for a furlough and Forrest had refused. When the officer applied the third time, Forrest took his pen in hand and wrote "I tole you twicst godamet know."[8] How do you think that would do? After all, it would be in keeping with the period of which I wrote. . . .

Later—

I seem unwilling to turn this letter loose, don't I? But I must pass this on to you. You recall how the "left wingers" romped on me? Some said with pity that it was unfortunate that I was only interested in plot and character and background. Because, it seems, I missed all the political and economic implications inherent in the period of which I wrote. Others, in wrath, shouted that I seemed totally unaware of "mass movements" (I've been wondering just what they were). Others that I was too small minded to realize that there were sociological matters that I entirely over looked.

Well. The English reviews have come in and, for the most part, are so good as to take my breath away. But one of them says "It is a pity that Miss Mitchell cannot handle character and plot as superbly as she handles mass movements." Another, after a whacking good review, remarks that it is obvious that Miss Mitchell is far more interested in the economic and sociological side of the period of which she writes than she is in mere story. Another announces, shrewdly, that I am at heart, a sociologist. It seems that there is some slight disagreement. I am rather afraid that the American left wingers are right, however. . . .

[7] *None Shall Look Back* (New York, 1937).
[8] In *General Forrest* (New York, 1902), p. 383, J. Harvey Mathes reported the incident with Forrest's spelling as Miss Mitchell gives it. Robert Selph Henry gives the endorsement as "I have tole you twict goddamit No!" *"First With the Most" Forrest* (Indianapolis, New York [c. 1944]), p. 14.

Mrs. Louella Parsons   Atlanta, Georgia
Beverly Hills, California   October 29, 1936

My dear Mrs. Parsons:

Everybody in the world reads your column and that is why I am appealing to you for assistance. I am appealing as an harassed and weary author, sadly in need of a rest and unable to get it because of the mail and telegrams that flood in on me due to rumors which seem to be circulating all over the country.[1]

I am the author of "Gone With the Wind." When I sold the motion picture rights to Mr. Selznick it was on the understanding that I was to have nothing to do with the movie production. I was utterly weary from the hard labor of getting my large book to press, I had lost a lot of weight, and I had been told to take a six months rest and try to regain all the weight I had lost. Therefore, it was understood that I would do no work on the adapting of the book for the screen, would have no voice in the casting and would not go to Hollywood. However, rumors are abroad that are very different from this. The story has even been printed that I am to select the entire cast! Mr. Selznick knows how to make movies and I most certainly do not and I have nothing to do with picking the actors, but these stories and rumors have brought down on me a deluge of requests that I get people into the movies. That foolish story about my "niece," Miss Betty Timmons, of Atlanta, being chosen by me for the part of "Scarlett," caused me endless trouble. It made people refuse to believe me when I told them that I had no part in the casting of the characters. They said if I could get my niece in the movies, I could certainly get them in too. The truth is, Miss Timmons is not my niece and is not related to me in any way. I have never even seen her and I have certainly never chosen her for anything, but the flood of letters, telegrams and personal calls have so distracted me and made my work so heavy, that I have been unable to get any rest for weeks.

On top of this, the persistent rumor which has appeared in many papers, and appeared in your column too, on October 22nd, that I am going blind has caused me much work and worry. You see, I'm not going

---

[1] In her column published in the New York *American* October 23, 1936, Miss Parsons had said: "These rumors of a cast for 'Gone With the Wind' are gradually getting David Selznick down. . . . No one has yet been chosen and will not be until the author, Margaret Mitchell, is consulted. . . . George Cukor will travel to Atlanta to interview Miss Mitchell, who is now confined to a darkened room by physicians because of severe eyestrain. For ten years Miss Mitchell wrote on this book, apparently a terrible toll, for she is now fighting blindness and so serious is her condition that her doctors will not permit her to come to Hollywood." In her column published November 8 Mrs. Parsons quoted at length this letter from Miss Mitchell.

blind and have no intention of going blind. I strained my eyes pretty badly in the final work on my book and they are still tired and so am I. My eyes will be all right again just as soon as I can get some rest. But whenever such an item appears in a paper, my friends and relatives scattered all over the United States write and wire me in panic. I have so many wonderful friends and naturally such items alarm them. When these letters come, I must get out of bed and write letters from morning till night, telling them that my eyes are all right, so you can see I do not get much rest!

I am begging you if ever again the rumor comes to your desk that I have something to do with the movie production of "Gone With the Wind" or that I am going blind, that you will deny them. I know I am taking a lot upon myself in asking this of you. My only excuse is that I have always read your column with the greatest interest and enjoyed it so very much and so I feel freer in writing to you than I would ordinarily to a stranger, which perhaps is presumptuous of me. My other excuse is that I am very tired and really do need a rest and I haven't been able to get it for months because I have been kept so busy answering letters and telegrams and telephone calls and personal calls.

I know you would laugh at some of the amusing things that have occurred. Several ladies have wired me that their little daughters tap dance beautifully and do the "splits" most elegantly and can't I get them into "Gone With the Wind"? (No, they haven't read the book, they admit.) People turn up with their colored cooks and butlers and demand that I send them to Hollywood to portray "Mammy" and "Uncle Peter." If I can ever get a rest, I can probably laugh at such things, too, but just now—

Miss Sara Helena Wilson   Atlanta, Georgia
Anniston, Alabama   November 3, 1936

Dear Miss Wilson:

Thank you so much for your review and thank you for sending it to me. If you only knew how I cherish reviews from my own section of the country! Before "Gone With the Wind" was published I felt that I would curl up like a salted slug if the people in the South turned their faces from my book. Of course I wanted the Northern reviewers to like it and humbly hoped that they would, but the good will of Southerners was what I prayed for. So, perhaps you can understand how very pleased your review made me.

Thank you for what you said about the negro characters—especially Prissy. I do not believe any other reviewer has mentioned her and Prissy was one of my favorite characters. Yes, as you wrote, she was "aggravating." She aggravated me unendurably while I was writing her and, when Scarlett slapped her,[1] it was really Margaret Mitchell yielding to an overwhelming urge. . . .

Miss Louella O. Parsons	Atlanta, Georgia
Beverly Hills, California	November 9, 1936

Dear Miss Parsons:

How can I thank you enough for your mention of me in your column on Sunday! Not a person has called me, either yesterday or today, and asked me to get them in the movies! And there was not a single letter in today's mail, asking the same thing. If you only knew what a load you have taken off of me. I certainly appreciate it more than I can ever tell you.

I thank you for your letter. I appreciated it so much and all the nice things you wrote me about "Gone With the Wind." If I ever do get to California (and I may come some day, for I have a sister-in-law[1] living in Los Angeles), I so sincerely hope that I can meet you. I have always read and admired and enjoyed your column so very much.

Thank you again for your courtesy and your help.

Mr. John Temple Graves, II	Atlanta, Georgia
The Birmingham News	November 12, 1936
Birmingham, Alabama	

Dear Mr. Graves:

I was just prepared to write to you when your letter and your "The Book of the South"[1] arrived. I was going to write you about your item concerning Mrs. Ward's testimony. You are right, I would have given a farm to have had that book while I was writing "Gone With the Wind." It would have saved me the trouble of reading several hundred books. While I knew from hearsay all the things I wrote in "Gone With the Wind," I wished to be able to have written references so that anyone who took issue with me could be answered. Mr. Ward was kind enough to send me a copy of his mother's testimony and my enthusiasm was

[1] *GWTW*, p. 366.

[1] Katharine Marsh Bowden (Mrs. A. O. Bowden).

[1] *The Book of the South* (Birmingham, 1936).

boundless. Mrs. Ward, to judge by her testimony, was a lady of great charm and sweetness and good common sense, and her lovely personality leaped out from the printed page. I wrote Mr. Ward of my enthusiasm and told him that I thought everyone should have the benefit of knowing the real truth of conditions during the war, and after, as his mother had related them. Mr. Ward was kind enough to send me several copies and I presented them to our libraries. What a gem the little volume is!

Sometime ago I had a letter from Mr. Cockrell, taking me to task for the use of the word "commandeer" and asking me why I had not used the term "impress."[2] I had used "impress" several times, as I wrote him, also the word "commandeer" appears frequently in military memoirs and diaries of the Sixties. Unfortunately, I have been too busy to reread all this material to find exactly where it is. You were so nice to send me that book. At present I have not been able to read it as the house has been full of out-of-town guests. I have only noted the wonderful job of typography and layout and the splendidly chosen pictures and their excellent reproduction. As you may have gathered, books about the South are my passion, and I know I shall like this and take pleasure in adding it to my collection. I am going to write Mr. Clabaugh.[3]

Mr. Herschel Brickell   Atlanta, Georgia
Ridgefield, Connecticut   November 13, 1936

My dear Herschel:
    I will tell you what your side of the bet in the Pulitzer affair will be. A copy of your "Don Quixote"[1] autographed to my two small nephews, Eugene and Joseph Mitchell. They are now aged five and two and I'm trying to assemble them a library. And what better gift than this book and your introduction.
    I've been reading a little lately. I can read for about a half hour before I get a headache, which is progress, I suppose, but maddening to me as I was accustomed to read ten hours on a stretch when I had the opportunity. And the first thing I read was your introduction. Good Heavens. It seems five years since you gave it to me and it hasn't really been five months!
    Herschel, why don't you write more? I mean more things besides your column—things like this introduction? Is it because you haven't the time

[2] Monroe F. Cockrell of Chicago. *The Oxford English Dictionary* cites "commandeer" as a South African word, and the first use it notes was in 1881.
[3] S. F. Clabaugh, publisher of the Birmingham *News* and of *The Book of the South.*
[1] Brickell wrote the introduction to the Modern Library edition of *Don Quixote* (New York, 1936).

—or haven't the inclination? You do it so well that you should—but there I go. Never again will I tell a friend that he "should" or shouldn't do anything. I've had to put up with too much of that myself recently. That I should write a sequel, that I should write a sweet lovely sappy Old South novel, etc. So I amend the "should" to "could." You see, you have charm in your writing and God knows that's a rare thing.

Today is Sunday and the foregoing has been interrupted about seventeen times. An editor down from N.Y. to pry a story out of me, the annual staff of a girls' school, the out-of-town friends who came over for the football game, reporters checking the rumors of my blindness and—the real nice interruption, Robert S. Henry who wrote that grand and readable "The Story of the Confederacy"[2] several years ago. We have mutual friends in town and for months I've been trying to catch him when he came through. With no luck. Why is it that the attractive people you want to catch are so elusive and the time stealers are with us always? Finally I sent word that if he didn't come I would wait till his new book about Reconstruction in the South[3] was off the presses and I would denounce it at the top of my lungs, if necessary, going to such lengths as accusing him of being a descendant of General Sherman. Yesterday he came for an hour and we inveigled him into staying the afternoon. He said he'd heard I'd been having a hell of a time and didn't want to add to it. So we fought Johnston's retreat, including the mess about the "high spot of ground" at Cartersville which was supposed to be untenable and was relinquished. And figured out just why Forrest didn't cut Sherman's line of communication behind his back. And argued about how long it did take Longstreet's Corps to get from Virginia to Chickamauga and *did* the artillery get there in time or was it just the cannon and no horses to haul them? And best of all, talked about his Reconstruction book. Seems that he does most of his work on trains for he is something-or-other in the railroad business in Washington and travels all the time. He had all his notes assembled three years ago and was all set to start the actual writing and had his bags and notes stolen while on a trip. He's just reassembled them again and is ready to start the writing. If I'd had that happen to me I'd have given up. I was so interested in his new work for heaven knows there's a need for such a book. Of course there are swarms of books on this subject but most of them cover only one state and are dull beyond belief. If his new book is one half as simple and charming and readable as the "Confederacy" was it should be a gem. However, he's run up against the same problem I ran up against. War can be made interesting and peace, a muddled peace, is hard to handle. I suppose it's because war has some design to it and reconstruction hasn't.

[2] Robert Selph Henry, *The Story of the Confederacy* (Indianapolis [c. 1931]).
[3] *The Story of Reconstruction* (Indianapolis [c. 1938]).

Anyway, I enjoyed him immensely and not the least item of my enjoy-
ment was the fact that he said he hadn't been able to catch me out,
historically speaking. When you understand that I have been waking up
screaming in the night after dreaming that someone *has* caught me out,
in spite of all my efforts to be accurate, perhaps you can understand my
pleasure. He said if I'd come on up to Washington, he'd get Captain
John W. Thomason, Jr. and Douglas Freeman over and we could choose
sides and really fight a campaign. It sounded marvelous and I all but
packed my bag then and there but didn't as I recalled that I had resisted
blandishments from that section—to come and make speeches, to visit
friends, etc. And wherever I've refused to go for one purpose, I can't go
for another. God, what a life. There is really no where I can go.

We did have a breathing spell a week or so ago—or did I write you?
We went down to the Georgia Coast, to the sea islands. We stayed at
Sea Island Beach, a part of St. Simon's Island, and it was heavenly quiet.
There is no place in the world so still. No one knew us, the phone didn't
ring and we rode and rode through long avenues of enormous trees with
yards of Spanish moss hanging down. After three days, it got around that
I was there and I saw speeches and reporters and photographers looming
up so we came home. I remember you said, you and Norma had been to
Charleston and I only wish you'd come a little further south. If you two
are ever in this section again, we must all go down there. . . .

Have you two any plans for a Southern trip? I should like to know
before John and I make definite plans. I do want you all to meet John. I
hope you'd like each other, if for no other reasons than a mutual admiration of the Marx brothers. Oh, heavenly day! "A Day at the Races"[4] is
being advertised! When it comes we will abandon all work and visitors
and spend the week at the movies. I can hardly wait.

To get back to your "Don Quixote"—I really did like it, Herschel—
But I clawed my memory over and over to try to recall what error you
said you'd made. Of course, I wouldn't know, being very ignorant of the
subject and of Spain in general. I was interested in your statement that
it was read now for its story and not for its "significance." Why will people persist in reading strange meanings into the simplest of stories? Is it
not enough that a writer can entertain for a few hours with a narrative
without being suspected of "significances" or symbolisms or allegories or
"social trends"?

Later—

I shall never get this off, I suppose, so I hasten to finish it up. Herschel,
did you review William Faulkner's latest?[5] I will not be able to read it

---

[4] A Metro-Goldwyn-Mayer release, c. 1937, with the Marx Brothers.
[5] *Absalom, Absalom!* (New York, 1936).

as my reading for months will be so limited. If you can get a copy of your review without too much trouble, please send it to me. I would go to the library and read it but I have abandoned the library. I know all the librarians and most of the regular visitors and when I go there I get backed in a corner or asked to autograph or have to stand for hours talking so that I come home exhausted and ready to weep. I'd be more interested in your opinions than anyone else's so I'd like to see them.

Stuart Rose of the Ladies Home Journal was down here. So was Kenneth Littauer of Collier's. Both were nice, both were entertaining. Both, I am sure, think I am insane for not promising to write them something and for not turning loose that lousy novelette I have.[6] I have been fending off some others, in a wild hope that my furniture which has all been sent to the upholsterers will come back before anyone else descends on me. Never was there a worse time for visitors. The apartment is bare as a cabin and while I don't give a hoot what people think it does get under my skin to have guests arrive and have no place to sit. I don't see why they can't wait until such a time as is convenient to me—but they don't—or won't. Perhaps I am a fool not to sign on the dotted line but I do not think so. I never have the time to get my hair washed much less write anything and if I had a contract hanging over me, I'd shoot myself. . . .

This is all—Clark Howell, for years editor of the Constitution, is dead[7] and his funeral is today and everyone in the state is in town and ringing the phone. I know this letter is choppy but I can't help it. I've always been able to work against pain but never against a constantly ringing phone.

Miss Georgia D. Trader   Atlanta, Georgia
The Cincinnati Library Society for the Blind   November 18, 1936
Mt. Healthy, Ohio

Dear Miss Trader:

You were so very kind to write me and send me the letter from Miss Matuseff. I cannot tell you how happy and excited I was when I learned that "Gone With the Wind" had been put into Braille. There is a library for the blind here in Atlanta and when they telephoned me to tell me

[6] Miss Mitchell's " 'Ropa Carmagin" was a story of novella length about a girl in love with a handsome mulatto. The manuscript was given to Harold Latham along with the *GWTW* manuscript. Latham thought it publishable except for its brevity (only 12,000 to 15,000 words). The manuscript was eventually destroyed.

[7] He died November 14.

that "Gone With the Wind" had arrived, I was indeed flattered and pleased. I love books so much myself and can think of nothing worse than not being able to read. So perhaps you can understand my pleasure in the knowledge that my book diverted, if only for a little while, those who are not able to read with their eyes.

Miss Katharine Brown   Atlanta, Georgia
New York, New York   November 18, 1936

Dear Miss Brown:

Your letter has just arrived and I'm trying to get you off a quick answer. If this letter sounds choppy, please over look it. This is one of those days when the phone is going like mad, autograph seekers arriving, and strangers calling "just to see what I look like.". . .

I think the whole idea of scouting through the South is a swell one for if you don't find anyone who will do, it will still be worth a million dollars in publicity.[1] And there's just a chance you will turn up a nugget. Count on me for any help you need.

Now, I come to the publicity business. I don't think you know anything of my back ground so I must explain. I worked here on the Atlanta Journal, an evening paper. My husband has worked on the Journal and the Georgian (it's Hearst and also an evening paper.) I have many good friends on the Constitution which is the only morning paper. In fact most of my friends are on these papers and they have been kinder than anyone can imagine to me since the book came out. I have found myself in the queer and not too pleasant position of being the best little bit of copy in town for the last five months and I've had to play ball honestly and faithfully with each paper, which isn't as easy as it sounds, especially when one of the papers is my old paper. They all look to me for news-breaks on everything connected with my business or the book or the movie. They don't want to be scooped by the opposition papers, nor if

[1] The idea of using an unfamiliar actress in the part of Scarlett seems to have originated with Miss Brown, though Selznick had conducted previous searches for unknown talent to play the title roles of *Little Lord Fauntleroy* and *Tom Sawyer.* Miss Brown wrote Miss Mitchell on October 13: "We, too, are being deluged with letters saying 'Don't put Clark Gable in the part but put Ronald Colman in.' Likewise in respect to Hepburn and Margaret Sullavan. My own personal theory is not to put a well-known actress in as Scarlett as everyone will be bound to say she is Katharine Hepburn, or Margaret Sullavan, or Joan Crawford playing Joan Crawford, and not Scarlett O'Hara. My feeling is that if we have a completely new person audiences will be more generally satisfied that she is their conception."

possible by the out of town papers on stories which they feel belong to me—and to them.

So I'd like, if possible, to give them a break on your trip south. Your trip may not be a big story up north but it *is* a big story in this section. The very idea that a movie company thinks enough of a story to send a talent scout and a director and an adaptor down here will go over big. And moreover, it makes people who've always refused to go to any movie about the south think very kindly of Mr. Selznick and makes them feel that he honest to God wants to do a real southern picture with real southern color. Oh, yes, it will be a big story. I know your outfit isn't averse to publicity and publicity will be a great help to you in your search for new faces (and also a great burden, too, I do not doubt!).

So this is what I want to know—

When will you arrive in Atlanta and where will you stay?

Will Atlanta be your first trip stop in the South or perhaps Richmond or Charleston? (You see if you go there first the news break would come from those towns.)

What is your full title with the Selznick Company?

And most important, do you mind this story being broken before you come South? Probably there will be some story out of N.Y. about your trip. If you do not want the first publicity in the Atlanta papers but want it to come out of N.Y. can you fix it so the Atlanta papers will get an even break by getting the news as soon as the N.Y. papers do?

Does all this sound very muddled? I am sure it does. I doubt if you make heads or tales of it! The reason I want to know when you will arrive and where you will stay (I advise the Biltmore, by the way) is that, if the story does break before you come here, I want to have an "out" for myself. I'm afraid the storm will break about my head and the countless scores who want me to get them in the movies will be back on my neck. And if this starts I'll just have to leave town for I couldn't go through it again and keep my sanity. So if it were known when you were coming and where you were staying, I could disclaim all connection and merely route people over to you. Yes, that's grief for you but I am becoming the most selfish of swine and derned keerful about my own hide!

So—could you wire me when you are coming, where you are staying, whether you are willing for me to break the story of your trip immediately and if Atlanta is your first stop on the way South? If it will hamper or embarrass you in any way to have the story broken before you get here, don't hesitate to tell me. But if you've already written some of the Southern colleges I imagine the story is already floating around.

I hope you'll let me give you a brawl of sorts—probably a cocktail party to meet the press. You see, I've been dying to give a party for them to thank them but had no excuse. And I wanted to have an excuse for holding it to the press because otherwise I'd have to give a huge reception and I don't want to do that. So please be my excuse! . . .

Miss Mary Moss   Atlanta, Georgia
Cambridge, Ohio   November 20, 1936

My dear Miss Moss:
I hope you will pardon the haste of this letter but out-of-town guests are descending on me in a little while and it may be days before I can write to you.
I am afraid I can be of little help to you in answering your question as to how I came to write the book. It was so long ago—back in 1926—when I began it that, of course, my memory is a little vague. I do recall perfectly, however, that there came a day when I thought I'd have to write a book and so I sat down and began "Gone With the Wind." I was *not*, as many rumors have had it, completely disabled from an automobile accident at the time, nor was I in plaster from heels to ears, as other rumors go. For how could I have used a typewriter if this were true? I did have a sprained ankle and that has been magnified into a broken back.
On the day when I thought I'd write a book, I decided I'd better write a book about something I was familiar with rather than something I knew nothing about. I was familiar with the period of the war and reconstruction so I decided I'd write about that period. I thought it would be easy. I was wrong. It wasn't easy! But then, no writing is easy.
May I wish you great success with your review? You cannot imagine how exciting it is know that someone, far away from Georgia, is speaking about "Gone With the Wind!"

Mr. Sidney Howard   Atlanta, Georgia
Tyringham, Massachusetts   November 21, 1936

My dear Mr. Howard:
I was so pleased to have your letter and am happy to know that you are coming South.[1] You were very kind to write me so many nice things

[1] Howard wrote on November 18: "It is about time I wrote you to say how much, how very much, and how sincerely I admire 'Gone With the Wind' and that I like the idea of making it into a picture as who would not. The rumor is that George Cukor, your director, is coming East about December first to see you in Atlanta, 'to

about "Gone With the Wind" and I especially appreciated your remarks about the negro dialect which was just about the toughest job in the book.[2]

But my pleasure at your coming is some what dimmed by the fear that there has been a misunderstanding about my part in the production of "Gone With the Wind." I hasten to write to you for I would not have you come South under a misapprehension.

When I sold the book to the Selznick Company, I made it very plain that I would have nothing whatsoever to do with the picture, nothing on backgrounds, costumes, continuity. They offered me money to go to Hollywood to write additional dialogue, etc. and I refused. I sold the book on that understanding. Not more than a week ago, I wrote Miss Katharine Brown of the Selznick Company and asked her if you were familiar with my attitude and she wired me that you were.

But now your letter arrives[3] and I realize that they have not told you and I am very distressed about it. I still have no intentions of doing anything about additional dialogue or even looking at the script. There are many reasons for this and I will try to list them as briefly as possible.

In the first place it would do no good for me to look over the script— any more than looking over a Sanscrit grammar. I know just as much about Sanscrit as I do about writing for the movies. A script would mean nothing to me and it would take me weeks or months to figure it all out.

In the second place, I haven't the time. I never dreamed writing a book meant losing all privacy, leisure and chance to rest. Since July 1, I've averaged an engagement every forty minutes from nine in the morning till long after midnight. And, between these engagements, I've had to handle an enormous mail and try to see my family.

The third reason is this. I know it sounds like a silly one but it is an important one to me. If I even so much as looked over the script, without even passing judgement on it, and there was some small item in the finished production that incensed or annoyed the people of this section,

---

confer,' as they say in Hollywood. If that is true I shall do everything in my power to make one of the company."

[2] Howard said: "I may also tell you that if I find myself obliged to write any additional dialogue for the colored folks you will have to lend me a hand. Those are the best written darkies, I do believe, in all literature. They are the only ones I have ever read which seem to come through uncolored by white patronising."

[3] In his letter of November 18 Howard said: "You know you have given me more story than I can compress into the two hours a picture is, at the outside, permitted. Some things will have to go because nothing is less adequate than a picture which tries to cover too much ground and so covers none of it properly. I shall ask you to look at our first lay-out of the material when it is in shape and, if you are willing, to tell me what you think of the script as it comes along. I have, on occasion, made Red Lewis do this for me and it has helped me with the script and eased the shock of the outcome for him."

then I'd get the blame for it. Southerners have been wonderful to my book and I am grateful indeed that they like it and are interested in the forthcoming picture. Not for worlds or for money would I put myself in the position where if there was something they didn't like in the picture, they could say "Well, you worked on the script. Why did you let this, that and the other get by?" I would never live it down and I could never explain that I really had nothing to do with the script. It won't matter to them if there is something in the movie they don't like that you may be responsible for. You didn't write the book and you do not live here in Atlanta and if they do not like something then you will be excused.

From the minute the news of the movie sale broke, I have been deviled by the press and the public for statements about who I wanted in the picture, who I wanted to do the adaptation, where I wanted it filmed. I have never opened my mouth on any of these subjects for it occurred to me that such statements [would] be the greatest presumption on my part as Mr. Selznick and you are most competent people and know how to produce good pictures. Moreover, having said I'd have nothing to do in any way with the production, I've published it in Ascalon [Askelon] and told it in the streets of Gath that I have no connection with the film of "Gone With the Wind." To be frank, I do not care who they put in it or where they film it. To be quite frank, I have all confidence in you and Mr. Cukor and Mr. Selznick so why I should I rush about issuing statements to the press on matters that are none of my business?

I did tell Miss Brown that I would be only too happy to do this for her—that if she, or Mr. Cukor or you came South I would do all I could in making contacts with them for finding new talent, for rounding up research workers and local historians who know what really went on down here in those days. I said I [would] take her from Dalton to Milledgeville, showing her old entrenchments, old houses and introducing her to people in each town along the way to help her. That's going to be a tough assignment in itself. But I can't do anything about the script or about additional negro dialogue. I just can't. I'm too nearly crazy now with the load I'm carrying to even consider it, even should I want to do it.

I know this foregoing doesn't sound hospitable nor obliging! But I had to write it for I realized that the Selznick Company had not explained the situation to you and I was very upset at the thought of you coming all the way down here in the belief that I was going to be of any assistance on the picture beyond making contacts.

May I tell you now how sincerely happy I was when I heard that you were going to [do] the adaptation? I did so want the book to fall into good hands and was so pleased when it did!

Speaking of Civil War monuments—you should see our Southern ones. I believe they were put out by the same company that put out the Northern ones. They are twice as ugly and three times as duck-legged!

Mr. John Macleay   Atlanta, Georgia
Liverpool Daily Post   November 23, 1936
Liverpool, England

My dear Book Taster:

I appreciated so very much the fine review you gave my book "Gone With the Wind" in your issue of October 7. I quite agree with you that the book would have been vastly improved had it been published in two volumes. Perhaps if I had not been a completely unknown writer it would have been brought out in two volumes. Here in Atlanta many of the old people who lived through the days of which I wrote, have had the book cut into five parts so that their feeble wrists would not be weighted down.

I've never written a critic before and taken issue with him (or her) on anything written about my book because I've always felt it was the critic's privilege to express his real opinion. But I have to speak up about what you wrote about my anachronisms, especially iodine.[1] You see, it took me about two weeks to run down all my references on iodine and its uses before and during the Civil War. And I did not, if you will read carefully, ever speak of iodine being used as an antiseptic.

Iodine as a drug came into use about 1818, I believe. During the war it was used in the treatment of goiter, taken internally for dysentery and externally for erysipelas, was used on "festers," bruises and wounds. As to whether they were aware of the antiseptic qualities, I cannot say but both Mrs. Gordon and Mrs. Pickett, in writing of those days refer to putting it on wounds, according to the doctors' orders. They were so ignorant of its properties that they painted the wounded every half hour and blistered them badly. "The Medical and Surgical History of the War of the Rebellion" gives its uses in dysentery and stomach complaints and remarks, in passing, that the mortality was quite high in dysentery![2]

[1] *GWTW*, p. 303.
[2] Mrs. La Salle Corbelle Pickett wrote of her wartime experiences in *Pickett and His Men* (Philadelphia, London, 1913) and *What Happened to Me* (New York, 1917). Mrs. John B. Gordon did not write her own memoirs, but her use of iodine in treating General Gordon after he was wounded at Sharpsburg is described in his *Reminiscences* (New York, 1903), p. 91: "My own confidence in ultimate recovery . . . was never shaken until erysipelas, that deadly foe of the wounded, attacked my left arm. The doctors told Mrs. Gordon to paint my arm above the wound three or four times a day with iodine. She obeyed the doctors by painting it, I think, three or four hundred times a day." The uses of ointment made with iodine and of tincture of iodine

Many old ladies with whom I discussed war experiences spoke of iodine. I tried to have four references against every statement of this nature in the book and I have more than four on this one. As to the other anachronisms—I wish you would write me about them for I am anxious to correct any in future editions. Practically all of the conversation in the book, especially the catch phrases etc., were taken from letters, memoirs, diaries, etc. So please let me know the other anachronisms.

May I thank you again for the kindness of your review? Naturally I was most interested in how English readers would react to "Gone With the Wind." The scene and the time are so far away from England of today that I felt that my book could be of little interest.

Mr. Russell Birdwell,   Atlanta, Georgia
Publicity Manager   November 24, 1936
Selznick International Pictures, Inc.
Culver City, California

THANKS FOR PROMPTNESS IN SENDING STORY BUT MUST SET YOU STRAIGHT ON MY CONNECTION WITH FILM JOB STOP MY CONTRACT SPECIFICALLY PROVIDES THAT I HAVE NOTHING TO DO WITH THE MOVIE AND I HAVE STATED PERSONALLY AND BY LETTER TO VARIOUS SELZNICK PEOPLE THAT I WILL HAVE NOTHING TO DO WITH TALENT SEARCH, CASTING, ADAPTATION OF STORY OR FILMING BUT APPARENTLY I MUST REPEAT THIS TO EACH NEW MEMBER OF ORGANIZATION I COME IN CONTACT WITH STOP WHEN MISS BROWN AND OTHERS COME TO ATLANTA I WILL FEED THEM FRIED CHICKEN, SHOW THEM STONE MOUNTAIN AND INTRODUCE THEM TO ANYBODY THEY WANT TO MEET BUT ALL PARTS OF FILM JOB ARE ON THEIR HANDS AND NOT ON MINE STOP AM RELEASING STORY TO ATLANTA AFTERNOON PAPERS TODAY AFTER DELETING REFERENCES TO ME AND MR BIRDWELL PLEASE MAKE THE SAME CORRECTIONS IN ANY RELEASES YOU GIVE OUT STOP ON THIS AND ANY FUTURE STORIES I WANT NO REFERENCES MADE TO ME EXCEPT AS AUTHOR OF THE BOOK.

---

in treating dysentery are described in *The Medical and Surgical History of the War of the Rebellion*, Medical Volume I, pt. 2 (Washington, 1879), pp. 823, 842.

Mr. Sam Doerflinger   Atlanta, Georgia
The Macmillan Company   Thanksgiving Day, 1936
New York, New York

My dear Mr. Doerflinger:

Thank you so much for your letter. Naturally I couldn't help being excited by the very notion of "Gone With the Wind" being among the nominations for the Pulitzer Prize.

I'll gladly tell you where I was born. I was born here in Atlanta, Ga. But I am not telling when I was born.[1] And this is the reason. I have never felt that a person's age was the concern of anyone except herself and her family. And my feeling on this matter has been considerably strengthened since "Gone With the Wind" was published. The day seldom passes but that seven complete strangers either phone me or call at the door and ask point blank, "Just how old are you?" The newspapers, news services, biographical reviews, etc. have been in a lather about the matter, too. The effect has been to arouse my stubbornness. My age is my own private business and I intend to keep it so—if I can. I am not so old that I am ashamed of my age and I am not so young that I couldn't have written my book and that is all the public needs to know about my age.

I am not, of course, finding fault with you for asking me the question, for you are one of the very few with a legitimate reason for seeking the information. But the others, the curiosity seekers, have made me stubborn on this point, and, if my reticence knocks me out of the nominations, then I guess that's just too bad.

Mr. Heyward Bowley   Atlanta, Georgia
Harpers Ferry, West Virginia   November 30, 1936

My dear Mr. Bowley:

Yours was a wonderful letter and I enjoyed every word of it. How nice of you to write me at such length. I felt, when I had finished it, as though I had read a chapter of a book which was far more interesting than "Gone With the Wind" could ever be because your story was about true happenings.

When I read a letter like yours I feel more than a little humble, for I realize that it is people like you, who lived through that era, who should

---

[1] November 8, 1900. Miss Mitchell's birth date had been noted in the Atlanta *Constitution* July 3 in Mrs. Bernice Denton Pearson's column "Let Your Stars Guide You."

be writing books about it instead of me. You write so excellently and so vividly that I hope you have at least written the memories of your childhood.

As to why I took the name of Rhett Butler—I wanted a two-syllable Georgia Coast last name and a one-syllable South Carolina Coast first name. Butler was a very prominent name in our State in the 1840's. I made him a Charlestonian because I had to make him a blockade runner, and there was little or no blockading done from Savannah. I checked hundreds of South Carolina records in an effort to ascertain that, during the period my book covered, there had never been anyone named Butler prominent in the blockade traffic. I did not wish to embarrass any family by seeming to use one of their family names. . . .

Mr. Sidney Howard   Atlanta, Georgia
Tyringham, Massachusetts   December 1, 1936

Dear Mr. Howard:

I was just as mortified as Jimmy Durante when I learned that the Selznick company had said nothing to you about my attitude on the film. They had assured me that you knew all about it. I know you must have thought my abrupt letter the height of discourtesy, but it was written in the belief that you already knew the situation. I hope you will forgive any seeming rudeness.

I am perfectly well satisfied to have my book in your hands and those of Mr. Cukor and Mr. Selznick. You all have taste and talent and intelligence. The truth of the matter is, as I wrote you before, that I haven't the time to work on the picture; I haven't the inclination; I haven't the experience—and moreover, I do not want to let myself in for a lot of grief. That is why I have been so obstinately "hands off" in this matter.

Reading your latest letter gave me the correct understanding of your previous letter, and I thank you most sincerely for the thoughtfulness and consideration of your offer to let me look over the script.[1] Now that the misunderstandings have been cleared away by your letters, I am even more confident than before that the book is in good hands.

I hope that you do decide to come to Atlanta, for I would be most

---

[1] Howard had written November 25: "My notion in writing as I did was chiefly to assure you—in so far as it is in my power to assure you—that you would have all possible measure of approval or criticism of your picture before it reaches the irrevocable stage of celluloid. The simple course, which I have twice followed with Lewis, is to submit the script to the novelist. I understand all too well how you feel. I should not dream of going near a play of mine after it has opened. . . . I take you at your word and shall not trouble you."

happy to meet you. The date of Mr. Cukor's arrival is still uncertain but is supposed to be around the 10th of the month. I have been planning to leave on a vacation trip on December 15th, but I am holding my plans in abeyance until I hear definitely whether you and he are coming.

Mr. Russell Birdwell   Atlanta, Georgia
Culver City, California   December 5, 1936

Dear Mr. Birdwell:

Your letter with the carbon of the story arrived today but as I have been away from the house since early morning, I have just read it.

I thought you understood my position in the matter of the filming of "Gone With the Wind." I've written it time and again to the Selznick Company, I've told it to its representatives and I've published it in many newspaper statements. I have nothing to do with the filming of "Gone With the Wind." I have nothing to do with the casting of it and have never once even hinted that I would like for anyone to play any role. I have never even said (as you quoted me in your story) that I would like to see a Southern girl in the leading role. I have no suggestions to make about the casting. I have no suggestions to make to Mr. Cukor and will make none. Of course, I will be charmed to meet him when he comes here and pleased to introduce him to anyone who may be of assistance to him. But that is as far as my connection with the film goes. I have said time and again that I will have nothing to do with the adaptation, with writing or even suggesting additional dialogue. I have written Mr. Howard and told Miss Brown and others of the Selznick organization that I will not even look at the script. I'll be very glad to meet Mr. Howard, for whom I have a vast admiration, but I will not read a line of the script.

If I had wanted to be tied up with the filming of my book I would have signed a contract and gone to Hollywood. But I didn't want to have anything to do with it, I said as much, I signed no contract. I do not wish to be tied up with the publicity of the film or the talent search in any way except when it is unavoidable—such as that I happen to be the author of the book.

Please do not misconstrue these simple courtesies. They have nothing whatever to do with your talent search and if they are going to be used in your publicity so as to link me with the talent search, then you will simply compel me to refuse to even meet Mr. Cukor and Mr. Howard when they come to Atlanta.

If your story goes out, making it appear that I am giving the tea for the Selznick representatives, I will have to recall my invitations and hold no tea. I am giving this party for my friends in the press who have been so kind to me and for my book. It is the only way in which I can show my gratitude to them. And it's *their* party and in *their* honor. I thought it would be very nice if Mr. Cukor and Mr. Howard and Miss Brown were here to attend it so that they could meet people who might be of some assistance to them.

But my invitation to them to attend the tea is purely a *social* courtesy, whereas your story makes it appear to be an important part of a business promotion and puts me in the position of taking a prominent part in the talent search. I am taking *no* part in the talent search and I must insist that my position shall not be misrepresented in publicity.

I have a very cordial feeling toward the Selznick company and all of its officials I have had the pleasure of meeting. Naturally when Mr. Cukor and Mr. Howard visit my home city, I wish to be hospitable to them. I would like to introduce them to my friends and do whatever I can to make their visit to Atlanta pleasant. This is exactly the same as I would do for any other visitor in whom I was interested.

Mr. Herschel Brickell   Atlanta, Georgia
Ridgefield, Connecticut   December 8, 1936

My dear Herschel:

I hate to write you, on occasions like this, when I am practically staggering with weariness and my mind too tired from the assaults of people I don't give a damn about to know what I am writing. But it seems that things are never going to be any different and if I wait till another day, a day of leisure, that day will never come and I will never write to you. So forgive this letter if it sounds abrupt. The cook is off, the secretary isn't here, the phone is going every minute, the door bell ringing and the door belching strangers who want autographs and want to see what I look like and want to make me make speeches and go to parties and tell what I like for breakfast and if I wear lace on my panties and why I haven't any children. It's only eleven a.m. and I've been going since dawn and feel as though it were midnight.

About the Guild.[1] Here's my situation. In my files I have over a thousand requests for autographed books, many coming from this section, many from most worthy causes. New requests by the score come in on every mail. I can't fill them all and so I've had to refuse them all. If I gave an autographed copy to the Guild, it would mean that (1) I'd make

[1] Newspaper Guild.

everybody around here mad as hornets (2) I'd have to go through my files and donate a copy to everyone who'd asked for one before I sent one to the Guild. And I can't do this. The request about pages of manuscript are about the same. All the Universities have been after me for all the manuscript or a part of it or a page of it; relatives, friends, collectors, etc. have come down on me about the same thing. So I've refused them all. I'd have to give away all my manuscript before I was able to have a page for the Guild or else make everyone around here sore as could be. Moreover, I want my manuscript and do not want it floating around for I intend to burn it just as soon as I get those leaves back which the MacM Co.[2] inveigled out of me when I was too exhausted to argue.

I haven't written any letters about my work in spite of about a million requests. First reason—because I don't want any letters about my work floating around. Second reason, I don't know how I work, haven't the slightest idea how I work and so couldn't write much of a letter. The proof sheets are going to be burned, too, just as soon as I get them back. I don't want anyone to see them, just as I did not want anyone to see ms pages but couldn't help myself. Don't ask why. I don't know. I suppose it is the same passion for privacy and resentment of strangers' prying that has made my life a Hell during the last few months. . . .

Miss Jessie Hopkins   Atlanta, Georgia
Carnegie Library of Atlanta   December 8, 1936
Atlanta, Georgia

My dear Miss Hopkins:

I am enclosing a check which I wish you would use in buying books on Georgia and Atlanta for the Reference Department. I am sending this check for two reasons. First, because the members of the Reference Department were of such great assistance to me during the months when I was checking the historical data of "Gone With the Wind." They were indefatigable, accurate, obliging and courteous. Their work for me did not stop when their day's work was done but they frequently phoned me at night and after their working hours to give me information they had patiently run down. What they could not find in their books, they found by telephoning local people and questioning them. I shall always be grateful to them for their assistance.

[2] In a story about the New York *Times* National Book Fair the *Times* noted on November 9: "Many persons were interested in seeing two pages of the manuscript of Margaret Mitchell's 'Gone With the Wind,' on display in the booth of the MacMillan [*i.e.* Macmillan] Company. The typed pages have been carefully and liberally corrected in pencil."

My second reason is that my father, Eugene M. Mitchell, was instrumental in acquiring for the Reference Department the beginnings of the present Georgia collection. He was Secretary of the Young Men's Library Association for eight years and was President for three years. He was President at the time Mr. Andrew Carnegie made his gift. He served on the Board of Trustees of the Carnegie Library from 1900 to 1905. It was during the period of his Trusteeship that he turned his attention to collecting volumes on Georgia and Atlanta and many of the books now in the Reference Department were his purchases. Notable among these was an almost complete set of the Legislative Acts of Georgia. Because of my father's interest in Atlanta and Georgia history, and my own interest, I wish to add to the Georgia Collection.

Mrs. L. H. Clark   Atlanta, Georgia
Fond du Lac, Wisconsin   December 9, 1936

Dear Mrs. Clark:

I know you'll think it sounds foolish when I tell you that I cannot give you the answer to your question about whether Rhett joined the Confederate army because his sympathy was aroused by the young boy who was being carried during the retreat from Atlanta. The reason I cannot tell you is that the whole book was written through Scarlett's eyes. What she understood was written down; what she did not understand— and there were many things beyond her comprehension, they were left to the reader's imagination, even as they were left to Scarlett's.

I know this is a very inadequate answer to write to someone who wrote me such a nice letter and who showed such a flattering interest in my book, but it is all I can think of to tell you.

1937

Mr. Sidney Howard
Tyringham, Massachusetts

Atlanta, Georgia
January 4, 1937

Dear Mr. Howard:

... You were nice to think of me and I appreciated it. I *did* have a nice Christmas, even if I was forced to spend it away from home. It was a quiet Christmas, spent driving through Florida orange groves, discussing with my husband abstract things like the gold standard (of which I know absolutely nothing), discussing many things which had, thank God, nothing to do with the writing of books or the producing of movies.

You see, in the early part of December, the Selznick company sent down a crew to Atlanta to "audition" people with the possible hope of picking up a new face for the cast of "GWTW."[1] As I wrote you before, I have nothing to do with anything connected with the filming of the book. I didn't want to have anything to do with it as I know that every one in the U.S. except me is movie crazed and yearns to act. And I knew if I had any connection with the film, life would be more of a burden than it has already been for six months. But, of course, when the audition crew arrived, the populace of six states descended on me, demanding that I endorse each and every one of them for the role of Scarlett, etc. The phone went every minute and wires and special deliveries deviled me and shoals of people camped on the doorstep and clutched me if I went out. No one seems to believe that I have nothing to do with the movie as it seems to be beyond human comprehension that any mortal does not yearn to be connected with movies. Even after the crew left things were terrible—so terrible that we had to leave town and spend Christmas away

---

[1] On December 2 Katharine Brown, "Eastern Representative of the David O. Selznick Picture Corporation," Anton Bundsmann, and Harriett Flagg arrived in Atlanta to hold auditions for possible screen tests. Harold Martin quoted Miss Brown in the Atlanta *Georgian* December 2: "We are holding auditions for only those persons interested in playing the parts of the four principal characters, Scarlett, Rhett, Melanie and Ashley. We won't be able to consider any character parts, though if there is a possible Aunt Pitty-Pat around we would be delighted to find her. We would also be delighted if we could find twins to play the parts of the Tarleton boys. But we won't be able to consider any of the numerous 'mammies' that have been recommended, nor any babies."

from home. Alas where has my quiet peaceful life gone? I will be so glad when the picture actually goes into production, then perhaps some of my problems will be over. Do you know when this will be? I probably know less about the whole affair than any one in the United States.

I hear vague rumors that Mr. Cukor, who did not come south with the audition crew, as he intended, may yet pay Atlanta a visit at some undetermined date. Is there any chance that you will come, too? I should so love to meet you. And I've been afraid, ever since that hasty letter I wrote you, that you would think me the rudest creature, for refusing point blank to have any thing to do with additional dialogue. I wish you would come. Then I could tell you to your face, much better than I can in writing, just how happy I am that "GWTW" fell into your hands and not into the hands of several others I could mention.

Dr. Douglas Southall Freeman   Atlanta, Georgia
Richmond, Virginia   January 4, 1937

My dear Dr. Freeman:

. . . How can I thank you enough for what you wrote me! To have you say such things about my book is the highest accolade the book or I can ever receive. You see, you are really the person the Confederate dead salute, for in your three [i.e., four] volumes are gathered not only the life of Lee but of the South and the Confederacy. I only wish that I could write as beautifully as you to tell you what your letter has meant to me. And I thank you for it very much.

I know you are a busy person and sought after by thousands of people, but I do hope, if I ever come quietly to Virginia, that I may have the opportunity of meeting you. I say "quietly" because I don't like crowds, nor do I take much pleasure in them. But meeting you would be something I should remember forever. When Mr. Robert Henry was here a month or so ago he said jokingly that I must come to Washington incognito, and that he would invite Captain Thomason and you over and we would pick a campaign and choose sides and spend an evening fighting. I was so overwhelmed at the thought that I sat like a newly gigged frog. I told him I wouldn't dare to do any fighting but would love to hear you three conduct a campaign.

Harry E. Ransford   Atlanta, Georgia
Los Angeles, California   January 4, 1937

My dear Harry:
     How good of you to write me and send me your good wishes and
those of your mother and your wife! It means a lot to have your kinfolks
approve of you, and so, I thank you for your letter. . . .
     I think it was awfully interesting that your mother "discovered" me
over the radio, and I take it as a great compliment to my mother and
father that she thought any daughter of theirs must have sense enough to
write a book! I do not know if you know it, but your father was just about
my mother's favorite cousin. She spoke of him so frequently.
     I, too, am interested in the coming picture version of my book, but I
have nothing to do with the filming either in writing the script or assisting
with the casting, so I do not think there is any chance of my coming to
Hollywood. The movie people offered me a good salary to come out and
work on the picture but I naturally refused. I like Atlanta too much and
[am] too devoted to my family to leave them. Moreover, I realise that an
author is never given a free hand in the filming of a book. I know, if the
movie people made some grievous error which offended Southerners, then
I'd be blamed for it. So I have kept my skirts free, but thank you just the
same for wanting me to come to see you all if I should come West.
     You asked about the character of Ellen and whether she was taken
from my great-grandmother. No, none of the characters were taken from
life, for I haven't much use for writers who use their own relatives for
copy. Moreover I'd always heard my great-grandmother described as
being a bright blonde with large blue eyes, pale gold hair—a vivacious
woman with a sense of humor who laughed all the time. Ellen in the book
was very dark, completely without humor and with no vivacity.
     I was somewhat upset when you said you recognized Tara as a real
place, for this is not so. Tara as I described it was built of whitewashed
brick, a square house set on a hill a quarter of a mile from the river, far
back from the road and with an avenue of cedars leading up to it. Rural
Home is a weatherboard house; L shaped; it is not on a hill; it is not far
back from the road; it has no avenue of cedars; and is nearly four miles
from the river. When I wrote of Tara I went to great pains to describe a
house which had never existed in Clayton County. At least, in all my
research through old records and the memories of old people I could find
no white-washed brick in the rural part of the County. I travelled the
roads of the County in the backwoods time and again to make sure of
this. In my imagination I located Tara on a road which I found in one of

General Sherman's maps of 1864. This road no longer exists and it has fallen to pieces and I had to travel it on foot.

It might amuse you and the family to know that five different house owners in the County are claiming their homes are Tara. I think some of them are mad at me for denying this. . . .

Dr. W. T. Oppenhimer   Atlanta, Georgia
Richmond, Virginia   January 6, 1937

Dear Doctor Oppenhimer:

Forgive my long delay in answering your nice letter. My husband and I were in Florida over the holidays and have just returned. The sight of your signature was like the sight of an old friend's face and I was very glad to see it. Of course you know how flattered I am that you are read-ing my book for the second time. It's such a long book and I can't help feeling swelled up when you write me such things.

And about that old parrot of yours—you aren't the only one to catch me out on this. Coming home from Florida I stopped in Macon, Georgia, and one of my friends said in a puzzled way, "My grandpa told me to tell you he liked your book so much, but he said Belle Watling certainly should have had a parrot. Now, just what could Grandpa mean?" Of course I couldn't help laughing, and I said, "You go home and tell your grandpa that he was a very wicked man, and, thanks to a Virginia doctor, I have caught up with him."

Mrs. Duncan McDonald   Atlanta, Georgia
Miami, Florida   January 8, 1937

Dear Irene:

This is a postscript to my letter of yesterday.

I was wondering how you had gotten the notion that I was in Miami. Last night John came home with an amusing and disturbing story that may explain this. He had met a man who had some connection with the airplane line between Miami and Havana. This man told John that around Christmas time a woman claiming to be me turned up at the air-port with two men who she said were her "managers" and demanded passage to Havana on a crowded plane. There were no seats, but she raised such a row and waved the Confederate flag so hard that they gave her passage immediately. I haven't been in Miami or Havana since around 1924, so this woman was an imposter. She is not the first to claim to be me. Not long ago a Milwaukee store long distanced me a woman had turned up in their book shop, claiming to be me and offering to autograph for a good price. The store became suspicious because my aversion to autographing is well known and widespread, so they communicated with me just to make sure. When the woman called the next day the detectives were waiting for her. I sometimes wonder how people get up the courage to do this sort of thing because they are so easily caught up with. I also heard of a woman on a cruise who pretended to be me and had a grand time for the duration of the trip.

If you have heard anything about this woman in Miami I'd certainly like to know the details.

Miss Katharine Brown   Atlanta, Georgia
New York, New York   January 8, 1937

Dear Katharine:
Thought the enclosed might interest you as it pretty well sums up the reaction to the announcements about Clark Gable and Tallulah Bankhead.[1] On the way back from Florida we sounded out every one we saw along the road. What they said is pretty well expressed in this clipping. Just between you and me, have they decided who will have the roles? I'll keep it quiet if you want to tell me but if it ain't any of my business, just don't tell me.

Has Mr. Cukor any further plans? Sorry about having to put him off. I expected him to come to Florida and so made many many dates for January with folks from out of town, mostly New York. And with two weddings in the family on top of it, I am in a state.

Mr. John Paschall   Atlanta, Georgia
Atlanta, Georgia   January 15, 1937

Dear Mr. Paschall:
For days I have been trying to get down to the Journal to see you, but each day letters and people descend on me and I never get out of the house.

---

[1] The enclosure was probably a copy of a story filed from Hollywood December 8 by Harold Heffernan. It reported that "authoritative channels indicate clearly there is hardly a doubt that Gable will play" Rhett. Heffernan declared that the fight for the part as Scarlett would be between Miriam Hopkins and Tallulah Bankhead. Atlanta *Constitution*, December 9.

I do not know if the enclosed little book will interest you. This is how it came into my hands. After GWTW was published Mr. George Ward, former Mayor of Birmingham, sent my father a leather-bound copy of this same book. It was the testimony of his mother which was made before a Republican investigating committee in Birmingham in 1885. The title page looked very dull and forbidding, but once I had gotten into the testimony I was delighted. Mrs. Ward told stories of Wartime experiences in Georgia, especially in Rome and some in Atlanta. She also gave testimony of the change in the Negroes after freedom came.

I was so charmed with the little volume that I wrote Mr. Ward, asking permission to have photostatic copies made, some for myself and some for the Carnegie Library's reference room as I felt it was really a valuable document.

Mr. Ward was more than kind. He refused to let me photostat the book, but had a number printed himself and presented several to me. Two weeks ago I heard that one of the Birmingham papers was running "Mrs. Ward's Testimony" as a feature and getting enthusiastic letters about it.[1] I do not know if you will be interested in this book in part or as a whole for the Journal. However, as so much of it is about Georgia, I thought you would like to see it. If you do not think it of any newspaper interest, please keep it anyway with my regards.

I imagine Mr. Ward would be only too happy to give his consent to publication. His address is the Brown-Marx Building, Birmingham. I do not believe the Birmingham paper copyrighted this material. But then, I am not sure of this.

Mr. Herschel Brickell   Atlanta, Georgia
Ridgefield, Connecticut   January 17, 1937

My dear Herschel:
    Each morning I rise, saying to myself that I'll write you in answer to your letter written around Christmas and that I'll write Lois Cole, too. And each morning Hell busts loose around eight thirty and I never get the letters written. We have been deluged and inundated, since returning from Florida, with people from New York. I had thought myself clever to stay away from N.Y. and avoid a lot of grief but it hasn't worked

---

[1] The Birmingham *Post* ran a series of articles (November 19, 20, and 21) by Lucia Giddens which were based on Mrs. Ward's testimony and quoted liberally from it. The series to which Miss Mitchell refers is an even fuller one edited by James Saxon Childers. It appeared in the Birmingham *News-Age-Herald* December 20 and 27 and January 3.

out that way. Of course, a lot of the people who come are charming and interesting people and people who, under other circumstances, I'd be proud and happy to meet but they come in such numbers, and I have to run them three or four a day and by three o'clock I'm too tired to remember whether they are authors, editors or critics or merely people actuated by violent curiosity.

We went to Winter Park hoping to God that no one but Edwin and Mabel[1] would ever know we were there. I knew so many people in the neighborhood who I would be forced to call on if they knew of my presence. Not that I minded calling but tired as I was the very idea of having to see people was appalling. With the best intentions in the world, Edwin let the cat out of the bag and we had to pack up early Christmas morning and get out of town, one jump ahead of newspapers and dinner invitations. The rest of the vacation we spent in small hotels in small towns and had a wonderful time and I gained six pounds which I lost within three days of my return home. . . .

Herschel, I know my book has been a freak, a runaway, a natural, one of those things that isn't supposed to happen but does happen ever so often. So I know its course is unpredictable. But can you make me any private predictions? You are in the center of things, you've been watching books for years. Do you know when it will stop selling? Do you have any idea when public interest in me, personally, will end? Of course, I cannot help feeling very proud at selling a million copies and I am grateful to people for liking it but I am neither proud nor grateful for the public interest in my private life or my personality. I resent it with a bitterness which I am unable to convey on paper. I have always believed that an artist of any type should be judged by their work alone. (I do not consider myself an artist, by the way, but only a craftsman but I use artist for want of a better word.) Personally, I would not walk two steps out of my way to look at my favorite writer, nor have I any interest in what he eats for breakfast and what his wife is like or if he sends her two dozen red roses every morning before breakfast (that is the latest legend about John and me).

If I liked his books, I liked his books and that's the end of it and unless he signified an overweening desire to make my acquaintance, I wouldn't have the slightest desire to meet him. And having met him, I'm sure I would not be so impertinent as to ask him personal questions. I have only myself to judge by and I find that I am in a small minority. And people cannot understand my lack of desire for personal questions, personal appearances etc. Not that it matters two damns whether they understand it or not but it makes it pretty inconvenient, some times, and makes it difficult for me to control my temper.

[1] Granberry.

I feel that public interest in me as a person will wane if the book ever stops selling. But when will it stop? The problem resolves itself around whether I can last till the book stops selling. At first I thought I'd go to Europe till it all blew over. But I realized that I couldn't do that. In the first place I loathe travelling and have no desire to see Europe and would be miserable away from John. In the second place, if I did go away a terrific load would descend upon John and he is already carrying far more of my load than I want him to. For instance, there are never less than forty letters a week wanting me to speak, invitations from very prominent organizations. It is not courtesy to ignore them, certainly it is not courtesy to send them abrupt letters, even though they must know from all the newspaper stories that I will neither speak nor make appearances. They must be answered and answered by me. And there are—oh, well, I won't go on. There are things I have to attend to personally because this happens to be my job, whether I like it or not, and I cannot put it upon any one else. Nor, as I think it over, can I run away.

Herschel, tell me something. I'm awfully ignorant about authors. I've known so few and so few of them intimately. Do all of them have to go through this? If so, how do they ever have the courage to write a second book? Are all of them put in such positions that they cannot go out of their houses? When they go to parties (I ventured to one tea) are their veils jerked off, their sashes torn loose, the seams of their skirts parted from their waists? Do people scream at them and poke them with their long finger nails? I know these people at that tea meant well enough and were trying in their way to tell me that they liked my book but Godlmighty, I will never go to another party. I should add that it wasn't Atlanta people who did all of this. My Atlanta friends stood aghast against the walls unable to help me while the out-of-town guests savaged me, knocked punch cups from my hands, overturned my plates of refreshments down my dress and tore my clothes in their efforts to obtain my attention.

Do other authors have to go through the miseries of seeing the most casual letters they write appear in print? Such has been my experience. I hate to go through my clippings because practically every letter I write finds its way into some newspaper. I regret to state that this is not confined to strangers. Some of my friends have turned over personal letters to papers. And then they write me aggrieved because the tone of my letters to them has changed! And when they do not actually print them they read them aloud at parties and the columnists comment on them, usually in garbled style. Does that happen to all authors? How do they ever survive it?

I know you must think by now that all my letters are full of bellyaching and, as I look back on them, I suppose they are. One would think from reading them that I was very unappreciative of my success. The trouble is that I've never been permitted time or opportunity to enjoy my success or even be proud of it or happy in it. John keeps me going by repeating that it can't possibly keep up much longer. Nothing could. I hope he's right. Atlanta friends and Atlanta papers have rallied in a campaign to let me alone. Friends refuse to introduce people who come to town and insist on meeting me. The papers have begged people not to devil me about getting them into the movies, reading their unpublished manuscripts, etc. And oh, how it has helped! But it's still rough going. Yes, my letters to you have been bellyaches but I know you understand. In a way, you've been in on this since the beginning. . . .

Mrs. Alfred L. Lustig   Atlanta, Georgia
Providence, Rhode Island   January 19, 1937

My dear Mrs. Lustig:

. . . You wrote me that you and Doctor Riggs had disagreed over how I had written "Gone With the Wind," Doctor Riggs saying that I worked hard over every sentence and re-wrote numerous times, while you said the book had written itself. You were both right, but I must confess Doctor Riggs was a little righter than you. There are many parts of my book which I will never be able to read because I become sick with the memory of the numbers of times I re-wrote them. One chapter, for instance, was re-written seventy times, many chapters at least thirty times. I do not write with ease, nor am I ever pleased with anything I write. And so, I re-write. There are, however, a few chapters which were never altered from the first way in which they were set down. If you are interested, I made no change in the text from page 398, when Scarlett is struggling home to Tara, to page 421, when she decided to take up her load and carry it. There were a few other passages which I did not change. For the most part, however, the book was sweated over.

I am glad you thought the ending logical and inevitable. I could not see any other end in view of the characters of the people in the book. However, you and I, and I might add, my husband, are very much in the minority in this belief. . . .

Miss Astride K. Hansen   Atlanta, Georgia
Laurel, Mississippi   January 27, 1937

Dear Miss Hansen:

Thank you so much for your letter and thank you, too, for your defense of Scarlett. You asked if it was my intention for her not to have "a
single honorable intention." To tell the truth, I did not wish, as the
author, to pass any judgment on any character but only to tell what they
did and said and let the readers draw their own inferences. Personally,
I cannot help feeling that Scarlett had good traits. Surely courage is
commendable, and she had it. The sense of responsibility for the weak
and helpless is a rare trait, and she had this, for she took care of her own
even at great cost to herself. She was able to appreciate what was beautiful in her mother, even if she could not emulate her. She loved her Negroes and looked after them. She had perseverance in the face of defeat.
Of course those qualities are balanced by her bad qualities.

Thank you for admiring her.

Mrs. Earl Taylor   Atlanta, Georgia
Angier, North Carolina   January 27, 1937

My dear Mrs. Taylor:

Thank you so much for your letter and the nice things you wrote me
about "Gone With the Wind."

In the matter of the poem, "Lines on the Back of a Confederate
Note"[1]—I find myself in a somewhat embarrassing situation, and in this
situation I can only be frank with you. I have known that poem since
childhood and have loved it. I have always heard it attributed to Major
S. A. Jonas of Mississippi. While I cannot tell you offhand of any particular book in which this poem is included, I have run across it countless
times in my research work in collections of Southern Poems. Sometimes
there were only four stanzas, sometimes as many as fourteen. I believe,
but am not certain (as I do not have the volume at hand), that Miss
Mildred L. Rutherford's book on Southern literature contains this poem
and attributes it to Major Jonas.

[1] The authorship of "Lines on the Back of a Confederate Note," generally attributed to Major S. A. Jonas, was claimed also for Mrs. R. E. Lytle of Louisville, Ky.,
and for Miss M. J. Turner of North Carolina. Mildred Lewis Rutherford, *The South
in History and Literature* (Atlanta, Ga., 1907), pp. 270–71. Mrs. Taylor had written
concerning the claim for Miss Turner. The poem appears in Rutherford, p. 866. Two
stanzas of it are quoted in *GWTW*, p. 514.

In the hope that I can be of a little assistance to you in running down this matter, may I suggest that you write to the reference department of the Carnegie Library nearest your city and ask them for any information about this poem and its author. If you do not have any luck in your North Carolina libraries, I am sure our Atlanta library might help you. I wish I could tell you the exact book in which this poem is included, but I cannot as I have read it in so many books.

Mr. Michael MacWhite   Atlanta, Georgia
Irish Legation   January 27, 1937
Washington, D.C.

My dear Mr. MacWhite:

I have delayed this long in thanking you for the inscribed copy of Mangan's poems[1] because I wanted to read them all first. Most of my reading these days is done very late at night, and how much I have enjoyed this book in the small hours! I am more than embarrassed to confess that, while I was familiar with some of Mangan's poems, I had never read "Gone In the Wind" until shortly after "Gone With the Wind" appeared and many people questioned if this was the source of my title.[2] I do not know how I had overlooked this sad and stirring poem, for I knew "Dark Rosaleen," "The Lament of Fitzgerald," "The Ode to the Maguire" and others. The truth is I had heard these poems orally and had never had a copy of Mangan's work in my hands.

Loving the poems and the songs and the history of Ireland as I do, there was really no excuse for my ignorance of "Gone In the Wind." I thank you so much for sending me the book, and your inscription makes it all the more valued. . . .

Thank you for writing that you found "Gone With the Wind" "delightful." Naturally, I was pleased, especially when such a word came from an Irishman and an Irishman in your position. I do not know how much you know of the part the Irish played in the building up of our

[1] James Clarence Mangan, *Poems* (New York, 1859), or one of many other editions.

[2] In his syndicated column prepared for release October 13 Dr. Phelps stated that Miss Mitchell "in all probability" got her title from Dowson's "Cynara." He suggested that Dowson may have got the phrase from Mangan's "Gone in the Wind." The first stanza of Mangan's poem reads:
> Solomon! where is thy throne? It is gone in the wind.
> Babylon! where is thy might? It is gone in the wind.
> Like the swift shadows of Noon, like the dreams of the Blind,
> Vanish the glories and pomps of the earth in the wind.

Southern section and in the Civil War. So many came to us in the 'thirties
and 'forties and they were a fine type of people. Reading the old records
as I did, they sometimes sounded like "The Annals of the Four Masters"
because of the many Irish names. As it was once said in Ireland of the
Fitzgeralds, "they became more Irish than the Irish themselves," so our
Southern Irish became more Southern than the Southerners. When the
trouble in the 'sixties began they went out with the Confederate troops
and did great deeds for their new land.

Mr. W. W. Watson   Atlanta, Georgia
Orangeburg, South Carolina   January 27, 1937

My dear Mr. Watson:
   I am so very glad you liked my book and gladder still that you wrote
and told me so. Thank you so very much for the many nice things you
said.
   When you asked me about the "most authentic books" on the lives of
the famous men of the War period, you have me out on a limb. You see,
I read so very many of them in trying to get my background straight that
it is hard for me to decide which were the best books. However, I must
say unhesitatingly that the four-volume "Lee" by Doctor Douglas Southall
Freeman is unsurpassed and unsurpassable. I found that the stories of
Generals Sherman and Johnston as told by themselves were the most interesting,—Sherman's "Memoirs" and General Johnston's "Narrative."
There are very many biographies of Lincoln, of course. Most people
seem to like the work of Mrs. Morrow on Lincoln.[1] Henderson's "Stonewall Jackson" is a standard work and one of great value.[2]

Rabbi Mordecai M. Thurman   Atlanta, Georgia
Wilmington, North Carolina   February 6, 1937

Dear Doctor Thurman:
   I only wish I were not pressed for time by illness in my family, for I
would like to write you a long letter of appreciation of the wonderful

   [1] Honoré McCue Willsie Morrow, *Great Captain: The Lincoln Trilogy of Forever
Free, With Malice Toward None, The Last Full Measure* (New York, 1935; 3 vols.
in 1).
   [2] George Francis Robert Henderson, *Stonewall Jackson and the American Civil
War* (London, New York, etc., 1898; 2 vols.).

letter you wrote me. You said so many things that were well calculated to warm this author's heart, and I thank you for all of them. I do not think you are "too ministerial" in your analysis. I thought it a very fair and broad minded summing up of the underlying currents of my story. I am happy to know that you intend to review it. . . .

I do not know if this will interest you but I will tell you about it. Many people have thought that I wrote "Gone With the Wind" as a parallel to the modern War and depression, but I had almost finished the book before the depression began. When I wrote it everyone thought the boom was here to stay. But I wrote about another world that blew up under the unsuspecting feet of our grandparents, without any idea that the world in which I lived would blow up shortly. Now that I look back on it I feel that the same qualities of courage are needed when, at any period of history, a world turns over. And the same qualities of gentleness and idealism are needed too.

Mr. Herschel Brickell   Atlanta, Georgia
New York, New York   February 8, 1937

Dear Herschel:

I intended answering your letter long ere this but added onto the ladies from Keokuk who want to see what I look like and the usual daily run of girls who intend to kill themselves if I don't get them into the movies and people who want to write books and don't want to work at it and feel that there must be some trick to writing one—I've had John in the hospital for ten days.

Did I write you that I'd at last gotten me an office? I'd wanted one for months but never had the time to take a day off and hunt for one. So I set our janitor a-prowl and he found me a one room and bath apartment in the neighborhood and I thankfully moved my files, typewriter, secretary and a sofa into it. I have no telephone but am close enough to home for Bessie to come and tell me in case of emergencies such as long distance phone calls, etc. And it's close enough to go home for meals. Best of all, when things get too bad, I can take a nap on the sofa while the secretary is getting out the mail, for, praise be, I can sleep through any amount of typing. It is marvelous to get uninterrupted sleep even if I do have to get it at odd hours.

Things are quieting down a little or if they aren't I don't know about them because I stay at the office till very late and let poor Bessie wrastle with things. But I think I'm through with the invasion of editors. They've all come down here and gone away with their minds made up that I'm probably crazy because I won't write short stories or articles for them. When I say with fervor that I wouldn't think of doing anything that would add to the present public interest in me or accept one penny that would run my income into a higher bracket—they just look at me. However, I think Kenneth Littauer of Colliers who was down here a second time when Edwin came up to talk about the article which is appearing in Colliers at some time in the near future[1] *did* get my viewpoint. Any way, he's a very nice person and we enjoyed him.

Honestly, Herschel, the amount of money editors offer is appalling. No literature even of permanent value is worth what they offer and they don't even want literature of permanent worth. I don't believe if Matthew, Mark, Luke and John offered to write some more Gospels, they'd be worth the prices that have been offered me. Perhaps some day when I am ending my days in the poor house I'll regret not writing some tripe and selling it but until I'm in the poor house I doubt if I'll do any regretting.

After each editor gets back to N.Y. rumors begin to float back—that I have sold them a million page story about the Revolutionary War, an article on my love life, an article on how I shall spend my money, that I am collaborating with Faith Baldwin on a Civil War play (I *did* tell you that she was down here to get an interview with me for Pictorial, didn't I?),[2] that Cosmopolitan has me sewed up on a ten year contract for a million dollars a year, etc. Good grief and here I sit not writing anything except interminable letters and not intending to write anything.

The reviews have begun to come in from South Africa and India and, Herschel, I give you my word, if they'd been written by unreconstructed Rebels they couldn't be better. I go cold chills up and down my back reading the Indian ones. . . .

By the way—just on the chance that anyone asks you if I'll autograph their book—tell them no. When the book hit the million mark the requests for autographed copies went up into the hundred thousand. They were being dumped on me through the mail (without even the courtesy of a letter of request) by the hundreds and the phone and door bell rang eternally. So I called a halt and I'm not even autographing for my kin folks. Of course, this seems very hardboiled to a number of people who get turned down and they resent it pretty bitterly for they do not understand why I should not give over my entire life to autographing. One more autograph won't hurt anybody is the burden of their lay. But when

[1] Edwin Granberry, "The Private Life of Margaret Mitchell," *Collier's*, XCIX, No. 11 (March 1937), pp. 22, 24, 26.
[2] Faith Baldwin (Mrs. Hugh Hamlin Cuthrell), "The Woman Who Wrote 'Gone With the Wind,' An Exclusive and Authentic Interview," *Pictorial Review*, XXXVIII, No. 8 (March 1937), pp. 4, 69–70, 72.

I checked up on it I found that every time I autographed one book, a hundred friends and relatives of the book owner descended on me. So it's self preservation with me. I know you won't believe me but recently as I was leaving the funeral of a cousin, a strange woman had the gall to stop me between the church and the car and ask me to autograph her book. Some people ain't got no notions of decency!

If only I wasn't so busy! The weather has been beautiful and we've had no winter. The jessamine has bloomed weeks ago, the peaches are out and the flowering quince, all the bulb flowers are on the wane. It would be marvelous to get out into the country. Of course, we'll probably freeze through March and me without a heavy coat!

Mr. Harllee Branch   Atlanta, Georgia
Second Assistant Postmaster General   February 9, 1937
Washington, D.C.

Dear Mr. Branch:

You cannot imagine how much your letter of congratulations meant to me, because I am sure you never realized the great admiration I had for you during the days when I was a reporter on the Atlanta Journal. You probably did not suspect that the height of my ambition was to do some work on the staff of the daily as well as feature stories for the Magazine. You have doubtless forgotten that several times you did call on me to cover stories for the daily, and I was made so happy and excited that I could hardly write them. Then, one day when you had sent me to interview a lady axe murderess who had refused to unburden her soul to crude male ears, you liked my story enough to say loudly so that the whole City Room could hear, "How would you like to come upstairs and work for me?" Nothing will ever again give me such a thrill, because I knew very well you did not care greatly about having women working on the City staff. I didn't go to work for you, but I always remembered your words with much gratitude.

Thank you so much for all the wonderful things you wrote me about "Gone With the Wind." I appreciated them all so very much. I appreciated, too, your invitation to come and see you and Mrs. Branch should I ever be in Washington. I do not know when such a trip will be possible as it is hard to explain on paper what a deluge of work has descended on us both since my book was published. It keeps us both busy night and day and, while, of course, I am so happy and grateful at the reception "Gone With the Wind" has received, I cannot help wishing that things would quiet down so that John and I would have the opportunity to do the things we would like to do instead of the urgent things we must do. For instance, we'd like to visit about with our friends and take little trips and have the opportunity to talk leisurely with the people we like instead of being constantly hurried and rushed by business matters. I know all this furore will quiet down soon, and the sooner it quiets down the better it will suit us, for, as you know, John and I like quietness above all things.

I am going to look for a photograph and if I have one I will certainly send it to you.

John sends his regards and I do too. With many thanks for your letter.

Miss Katharine Brown   Atlanta, Georgia
New York, New York   February 14, 1937

Dear Katharine:

Yesterday I had to go to Macon on the saddest trip I'll ever make to that town. Aaron Bernd,[1] who was your and my host at Teteer-on-the-Jitters during your trip to Macon, had died of pneumonia and I went over for the funeral. As he was as good a friend as John and I had, it was a pretty desolate day. He had so very many friends, both Jewish and Gentile, and we all hung together after the funeral and went out to Teeter that night for the last time. In an effort to divert ourselves we fell to talking about the coming production of *G. W. T. W.* (as you probably know wherever two or more of ye are gathered together these days, the two or more talk about the movie). As I listened to Susan Myrick talking an idea dawned on me that made me wonder why I hadn't thought about it before. I spent the night with her and encouraged her far into the night to talk about the picture. She had such good ideas (at least I thought them good) that I came home determined to write you.

You know what my attitude has been all along in the matter of not making any suggestions to any of you Selznick folks about the film. You know the fight I have put up against the general public who wanted to get in the picture as actors, script assistants, costumers, advisers, etc. Half of my fight has been, frankly, because I didn't want any more grief than I already had. The other half was because I sincerely believe that you people know your business far better than I'll ever know it and I did not want to hamper or embarrass you with suggestions that were useless or impractical. I've even refused as much as five hundred dollars to name the cast *I'd* like because I thought it might embarrass y'all in some way. So this is my first suggestion and for Heaven's sake, if it sounds foolish

[1] Book reviewer for the Macon *Telegraph.* He reviewed *GWTW* June 30, 1936.

to you, don't mind telling me because it won't hurt my feelings and no one else except John will ever know about it.

My suggestion is—why not take Susan Myrick out to the Coast in some capacity while the picture is being made? (I say "in some capacity" for I do not know just what sort of title such a job would carry.) You said that you'd like to have me there to pass on the authenticity and rightness of this and that, the accents of the white actors, the dialect of the colored ones, the minor matters of dress and deportment, the small touches of local color, etc.[2]

Well, I can't go and you know why. But I thought if you really wanted a Georgian for the job there wouldn't be anyone better than Sue. In fact, she'd be a better person for the job than I would because she knows more about such matters than I do. I hope you will not gag when I explain why. I know you are sick and tired of people who want to get into the picture "because of their lovely Southern background." I know I am. But I have to drag in Sue's background for explanation.

Her Grandpa, old General Myrick,[3] had the biggest and whitest colyumned house in Georgia, at Milledgeville. It's still there, a lovely place but no longer in Myrick hands. The family lost it due to hard times. Sue is the youngest child of a Confederate soldier[4] and God knows she's heard enough about the old days. Being poor as Job's turkey, she was raised up in the country and she knows good times and bad, quality folks and poor whites, Crackers and town folks. And good grief, what she doesn't know about negroes! She was raised up with them. And she loves and understands them. Since going on the paper, she has been the paper's official representative at most of the negro affairs of her section. Mr. W. T. Anderson, owner of her paper (I wish you could have met him), is strong for the colored folks and tries to get a square deal for them and the saying among the colored folks in the district is that "De Race is got two friends in dis County, sweet Jesus and de Macon Tele-

[2] W. T. Anderson, editor and publisher of the Macon *Telegraph*, wrote Miss Mitchell December 9: "Sue tells me about Hollywood wanting you to come out there and see that your book is properly filmed, and that you won't go. . . . If you don't think of anything better I should like to see Sue Myrick deputized to supervise. She has studied stage business, knows Southern dialect, has Southern background and understands the characters and the qualities every foot of the way. I think you would do the best job, and think Sue would do the second best. She'd fight to keep the picture off the rocks. If you are asked what to do about the job you don't want, keep this idea in mind."

Miss Mitchell replied on December 12: "I hadn't thought of Sue for the purpose you mentioned because, to tell the truth, my only thought was to get from under it and without being killed. However, now that I do think about it, it sounds like a swell idea, and I promise you if these people come back (as I fear they will), I will certainly beat the drum for her."

[3] General Stith Parham Myrick.

[4] James Dowdell Myrick.

graph." So whenever there's a colored graduation if Mr. W. T. can't be there to make a speech, Sue goes and if the colored P.T.A. wants to be addressed by Mr. Anderson and he can't make it, Sue does the addressing —The same holds for funerals and awarding of prizes.

Moreover Sue is as competent a newspaper woman as we have in this section. She can-and does-do everything from advice to the lovelorn and the cooking page to book reviews and politics and hangings. But the main thing that recommends her to me is her common sense and her utter lack of sentimentality about what is tearfully known as "The Old South." She knows its good points and she doesn't slur over its bad points. She knows her section and its people and she loves them both but she is not unaware of either the faults or the charm of both people and section. In other words she's a common sense, hard headed person with an awful lot of knowledge about Georgia people and Georgia ways, not only of this time but of times past. So I'm handing the idea on to you of using her on the picture.

Now, Katharine, please don't think you've got to consider her seriously just because I suggested her or just because she's a friend of mine. If the idea doesn't seem good to you, just tell me so. It won't bother me and Sue will never know that I've ever written you so there'll be no skin off anyone's nose. . . .

Mr. Jackson P. Dick, Jr.   Atlanta, Georgia
St. Paul's School   February 16, 1937
Concord, New Hampshire

My dear Mr. Dick:
    Your father sent me a copy of your review of "Gone With the Wind" and I am very happy that he did so, for I enjoyed it so much and it interested me so much. And more than my interest in the review itself is my interest in the mind behind the review. You see, I do not know you and I do not know your exact age, but there is a maturity of thought and judgment in your article that, to be quite frank, I have never seen in a boy still in school or college.

    As you perhaps have guessed, I have read a number of reviews of my book. What has impressed me and my husband about many of these reviews is that the writers did not take the trouble or were not mentally capable of thinking out ideas for themselves. Instead, they read the reviews of well known critics and swallowed them whole and re-wrote them. In your review it was obvious that all you wrote was out of your own head. You may not know how rare this is, but I do. I will point out just one example of many: it is where you sum up Ashley Wilkes. I have become somewhat weary of reading reviews which call Ashley "weak," "idealistic," "a dreamer," "a coward" et cetera. I never thought of him in this way and always considered him the greatest realist in the book because his eyes, like those of Rhett, were always open. He saw things with a cruel clarity but, unlike Rhett, he was not able to do anything about them. You are the only one of thousands of reviewers who has summed him up right, and you expressed it all so well and so beautifully, for he was a tragic character.

And, so far as I know, you are the only person who has mentioned what seems to me to be a simple and obvious fact,—that Scarlett was "a pitifully unhappy woman in love." This one thing motivated her as much as hunger.

I could go through your review paragraph by paragraph telling you how good it was, but that would make this a very, very long letter! So, I will just congratulate you on the clarity of your ideas, the smoothness of your expression of them, and your most excellent choice of words. May I thank you, too, for the many fine things you wrote about "Gone With the Wind"? Such things, coming from a Southerner and an Atlantan, make me very happy. . . .

Mr. Stark Young   Atlanta, Georgia
New York, New York   February 16, 1937

Dear Mr. Young:

For weeks I have been searching for the opportunity to write you a long letter about your wonderful article in the Quarterly.[1] But the opportunity for a long letter never seems to arrive, so I am writing you a short

[1] In his letter of September 14 Young wrote: "I'll take this up with Malcolm sooner or later (and perhaps in the January Virginia Quarterly . . .)," and so he did. In "More Encaustics for Southerners" Young creates an imaginary colleague "S——" on the model of Cowley and proceeds: " 'My dear fellow,' he says, 'you Southerners live on romantic nursery tales.'

"You can see that from how the poor South comes off when S—— sets out to review a book about it. The kind of book that fares worst is not so much the share cropper, lynching variety, but a novel that assumes a certain air of old custom, breeding, sentiment, or romance. He will turn on a book like that and lay it out, author and South together. I have sometimes wondered whether it is not that S—— feels instinctively that he could never be a part of the life the book portrays, and this unconsciously is what drives him wild. . . .

"One thing I do have sense enough to see: it would be worse than useless to try to describe to S—— a kind of society that I grew up to admire, whether I ever saw any perfect expression of it or not. In such a society people value greatly only those opinions they have put into action or are willing to pay for, sometimes even with their lives if it comes to that." *The Virginia Quarterly Review*, XIII (1937), 47.

one just to let you know how very fine I thought the article was and how much I enjoyed it.

There was one statement that impressed me so very much—"in such a society people value greatly only those opinions that they have put into their lives, if it comes to that." This seems so very true to me and so well summed up. It brought back to my mind a conversation I had with my brother some years ago. I had gone through hundreds of daguerreotypes of the fifties and sixties and I was struck by the expressions on the faces of the Southerners in the daguerreotypes. There was a certain expression common to old and young, men and women—an expression which you will not find in many modern pictures. It baffled me for I could not analyze wherein the difference lay. I spoke of this to my brother and he, looking at some of the daguerreotypes, said, "The reason those people look as they look is because they all believed in something. So few people these days believe in anything and it shows in their faces."

Are you ever going to write another book? I know from personal experience that that is a question no writer likes to hear. But I would so love to know that you are writing something else for I know how much I would like it.

Mr. Herschel Brickell   Atlanta, Georgia
New York, New York   February 22, 1937

Dear Herschel:

In your last letter you asked me how the English sales were going. I had a letter from Macmillan and Company, Limited, of London, dated the 26th of January, and they said the book was in its fifth impression and 38,000 copies had been sold three months after publication. About the translation rights, everybody except the Chinese and Albanians have put in a bid. We've been working on them for some time and they ought to be closed up within a couple of weeks if we don't hit any more snags. And, good grief, the number of snags we have hit! I'll let you know about these if they ever get settled. . . .

I am hoping against hope to get to Washington on March the 1st to the press ladies' gridiron dinner. Lois Cole is spending the week-end in Washington and, of course, I am very anxious to see her. I would enjoy the party so very much but so many things—wearying things—enter into such a trip. I know scores of people in Washington and I would have to call on them all, for my name will probably be in the papers and they will know that I am in the city. These days I am too tired to see a lot of people, but I want to go to the dinner for they have been kind enough to invite me especially, and I do want to see Lois. If John continues to improve I may make the trip and stay a couple of days. I wish I could go over to Richmond and see Douglas Southall Freeman, but I know just as many people in Richmond and the same situation prevails. If it were only possible for me to make one move without it getting in the papers life might hold some amusement. . . .

Hon. Robert W. Bingham   Atlanta, Georgia
Louisville Courier-Journal   February 23, 1937
Louisville, Kentucky

My dear Judge Bingham:

I have received many letters since "Gone With the Wind" was published, but none that I will cherish like yours. To have praise from a person like you is praise indeed, and I only wish there were some way I could tell you adequately how much I appreciated your words.

Your letter arrived at a fortunate time. On the day it came I had been harried and upset by totally false rumors that I was in Reno divorcing my husband. Naturally, all the news services had me on the wire for a confirmation or denial of this rumor. As I have had no thought of divorcing John and was not in Reno, I was greatly disturbed. That morning I began wishing that I had never written "Gone With the Wind," because its success has disrupted the peace and quiet of my old life which was so dear to me. Then your letter arrived, and after I read it I was so very proud and so very glad that I had written a book that could call forth such a response. I felt that the years of labor that went into "Gone With the Wind" were years well spent.

May I thank you for insisting to me that Melanie was beautiful? Of course, I had pictured her as a very plain little person but in my heart I thought her beautiful too. I had known so many plain faced elderly ladies when I was a child who were beautiful from the inner glow of their lovely souls, so I am glad if the inner glow of Melanie was apparent. You could not have complimented me more than by putting Melanie in the same class with your mother.

So many people, Southerners among them, have chided me for drawing "a bad woman" for my heroine and have said that I set up Scarlett as a "typical Southern woman" and thereby cast aspersions on all Southern ladies of bygone days. Of course this was not my intention and I could not help finding such remarks a trifle upsetting. I was bothered because these people fastened their eyes on Scarlett and her didoes and seemed to miss Melanie and Ellen and the stout-hearted Atlanta matrons who defied the shells and took care of the wounded and defied poverty to rebuild on their old foundations. Thank you for seeing this side of my picture. I shall long remember your phrases, "the poverty and the pride, the gentility, the gracious manners, the romance, the preservation of dignity and high and generous humanity in rags and semi-starvation." I, too, had heard those stories. I was raised upon them as a child. Visiting about the South I had seen many old ladies and gentlemen who were poor in purse and rich in everything that mattered. I wanted to write them into my story, and your letter made me feel that I had succeeded.

I saw Willie Snow Ethridge at the Press Institute at Athens, Georgia, this week-end, and told her of the great pleasure I had had from your letter. I hope she will tell you how much I appreciated it. We are devoted to the Ethridges and we feel that you are to be congratulated for having Mark on your paper.

You wrote of your father's imprisonment on Johnston's Island.[1] I, too, was raised on stories of that dreadful place, for some of my relatives had the bad fortune to be imprisoned there. I am still haunted by the stories of the freezing weather, the insufficient blankets and the smallpox epidemics. My relatives told how the only way they kept themselves from freezing to death was by rolling themsleves in the filthy blankets of men who had died of the disease. There was so much in your letter about your family that paralleled experiences of my own kinfolks and made me feel almost as if I had had a message from a distant relative. But perhaps the experiences of all of our ancestors were somewhat similar, and so we Southerners can share in a common tradition that binds us closely together.

Mr. Ed Danforth   Atlanta, Georgia
Atlanta Georgian   March 1, 1937
Atlanta, Georgia

Dear Ed:

I am desolated about the omission of the accordion hatrack in the hall of Belle Watling's establishment. I must admit that once before I have been taken to task about Belle's house. An old gentleman in Richmond, who had been a sad rip in his day, I fear, wrote me in sorrow because Belle did not have a parrot. He said she should have had a parrot, so her establishment was spoiled as far as he was concerned. The truth of the matter is, Ed, I spent most of my time looking up references in books

[1] Johnson's Island, Union prison camp at Sandusky Bay, Lake Erie.

when I should have been consulting authorities now living who knew about hatracks and parrots.

Thank you for that letter. You do not know how I will treasure it. I know the feeling you must have had before you read my book. I am always prejudiced against books written by my friends. My feeling is "hell, it can't be worth much because I know them." So thank you for liking it and thank you for telling me so. . . .

Mr. Olin Miller   Atlanta, Georgia
Thomaston, Georgia   March 3, 1937

Dear Mr. Miller:
. . . How much I thank you for what you said about my sentence structure and the rhythm of it. You cannot imagine what balm your words were to me. So many critics have said nice things about my plot, narrative and characters, and then they finish off with remarks about my "undistinguished style," or they say the story gets across in spite of the way it is written. I do not mean that I am not grateful for the nice things they wrote about characters et cetera, but I did work so hard on the style. I wanted it to be simple enough for a child of five to understand, and I did not want the style to intrude upon the story. I worked to secure a style which I called "colloquial" for want of any other term. I have a fairly good ear for voices and the intonations of voices, and it has always seemed to me that there is beauty and poetry in the Georgia voice and the Georgia way of expressing things. It shows up even in the conversation of people who have little or no formal education. I thought, as I was writing a book about Georgia people, that I would write it in the style a Georgian would use in speaking the story. I do not mean just in conversation but in the expository parts as well. To this end I labored, frequently shifting words and making sentences somewhat ungrammatical, but shifting them just the same because to my inner ear the accent of a Georgian's voice would fall at that place. I do not know if I am making myself clear in what I write—I have never talked about this before to anyone except John. But I had to tell you about it because your remarks made me so very happy. Of course there were many parts where I did not shift words and juggle phrases because, thank Heaven, occasionally I did not feel that they needed shifting. One instance which comes to my mind now is that part at the end of the chapter where Rhett Butler goes off to the War leaving Scarlett in the dark road.

I was sorry that I did not get to see more of you at Athens. I have always wanted to tell you at great length how much I enjoyed your work.

I, who am so verbose, always marvel at how much you can get into a line and how full of meaning that line is. May we meet at another Press Institute when I am not so flabbergasted at finding myself unexpectedly a guest of honor.

Very Rev. Mons. Jas. H. Murphy   Atlanta, Georgia
Ellicottville, New York   March 4, 1937

My dear Monsignor Murphy:

Thank you so very much for your letter and for the copy of the letter to the editor of "America."

Yes, I had read the Reverend O'Flaherty's item entitled "Banned for Youth."[1] Of course your answer made me very happy, and I hope I can make you understand how much I appreciated your defense. A number of times the character of Scarlett O'Hara has been attacked and I have been accused of portraying "a bad woman" who by her wickedness cast into disrepute virtuous Southern ladies of a bygone day. I am not one to rise up in defense of my book, but I frequently feel downhearted at such remarks for this reason. I had tried so hard to portray the wonderful women of the old South. I had striven to show that Ellen O'Hara was indeed a woman whose children rose up and called her blessed, a woman whose ideals prodded the hardening conscience of Scarlett, even though Scarlett did not obey the prods. I had tried to show Melanie as a Christian character so honorable that she could not conceive of dishonor in others. Mammy was as uncompromising about right and wrong as was possible. The stout-hearted matrons who knew right from wrong refused to tolerate Scarlett. Having put a great deal of work upon these ladies, I naturally felt a sense of disappointment that the eyes of many of my readers focused entirely upon the bad woman and paid no heed to the many good women. That is why I thank you so much for your answer, because you brought out the things that I was trying to express.[2]

[1] Father Raymond J. O'Flaherty excoriated *GWTW* in a letter to the editor of *America* printed in its issue for January 23. He expressed surprise "that a high-school teacher has assigned it to be read by the class." In a note following Father O'Flaherty's letter Thomas F. Meehan of *America*'s staff suggested that the novel "Might be rated according to the classification used for movies: Class B. 'Objectionable in parts.'" Despite the headline "Banned for Youth," neither O'Flaherty nor Meehan suggested banning *GWTW*.

[2] In his letter to his editor of *America* Msgr. Murphy wrote: "The most beautiful character in the book is Ellen O'Hara, the mother of Scarlett, an embodiment of the valiant woman of scripture, a woman whose Catholic life and ideas spread the good odor of sanctity about her and who dies a martyr to charity. After her, for eminence of character, stands Mammy, that black diamond in the rough, who imbibed her

To be quite frank, I do not think that "Gone With the Wind" should be "given indiscriminately to children." As you can imagine, I did not write it for children, but for mature people who realized the truth of "as ye sow—." I must confess to a sense of shock at finding that any number of children were reading my book and seemingly enjoying it. To some mothers I said, "My mother would not have permitted me to read that book until I was eighteen. She did not permit me to read 'Tom Jones,' 'Moll Flanders' and other books of that type until I reached that age." But the mothers laughed at me and said, "The education of children has changed since your day. Children know things at a much earlier age now. Much of your book goes over the heads of children between the ages of ten and thirteen, and the adolescent readers already know far more than what you wrote in your story."

It was my pleasure not long ago to talk with Sister Loyola,[3] who was until recently in charge of Saint Joseph's Infirmary here in Atlanta. I was discussing with her some of the matters I have mentioned above. She made me very happy by saying that she thought that "Gone With the Wind" was a basically moral book in that it showed that people pay inevitably for the wrong they do, and that certainly there was nothing in Scarlett's character that would induce any young girl to copy her.

Thank you, too, for the kind things you wrote me about my book. Nothing makes me happier than to be told that "Gone With the Wind" has brought some understanding between the two sections of our Nation.

Mrs. Allan Taylor   Atlanta, Georgia
New York, New York   March 5, 1937

Dear Lois:

I came in so late last night and, as a result, received your air mail letter too late to answer it so I have just wired you about the business of the facsimile in the books. Here are the reasons for my refusal.

I have already been through the mill on the matter of facsimile and "rubber stamp" autographs. It is incredible, the number of different things the public can imagine, just to harass a person. And one of the incredible rumors that I've been fighting for months is the one that I have never yet autographed a single book—The Macmillan Company or I

---

standards of fidelity and learned her rigid code of conduct from her long years with Catholic Ellen O'Hara. Gone With the Wind is true to life. It may be sordid in spots; so is life. It, nevertheless, conclusively proves that true religion is its own reward and, in time of calamity, man's only solace."

[3] Sister Mary Loyola.

have merely used a rubber stamp. For weeks the day never passed but that I had queries about this matter. People who had autographed copies got into frenzies when the rumor reached them and rushed to me to know the truth (though why in God's name it should matter, I can't understand). People who were dickering for autographed copies threw up the trade at the news and wrote or wired me to know the truth. Second hand book shops wanted my word of honor that I had honest to God autographed the volume they were trying to sell. I've had to say so often, with what patience I could muster, that I had never used a rubber stamp or a facsimile signature and that I never would—that anyone would be perfectly safe in buying an autographed copy because, short of forgery, the signature would really be mine. Yes, I know all of this sounds incredible but then this last year has been so full of incredibilities that, with ease, I now believe six impossible things before breakfast every morning.

If the proposed facsimiles went out on sale, this whole business would start over again. More than that, the rumor would get around that I had started autographing again and that would be Hell indeed. I haven't autographed a book since December and have no intentions of ever autographing another. You see, the requests have risen into the hundreds of thousands, to the point where I couldn't have done anything about it, even if I had wanted to. And I didn't want to. Ever so often the rumor gets out that I have autographed some one's book and then for a week, life is unsupportable because everyone I have refused comes down on me, just terribly, terribly hurt—and now people are spurred on to camp upon my trail and jump out at me from under park benches, cracks in Stone Mountain, the Cyclorama and hot dog stands at Jonesboro.

I feel pretty violently about autographs and always have. I don't know if you know it but I never would have autographed the end sheets you sent me before *GWTW* was published if you hadn't asked it. And I would never have done the few I did here in Atlanta except for Norman Berg. He had been so swell to me and he said it would help him make a better showing so I did it against every instinct in me. If I could buy back every autographed [copy] and destroy it, I would. (I mean the ones which are in the hands of strangers. Of course, I'm pleased to death about the ones friends wanted.) Long before *GWTW* was published I felt violently about autographs. So I cannot understand other people's feelings about them. I can only judge by my own feelings. And I never once wanted the autograph of a stranger. When I was a reporter, I met practically every author who came to town, some very great ones whose books I loved and cherished. And I never once asked for an autograph and never once wanted one. For of what value is a signature if you do not know the person who writes it? Of what value is it even if you *do* know them and you do not love them or at least respect them highly? Frequently when I have bought books which I liked a lot and the captive author was in the book store autographing, I refused to have the book autographed. When a stranger asks me for an autograph I feel just as if he (or she) had asked me for a pair of my step-ins and it makes me just as sore. I realize that other people do not feel this way and that they do not intend to be insulting and are being just as nice as they know how but my feeling only grows stronger. And this feeling is one of the reasons I never go anywhere except to my office or to the Library. I do not want to hurt people's feelings but, on the other hand, I do not want to get furious forty times a day.

Of course, the result of this has been that people go to the most re- remarkable ends to get autographs. John turns them down by scores every day, poor Father's life has been made a misery by the people who sit in his office and take up his time telling him that he should force me, by parental authority, to sign their books. Steve and Carrie Lou[1] and all of my relatives lead hunted lives because perfect strangers descend upon them, leaving copies with them and instructions that they *make* me sign them. When I make a business appointment with someone they usually turn up staggering under a dozen copies which their friends have wished upon them, in the frank hope that the caller can "embarrass" me into signing them. And oh, my God the pressure that's brought to bear by charitable organizations wanting an autographed copy for raffling pur- poses! And they talk at great length about the worthy cause. Usually I can get them told by asking how much they have contributed to that worthy cause in hard cash and show that I have already contributed fifty times as much and will contribute again but I will not autograph.

So I know that if the facsimiles got out it would probably start a rumor that I was autographing again and the trouble would break out afresh. It takes practically nothing to start a rumor, I've found. John and I collect rumors and see who can collect the most in one day. My yester- day's crop were (1) That I had a wooden leg. (2) That I've had a suite at the Piedmont Hotel for weeks and have been drunk the entire time and throwing my money away. (3) That I am dressing dolls like *GWTW* characters and selling them for twenty five dollars a doll and making mil- lions. (4) That I have purchased the old General Gilmer home near Clarkesville, Ga. (that's up by Tallulah Falls) and have restored it and the movies will use this place for a background. (5) I am to play Melanie in *GWTW*.

Oh, Lois, if I could have only met you in Washington! It would have been marvelous! I had my mouth all set and after I talked to you I was

[1] Carrie Lou Reynolds Mitchell (Mrs. Stephens Mitchell).

so excited. Then the old cautious instinct reasserted itself and I called
Steve just to check up on the laws of the District of Columbia. The firm
went into a huddle and jerked down a lot of books and rendered a decision against me. We discussed the pros and cons and while there was
a chance of it turning out all right, it was just a chance. Of course I do
not want this suit[2] to come up there and I know Mr. Brett doesn't either.
It would be much better to be sued either in N.Y. or Atlanta. (Of course,
Atlanta would be ideal, if for no other reason than the perfectly natural
one that here people know more about the history of this section than
people in N.Y. or D.C. do.) I did not want to throw a monkey wrench
into the proceedings so decided to stay home. Lois, I do not know
whether or not you saw the lady's "brief" but it was almost as funny as
P. G. Wodehouse at his best. One thing especially charmed me. She
stated that I got Rhett Butler's name out of her book because she mentioned General Ben ("Silver Spoon") Butler. Either she thought she
made up Spoon Butler or she thought no one but herself had ever heard
of him. And General Butler is as well known and cordially hated in this
section as Sherman was as he not only got away with all the Silver spoons
in New Orleans but he issued the famous order that any New Orleans
women who did not treat his troops with cordiality should be considered
as public women and used as such.

To tell the truth, I was relieved when the letter announcing her claim
arrived.[3] I had been waiting for months for the first racketeer to open
fire. It had been a marvel to us all that some chiselers hadn't opened up
on me sooner. We didn't know what form it would take, extortion, attempted blackmail, suits of every kind. It seems the natural thing when
a person has got on the front page and made a lot of money. We were
glad that the opening gun was a pop gun. It might have been one of
those bad affairs where some one alleges that you've run over them and
permanently injured them—on a day when you weren't even in your
car. . . .

P.S.

You know that letter you sent me—the one where the man asked if
Melanie had not had carnal relations with Rhett? The first letter asking
that question came in to me two weeks ago. I thought, of course, that
someone was trying to pull the old Mitchell leg. But then, the same letter
began coming in, and strangely enough from all parts of the United
States. One came from a Y.M.C.A. secretary who said that the boys [at]

---

[2] By Susan Lawrence Davis.
[3] That *GWTW* plagiarized her *Authentic History of the Ku Klux Klan, 1865–1877*
(New York, 1924).

the Y. had been discussing the matter for days and so heated had the discussion become that he feared blood shed and was appealing to me to settle the matter. A number of ladies' literary and bridge clubs have been rent asunder about this scandal and letters from patriotic societies ask the same question. Dear me, even the most chaste women must avoid the appearance of evil and Melanie should never have closed that door. It is interesting to see how the same idea will break at the same time in places thousands of miles apart. A month ago the burden of letters was whether or not Rhett hadn't really been in love with Melanie all the time and that was why he had no love left for Scarlett in the last chapter. Before that the mail demanded was Scarlett's name pronounced "Scar-LETT." Before that it was did Tara rhyme with Sara or Laura. It rhymes with neither and that had me up a stump.

Miss Katharine Brown Atlanta, Georgia
New York, New York March 8, 1937

Dear Katharine:

It will be marvelous if you and Harriett can come to Atlanta with Mr. Cukor. I hope nothing happens to upset your plans to come. John and I will be so happy to see you again.

I have thought over the matter of Mr. Cukor and his visit and the inevitable aftermath and, as I believe I wrote you before, I have decided that the best thing is for him to come with all the loud trumpets possible. You are absolutely right about the press and the public being offended if he attempted an incognito visit. It would be bad on the Selznick Company and the picture, and, as you know, I am most anxious for people down here to like the film. There is nothing I can do to stave off the public and I realize it and am resigned to it. There is only one thing I can do. That is when I know the date of Mr. Cukor's arrival and the hotel at which he will stay, I can throw myself on the mercies of the Atlanta newspapers and ask them to run appeals to the public not to devil me but to devil Mr. Cukor. This will help a little, but, of course, there will be no defense against the various organizations in the small towns of Georgia which will bring pressure to bear on me to make Mr. Cukor come to their towns and give screen tests to their hopefuls. But I am feeling fine now and have gained weight, and so this will not bother me so much. If things do get tough I can always leave town after seeing Mr. Cukor, and let Bessie handle the movie aspirants. I wish to God you could have seen the white woman who turned up last week with a can of blacking in her pocketbook and the determination of playing Mammy. I sat on the blacking so she couldn't put it on her face, and for forty minutes watched her play Mammy up and down the rug.

So tell Mr. Cukor to come on at any time convenient to him and let me know as far in advance as possible. Let me know too, if you can, just what he would like to see in this neighborhood. For instance, if he wants to see the line of old fortifications between Atlanta and Dalton or those at Jonesboro, I want to get hold of Wilbur Kurtz who, as I told you, is about the only living authority on these campaigns. He knows every foot of ground in two hundred miles, the old houses, who lived in them, what generals died in them, et cetera. As a matter of fact, if you wanted an honest to God expert on the War part of the picture, you couldn't do better than kidnap Mr. Kurtz and take him to Hollywood.

Of course we'd love to see Mr. and Mrs. Howard, and I would not tip the newspapers off to his presence here or even breathe it to anyone. Please tell him to let me know as far ahead as possible when he would be here so that I would not be entertaining the senior class of some high school on that day. Tell him we would want them to spend the afternoon with us and see Atlanta's few sights and have dinner with us. . . .

Miss Alice Dean   Atlanta, Georgia
Woodstock, Georgia   March 12, 1937

Dear Miss Dean:

I am very glad to tell you about the pronunciations of the names in "Gone With the Wind." Tara is pronounced "TA-ruh" with the accent on the first syllable, the first a short and the second a modified broad a. It is not pronounced with the first a as in "arm." Melanie is pronounced with the accent on the first syllable and both e's are short. Wilkes is a one-syllable name, pronounced as though it were spelled "Wilks" to rhyme with "silks."

Mrs. Lutie Marshall Bradfield   Atlanta, Georgia
St. Louis, Missouri   March 16, 1937

My dear Mrs. Bradfield:

. . . In the matter of Sherman's visit to Atlanta after the War—you were quite right in saying that he paid Georgia a second visit. For your information I am writing you quoting from a letter written by the late Clark

Howell, Editor of the Atlanta Constitution. Perhaps you knew him when you lived here in Atlanta.

Mr. Howell's letter (now on file in the reference department of the Atlanta Carnegie Library) stated that Sherman had been very anxious to revisit the South and to make a trip from Chattanooga to Savannah. But he did not do this until about 1878 or 1879 when "he was assured that he would be civilly received."

Mr. Howell wrote, "I was a boy at the time—fifteen or sixteen. My father, who was a Confederate Artillery Captain, considered the War over at its finish and he believed the best policy of our people would be to proceed along a reasonable line and re-establish our relations with the North. When General Sherman was dated for Atlanta, my father, Captain Evan P. Howell, organized a committee of some fifteen leaders of the Confederate business men to make a formal call on the General at the Kimball House. The committee was to meet in my father's office, and as a boy I happened to be there at the time. So I went along with the committee.

"I recall distinctly a question asked by Captain Jim English, who had fought all through the War with the Confederates. 'Why,' he said to General Sherman, 'were you so hell bent on capturing Atlanta? You had established your base at Chattanooga. Wasn't that enough?'

"The General rose from his chair and, holding up his left arm with the fingers of his hand spread out, he said, 'The answer is simple. Atlanta, say, is on my wrist. At the end of each of my fingers are Norfolk, Savannah, Jacksonville, Pensacola and New Orleans. Atlanta was the only place in the South from which every city on the South Atlantic and the Gulf Coast between Norfolk and New Orleans could be reached over night. From no other place could this be done. I knew when I had Atlanta the War would be at an end.' "

Thank you so much for the many nice things you wrote me about "Gone With the Wind."

Mrs. Caroline Miller　　　　　　　　　　　　　　　　Atlanta, Georgia
Care of Harper Brothers　　　　　　　　　　　　　　　April 7, 1937
New York, New York

My dear Mrs. Miller:

Your letter made me very happy indeed, for your book is undoubtedly the greatest book that ever came out of the South about Southern people, and it is my favorite book.[1] I think I was among the first in the State to

---

[1] Caroline Pafford Miller, *Lamb in His Bosom* (New York and London, 1933).

read it, for Susan Myrick, who had to review it for the Macon Telegraph, rushed up from Macon with it, insisted that I read it that night, and I did. I became as violently enthusiastic as she was about it, and went about buttonholing people for weeks, telling them they had to read it so that they could talk to me about it.

I never wrote to tell you how fine a thing I thought it was for, even though I was not a front page celebrity myself then, I realized what you were going through and did not wish to add another letter to your burden. But I went over to Athens to hear you speak to the Georgia editors, and my enthusiasm doubled, if possible. All of my family were mad about "Lamb in His Bosom." They loved it. My father, who frequently says nothing worth reading has been written since the good Queen died, now says that two Georgia books are worth reading, yours and mine.

No, my husband and I will not take coffee with you should you ever come to Atlanta. But you must have dinner with us. You are one of the few people in the world we would love to have at our table and for an evening. If possible, please let me know a few days in advance of your visit. I should hate to have some engagement that I could not get out of when you arrive. . . .

Miss Katharine Brown   Atlanta, Georgia
New York, New York   April 7, 1937

Dear Katharine:

The enclosed clipping about the latest adventure of the charming madcap, Honey Chile,[1] does not tell all, and I thought you might be interested in the rest of it. My long-suffering aunt called me on Sunday and told me that Honey Chile, who had heretofore never honored her with a visit, had flown from New York and was staying with her. "She says if they put anyone else in as Scarlett the picture will be ruined. Lots of people have the gall to think she is my daughter. Good heavens! She intends to see Mr. Cukor and that is why she has come. She intends to see you too."

Well, she didn't see Mr. Cukor or me. But, while I was at lunch with him and Erwin[2] and Darrow[3] yesterday at the Biltmore, she had sixteen

[1] Yolande Gwin's story about the latest escapade of "Honey Chile" Timmons appeared on the first page of Atlanta *Constitution* April 7 with the headline "Socialite, With O'Hara Dash, Races Madly to See Cukor."
[2] Hobart Erwin, set designer.
[3] John Darrow, Cukor's assistant.

bellboys paging him. Mr. Cukor told each bellboy to tell her that he was not in the hotel. Finally, Erwin and Darrow went out to lure her upstairs for an audition while Mr. C. and I made our escape.

Last night Yolande called me, practically incoherent. Honey Chile had phoned her at a quarter to six at the Constitution, a short while before the paper went to press. This merry romp screamed over the phone that she had discovered the train on which the badgered George was to leave and she had bought a ticket and was going to New Orleans.

"If I talk to him he will realize I am the only Scarlett. I must see him. I *will* see him. I will go all the way to Hollywood with him if necessary. I am now at the Terminal Station." Yolande said that she was overcome with horror and pity for the Selznickers. All of you had been so wonderful to her that she could not bear to think of the weary trio being captured by this determined belle. She rushed to the city editor and asked for fifteen minutes off so that she could go to the Station and warn the unsuspecting George. The city editor roared like a bull, snatched a photographer out of a trash basket, called a taxi and threw Yolande and the photographer in.

"Warn Mr. Cukor! You cover that story if you have to go all the way to New Orleans."

In the taxi Yolande wrote a note on a bank deposit slip to give Mr. Cukor if time was short. When she arrived at the Station Honey Chile was racing up and down beside the train, and she yelled to Yolande, "Either they aren't on the train or they are in hiding, but I will find them." She leaped on the train and the photographer banged away. Thereafter for ten minutes Yolande said Honey Chile tore through the train jerking open stateroom doors, disconcerting honeymoon couples, arousing sleeping children, and catching several gentlemen who had taken off their pants. The train was in an uproar, and the whole crew was pursuing her. Convinced that they were not on the train, she leaped off and rushed up and down the tracks, telling her troubles to all and sundry, announcing that she would make a perfect Scarlett. Yolande said that, personally, she was mortified as the Station was packed and everyone showed an appreciative interest. One old lady sat down on her suitcase and said, with enthusiasm, "This is every bit as good as a movie!"

Then Yolande had an idea. The train was very long and she suggested that Honey Chile wait at the end of the Pullmans while she, Yolande, watched the stair. Honey Chile took off like a rabbit at the suggestion. In a few minutes down the stairs came the trio, all unsuspecting and very weary after seeing hundreds of applicants. Yolande jumped at them crying, "Something dreadful has happened." All three, bless them, questioned, "Is Mrs. Marsh hurt?" "No, something far worse, Miss ——— is going to New Orleans with you."

Yolande said they evidently agreed with her that this news was far more dreadful than hearing that I had been mangled by a truck. And George positively paled. He told John Darrow to hold Honey Chile off the train at any cost, and the weary John sprinted for the end of the train with Yolande and the photographer close behind. Yolande peeped over her shoulder and she took oath that George and Hobe Erwin dived into the coal car. Miss _____ leaped upon Darrow, crying, "I don't want to see you. I have already seen you. My God, anybody can see you. I must see Mr. Cukor. This is the turning point of my life!" John soothingly took her hand and addressed her as sweetheart and told her Mr. Cukor had gone to New Orleans by motor. "Then, I will go to New Orleans," cried the determined Honey Chile. "What would you advise me to do?" "I would advise you not to chase him. Men don't like to be chased. The more you pursue him the less chance you have. Go home and forget about it, and perhaps when we come back to New York we'll see you." He held her hand till the whistle blew and then leaped aboard.

Yolande said the young lady had given no one any intimation that your company had already seen her in New York.

When Yolande got back to the paper the city editor almost threw a slug at her. "If you had been worth your salt you'd have pushed her on that train and we'd have had a fine story." "But Mr. Cukor had been so nice to me." "Bah," said the city editor.

All this is to let you know that this charming Dixie belle hasn't given up and will probably be on your neck ere long.

I so enjoyed seeing you, but I wish our visits together could take place in quieter times. I hardly felt that I had seen you, and I didn't tell you 1/100 of the things I wanted to tell you. Judging by the Southern clippings, your outfit went over like a breeze and everyone fell in love with you. I do not know if your trip had any value in a material way, but in good will and advertising it must have been worth a million. You are all charming people.[4]

---

[4] Miss Brown answered this letter in a wire of April 8 from New York: "DEAR MRS. MARSH SELZNICK INTERNATIONAL PICTURES JUST RECEIVED YOUR LETTER AND WANT TO KNOW IF THE MOVIE RIGHTS TO THE SAGA ENTITLED 'THE LIFE STORY OF THE ADVENTURES OF HONEY CHILE' ARE AVAILABLE WE CONSIDER THIS A NARRATIVE COMPARABLE IN SCOPE TO YOUR ILLUSTRIOUS 'GONE WITH THE WIND.' "

In a letter of April 19 Miss Brown added: "Your letter completely upset the office. I don't ever recall getting so much fun out of a communication. . . . My rough guess is that Miss _____ has cut herself out of serious consideration by this last gesture."

Mr. Herschel Brickell   Atlanta, Georgia
New York, New York   April 8, 1937

Dear Herschel:

. . . Everything is marvelous here in the country now. Mr. Cukor, who is to direct "Gone With the Wind," has been here with his technical staff, and I took them over all the red rutted roads of Clayton County. The dogwood was just coming out and the flowering crabs blooming like mad. The movie people wanted to see old houses that had been built before Sherman got here and I obligingly showed them. While they were polite, I am sure they were dreadfully disappointed, for they had been expecting architecture such as appeared in the screen version of "So Red the Rose."[1] I had tried to prepare them by reiterating that this section of North Georgia was new and crude compared with other sections of the South, and white columns were the exception rather than the rule. I besought them to please leave Tara ugly, sprawling, columnless, and they agreed. I imagine, however, that when it comes to Twelve Oaks they will put columns all around the house and make it as large as our new city auditorium.

The "Hollywood girl" you mentioned meeting, whose name is Katharine Brown, was down here with them. She is a charming person and I like her very much. I am always amazed that anyone so young and pretty can hold such a responsible position. By the way, she isn't in the Hollywood end but the New York end of the Selznick company. . . .

In your last letter you said something about planning "a birthday celebration" for "Gone With the Wind." That will be marvelous, and I thank you for the thought. I am enclosing a clipping about the first two translations, and as other contracts are signed I will write you about them. I have had offers from practically every country, except Albania, so far, and we are struggling through the mazes of foreign contracts and expect to close them up fairly soon if we do not strike more snags. If there is any other information you want, do, please, ask me for it.

I feel perfectly wonderful these days, and have for the last couple of months. As a matter of fact, I am looking for a wildcat so that I can offer the wildcat the first bite before we mix up. I have almost regained all my lost weight and my mirror tells me that I am looking like a human being again. The main reason for this wonderful state is my office, which I think I wrote you about. I took it in January. It is a small room and jammed with file case, desk and sofa. Clippings and letters are kneehigh. I go there early in the morning and stay most of the day. There is no

[1] *So Red the Rose* had been made into a film starring Margaret Sullavan in 1935.

telephone and no one except the family knows my address. The admirable Miss Baugh keeps house for me in the office and has contributed at least seven of my ten missing pounds by her good work.

By staying in the office I am practically inaccessible. The autograph hunters can't get me and the tourists who ring the doorbell and ask "just a peek at her" only get a peek at Bessie through a crack in the front door. At night John handles the telephone and I do not talk to anyone except old friends. Of course, on my infrequent visits to the reference department of our library I get nabbed, but I do not mind that so much now that I am feeling better. The nabbers are all very kind and polite people and, now that I feel so well, they don't bother me so much.

The editors have stopped coming to see me and most of the would-be interviewers have been discouraged and people in Atlanta have discovered that I won't go to cocktail parties to meet their interesting friends who just love to write. So you can see that, in spite of having to stay in the office most of the day, life is pretty normal and quiet again.

Recently I had a letter from Caroline Miller. I have never met her but perhaps you will recall my enthusiasm for her book. I have wanted to meet her for a long time and could have done so easily for we have many mutual friends, but, even before I landed on the front pages, I realized that people in the public eye have no particular desire to meet anyone they can get out of meeting. So I was glad to hear that she might be in town sometime and would come to see us. As you may have heard, she divorced her husband last fall and they are having some kind of row about the custody of the three children. I wish to heaven Mrs. Miller had delayed the airing of her domestic difficulties for a year at least, for the addle-brained public has mixed me with her. For some time the rumors were hot that I was in Reno divorcing John and fighting for the complete custody of my three non-existent children. At the peak of this rumor all the news services cornered me for a denial, but little good did this do. I am continually meeting strangers who ask me if I am sure that I am doing the right thing in taking my children completely away from their father. This rumor is the favorite one with the dear public and is just a few votes ahead of another rumor—that I have a wooden leg. Would you ever have suspected this last? I managed my wooden leg very neatly when I was climbing the mountains at Blowing Rock with you and Edwin, didn't I?

I often wonder if you ever heard from any of your friends in Spain. That war seems to get no better faster.

Saturday

This letter is rapidly assuming the proportions of GWTW, isn't it? But the clipping you sent me from the negro magazine has just arrived and

I want to thank you for it and tell how interesting I found it. I have followed the course of GWTW in the "Daily Worker" (that is the name, isn't it?) with much enthusiasm.[2] They do not like it at all, to put it mildly, any more than any radical periodical likes it. On the negro angle they disliked it so much they called on negro readers to write to Mr. Selznick, owner of the movie rights, and forbid him to produce the picture, threatening to boycott the picture if he did—and do worse things. They referred to the book as an "incendiary and negro baiting" book. Personally I do not know where they get such an idea for, as far as I can see, most of the negro characters were people of worth, dignity and rectitude—certainly Mammy and Peter and even the ignorant Sam knew more of decorous behavior and honor than Scarlett did.

The negroes in this section have read it in large herds and while I have not heard as many comments as I would like to hear, my friends are continually telling me what colored elevator operators, garage attendants, etc., tell them and these colored people seem well pleased. Our washwoman,[3] a middle aged woman and a worthy citizen if ever there was one, the owner of three houses, a tax payer and a pillar of rectitude, remarked about the book, "It just goes to show that white folks in the old days had more sense than they have now. In those days white folks raised fine colored folks and they had sense enough to let fine colored folks raise the white children. And the colored folks knew what was what and they didn't ever let the white children forget it. Now days, the white folks don't let the colored folks have any say-so in the raising of the children and look at them—sassing their elders, saying bad words, disobeying. Let me tell you, no old fashioned mammy would have let a child 'express itself' like children do now. 'Express itself'!" . . .

Captain Achmed Abdullah   Atlanta, Georgia
New York, New York   April 14, 1937

My dear Captain Abdullah:
    Thank you for your letter and the entertaining anecdote. Of course I laughed, as you knew I would.
    As to your question about where I learned about strategy and tactics

[2] Most of the articles in the *Daily Worker* derogating *GWTW* were by David Platt. In a story of October 29, 1936, Platt wrote of "Margaret Mitchell's reactionary novel of the South, the best-selling, black-baiting 'Gone With the Wind.'" He declared: "The film must be stopped. The Klan must not ride again. Send your protest to Selznick International Pictures, Hollywood, to make sure that it doesn't." New York *Daily Worker*, October 29, 1936.
    [3] Carrie Holbrook.

—I certainly thank you for the compliment. Honesty forces me to admit that I do not know anything about them and have long been the despair of my military-minded friends. When they talked about "enfilading" and being "bracketed" and other military phrases I can only suck my thumb.

As to the military part of "Gone With the Wind,"—well, I know the country between here and Dalton, Georgia, through which the Sherman-Johnston campaign was waged. Many of the old entrenchments are still there if you know where to find them, and to anyone interested in history the sad tale of that retreat is plain in these earthworks. Having the valor of complete ignorance, I wrote about the Sherman-Johnston affair without ever referring to a reference book. I never thought I would sell "Gone With the Wind" and I saw no reason why I should plague my brain by studying military matters which I cannot comprehend. So I fought that campaign from memory and wrote it at far greater length than it appeared in print. When the Macmillan Company bought my book my emotions were compounded of pleasure and horror, for I realized that I had not checked a single fact in that long manuscript. I put in eight months thereafter on the memoirs of Sherman, Johnston and Hood. I studied Cox's Atlanta campaign[1] harder than I ever did Caesar's Gallic Wars. And, if there was even a sergeant who wrote a book about that retreat, I read it. I know it sounds like bragging, but I do not mean it that way for the credit is only due an exceptionally good memory,—but I only made two errors in the draft of my manuscript Macmillan bought. I placed the Battle of New Hope Church five miles too close to the railroad, and I had the final fortifications of Atlanta completed six weeks too soon. You see, as a child I had climbed all over those old earthworks and had heard veterans of the campaign talk about fighting and, as I remarked above, I have a long memory.

I recently had a clipping from a Miami paper, showing you sunning yourself luxuriantly and saying that you liked "Gone With the Wind." Thanks for that remark. I have always liked all of your stories.

Miss Katharine Brown   Atlanta, Georgia
New York, New York   April 22, 1937

Dear Katharine:
    Thanks so much for your long letter and the details about Mr. Sinclair[1] and the set-up for the actual tests. Of course, I was very inter-

---

[1] Jacob D. Cox, *Atlanta* (New York, 1882).

---

[1] Robert Sinclair, a stage director for Selznick International Pictures.

ested. I do hope Alicia Rhett[2] turns out well. I liked her pictures very much and she has a lovely air about her.

Thank you for offering to send the preliminary tests to Atlanta for us to see.[3] Of course, you can imagine how much we would like to see them, but I do not think you had better ship them. The reason is that, despite all of our efforts to keep it quiet, it would get around because the theatre people and the newspaper people live in each other's pockets. When the news did get around we would have both press and public on our necks asking exactly what we thought about the girls and their possibilities. But thank you for offering to send them. . . .

I had heard nothing about an article about me for the Ladies' Home Journal.[4] I wonder if this is another one of those rumors that are continually rising up about me? I keep hearing that I have sold manuscripts for several million dollars to various magazines, and I wonder if this is an allied rumor. No one has interviewed me for the Journal, nor has Mr. Stuart Rose, of that publication, intimated anything about it in a letter to me. Next time you write me, please tell me where you heard this news. . . .

Mr. Frank D. Fackenthal   Atlanta, Georgia
New York, New York   May 4, 1937

THANK YOU FOR YOUR WIRE STOP PLEASE CONVEY TO THE PULITZER AWARD COMMITTEE MY ENORMOUS THANKS AND GRATITUDE[1]

---

[2] An actress discovered by the Selznick search in Charleston. Miss Brown wrote on April 19: "George saw Alicia Rhett give a rehearsal in *Lady Windermere's Fan* and he thinks she has talent. We are probably going to bring her up for a month's work with Sinclair and make a test of her as Melanie on the hundred to one shot that she will be able to play it. If she can't play Melanie, which from our point of view is the most exacting acting role, then there is a chance that she will play Carreen." Miss Rhett played India Wilkes in the film of *GWTW*.

[3] These preliminary tests were of Alicia Rhett as Melanie and of Susan Falligant and Louisa Robert as Scarlett. Selznick International did not exercise its options on these two aspiring actresses from Atlanta.

[4] Miss Brown mentioned that an article about Miss Mitchell was scheduled for the September issue of the *Ladies' Home Journal*. No such article appeared.

[1] Fackenthal had wired on the evening of May 3: TAKE PLEASURE OF ADVISING YOU IN CONFIDENCE AWARD BY TRUSTEES OF COLUMBIA UNIVERSITY OF PULITZER NOVEL PRIZE TO GONE WITH THE WIND   ANNOUNCEMENT PRESS TUESDAY MORNING   HEARTY CONGRATULATIONS.

Mr. Hendrick Willem Van Loon   Atlanta, Georgia
New York, New York   May 5, 1937

Dear Mr. Van Loon:

Thank you so much for your telegram. Thank you again for giving me
the opportunity to speak my little piece over the air. I am no speaker, and
have refused any number of offers to talk because I have sense enough
to know that speaking is not my strong point. But after the news of the
Pulitzer Award I was so anxious to express my gratitude to everyone who
has helped make "Gone With the Wind" a success that I took my courage
in my hands and, supported by my husband, my ex-managing editor on
the Atlanta Journal, and several friends in the radio station, I managed
to say something. I wish that I had had more time in which to prepare
for this, but the request came so suddenly and I was having a rather
full day, so I did not have the opportunity to prepare an adequate statement. That is my last radio appearance and I thank you for giving me the
opportunity.

President Nicholas Murray Butler   Atlanta, Georgia
Columbia University   May 8, 1937
New York, New York

My dear President Butler:

I expected so little of "Gone With the Wind" when it went off to New
York with Harold Latham two years ago. Since that day I have watched
its career with steadily growing amazement, wondering if that book with
my name on it could be, in reality, the enormous stack of dusty copy
paper which lay around our apartment for so many years. So perhaps
you can understand that I was genuinely surprised, and most happy and
proud, when the Pulitzer Award Committee gave the prize to "Gone
With the Wind." It is an honor far beyond any I ever expected for my book,
and I thank you and the other members of the Committee.

I hope that I will some day have the pleasure of meeting you and
thanking you in person.

Mr. Herschel Brickell   Atlanta, Georgia
New York, New York   May 9, 1937

Dear Herschel:

I've been wanting to write to you ever since getting your wire but this afternoon is the first opportunity. Officially, I'm out of town. The papers have said so and Bessie and John have said so over the phone so we are beginning to get a little rest and quiet. These last few days have been wild ones indeed.

I was so sorry to have missed your phone call. I would have loved to hear your voice bearing the glad tidings. But I wasn't at home as you doubtless gathered. It so happened that Harold Latham, by a fine co-incidence, arrived in Atlanta on his annual trip to the Atlanta branch office, on the day the Award came through. Having no idea that I'd get the award, I made plans for his visit. They included going out to supper, a call at Father's house for him to meet the family and then to the church of our cook, Bessie, to hear her choir sing. Harold L. is very fond of negro spirituals and the choir was obliging enough to invite us to hear them. So I wasn't home to get the official wire and I wasn't home to get your call. Along about eight-thirty the city editor[1] of the morning paper who had gotten an A.P. flash on the Award managed to run me down at Father's and he (the editor) was in a taking as he'd trailed me all over town for a statement. Lamar is a blood hound if ever I saw one and he was highly indignant because I hadn't stayed at home where he could catch me easily. He asked for a photograph. I haven't been giving any since last September but somehow in the excitement said I'd give one and the next thing I knew Lamar and the photographer had both arrived at Father's house. I don't know which impressed me the most—winning the Award or having the City Editor leave his desk. John said Lamar came because he expected me to take flight or refuse to be photographed and he wasn't taking any chances on my getting away from the camera. Anyway I was terribly impressed at having a City Editor off his desk on my account just at the rush hour.

While it was an honor indeed to have him there I was in a state because we were late for the negro singing and I didn't dare intimate where we were going because old blood hound would have accompanied us with great pleasure, shot forty pictures of us and the colored choir and written a hell of a story about where Miss Mitchell went to celebrate winning the Pulitzer Award.

We finally made our escape but I was uneasy all during the singing

---

[1] Lamar Q. Ball, city editor of the Atlanta *Constitution.*

144]   MARGARET MITCHELL

for fear he was lurking somewhere in the back of the church and I was afraid to pick up the morning's papers. The choir was marvelous and half the congregation turned out. The whole affair was so sweet, so simple and dignified and in such good taste. Bessie presided and introduced us (John, Harold, Steve and Carrie Lou) and we all made little talks. The colored folks were pleased to have us but they didn't slop over. They just took it for granted that naturally Bessie's Madam and Bessie's Madam's publisher wanted to hear them sing and oh, how they sang! One old sister got to shouting and I thought Harold Latham would have a spasm he enjoyed it so much. Anyway, we didn't get home until one a.m. and that's why you didn't get me.

I have a very good memory and I remembered that you said last summer that you were going to sit next to the door at the Pulitzer dinner so you wouldn't have to walk very far to telephone the news to me. I don't know how you knew it would happen anymore than I know how you knew it would sell so well. It will always be a mystery to me. I thought when you made the above remark that you were just bolstering me up and trying to make me feel good but I thought at the time, that by the time the Pulitzer Awards were made no one would remember that I'd written a book. Even when the thing kept on selling, I didn't think they'd give the Award to me because I thought the Committee would think I'd already had enough (and Heaven knows I have!) and that someone else who'd written just as good a book but not had as good a sale should get the prize. I couldn't really take it all in until the check arrived yesterday.

You did a lot for me in this matter. You pulled for that book from the day it was published and I can't ever thank you enough. One tangible evidence of my appreciation will arrive at your house in a few days for the Burgundy is on the way. (Bad 'cess [to] you for refusing to answer my question where to order and what brand.) And as soon as I can get out of the house I'm sending you my end of the wager on the winning of the Award. No, I hadn't forgotten it.

Herschel, you mentioned in the penciled note you wrote several days ago that you had met Miss Susan Lawrence Davis, the old lady who is suing the Macm. Co. for plagiarism. For Heavens sake tell me what you know about her, or if you do not know anything about her, tell me if you know anyone who does. Of course, I do not anticipate any difficulty in winning the case if it comes to a trial but it is annoying and will cause me a lot of trouble and perhaps make me go to N.Y. which I do not want to do at present. And as the costs of the affair are on me, even if the Macm. Co. is the one being sued and not me, it will probably be expensive. I never heard of the lady or her book till she made her claim and even then had the world's worst time trying to locate a copy of her "Authentic History of the K.K.K." for no book store or library had it and no one could order it as her publishers[2] had gone out of business some years ago. Finally the Macm. Co. located a copy for me. I hate to sound catty but it was impossible to read. Try as I might I couldn't get more than a quarter through it. I am somewhat at a loss as to what she is basing her claim upon. If you know any thing about the woman personally—that is, is she in the habit of suing people, etc.—please let me know. Of course we hope to have the case thrown out before it ever comes to trial.

In a way, I was relieved when the claim was brought. All of us, having been born with our eyes open, and having observed through legal practice or newspaper work, the difficulties into which front page celebrities run, knew that something like this was bound to happen as soon as the news got around that I had made some money. We didn't know whether it would be an infringement suit or a damage suit alleging I'd run over someone or that someone had slipped on a banana peel in front of my house and broken their back or an extortion scheme or what. But we knew something would turn up just as sure as gun's iron. I was lucky to go so long but I've been waiting for something to pop and was glad when it did at last. I suppose it would have happened sooner in some disagreeable way if I hadn't stayed so close at home and refused to go places and meet people. . . .

I recall that your parting words to me were a solemn injunction "Don't let the so-and-sos get you." For your information, they haven't got me but they've come derned close several times!

Mr. George Brett, Jr.   Atlanta, Georgia
The Macmillan Company   May 10, 1937
New York, New York

Dear Mr. Brett:
I've been trying to write and thank you for the orchids ever since they arrived. I never saw so many or such big, gorgeous ones except perhaps around the neck of a Kentucky Derby winner. Perhaps that's an apt remark for I felt as wild and full of prance as a Derby winner when I wore them out to the party Mr. Latham gave. I still could not convince myself that I had actually won the award but I kept slewing my head sideways and looking at the corsage and telling myself that certainly I wouldn't be wearing those orchids if I hadn't won something! You were grand to send them and they added very greatly to the pleasure and happiness of the

[2] American Library Service.

event. I thank you, too, for the phone call. It was nice to hear your voice and Lois' and I am sorry if you had trouble tracking us down. Before I ever knew that I would get the Award, I had made plans for Mr. Latham's visit and I couldn't change them. So I was not at home to get my official wire or your phone call. The editors of the various papers were looking for me, too, that night as they wanted a statement and they were indignant because I hadn't stayed home where they could catch me with ease. The City Editor of the morning paper came out to Father's house, in person, and to this day I don't know which impressed me the most—winning the Pulitzer Prize or having a City Editor leave his desk at the rush hour! . . .

Mrs. Louis Davent Bolton   Atlanta, Georgia
Mansfield, Georgia   May 10, 1937

Dear Mrs. Bolton:

When the copy of Dolly Sumner Lunt's book[1] arrived this morning I was utterly convinced that there is such a thing as mental telepathy! I had been trying for some time to locate a copy and had had no success. I owned a copy and treasured it and it was with reluctance that I gave my copy to Mr. George Cukor, who is to direct the film of "Gone With the Wind." When he was here in Atlanta he asked me hundreds of questions about life in the old South and I did my best to answer them. I also gave him that book and one or two others dealing with the same period. After I had done so I had all the impulses of an Indian giver and wanted the book back. However, I felt I had given it away in a good cause because it showed more clearly than I could personally tell him what the attitude of ladies of another day had been. How very kind you were to send the book to me. Thank you a thousand times. No one will ever get this copy away from me.

Is it true that you are thinking of bringing out a larger edition of this wonderful Journal? I think it would be most interesting. For some time I have had it in my mind to journey to see the old Burge Plantation. I had my plans all arranged and then many things rose up to keep me at home. The recent Pulitzer Prize plunged me into a great deal of correspondence, so that I do not know when I will be able to leave Atlanta. But, may I come to see you sometime? It would be a great pleasure.

[1] Dolly Sumner Lunt Burge, *A Woman's Wartime Journal* (New York, 1918). This was published with an introduction by Julian Street. It was reprinted in Macon, Ga., in 1927. The complete journal was published as *The Diary of Dolly Lunt Burge* (Athens, Ga. [c. 1962]).

Mr. Louie Morris   Atlanta, Georgia
The Sun   May 24, 1937
Hartwell, Georgia

Dear Louie:

It is worth being sued for $6,500,000,000 to have a friend come to my defense as you did! You were awfully kind to print that statement and to go on record as having faith in my honesty and integrity. You could have knocked me over with a fern frond when the old lady made her claim, for I had never heard of her or her book either until her lawyers wrote me. Then I managed to get a copy of her book after considerable difficulty, and I am still more at a loss after reading it as to what she bases her suit upon. Her book purports to be history while mine is fiction. I do not anticipate any difficulty in proving that I did not infringe her copyright, but just the same, a suit like this can be troublesome and expensive. But if it takes all the royalties "Gone With the Wind" has earned I intend to prove my point.

Wasn't it a pity the press trip was called off! We are waiting to learn when and where it will be held.

Miss Adrienne Fertig   Atlanta, Georgia
Miss Helene Boetzel   May 24, 1937
Beechhurst, New York

My dear Miss Fertig and Miss Boetzel:

I am sorry that I cannot tell you Scarlett's original name for that is a deep, dark secret shared only by my husband, my publishers and myself.

Thank you both so much for writing me that you liked "Gone With the Wind." Of course, I was glad to know that it was interesting to girls twelve years old. I believe you are my two youngest readers.

Mr. Herschel Brickell   Atlanta, Georgia
New York, New York   May 28, 1937

Dear Herschel:

Of course I was very interested in what you wrote about Miss Susan Lawrence Davis. Your experiences with her parallel those of several other people who have written us since she made her claim. She seems to have a genius for devilling people, and she probably perfected the sitdown strike long before it became popular. One man who was bursting with the desire to testify against her wrote that she had sat down in his office for nearly three months.

You asked how far her suit had gone and just what the legal status of it was. I'll begin at the beginning. I had never heard of her or her book and this despite the fact that I read hundreds of books on this period. Several months ago her lawyers wrote me that I had infringed her copyright and made a demand for accounting. Simultaneously they wrote to The Macmillan Company. They demanded that I and some official of The Macmillan Company come to Washington so that Miss Susan could explain to us in detail the enormity of my offence. Of course, the Macmillans and I refused to come and demanded particulars. She insisted for some time that I must come to Washington but, finally, one of the lawyers went to New York, bringing the particulars. These particulars, legally known as a brief (though Heaven knows why, as they were far from brief and ran to something like 240 pages), were presented to the Macmillan lawyers and me. On one page of her brief she would list words and phrases and page numbers from her book: on the opposite page she would itemize words and phrases which she alleged I had stolen from her. The very first accusation was that she had bound her book in Confederate gray and I had dared to do likewise. Among many other claims were the following: that I had mentioned the poet-priest, Father Abram Ryan, Fort Sumter, States' Rights, the Freedmen's Bureau, General Wade Hampton, General John B. Gordon, scallawags and carpetbaggers, and the Federal commissioners who tried unsuccessfully to see Abraham Lincoln directly before Fort Sumter fell. It would seem that these phrases and historic events were the product of her own creation and had never been heard of until she wrote her book in 1924. There were hundreds of other claims of infringement which were just as absurd.

Of course, The Macmillan Company and I refused to settle and cried aloud, "Millions for defense but not one cent for tribute." After this she brought suit, not against me here in Atlanta, but against The Macmillan Company in New York. In this suit she made a blanket accusation of infringement and did not particularize, nor did she file the brief I described above. The fact that she did not sue me and did not file this brief, naturally, muzzled me when it came to answering questions fired at me by the newspapers. I could only say that I had not committed plagiarism, and could not cite any of the absurdities of her brief.

However, despite the fact that she had not put this brief into her suit, The Macmillan Company gave out a press statement citing some of her foolish claims. Then The Macmillan Company lawyers put in a legal demand that she file her particulars (meaning the before-mentioned brief). At this time I have not heard whether she has introduced the brief with its particular accusations into the case. In fact, I have heard nothing from the case for several weeks. It is our belief that when it comes to trial there will be no trial and we feel that the judge will throw the case out of court because of its obvious baselessness. However, it does not pay to count your chickens too early in legal matters, and it may not work out this way. For my part, despite the trouble and expense involved, I would prefer that the case went to trial. If there was a trial and I got a just verdict the news would spread widely and the details would be known and my reputation would be cleared. If the case is non-suited no one would ever know anything about it and several million people would think I bought the old lady off quietly.

Of course, the above is told in confidence because, as I am not being sued and the brief has not been filed, I am not supposed to say anything about it.

I have just finished "Bugles Blow No More,"[1] and my enthusiasm is running high. I wish you were here to discuss it, for John has been too busy to read it and all my friends too busy with summer plans to do any reading. He has certainly done a wonderful job and Richmond comes to life in a marvelous way. The man's research makes me feel very humble, and the fighting in the Seven Days battle is the best thing of its kind I have ever read. He ought to have a wonderful sale and I hope he has it. . . .

Mr. Sidney Howard   Atlanta, Georgia
Tyringham, Massachusetts   June 9, 1937

Dear Mr. Howard:
When Mr. Cukor talked to me over long distance from New York about your proposed trip to Atlanta I was sorely tempted to tell him that I would do anything he wanted if only you and your wife would come to see us! Because, seriously, my husband and I looked forward to meeting you. I hope you will understand me—what stiffened my spine was a hunch that you personally were not very anxious to make a wild, flying one-day trip to Atlanta for no particular reason. I thought that when you decided to come to Atlanta you would like to come in peace and at leisure. I hope I read your mind correctly. I kept trying to discover exactly why they wanted you to come, but I did not learn the reason and I was somewhat puzzled. Your letter clears up that puzzle.

[1] Clifford Dowdey, *Bugles Blow No More* (New York, 1937).

I know so little about the movies that I thought the script was already finished. If it wasn't finished what was that thick pile of manuscript that lay on George Cukor's desk during his visit to Atlanta?[1] By heroic self-control I did not look at it. I knew if I did I could not honestly tell newspaper reporters and friends that I had no idea what the script was like. I wanted to be in the position of complete ignorance when asked whether my ending had been retained and what characters and episodes had been omitted. I am not an extraordinarily good liar, and I knew if I looked at the script I could never say with any plausibility that I didn't know anything about it. Of course, I was terribly interested, and I hope to have the opportunity in the not too far distant future of discussing it with you.

I gather from your letter that you have no more idea than I when the production will start.

I hope you will understand when I say that I felt very comforted when I heard that you had had two plagiarism suits.[2] Being new to this writing profession, I had an uncomfortable feeling as though I had contracted the itch, no matter how innocently acquired. I was glad to learn other writers were similarly afflicted. I do not anticipate any difficulty in the winning of this suit and I doubt if it will ever come to trial, for I imagine any judge would throw it out of court. The suit is based, among other things, on the fact that my book was bound in Confederate gray and so was Miss Davis's book. And it seems that the lady has a copyright on every Southern general from Lee on down, for, among her other accusations, are some stating that I mentioned General Gordon and General Wade Hampton and she did too. However, the suit will be a bother to me and an expense too. It seems a pity that people cannot be forced to post bond for court costs and attorneys' fees before they file a plagiarism suit.

I was glad to learn that you do intend to come to Atlanta sometime,

[1] Howard wrote June 14: "Picture scripts are written and later rewritten in collaboration with the director, who has, after all, to make the picture. The script of GONE WITH THE WIND is written but not yet re-written."

[2] On June 5 Howard wrote: "I hope that the plagiarism suit is not too troublesome. The Authors' League tells me that it is really nothing but I have had two myself and don't like them." On June 14 he added: "As to plagiarism suits, there seems to be a form of persecution mania which rushes to express itself against every outstanding literary success. It is encouraged, I think, by the fact that the picture companies find it cheaper to settle such suits than to defend them. Be sure your attorney knows the circumstances of the suit against O'Neill's STRANGE INTERLUDE. In that case one of the Federal judges soaked the plaintiff for the defendant's legal fees. I was grateful for that decision because it caused a Wisconsin cheese manufacturer to withdraw support of his wife's suit against my play THE SILVER CORD. Apart from the expense, it is not pleasant to be called a thief. But there you are, and I can't think of any startling success which has enjoyed immunity."

but do not think you can buy us a dinner. It is going to be our dinner or nobody's. So get ready for it.

Mr. Charles Smith   Atlanta, Georgia
Concord, Georgia   June 12, 1937

My dear Mr. Smith:

Yesterday my brother, Stephens Mitchell, told me that he had had a very enjoyable conversation with you. He said that in the course of this conversation you had remarked that you had been to a house which was represented to you as being "Tara," and that, furthermore, the owner of the house, Mr. Stephens,[1] had even pointed out the banister from which Scarlett had shot the Yankee straggler. Stephens is always such a great one for joking that I could not make up my mind whether or not my leg was being pulled—or whether, indeed, it had been your leg which had been pulled! While I hate to put you to the trouble, I would appreciate it very much if you would let me know whether or not Mr. Stephens is passing off his house as "Tara."

I will explain my reasons for wanting this information. During the ten years when I was working on "Gone With the Wind" I went to an incredible amount of trouble to keep from portraying actual people or houses, and from using the names of anyone who had really lived in that section during the period of which I wrote. I did not wish to embarrass anyone by making it appear that they had had a kinswoman of the type of Scarlett O'Hara. I searched Clayton County and the old records to make sure that there had never been a white brick house on a high hill close to the river and approached by a long avenue of cedars.

Shortly after the publication of "Gone With the Wind" I was annoyed and disconcerted by the reports brought me by Northern tourists that several families in the Jonesboro section were passing off their houses as "Tara." Of course, the people who were doing this were liars of the first water and I have never been able to understand their motives, for I would not think anyone would like to claim kin with a character like Scarlett. I made a trip to Jonesboro incognito and was shown three or four "Taras," and none of them tallied with my description. Now I learn with interest of Mr. Stephens's allegations. On the fact of it it is foolish for him to claim that the house he lives in is "Tara," for that house is of wood, not brick, and has an 1880 jigsaw front on it. Moreover, I do not know how he would have known what was in my mind when I was

---

[1] Alexander Stephens.

writing, as neither I nor any of my family has seen Mr. Stephens since 1920. Nor have we held any communication with him.

It would be a great favor to me if you would tell me whether he is falsely passing off his house as the non-existent "Tara," for I am very anxious to lay this rumor as I have laid others about my book and its characters.

Rev. Robert W. Burns   Atlanta, Georgia
Peachtree Christian Church   June 14, 1937
Atlanta, Georgia

My dear Doctor Burns:

Thank you so much for sending me the copy of "The Peachtree Tower" which contained your sermon on "Gone With the Wind."[1] I had intended hearing this sermon personally and it was a great disappointment to me when the unexpected arrival of out-of-town guests kept me from your Church. I heard so many complimentary things about this sermon that I was, naturally, very glad to have a copy of it.

First, let me thank you for all the wonderful things you said about my book. Coming from a minister, I appreciated them especially. One remark of yours interested and pleased me so very much—that was when you spoke of "the sense of honor in Ashley." It has seemed strange to me that of the many people who have spoken of my book during this past year so few have liked Ashley or given him credit for having honor and for trying desperately to be true to his sense of honor. It seems that people do not like failures and give no credit to the honest struggles that precede failure. Most people thought Ashley weak because at times he could not completely withstand the onslaughts of Scarlett. It has amused me that generally the very nicest ladies have been most outstanding in their criticism of him.

Thank you for summing up so beautifully Scarlett's procrastinating philosophy. After reading your sermon I am doubly disappointed that I did not actually hear it.

---

[1] *The Peachtree Tower*, II, No. 8 (June 1937), pp. 3–4, printed "Gone With the Wind, A Sermon Preached in Peachtree Christian Church, November 8, 1936, by Rev. Robert W. Burns." Dr. Burns repeated this sermon several times.

Mrs. Winifred Lawrence Atlanta, Georgia
Newton Falls, Ohio June 18, 1937

Dear Mrs. Lawrence:

Thank you so much for your letter. Of course, nothing could have given me more pleasure than the idea implied in your letter that "Gone With the Wind" had given you a new understanding of the old South and its problems.

In the matter of the tune "Marching Through Georgia,"[1] I recall an amusing story related to me many years ago by an old gentleman who had fought in the Confederate army. He was a very prominent man and after the war was sent to various European countries on government business and was extensively entertained. He said that in every foreign country the people were so kind and they always wanted to show him honor, so, as a delicate compliment, they always played "Marching Through Georgia" for his benefit, believing that it was the Georgia State official anthem. Not wishing to embarrass his hosts, the old gentleman had to carry this off as best he could, and frequently good manners forced him to stand while this tune was being played.

Mr. Herschel Brickell Atlanta, Georgia
New York, New York June 28, 1937

Dear Herschel:

The item you enclosed about Margaret Mitchell, a Southern belle before, during and after the Civil War,[1] is not so remarkable as you think. For a long time the rumor has been afloat that I am far advanced in years and that "Gone With the Wind" was really a verbatim account of what happened to me in my youth. The strangest thing I have encountered during this last year is the inability of the public to conceive of creative writing. People cannot or will not believe that a story and characters can be manufactured from whole cloth. The story must have been the author's life story or that of someone the author knew, or it must have

[1] *GWTW*, p. 801.

[1] Brickell wrote on June 25: "I picked up the New International Year Book for 1936, published by Funk and Wagnalls, and naturally turned straight to the fiction survey. It begins with this marvelous remark: 'The year's sensational success was "Gone With the Wind," by Margaret Mitchell, a Southern belle before, during, and after the Civil War'!!! All I can say is that for one who has been a belle for so many decades, you are remarkably well preserved."

been taken from old diaries or letters. And characters, of course, are always "taken from life." I do not know why it is so difficult for people to believe in the possibility of complete creation. As far as I am concerned it is very easy to think up plot and characters and utterly impossible to take plot and characters from life. Had you ever thought of this idea? If so, I'd like to discuss it with you when you come to see us.

We are in a twit about your visit and will be glad to know when to expect you. At present we have given up the idea of going to the Coast. We have heard that it is beastly hot there and the mosquitoes are as large and voracious as vultures. However, we hope to make your stay here an entertaining one, even if it isn't a time of mad and abandoned excitement and revelry. By the way, when you come to Atlanta, if you come by Asheville (and I suppose that is the only way you can come if you are traveling by train) get off at the Peachtree Station (sometimes called the Brookwood Station) instead of the Terminal Station. The Peachtree Station is only a few blocks from our apartment. . . .

Mrs. Lewis Edward Gibson   Atlanta, Georgia
Atlanta, Georgia   July 22, 1937

My dear Mrs. Gibson:
    I only wish I did know the origin and meaning of "layovers catch meddlers"![1] And I hope if you or your friend discover the meaning you will tell me. I've heard it all my life and my grandmother told me that she had heard it all of her life. But she did not know the meaning. It was one of those phrases used to put children in their proper places when she was a little girl.

    When I started to use this phrase in "Gone With the Wind" I made a number of inquiries among elderly people about the pronunciation and spelling. None of them had ever seen it in print. Some of them used slight variations such as "larovers catch meddlers" and "lareovers catch meddlers." The majority used "layovers" and, wanting to write a "colloquial" type of book, I used this phonetic spelling. . . .

[1] The *O.E.D.* gives this term in the sense in which Miss Mitchell used it as dating from 1785 (under "lay-over").

Mrs. Louis Davent Bolton   Atlanta, Georgia
Mansfield, Georgia   July 22, 1937

My dear Mrs. Bolton:

Your letter with its cordial invitation arrived several days ago and has lain heavily upon my conscience because I did not answer it immediately. But we have had a deluge of out-of-town guests, among others, Mr. Herschel Brickell, the book critic of the New York "Post." He is a Southerner and was most kind to my book in his column long before it went up like a sky rocket and we did our best to "put the big pot in the little one" for him, during his visit. Now, he has returned to New York and I can hasten to answer your letter.

How good of you to issue so warm an invitation to my husband and me! I only wish we could come down this week end. But we can't and to tell the truth, I do not know when it will be possible. When your letter first arrived, I was certain that I could come down on Saturday but in the light of recent developments in my life, I find that I will be chained to my desk and my research books for many weeks to come.

Perhaps you have read in the papers about the old lady who is suing me for $6,500,000,000. She alleges that I have stolen from her history of the Ku Klux Klan and, among other things, states that I brazenly wrote "Stonewall Jackson was dead" when the same words had appeared in her volume, that I had used the terms "Freedmen's Bureau," "Carpetbagger," "Scallawag," "Fall of Ft. Sumter," and had also stooped to such depths as to mention the names of General Gordon and General Forrest, even as she had done. She sent me four hundred typewritten pages of alleged plagiarisms and every page is just as funny as Mickey Mouse. However, the matter has gone to court and I will probably be called upon to prove that every one of the many thousands of historical references in my book were matters of common knowledge before her book was printed. This will take an endless amount of research for I want to cite ten authorities on every reference.

My brother, also my attorney, returned from New York yesterday with the news that a Dutch publisher[1] was starting to "pirate" my book and we must open suit to protect it. And Mr. Billy Rose, the impresario of the "Fort Worth Frontier Fiesta," has infringed my rights by a panto-mime dramatization of "Gone With the Wind" without so much as asking my permission. So suit has been entered against him.

As you can see, to misquote Gilbert and Sullivan, "An author's life is not a happy one!"

---

[1] Zuid-Hollandsche Uitgevers Maatschappij.

As you can judge by the foregoing, life is going to be a trifle complicated for some time to come and I do not want to make an engagement with you and then have to break it at the last minute because a telegram from New York makes it necessary for me to drop my pleasures and go to work on stuff needed immediately by lawyers.

So please go on your trip to the White Mountains and let me know when you return. I hope by then things will have quieted down enough for me to do a few of the things I'd love to do—such as meeting you and seeing your plantation.

I was so interested in learning that you plan to publish the entire Journal. I know it's none of my business but may I make a suggestion? I'd try to get it in the hands of a publisher as soon as possible because with the reawakened interest in that period of our history, there are bound to be other reissues of books of a like nature. For instance, I know that "Dixie After the War" by Myrta Lockett Avary, of Atlanta, is to be reissued by Houghton Mifflin this Fall and it may bring others in its train. And the sooner you get yours to a publisher, the better chance it will have.

I am sorry that I cannot write the foreword to the Journal as you requested and I hope you will understand my reasons for refusing. When my book made its first success I was swamped with requests for endorsements, forewords and "jacket blurbs" from publishers and also from many friends who were publishing books last season. They came in in hundreds, in far greater volume than I could possibly handle. My publishers besought me in the strongest terms not to oblige anyone in this matter, no matter how ungenerous and ungracious it might appear to the public. They were so insistent in this matter that I finally promised them I would not, until they gave me permission. Now, having refused a number of my close friends, I could not write a foreword for the "Journal" without making them feel that I had slighted them. Everyone has been so wonderfully kind to me that not for worlds would I hurt the feelings of any of my friends by seeming to slight them.

May I hear from you on your return? I hope sincerely life will have quieted down for me by then and I can come calling. I hope you have a wonderful trip and I can't help envying you!

Mr. Clifford Dowdey   Atlanta, Georgia
Blowing Rock, North Carolina   July 22, 1937

My dear Mr. Dowdey:

This is the third letter I have written to you. Of course, the other two were never sent. The first, written within the hour I had finished "Bugles," was my first "fan letter" and it found its way into my waste basket. I couldn't send it because I wanted the author of "Bugles" to have some faint respect for me and he couldn't have had had he read that incoherent letter of praise.

The second letter was most dignified and formal and I pondered long over words and phrases and it was a pretty pompous and dull letter. Just when it was going into the mail I read a foolish statement in the column of a New York critic about the fancied similarity between your title and mine and it made me mad and embarrassed me so I held up the letter. Then I read your highly justified complaint to the columnist and the second letter went into the waste basket. Foolishly, I was afraid you were exasperated at me as well as the critic (and I wouldn't have blamed you!) and I feared you might bite me. Herschel Brickell has probably told you that I'm a bit shy and do my best to avoid being bitten.

Then Herschel came to visit us several days ago, so full of you and your wife, saying so many wonderful things about you two, that I have plucked up my courage and decided to tell you that never in my life have I read a book that held me as "Bugles" did. I knew I would like it, ever since Stuart Rose told me about it many months ago when he was here in Atlanta. But I never dreamed I'd like it so much. There were times, in the battle chapters, when my mouth grew so dry from the dust the soldiers' feet kicked up that I all but choked but I wouldn't go get a drink to ease myself for fear of losing the spell.

How wonderfully you made Richmond your heroine—she *was*, wasn't she? At least the city was the heroine for me and when you had finished with her I felt that I knew her mind and her heart and could find my way about her streets blindfolded.

Having done some research and knowing some of the miseries of making dry dust come to life and the struggles to clothe dead facts with living reality, I admired especially the way you handled your background. Never once was there the feeling, so often felt in historical novels, "Well, he sure dragged *that* bit of research in by the hind leg and you can hear the bones rattle." No, there was living and breathing newness and reality to your background, just as there was passion and fire as fresh as today in your people.

I'm no critic but one of those scorned wretches who "just know what I like" and I liked your book more than I can tell you on paper. And I don't like many books. Thank you for writing it; thank you for the pleasure it gave me; thank you for the new friends who walk about in my mind and make pleasant conversation with me.

I came within an ace of meeting you and your wife. My husband and I had intended to come to B.R. when Herschel was there but between being sued by an old lady on a plagiarism accusation for $6,500,000,000 and suing a Dutch publisher for trying to pirate "Gone With the Wind" we couldn't make it. And speaking of Miss Susan Lawrence Davis, the lady who is bringing the suit, I may as well warn you that she'll probably sue you next! I'm sure she will for you are as guilty of her charges as I am. Among other allegations she makes against me are—I brazenly bound my novel in Confederate gray and her book was bound in gray. (And so was yours!) And I came right out in the open and said "Stonewall Jackson is dead" and so did she and it is obvious I would never have known he was dead had I not pilfered the fact from her book. Alas, you said he was dead, too! How could you rob an old lady, Mr. Dowdey? And there are other charges of which you are guilty along with me. You mentioned General Lee, just as I did and so did she and it seems she had a copyright on the General and all the War, too and all of Reconstruction. How lucky you were to stop at the surrender. Miss Davis evidently owns the rights to "Carpetbagger," "Scallawag" and "Freedmen's Bureau" and I was low enough to steal them from her. Seriously, I'd really like to know if she has started any proceedings against you. But perhaps she's been too busy with the suit against me to start on you.

Herschel told us that you'd had eye trouble. I hope that a rest will fix them up. Old newspapers are the devil and all on eyes and I often wonder why all our grandparents weren't blind from reading agate type. And the faded ink of old letters is even worse. And what the newspapers and the letters don't do to eyes, proof reading does do. I had to get new glasses and take a two months rest from all reading after I'd finally gone to press. I hope new glasses and rest will bring about as happy a state of eyes for you as they did for me.

Now, I cannot resist any longer writing the true fan's plea—Please write another book! I'll be waiting for it.

Mr. Clifford Dowdey   Atlanta, Georgia
Blowing Rock, North Carolina   July 29, 1937

My dear Mr. Dowdey:
    . . . When Herschel first alighted from the train he said, "The Dowdeys told me to tell you that they were prepared to forgive you even though you have ruined their lives." To which I replied, "You must be indeed an ambassador of good will." Then I told how I had wanted to write to you and why I had not done so, and he told me how nice you were and that you would not bite me. Herschel is a very clever man and he avoided telling me that I would like you and your wife, because he knew if he

did natural perversity would make me decide that I wouldn't like you. He just went on and on about how much he had liked you. It shows that he had indeed the wisdom of the serpent.

I was glad to learn that I had ruined your life because my own life was ruined a number of times by authors during the ten years when I was working on "Gone With the Wind." Misery loves company and, while you have my sympathy, of course I couldn't suppress some satisfaction at knowing that someone else had suffered a little bit of what I endured.

I am singularly a prey to a disease known in this family as "the humbles." Everybody's stuff looks better than mine and a depressing humility falls upon me whenever I read stuff that I wish I could have written. Temporarily the humbles kept me from doing any writing at all. My life was ruined for three months after "Marching On"[1] and when I finally got back to my typewriter I swore I would never read a book on the War until I had finished my own. Then Mr. Stephen Vincent Benet struck me a body blow. A friend brought "John Brown's Body" and insisted on reading me the "This is the last—this is the last" part, in spite of the fact that I had flung myself on the sofa and stuck my fingers in my ears and screamed protests. I had to read it all then. The result was that I wondered how anybody could have the courage to write about the War after Mr. Benet had done it so beautifully. Recovery was slow, and scarcely had I tottered to my desk when Mr. Stark Young arrived, terrible as an army with banners, and annihilated me with "So Red the Rose." My husband took me in hand brutally at that point and extracted from me a promise that I would not read any books on the subject except reference books. But in the course of my reference work it became necessary for me to discover on exactly what day of Johnston's retreat the rain began to fall. I knew where I could find it, although I had not read the book in twenty years. It was in Mary Johnston's "Cease Firing." If I had contented myself with merely reading the item about the rain I would have escaped. But I am a weak vessel and before I knew it I had read the whole book and was down with another bad case of humbles. I could go on indefinitely about people who ruined my life, but I will spare you any more. I have gone into these details just to show you that I realize we do have "so very much in common"—far more than friends in common.

Yours was a very fine letter and I appreciate it more than I can tell you. I am glad the things I told you about "Bugles" pleased you and sometime when I meet you I will tell you why I knew Richmond was your heroine. And I will tell you several thousand other things about

---

[1] James Boyd, *Marching On* (New York, 1927).

your book. If I tried to do it in any letter it would run as long as my own opus. I especially want to tell you about the conclusion of your book.

You should have known better than to invite me to come to visit you and Mrs. Dowdey at Blowing Rock because I will probably take you up on the invitation. Then if I turn out a ghastly bore you will have only yourself to blame. Seriously, my husband and I would like to come to see you for two or three days sometime after the Summer School[2] is over. You were more than kind to invite us and I hope you will write me again when the Summer School has folded its tents and when it is convenient for you to have us. I do not know whether my husband can accompany me at this time. He is handling my business matters and it takes all of his time which is not claimed by his heavy work at the Georgia Power Company. It may be impossible for him to get away this summer, but he thanks you for inviting him. I should tell you that I am the world's worst house guest. I do not play bridge or parlor games, get drunk, make love to the hostess's husband, play golf, take nice long walks in the rain, or fish. Moreover, I am immoderately talkative. . . .

Miss Ruth Tallman　　　　　　　　　　　　Atlanta, Georgia
Lakefield, Minnesota　　　　　　　　　　　July 30, 1937

Dear Miss Tallman:

Thank you so much for your lovely letter and the interest in "Gone With the Wind" which prompted you to write it. Thank you, too, for the many fine things you said about my novel. I appreciated them all.

I will do my best to answer your questions— 1st—"Why did you interweave the lightness of a novel with something of so serious a nature as the War and Reconstruction"? I do not know if I correctly understand the meaning of this question, but the reason why I wrote a novel instead of an out and out history book was that I am not a historian by profession but am only a story teller.

2nd—"Were there Confederate soldiers who felt toward the War as Ashley Wilkes in his letter to his wife"? Yes, there were many like Ashley, if I can judge from the scores of old letters I read and the many veterans to whom I have talked. The general opinion seems to be that every Confederate soldier felt exactly alike and all were fighting for the same things. This is not altogether true. About the only thing most of them had in common was a love of the South, a desire to defend the South from invasion, and a resentment of what they felt to be Northern meddling in Southern business. In one squad of Confederate soldiers you could find

[2] The Blowing Rock School of English.

the wealthy planter who was a large slave owner who believed in slavery; the poverty stricken mountaineer who owned no slaves but who didn't like to be dictated to by Northerners; young men who were ardent secessionists and who were fighting to establish a Southern nation; men who believed in the Union and loved it but who loved their own section too and went with their own fellow Southerners; wealthy men who did not believe in slavery and who had freed their slaves, yet who resented the desire of the North to free the slaves of other men without making payment for them. The army of the Confederacy was an army of individualists and there was seldom found any unanimity of opinion wherever a group of soldiers were gathered together. But, as I remarked above, they were one and all animated by a love of the South and a conviction of the rightness of the Southern Cause.

3rd—"Did blockaders actually secure war supplies from Northern ports"? This is a matter of historic record and can easily be verified from the many books written about blockading and by blockaders. Not only were war supplies brought in from the North by boats, but a brisk trade was done on land. War supplies were slipped through the lines from the North via the border states like Kentucky and Maryland. Many of the old books of personal reminiscences of that era speak in a matter of fact way of getting supplies through the lines.

4th—"Did men as old as seventy and as young as sixteen fight in the Confederate army"? This was so well known a fact that General Grant in commenting upon it remarked that the Confederacy was "robbing the cradle and the grave and grinding the seed corn." I have in my possession copies of the proclamation of the Adjutant General of Georgia, calling on the Militia reserve for all men between those ages and stating that even tuberculosis, hernia, chronic rheumatism, loss of one eye, one arm, one leg or all the fingers from one hand did not permit a man to claim exemption from army service. In my own family my great-grandfather, who was far above the age for military service, went out in the last days of Sherman's campaign and was shot through the lungs with a minie ball in a brisk skirmish, and a number of my great-uncles and cousins who were around sixteen or seventeen also saw active service.

5th—"Did the Yankees truly loot the cemeteries of the Confederacy"? The cemeteries were the first places they went. I am enclosing a letter written by me to Time Magazine about this matter. In it I quoted only a few references. Should you or any of your friends be interested in further information on this subject, write to Miss Alma Jamison, Reference Department, Carnegie Library, Atlanta, Georgia. She has on file scores of references as to Federal looting of Southern cemeteries. A number of these references are taken from reminiscences of Federal soldiers who were in Georgia with Sherman.

6th—"Were there Southern women who actually suffered the degradation that fell to Scarlett"? Starvation, deprivation and suffering were the common lot of Southern women in those parts of the South where the Federal army had been. I am enclosing a list of books of reminiscences of Southern women which throw some light on this situation and also a newspaper article recently published in the Atlanta Journal.

7th—"Was the sole purpose of the Ku Klux Klan to protect Southern women"? There are many histories of the Klan which will tell you all about its origin and it would take me too long to quote them all or part of them. One of the earliest purposes of the Klan was to protect women and children. Later it was used to keep the Negroes from voting eight or ten times at every election. But it was used equally against the Carpetbaggers who had the same bad habit where voting was concerned. Members of the Klan knew that if unscrupulous or ignorant people were permitted to hold office in the South the lives and property of Southerners would not be safe. South Carolina suffered exceptionally from corrupt and ignorant officials during the Reconstruction era, and practically any history of South Carolina or biography of General Wade Hampton will give you an excellent idea as to why the Klan did not want Negroes on Judges' benches or in the governor's chair.

8th—"I take it that there is nothing fictitious about your book except the characters"? My characters, their own personal lives, the houses they lived in, the parties they attended are all fiction. The historical background of War and Reconstruction are as accurate as I could possibly make them after ten years of reading thousands of books, documents, letters, diaries, old newspapers and interviewing people who had lived through those terrible times.

I appreciate more than I can tell you your interest in these matters. I only wish it were possible for me to let you have access to all the material upon which I worked while writing my book, but, as I said before, my material was very numerous!

Mr. Clifford Dowdey   Atlanta, Georgia
Blowing Rock, North Carolina   August 10, 1937

Dear Mr. Dowdey:

As soon as I learned that the plagiarism suit had been dismissed I left Atlanta for a short visit. I have just returned and that explains my delay in receiving and answering your letter.

I cannot tell you how much I appreciate your invitation and that of your wife. Please tell her I don't climb mountains either, and sedentary vacations are my dream of Heaven.

I wish I could say in this letter that I was coming immediately to Blowing Rock, but I cannot. On my return I discovered that I will have to remain in Atlanta for an indefinite period on account of two more lawsuits—one which I am filing against a Dutch publisher who is pirating "Gone With the Wind" and another against an infringement of my dramatic rights. I am up to my ears in long distance calls and lawyers, and I will have to remain here until the suits are formally filed. I do not know when this will be, but I should be free within a couple of weeks. When I see daylight may I write or wire you immediately, setting a proposed date for my visit? And may I count on you to be very frank in your reply if the time I set is not convenient for you due to the arrival of other guests or for any other reason? I realize that there is nothing more maddening than a guest who intends to come avisiting but who will not set the date for the visit. If there were some way by which I could tell when these legal messes would be over I would set the date definitely.

My husband will not be able to accompany me, regardless of the time I decide to go to Blowing Rock. He has a heavy schedule at the Power Company which will prevent a vacation until around Christmas. . . .

Miss Katharine Brown   Atlanta, Georgia
New York, New York   August 13, 1937

Dear Katharine:

. . . Your item about the possible Prissy whetted my interest. I have been especially interested in who would play this little varmint, possibly because this is the only part I myself would like to play. For this reason whoever plays Prissy will be up against a dreadful handicap as far as I am concerned, for I will watch their actions with a jealous eye.

Lizzie McDuffie, Mrs. Roosevelt's maid, who tried for the part of Mammy, was the nurse of one of my good friends, Elinor Hillyer, formerly on the staff of Delineator and now with Altman's. Elinor told Lizzie to phone me when she came to Atlanta recently, and Lizzie did and I had a most pleasant and interesting visit with her. She is a woman of great dignity and intelligence and it was a relief to sit and talk with someone who didn't ask me if it was hard to write a book. She was very reticent about her experience in your studio, but said with great enthusiasm how nice you had all been to her.[1] . . .

[1] The Atlanta *Constitution* published an interview with Mrs. McDuffie by Yolande Gwin July 30. Mrs. McDuffie was born in Covington, Ga., and grew up in Atlanta. She related that she had been given a screen test for the part of Mammy in the fall of 1936 and that "Miss Eleanor" had written a letter recommending her for the role.

I enjoyed the article about you in the August 1st New York Mirror but, being an ex-feature writer, I wanted to add to this story. To tell the truth, ever since I laid eyes on you my old newspaper blood has been surging again through my veins. You are, as you probably know, the world's best copy. The trouble about writing a story about you would be that there is of a necessity a great deal of material that would have to be omitted. That sounds as though I were accusing you of having a lurid past, but I hasten to correct that impression. As I have sized you up, you are the best "public relations" woman I have ever seen and about the smartest. But three-quarters of the value of a public relations expert lies in the fact that no one knows they are a public relations expert. So, in any story written about you that would have to be omitted. The nice part is that you do "look like a debutante" and not like someone who keeps this, that and the other warring element and temperamental personality smoothed down.

I do not know when I enjoyed a book as much as I did "A Mind Mislaid."[2] When I read it I did not know the author was your father, so, you see, that knowledge did not influence me. It was not only interesting but it should do an enormous amount of good. Certainly, it will help take out of the public mind the superstitious horror of asylums and will help make people realize that mental troubles are very much like any other disease and should be treated as such. . . .

Mr. Clifford Dowdey   Atlanta, Georgia
Blowing Rock, North Carolina   August 24, 1937

Dear Mr. Dowdey:
Thanks so much for your letter. I was just preparing to write to you when it arrived. The first of September will do splendidly for me—that is, if hell doesn't bust loose in some other quarter between now and the first. Will you please wire me definite information as to the date of your wife's return to Blowing Rock, and I will come as soon as possible thereafter?

I hate to impose on you and Mrs. Dowdey by asking you to meet me in Hickory when I could come up to Blowing Rock by bus, but I will have to ask you to do this. The reason is—I shall probably get distressingly sick at my stomach from the altitude, and I do not know how I could manage this in a dignified manner in a bus. I doubt if I can manage

---

[2] Henry Collins Brown, *A Mind Mislaid* (New York, 1937).

it dignifiedly even with the aid of you and Mrs. Dowdey, but I believe I could do it better in an open car than in a closed bus.

I sound as though I confidently expected an upheaval, and I do. When Herschel and Edwin Granberry met me at Hickory last summer I was attempting to act as a "coming author" should act, and so, I began our acquaintance with a dissertation on the future of the experimental novel, a subject I know nothing about and care less. Halfway to Blowing Rock I abandoned the experimental novel and the gentlemen held my head over a 5,000-foot valley. I was ill with an abandon seldom seen in those hills, and the combined eight handkerchiefs of the party were not enough. So, if you will meet me at Hickory I will arrive with four bath towels and hope to be as little trouble as possible.

My conscience smites me at even contemplating visiting you when you tell me you are not through with the story for the Journal. I have no business dumping myself upon you when you are so hard at work. I can only salve my conscience with the thought that a little vacation from work may help your eyes.

Let me know the exact date of Mrs. Dowdey's return and I will let you know what train to meet.

Dr. Henry O. Smith   Atlanta, Georgia
Hudson, New Hampshire   August 28, 1937

My dear Doctor Smith:

Thank you so much for your letter. Thank you, too, for saying such nice things about "Gone With the Wind."

In the matter of my use of the term "la grippe"[1]—I bent every effort to have the small details of my novel as accurate as the more important historical facts. To this end I gave a great deal of thought and time to the matter of the term "la grippe." Many people who had lived through the sixties assured me that the term was in use; several doctors who had served in the Confederate Army also made this statement; the term is found in letters of the day. Should you wish medical reference, I would give you the following, taken from the Journal of the American Medical Association, April 3rd, 1937:

> In France 'la grippe' has been used since the epidemic of 1743 (Townsend, J. G.: A Review of the Literature on Influenza and the Common Cold, supple-

[1] *GWTW*, p. 566. The *O.E.D.* cites a use as early as 1776.

ment 48 to Public Health Reports, 1924). The term was used in the United States even before the Civil War, as shown by the following references:

McCall, A.: Some Account of the Epidemic 'Grippe,' Boston M. & S. J. 31: 254, 1844–1845.
Stewart, F. C.: An Account of the Epidemic Influenza Prevailing at Paris, Known There Under the Name of La Grippe, M. Examiner (Philadelphia) 1: 353, 1842.

Mr. Herschel Brickell   Atlanta, Georgia
New York, New York   September 4, 1937

Dear Herschel:

I had a not too far distant ancestor who was a very godly man. He was a loving father and husband, a kind master and an honorable friend. If ever a man's life was an open book his was, and his nature was simple and candid. But he had one eccentricity and this eccentricity caused great though suppressed indignation among the females of his family. He could not endure to have any questions asked about his business, either private or public. Nor did he suffer any questions about his activities. It is related that an addled female cousin, visiting at the plantation for the first time and totally unaware of this eccentricity, observed him putting on his hat and asked politely, "Oh, cousin, are you going out?" It is reported in the family that the look he gave her hastened her death. Once his wife asked him where he was going. This was on their honeymoon so it was pardonable. He said simply, "Out," and he gave her a look. Though she lived with him some fifty years thereafter, she never again asked any questions. Father told me that when he was a very little boy and the old gentleman in his nineties, he (Father) peeked through the shutters as the old man left the house, saw him walk down the side of the road and out of sight around a clump of trees. Father scuttled out and followed him unseen. He noted that the old gentleman walked a quarter of a mile down the road before crossing the road to get to the pasture. His desire was simple: he wanted to get to the pasture. He could have crossed the road directly in front of the house but he had no intention of letting anyone in the house have the satisfaction of knowing where he was going.

As you can imagine, such an eccentric was not bragged about in my presence when I was young. However, when I had turned twelve and had goaded Mother about something she burst out with the fact that there was only one person in the family I had ever showed the slightest resemblance to, and it was that bewhiskered old wretch who didn't want anyone to know about his business and who couldn't bear to have a house full of women gabbling and quacking about his activities.

The older I grow the more I believe in heredity, and I find myself feeling very sympathetic to the old gentleman. All this may explain in part some of my reactions to some of the stories about me. Probably I'd resent them whether they were true or not. The resentment is doubled, of course, when they aren't true. . . .

Well, you were good to call. If I sounded abrupt when I answered it was because I expected it was a call from the N.Y. lawyers who are alleged to be handling the Billy Rose case. They have delayed till I am nearly crazy and from day to day wire us that they've put the papers in the mail. And then they do not put them in the mail. Anxious as I am to get off to B.R. and unable to go until I sign the legal papers, I have been figuratively dancing up and down. When the phone said New York, I leaped from bed hotly, thinking it was the lawyers and that at last I could go into my opinion of them at length (Steve and John, knowing my state of mind have carefully done all the long distancing down town). So I had to rapidly go into a different gear when I realized it was you. . . .

Sunday.

God willing I leave for B.R. at midnight. The papers finally arrived and Steve and I have put in the day on them. Whether they are right or not, I'm past caring. I'm leaving town. I do hate to put myself on the Dowdeys in the shape I'm in but if I stay here the doctor intends to put me in the hospital, and the Dowdeys are preferable. Once in the hospital, the mildest rumor about me would be delirium tremens or nervous breakdown. But the Dowdeys have never seen me and so probably they'll think my present looks and mentality and conduct is perfectly normal. . . .

Dr. C. Mildred Thompson
Vassar College
Poughkeepsie, New York

Atlanta, Georgia
September 27, 1937

Dear Miss Thompson:

I have returned home from a long vacation and find a clipping from an Atlanta newspaper which said that you had been visiting your sisters here. I regret so much that I was out of town during your visit, for it would have been a pleasure to see you again. Our other visit, as far as I was concerned, was far too brief. I hope when you are in Atlanta again you will let me know.

During the last few months I have thought of you frequently as I recalled a remark you made when we met. You said you were thinking of writing about the Ku Klux Klan in Georgia. Every time I thought of your remark I smiled and the smile was a little rueful. I do not know whether you noticed in the papers during the last few months that an old lady, named Miss Susan Lawrence Davis, had been suing The Macmillan Company on the ground that "Gone With the Wind" was swiped bodily from her "Authentic History of the Ku Klux Klan." She was suing for the mere trifle of six billion dollars. Her case was recently thrown out of court before trial. Among other allegations in her bill of complaint was this one,—that she had said the Klan regalia gave a "ghostly effect" and that I had said Carreen was so thin as to be "wraithlike"! It appeared that Miss Davis had a copyright on all historical facts of the War and Reconstruction, and for a time it appeared that I might have to prove in court that the facts of the War and Reconstruction were matters of public knowledge long before her History appeared in 1924. If she appeals and wins a trial I may still have to prove these facts, and I just wanted to warn you that should this occur I intend to go to court with your marvelous book[1] tucked carefully under my arm! . . .

Mr. Sidney Howard   Atlanta, Georgia
New York, New York   October 8, 1937

My dear Mr. Howard:
    As you and I are inextricably entwined like Siamese twins in the newspapers, I am able to keep up with you through my clipping service. Recently my heartfelt sympathy went out to you when I learned that the entire Selznick organization had descended on you at the same time you were rehearsing your new play.[1]
    Offhand I cannot answer your questions for this reason. The decorators are running mad in my apartment and I cannot get my hands on any notes or books, as everything is piled helter-skelter under tarpaulins. However, this afternoon I will go to our reference library and see what I can dig up for you. I have a vague memory of a half-page newspaper advertisement in an 1864 paper about the arrival of new blockade goods. If I can find it I will get a photostat for you.
    Some of the things I am going to say now may upset your plans. For

---

[1] Clara Mildred Thompson, *Reconstruction in Georgia* (New York, 1915).

[1] Of this visit Howard wrote Miss Mitchell October 7: "Cukor is here again; so is Selznick. Some spirit of madness moved Selznick to load the whole kit and kaboodle on a private car and bring them East to work with me here, which is just fine, because I am rehearsing a play [*The Ghost of Yankee Doodle*] at the same time. But Selznick likes to be as complicated as possible and believes that our script will be ready to shoot some day. I am beginning to wonder."

instance, you wrote of "cast iron balconies." If ever there was a cast iron balcony in pre-War Atlanta I never heard of it or saw a picture of one. That type of architectural decoration was not peculiar to this up-state section. It is found two hundred miles away in the coast section around Savannah and, of course, reached the height of its beauty in New Orleans. Moreover, most of the iron in Atlanta had been donated for munition purposes long before Gettysburg because the pinch of the blockade was felt before the summer of 1863.[2]

About the depots for feeding and clothing refugees from Tennessee— if there were such depots I never heard of them, but this afternoon I will query not only the library but my elderly friends who would recall them if they existed. This was the way the refugee problem was generally handled. Practically everybody in the South was vaguely kin to everybody else and if they weren't kin they had friends in other states. The idea of anything like organized charity would have been abhorrent to refugees. Generally the refugees arrived in a strange town and were taken into the houses of relatives, friends or kind-hearted strangers. I recall that one of my relatives, when refugeeing to Macon, was taken into the house of a stranger and this stranger already had under her roof twenty other refugees who slept on pallets in the halls and in the linen closets. The various churches had circles for the relief of refugees. It is my impression that the ladies took the garments they had made and the food they had collected and went about in little groups calling on the refugees and giving where gifts were needed. However, I may be wrong and I will check this point, and also look in the newspapers for names of ladies' auxiliaries and church organizations, as you requested.

And about Doctor Meade blowing up the blockade runners—would it be possible for him not to blow up the whole tribe of blockaders? If he damns them all there will be a wild howl of rage from the South for many of the blockaders were honest patriots who obeyed the government rules and came out of the War poor as church mice.

I'll write you more as soon as I can dig it up.

Mr. Sidney Howard   Atlanta, Georgia
New York, New York   October 11, 1937

Dear Mr. Howard:

As the paper hangers still obstinately refuse to remove furniture from in front of the door of the closet in which my reference books and notes

---

[2] "There were no iron picket fences, iron summerhouses, iron gates or even iron statuary on the lawns of Atlanta now [1862], for they had early found their way into the melting pots of the rolling mills." *GWTW*, p. 146.

are stored, I still cannot cite you "page and line." However, I will add some more information (from memory) to that which I sent you Saturday.

I telephoned all the old people of my acquaintance yesterday and not a one of them recalled a single iron balcony in Atlanta during the War period. Nor did any of them recall any signs on churches calling for iron or, for that matter, calling for anything. The churches did not ever have such signs upon them. Any appeals of this type would have appeared in the Atlanta papers. I doubt if there would have been handbills bearing such appeals, as the paper shortage was always acute. There may have been placards bearing appeals on the office of the provost marshal but I cannot establish this definitely.

As far as I know, the last appeal for old iron was in 1862, a year before Gettysburg. General Beauregard issued this appeal throughout the Confederacy and he was asking for church bells. I cannot tell you the exact date of Beauregard's appeal, but I am having it looked up in the old newspapers at our library. It may also appear in the Records of the War of the Rebellion. I do not know about the general response to this appeal: I only know that the Methodist Protestant Church in Atlanta, of which my great-grandfather was minister, gave their bell in 1862.

The memories of old timers agree with what I had heard about there being no charitable centers for refugees. The best help I can give you on this matter is as follows. Adjoining the railroad tracks and the depot was the city park. It would be in this park that refugees who came by train would pause. Here they would wait with their baggage until friends and relatives came in their carriages to get them. The refugees who had neither friends nor relatives would probably sit here for a while until some kind-hearted citizen offered them shelter, or they would sit in the park for a while until they started the weary tramp around the town to find what already over-crowded boarding houses could take them in.

About the blockaders' stores—blockade goods was sold in several ways. Many storekeepers (retail merchants) went to Wilmington and bought goods on the docks at auction and shipped them back to Atlanta to their stores. Others had large warehouses in Atlanta. They had their agents in Wilmington ship the goods to the warehouses and they held auctions in these warehouses for the benefit of retail merchants and any citizens who wished to bid. Men engaged in blockading cotton to England had offices here in Atlanta for the purpose of purchasing cotton from the rural districts around the city. These establishments—wholesale, retail and cotton offices—would probably have borne no other signs than the names of the proprietors. As I wrote you Saturday, the stores usually announced the arrival of new blockade goods by advertisement in the newspapers, although I have seen a handbill which ran vaguely like this,

"Blank & Blank beg to announce that they have just received a consignment of goods through the blockade,—toothbrushes, ladies' merinos, fine tarlatans, etc." I am still hunting for one of these ads so I can send you a photostat.

The only names of ladies' charitable societies that I know of are: The Soldiers' Friend, The Soldiers' Aid, The Volunteer Aid Society, The Thimble Brigade, The Ladies Defense Association, The Wayside Homes, The Ladies' Clothing Association, the Ladies Industrial Association, The Ladies' Christian Association. I never heard that these organizations had anything to do with refugees. They correspond somewhat to the ladies' canteen workers of the last war in that they met all troop trains with baskets of food, socks et cetera. They also cooperated with the doctors in getting the wounded off the trains, nursing in the hospitals and taking convalescents into their homes.

I hope this is some help but a very large bird tells me in a loud, squawking voice that it probably isn't helpful but is very upsetting to things you had already decided to do!

Tuesday, October 12th

General Beauregard's appeal appeared sometime shortly before March 27, 1862. The original is in the Beauregard Collection of the Confederate Memorial Museum, Richmond, Virginia. The Confederacy was placarded with it and it appeared in newspapers too. I am quoting a part of it below:

> "More than once a people fighting with an enemy less ruthless than yours . . . have not hesitated to melt and mould into cannon the precious bells surmounting their houses of God, which had called generations to prayer.

> "We want cannon as greatly as any people who ever, as history tells you, melted their church bells to supply them; and I, your General, entrusted with the command of your army embodied of your sons, your kinsmen and your neighbors, do now call upon you to send your plantation bells to the nearest depot, subject to my orders, to be melted into cannon for the defense of your plantations.

> "Who will not cheerfully and promptly send me his bells under such circumstances? Be of good cheer; but time is precious."

Today I had every historical organization in the city, as well as the WPA research workers, looking for the refugee center references. As we have found nothing at all, I would imagine my first report to you on **this** subject was correct. I would also say definitely that no church ever **bore** a placard of a secular nature. No appeal for iron was made in Atlanta in midsummer of '63.

The photostats of blockade ads will go to you tomorrow, as well as a picture of The Calico House. (So called because it was painted to resemble that material. And very dreadful looking it was, too, as it looked like a modern camouflaged battleship.) The Calico House was the closest approach to a relief center the town had. All garments, packages, bandages and food for soldiers and the needy were assembled there.

My husband and I look forward to seeing you in Atlanta some day when this cruel war is over.[1]

Mr. Gilbert E. Govan   Atlanta, Georgia
Chattanooga, Tennessee   October 15, 1937

Dear Mr. Govan:

The Library Journal arrived this morning and I ate your editorial[1] along with the breakfast eggs. Of course, I liked it, but then you knew I'd like it when you wrote it! Only a person who grew up in the Atlanta section could have written this article. I am so glad you wrote it because it backs up in an authoritative manner the things I tried to put over about this North Georgia section.

Most Southerners (and most North Georgians too) find it difficult to understand how the Atlanta neighborhood differed from the rest of the South. People persist in believing that magnolias, moonlight, Spanish moss and enormous white columns were to be found everywhere in the old South. Some people became incensed at being told that the old South was not a hundred per cent white columns. This section of North Georgia, as you know, was undeniably crude in spots. Another generation of cotton money would perhaps have given us a lot of white columns, but during the period of which I wrote the cotton money was going back into the land and into Negroes, and not into architectural gems. It was this very circumstance which made me want to write my book. The white columns and the Spanish moss has been done many times and done beautifully, but this "new South" was almost untouched. As you ex-

---

[1] Howard wrote in his letter of November 26: "I have shot the photographs and your letter out to George Cukor. I think that we can take one small historical liberty and see an iron fence wrecked in the summer of '63 because, for picture reasons, it seemed to be convenient to give the camera a long walk through Atlanta and let the audience see how things are going in the city just before the battle of Gettysburg and because it is extremely difficult to do this earlier in the picture. I took care of the refugees in the course of this walk by showing a farm wagon of them unloading along the street into the welcoming arms of Atlanta ladies. Your suggestion of seeing them in park is good, too, but the action of climbing out of a wagon may be more pictorial."

[1] Mr. Govan's "Why 'Gone With the Wind'?" appeared in the "Editorial Forum" of *Library Journal* for September 15.

pressed it so well, it was a new South long before Henry Grady and Ben Hill raised their voices.

I didn't mean to run on at such length, but I am just so happy at reading something by someone who had red, North Georgia clay on his heels and an understanding of this odd town.

About the title, I think I told you that it came from Ernest Dowson and sheer desperation. During the many years when I was working on the book it had no title and, as it did not occur to me that it would ever be published, I saw no reason for clawing my brains about a title. When I chose "Gone With the Wind" I did not think it especially good, but since we were going to press I let it go. It seems that it was a better title than I knew. While it was "Cynara" which suggested it to me, the phrase appears in the book on page 397.

Mr. Herschel Brickell   Atlanta, Georgia
New York, New York   October 20, 1937

Dear Herschel:

I'd like to see your review of Hemingway's book[1] if you can get a clipping without too much bother. I read an advance copy and, dumb creature that I am, I read it for the story and the characters. Now I read solemn reviews about it which speak at length of profound social implications, sociological portents, et cetera. I seem to have missed them all! I think I need a practicing left-winger at my elbow to point to me what is what in modern literature.

I believe I told you once of the excellent word our family used to denote the condition of our house when painters, paperers and upholsterers were ravaging it—"choss." We have been in a state of choss for some time, and the smell of newly painted woodwork was so bad that it gave both of us colds and bronchial coughs and sent us to the Biltmore for a week until the house had dried out. As always, when the apartment is torn up, visitors descended in swarms and we have just come up for air. The apartment is straight again except for draperies and the dining room carpet, and I am thankful, for my old friend of Journal days, Elinor Hillyer, whom you met at the Pulitzer dinner, arrives in Atlanta today. I am glad to have a sofa on which to sit her. I only wish more of my real friends would travel in this direction, as they are so much fun. . . .

The Danish edition, which has delightful illustrations, has arrived and also the first of the Danish reviews. They are so good that you could

[1] Ernest Hemingway, *To Have and Have Not* (New York, 1937).

knock me over with a cork, and when I get them translated into better English I'll send you a sample. The Danish publisher, Steen Hassel- balchs, is an up and coming gent and he has offered a prize to his readers —a trip to New York and five days in Atlanta "to see the 'Gone With the Wind' country." Of course, I wrote Mr. Hasselbalchs that I'd try to help the winner have a good time and at present our greatest concern is that the winner may not speak English. Atlanta seems as much without Danes as without duck-billed platypusses. I know the winner will be disappointed if he expects white columned mansions and darkies singing "Old Black Joe." I guess I'll have to take him to Bessie's church and let the congregation shout "Swing Low" for him. . . .

Mr. Herschel Brickell   Atlanta, Georgia
New York, New York   October 30, 1937

Dear Herschel:

Thank you for the Hemingway review.[1] John and I read it with great interest. You certainly went for him with a tomahawk in one hand and a scalping knife in the other. In fact, I don't recall ever having read a review by you which so completely massacreed a book. Your review did a great deal toward clarifying my own feelings about the book, for, while I was fermenting with ideas—for the first time in years, I was not able to straighten them out, and while discussing the book with John I had to fall back on helpless wavings of hands. The tragedy of it is that he can write so well, and "Farewell to Arms" still remains my favorite modern novel in spite of this confusing work of his.

The first time I had any idea of Hemingway's brutality for its own sweet sake and sadism for the joy of sadism[2] was when I [realized] . . . that neither "Death in the Afternoon"[3] nor "Africa" interested me very much. . . .

There's too much sadism for its own sweet sake in the world today without having sadists deliberately titillated. I know that sounds very old fashioned and moral—just like those loathsome people who say,

---

[1] Brickell wrote a long and scathing review of *To Have and Have Not*. "I con- sider," he said, "Mr. Hemingway's novel a poor piece of work and . . . I can see no reason at all why intelligent readers should bother with it."

[2] Brickell declared: "The sadistic streak that frankly disgusted me—and some others—in 'The Green Hills of Africa' [New York, 1935] comes out often in the novel; too often the author himself seems to be reveling in the hideous brutality of his characters."

[3] *Death in the Afternoon* (New York, 1932).

"Why can't authors write about sweetness and light? There's so much of the sordid that we do not like to be reminded of it."

From the viewpoint of technique its brutality defeats its purpose where one strong passage in a long book can set the reader's scalp atingle. That was why I asked you about "Lena."[4] I read it immediately after Hemingway and was impressed by the punch which arrived at the end of an almost casually written narrative.

Elinor Hillyer has come and gone. Every one of her 250 first cousins and half of her second cousins entertained for her. I went to most of the parties—my first round of parties in nearly three years. My complexion looks like a relief map of the Himalayas. It was wonderful seeing her again but I hardly had a chance to talk to her. Her situation as a "feted guest" made me realize stronger than ever what I would be up against if I came to New York for a short visit to see a few friends....

Mr. Herschel Brickell   Atlanta, Georgia
Ridgefield, Connecticut   November 4, 1937

Dear Herschel:

I may have let you in for a job that will be troublesome to you, so, if you do not wish to undertake it, have no hesitancy in refusing. Here is the how-come of it.

I had a long telephone conversation with Katharine Brown, of the Selznick International Pictures in New York. You wrote me some time ago that you had met her at a tea. She said they were testing a well known actress[1] for the part of Belle Watling. The actress was born in Wisconsin and, naturally, did not have a Southern accent. In the midst of the test it suddenly occurred to the studio that Belle Watling not only had a Southern accent but probably a different accent from the more educated characters. So, Miss Brown got me on the phone and asked if Belle's accent would have been different from Scarlett's and Melanie's and in what way. I did the best I could over the phone. I told her that the accent would have varied as it always does between the educated and the illiterate. I told her too that most of the prostitutes of the day were recruited from freshly landed immigrants or (here in the South) the daughters of small farmers who had been led astray, cracker families and poor white mountaineers. I said that in pronunciation they generally changed e's and i's—calling a pen "a pin," men "min" and accenting such

---

[4] Marcia Gluck Davenport, *Of Lena Geyer* (New York, 1936).
[1] Ona Munson.

words as settlement and government on the last syllable, "settle*mint*" and
"gover'*mint*." In many cases they changed i's to e's, such as "*se*ngle" for
single. I told her the voices would be flat and slightly nasal.

I realized as I was speaking that all I said was confusing. Katharine
then asked if I could suggest any Southerner in New York who would be
able to sit in on an audition for Belle and correct the accent. I know very
well that an ear for accents is born in one like an ear for music. And the
only people I could think of were you and Norma and Elinor Hillyer, and
Katharine crowed with delight at the mention of the Brickells and
said she would get in touch with you. Knowing the movie people and
their ways, I would not be at all surprised if they had dispatched Rolls-
Royces with couriers and outriders to Ridgefield last night to kidnap
you and Norma.

So, the purpose of this letter is to tell you and Norma that it won't
hurt my feelings if you refuse to have anything to do with the matter.

Mr. George Brett, Jr.   Atlanta, Georgia
New York, New York   November 17, 1937

Dear Mr. Brett:
I have your letter of the 15th which quotes from the letter of Mr.
Harold Macmillan about a Young People's Edition of "Gone With the
Wind." In your letter to Mr. Macmillan you set forth excellently my own
idea on the subject. In the first place, I would not want the book
bowdlerized. In the second place, a vast number of children have read the
book already and their parents and teachers say that they have no difficulty with it as the language is simple. I must admit to a feeling of
alarm when I learned that children of ten and eleven years were reading
it. I had a guilty feeling that my mother would never have permitted me
to read such a book until I was eighteen. I even remonstrated with the
mothers of some of the children who were eating it up, and was sat upon
firmly. The youngest reader, to my knowledge, is my nephew Eugene,
age six, whom you met. He has had most of it read to him three times.
The book is on the required collateral reading lists of many schools in
the South, and even a number of junior high schools and grammar schools
are using it. I cite the foregoing merely to back up my contention that it
does not need to be cut for children.

I discovered with relief that the sex angle either went over the heads
of the young or was accepted because the movies had already prepared
their innocent little minds. I discovered, too, that children interpret

things in the light of their own knowledge. One eleven year old girl, giving an oral book review in school, chose "Gone With the Wind," and when she reached the part about the Ku Klux Klan using Belle Watling's establishment as their alibi, this bright child referred to Belle's house as "the swankiest night club in Atlanta, run by a lady named Miss Watling who, I think, was sorta like a blues singer." After that I had no fears that I was polluting the youthful mind.

Please tell Mr. Macmillan that I appreciate his letter of inquiry, but I do not want "Gone With the Wind" abbreviated or re-written.

Sen. Walter F. George   Atlanta, Georgia
Washington, D.C.   November 20, 1937

Dear Senator George:

I am planning to be in Washington Tuesday afternoon and evening en route with my husband to spend Thanksgiving Day with his mother. Since I last saw you in Washington I have been learning things about the international copyright situation which I never dreamed of before and I have learned that a treaty which would put the United States in the Berne Convention is now pending before the Senate. If it should be ratified it probably would not help my situation in Holland, but it might prevent piracies of my book in other countries. For that reason and because I am thoroughly angry over the treatment I have received in Holland, I have become much interested in this matter, and I have been wondering if I personally could help even in a small way in getting the treaty ratified. Would anything be gained if I talked over the situation with some of the members of the Senate Committee on Foreign Relations? I am wholly inexperienced in dealing with such important matters of state, and I will not do it if you recommend against it. On the other hand, if you think it would be desirable, I would be very grateful if you could make engagements for me with some few members of the Committee on Tuesday, anytime after four o'clock. If necessary, I could remain over in Washington Wednesday morning.

You understand already my desire not to get into the newspapers. And, if you do make the engagements for me, please ask the other gentlemen if I may see them privately.

You were so courteous and helpful to me during my recent visit in Washington that I hesitate to impose further on your good nature, but I find myself in a new and strange situation and I do not know to whom else I can turn for assistance.

I will telephone your office as soon as I reach Washington, sometime around noon Tuesday, to learn what plans, if any, you may have made for me.

Miss Katharine Brown   Atlanta, Georgia
New York, New York   December 10, 1937

Dear Katharine:

. . . Of course I am interested in the fate of Lizzie McDuffie.[1] I have not had a great number of pleasant occasions during the last year, but the time I spent talking to Lizzie was most enjoyable. Of course business at the White House will be at a standstill until Lizzie's fate is known! If our Bessie was up for a screen test I know John and I would be so a-twit that the Power Company, Dutch publishers and the raids of autograph hunters would be as nothing.

I haven't mentioned the young lady you told me about over the phone and will not, of course. I immediately forgot her name,[2] which is a help. Of course I'd love to know what happens to her or to any of the Scarletts and think it would be grand if you did telephone me about it. . . .

About the manuscript of "Gone With the Wind" which Mr. Whitney[3] wants to buy—here is the situation. I do not even know if it is in existence, for I intended to destroy it and probably did nearly two years ago. Time has telescoped during these two years and so many things have happened that many past events are a blur. It may be that all or part of the manuscript is in the basement, inextricably mixed with thousands of sheets of re-writes. Some day I pray I will have the time to get into the basement and burn all papers connected with "Gone With the Wind." At present I do not have the time to wash my ears more than once a week.

Even if the manuscript is in existence it isn't for sale. But I wish you would thank Mr. Whitney for his interest in it. I think it's a wonderful

[1] Miss Brown wrote on December 6: "Mrs. Elizabeth Mammy White House McDuffie will be tested on the 13th. I am quite sure that the nation's business will be stopped until the household sees this test. I am writing to David [Selznick] today to suggest that we have an extra copy struck off and sent to Mrs. Roosevelt who, as I think you know, wrote me a personal letter about Lizzie McDuffie. We are really getting a great kick out of making this test and I, for one, should be very pleased if she got the job."

[2] This was probably Edythe Marrener, whom Irene Mayer Selznick had "discovered" at a fashion show. Miss Marrener soon afterward changed her name to Susan Hayward. Gavin Lambert, *GWTW: The Making of Gone With the Wind* (Boston; Toronto, 1973), p. 40.

[3] Jock Whitney.

compliment. Even if it is in existence I am afraid I could not sell it to him as almost every university, historical organization and library here in the South have been after it too, as well as my family, and I should be outlawed if I let it cross the Mason-Dixon Line. The whole truth of the matter is that I do not care where my book, as a book, goes, but I do not want even one sheet of manuscript or one line of notes to survive.

Just for your own ear, there is a slight rise in feeling against Clark Gable for Rhett. However, I gather he is the one slated for the job. Is it definite that Dorothy Jordan will be Melanie?[4] I have heard nothing but enthusiasm for the choice.

I had hoped that long ere now normal life would have returned and that John and I would be taking a winter vacation in New York, and we looked forward to seeing you. But, if it ain't one thing it's another, and this unauthorized publication of "Gone With the Wind" in Holland has kept us busy recently and will continue to do so until I win out. As you may have seen from the newspapers, I went to Washington to the Department of State to get aid in stopping the publication. I do not yet know what will come of it. . . .

[4] A story from Hollywood signed by Louella O. Parsons declared December 8: "You may expect David Selznick to announce within a day or two that Dorothy Jordan has been signed for the role of Melaine[!] in 'Gone With the Wind.' . . . Dorothy, Mrs. Merian Cooper in private life, retired from the screen after her marriage and is now the mother of two children. Her home is Clarkesville, Tenn. Cooper was active in Selznick International when it was first formed and is a close friend of both David and Jock Whitney." Atlanta *Georgian*, December 8.

1938

Dr. Anderson M. Scruggs
Atlanta, Georgia

Atlanta, Georgia
January 5, 1938

My dear Doctor Scruggs:

Of course, I was itching to get you apart at Ruth Carter's the other night, for I was hanging on your words. I was so very sorry that business matters called me home from the party at such an early hour, for I did want to talk further with you.

You were kindness itself to write me all the wonderful things in your letter. My vanity simply blossomed. It is true that some English and Irish reviewers had mentioned vague poetic quality in "Gone With the Wind" but they did not amplify. Practically all of the American reviewers thought that my style left much to be desired. Honesty forces me to admit that these remarks bothered me not at all, as my style was precisely what I wanted it to be—simple, unadorned, colloquial. I thought that in a narrative such as mine the style should not obtrude into the story.

I cannot help feeling very set-up that you, a poet whose work I have always admired, should say such generous things. Thank you again.

Dr. William Lyon Phelps
Augusta, Georgia

Atlanta, Georgia
January 21, 1938

My dear Doctor Phelps:

I hope you will forgive my delay in answering your letter, but practically as soon as you left our house my piracy problem in Holland began boiling over, and from that moment until this John and my brother and I have been on long distance to Washington and have been writing interminable letters to New York and The Hague. So I delayed writing because I wanted the leisure to set forth my ideas about my letters. I feared that if I wrote you briefly and hurriedly you might think that I was very abrupt and unappreciative.

I am far from being unappreciative. In fact, I was never so flattered in my life as when I learned that you wished to include letters of mine with those of the truly great, like Barrie.[1] I do thank you for wanting to do this, and I hope you will not be irritated at me for not wanting them included. You have been so wonderfully kind to me and "Gone With the Wind" that I am embarrassed at not acceding to your request and thus repaying your kindness in this small way.

Here are my reasons for not wishing my letters included in your volume. The first letter had to do with my eyestrain. You cannot imagine what a desperate time I have had with the legends about my "blindness." I wish to Heaven I had suffered in silence and never admitted to anyone that I had had a minor case of strained eyes, for from that small beginning grew the most pathetic stories about my "blindness" and dramatic legends that an operation had restored my eyesight. I like truth and I like accuracy and it infuriated me for people to say and write such things about me. I have fought that rumor for a year and a half and have about laid it. But if that letter appeared in your book it would start the rumors all over again, for it has been my sad experience to learn that so many people read carelessly and hastily. Instead of reading, they merely glance at the page. They would see that phrase "black bandage" and then the story that I am blind would get a fresh start—probably with some folks saying "I *know* it's true; Dr. Phelps said so!"

But I have an even stronger reason for not wanting any letters of mine ever to appear in print anywhere. My reason is that I have a passionate desire for personal privacy. I want to stand before the world, for good or bad, on the book I wrote, not on what I say in letters to friends, not on my husband and my home life, the way I dress, my likes and dislikes, et cetera. My book belongs to anyone who has the price, but nothing of me belongs to the public. This may seem a very extreme view to you, but it is the way I feel.

As I told you when you were visiting us, I have had to refuse in the past year and a half countless requests from people, many of them very old friends, who wished to include letters from me in newspaper articles, magazine stories, anthologies, textbooks, memoirs, et cetera. I am afraid I would get into more hot water than I could ever get out of if I gave my consent to you to use my letters when I had refused the same request of old friends.

I hope you will not misunderstand and think that I am classing your autobiography with the newspaper articles that reportorial friends wish to write. I know the worth of your book and the value of it too. I know your book will be like you, scholarly, dignified and gay as you are gay. I know that an invitation to appear in your book is as great an honor as I am likely ever to get. The difficulty is that I do not want *any* of my

[1] In Phelps's *Autobiography with Letters* (New York, 1939).

letters to be published *anywhere*. My letters belong to me and to the friends to whom I wrote them—and not to the public at large.

I hope you will understand my viewpoint and will not think me a singularly tough-mouthed individual. And I hope that my refusal will not cast any shadow over a friendship which has made me very proud and happy. . . .

Mr. Joseph Henry Jackson   Atlanta, Georgia
San Francisco, California   February 15, 1938

My dear Mr. Jackson:

Thank you so much for your interesting letter. I know how busy you must be, so I appreciate all the more the length of it. I am so grateful to you for having explained a mystery that has puzzled me for over a year— my alleged presence in California. When you wrote me of Ruth Comfort Mitchell and the way people mixed us up, the mystery was explained.

Yes, I, too, hear persistent rumors that I have written a sequel to "Gone With the Wind" and that I am now in Hollywood assisting in the motion picture. But neither of these rumors is true, for I am not doing any writing at all these days, nor do I intend to go to Hollywood.

I am not very well qualified to answer the question in your last paragraph as to what might be done to bring about ratification of the Berne Convention treaty by our country. The obvious answer, I suppose, is that the cause would be helped by anything which would impress upon the senators the fact that there is a public demand for ratification of the treaty. But I am wholly inexperienced in legislative affairs and I wouldn't attempt to say what methods should be employed in doing this. The basic thing, however, is public education, and there is a great need of public understanding of this matter because so few people know the truth of the situation. This applies not only to the general public, but to a great many authors as well. Until comparatively recently I myself thought that an American copyright gave protection all over the world. Painful experience has taught me differently, and it is that which has aroused my interest in this matter. I wouldn't like to see other writers subjected to the same troubles I have had.

This is a matter of interest to the public as well as to the writers themselves. For one thing, it will encourage the development of American literature if writers in this country are protected by their government and do not have to waste their time, energies and money in fighting for their rights in foreign countries. Still another angle to the situation is this—in all of my foreign contracts it is provided that the translation must be faithful and accurate and the book must not be altered in any **way** without my written permission. But a pirated edition could be changed in any way the publisher saw fit. Naturally, this is a bad thing from an author's standpoint, but it is also a bad thing from the standpoint of the American public as I see it. It makes it possible for foreign publishers to take American books and twist them around any way they please. If such publishers did not like the picture of American life presented in the books, they could change it around in conformity with local prejudices and thereby present a distorted picture of our country to their readers—with the author of the book made an unwilling party to this deception.

I could mention many other bad features of this situation, but I won't trouble you with them. As I said before, the most important thing is to bring about a better and wider public understanding of this problem, and I am happy to note that you are planning to make some further comment on it. That is the best possible thing that could be done for, if men of your influence take an interest in this problem, I am confident it will be solved. I am looking forward with great interest to the clipping of your article you said you would send me.

Mrs. Mark Ethridge   Atlanta, Georgia
Prospect, Kentucky   March 10, 1938

Dear Willie:

It was so good to hear from you, even if your letter did give me a too sharp memory of how I felt a month or so before "Gone With the Wind" was published—(when you wrote that you almost wished it[1] wasn't ever coming out). I recall very vividly those identical sensations, which were accompanied by knee joints turning to boiled custard and a tendency to run and hide when I saw any of my friends on the street. I also perspired suddenly and excessively and plaintively wondered if the Lord couldn't manage an especially loud thunderbolt which would strike me (but do no damage to anyone else) before publication date. I think authors should be given a total anesthetic immediately after the last galley proof is read and should be kept under mercifully until six months after publication.

I know your book is going to be good and John knows it and I daresay Mark knows it. And I hope a year from now you will think it is good too.

Selfishly, John and I want to urge you to come to Rich's tea because, of course, we want to see you. But, as to serious advice about your coming, I hardly know what to tell you. This was my own attitude. In spite of

[1] Willie Snow Ethridge, *Mingled Yarn* (New York, 1938).

what you wrote about my not needing publicity before publication, I did need it, for every new author needs it. Mine was a first book and I was utterly unknown. In spite of this, my mind was made up that I would not attend any autographing teas—I did not care if I never sold a single copy. I had many reasons for feeling like this, but I will spare you all of them except one which may bear upon your case. I was not a professional writer and I never intended to be one. I do not at present consider myself a professional writer but only a lucky amateur. The reason I gave in and went to two teas, one at Davison's and one at Sears-Roebuck's, was as follows. The Atlanta book stores had plunged heavily on advance orders, far too heavily I thought, and I was perfectly certain they were going to get stuck with at least half of them. Norman Berg, manager of the Trade Department of the Atlanta branch of Macmillan Company, had sold these orders and it meant a great deal to him that the stock should move. I personally did not feel that the presence of an author at a book store did the slightest bit of good. But if Norman and the book stores thought it did good and wanted my presence, then I was willing to help. I may add I would have gone to Rich's too, except for an unfortunate mixup. I asked the young man who was formerly in charge of Rich's books if he wished to have me there. I told him that after the first week of publication I never intended to make a public appearance anywhere at any time or for any reason. Because he could not have me first, as I had already promised Davison's, he turned me down. Shortly thereafter he left Rich's and was replaced by the very charming Mrs. Markowitz[2] whom you met last year. Rich's wanted me to come for a tea, but my week was up then and if I had accepted their invitation I would have had to accept a thousand others. And so, I refused.

You are a professional writer and have been writing steadily for years, and you are doubtless going to write other books for you have a number of books under your hair. Therefore, I feel your situation is somewhat different from mine, and I do not feel capable of giving any advice. I only know that coming for the tea won't do you any harm! Moreover, to a professional writer it is valuable to be known, and public appearances make one known. Regardless of what you say, you make an excellent public appearance. You handle yourself well and you go over in a big way. Moreover, you might have a good time out of it. You know your Wesleyan friends will rally around and it might be a lot of fun. If you do decide to come, please give us some advance warning, so that if you decided to stay over John and I could invite in some of the newspaper folks for a party. We would dearly love to have a real, live, roaring lioness for a party.

[2] Mrs. Lillian Markowitz.

I can give practical advice on one subject: wear shoes to the tea that are easy on the Ethridge dogs. Floors are mighty hard on an author's feet and four-inch heels have a way of boring clear up to the skull, and that ruins one's pleasant expression. I put my vanity in my pocket and wore sandals, and I certainly got off more easily than I expected.

There isn't much news with us, except the same old sixes and sevens, which means piracy suits and infringement suits. I have been fighting for six months a piracy case in Holland, where I was published without a by-your-leave. The United States has never seen fit to join the international Berne Convention which protects authors. Therefore, American authors have to be published simultaneously in the United States and some other country which is a member of the Berne Convention. I was published simultaneously in Canada and am legally entitled to protection, but that didn't bother the Dutch at all. If I lose my case in Holland it will not only affect me personally and cost me thousands of dollars for legal fees, but it will affect every American author, and will affect Canadian publishing very seriously. It seems a pity, as the bill to get the United States into the Convention has been up before the Senate so often, that it should not have passed. This Dutch business and the lady who sued me for six billion dollars and the dramatic infringement case against Billy Rose in Texas have taken all of our time in recent months, and have been very expensive and worrisome. However, I have always felt that people who would not fight for what they had deserved to lose it. So, I intend to keep fighting.

Do give my love to Mark and the children, and see if you can't go into a coma until publication day. I'll bet you feel much worse than when you were waiting for the children to get born.

Miss Katharine Brown　　　　　　　　　　　　Atlanta, Georgia
New York, New York　　　　　　　　　　　　　March 16, 1938

Dear Katharine:

I haven't seen Wilbur Kurtz since his return from the West Coast, for John and I have been busy and Mrs. Kurtz has been laid up with a cold and we have been unable to get together. I hope to see him in the next day or so, for, as you can imagine, I am simply hopping with excitement to hear all. Wilbur is a close-mouthed individual and would not even tell me anything interesting over the telephone. When he left Atlanta he told no one where he was going and why, except John and me. The news leaked out from Hollywood, and when he returned he gave a very nice interview to The Journal. But I am anxious to hear about the script and the background and the plans, and the cautious Wilbur does not even trust the telephone operators.

I did hear one amusing story from Hollywood, that spawning-place of rumors. Another friend of mine has recently been there visiting a relative who is a director. At a party given him he asked the everlasting question, "but who is going to play Scarlett?" and the assemblage set upon him with derision. They told him that he, being from Atlanta, should know better than anyone: the author, Margaret Mitchell, was to play the part, and she had been in Hollywood for four months being groomed and tutored. They all thought Mr. Selznick had been clever as hell to keep her so quiet. My friend's jaw dropped on his chest, for he'd been seeing me at least once a week for the last six months. He told them so and remarked that I had no histrionic ambitions. I gather, too, that in his indignation he ungallantly stated that I was something like fifty years too old for the part. But the movie people merely patted him kindly and told him that he did not know what he was talking about. This rumor caused John and me to roll on the floor with delight. I just hope my relatives in Los Angeles and my friends there don't believe it, for they will think I am mighty high-hat not to have called them up.

I think the cards Selznick International hands out in answer to the everlasting question are a fine idea. I only wish I could have had 150,000 of them to hand out myself during the last year.

I hear by the grapevine route that some Northern organization whose title is, I believe, The Society for the Dissemination of Correct Information About the Civil War,[1] has been flooding the California office with their mimeographed stuff about what a horrible and unladylike person I am and how utterly false is the picture I presented in my book. This outfit never had the courage to send me any copies, but they had been circulating them sub rosa. I got a copy a year ago from a gentleman whose sister-in-law is a well known slick writer. This gentleman, a Northerner by birth, was furious because I had out-sold her, and he annotated this mimeographed stuff for me. The annotations showed obvious indication of violent indignation at my sales records. Most of the material consisted of "letters from subscribers" which appeared a year ago in the columns of a Boston newspaper. A majority of them were pitched on a personal angle—that is, personal about me, referring to me as "the Atlanta midget." Many of them were along this general line: "A Northern lady (they were very careful not to give her name), recently returning from a trip South, says that Southern people are indignant at 'Gone With the Wind'

---

[1] The Society for Correct Civil War Information, an organization in Evanston, Ill., run by Lucy Shelton Stewart.

and say that the author is not a person of good family" et cetera, et cetera. Most of the stuff was pure mouthing, and there never was a direct accusation of inaccuracy which I could answer with about sixteen references from Northern and Southern authorities. Ever since a woman wrote to *Time* magazine saying that I lied about Federal soldiers looting and desecrating Southern cemeteries, few people have had courage to give me the lie direct. I nailed this lady in a large way with four or five references, and offered to send forty more if *Time* would give me the space. These people have no scruple about twisting angles to suit their own purposes. For instance, Mrs. Wilbur Kurtz wrote an article for an Atlanta paper about the horrors of Reconstruction and, like a good historian, she quoted direct from an eyewitness, Princess Salm-Salm, wife of a Northern officer stationed in Atlanta shortly after the War. The Princess exclaimed in horror at what she saw.[2] The people who got out the mimeograph dropped out the Princess and declared that Mrs. Kurtz, *A Southern woman*, had made these statements and how could they expect truth from a Southern observer.

I've been very careful to keep any news of this brochure from getting into the hands of various Confederate organizations, for I knew it would start the War all over again. The one thing I have always wanted to avoid is the stirring up of old hates and prejudices, because I wrote my book with no hate and no prejudice. I've been made very happy by the graceful and generous praise from Northern people, and in the thousands of letters I have received from Northerners there have been only one or two who disagreed. Their disagreements were based on the one fact that I did not show any Negroes being beaten to death.

By another grapevine I learn that there are chain letters circulating here in the South (and in the North, too, for all I know), asking that correct Southern accents be used in the picture. I haven't seen one of these letters yet, but I will try to secure one and send it to you. Frank Daniel, on the Atlanta Journal, is using these letters as a springboard for a story entitled "Just What Is a Southern Accent?" He is pointing out, and very truly, that there is no definite Southern accent. Here in Georgia alone there are at least five different accents, and a native Georgian can spot someone from the mountains or coast or wiregrass

---

[2] Princess Agnes Elizabeth Winona Leclercq Joy Salm-Salm, wife of Felix Constantin Alexander Johann Nepomuk, Prince Salm-Salm. From July to October 1865 General Salm-Salm served as military governor in Atlanta. The princess's recollections of her months in Atlanta are detailed in her *Ten Years of My Life* (London, 1876; 2 vols.). A story quoting at length Mrs. Kurtz's letter concerning the princess's experiences and comments appears in the Atlanta *Constitution* for January 24 under the headline "Wife of the Military Governor of Atlanta in 1865 Verified 'Gone With the Wind Facts.'"

section by the time they say "how do you do." I will send you a copy of the story.[3]

Things are somewhat quieter now and we do not get as many tourists and phone calls. The problem at present involves Prominent Visitors. Atlanta has a score of Prominent Visitors in a day, and the organizations entertaining them all try to lure me out to banquets, et cetera, "just to say a few words." As I decided the week the book came out that I would not go to banquets or any public gatherings, and would never say "just a few words," it's been a tug-of-war. So far, I have won the tug, although my hands are skinned from rope burns. With the subsidence of public interest in me as a person, I have high hopes that in the next six months I can perhaps come to New York and quietly see the people I want to see without being devilled by autograph hunters, people whose daughters write divine poetry and presidents of organizations who want me to speak. Hasten the day! I will be glad to go atraveling again like a human being.

If you have any news about the casting of even minor characters, such as Miss Pittypat or Mrs. Merriwether, of course, I'd love to know about them, and I would not spread the news. I have been credited for months with knowing who was to play Scarlett and being plain dog mean and close-mouthed for not telling anyone. Did you ever dream when you bought the movie rights from me that there'd be this public interest? Heaven knows I didn't.

Mr. Herschel Brickell
New York, New York
Atlanta, Georgia
March 19, 1938

My dear Herschel:

We are leaving for Florida tonight and probably will be away until at least the middle of April, when, worse luck, I must return. In a weak moment I promised to do something for the Dane who won my Danish publisher's "Gone With the Wind" contest.[1] The prize was a trip to New York and Atlanta, so I will have to return and take him to Jonesboro and Kennesaw Mountain. He has been studying English for several months but confesses he cannot understand American at all. This will make things very jolly for everyone. There is a Viking Society here in Atlanta composed of Scandinavians. Pray God there is a Dane amongst them! So, picture me with the Dane, local historians, an assortment of

[3] Published as "Is There a Southern Accent?" *The Atlanta Journal Sunday Magazine*, March 27, 1938, pp. 1–2.

[1] Emanuel Christensen.

Swedes and Norwegians and probably photographers and reporters from the local papers, trying to explain troop movements around Jonesboro.

Misery loves company and that is why I cannot feel too dreadfully sorry about the jump in your mail since the Holland's article.[2] I really do feel sorry, for I know how hopeless and maddening such correspondence is. But, as I remarked above, it is pleasant to have company, and such good company! In the beginning I put my foot down flat on manuscripts. If an envelope is suspiciously thick I do not open it. John or my secretary opens it and we try to have witnesses to prove that I never read it and that it was returned immediately. While I do not imagine I will be doing any more writing, I do not want to give anyone the chance to hold me up on a plagiarism charge. What these writers do not understand or do not care to understand is that to do a conscientious job on a novel mansucript takes about six months. When you have finished the novel doesn't belong to a writer, as it has been practically rewritten. Sometimes I feel guilty at my conduct in this matter, for I have been so fortunate. However, I steel myself with the memory that I not only did not ask anyone to assist me but fought violently against letting even close friends read as much as a line.

No, I hadn't heard the good news about Marjorie Rawlings' new novel,[3] but I am very happy to know that the Book of the Month Club has chosen it, and I will buy it as soon as it comes out. If it's even half as good as "South Moon Under"[4] I know I will like it a lot.

Mr. Herschel Brickell   Atlanta, Georgia
Ridgefield, Connecticut   April 14, 1938

Dear Herschel:

I might as well break the news to you brutally. I weigh 120 pounds and have to unzip all my dresses to breathe. I am breaking ground for my third chin and I never felt better in my life. I recall your remarks that you never could hand fat people a thing. I do not wish to go under false colors for I am as hefty as a hog at killing time.

We had a wonderful vacation, drifting about small Florida towns. No one knew who I was and no one asked for autographs. We went to see Mabel and Edwin, of course, and had a most enjoyable two days with

---

[2] Grace Leake's "Herschel Brickell, Literary Outpost of the South," an article in a series called "Southern Personalities," appeared in *Holland's*, LVII, No. 2 (February 1938), pp. 15, 43.

[3] Marjorie Kinnan Rawlings, *The Yearling* (New York, 1938).

[4] *South Moon Under* (New York, London, 1933).

them. Edwin, after the peculiar manner of authors, has junked everything he wrote on his novel and started afresh. I was appalled at this until he went into details and then I felt very enthusiastic. I think he has many things clear in his mind now which were foggy when I talked to him last summer. It was this fogginess that kept him from really doing any work. . . .

Edwin and Mabel were very excited about Marjorie Rawlings' book though they had not read it. I am looking forward to it as soon as I have cleared away the accumulated mail. It sounds as if it would be a marvelous piece of writing and I hope she sells a million copies.

Of course I was so pleased about Clifford getting the Guggenheim award. There was a note from him waiting for me when I returned and, although he barely mentioned the Guggenheim, the tone of his letter was much better than usual and his attitude toward his work excellent despite his sinus trouble and Helen's cold. I am going to look up the Saturday Review attack on him which you mentioned. It sounds very much as if a good U.D.C. friend of mine wrote it.[1] I saw her on our trip and she was high in her praise of McElroy's book.[2] She also told me she thought Clifford had been unfair to President Davis. I believe it is part of this year's U.D.C. program to concentrate on President Davis and try to clear up matters surrounding him. With all due respect to them, they will have a hard job making President Davis as magnetic a figure as Lee, Stephens and others.

You harrow me when you tell me that the ladies at White Plains were still interested in me. While we were away the Herald-Tribune's best seller list included me out except for two stores and last Sunday I was included completely out. I thought this a definite indication of waning interest and I am going to continue to believe this as it makes me feel more comfortable.

You asked about news of the movie. Here is the latest I know, and it is six weeks old. I have a friend who is perhaps the world's leading authority on the Atlanta campaign and all historic events centering around Atlanta. His knowledge is not just book knowledge. As a young man he went over battlefields when veterans were still spry enough to take him. He knows where every battery stood and where every mule got its ears shot off; he is an architect and an artist; he has also written a number of historical articles and is now writing a military book on the Atlanta campaign. When the movie folks were here a year ago I per-

[1] Mrs. Eugenia Dolly Blount Lamar of Macon, President-General of the United Daughters of the Confederacy, attacked Dowdey for his unsympathetic portrayal of Jefferson Davis in her letter published in *The Saturday Review of Literature*, XXVII, No. 22 (March 26, 1938), p. 9.

[2] Robert McNutt McElroy, *Jefferson Davis, the Unreal and the Real* (New York, London, 1937; 2 vols.).

suaded him to take them about the countryside. They were impressed by him and in February sent for him to come to Hollywood for "a preliminary conference" on the background of "Gone With the Wind." I saw him last night and he told most interesting stories. Evidently, the ground has been broken for the production, even if the four main characters have not been cast. His job was picking flaws in the old Atlanta sets, fighting to keep too many tall, white columns off of houses, et cetera. He said the research department was working overtime, as were the art department and the set-building department. But no one had any idea when the actual shooting would begin. It can't begin until all this preliminary work is done and the costs of production estimated. He said that if there had been anyone definitely chosen for Scarlett or Rhett he believed the news would have leaked out on the lot. He said that Sidney Howard had adhered very closely to the book. Naturally, he had had to drop out many characters and situations to shorten the script and he had been forced to condense. I gathered that it was a good script and that the ending was as I had written it. Of course, the script may be re-written twenty times more before it is shot.

Yes, we closed the Billy Rose affair before leaving town.[3] You spoke of hearing of it on the radio. If you remember on what broadcast it appeared I wish you'd let me know.

While away I frequented hotel lending libraries. I am two years or more behind on my reading and instead of reading new books I endeavored to catch up on those I had missed. I read "Appointment in Samarra," "Butterfield 8," "The Postman Always Rings Twice," "Serenade," "Imperial City,"[4] and dozens of others. By the time I came home I had bad emotional indigestion. If I had read these books over a long period of time as they appeared it would have been a different matter. Reading them close together as I did, the impact was strong. I hope you will understand that my emotional indigestion did not arise from any sense of shock or disapproval at the goings-on of these characters. What depressed and bothered me was the tiredness of everyone concerned. These characters did not leap gaily in and out of strange beds as did the characters of the jazz age, nor did they commit murder, forgery et cetera with passion, enthusiasm or regret. They did all these things—for what reason I cannot say. Certainly, they got no pleasure from any of their sins, nor did they have any sense of remorse. We came

---

[3] Rose paid $3,000 in damages, promised to pay an additional $25,000 if Miss Mitchell's rights were further violated by him, and wrote a letter of apology. Finis Farr, *Margaret Mitchell of Atlanta* (New York, 1965), p. 177.

[4] John O'Hara, *Appointment in Samarra* (New York [c. 1934]); O'Hara, *Butterfield 8* (New York [c. 1935]); James M. Cain, *The Postman Always Rings Twice* (New York, 1934); Cain, *Serenade* (New York, 1937); Elmer L. Rice, *Imperial City* (New York, 1937).

home slowly, visiting our friends in the small towns of Georgia and Florida, and I looked upon my friends and their friends with new eyes. I think the novelists, especially in the New York area or those who write about New York, have cut themselves off from the realities of America. For I could see that the old morals persist and the old ways of looking at sin and such have not changed. Remorse for ill-doing is as strong as ever and social pressure toward ill-doing as it was a hundred years ago. There was a vitality and enthusiasm for life in both its good and bad aspects in these small town people. I hope you know what I am getting at, as I do not know if I am making myself very clear. After reading all these books I was seized with a violent desire to write a story about a girl who went wrong and certainly did regret it. I think it would be colossal and sensational. I could not find in any of the books I read the perfectly normal feminine reaction of fear of consequences, of loss of reputation, of social disapproval or of that good old-fashioned Puritan institution, conscience. I suppose my desire to write such a book puts me definitely in the Victorian era. But then, "Gone With the Wind" was probably as Victorian a novel as was ever written, in spite of anything anyone may say.

I read about the eight inches of snow in Connecticut and thought of all the bulbs you and Norma had put out. I hope it was not love's labor lost.

Mr. Kenneth Roberts   Atlanta, Georgia
Kennebunk Beach, Maine   April 14, 1938

My dear Mr. Roberts:

I *did* think you owed me $10.00. I still thought I deserved it until my husband and I went on our recent vacation. During our trip my husband read "Northwest Passage."[1] He had been too busy to read it when I read it and he had heard me going on enthusiastically about it. He enjoyed it as much as I did and he told me that he thought I should cancel out the $10.00 because he had received many times that amount in pleasure from your book. I am, I hope, a fair-minded person and this seems reasonable to me. So I am notifying you that I consider that you and I are square.

I appreciated your letter so very much. When I told Mr. Vose[2] the sad story of the effect of "Northwest Passage" upon me I did not know that he was going to pass the information on to you, but I am glad he did

---

[1] *Northwest Passage* (Garden City, N.Y., 1937).
[2] Robert C. Vose.

because it gives me the opportunity to tell you what a wonderful book you wrote. I know that thousands of people have already told you, but I want to be among those thousands. "Northwest Passage" was not only intensely interesting reading, it taught me much about a period of history of which I am ignorant. I know something of our Seminole Wars in this section, as I had relatives who were incautious enough to get tomahawked and scalped and other relatives who fought Chief Osceola. But I knew so little about the section of which you wrote and it made the book doubly interesting. While I was recovering from my midnight ice box raid I re-read "Arundel"[3] and liked it just as much as I did the first time.

As to the note to Mr. Vose, which you enclosed, and the suggestion about the autograph—you have me in a somewhat embarrassing position and I can only be frank about it. I know you, of all people, will understand, for your experiences doubtless have been similar to mine. I have not autographed anything—books, albums, pictures, bed quilts et cetera —since December 1936. At that time the autographing situation had gotten completely out of hand. Every tourist in Atlanta between trains called for an autograph and, unfortunately, their trains usually arrived in Atlanta around two o'clock in the morning, and everyone whose grandfather was in the Confederate army called too. It was not that I was unappreciative of their interest, for I was and still am breathless and incredulous at the career of "Gone With the Wind." But I was having no time to sleep or to eat uninterrupted meals or to attend to my household duties and to my mail. So, I decided never to autograph again. Unfortunately, when I came to this decision I had not even inscribed the copies belonging to my brother and other relatives. I have never autographed these copies, for I discovered that I could not pick and choose without offending many people. So, that is why I am returning your note to Mr. Vose. I am very sorry.

Mr. Vose said so many interesting and charming things about you personally and your note bears them out. I am so glad to have the opportunity to tell you that I no longer carry that $10.00 on my mental books against you!

Mr. Harold Latham   Atlanta, Georgia
New York, New York   April 18, 1938

Dear Harold:
Thank you for your telegram about Mr. Christensen and for your **letters** of April 14th and 15th. You were very kind to wire me about

[3] *Arundel* (Garden City, N.Y., 1930).

"the gainer" and to give me advance information. I did not see him the day he arrived, as Stuart Rose, of The Saturday Evening Post, landed in town at the same time and John and I were with Mr. Rose all day. However, Mr. Christensen was well taken care of. Mr. Born,[1] the travel agent who had him in charge, had secured the services of Wilbur Kurtz, our well known authority on Atlanta and Georgia history, and also an elderly Danish lady to interpret. I gather that "the gainer" must have seen most of North Georgia that day, as the indefatigable Mr. Kurtz showed him Stone Mountain and Kennesaw Mountain (They are forty miles apart.), all of the old entrenchments around Kennesaw, the line of retreat from Kennesaw to the battlefield of Peachtree Creek (another twenty miles), the Cyclorama, the old houses, et cetera. The elderly interpreter pronounced herself completely bushed and she was unable to go with Mr. Kurtz, Mrs. Kurtz, Mr. Christensen and me on an expedition next day to Jonesboro and Clayton County. We found that we did not need the services of an interpreter, as Mr. Christensen understood far more English than he spoke. He was amazingly quick at understanding things and we had a delightful morning.

Mr. Born took him to a baseball game that afternoon. It seemed to bewilder him as it went so fast—"not at all like cricket," he told me. That night we had him to dinner in a private room at the Athletic Club, with my father and brother and seven other guests, and we had the Negro quartet from Bessie's church to sing spirituals for him. I ardently wished for your presence because the quartet sprang several new songs on us. I was especially taken with one named "I have just got to Heaven and I can't Sit Down." There was a great deal of pantomime in this song. The tall, bespectacled Negro kept insisting in deep bass that he couldn't sit down in Heaven; the other three urged, pleaded and entreated that he sit down. They would almost get him into a chair and then he would leap up, pointing to various saints and prophets who were standing around watching him. The denouement was that in a fury the bass Negro picked up a chair and knocked the other three to a sitting position. I tried to translate this to the Dane, but with little success, I fear.

During this dinner there occurred a most unpleasant happening which I hope the Dane did not understand, as I should not like for him to lecture upon it in Denmark. For nearly a year I have had no photographs taken by the newspapers, nor have I given any interviews unless on matters of "news." By that I mean winning prizes, suing and being sued, et cetera. I know what constitutes news and I am very glad to cooperate with the papers whenever a real story breaks, but I see no reason why my face should appear in the papers three times a week for no good

[1] John M. Born.

reason. Every time some "important visitor" comes to town an effort is made to have me photographed with these visitors, and I have always declined. The Journal and The Georgian have been most understanding about this, and The Constitution understanding, but in a lesser degree. I notified all three papers of Mr. Christensen's arrival. The Journal and Georgian photographed and interviewed him merely stating that I would entertain him during his stay. The Constitution, however, was hellbent on getting a picture of both of us together, and for twenty-four hours I told them that it could not be done. Just when our dinner was beginning a reporter and photographer showed up and forced their way into our private dining room. John took them and Mr. Christensen out and told them that I had already discussed the matter with the City Editor. They phoned the city editor and he left his desk and arrived at the Club. He said he would have a picture of us both or else we would be "pretty damned sorry." The fact that the other two papers did not have a picture made him all the more determined. He tried to break up the dinner and he departed saying that he would make us so sorry that we had refused this one that we would be glad to give any future pictures he asked. Our reply was that we did not jump through hoops for anybody. Mr. Christensen was a witness to all of this and I do not know how much he understood. . . .[2]

I am overjoyed that you liked the foreign editions. As I wrote you before, I always wanted you to have copies but I hesitated, fearing they would be a burden. You see, I have lived in an apartment with limited book space for so long that I forget that other people have more room.

Mr. Will Stripling, President   Atlanta, Georgia
Frontier Fiesta Association   April 18, 1938
Fort Worth, Texas

Dear Mr. Stripling:

I am asking Mr. Sterling Holloway, of Thompson and Barwize, to present to you the copy of "Gone With the Wind" which was used in recent infringement action against Billy Rose. Naturally, I am pleased that the case has been satisfactorily concluded, with the recognition of my rights for which I was contending. The settlement has released this copy

---

[2] Wilbur Kurtz was one of the guests at the dinner for Mr. Christensen. He wrote in his private notebook: "During the evening a couple of Constitution representatives came up to interview and photograph. John Marsh talked them out of photographing Margaret—as she will not permit pictures of herself to be taken. John just about missed his dinner because of this affair." MS at the Atlanta Historical Society.

of my book, which had been filed with the court as an exhibit, and I would like for you to accept it as an expression of my thanks for the friendly and sympathetic attitude displayed by you and the other members of the Fiesta board during these unpleasant proceedings.

As you may know, my grandfather, Russell Crawford Mitchell, was living in Alto, Texas, when the War began. He enlisted in Company I, First Texas Volunteers, and served with this company until he was wounded at Sharpsburg. After the surrender he returned to Atlanta and spent the rest of his life here. He loved Texas and Texas people and he passed on this feeling to his children and grandchildren. His memories of Texas were so vivid and so pleasant that when he bought a great tract of land in North Georgia and established a town there he named it Alto after his Texas home. Our State tubercular hospital is now located there. I have never been to Texas but I have, by inheritance, an interest and a warm feeling toward that State and its people. So you can understand that it was embarrassing to me to bring action against the Fiesta as well as Billy Rose. The technicalities of the law, however, made this necessary. And I am grateful that the members of the Fiesta board and the citizens of Fort Worth understood my position and permitted me to retain their friendship which I value so highly. . . .

Mr. Joseph Henry Jackson   Atlanta, Georgia
San Francisco, California   April 19, 1938

My dear Mr. Jackson:
    I have returned home after a long vacation and I found your letter and clipping, about the pirating of "Gone With the Wind," waiting for me.[1] Thank you for both and thank you, too, for the interest which prompted you to write the column. It was kind of you to go to this trouble. So very few people realize that authors of the United States have no copyright protection abroad, and so, I was glad, for my sake as well as for other authors, that you gave publicity to this situation in your column.
    News and clippings from Holland concerning my fight in the Dutch courts keep me torn between indignation and grim amusement. I understand now why that expression "you can't beat the Dutch" arose. As I told you in my previous letter, the Dutch publishers of "Gone With the Wind" defended their action in publishing my book without paying me

---

[1] Jackson's column, "A Bookman's Notebook," of February 19 was devoted to Miss Mitchell's copyright difficulties, quoting at length her letter to him of February 15.

for it, by saying that I had not had simultaneous publication in the United States and in Canada. My latest information is that they have abandoned this stand and have taken another one. They claim that I was not "published" in Canada under the terms of the Berne Convention. The argument centers around the meaning of the word "editee" in the Berne Convention treaty. The Dutch publishers assert that The Macmillan Company of Canada (my Canadian publishers) did not really "publish" "Gone with the Wind," but were merely a distributing agent of The Macmillan Company of New York. The two firms are totally independent of each other but the Dutch are using this as the basis of their suit. The few Dutch newspapers I have seen support the claims of the Dutch publishers and say that I should not expect protection in Holland when the United States is not a member of the Berne Convention. If I lose my case in Holland a precedent very dangerous to all American and Canadian authors and publishers will be established.

Ordinarily I am a mild individual, but my blood is up on this matter and I intend to take it through every court in Holland. Mr. George Brett, President of The Macmillan Company of New York, is now in Europe and he is going to The Hague to testify personally at the trial. As you can imagine, I am awaiting with great interest the outcome of his testimony.

While my husband and I were away we picked up a Modern Library Edition of "Of Mice and Men."[2] I had read it when it first appeared and thought it wonderful, but my husband had not had the opportunity to read it. To our great pleasure and interest, we found your Introduction and we were delighted with it.

Mrs. Gilbert E. Govan   Atlanta, Georgia
Chattanooga, Tennessee   April 21, 1938

Dear Christine:

As Margaret Baugh wrote you, John and I took a long vacation—the first real vacation in thirteen years. We had no mail forwarded and we devoted our time to regaining the weight we had both lost in the last two years.

When I came home I found your book and your letter to Margaret Baugh and I wanted to write you immediately. However, at that very moment there arrived a Dane bearing letters of introduction from my Danish publishers. The Dane had won a "Gone With the Wind" contest in Denmark and the prize was a trip to Atlanta. He was here for five days

[2] John Steinbeck, *Of Mice and Men* (New York, [c. 1937]).

and during that time I showed him about the countryside, lecturing as best I could on historic spots. He has gone now and I hasten to thank you for "Plantation Murder."[1] No, I have not read it yet but I intend to during the coming ten days. John's vacation lasts till the end of the month and we are going away again immediately to a quiet spot. I know I will enjoy your book for Margaret has told me what a grand story it is.

I do not recall whether I told you, that night you were with us, that murder stories are my meat. I have often wondered why so few people lay the scenes of their murder stories in the South. Of course, I like murders in London with Scotland Yard in hot pursuit, and I am not one to turn up my nose at murder in New York with scientific criminologists on the trail. But how wonderful to have a murder here in the South and to see vividly depicted on the jacket a brace of bloodhounds! That's bringing murder close to home. You were so very sweet to send it to me. And please think of me enjoying it during the coming few days.

Margaret let me see your letter to her and I certainly enjoyed your descriptions of writing during the re-plastering and painting. I remember having a sanding machine roaring in the next apartment for two weeks while I was attempting a particularly tender chapter. I don't see how anyone with three children manages to write a line. And so, my opinion of you rises mightily. One of my worst periods occurred shortly after the movie "Tarzan"[2] appeared and all of the innocent little ones in the neighborhood congregated under my window, beating on thin breasts and screaming, "Wa-oo! Wa-oo!" I descended to bribery and dropped pennies and pieces of chewing gum like manna for weeks.

Please give Gilbert our best. And many, many thanks again for the book.

Mr. Kenneth Roberts   Atlanta, Georgia
Kennebunk Beach, Maine   April 21, 1938

Dear Mr. Roberts:

Your autographed bookplate arrived and it gives me great pleasure. You are a most understanding and generous person and you make me feel ashamed of my own "no autograph" stand—even if that stand was taken in self-defense.

---

[1] Christine Noble Govan, *Plantation Murder* (Boston, 1938).

[2] Tarzan was introduced to the screen with Elmo Lincoln as *Tarzan of the Apes* in 1918. Miss Mitchell's letter probably refers to the Tarzan of the exceedingly popular Johnny Weissmuller, who first appeared in that role in *Tarzan the Ape Man* in 1932.

Thank you for the offer of a view of your contract. That is generosity too. Just between you and me, I do not know when, if ever, I will sign another contract. Like most writers, I loathe writing above all other occupations and will go to any lengths to keep from writing. Moreover, I have not had the time since June 1936 even to think about writing, and I do not know when the pressure will let up. I was very cheered when I got off the best seller list last month, for I hope that is an indication of a return to normal life.

I daresay your suggestion about keeping "a few cans of Friends' oatmeal in the ice chest" is an excellent one, but when I am reading a book and am at fever heat I need rich and varied viands. The kinds of things that Mr. Booth Tarkington's Florence Atwater[1] (my favorite female character of all fiction) would refer to as "rare, exquisite: obs., uncouth." By this I mean apple pie, cold boiling bacon, a tasty dish of ambrosia or a jar of pickled peaches. I can think of a number of authors whose work would make me turn to oatmeal, but never yours.

Mr. Herschel Brickell   Atlanta, Georgia
Ridgefield, Connecticut   May 3, 1938

Dear Herschel:

Ordinarily I do not think that stories based on Negro mispronunciations are very funny, but I have heard one which appeals to me. My friend, Beth Williams, on the Quitman Free Press, reports that she was golfing recently and using as a caddy a little pickaninny fresh out of the briarpatch. He was very anxious to appear as knowing about the fine points of golf as the more experienced caddies. Beth was having a bad round and getting madder as time went by. There was something wrong with her stance. This was obvious even to the caddy for, when she lamented loudly, he said soothingly, "Don't you bother, Miss Bess, your game's all right. It's just your stench that's so horrible." If you can understand just how warm it gets in Quitman you will realize that the little boy was probably right in what he said and what he intended to say.

I keep laughing about you and your thirteen cat mouths to feed. My long-suffering mother permitted us to have thirteen cats once, but seven of them were yard cats and not so pampered as the house cats. I hope you've managed to work off a few cat mouths on your friends. I only wish we had a house instead of an apartment, for I would gladly take one off your hands myself.

[1] A character in *Gentle Julia* (Garden City, N.Y., and Toronto, 1932).

Willie Snow Ethridge, wife of Mark Ethridge, editor of a Louisville paper, is giving birth to a book this month and is coming down to Atlanta for the accouchement, as it is a Georgia book and a Macmillan book and should be born in the Atlanta Macmillan office. She wrote me that Marjorie Rawlings had been in Louisville and everyone had enjoyed her so much. Norman Berg, of the Atlanta Macmillan office, told me over the phone yesterday of visiting Mrs. Rawlings recently in Florida and having a perfectly wonderful time. He, too, thought her delightful. I simply must meet her myself. No, I haven't gotten to "The Yearling." . . .

I am glad my remarks on the James Cain–John O'Hara books interested you. But don't get me wrong—I read them in gulps, just as I read "The Three Musketeers." That type of book makes fast reading. As I told you, I haven't any literary critical sense and all I ask is that a book hold my interest. If it does that I never stop to think if I am reading hokum or melodrama. It's generally two weeks before such ideas come to mind.

I recently read in the Saturday Review of Literature an article on these writers, and the author used a phrase which I was struggling for when I wrote you last. He spoke of the lives and tragedies of the characters of such books as "Being Lived in a Moral Vacuum."[1]

What did you think of the Pulitzer Awards? If you wrote a column about them please send me a copy. "The Late George Apley"[2] is one of those books which appeared when life was frenzied, and so, I have not read it.

Sometime soon I am going up the road to Dalton, Georgia. This town was one I mentioned as being near the spot where Sherman launched the Atlanta campaign. I am going to start at Dalton and try to cover the battlefields and the line of march. Not all of it, of course, as a great part of it lies in the roughest country imaginable, and I have no fondness for rattlesnakes or breaking my neck in hidden ravines. It's been some years since I covered this route and, as people are always asking me questions about military strategy (in the innocent belief that I am an authority and an historian as well as a novelist), I think I'd better review the campaign on the hoof. I wish you could come, for, while you might not be interested in who fought who and where, it would be a change from the

---

[1] Here Miss Mitchell seems to have conflated two pieces, an editorial in *The Saturday Review of Literature*, XVIII, No. 1 (April 30, 1938), p. 8, concerning the novels of James Cain, Ernest Hemingway, John O'Hara, John Steinbeck, and others, and an article, "Watch Out for Mr. O'Hara," by Wolcott Gibbs in the *SRL*, XVII, No. 17 (February 19, 1938), pp. 10–12. This article includes the sentence (p. 12): "If he should decide (as a great many critics seem to feel he did in 'Butterfield 8') to write skillful, rather melodramatic novels about people whose inevitable tragedies take place in a moral vacuum and are therefore not tragic or moving in any final sense, he will still be successful, but it won't be what his friends want from him."

[2] John Phillips Marquand, *The Late George Apley* (Boston, 1937).

reading of many books. I have often wondered how you managed to read so many books and still keep a fresh viewpoint.

Mr. Kenneth Roberts   Atlanta, Georgia
Kennebunk Beach, Maine   May 6, 1938

My dear Mr. Roberts:

Thank you so much for being a "sour New Englander" and for refusing Mr. V's offer of good clean fun and a jolly time had by all. I appreciate more than I can tell you your diplomatic handling of this matter and I thank you for your thoughtfulness. As Mr. V. remarked, I *am* "a great admirer" of yours. Never more so than now! I am returning the two letters you sent me.

Yesterday I read in a movie column that some actress had made herself a cocktail jacket or a lounging coat or some such useless garment and had modeled it along the lines of those worn by Rogers Rangers. I have no objection to this, and, in fact, if they become fashionable I might step out in one myself. But I can see where this trend will lead, and I think that you should take steps before something dreadful happens. It will be only a matter of time before the designers start copying Rogers's hat. While this hat was doubtless very becoming to him, it would be dreadful upon the heads of several million American women and would look worse upon my head than anyone else's. We have suffered a lot from strange hats during the last few years, and I personally do not know whether I could bear it if I had to wear that squirrel tail effect at the back of my head. I have just gone through the Scarlett O'Hara bonnet era, and I was so mortified at the way they looked on women's heads (though God is my witness I had nothing to do with the design) that I felt ashamed to look at a woman on the street.

Mr. Herschel Brickell   Atlanta, Georgia
Ridgefield, Connecticut   May 16, 1938

Dear Herschel:

. . . Thanks for the column about the Pulitzer awards. I liked it so very much. I'm so glad you spoke up for "Paradise."[1] I read it when it first

[1] Esther Forbes, *Paradise* (New York *c.* 1937).

came out and liked it so very much. It had solidity and a three dimen-
sional quality not often found in historical novels, and the characters
were as real and solid as the background.

When are you going to Bread Loaf? I hope you get away soon for you
sound tired and in need of a change. This isn't so much of a letter for I
must gallop down to The Macmillan Company office to confer about the
visit of Willie Snow Ethridge, wife of Mark, whom I think you knew in
Mississippi. The Macmillan Company is bringing out Willie's first novel on
Tuesday and she is arriving Monday. There will be the usual publisher's
dinner and book store teas and private entertainments as well. John and I
expect to participate in the latter. Everything is in a stew, as we do not have
bushels of authors in this section as you do in New York.

Wednesday, 18th

I expected to get this off the day I started it, but Willie arrived and
the excitement began. She is still here and the excitement is continuing.
I cannot tell you of my heartfelt pleasure that it was Willie and not me
who was having to undergo all of this. She has unbounded energy and
enjoys bushels of teas and parties and she is never at a loss for "a few
words," and she makes those words very charming ones. This is a gift—
and one I do not possess. . . .

I suppose you know about the expected baby at the Lois Cole–Allan
Taylor apartment. It is due in the next couple of weeks and I would give
a lot to come up either for the event or after it, but I see no chance. However, as life is getting normal by leaps and bounds, I hope the time is not
far off when we can come to New York. Since our return from Florida
life has almost reverted to its pre-War Between the States status—the
phone does not ring, the tourists come no more, the mail has dropped off.
I felt certain that this would happen when I got off the best seller list,
and I only hope the movie does not cause a recrudescence.

By the way, I had a letter from Mr. Selznick recently, saying that he
would go into production positively "between now and September." Did
you see "Jezebel"? I liked it so very much but have found few people who
agree with me. I did not see similarities between it and GWTW except
for costumes and some dialogue about the approach of the War. I do
not feel that I have a copyright on hoop skirts or hot-blooded Southerners.[2]

[2] Selznick was more concerned than Miss Mitchell about *Jezebel,* a Warner
Brothers–First National film starring Bette Davis based on a 1933 play by Owen Davis.
In a letter to Harry M. Warner dated December 1, 1937, Selznick cautioned against
publicizing *Jezebel* on the strength of *GWTW.* On March 8 he wired Jack Warner:
"Dear Jack: Reiterating what I told you last night. I think it would be a very great
pity indeed from your own standpoint if so distinguished a picture as 'Jezebel' should
be damned by the millions of readers and lovers of 'Gone With the Wind.' And I am

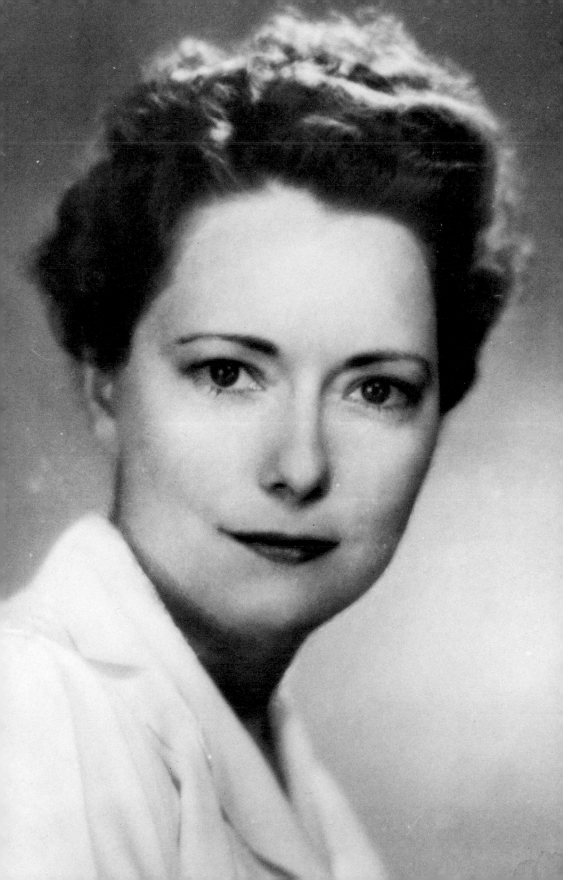

"Being a product of the Jazz Age, being one of those short-haired, short-skirted, hard-boiled young women who preachers said would go to hell or be hanged before they were thirty, I am naturally a little embarrassed at finding myself the incarnate spirit of the old South!" JULY 8, 1936

GONE WITH THE WIND

By MARGARET MITCHELL.

The stirring drama of the Civil War and Reconstruction is brought vividly to life in this really magnificent novel.

Scarlett O'Hara, born of a gently bred mother from the feudal aristocracy of the Georgia coast and an Irish peasant father, inherited charm from the one, and from the other determination and drive.

As the belle of the county, spoiled, selfish, Scarlett arrives at young womanhood just in time to see the Civil War sweep away the life for which her upbringing has prepared her. After the fall of Atlanta she returns to the plantation and by stubborn shrewdness saves her home. But in the process she hardens. She has neared starvation and she vows never to be hungry again. In the turmoil of Reconstruction she battles her way to affluence.

Scarlett's friend, Melanie Wilkes, of finer fiber, meets the same hardships with equal courage and better grace. Scarlett uses any available weapon; Melanie refuses to break with her ideals. Side by side with Scarlett and Melanie are the two men who love them: Ashley Wilkes, for whom the world died when Appomattox fell; and Rhett Butler, blockade runner and charming scoundrel.

The story epitomizes the whole drama of the South under the impact of the War and its aftermath. The ruggedness and strength of north Georgia's red hills are in the characters—bluff, blustering Gerald O'Hara; Ellen, his wife; Mammy, who both loved and chastened Ellen's daughters; the rollicking Tarleton twins; the quick-tempered and murderous Fontaines; stately John Wilkes, and a host of others, white and black, forming a rich picture of Southern life.

The author is descended from people who have loved and fought for Georgia since the Revolutionary War. She was born and raised in Atlanta and was for several years feature writer on the Atlanta *Journal*.

Cloth, 12mo. $2.50. To be published April 21.

The novel as it was described in Macmillan's spring 1936 catalog

4

With this backwash of wounded (and the increase of frightened refugees crowding *hearing conflicting reports*

into the already crowded town, Atlanta was in an uproar. The small cloud on the

horizon had blown up swiftly into a large, sullen ~~storm~~ cloud and it was as though

a faint, chill wind blew from it. No one had lost faith in the invincibility of

the troops but everyone had lost faith in the General. New Hope Church was only

57 miles from Atlanta! The General had let the Yankees push him back sixty three

miles in three weeks! Why didnt he hold the Yankees instead of everlastingly retreat-

ing? He was a fool and worse than a fool. Every grey beard in the Home Guard and

every member of the State Militia, safe in Atlanta said they could have managed

the campaign better and the less well bred of them drew maps on table cloths to

as his lines grew thinner and as he was forced further back

prove their contentions. The General ~~was~~ call~~ed~~ desperately on Governor Brown for

~~these very men~~ x _____ But the State

Troops felt reasonably safe. After all, the Governor had defied Jeff Davis' demand

for them. Why should he accede to General' Johnston ~~_____~~

(For seventy miles and twenty five days they had fought almost daily.)

Fight and fall back! Fight and fall back! New Hope Church was behind the

grey troops now, a memory in a mad haze of like memories, heat, dust, hunger,

the

weariness, tramp- tramp on the red rutted roads, slop- slop through ~~_____~~ red

mud, retreat, entrench, fight- retreat, entrench, fight. ~~_____

_____~~ New Hope Church was a nightmare of

another life and so was Big Shanty_ miles below, where they turned and fought

the Yankees like demons. But, fight the Yankees till the fields were blue with

sinister

dead, there were always more Yankees, fresh Yankees; there was always that ~~_____~~

south east curving of the blue lines toward the Confederate rear, toward the railroad

and ~~_____~~ Atlanta. ~~_____

_____

_____~~

"Unfortunately, I still do not have my manuscript as the publishers have not returned it, and unfortunately, too, I want to keep the manuscript; and if I did not
want it, John and my father would skin me alive if I parted with it. I do thank you
for the honor of being invited, for it is indeed an honor, but I just cannot part with
my first 'baby'." JULY 11, 1936

P2

"All I *knew* personally) was a fine old gentleman who was a mite addled. But I've heard tell from all of you about what he used to be *like* And I want to say this. He was a fightin' Irishman and a Southern gentleman and *as* loyal Confederate as ever lived. You can't get no better combination than that. And we aint likely to see any more like him because the times that bred men like him are as dead as he is. He was born in a furrin country but the man we're buryin' here was more *of a* Georgian than any of us here mournin' him. He lived our life, he loved our *land,* and, when you come right down to it, he died for *our Cause* just the same as our soldiers did. He was one of us and he had our good *points* and our bad *points* and he had our strength and he had our failings. He had our good *points* in that ~~he had~~ couldnt nothin' stop him when his *warnt* mind was made up and he ~~was~~ afraid of nothin' that walked in shoe leather. There wasnt nothing that come to him *from the outside* that could lick him. He wasnt *scared* of the English *government* that wanted to hang him, And when he come to this country and was *poor scared* that didnt *scare* him a mite. He went to work and he made his money. And he wasnt *scared* to tackle this section of the country when it was wild and the Injuns had just been run out. He made a big plantation out of a wilderness. And when the war come on, and his money began to go, he wasnt *scared* to be *poor again* And when the Yankees come through Tara and might *of* killed him or burned him out that didnt neither ~~scare~~ *He just planted his feet and stood his ground.* him or lick him. That why I say he had our good *points.* There aint nothing *from the outside* *(cause he could be licked from the inside)* that can lick any of us..... But he had our failings, too! I mean to say that what the whole world couldnt do, his own heart could. When Mrs. O'Hara died, his heart died , too and he was licked. And what we seen walking around here wasnt him."

Will paused and his eyes went quietly around the silent circle of faces. They crowd stood in the hot sun as though enchanted to the ground and what ever wrath they had felt for Suellen was forgotten. Will's eyes rested for a moment on *Scarlett's* and they crinkled slightly at the corners as though he were inwardly smiling comfort to her. And *Scarlett,* who had been fighting back *rising* tears did feel comforted. Will was talking common sense instead of a lot of tootle about reunions in another and better world and submitting her will to God's. And *Scarlett* had always found strength and

Friday July 3, 1936

Dear Mr. Burnet:

You said in your nice letter that "this requires no reply." But I must reply to thank you for it and to tell you that I haven't sold the movie rights for three or ten million dollars, as rumor has it. In fact, I haven't even had an offer from the movies. I don't know where this rumor started but its about run me

crazy. Of course, I'd like to sell it but don't see how the book could be made into a movie. You can help me a lot by denying the story. As you can imagine, every one in Georgia on the Relief Rolls is after me & give them a thousand dollars and they get mad when I say I've never had the three million and, much less three million!

Sincerely
Margaret Mitchell Marsh

"As to how I got started on Civil War material, I suppose I started in my cradle. Father is an authority on Atlanta and Georgia history of that period and Mother knew about as much as he did." APRIL 28, 1936

"I left town three days after I was published. . . . I couldn't stand limelight. I had not expected the book to be a bestseller. In my wildest imaginings I never thought that anyone except my friends and my relatives would read it. . . . So when the book went over, my surprise and alarm and confusion completed what standing in line at interminable receptions had done. So I went away to Blowing Rock. I went for three reasons, Mr. and Mrs. Edwin Granberry (he reviewed the book for the N. Y. 'Sun') promised me sanctuary, Herschel Brickell of the N. Y. 'Post' would be there and, most important, I had heard that you [Julia Peterkin] would be in Blowing Rock." JULY 25, 1936

With Granberry and Brickell at Blowing Rock, North Carolina

"I suppose you know that casting this picture is the favorite drawing room game these days and every newspaper has been after me to say just who I want to play the parts. It has been difficult but so far I have kept my mouth shut. I wish to goodness you all would announce the cast and relieve me of this burden." OCTOBER 6, 1936

On the following pages, Rea Irvin's cartoon that appeared in *The New Yorker*, February 20, 1937, p. 14–15 (*Drawings by Rea Irvin;* © *1937, 1965, The New Yorker Magazine, Inc.*)

OUR OWN PREVIEWS OF HOLLYWOOD ATTRACTIONS

Joan Crawford and Clark Gable in "Gone With the Birth of a Nation, or The Gold Diggers of 1860"

1

2

3

Gerald O'Hara (Freddie Bartholomew), a barefoot boy, leaves his home in Ireland to seek his fortune in America.

Here he becomes quite a man (Walter Connolly) and owns Tara, a fine plantation, and some fancy jumpers.

The darling of his heart is his daughter Scarlett (Joan Crawford), who loves to play with her father's gold watch and chain.

4

5

6

She strives in every way to improve her appearance,

for she is in love with the bookish, golden-haired Ashley Wilkes (Franchot Tone) and,

finding him alone in his library, she confesses her love. Ashley, however, is more interested in his book.

7

8

Rhett Butler (Clark Gable) overhears her confession and

propositions her.

9

In the meantime, Ashley has married his cousin Melanie (Janet Gaynor) and the Civil War breaks out.

10

Scarlett's sorrow at Ashley's marriage is mitigated by the sight of so many gold buttons.

11

Meanwhile Rhett has become a wealthy man through blockade running and

12

keeps Scarlett supplied with furbelows and gewgaws.

13

He is, however, often seen in the company of Belle Watling (Mae West), the bad woman of Atlanta.

14

Scarlett's father dies and she carries on at Tara in his place.

15

Ashley is brought back wounded and Scarlett nurses him. She resumes her wooing but, on his death bed, Ashley repulses her with a few well-chosen quotations from the classics.

16

She joins the army as a vivandière, crosses the Delaware with General Beauregard (George Arliss), and Atlanta is saved.

17

Scarlett decides that after all Rhett is Her Man. They are married and live in luxury and happiness ever after.

WESTERN UNION

Received at

RXAA330 TWS PAID 3 TO BE DLVD IMMEDIATELY=   1939 JAN 13 PM 8 08

TDS CULVERCITY CALIF 13 551P

MRS JOHN R MARSH=

4 EAST 17 ST NORTHEAST ATLA=

DEAR MRS MARSH: WE ARE ABOUT TO GIVE STORY ON SCARLETT,
ASHLEY AND MELANIE TO THE PRESS AND ARE HOLDING IT UP FOR ONE
HOUR IN ORDER TO GIVE YOU TIME TO RELEASE IT TO ATLANTA PAPERS
AND CORRESPONDENTS. WOULD ACCORDINGLY APPRECIATE IT
ENORMOUSLY IF YOU WOULD IMMEDIATELY UPON RECEIPT OF THIS
TELEGRAM SEND FOR THE PRESS. SENDING YOU FULL STORIES IN
SEPARATE WIRES. I DO HOPE YOU ARE AS HAPPY ABOUT THE FINAL
OUTCOME AS WE ARE. ONE OF MY GREATEST HOPES AND DREAMS IS
THAT YOU WILL BE COMPLETELY SATISFIED WITH THE FILM VERSION
OF YOUR MAGNIFICIENT WORK. CORDIALLY AND APPRECIATIVELY=
DAVID O SELZNICK.

"Around nine o'clock your first wire came and the Western Union girl told me a long wire was on the way and segments of it would arrive at fifteen minute intervals. . . . I knew our morning paper was going to press and of course I wanted the home town newspaper to have the break on this story, so I left John at the Western Union office to wait for the remainder and I went to the Constitution office. . . . It was all very exciting and reminded John and me of our own newspaper days." JANUARY 14, 1939

On the preceding page, Margaret Mitchell during a press conference at Macmillan, 1937. (*Copyright © 1937, 1965, Robert Disraeli*)

"Yes, I know Rhett Butler is 'the stock figure of melodrama.' Thank you for saying I made him credible. I knew when I picked him just what he was." JULY 9, 1936

"[Clark Gable] has never been the choice for Rhett down here. . . . In looks and in conduct Basil Rathbone has been the first choice in this section, with Fredric March and Ronald Colman running second and third." JULY 13, 1938

"May I thank you for insisting to me that Melanie was beautiful? I had pictured her as a very plain little person but in my heart I thought her beautiful too." FEBRUARY 23, 1937

From a letter to Olivia De Havilland: "The letters I have received and personal comments I have heard indicate that your selection for the part of Melanie has met with general approval." JANUARY 30, 1939

"Nothing could have pleased me more than to have a psychiatrist praise the pattern of Scarlett O'Hara's emotional life." AUGUST 22, 1936

"I am impressed by the number of different faces Vivien Leigh has. In the stills you have been good enough to send me, she looks like a different person every time she is shown in a different mood." MARCH 24, 1939

"I . . . always considered [Ashley] the greatest realist in the book because his eyes, like those of Rhett, were always open. He saw things with a cruel clarity but, unlike Rhett, he was not able to do anything about them." FEBRUARY 16, 1937

"Mr. Howard has always been the almost unanimous choice of Southerners for the role of Ashley." JANUARY 14, 1939

Hattie McDaniel (Mammy) won an Academy Award—the first ever won by a black performer—as best supporting actress in 1939. Eddie Anderson, above right, played Uncle Peter; Everett Brown, below left, played Sam.

". . . the negro characters were people of worth, dignity and rectitude—certainly Mammy and Peter and even the ignorant Sam knew more of decorous behavior and honor than Scarlett did." APRIL 8, 1937

"You asked if Tara and the characters really existed. No, they all came out of my head with the exception of the little black maid, 'Prissy'." JULY 11, 1936

". . . this is the only part I myself would like to play. For this reason whoever plays Prissy [Butterfly McQueen] will be up against a dreadful handicap as far as I am concerned." AUGUST 13, 1937

"I have always loved old people, and from childhood listened eagerly to their stories—tucking away in my mind details of rickrack braid, shoes made of carpet, and bonnets trimmed with roosters' tails." AUGUST 7, 1936

"They were a pretty outspoken, forthright, tough bunch of old timers and the things they said stuck in my mind much longer than the things the people of my parents' generation told me." JUNE 1, 1936

Mrs. Merriwether (Jane Darwell), Aunt Pittypat Hamilton (Laura Hope Crews), and Mrs. Meade (Leona Roberts) at the Atlanta Charity Bazaar

"Miss Crews . . . looks too cute to be true. She sounds as if she'd be so much fun." APRIL 17, 1939

"My suggestion is—why not take Susan Myrick out to the Coast in some capacity while the picture is being made? . . . You said that you'd like to have me there to pass on the authenticity and rightness of this and that, the accents of the white actors, the dialect of the colored ones, the minor matters of dress and deportment, the small touches of local colors, etc. . . . Sue is as competent a newspaper woman as we have in this section. . . . The main thing that recommends her to me is her common sense and her utter lack of sentimentality about what is tearfully known as 'The Old South.'" FEBRUARY 14, 1937

Susan Myrick with Clark Gable, Leslie Howard, and Ona Munson

Photographs taken on the set by Wilbur G. Kurtz, Atlanta artist and historian, "perhaps the world's leading authority on the Atlanta campaign and all historic events centering around Atlanta. His knowledge is not just book knowledge. As a young man he went over battlefields when veterans were still spry enough to take him. He knows where every battery stood and where every mule got its ears shot off." APRIL 14, 1938

"The last stills which Miss Rabwin sent me showed the exteriors of Tara and, so help me God! there were white-painted, barred fences. Not a split-rail fence was to be seen. Everyone who saw the pictures spotted that immediately and yelled bloody murder. Couldn't Mr. Selznick have rented the elegant split-rail fences from the 'Jesse James' company?" APRIL 17, 1939

"I had feared, of course, that [Twelve Oaks] would end up looking like Grand Central Station, and your description confirms my worst apprehensions. I did not know whether to laugh or to throw up at the *two* staircases. . . . When I think of the healthy, hardy, country and somewhat crude civilization I depicted and then of the elegance that is to be presented, I cannot help yelping with laughter." FEBRUARY 10, 1939

"The ladies' organizations of Confederate Atlanta correspond somewhat to the ladies' canteen workers of the last war in that they met all troop trains with baskets of food, socks, et cetera. They also cooperated with the doctors in getting the wounded off the trains, nursing in the hospitals and taking convalescents into their houses." OCTOBER 11, 1937

"Far from 'okaying' the pictures [especially the production still overleaf], I cried 'Godlmighty' in horror before I caught myself. My eye lighted on Scarlett's widow's bonnet and long veil in the midst of the decollete gowns of the Atlanta belles. I cannot imagine even Scarlett having such bad taste as to wear a hat at an evening party, and my heart sank at the sight of it. . . . A quick view of the uniforms showed not a one that looked as if it had seen active service. Nor was there a wounded man to be found with a microscope. The Armory looked vaguely like Versailles and not like the rough room in which drills are held. . . . I have an idea that Mr. Kurtz and Susan were overridden on these points." FEBRUARY 17, 1939

"I was especially interested in your paragraph about the lack of applause when the Confederate battle flag was shown fluttering over the acres of wounded Confederate soldiers at the car-shed. Here in Atlanta at the premiere there was a great deal of applause early in the picture, and later on where Scarlett shot the Yankee deserter on the stair the tense audience practically yelled. But during the scene you mentioned there was a deathly stillness, just as you noted in the Raleigh theatre. Afterward a number of us were talking it over, each giving reasons why the audience had been so still. One man summed it up this way—'Have you ever felt like applauding in a Confederate cemetery on Memorial Day? No, you haven't; you feel something too deep for applause." MARCH 15, 1940

"There is to be a civic festival with every kind of whoop-te-do you can imagine, including a parade with a brass band stationed at every corner for a mile. The papers have been full of it and, of course, everybody in Christendom has been on our necks demanding tickets for the premiere." NOVEMBER 30, 1939

"The movie people were all charming and the Atlanta people who met them fell in love with them. I wish you, as an old Atlantan, could have been here, for we will never see the town so excited again. The crowds on the streets were larger than those which greeted Lindbergh and President Roosevelt, yet everything was so orderly and well-bred and people did not mob the stars or try to snatch off their buttons for souvenirs. I was so proud of the town I nearly burst." MARCH 26, 1940

At Loew's Grand on premiere night, from left to right, Olivia De Havilland, John Hay Whitney, Margaret Mitchell Marsh, and John Marsh

UP FRONT WITH MAULDIN

Somewhere in Italy

Dear, Dear Miss Mitchell,
You will probably think this is an awful funny letter to get from a soldier, but I was carrying your big book, "Gone with the Wind," under my shirt, and a

"I am so flattered by the drawing that I must write and thank you. It has done me a great deal of good here in Atlanta, for it has raised my stock with the small fry to extravagant heights. I have been out ringing doorbells for the Seventh Bond Drive and have met any number of children. I cannot tell you how respectful they are to me because my name appeared in your cartoon, and they believe that I really did get such a letter." MAY 14, 1945. *Copyright © 1945, Bill Mauldin*

Margaret Mitchell with Vivien Leigh, Clark Gable, and David O. Selznick.

Dust jackets from foreign editions of the novel

Illustrations from foreign editions of the novel

"Have you any suggestions about the technique of smashing bottles on battleships? . . . Does the champagne usually spray the sponsor as well as the battleship?" JUNE 23, 1941

"After the launching of the 'Atlanta,' Admiral Marquart said that the bottle was the most thoroughly broken bottle he had ever seen, and I did not get a drop of champagne on me. Having played baseball as a child, I swung low from the hip. . . ." APRIL 26, 1943

Margaret Mitchell christening (above) the first U.S.S. *Atlanta* on December 24, 1941, and (below) the second U.S.S. *Atlanta* on February 6, 1944. On the latter occasion the Navy presented her with a gigantic bouquet of roses.

"My Red Cross uniform seemed to fox everybody, especially the New York reporters. It was referred to as that of an ambulance driver, a Red Cross nurse, canteeneer, home defense, AWVS, et cetera." MARCH 7, 1942

Still no news about when and if I go to Washington. Political matters have overshadowed such unimportant things as copyright protection for authors. By the way, when George Brett was recently in Europe he went to Holland to testify in my behalf. The piratical publishers prodded the Dutch court not to let him testify and the court obligingly refused to let him speak his piece. They did let him file a deposition. Holland must be a wonderful place.

Harold Latham dug up a manuscript here about which The Macmillan Company is quite excited. Harry Lee, the young author, is only twenty-four years old and doesn't look a day over sixteen. The contract has just been signed and we are all looking forward to the book. I believe it is a story of adolescence in Atlanta and the name is "Fox in the Cloak," referring to that misguided Spartan boy who let the fox nibble his gizzard. As the manuscript stands now it is terrifically long and the author is engaged in cutting. We hear rumors of other Atlanta manuscripts that Mr. Latham has under consideration and, as one Journal reporter remarked at the dinner for Willie Ethridge, it looks like Macmillan is taking Atlanta like Sherman took it.

Mr. Herschel Brickell   Atlanta, Georgia
Ridgefield, Connecticut   May 25, 1938

Dear Herschel:

Thanks for your note and the enclosure of your review of Willie's book. John and I wished that you could sit down and talk with us on the

---

fearful that this is what may happen due to a few completely unnecessary bits. The picture throughout is permeated with characterizations, attitudes and scenes which unfortunately resemble 'Gone With the Wind,' regardless of whether or not they were in the original material. But I am referring to a few specific things, such as the very well-remembered piece of business in which Scarlett pinched her cheeks to give them color. More importantly, there is the scene of the men around the dinner table, which actually is a slow spot in your picture, if you will forgive my saying so. I refer to the dialogue scene dealing with the difference between the North and the South, the discussion of an imminent war, and the prediction by the Southerner that the North will win because of its superior machinery, et cetera. This scene is lifted practically bodily out of 'Gone With the Wind,' in which it is an important story point leading to Rhett Butler's entire behavior during the war. . . ." David O. Selznick, *Memo from David O. Selznick* (New York, 1972), pp. 153–154.

Bette Davis was an eager candidate for the role of Scarlett. Lambert says: "Davis's inconsolable desire for the part . . . was indirectly rewarded. Discovering a story whose southern heroine had obvious affinities with Scarlett, she persuaded Jack Warner to let her make it in 1938. The year before *Gone With the Wind* was a candidate for awards, she won her second Oscar for *Jezebel*, to Selznick's considerable annoyance." Lambert, p. 38.

subject, for, naturally, the book has been under discussion at our house
for several days. My spies in Macon report that most of the characters
are not even thinly veiled, for all the disclaimer in the front of the book.
We hope to stop in Macon on our way to the annual editors' convention
to be held ten days from now. I imagine by that time the town will be
seething. As you perhaps know, Willie and Mark are Radicals or Liberals
and they are strange bedfellows for such Tory Conservatives as John
and me. Willie does not like the paternalism of the cotton mill she wrote
about. This dislike is contradictory to her violent espousal of the New
Deal, which is, God knows, paternalistic. But Willie does not see her
contradiction. She wanted to be completely fair to both sides in her book
and to give that ole davvle, Capitalism, its due. We wouldn't like to tell
Willie this because we don't want to hurt her feelings, but we finished the
book with a much higher opinion of mill owners than we had before and
a far greater approval of the paternalism.

I have just finished Mrs. Rawlings's "The Yearling." You did not tell
me one one-hundredth of how beautiful it was and, as I had read very
few reviews of it, I was not prepared. That was just as well for it came
freshly to me. You can't put a book like that into any category, which I
think will annoy people who like to paste labels on literature. Books like
this are just what they are, and we can only be grateful that they come to
us. When I had finished it I had the horrors as I thought of what could
have happened to such a simple chronicle in the hands of a writer bitten
with "social consciousness" and the "have-and-have-not" feeling. Can't
you just see what an underprivileged child Jody would have been? And
what wouldn't a socially conscious writer have done with those gorgeous
bewhiskered Forrester boys? That scene where the boys get up early
and, stark naked, tune up and have a "hoe-down" is something I will
cherish.

To eveyone who, as a child, has run wild in the woods it must bring
back a thousand memories, even as it did for me. My memory for smells
is very strong and this book brought back smells years old so strongly. I
remembered especially the way the swampy bottoms of the Warrior
River smelled and the steaming sweat on me and the colorerd boys when
we crawled through the underbrush hunting wild hogs, and the river
smell and the rotting vegetation and the sharp smell of a wild boar at
far too close quarters. Do you see any reason why this book shouldn't
have the Pulitzer award this year? I don't.

There's no news in particular, which in my case means good news.
Things continue to be quiet and normal and very happy. I have been to
a few social gatherings during the last month and had a most enjoyable
time, as no one tried to pull my clothes off for souvenirs, and few asked for

autographs. It is due to this happy state of affairs that we are going to the editors' convention. Of course, the Georgia press has been wonderful to me since the beginning, not only in their reviews and kind remarks but in their sheltering attitude, which has gone far toward making life endurable. Two years ago when I went on one of the conventions the president arose in open meeting and declared that none of them wanted my old autograph and that none of them thought a bit more of me than they did before. Such an attitude has made it possible for me to live in Georgia and jaunt about the State with the freedom I formerly enjoyed. Now that the wind has blown over I am certainly grateful to all Georgia editors for what they did for me. It has been my lot to meet a number of skunks during the last two years, but, as I balance my books, I find I've met with far more understanding and kind people than skunks.

While I am gossiping along I'll tell you something else that may or may not lead to something. I believe I told you of the women who have popped up all over the country pretending to be me. They have signed autographs, given lectures, gotten drunk, picked up gents and done other things not salutary to mention on paper. To date I have been unable to catch a one of them, which is a source of great regret to me. Up until the incident I am now going to relate I do not believe my name has been used for swindling purposes. Recently there came to me, third hand, a story that made me boil. An old Indian, whose memory went back to the days of frontier fighting, had written his memoirs. He had been all over the world and, from what I can learn, had had a most interesting life. He was approached by two men who offered to get his memoirs published. The old man was somewhat suspicious until they introduced him to a woman in New York who said she was Margaret Mitchell. He surrendered the manuscript to her, and since that day has not laid eyes on the manuscript or the men or the woman. I do not know what motive these crooks had unless they are waiting for the old man to die so that they can sell the manuscript. I think I now have the chance to nail one of these impostors, and by doing so scare off the others. Indians are government wards and I am hoping the government will take a hand in this case. I am now in communication about the matter and I am hoping the government will do something about it. If I could just get one of these women behind the bars it might make a few others think twice before they said they were me and picked up gentlemen on trains. One of them seems to have a regular beat on the Washington-to-New York train.

My, how I do travel! A recent clipping from Dublin, Ireland, reports that I spent Christmas in County Meath and that a number of people met me at a party in a Dublin hotel. Ireland is one country I wouldn't mind seeing. So, it was nice of this lady to see it for me. . . .

Mr. Herschel Brickell   Atlanta, Georgia
Ridgefield, Connecticut   May 31, 1938

Dear Herschel:

I am writing you immediately about your request to quote from my last letter about "The Yearling" to Marjorie Rawlings. Yes, do this if you like—only I did not say even a small amount of what I thought of the book.

During the last two years I have had to restrain myself both in speech and in print from saying anything, good or bad, about any book. The bad was always garbled and made worse and the good inevitably led to a demand from the author and publisher of the book for an endorsement on the dust jacket. I think you know me well enough to realize that it is not a lack of generosity which has led me into refusing point blank to endorse any book—even the Four Gospels. The requests for endorsements have come in in such stupefying numbers that if I had given in to them I would have spent the last two years doing nothing but reading books and writing blurbs. If I had endorsed one I should have been forced to endorse all, or else infuriate everyone concerned, including some of my best friends. Alas, since 1936 most of my friends have published books. I had the choice of appearing to be very selfish, critical and ungenerous or else of endorsing some of the world's worst efforts. (Of course, all of them weren't the world's worst, and there were many books which I loved and admired.) So, I took the first choice and all the criticism that went with it. I know in the case of Mrs. Rawlings that nothing like this will happen—if for no other reason, because, Heaven knows, she needs no words of commendation from me, as she is a fine writer and one who has shown that she can grow. I noticed with pleasure that she was at the top of the best seller list on Sunday. While John and I do not know her, we felt as pleased and proud as if we had had a personal hand in the matter.

Norman Berg, who is head of the trade department of the Atlanta branch of The Macmillan Company, met Mrs. Rawlings several weeks ago and visited at her home. He returned boiling with enthusiasm, and he is a young man not given either to boiling or enthusiasm.

Just at present I am playing with an idea which I hope you will keep under your hat for a while. I am considering coming to New York around the end of June, probably leaving Atlanta on or around the 25th. I would come earlier, but the annual outing of the Georgia editors comes in mid-June and we are going. While I have some small business affairs to attend to in New York, the real basis of my trip is scientific investigation. Of course, I want to see Lois's baby (which I hope will be born long before

I get there) and to pleasure myself with the sight of the faces of my friends. However, I mainly want to prove that my "Gone With the Wind" problems are over, or mostly over, and that I can walk like a natcherul woman again. On this trip I would have to see several million acquaintances and people with whom I have business relations. I feel, however, if I could make this trip and work off these people it would break the trail for later trips for John and me. Then we could come up to New York occasionally in the fall and winter, see the people we wanted to see, have time for shows, and not have to bother with the people I did not want to bother with.

Of course, something may come up which will keep me from making this trip. But I wanted to know before I made my plans whether you and Norma and the Dowdeys and one or two others would be home around that time. Please let me know. I haven't written the Dowdeys et cetera yet, so, if you see them do not mention it. I have hopes that I can make this trip without being deviled by the numerous New York organizations who have wanted me to speak or to make what is quaintly known as personal appearances.

Mr. Jack Williams   Atlanta, Georgia
Waycross Journal-Herald   June 16, 1938
Waycross, Georgia

Dear Jack:
    That was a sweet note you sent me. But it should be I who thank you and all the Georgia press instead of you thanking me. John and I look forward from year to year to our trips with our newspaper friends, and since the publication of "Gone With the Wind" we have enjoyed them even more. The reason for this is that my friends in the Press Association have been so wonderfully kind and thoughtful and understanding that when I am with them I can enjoy myself as John Marsh's wife, and not be regarded purely as the author of a book. I do not doubt that that sounds very strange, but I know you understand.

Mr. and Mrs. Herschel Brickell   Atlanta, Georgia
Ridgefield, Connecticut   July 6, 1938

My dear Miss Sally and Norma and Herschel:
    I went to sleep as soon as the train started and when I woke up it was ten o'clock in the morning. No nicely tamed Connecticut hillsides were

outside the window. Instead there were red rivers and coffee colored swamps with white wading birds in them and mimosas and willows and water melon-pink crepe myrtles. It scarcely seemed possible that I could whisk so quickly from one land to another.

Bessie had the fatted calf ready—fried chicken and every other dish which ruins my complexion—and we opened the Burgundy. John will write you about the Burgundy, Norma. He says I have no palate and no comprehension of good wine. I only know it was the very best Burgundy I ever drank and we drank the first three toasts to you all.

John appreciated the wire too, but he will write you about that. In fact, he appreciates all that you did for me, and so do I. You three were so wonderfully kind and I am sure I was not the very best of guests. Sometime I hope to see you all when I have the correct quota of sleep behind me, so that I will not be as stupid as a gigged frog. Thank you for being a haven of retreat. And thank you for being exactly what you are and staying that way.

Miss Katharine Brown   Atlanta, Georgia
New York, New York   July 7, 1938

My dear Katharine:

As you may have gathered from the New York newspapers last week, I was in the modern Babylon. It was my intention to have you for lunch or dinner if you could work me in, for there were—and are—so many things I wanted to talk over with you. Unfortunately for my plans, I had to come home almost immediately after the newspaper stories broke, for once I get into the papers in a town I find it high time to retreat home. I thought, as I packed madly for the Southern retreat, that I would at least talk to you over the telephone, but than I ran up against the long week-end and the Fourth of July holiday with everybody in New York out of town.

John and I hope to get North in the fall for a little while and we want to see you.

I got out of Atlanta with every newspaper and press association on my neck about the Gable-Shearer announcement, and I ran head on into the same situation with the New York press. It has been my policy since I put the movie rights into Selznick International's hands not to issue any statement of any kind on the subject. Personally, I have always felt it was not my place to state preferences or dislikes or opinions as to how the film was being handled. The result was I did some pretty fancy footwork last week and said nothing at all. Some New York newspapers said as much, but others quoted me as bridling and blushing and saying that Mr. Gable should be a landslide. The truth is I made no such statement.[1]

Do, please, tell me if it is true that George Cukor is out of the picture. I have very little interest in who will act in the picture, but I am sorry if George will not direct. I thought him a grand person and a brilliant one. Of course, if the answer to that question is a confidential matter, just skip it. However, I can keep my mouth shut on such matters if you care to tell me about it.

I was so tremendously glad that the two leading characters were announced, even if the press did give me a fine badgering about it. And I will be gladder still when the whole cast is announced and the picture goes into production. Selznick International may think GWTW is a headache to them, but dearie, the film has been a Grade A headache to me! And, alas, I have nothing to do with the matter. As you doubtless know, I am lots more interested in who will play Ashley and Melanie than in any other characters. I always felt that any competent actor and actress could do Rhett and Scarlett, but it is difficult indeed to portray complex people who think instead of act. If you have any advance dope on who will play these parts I would love to hear about it.

While in New York the press hammered one question at me above all others. They wanted to know how I would feel if the character of Scarlett was completely changed and tailored to fit Norma Shearer, thereby making Scarlett a poor put-upon creature instead of a hellion. As such an idea had never occurred to me I simply hung my mouth open and said that I had had no information that such a change had been made in the script. Since coming home this rumor has risen up and roared in my ears from every side. I thought I would pass this along to you for what it's worth, for in your job you have to know about ten thousand rumors. . . .

---

[1] A story by Harold Heffernan dated from Hollywood June 23 begins: "Clark Gable and Norma Shearer appeared today to be cinch nominations as an all-star battery to carry the colors of 'Gone With the Wind' into the screen field when the picture goes into production, probably next December." An "add" printed with this in the Atlanta *Constitution* June 24 quoted Miss Mitchell merely as saying she thought the two would be "grand" in the roles of Scarlett and Rhett. In an International News Service story dated from New York July 2 Miss Mitchell was quoted on Miss Shearer as Scarlett: "She is a good actress," and on Gable as Rhett: "He ought to be a landslide." Atlanta *Georgian*, July 2.

Public reaction to the announcement about Miss Shearer was less than overwhelmingly favorable, and the papers of August 1 reported her withdrawal from consideration for the part. "I have decided," she said, "that I should not play Scarlett. I am convinced that the majority of fans who think I should not play this kind of character on the screen are right. I appreciate tremendously the interest they have shown." Atlanta *Constitution*, August 1.

Gable signed the contract for his part August 26. Atlanta *Journal*, August 26.

Miss Isabel M. Paterson   Atlanta, Georgia
New York Herald-Tribune Books   July 13, 1938
New York, New York

My dear Miss Paterson:
  . . . When I read your column of July 10th I yelled with appreciation.
No one but you could have gotten such a story out of Mr. Young and me
and "Uncle Henry."[1] To be quite frank, I am skulking in doorways and
running across intersections lest I meet some of "Uncle Henry's" conservative relatives. They, quite naturally, fail to share Atlanta's appreciation of the old gentleman's antics.
  All the things Norma and Herschel told me of you were absolutely
true. I should have known they would be, for the Brickells have a
wonderful knowledge of people. But it's always a pleasure to discover for
myself the truth of my friends' opinions. . . .
  Many thanks for the "turn of the bookworm" in my direction. I appreciated it and enjoyed it so very much, and so did my husband.

Miss Katharine Brown   Atlanta, Georgia
New York, New York   July 13, 1938

Dear Katharine:
  . . . It wasn't Louella Parsons or Jimmie Fidler who started the rumor
about the change-in-script in Norma Shearer's behalf. The New York

  [1] "[Mr. Young] mentioned that he had a fatal gift for saying exactly the wrong
thing when he first met people. If he told a joke, it was on the nearest and dearest of
the listener's friends or folk. . . .
  "He wanted to tell a story of some Southern eccentric who used to walk backward all the time, but Mr. Young said, 'Maybe you knew him?'
  " 'Knew him?' Mrs. Marsh said of course she did; she used to consult him for
historical data; he was a brilliant scholar. Uncle Henry somebody, a close friend of
her father's. 'I was sure of it,' said Mr. Young. 'He would be.'
  "Thereupon they both launched into the extraordinary career of Uncle Henry,
whose backward strolls seem to have been punctured by shot-gun salutations of rock
salt and pork fat from residents who objected to being walked past in reverse. . . .
  "Aside from that, Uncle Henry had few outstanding peculiarities except his habit
of sleeping in an open field. He was well-to-do, but wasn't going to put property rights
above human rights. One time he sat on top of a chimney to keep warm, and was
brought down by the customary charge of rock salt and pork fat. We inquired, why
mustn't a man sit on his own chimney if he chose? but Miss Mitchell explained it
wasn't his own; he had elected to perch above a friend's roof, and probably blocked
the draught. He usually ate lunch while sitting on the base of a statue in the public
square, but nobody payed any attention to that. It was handy, if one required general information; one could step into the square and ask Uncle Henry, instead of
going to the library. Uncle Henry had every imaginable fact in his head." *New York
Herald-Tribune Books,* July 10, 1938, p. 15.

reporters had that item several days before those two commentators signed off, and they nearly ran me ragged about it. They also had the dope that the actual contracts with Shearer and Gable had not been signed, and they tried to get it out of me whether I thought the announcement was a trial balloon. As if I should know!

Here is what has come to my ears about these two. I get reactions from letters, phone calls and people who catch me in department stores and beauty parlors. I haven't heard a word against Norma Shearer as an actress or a woman. She is, of course, enormously popular and everyone prefaces their statements with the remark that they think she is a wonderful actress. However, everyone thinks she is sadly miscast in the part of Scarlett. They think she has too much dignity and not enough fire for the part. As to Clark Gable—I believe I told you once that he was not as popular here in the South as in other sections of the country—in tough and hardboiled roles, yes; but in other roles, no. He has never been the choice for Rhett down here. People think he is a very fine actor, too, but they think he does not look Southern or act Southern and in no way conforms to their notion of a Low-Country Carolinian. In looks and in conduct Basil Rathbone has been the first choice in this section, with Fredric March and Ronald Colman running second and third. All of the foregoing is confidential, of course. I thought you might want to know the reaction of this section.

Lois Cole did not know that I was coming to New York till I was practically there. She was so busy producing a new son shortly before my trip that I did not know whether I'd be able to see her. She was doing fine and I did see her and the baby too. He is a fine child and I am to be his godmother, which, naturally, makes me quite setup about myself.

Between eleven and twelve at night we get phone calls from people who have been arguing about the cast (and probably drinking about it too) since dinnertime. They call us up in a fury to find out whether or not we like Gable and Shearer. John is patience itself and soothes indignant ladies who just can't bear Mr. Gable's dimples. He tells them that Mr. Selznick would dearly love to have a letter from them on the subject. I know Mr. Selznick must appreciate our urging people to write to him.

Mr. & Mrs. Herschel Brickell   Atlanta, Georgia
Ridgefield, Connecticut   July 21, 1938

My dear Miss Sallie and Norma and Herschel:

This is to thank you for your wonderful letters and to warn you that very shortly a box will arrive. I hope it arrives in good condition for it will contain some jars of pickled peaches which Bessie put up during my absence. Of course, Norma, Bessie was pleased with your message and should you ever come to Atlanta the chicken population of the town will be exterminated in your behalf.

While I was away a friend in Macon, known as "the Dowager Duchess of Georgia" (she is President-General of the U.D.C.).[1] sent me a hamper of peaches from her orchard. The frugal Bessie pickled them. I want you to try an experiment sometime. When Clifford Dowdey calls feed him a peach and see if he goes into convulsions. The reason is the Duchess laid him out in the Saturday Review for being unfair to Jefferson Davis in "Bugles Blow No More." Clifford, of course, had taken his tone from contemporary newspapers and letters, but the Duchess would have none of it. I just wondered whether a peach from her orchard would stick in his throat.

I enjoyed Isabel Paterson's column so very much and thought it very clever. She wrote me a grand letter too, which I appreciated. As you all doubtless suspected, I liked her so very much and I will always regret that I was so sleepy the night we went to see her.

Speaking of Isabel Paterson's column, I had an "add" on the "Uncle Henry" story. After an uneasy week, when I feared the Atlanta papers might pick up the column verbatim (but they didn't), I drew a long breath and thought I might discuss the matter with two of our best friends. There are so few friends with whom I can talk about meeting prominent people in the literary world. Most people rush out and repeat what I have said and it eventually gets into the newspapers in a beautifully garbled manner. And makes me appear to be bragging about life-long friendships with well known people whom I have only met slightly.

We sat on our friends' porch. Edith's mother lives with them and on Sunday afternoons she always takes an alleged beauty sleep. I say "alleged" because her bed is right by the window and only Venetian blinds separate her from callers. She acts as if she were non-existent and, while we know she is existent, we never make reference to her presence because we know a lady of the old school speaks to no one from her bedroom. I had launched out into Stark Young and Isabel Paterson and "Uncle Henry" and had reached the place where "Uncle Henry" was shot for walking backwards. An anguished moan sounded from behind Venetian blinds and Mrs. Mac wailed "You didn't tell that reporter Papa's name, did you?" Then I was the anguished one, as my brain went helter-skelter trying to remember if, by any chance, Mrs. Mac could possibly be "Uncle Henry's" child. I could remember no connection and I said feebly, "Mrs. Mac, 'Uncle Henry' wasn't your father, was he?" "No, but

[1] Mrs. Lamar.

Papa was the one who shot 'Uncle Henry' for walking backwards." I thought John would roll down the hill into the lake at this, and Edith and her husband nearly choked. Mrs. Mac was so moved that she even opened the Venetian blinds an eighteenth of an inch. "No, really, Papa didn't shoot 'Uncle Henry.' People just said he shot him because they were such good friends." To a Northerner such an explanation would hardly be satisfactory, but we all understood it. Edith said, "Mama, you know Grandpapa did shoot him—regularly. The old gentleman used to brag about it." Mrs. Mac, forgetting her recent denial, spoke with some heat: "Papa really shot him for his own good and for Papa's peace of mind. Papa used to take a nap on the front porch before supper every night and it made him nervous for 'Uncle Henry' to come charging along backwards at such a rate of speed. He couldn't sleep for waiting for him to go by. Then too, he felt that a gentleman of 'Uncle Henry's' scholarly attainments and bank account was doing an unbecoming thing and just showing off. As they had been college mates and were dear friends, he felt no hesitation about shooting him, and 'Uncle Henry' never had any hard feelings." We all tried to smother our laughter, and I said, "Did it stop 'Uncle Henry'?" "Yes, it stopped him from walking backwards by *our* house."

This goes to prove that Stark Young and I have something in common. You remember he said that he never told a story but that he discovered in his audience a blood brother of the subject of his story. . . .

Herschel, thanks for the review of Minnie's book.[2] I enjoyed it a lot and I have mailed it to her. She is in Ohio for the summer.

Mr. Kenneth Roberts   Atlanta, Georgia
Kennebunk Beach, Maine   July 21, 1938

My dear Mr. Roberts:

Your obstinate refusal to aid Mr. V. in his little scheme has won my everlasting gratitude. He certainly belongs to the bulldog breed. I notice he writes that his lack of my receipt is interfering with his nightly rest. If I (or my husband) ever lay hands on him by mail or in person, his nightly rest is going to be even more disturbed. I have run into a number of very thick-hided people of his type in the last two years, and I have discovered, to my sorrow, that my old fashioned upbringing did not teach me how to handle them. My husband recommends a niblick or a short-handled tomahawk. Perhaps he is right; after all, I am not quite five feet

[2] Minnie Hite Moody, *Old Home Week* (New York [c. 1938]).

tall and have never been at my best with large or long-handled weapons.

I was preparing to write to you when your note came. I had just finished "Trending Into Maine"[1] and I enjoyed it so very much. I have tried to analyze the charm of it, even as I tried to analyze "For Authors Only,"[2] and I have come to no conclusion other than that the charm comes from the person back of these books. I must thank you for a laugh that came from deep down. I know I should have been prepared for the stewing of the coot. A recipe similar to that was sprung on me during my first week at Smith College and I should have remembered, but I didn't, and my yells of joy were the kind I generally reserve for Donald Duck and the Marx Brothers.

I re-read "Trending" with care, and came to what may seem a strange conclusion—Maine people of a past day seemed very much like Georgians of the same era—an era before the doctrine was promulgated that the world not only owes a man a living but a lot of fun too. The obstinate independence, the insistence on integrity and thrift, and the many other qualities you brought out of your Maine people have a familiar sound to me when I recall reading old letters, documents and diaries which Georgians wrote.

Physically, too, the book was a joy; the type is so good, the illustrations perfect, the binding all a binding should be. It is a book to be proud of.

Many thanks for your "united front" in the matter of Mr. V. He certainly had gall to bother Mr. Tarkington.[3]

P.S.

Your note enclosing Mr. Tarkington's bit of art work has just arrived and, after one look, I lay on the floor in exactly the position Mr. Tarkington pictured Mr. V. "expired of mirth." Not since little Orvie Stone[4] leaped into Grandma's punch bowl have I enjoyed such a good laugh. I enjoyed it so much that I even forgave Mr. Tarkington for depicting me as a cross between Alice in Wonderland and one of the vampire ladies of "Dracula." I should like to keep this bit of art work, but I am exercising great self-restraint so I can feel smugly superior to Mr. V. who wishes to collect literary items. Please give Mr. Tarkington my thanks for a grand laugh.

---

[1] *Trending Into Maine* (Boston, 1938).
[2] *For Authors Only* (Garden City, N.Y., 1936).
[3] Booth Tarkington.
[4] The title character in Tarkington's *Little Orvie* (Garden City, N.Y., 1934).

Mr. Stark Young   Atlanta, Georgia
New York, New York   July 21, 1938

My dear Stark:

I knew it would be a pleasure to meet you, but I did not know how great a pleasure. Of course, I enjoyed the visit to your lovely house. I have tried to analyze since coming home just how the house manages to look so perfectly New England on the outside and so perfectly Mississippi on the inside. I haven't figured it out yet and probably never will, but the combination gives an added charm.

I have been skulking furtively in back streets since Isabel Paterson's column appeared, as I feared the relatives of "Uncle Henry" might catch me. But either they do not read the New York papers or else they realized with relief that the whole affair had been handled with great tact and many of the old gentleman's most outstanding eccentricities had been omitted.

Now that I think back on it, I suppose to Northerners our meeting and our sudden wholehearted conversation about "Uncle Henry" did seem strange. Northerners always wonder how Southerners manage to know so much about other Southerners whom they have never met and probably never will meet. For my part, I pity Northerners. Evidently, the grapevine does not work in the North, and I think people above the Mason and Dixon line miss many choice bits because they must depend on such crude devices as the radio and the newspapers for their information.

You were so nice to have me over for tea and the memory will always be a pleasant one. . . .

Mr. Alexander L. May   Atlanta, Georgia
Berlin, Germany   July 22, 1938

Dear Mr. May:

I enjoyed your interesting letter of June 30th so very much and I am glad that you and your friends found entertainment in my letter and the pamphlet I sent you. . . .

As to your question about titles and authors of some books concerning the history of Georgia and the history of the Confederacy written by Southerners—I am going to give you the following titles, but I do not know whether you will find them in your State Library. Most of them are out of print here in the United States. First, I want to mention two books written within the last five years. The author is Robert S. Henry who was born in Nashville, Tennessee. He wrote "The Story of the Confederacy" several years ago and Bobbs-Merrill published it. It is far from being a dull history; it is quick, entertaining reading, unbiased and accurate. I would send you a copy except that I fear the duty you might have to pay would be enormous. Several months ago Mr. Henry published a companion volume, "The Story of Reconstruction." It is a detailed work on reconstruction in all Confederate states. Another recent book on reconstruction was "The Road to Reunion," by Professor Paul Herman Buck, which won this year's Pulitzer Award for History.[1]

Among the older books there are:

"Reconstruction in Georgia" by Mildred Thompson, an Atlantan
"Reconstruction of Georgia" by Edwin C. Woolley, published by Macmillan
"Dixie After the War" by Myrta Lockett Avary of Atlanta, recently reissued by Houghton, Mifflin Company
"Life in Dixie During the War" by Mary Gay of Atlanta, published by Foote and Davies, Atlanta, 1897
"The War Time Diary of a Georgia Girl" by Eliza Frances Andrews
"Advance and Retreat" by General J. B. Hood
"Narrative of Military Operations" by General Joseph E. Johnston, Appleton publishers, 1874
"In and Out of the Lines" by Frances Howard
"Reminiscences" by General John B. Gordon
"Georgia Land and People" by Frances Letcher Mitchell
"Official History of Fulton County" by Walter G. Cooper
"History of Georgia" by Clark Howell
"History of the State of Georgia from 1850 to 1881" by Colonel I. W. Avery, published by Brown and Derby, New York, 1881
"History of Atlanta" by Wallace P. Reed, 1889
"History of Atlanta and Its Pioneers" by the Pioneer Citizens Society of Atlanta, Byrd Printing Company, 1902
"Georgia and Georgians" also "Georgia Landmarks and Monuments" by Lucian Lamar Knight of Atlanta
"Atlanta and Its Builders" by Martin[2]

I hope you can find some of these, but most of them are out of print and are rare.

[1] *The Road to Reunion* (Boston, 1937).

[2] The titles in this list not previously noted are Edwin Campbell Woolley, *The Reconstruction of Georgia* (New York, Columbia University Press, 1901); Frances Thomas Howard, *In and Out of the Lines* (New York and Washington, 1905); Frances Letcher Mitchell, *Georgia, Land and People* (Atlanta, 1934); Clark Howell, *History of Georgia* (Chicago, Atlanta, 1926; 4 vols.); Lucian Lamar Knight, *A Standard History of Georgia and Georgians* (Chicago, New York, 1917; 6 vols.); and Thomas H. Martin, *Atlanta and Its Builders* (Atlanta, 1902; 2 vols.).

Of course, I was very interested in your story of your argument years ago about "Uncle Tom's Cabin" and I enjoyed the details. It makes me very happy to know that "Gone With the Wind" is helping refute the impression of the South which people abroad gained from Mrs. Stowe's book. Here in America "Uncle Tom's Cabin" has been long forgotten and there are very few people today who have read it. They only know it as the name of a book which had a good deal to do with the bitterness of the Abolition movement.

It was kind of you to offer to send me the book cover of the German edition of "Gone With the Wind." Thank you for your offer, but I have a copy of the book which the German publishers sent me. It is a very striking cover. My friends have teased me a great deal about it, for they say that the Scarlett depicted on the cover resembles me! But I was never that sweet and pretty looking.

Mr. Herschel Brickell   Atlanta, Georgia
Ridgefield, Connecticut   August 12, 1938

Dear Herschel:

The political races are on and the air thick with campaign speeches. Yesterday Mr. Roosevelt invaded Georgia to try to swing the senatorial election from the Conservative Democrats. I listened to the speaking and I hope sincerely that the Selznick company was not listening. The reason is this—many Southern newspapers have been running campaigns urging Mr. Selznick to use real Southern accents in GWTW. They've raved about the beauty of the Southern voices, the accuracy of pronunciation and enunciation; they've threatened to boycott the movie if the Southern accent isn't right. Yesterday, after listening to a vast number of Southern accents, I thought how bewildered Mr. Selznick would be. I don't believe Southerners realize how they sound. Those on the air yesterday were not illiterate country folk—they were college graduates and the flower and chivalry of our dear Southland—and they said: "Sarroldy" for Saturday, "yestiddy" for yesterday, "neye-eece" for nice, "guh-munt" for government, "intehdooce" for introduce, "instuh-ment" for instrument, and "puhzuhve" for preserve.

If the bewildered Mr. Selznick made his puppets speak like this the South, suh, would secede and declare that we had all been insulted.

I wish I could have been with you and Jim Still[1] when you spent the

---

[1] James Still was a "mountain poet" whom Brickell had met at Blowing Rock. His *Hounds on the Mountain* had been published in New York in 1937.

day with Kenneth Roberts. I'm sure he must be a fine person and it would be a pleasure to meet him. I wonder if the subject of me and Mr. Roberts and Mr. Tarkington and a persistent gentleman named Mr. Vose came up? It was through Mr. Vose that my correspondence with Mr. Roberts began. Six months ago I went to dinner with friends; after they had promised that no strangers would be present, they sprung Mr. Vose on me. He had been burning the woods for two weeks to get an introduction and I had refused. He was so obviously a lionhunter and bragged unendingly of his chumminess with Tarkington, Roberts, Helen Wills and others. Through a dreadful evening I kept pretty quiet. Then, in one of those conversational lulls which drive hostesses to take cyanide in the butler's pantry, I rescued the conversation by telling Mr. Vose, jokingly, that Mr. Roberts owed me $10.00 because I was ill of a minor digestive complaint while reading "Northwest Passage" and the starvation scenes were so vivid that I ate everything in the ice-box and the doctor had to come to see me twice.

Thereafter Mr. Vose wished to come to see me but I did not see him. And the next thing I knew he was urging Mr. Roberts to send me $10.00, and he wanted me to send Mr. Roberts a receipt for the money. Mr. Vose then wished to purchase the correspondence and the receipt and either hug them to his own bosom or show them to friends or else sell them. This sort of goings-on annoys me as few things can, and it made John more furious than me. Mr. Roberts was swell and understood about it and he sent me a grand autographed book mark for my copy of "Northwest Passage." He refused Mr. Vose's pleadings, writing him curtly that he (Roberts) had "paid me off with Revolutionary shinplasters." Mr. Vose has tried time and again to get Mr. Roberts interested in this, Mr. Roberts continues to write him that he (Roberts) is a sour old New Englander and a spoilsport and a closefisted miser. The insensitive Mr. Vose is madly trying to make Booth Tarkington bring pressure to bear on Roberts to enter into this singular arrangement with me. I saw the correspondence (for Mr. Roberts evidently dearly loves to torment Mr. Vose and so does Mr. Tarkington) and Mr. Tarkington had written Vose that it was useless to try to get Roberts to pay me my just due. Mr. Tarkington said Mr. Roberts had owed him $2.80 for eight months for teaching him backgammon and, in conclusion, he could only point out to Vose that Roberts was born in Kennebunk.

You'd think Vose would be stymied, but no. He is so desperate to get this little literary item that he even wrote me last week, sending me the check for $10.00 which he had sent to Roberts. John, who wants to hit him with a short-handled tomahawk, would not even let me acknowledge it, for he did not wish Mr. Vose to have my signature. He returned the check, et cetera, by registered mail with a curt note. Throughout all this foolish business Mr. Roberts has seemed such an understanding person, and a humorous one. And, here I fall back again on old fashioned words, a gentleman. All this foregoing is to explain why I wish I'd been with you that day.

Medora Perkerson, whom you met, recently signed a contract with The Macmillan Company for a mystery novel.[2] She had written only six chapters. The scene is laid in the old and historic town, Roswell, which is twenty miles north of Atlanta. I am happy about this, not only for Medora's sake, but for the grim pleasure I will have at seeing one of my friends in the toils. Even the most understanding of my friends here have little comprehension of what I've been through, and I am glad for Medora to be in the soup with me.

Things are almost normal now. The mail is off. It is true John works four nights a week on odds and ends left over from those chaotic months, but another two months should see the end of them. We felt so cheered about the return of peace and quiet that last Sunday we hauled Sue Myrick, of the Macon Telegraph, up here and used her as an excuse for a debut party. We had between fifty and sixty newspaper folks and it must have been a good party because one editor held on to the kitchen table and refused to be dragged home by his wife, declaring that this was the first good time he had had since the bank holiday in the first Roosevelt term. Sue is a grand person and a good storyteller. Unfortunately, she is full of dialect stories about Negroes and Crackers. She inspires John and me to similar stories. After an hour of this we are unable to talk grammatically in normal social intercourse and for days after Sue had been here we sounded like a group of Erskine Caldwell's characters having a reunion with the characters of Joel Chandler Harris. . . .

Mr. Herschel Brickell   Atlanta, Georgia
Ridgefield, Connecticut   August 15, 1938

My dear Herschel:

It will seem strange to me and your other author friends to have you over on our side of the fence—strange and a lot of pleasure for us— strange and not much pleasure for you. Writing books ain't no pleasure and ditch digging is a far easier profession. However, I hope I'm the first to welcome you to our side of the fence seeing as how you were practically the first to welcome me.

[2] Medora Field Perkerson, *Who Killed Aunt Maggie?* (New York, 1939).

I still haven't gotten my breath after reading the news that you **and** Post had parted doll rags. I still haven't taken it in. I'm glad that you **feel** happy about it and I give three cheers if forces outside of your **control** have pushed you into doing something you've been wanting to do **and** haven't done. I wish you had written me more of your plans. When you have the time please do so for you know I'll be interested. I can't figure from your letter whether you intend to write a book as well as take some other job or whether you are just going to write a book. "Just going to write a book!" Good Heavens, cold sweat breaks out on me at the thought of doing such a thing and here the temperature is at a hundred degrees!

Will it be a novel or non-fiction or what? And have you started it? And does it go easily? And what does Norma think of it? There is no reason in the world why you shouldn't write a bang-up book; you know people for you've been observing them quietly for a long time; you have mature judgement; you aren't et up with any rabid theses; you've been stringing words together most successfully for a number of years; you have excellent writing habits and are disciplined to hours of writing and best of all, you are an adult. There are too few adults in the literary profession.

I wish all this had happened while I was up North so that I could have heard the details. Do take the time while you are at Bread Loaf to write me some of them. Whatever your venture, all good wishes go to you.

Mr. and Mrs. Clifford Dowdey   Atlanta, Georgia
Norwalk, Connecticut   August 22, 1938

Dear Helen and Clifford:
   I felt awfully good about the run of writing you two have had since your vacations. Thank you both for reassuring me that you didn't mind my putting in my oar. After leaving you I had a guilty feeling that I must have acted very horsey and know-it-all. I know in my heart that I know less about writing—and still lesser about criticism—than anyone you could pick up in the street. I'm glad if I served my purpose successfully, for my purpose was to be a sounding-board. . . .
   About the Southern Literary Messenger—I heard from Mr. **Dietz** two or three weeks ago. He sounds like a very fine person. He **wanted** an article or a sketch or a paragraph. I couldn't let him have it **for a** thousand reasons—the two main ones being lack of time to write (and lack of inclination) and the many promises I have made to editors to give

them all the chance to look over whatever I wrote. I am going to sub-
scribe to the magazine and will write him that today.[1]

Of course I'm interested in the piece you are writing for him and
I only wish you'd told me more about it in your letter. When I read
the title, "Are We Still Fighting the War?," I laughed aloud. Ever since
Roosevelt's Barnesville speech Senator George and his supporters have
been on the air. I have heard so many yells of "states' rights" and
"Northern oppression" and "sinister centralization of power" and so many
bands playing "Dixie" that I have wondered whether this was 1938 or
1861. I feel that if I look out of the window I will see the Confederate
troops, headed by General John B. Gordon, marching toward Washington. When I read Heywood Broun's sneering remarks about Senator
George "arousing sectionalism" and his other remarks about some Southerners acting as if Appomattox had never occurred I wondered whether
he was just plain dumb. His ideas, and those of a number of Northern
commentators of pinkish tinge, seem to be that Appomattox settled
beautifully and peacefully and justly all the problems, economic and
social, for which the South was fighting. Their idea seems to be that
might made right in 1865. Common sense should show that many of the
problems that sent us to war have never been settled, and the same
injustices persist—tariff, freight rates, et cetera. As far as I can see,
Appomattox didn't settle anything. We just got licked. Our situation is,
in spots, much worse than it was then and the problems are raising their
heads once more. This seems to annoy Mr. Broun and his playmates.
After all, when a section has been held in economic slavery for over
seventy years that section should have the delicacy of feeling not to
squawk.

There is a good paragraph on this subject in Jonathan Daniels' "A
Southerner Discovers the South." It's where he compares the South with
Carthage and remarks that the Romans, after all, were politer than the
Northern conquerors, for after they had sown Carthage with salt they
never rode through it on railroad trains and made snooty remarks about
the degeneracy of people who liked to live in such poor circumstances.
Please read that paragraph. You may not like the rest of the book, but
I think this will appeal to you.[2]

---

[1] Plans by Frieda Meredith Dietz to revive *The Southern Literary Messenger* were
under way by this time. The first issue of the new *Messenger* is that for January
1939. Miss Dietz signed her letters F. Meredith Dietz, and Miss Mitchell mistakenly
identified her as a man.

[2] Daniels wrote: "Cato the Elder was no more implacable than the Brahmans of
Boston who came after the Abolitionists with considerably cooler heads. The South
was not plowed up and planted with salt as Carthage was. If no more generous,
Bostonians (citizens of a region and an attitude and not a town) were less waste-

I want to serve warning on you that there is absolutely no use for you to assault me fore and aft in the belief that you can prod me into writing an article along the lines you suggested. It will do you no good to break out the Southern Cross or send a fife and drum corps under my windows to play the "Bonnie Blue Flag." It will do you less good to throw my grandfathers in my teeth. I will not even respond if you throw my great-grandfathers in my teeth. My emotional setup at present is probably closely akin to the setup of the above mentioned ancestors after they had tramped all the way home to Georgia from Virginia. I imagine that all they wanted, after four years of rampaging around and getting no sleep and eating at irregular times and being targets for Yankee sharpshooters, was a little bit of peace, and that—to quote an old New Bedford whaling story—of the damn cheapest variety.

What the foregoing means is that I've been in the front line for over two years and am just now getting into the rest area. Peace and quiet are not far off, I hope, and not for anything in the world would I write one line on any subject which would bring one stranger panting to my door or add one letter from one Ph.D. student writing a thesis which he hopes I will write for him. There, O'Dowda, get as aroused as your Catalan ancestry will permit. Waggle your finger in my face and ask me what has happened to the fighting blood of my ancestors. If you ask loud enough I may tell you what has happened—in words of one syllable.

Seriously, I do appreciate your belief that I could write such an article. I don't think I could do it. I do think you can. I think you could write it with passion and fervor and yet with a restraint that would give the Radicals no hook on which to hang their sneers.

I was more interested in your remarks, Clifford, about your emotional allegiances going home. That is a subject which John and I will take great pleasure in hearing about when you and Helen come down here. I'm glad you got straightened out about Richmond. As you know, I couldn't live any other place in the world except the South. I suppose, being adaptable, I *could* live anywhere, but I would probably not be very happy. I believe, however, that I see more clearly than most people (because of my experiences during the last two years) just what living in the South means. There are more rules to be followed here than any place in the

---

ful. They recognized that the South kept in its place (a place in the nation geographically similar to that of the Negro in the South) might be useful and profitable. It was. . . . I ask now only that they recognize the poverty of the South as a part of the same civilization as Harvard and in a measure as the creation of the same people. Cato did not ride through Carthage on the train and blame its condition on the Carthaginians. That much only I ask of the Yankees." *A Southerner Discovers the South* (New York, 1938), p. 345.

world if one is to live in any peace and happiness. Having always been a person who was perfectly willing to pay for everything I got, I am more than willing to pay for the happiness I get from my residence in Georgia. You are more impatient than I am, or perhaps I should say I have been schooled in patience more than you have. I do not know whether the following of many rules which seem nonsensical would annoy you to the point of making you irritable at Southern life. I realize the foregoing is not very clear, but I would have to write a book to tell you what I mean, or else talk to you for many hours.

No, we haven't withdrawn our invitation and we do hope you will stop over in Atlanta. John hopes it as much as I do. . . .

Mr. and Mrs. Herschel Brickell   Atlanta, Georgia
Ridgefield, Connecticut   September 4, 1938

Dear Norma and Herschel:

In accordance with the request that all news about the book and the Natchez trek be kept grave yard, I have told no one except John and he isn't likely to reveal it! Witness the fact that I'm writing this letter on Sunday in the absence of Miss Baugh, my secretary, and you'll understand that even she doesn't know about it and she is one of the most discreet of mortals. I can understand that you do not want the news of your plans to get abroad until you are good and ready to tell it yourselves. . . .

Changing the subject abruptly, we sho' Gawd got a flourishing crop of authors in Georgia now! Not so long ago we could only point to Frances Newman[1] and then hastily brag about Uncle Remus. But Now! It looks to me like Georgia's got another money crop and it's writers. When the boll weevil hit the state we were a one crop state. When we were about bankrupt, county agents went around preaching diversified crops. Well, we got the goober crop in and the pecans and upped the peach quota. We de-ticked the cattle so the hides could compete with the Western and Argentine hides. We did things with soy beans. We managed enormous tobacco crops. We even learned to grow slash pine for paper. That looked like the end of our resources and our diversification. But now come the authors. It seems that every one I know has

---

[1] Frances Newman was an Atlanta librarian and author, best known for her novels *The Hard-Boiled Virgin* (New York, 1926) and *Dead Lovers Are Faithful Lovers* (New York, 1928). For several years she conducted a column for *The Atlanta Journal Sunday Magazine* called "Elizabeth Bennet's Gossip." After Miss Newman's retirement from the *Journal* this column was, for a while, written by Miss Mitchell.

written a book or is writing one. Tuther day, I went to a party for our newest Georgia author, Evelyn Hanna of Thomaston, whose "Blackberry Winter"[2] had just gone on sale. Most of the people there were people I'd known for years, sensible people who like me (some years back) you'd never have suspected of a book or books. And practically every one had just signed a contract, was waiting for a publication date or whispered to me that they "wanted me to be the first to know." It looks like a renaissance to me and it makes me feel good. I remember all too well the truthful remarks Mencken made in his "Sahara."[3] I remember especially that he quoted the immortal words of the late and unsung poet Gordon Coogler—

> "Alas for the South! Her poets are gittin Fewer!
> She never was given to Literature."[4]

Whether a book crop is a good one or a bad one doesn't matter so much now. The point is that people are writing and probably will keep on writing. Atlanta has always had a lot of poets and some good ones. Now come the prosers.

As you've doubtless gathered from the papers Georgia is a political cock pit now. Since Mr. Roosevelt came down to put in a good word for Mr. Camp and to remark that our veteran Senator George didn't see eye to eye with him, there has been great excitement. All the conservatives lined up behind George and the new dealers behind Camp[5] (and every body who was sucking a Government tit or hoping to suck one if they could bump another sucker out of the way). Then former Governor Gene Talmadge came into the race. While he yells awfully loud and wears red galluses and, like Judge Priest,[6] knows when to say "ain't," he is even more conservative than George. We are afraid he may split the conservative vote. For the first time in more years than I can remember, there's a real issue in Georgia politics, and a bitter issue. People who were for Roosevelt before go around muttering "I'm damned if any Yankee is going to tell me how to mark my ballot!" and "I don't like no Yankee to tell me who to vote for." I guess Southerners never change. You can coax and gently lead them almost anywhere but try

---

[2] *Blackberry Winter* (New York, 1938).

[3] Henry Louis Mencken, "The Sahara of the Bozart," in *Prejudices, Second Series* (New York, 1920), pp. 136–154.

[4] Miss Mitchell was quoting from memory lines from J. Gordon Coogler's *Purely Original Verse* (Columbia, S.C., 1897), p. 36: "Alas! for the South, her books have grown fewer— / She never was much given to literature."

[5] Lawrence S. Camp.

[6] A character in stories by Irvin S. Cobb.

to drag and bully them or tell them how to mind their own business and they get very stiffnecked. Roosevelt lost an awful lot of personal popularity by that Barnesville speech endorsing Camp. And more popularity by forgetting to throw the switch that was to turn on the electricity into that section of rural Georgia. He'd been invited for the purpose of throwing the switch and after he got through lambasting George it slipped his mind. Two weeks more and we'll know how the state stands. It's something no one can predict now and most people who do predict are indulging in wishful thinking. . . .

Miss Evelyn Hanna   Atlanta, Georgia
Thomaston, Georgia   September 6, 1938

My dear Evelyn:

It was my intention to write you at great length about your book, for I read it at one sitting (or should I say "at one lying"—for I did not finish it until two o'clock in the morning?). I wanted to tell you in detail how interesting I found it, how much I enjoyed it and, in particular, which passages appealed to me the most. But this discussion will have to wait, and I am sorry for there is nothing I enjoy more than talking books. The reason for this sincere but hasty letter is that there is illness in my family and business matters from New York have dumped a new mess of problems in my lap. I hope with all my heart that you do not have problems of copyright infringement, lawsuits and "Foreign entanglements" because of "Blackberry Winter." You've written such a fine book and I hope no such unpleasantnesses arise to take any of the edge from your pleasure in your accomplishment—for you should be pleased!

Come to see us when you are next in Atlanta. Give us a little warning so that you can come out and have supper with us.

Miss Evelyn Hanna   Atlanta, Georgia
Thomaston, Georgia   September 8, 1938

My dear Evelyn:

I was distressed to learn that you had been ill last Saturday and are still feeling po'ly. I am very sorry you did not telephone me Saturday for I would have brought you out home and we would have looked after you. I hope you are much better now. . . .

And now I am going to do two things I rarely do. I am going to give advice, unsolicited, and I am going to express myself frankly and openly. The former I have never liked in other people so I try to avoid it in myself. The latter I have had to learn to avoid since "Gone With the Wind" was published. I will probably sound conceited when I say that after my book was published, many of my letters were printed in newspapers or passed from hand to hand or publishers wanted to put excerpts from them on book jackets. It did happen, however, and it took away a lot of my freedom of speech. It made me guard my remarks at all times, especially those in writing. But I am going to break that rule because I want to write you a very personal letter, not a formal, official one. You are in the same frying pan as I am now, and I know you will keep our correspondence confidential, thereby making it possible for me to write you freely and openly.

The unsolicited advice is this—the *important* thing is your book and not the reviews of your book. Don't be too elated when you get a good review and don't be too depressed when you get a bad one. The important thing is the creative ability inside of you, and your book shows you have got it. Too much sugar in good reviews is just as bad for it as too much vinegar in bad reviews—provided, of course, you make a meal on either the sugar or the vinegar. Take them sparingly, if you wish, as flavoring, but don't take them at all if they threaten to spoil the really important thing, the creative ability inside of you. Don't let it get warped or twisted or inflated or suppressed. Hold on to it, guard it, protect it. Don't read the reviews at all if they threaten to damage it.

You remember what Olin[1] said, "She'll have to develop a tough hide, won't she?" Olin is very wise about people and he also knows how to say in a homely phrase what I have labored to say in a paragraph. Anyone who gets into the public eye needs a tough hide. Even if your book proves to be a tremendous success, it will nevertheless bring you unpleasant experiences. So do try to develop a tough hide for your own sake. Don't let the things outside of you injure and damage the many good things inside of you. Shield and protect them with a tough hide.

Whether a book is good or bad is wholly a matter of opinion. Some will have one opinion, some the other about any book. But those opinions (of outsiders) are not the true criterion of an author's merit. It is—have you written sincerely? Your book shows on the face of it your sincerity and honesty. Don't let those qualities be crushed or warped by unfavorable outside opinions.

When you have published a book, you have given a hostage to fortune, a hostage which makes you as vulnerable as though you had given

[1] Olin Miller.

husband or child. People will like or hate or be indifferent to your book or your husband or your child and there is nothing you can do about it except to continue in your own serene belief in these three possessions and your love for them.

I was afraid that you were not prepared for some of the things that come the way of every author. That is why I took my courage in my hand and called on you at the Biltmore. Perhaps I was luckier than most people, for I expected nothing but [bad] when my book was published. I had had years of experience on a newspaper and had been associated with people who associated with authors. Nothing that was said about me or "Gone With the Wind" was one one-hundredth as bad as I expected and I was—and am—humbly grateful for my good fortune.

I know of a number of Southern authors who had dreadful criticisms of their first books. These authors put a buckler between them and the "slings and arrows of outrageous fortune" and by the time their second or third books were published the whole nation was acclaiming them.

I know that giving advice is a useless and usually a thankless affair, but, for your own sake and the sake of your future books, I would like to beg this of you: don't get bitter and don't let anything drive you into a defensive position. To be trite, bitterness never does any harm to anyone except the person who is feeling it. It also keeps a writer from getting the true perspective on his work. The same is true about writers who are forced into a defensive position. Unfortunately, a number of Southern writers have had this happen to them, and the South is the loser. The South can use all its talented young folks now. I love my section and I know you do too, for it stands out in every page of your book. Many people cannot understand how you can love your section and yet be honestly critical of it. Well, I can understand that and so can you, so please don't get a hate on the South because a few reviewers may misunderstand your intentions. You will read a few reviews but you will never hear from the rank and file of people who read your book and like it. Try to realize that there will be many in this latter class.

I do sound very dull and preachy, don't I? Forgive me if I do. My excuse is something that happened in the first few weeks after "Gone With the Wind" was published. Several Southern authors with years of experience and several novels behind them wrote me unsolicited letters warning me of some of the things that were ahead of me and suggesting how I might be able to meet them. I shall always be grateful to them. I had entered a strange new world and they gave me invaluable help. I don't know that this letter will be of any help to you, but I hope it may give you some encouragement. At least, it will tell you that I appreciate the problems you are facing and that I want to see you meet them courageously and successfully. But even if my letter fails to accomplish any of these things, I wanted to write you anyhow, because I feared you were unhappy and I hoped I might help you to see your situation in a pleasanter light.

Thanks for the invitation to come and sit on your front porch. I would love to do this if I were not tied to a basket of mail and lawsuits. Perhaps they will be finished some day and then I can join you on the front porch.

Miss Katharine Brown   Atlanta, Georgia
New York, New York   September 12, 1938

Dear Katharine:

Your letter of September 6th, with its request for the loan or purchase of all or part of the manuscript of "Gone With the Wind" for exploitation and advertisement of the picture, has arrived. Far from being "cross" at you or Mr. Selznick or Mr. Whitney, I am naturally flattered to death by their interest. But I can't let you have all or even a part of it.

The truth is that I set out to destroy the original manuscript right after the book was published two years ago and I think all of it went into the furnace. If any part of it survived, it was only because it got buried under the avalanche of things that descended on me in those days, and if any stray sheets turn up in the future, I intend to destroy them too. I never wanted any part of it to pass out of my hands for addition to literary collections or for display purposes, so the sensible thing seemed to be to burn it up. I felt and still feel so strongly about the matter that when I was making some revisions in my will last month I included a stipulation that should any pages of manuscript or notes et cetera turn up after my death they should be destroyed immediately and should neither be sold nor given away nor exhibited. I do not care who gets "Gone With the Wind," as a book, but I do not want manuscript sheets floating about.

Someone misinformed you about the manuscript of "Gone With the Wind" being shown at the Book Fair, but it is easy to see how such an error got about. The Macmillan Company wanted the manuscript and when I could not produce it they asked for any part of it for the exhibition. I had not completed my work of destruction then and I let them have one or two pages which they returned to me after the Book Fair.[1] About that same time Collier's Magazine was running a story about me, and they asked me for a page from one of the several chapters I had

---

[1] See note to the letter of December 8, 1938, to Herschel Brickell.

eliminated from the book before it was published. After considerable searching, I managed to find one and they used it in their lay-out.[2]

Those three pages are the only part of my manuscript that have ever been exhibited and I have always regretted that I let those sheets go out of my hands, even temporarily, for they caused me an enormous amount of labor and inconvenience. Libraries and private collectors bombarded me with offers for the manuscript; editors of many magazines descended on me and are still descending, trying to buy the chapters I had eliminated from the published version of "Gone With the Wind." For a long time it seemed as if no airplane landed here without an editor determined to wrest one of these chapters from me. Bessie was kept so busy frying chickens and I so busy saying "I'm sorry but I can't" that we were practically exhausted. The public arrived by mail and in person, wanting to view the original manuscript, demanding to know in detail what had been in those unpublished chapters; newspapers wanted to print them; the rumor arose that I had written a final chapter (after the published one) which I or The Macmillan Company would sell for a dollar. You cannot imagine the uproar in which we lived, and we were already having uproar enough to keep us busy. There were editors to see and newspaper stories to deny and hundreds of letters to be written and tourists to be gotten rid of as gracefully as possible. I wouldn't go through all that again for a million dollars.

Even if some remnants of the manuscript or the discarded chapters were to show up some day, I don't see how I could let Mr. Selznick have them after I have refused them to universities and historical societies and like organizations here in the South. By this time, he has had enough experience with the South and Southern people to know that that would never do.

As you can gather, I have been in a strange and difficult situation about this matter and it has been made more difficult by the fact that many people do not understand that I really have violent objections to letting even a page of corrected galley proof get out of my hands. I object for the same reason that caused me to resist the many efforts to publish "intimate" stories and pictures of my private life. I want to keep my private life private if there is any way possible to do so, and I always regarded my manuscript as an intimate and personal thing.

Please tell Mr. Selznick and Mr. Whitney how sincerely I appreciate their interest and their requests. I do think it is grand of them both to want the manuscript even if I can't let them have it.

[2] A photograph of "a page of the original manuscript of Gone With the Wind, from a section omitted in the printed version" appears on p. 22 of *Collier's*, XCIX, No. 11 (March 13, 1937), as an illustration for Granberry's "The Private Life of Margaret Mitchell."

By inference I gathered that plans for the beginning of production must be under [way] and, of course, I was interested. And of course, too, I will be interested in knowing how Alicia Rhett's tests turn out if you decide to bring her up from Charleston. I was sorry the young lassies of the Barter Theatre did not work out very well. I hope you had a good time in Virginia even if you didn't pan any pay-dirt.

I did my best after your (Mr. Selznick's) telegram came but the sum-total of the newspaper publicity was the enclosed clippings. If I can find another clipping I will send it too. It was by an Atlanta columnist who stated briefly that he had seen a telegram from Mr. Selznick to me officially confirming Clark Gable. The truth is the Atlanta papers (and probably many others) are waiting for the first official break on the casting of Scarlett and the first official news on the beginning of produc-tion before they turn loose any publicity. I do not believe that they would run another line unless I eloped with Mr. Selznick to Tahiti, and as he is very busy at present, and I am too, I don't know how we could manage it just now.

Mrs. Clifford Dowdey   Atlanta, Georgia
Norwalk, Connecticut   September 16, 1938

Dear Helen:
    . . . I infer from your remarks about Clifford's deep immersion in Wil-liamsburg and various other statements that he is rapidly approaching the end of the book.[1] I hope I've guessed right and I hope, too, that he manages to get the revision done (if revision is necessary) before you two hitch up the oxen and get into the covered wagon for the cross-continental trip. I am sure you both needed a vacation and it would be grand if you could go West with nothing on your minds except your hair. Why don't you two go to Taos? I'd love to see how you would look in Volume XX of Mabel Dodge Luhan's Memoirs. If you two worked at it you should be able to give her three or four hair-raising chapters.

Tell Clifford I'm looking forward to his article in The Messenger with great interest. By the way, I am worried about The Messenger. I don't think they will make much money because they are so generous. I wrote Meredith Dietz and asked the price of a year's subscription and he re-plied that he had already put me on the free list. Folks don't never get rich thataway!

Helen, if you haven't sold that story by the time you come South, please let me read it for I can't help being curious. Perhaps if you plowed it under till next year and then exhumed it you might get a new slant

[1] *Gamble's Hundred* (Boston, 1939).

on it. You say you are lying fallow: me—I am in favor of bigger and better fallowing. In answer to your question about whether I have felt "any of the old compulsion to write during these last two years"—no, I have not. To tell the hideous truth, I have never once in my life felt a compulsion to write anything. The exact opposite has been my problem. I loathe writing and will go to any lengths to keep from writing. Having a definite antipathy for putting words on paper, the only reason I ever wrote any was because I had nothing to do at that particular time and, having started something, was goaded on by the Puritanical adage that one should finish what one had begun. John's large shoe placed on the metaphorical seat of the pants of my soul accelerated some of my efforts. I think it would be a wonderful thing to have a creative urge. At present, seeing the enormous amount of work and worry I have brought on my family and myself, I would think several times before really trying to publish a book. . . .

I have just read about Thomas Wolfe's death[2] and, while I never knew him, I had a distinct feeling of shock. If ever there was a comet in these Southern skies, he was it. I imagine his family is glad he made his peace with Asheville before he died.

Mr. Herschel Brickell   Atlanta, Georgia
Ridgefield, Connecticut   October 31, 1938

Dear Herschel:

The last week has been a nightmare such as one has during malaria or beri-beri or scurvy. Father took a bad turn and gave us four anxious days and nights. As he was delirious a great part of the time and wished to get out of bed, it was necessary for us to spend most of the nights with him. It was impossible to sleep by day as every friend I ever had arrived in town and telephoned. There was also a librarians' convention in progress and one of the book stores was giving a juvenile book fair with authors, including Munro Leaf, and speakers like May Lamberton Becker. All day long people phoned saying they just knew I would love to meet these juvenile authors. To complicate matters, Mrs. Ogden Reid, of the Herald-Tribune, announced blatantly in New York that I had endorsed Katharine Hepburn for the role of Scarlett. I had done no such thing but that did not prevent all the news services in the country from querying me and getting denials. On top of it all, I was awarded a medal[1] and

[2] September 15.
[1] The Carl Bohnenberger Memorial Medal given by the Southeastern Library Association for "the most outstanding contribution to Southern literature" in the two years previous. Atlanta *Constitution*, October 29.

had to write a speech and alter an evening dress. However, that's in the past, for Father is better and I got twelve hours' sleep last night for the first time in ten days. Yesterday he sat up in bed and he is very cross and irritable, which are excellent signs. He should be home in three days and you can imagine our relief.

I am wiring Clifford and Helen in Richmond to come on this next week-end, and we are looking forward to their visit with great pleasure for they are like homefolks. I had intended giving some parties for them but, under the circumstances, I do not believe that I will. We are looking forward to your visit, too, because you, too, are homefolks. We were going to partify you too if you wanted it, but I know you will understand when I tell you that we aren't going to do it. We want to see you for a quiet visit for just as long as you can stay for you put no strain upon us, whereas, if we had to have a party or strangers in the house we'd both go berserk.

So, you wire us when you are coming and we will make your reservation at the Biltmore and when you get to town telephone us. It will be so much fun to see you, and if you are any friend of ours you will give us one of those Shakespeare speeches and with gestures. Don't try to tell me you never had elocution rammed down your throat before—and you born in Mississippi! Didn't you have to learn "Spartacus to the Gladiators"[2] with gestures? And "Little Giffen of Tennessee"[3]? Why, I even remember the gestures proper to "The Blue and the Gray"[4] and, if you ask me prettily enough, I will render them after you give Hamlet's Soliloquy. Seriously, you have all my admiration. Everybody ought to know how to speak publicly, but how few people are willing to take the trouble? The other night when I was being awarded the medal I wished fervidly that I had studied public speaking, especially when May Lamberton Becker followed me and laid the audience in the aisles with apparently no effort. . . .

Col. Telamon Cuyler   Atlanta, Georgia
Wayside, Georgia   November 9, 1938

My dear Colonel Cuyler:

I was sorry that I had to leave the costume party but our New York guest had to return to her hotel. I had hoped to see you on Sunday but it appeared that Father needed me on that day. I have given him your good wishes and he thanks you. He has been home from the hospital for

2 By Elijah Kellogg.
3 By Francis Orrery Ticknor.
4 By Francis Miles French.

several days and is recovering nicely. He is, however, still weak enough to need the services of a nurse. He is still unable to do any reading, as he is easily tired, and this is an annoyance to him for, as you know, he has spent the greater part of his life reading.

Thank you for the kind words about my schoolgirl costume. It was a jumped-up affair for I was not sure until the last minute that Father's condition would permit me to attend the party. I enjoyed the whole affair so much and I think Miss Blair[1] deserves all compliments possible on the way she handled it. I thought you dashing and distinguished, and I must tell you that Mrs. Becker, our guest, was impressed by you immensely. She is a book critic on the New York Herald-Tribune, and I do not think she had ever been South before. The party was something new in her life. And how wonderful that I could show her a real Confederate in a real Confederate coat![2] She talked about you all the way back to the hotel. I am always happy when I can display "old Atlanta" at its best to visitors, and I thank you for your assistance in doing this. . . .

Friends who came through here last week-end had seen "Kiss the Boys Goodbye."[3] They said it was a burlesque on Selznick's search for Scarlett. They said that it was amusing in spots but that the author evidently hated every one of her characters so much that it was impossible to feel sympathy for them. It was a malicious comedy all the way around. In the end, however, the apparently dimwitted little Southern girl who had been chosen to play "Velvet O'Toole" turned on her Northern tormentors and routed them, butting one anti-Southern columnist in his fat stomach, shooting an amorous movie producer, telling the literati what bad manners they had, winning the heart of a millionaire polo player, et cetera. They said, though the girl who played the part was an Alabama girl, the Southern accent was laid on with a trowel. . . .[4]

[1] Ruth Blair, executive secretary of the Atlanta Historical Society.

[2] To the costume party of the Atlanta Historical Society Colonel Cuyler wore the Confederate uniform of his great uncle, Col. Algernon S. Hamilton of the Sixtysixth Georgia Volunteers.

[3] *Kiss the Boys Good-Bye*, by Clare Boothe, was produced by Brock Pemberton at Henry Miller's Theatre, New York, September 28, 1938. It was presented at Atlanta's Erlanger Theatre by a touring company March 31 and April 1, 1939. The play was published by Random House in 1939 with "A Tribute to Miss Boothe" by Heywood Broun as a foreword and with a long introduction by Miss Boothe. "This play," she began, "was meant to be a political allegory about Fascism in America. But everywhere it has been taken for a parody of Hollywood's search for Scarlett O'Hara." (P. vii.) Inez Robb interviewed Miss Mitchell in New York in September 1941: "The Atlanta author said she had seen Clare Boothe's 'Kiss the Boys Goodbye' and 'just whooped with laughter' over it. But she was at first incredulous and then doubled up with merriment when told that Miss Boothe regarded her play as a serious exposé and indictment of the south as the stronghold of Fascism." Atlanta *Constitution*, September 6, 1941.

[4] Cindy Lou Bethany, aspirant for the movie role of Velvet O'Toole, was played by Helen Claire.

Mr. Alexander L. May   Atlanta, Georgia
Berlin, Germany   November 18, 1938

My dear Mr. May:

I received your letter of October 30th, and found it as interesting as your other letters. I am very sorry to learn that you could not obtain the books on the South and the Confederacy which I listed in a former letter. I am mailing to you today a copy of Robert Henry's "Story of the Confederacy." It is a cheap reprint of the original edition. The price is $1.00 and the postage 30¢—I am telling you the price and the amount of postage because you requested it, but I would take it as a favor if you would let me present this volume to you as a gift from an Atlantan to an ex-Atlantan. Instead of sending me the money for it, please ask Mrs. May to send me a handkerchief or some other little souvenir which you can put into a letter. I will be more than pleased to have it in exchange. I will see about Mr. Henry's "Story of Reconstruction" when I have the opportunity of going downtown to the book stores.

I am very glad to answer the questions you asked, for, of course, the knowledge that German readers were interested in details of "Gone With the Wind" pleased me. So, I will arm you with the answers to questions asked you by your German friends.

Atlanta *claims* 300,000 population now. This includes what is known as the "metropolitan area." In the metropolitan area are many far-off residential sections which probably did not exist when you lived in Atlanta or else were little towns on the outskirts of Atlanta. Buckhead, which lies to the north of the city out Peachtree Road, is part of the Metropolitan area; Hapeville, to the south between Atlanta and Jonesboro, is another; East Point and College Park, lying between Hapeville and the city, are two other settlements which Atlanta now claims. Atlanta has spread out until the houses are continuous to Decatur on the east, and almost to Marietta on the west. The fine residential section which centered around Capitol Square on the south side of town jumped the railroad tracks many years ago. Now many wealthy people have built homes as far to the north as the Chattahoochee River, near Roswell which is nearly twenty miles from Five Points. The territory between Buckhead and Roswell is built up with beautiful homes and large estates.

About the Geechee dialect—you were correct when you said it was the dialect used by the Negroes in Savannah and the Sea Islands. The derivation is from the Indian name of the Ogeechee River. It is almost impossible for a person not born near Savannah to understand this dialect. I have just returned from a trip to that section and I heard some of the Negroes using this dialect. It was with difficulty that I understood them at all. Many of the words they use are African words which have survived from the days when slave traders sold Negroes fresh from the jungles to the Sea Island plantations. These Sea Island Negroes were isolated from the mainland, and so, they kept some of their native African words. For your information, the Negro dialect spoken around Charleston, South Carolina, is called the Gullah dialect. It is somewhat similar to Geechee.

You were right when you told your friends that I was not writing a continuation of "Gone With the Wind." Ever since it was published, in the summer of 1936, the rumor has been afloat that I had written or was intending to write a sequel, but there is no truth in this rumor. Even if I wished to continue it, I would not have the opportunity or the time. I have had no leisure in which to do any writing at all, as the success of my book has brought such a multitude of problems, of both business and social natures, that I scarcely have time to buy myself winter clothes. I know that sounds incredible, but you must take it as the truth. To give you only one example of the reasons why I am unable to do any more writing—when I sold the moving picture rights to my book the Selznick company announced that they wished to secure a young and unknown Southern girl to play the part of Scarlett. Young Southern girls by the hundreds have been after me during the last two years, pleading with me to endorse them for this part. I have nothing to do with the production of the film and cannot be of assistance to any of them. Nevertheless, these young ladies have taken up two years of my time with their importunities. Until the film is actually produced I will have this problem to face. As you can imagine, I will be very happy when the film is finished. . . .

Mr. and Mrs. Clifford Dowey   Atlanta, Georgia
Fort Worth, Texas   November 30, 1938

Dear Chillun:

Helen, you are the most honest person I know. I do not recall ever getting back a handkerchief which I have loaned to a friend. This morning I received not only my own handkerchief but the three other lovely ones which you sent. If that ain't compound interest or bread cast on the waters or a rolling stone gathering a stitch in time, I don't know what is. The handkerchiefs are beautiful, and much needed due to the numbers I have lost recently by lending mine to wet-nosed friends. So, thanks an awful lot.

Shortly after your visit my father seemed well enough for us to get away for a week-end. After the long strain of his illness we needed a change so we went to our favorite place, Sea Island, off the coast of Brunswick. It lies next to St. Simon's Island, where Fanny Kemble lived.[1] Herschel had been so indefinite about when he was coming that we wired him saying we were going to the coast. To our pleasure, he long-distanced us that he would come down and spend the week-end with us, and he did. It was lots of fun, although a very quiet affair. We sat around talking endlessly and rode many miles under the big trees with Spanish moss. . . .

Herschel came back to Atlanta for one day and Marjorie Rawlings came up from Florida. Herschel's lecture agent had sent him to try to lure her into a lecture tour. We four had lunch together and it was a very gay affair. She knew as many backwoods stories as we did and told them most excellently. She invited us to drop in on her should we go South to visit the Edwin Granberrys in Winter Park this winter, and perhaps we'll do it. She was a lot of fun.

I have just finished John Thomason's war story in this week's Post[2] and I am meditating just how to blast him. Do you know that he said that no one knew exactly how the First Texas Volunteer Infantry got to Virginia except that General Hood said they just "straggled to the front." Them is fightin' words, as Grandpa Mitchell organized the First Texas and was one of the "stragglers." I will bet a wad of Confederate money that the only way the Second and Third Texas got to Virginia so quick was that they stole horses and mules all the way from East Texas to the railroad at the River. I liked the story anyway, even if he did throw off on Grandpa's bunch of wildcats.

Dr. William Lyon Phelps   Atlanta, Georgia
New Haven, Connecticut   December 29, 1938

My dear Doctor Phelps:

John and I enjoyed hearing you over the radio last night[1] and we were as proud of your unstumpability as if we had had something to do with it personally. . . .

I cannot tell you how Melanie came to be named Melanie, because that has always been her name ever since I first thought of her. As I believe

[1] Frances Anne Kemble, an English actress of great beauty and fame, was for several years married to Pierce Butler of Philadelphia and Saint Simon's Island, Ga. As an author, she is best remembered for her *Journal of a Residence on a Georgian Plantation in 1838–1839* (New York, 1863), a book published as antislavery propaganda.

[2] John William Thomason, "Preacher Goes to War," *The Saturday Evening Post*, December 3, 1938.

[1] On the NBC program "Information Please." Atlanta *Constitution*, December 28.

I told you, I checked the names of all my characters against names in records in Fulton County (Atlanta), Clayton County and Fayette County to make sure I did not use names of actual people. I remember with what dread I looked for the name of Melanie Hamilton or Melanie Wilkes in old Atlanta records. I knew if I found a duplication I would be forced to change her name, and I knew I could not change her name because it belonged to her.

To the best of my knowledge, the name Melanie is a peculiarly Southern name, and Coast Southern at that. As it was brought to the United States by French people or people of French descent, the name was popular in towns such as New Orleans, Mobile, Savannah, Charleston. I have been told that the popularity this name enjoyed during the thirties, forties and fifties was due to Melanie, Princess Metternich. I suppose the delegates at the Congress of Vienna were impressed by her charms and carried the name back to their homes. Ever so often I receive letters from the West and the Middle West, telling me that the name is pronounced MEE-laney there, and I want to choke somebody when I hear of such a perversion of a lovely name. . . .

1939

Mr. and Mrs. Clifford Dowdey　　　　　　　Atlanta, Georgia
Fort Worth, Texas　　　　　　　　　　　　January 2, 1939

Dear Helen and Clifford:

I think you may be interested in the latest Marsh mangled metaphor. Someone asked John recently if I intended to write another book and he replied, "A wet hen avoids the fire."

The Literary Messenger arrived and, while I have only skimmed most of the articles, of course I read yours,[1] Clifford, with leisure and appreciation. (John has not had the chance to read it, as we were trying to close the books for the year and start in on the income tax matter. He has scarcely had time to breathe during the last two weeks.) I liked the article very much and I would have liked it even if you had not written it. I would have liked it even if it had been written by one or two Southerners who shall be nameless but whose works are anathema to me. You said things that should be said, not once but over and over until by repetition they penetrate the minds of people who wonder why the South still licks its wounds. I was glad you brought in the idea of not lying back on grandpa's war record. . . .

There's no particular news from us. The end of the year always means a lot of hard work but it's about over now. We had a fine Christmas and after a family dinner we went calling and eggnogging. It has been four years since we did that and it was so much fun. A great part of the fun lay in the heartening fact that people no longer treated me as a curiosity but took me for granted just as if I had been a successful lady embalmer or life insurance salesman. I expect there will be one more upsurge of public interest and then I think it will all be over. The upsurge will come during the next two weeks when Mr. Selznick will announce to the popeyed world just which little lady will play Scarlett. . . .

---

[1] "Are We Still Fighting the Civil War?" *The Southern Literary Messenger*, I (1939), 12–15.

Mr. David O. Selznick   Atlanta, Georgia
Culver City, California   January 14, 1939

My dear Mr. Selznick:

I would have telephoned you last night to tell you of my pleasure in your announcements but, after spending three hours between the Western Union office and the offices of the Associated Press and our morning newspaper, The Constitution, I was rather tired. I am sure the excitement of the evening contributed to this tiredness! But I didn't mind being weary in so good a cause.

Yesterday afternoon (Friday) The Journal, one of our afternoon papers, carried a copyrighted UP story about Miss Leigh, which I am enclosing. It bore the earmarks of being an "official release" but, on second reading, appeared to be a news leak. None of our three papers queried me about it. Around nine o'clock your first wire came and the Western Union girl told me that a long wire was on the way and segments of it would arrive at fifteen minute intervals.[1] It seemed sensible to avoid delay in delivery by going to the Western Union office, so John and I did this. Three sheets telling about Miss Leigh had arrived by the time we reached the office; I knew our morning paper was going to press and of course I wanted the home town papers to have the break on this story, so I left John at the Western Union office to wait for the remainder and I went to The Constitution office. By good luck, they had a photograph of Miss Leigh and they tore out part of the front page, put her picture in, and began setting your wire. At intervals the rest of the wire came in. It was all very exciting and reminded John and me of our own newspaper days.

As you will notice from the enclosed clippings, Scarlett's home town

---

[1] After a preliminary, warning wire Selznick sent three long telegrams to Miss Mitchell: one detailing the casting of Vivien Leigh as Scarlett, one the casting of Olivia de Havilland as Melanie and Leslie Howard as Ashley, and one spelling out a long biographical sketch of Miss Leigh that was being released along with the announcement of the casting. Atlanta *Constitution*, January 14.

The selection of Vivien Leigh to play Scarlett had been, except for an intentional leak to Ed Sullivan, a well-guarded secret. Susan Myrick wrote from Santa Monica January 11: "To your ears alone can I say the following. I have not written it to a soul and the studio is so secretive about it all I'm almost afraid to write it to yall. But I have seen the girl who is to do Scarlett. I am even yet afraid to say her name aloud. Will Price (who used to be with Fed Theater in Atl) and I speak of her in hushed tones as 'That Woman' or as 'Miss X' and we have spent several mornings with her, talking Southern just for her stage-taught ears. She is charming, very beautiful, black hair and magnolia petal skin and in the movie tests I have seen, she moved me greatly. They did the paddock scene, for a test, and it is marvelous business the way she makes you cry when she is 'making Ashley.' I understand she is not signed but far as I can tell from George [Cukor] et al, she is the gal."

is very interested in her progress and equally interested in Mr. Howard and Miss de Havilland. I am very grateful to you for sending me so long and detailed a wire, for I am grateful to the Atlanta papers and Atlanta people for their interest and I was glad to have so much information to give them.

If I can judge from the reactions of the newspaper men last night and that of the men on the afternoon papers who have called me this morning, they are well pleased with the choice of Miss Leigh. Everyone thought it was a fine thing to have a girl who was comparatively unknown in this country because her rendition of Scarlett would not be mixed up by past performances of roles of a different type. Mr. Howard has always been the almost unanimous choice of Southerners for the role of Ashley. And the announcement of Miss de Havilland was hailed with pleasure. (For a bad five minutes it looked as if a picture of Miss de Havilland in a scanty bathing suit was going to appear in the morning paper, bearing the caption "Here is Melanie, a True Daughter of the Old South." That picture was the only view of her the file clerk could find at first. I made loud lamentations at this, especially when the editor said, "We can explain that Sherman's men had gotten away with the rest of her clothes." Finally we found the sweet picture with the old fashioned bangs.)

I know that you must feel a great sense of relief this morning—a relief far greater than mine. It is fine to have the announcement over and the picture ready to go into production. As always, you have my heartiest good wishes for the success of the film.

Mrs. H. P. Redwine   Atlanta, Georgia
Fayetteville, Georgia   January 28, 1939

Dear Mrs. Redwine:

Your "love letter" made me so very happy and I think you are the kindest of people to write such nice things. If I could believe one-half of them were true I would become so swollen with pride that neither you nor my other Fayetteville friends could endure me.

I am so glad my Christmas check to the Library helped. I suppose you can tell how interested I am in books. They have always been almost as necessary to me as food. So, of course, I can't help feeling a warm interest in the Fayetteville Library and its career. Yes, I do know the financial situations of our Georgia counties which are mainly devoted to agriculture. I know that since the days when the boll weevil first struck our section the agricultural communities have been hard hit—so hard hit that things like libraries must occupy subordinate places. I hope when times are better that we will some day see the Fayetteville Library a large and flourishing affair, with thousands of volumes for the people of the County. When that day comes I will be very proud to think that I had a part in it.

For weeks I have been intending to come to Fayetteville for another happy visit but something always turns up to prevent it. The current excitement over the selection of Vivien Leigh has kept me busy recently, but I hope when this upsurge has subsided I will have the opportunity of calling at the Library again—and I hope I will see you there.

Mr. David O. Selznick   Atlanta, Georgia
Culver City, California   January 30, 1939

My dear Mr. Selznick:

I am sorry I have delayed so long in answering your three letters— the one written shortly after the announcement of the cast, the letter of January 24th about the difficult scene at the barbecue, and your last letter concerning the Associated Press dispatch about the Ocala ladies.[1] I realized that you wanted an immediate reply to the one about the barbecue scene, but this is the first time in more than two weeks that I have had the opportunity or the leisure to think coherently. Since the announcement was in the papers my life has been a bedlam. Of course, my life during the past two years has been lived in practically the same circumstances, very largely because of the thousands of people who thought I was producing "Gone With the Wind" single-handed in my back yard and who believed that I, and I alone, could give them parts in it. But the last two weeks have broken all records. I have been living in the pockets of the newspapers for days and they telephone at all hours about all subjects; requests for minor parts in the picture come in every minute; people who wish to sell me their grandparents' furnishings to be used in the picture have swamped me; anxious folks who want to know if you are going to do right by the South must be soothed; and, on top of it all, an incredible number of people want personal letters of intro-

---

[1] An Atlanta *Journal* story by Frank Daniel reported on January 20: "The Dickinson Chapter, United Daughters of the Confederacy, celebrated General Lee's birthday Thursday [January 19] by deploring Vivien Leigh, and announcing the chapter's secession from Selznick International because that studio had chosen an English actress to play the Southern heroine of 'Gone With the Wind.' . . . The Ocala Daughters, in a resolution, protested vigorously 'against any other than a native-born southern woman playing the part,' and added, 'we resolve to withhold our patronage if otherwise cast.' "

duction to you so they can get on the lot and watch the entire proceedings. As you can imagine, the handling of such people calls for endless time, patient explanation and greater understanding and tact than I possess. So, please forgive my delay in answering your letters.

About the scene at the barbecue where Melanie is first introduced—yes, I see your problem perfectly, for you set forth the difficulties so clearly.[2] I understand, too, the reason why you must make Melanie's

---

[2] Selznick wrote on January 24: "At the risk of incurring your displeasure, and with what amounts to almost a depressing conviction that you will refuse, I have decided after a long debate with myself to call upon you for help in connection with one extremely important scene in the picture.

"It looks as though we are going to be able to accomplish what I have hoped, which is a minimum of original dialogue. Throughout the work on the script I have refused to permit re-writing of your own lines in the book and the result I think will be that between ninety and ninety-five percent of the dialogue in the picture will be identically as originally conceived and written by you. Naturally, and unfortunately, and with great beating of breasts and letting of blood, we have had to make a great many cuts of scenes which we all love; but this is forced on us by the limitation of the length of any motion picture. In what remains, however, we have been as faithful as possible; and even where we have had to make transpositions and alterations we have usually been able to find lines out of the book.

"It is for this reason that I am distressed that one highly important scene in the picture has no dialogue parallel in the book which is what leads me to write in the hope that you would consent to write a version of this scene for us.

"I am referring to the scene in which Ashley and Melanie are both introduced in the picture for the first time—the scene at Twelve Oaks in which Scarlett greets both of them.

"In the book there is simply a reference by you, in retrospect, of the fact that Scarlett found it difficult to be civil with Melanie. Now, we have found it very difficult to bring Melanie to life in the first part of our script and this is really our only opportunity to invest her with the graciousness and sweetness and charm which we hope the character will possess. There is the additional factor that it is highly important that we immediately stamp her for what she is, for in a film an audience's first impression of each character is the lasting one, even more so than in any other medium.

"The same is true of Ashley. We will have had scene after scene building up Ashley's introduction and when we first see him it is important that we characterize him also for exactly those traits that we want the audience to absorb.

"We have made several attempts at a scene in which Scarlett behaves in rude fashion with Melanie in this scene and in stupid flirtatious fashion with Ashley—with Scarlett's behavior going completely over the head of Melanie, who in turn behaves with such generosity and charm that quite unconsciously she scores on Scarlett who is further infuriated; and with Ashley controlling and handling the situation in a charming and civilized manner. But our attempts frankly lack the flavor of your own writing and do not seem of a piece with the picture as a whole.

"It would be a great pity indeed if this scene in which we first meet two of our four most important characters and in which we first start the relationship between Melanie and Scarlett, and in which further we have the first contact between Scarlett and Ashley, did not come off. I think you will understand why I am so worried that this will materially hurt the whole picture and the relationship of the three principals throughout the entire story. And if you do understand, and if you sympathize with our plight, I hope that if you still feel that you want to steer clear of the script you will at least understand and forgive my cry of distress."

first entrance a telling one—an entrance which will establish her for exactly what she is. To tell the truth, difficulties of this nature had not occurred to me until I read your letter, for I know so little about script writing. The technique of novel writing is, I now observe, a very different one. As Melanie was one of the characters which I wished to build continually throughout the book, I intentionally did very little with her in her opening scenes—merely introduced her and thereafter let her grow. But I can see your problem very clearly.

I am so very sorry that I cannot help you with this problem. No matter how much I might wish to help you, by writing the dialogue or sketching the scene, it would be impossible. I am a slow writer and writing takes time, uninterrupted time. For nearly three years, I have had no time for writing of any kind. With hundreds of letters coming in, with the telephone constantly ringing, with people clamoring for "introductions to Mr. Selznick" and newspapers bedeviling me for statements on subjects which do not concern me, I have had no time even to think about creative writing, much less attempt it.

Some time ago I abandoned any thought of writing, at least until after the "Gone With the Wind" storm subsided, and it shows no signs of subsiding, for the remarkable public interest in your film is constantly stirring it up again.

So I must ask to be excused but not without regret that I am in no position to help. I am proud that you wish to keep the whole film true to the book and I would help if I could.

I want to take this occasion to correct a wrong impression of my attitude which you may have gained from the newspaper stories published at the time of your announcement of the cast. I was quoted as saying that I thought Miss Leigh could easily learn to talk like a Southerner because she is English. I have forgotten the exact words, but that was the general meaning of the statement credited to me.

I did not say this. I said that Miss Leigh's nationality was not in itself a disqualification, because Southern voices and English voices are frequently similar, and often more similar than the voices of Southerners and those of people in other sections of the United States.[3]

I did not attempt to get the misquotation corrected because I know how futile it is to try to get statements like that changed after they have been published, but I do not wish you to be left under the misapprehension that I think Miss Leigh or any of the others should try to "talk

[3] Apparently Miss Mitchell was correctly quoted in Daniel's story: "Mr. Selznick seems to me to have acted wisely in selecting an English girl for the role, since southern people consider their intonations more closely akin to English speech than to the harsher qualities of natives in different parts of America." Atlanta *Journal,* January 20.

Southern." I have scrupulously avoided interfering in your business by offering suggestions about your film but the misquotation forces me to state what my real attitude is.

Good quality stage voices are not distinctively Northern or Southern or Eastern or Western, and natural voices of that kind will be far more acceptable to the South than any artificial, imitation "Southern" talk. Of course, a voice with distinctively un-Southern qualities, a New England twang or a Mid-Western rolling "r" would be out of place in a Southern film, but I don't believe even that would be as offensive as pseudo-Southern talk in the mouth of a person who did not come by it naturally. If Miss Leigh says "bean" for "been" and uses a broad "a," naturally it would be desirable to attempt to eliminate such distinctive Britishisms, but I doubt the wisdom of attempting to go much further. Eliminating distinctively un-Southern accents or pronunciations of words will be fine, but attempting to teach her to "talk like a Southerner," as I was misquoted as saying, will probably do more harm than good.

This is partly because Southerners have been made sensitive by the bogus Southern talk they have heard on the stage and screen so often. But it is also due to the fact that there is no one "Southern accent." There are at least five different Southern accents in different sections of Georgia alone, and Georgians talk differently from other Southerners. Virginia people have a very distinctive accent and Charlestonians speak differently from everybody else. Louisiana and Mississippi lie side by side but the people in the two states do not talk alike. And so it goes.

So many Southern people have expressed the wish that your actors will talk in good quality natural stage voices, instead of imitation "Southern," leaving the atmosphere to be built up by the Negroes and other actual Southerners who may be in the cast. I believe this is the dominant public sentiment and it conforms directly with my own ideas. I would be so embarrassed if you were given a wrong impression of my attitude by reason of a misquotation in the newspapers.

You were kind enough to offer to send me stills of the cast in costume. Of course I will be very happy to have them and thank you so much for offering to send them. . . .

Miss Vivien Leigh   Atlanta, Georgia
Selznick International Pictures   January 30, 1939
Culver City, California

My dear Miss Leigh:

I realize that my long delay in acknowledging your telegram[1] must seem discourteous to you. But you yourself are the cause of the delay! Ever since January 13th, when the announcement came that you are to play Scarlett, you have been such an active subject of discussion I have had no time to write. Here in Atlanta, where Scarlett was supposed to have lived, interest in her and in you is very high. The newspapers have been full of stories about you and they telephoned me every five minutes, it seemed. Friends, relatives and strangers also telephoned to ask me questions, most of which I could not answer, and every time I went to town to shop I could never do any shopping because people stopped me on every corner to talk about you and to say how pleased they are that the film is at last getting under way.

I have read that some people have protested your selection because they believe that an American girl, and not an English girl, should portray Scarlett. You will be pleased to know that I have encountered none of this sentiment in Atlanta and very few letters of protest have come to me from other places. Most of the letters I receive are favorable, and the people who stop me on the streets to talk about you seem very pleased with your selection and charmed by your appearance in your photographs.

Your telegram to me, which was printed in one of the Atlanta newspapers, pleased everyone so much. I hope you do not mind the fact that it *was* printed. I will tell you how that came about. I am a former newspaper reporter and when Mr. Selznick sent me an enormously long telegram announcing that you had been selected, I knew my friends on the paper would want to see it and I carried it to them myself. While this story was being set up in type my husband arrived with your wire. He called across the city room to me that he had a wire from you, and the editor who was putting the story into the paper simply snatched it from him and rushed to the composing room with it. *I* did not get to see it till two hours later.

Thank you again for your wire and for the sentiments you expressed in it. Please know that my sincere good wishes go to you. While I have

[1] Miss Leigh telegraphed January 13: DEAR MRS MARSH: IF I CAN BUT FEEL THAT YOU ARE WITH ME ON THIS, THE MOST IMPORTANT AND TRYING TASK OF MY LIFE, I PLEDGE WITH ALL MY HEART I SHALL TRY TO MAKE SCARLETT O'HARA LIVE AS YOU DESCRIBED HER IN YOUR BRILLIANT BOOK. WARMEST REGARDS. Atlanta *Constitution*, January 14.

nothing to do with the production of the film of my book, I cannot help feeling a thoroughly normal pleasure that the role of Scarlett has fallen into the hands of a girl whose photographs show her to be so charming.

Mr. Leslie Howard   Atlanta, Georgia
Selznick International Pictures   January 30, 1939
Culver City, California

My dear Mr. Howard:

Thank you so very much for the wire[1] you sent me on January 13th when Mr. Selznick announced your selection for the part of Ashley Wilkes. Your telegram pleased not only me but thousands of others (if I may judge by the comments I have heard), for it appeared in our morning paper the day after the announcement.

I have little privacy these days and, whether I like it or not, almost everything that happens to me becomes public property—as your telegram did. I feebly told the newspaper editor that yours was a personal wire, but little good that did! Now I am not sorry that it was published for everyone thought it amusing and charming. I suppose you know that from the beginning you have been the choice of the people of this section for the part of Ashley. Here in the South a sigh of relief went up when the announcement about you was made.

I have enjoyed your work in many other roles and I look forward with intense interest to the time when I can see you as Ashley Wilkes. My very best wishes to you.

Miss Olivia de Havilland   Atlanta, Georgia
Selznick International Pictures   January 30, 1939
Culver City, California

My dear Miss de Havilland:

Certainly, it was not my intention to wait two weeks to thank you for your charming wire.[1] I was so pleased with it that I intended to acknowl-

---

[1] Howard wired: DEAR MRS MARSH: I AM NOT AT ALL ENVIOUS OF RHETT BECAUSE THANKS TO YOU, IT WAS MELANIE, MA'AM, THAT I WANTED. BUT SERIOUSLY, I FEEL IT A GREAT HONOR TO HAVE BEEN SELECTED TO ENACT ONE OF THE ROLES OF YOUR BOOK, THE TITLE OF WHICH ESCAPES ME AT THE MOMENT. Atlanta *Constitution*, January 14.

---

[1] Miss De Havilland wired: DEAR MRS MARSH: THE NEWS THAT I AM TO PLAY MELANIE MEANS A LONG CHERISHED DREAM REALIZED. NOW I HOPE FOR ONE THING MORE IMPORTANT, THAT IS TO PLAY THE ROLE TO YOUR SATISFACTION. Atlanta *Constitution*, January 14.

edge it immediately. However, the sudden upsurge of public interest in "Gone With the Wind," as a result of the announcement of the cast, has kept me busy night and day. I realize that interest in the forthcoming film is national, but here in Georgia where the scenes are laid, practically everyone takes a personal interest in each new development, and such a flood of letters and telephone calls came in, I have not had a moment of my own.

Your wire to me, which was printed in our morning paper the day after the announcement, delighted everyone—as it did me. The letters I have received and personal comments I have heard indicate that your selection for the part of Melanie has met with general approval. It will interest you to know that the neighborhood theatres in Atlanta are re-running your picture "Captain Blood"[2] to full houses.

I am sending my sincere good wishes to you. I know better than anyone else how difficult a part Melanie's will be. She is one of my favorite characters in the book and I am looking forward to the day when I will see you portray her on the screen.

Miss Katharine Brown   Atlanta, Georgia
New York, New York   January 31, 1939

Dear Katharine:

...The excitement about Vivien Leigh is subsiding, which is a blessing. I do not believe the Selznick company need worry about the picture being boycotted. At least, not here in the South. I believe even those who protested about Miss Leigh will attend so that they will not feel left out when the matter is discussed. After all, if they do not see the picture how will they be in a position to criticize it? ...

I am enclosing a clipping from this morning's paper about Mr. Whitney. You will note that he was questioned about the possibility of the world premiere of GWTW being held here in Atlanta. In the past two months, Atlanta has been in quite a stew about this. It all started, so far as I can tell, from a newspaper story out of Washington[1] which stated flatfootedly, but without quoting any authority, that the premiere would be held here. ...

Organizations and individuals may write you about premiere matters, because I intend to push them all off on you, just as I have done with the would-be Scarletts. But don't believe it if any of them tell you that I

---

[2] A 1936 film release by First National Productions and the Vitaphone Corporation; based on the novel of the same title by Rafael Sabatini (New York, 1925).

[1] The Associated Press carried a story on December 26, 1938, stating that the premiere would be in Atlanta. Atlanta *Journal*, December 26, 1938.

have endorsed or recommended their plans. And don't let any of them give you the impression that I am urging, promoting or sponsoring the idea of having the premiere staged here.

I have told everybody simply that "I know nothing about it and I have nothing to do with it," but often people think I am not telling the truth about matters like this (they just can't believe I know as little about the movie as I do), and probably I will be credited with having said a lot of things that never entered my mind.

I really dread the months ahead until the picture has actually been produced, for literally hundreds of people have already come down on John and me for seats at the premiere. Some of them want passes but the great majority want our promise that they will get seats, that they won't be crowded out. With interest already so high, this coming year may be even harder on us than 1936 was. I think you know that attending any premiere would be an ordeal for me, so don't believe any stories you may hear that I am the one who is promoting the idea of holding the premiere in Atlanta.

Mr. and Mrs. Clifford Dowdey   Atlanta, Georgia
Tucson, Arizona   February 9, 1939

Dear Helen and Clifford:

We were glad to have the letter from Tucson for we had been wondering where you were. So it rained when you arrived, did it? Take my advice and don't let any Indian tribe adopt you two, or you'll find yourselves known as "Rain In the Face" and "Weeping Skies." Why don't you two hire out as rain makers? I hear there's a great future in that business.

If the deadline is March 1st, I suppose you, Clifford, are now in the death throes. What a relief it will be to have "Gamble's Hundred" out of the house. I recall that "Gone With the Wind" assumed all the attributes of a corpse too long unburied right before my deadline. You both must be fagged and I hope you take a vacation as soon as the manuscript has been popped into the mail. Of course I'm a fine one to give such motherly advice because I didn't take such a vacation, and I have regretted it for three years. I was so tired I was seeing double and I was expecting to go away for a rest and then the Book-of-the-Month Club publicity broke and the mail jumped and I couldn't get loose. It was two years before I had the opportunity to regain the weight I lost and to get a three weeks' vacation. Why don't you two take a few weeks off and MEET CUTE PEOPLE? Or shoot skis or trap dingoes or wombats? I hear you go after them with a lighted candle and a needle and a haystack, and they are very tasty with marshmallows.

Seriously, Clifford, I hope you take some time off to let the well fill up.

I've been sick abed with a cold for some time and with complete weariness. We had thought our troubles over until the moving picture was released next year, and we never thought that the mere announcement of the cast would cause such a to-do. For three weeks life was a hell on earth, with the newspapers and the public and the pros and cons of Vivien Leigh. I neither endorsed nor objected to the pretty lady. Even had I wished to do so, it would have been impossible as I had never seen her on the screen. My first view of her was a none too good newspaper picture shown me at the time of the announcement. I noticed, however, that my noncommittal statements got me nowhere, as the headlines announced blandly, "Author OK's Vivien."

With the picture actually going into production, there was a last maddened rush of people who wished to play bit parts and extras and who were determined that I could—and should—secure such work for them. It is quieting now and we are beginning to crawl from under and try to take care of the business matters which accumulated during the avalanche. . . .

Now, write and tell me that the book is done and that it is the sorriest piece of work you ever did and you are utterly ashamed of it and wonder what publishers are thinking about to publish it. That will be the best of signs. And write me, too, that you are getting a rest and a vacation.

Miss Susan Myrick   Atlanta, Georgia
Santa Monica, California   February 10, 1939

Dear Sue:

Laughs have been few and far between recently, as I have been laid up with a cold and a persistent fever. But your letter had a laugh in every line. I must admit some of my laughter was on the wry side—especially when you described Twelve Oaks. I had feared, of course, that it would end up looking like the Grand Central Station, and your description confirms my worst apprehensions. I did not know whether to laugh or to throw up at the *two* staircases. Probably the Twelve Oaks hall will be worse than the one in "So Red the Rose." People here in Atlanta got up and left the theatre in herds when that hall was shown. And I will never forget the pungent remarks about the level of Hollywood brains. God help me when the reporters get me after I've seen the picture. I will have to tell the truth, and if Tara has columns and Twelve Oaks is such an elegant affair I will have to say that nothing like that was ever seen in Clayton County, or, for that matter, on land or sea. This would be somewhat embarrassing to me and perhaps to the Selznick company, but I am not going on record as telling a lie just to be polite. When I think of the healthy, hardy, country and somewhat crude civilization I depicted and then of the elegance that is to be presented, I cannot help yelping with laughter.

I wish you'd write something about Scott Fitzgerald when you get the time. If anyone had told me ten or more years ago that he would be working on a book of mine I would have been stricken speechless with pellagra or hardening of the arteries or something.[1] I dearly loved his books and still do and re-read them ever so often. "This Side of Paradise"[2] is the most perfect crystallization of an era in all American fiction. It makes me feel sad when I think how utterly past that era is now. I'm sure Mother and I picked him up in our car one day when he was at Camp Gordon during the war. The streetcar tracks had not been laid that far at that time and we usually hauled twelve soldiers to town every time we went out to see Stephens. After he got famous and I saw his picture I remembered him.[3]

Sue, it does sound incredible that the script is not yet finished. I have an idea (and correct me if I'm wrong) that they are using Sidney Howard's script for the first part of the movie—and it followed (so I was told by Mr. Howard) the book closely. I imagine they are following the book up to the end of the War with few changes, but telescoping the Reconstruction period as much as possible.

[1] In a memo to Daniel T. O'Shea, vice president of Selznick International Pictures, David O. Selznick wrote January 6: "Fitzgerald starts with us today, 1/6/39, at $1250 week on loan from MGM. He will work on GWTW dialogue." Rudy Behlmer states in a note to this memo: "Author F. Scott Fitzgerald worked on a few scenes, contributing criticisms, suggestions, and some revised dialogue until on or about January 24, 1939. Virtually none of his material appeared in the final version of the script." Selznick, p. 184. Gavin Lambert credits him with a larger contribution: "Instructed . . . to use only Margaret Mitchell's dialogue, Fitzgerald seems to have been the first to caution Selznick that there was already too much of it. He reminded him that in movies it's dull and false for one character to describe another," and recommended that long speeches—such as Ashley's account to Scarlett of the desperate state of the Confederate army—should be reduced to a minimum, because the audience had already been shown what he was talking about. Fitzgerald would indicate, too, how an image or the expression on an actor's face would replace dialogue. . . . Fitzgerald also discovered, rather to his surprise, that Margaret Mitchell's original dialogue was usually better than other writers' reworking of it." GWTW, The Making of Gone With the Wind (Boston, Toronto, 1973), pp. 71–72.
[2] Francis Scott Fitzgerald, This Side of Paradise (New York, 1920).
[3] Fitzgerald, a lieutenant in the Forty-fifth Infantry, was stationed at Camp Gordon, near Atlanta, from mid-April to mid-June 1918. Andrew Turnbull, Scott Fitzgerald (New York, 1962), p. 82.

God forbid that Scarlett's Reconstruction house should be a poem of good taste. That would throw out of balance the whole characterization of the woman. Hurrah for George[4] and Mr. Platt[5] for standing up for a bad-taste house. Hobe Erwin had some swell ideas on that house and we had a hot correspondence on wallpaper and many other details, including a perfectly ghastly gas lamp fixture which stood at the bottom of the stairs (my own idea), a large brass nymph, discreetly draped and bearing aloft the gas fixture. . . .

Dearie, your Georgian articles[6] are fine. Not long ago my barber, who does not know I know you, talked about them during an entire hair-setting. Everybody enjoys them so much.

Later—

Wilbur Kurtz, junior, just phoned and told Margaret Baugh that his father had wired him that SIP was keeping him on for another ten weeks. For a number of reasons besides my personal liking for the Kurtzes, this news cheered me. On the chance you are interested, I will give you the reasons.

You are clear across the continent and living a very sequestered life, so I know it is hard for you to understand what turmoil and excitement has been going on in the South (and in the North, too) since the Vivien Leigh announcement. I should add that the Selznick company is not out of the woods yet on the matter of giving two leading parts to foreigners after all their talk about getting Southerners. My clipping service keeps me in touch with public reactions and I imagine I know more about them than even Selznick's publicity department. A number of people from out of this section smiled in a superior manner at some statements I made in "Gone With the Wind" to the effect that Southerners were violent people, still untamed, though very polite. They have changed very little, and there has been plenty of violence recently. There I was caught between the lines. I had nothing to do with the picture and little interest either, except that I be let alone, but I caught the barrages from both sides. The final statement I gave out to the papers seemed to have a very quieting effect; the Associated Press carried it all over the country. I said that Miss Susan Myrick, well known newspaper woman of Macon et cetera, and Mr. and Mrs. W. G. Kurtz of Atlanta, well known et cetera, have been taken to Hollywood for the express purpose of passing on the

[4] George Cukor.
[5] Joseph B. Platt, designer of interiors for *GWTW*.
[6] Miss Myrick wrote a series of more than two dozen articles about the filming of *GWTW* which appeared in the Atlanta *Georgian* beginning January 16. A longer series, "Straight from Hollywood," appeared in the Macon *Telegraph* January 12 through July 13.

accuracy and authenticity of Southern backgrounds; I said that your presence in Hollywood, at Mr. Selznick's invitation, was the surest guarantee of his good faith and his desire to do right by our much maligned Southland. People have been chewing that over and it tastes very well. With no disrespect meant to Mr. Selznick or Mr. Cukor, the fact remains that all that stands between them and a violent Southern revolt is you and the Kurtzes in Hollywood and, I may add, my own noncommittal but pleasant attitude. If two weeks after such a statement appeared in every small town paper in the South the Kurtzes came home, I know exactly what would happen. Every paper would rise up editorially and denounce Mr. Selznick, saying that all he wanted was the use of your name and the Kurtzes' name for publicity and when he had gotten that publicity he let you out. They would point out that this was perfect evidence that Mr. Selznick had no desire to do a true Southern epic but intended to produce another Hollywood Southern horror full of boners, bulls, inaccuracies and material offensive to the South. Next people would begin writing letters to the newspapers, then boycott would raise its head months before the picture was half shot. I'd be between the lines again, pulled hither and thither by papers and public who would want to know just what I thought about the whole affair. There would be no other thing for me to say except that I had no idea why you three were let out when the picture had hardly begun. The headlines above such an innocuous statement would read "Author Denounces Selznick for Double Dealing." This may sound fantastic but it fits in with my past experience. I made the most non-committal statement about Vivien Leigh but hundreds of papers head lined it "Author Okays Leigh" and "Author Satisfied with Leigh." Some were even stronger.

You know me well enough to know that I am not an alarmist nor do I borrow trouble. But I have always been one to take "the long view." Moreover, for nearly three years I've had a box seat with an excellent view of the reactions of the public mind especially the Southern mind. It sometimes seems to me that "Gone With the Wind" is not my book any longer; it is something about which the citizens are sensitive and sore at real and fancied slights and discriminations and are ready to fight at the drop of a hairpin. With public emotions barely cooled about Vivien Leigh, I think it would have been complete folly if Mr. Selznick had let Wilbur and Annie Laurie come home. Mr. S. is not a Southerner, of course, and knows practically nothing of our psychology and he would have, unwittingly, let himself in for more trouble and wrangling than he or his publicity department could ever handle.

I feel certain that if he had let the Kurtzes out and a storm broke over him, he or Katharine would have been on the phone in no time asking me to help them or give them advice. And, of course, there would have been no help to give and no advice either.

After more than two years of having my life upset by this movie, I shudder to think what I would have gone through with if the embattled South had gotten sore about the Kurtzes being let out. I am so desperately tired of standing in the middle ground between the movie folks and the public and I do not know if I could have gone through with another barrage so close to the Vivien Leigh barrage.

Annie Laurie wrote that you had met Katharine Marsh Bowden. I hope you get to see the family as they are swell people. Annie Laurie also included casually a bit of information that turned my few remaining hairs white. She spoke of the bazaar scene with Scarlett and Rhett dancing together, and mentioned that Scarlett had on a bonnet and veil. In the name of God, what was she doing with a hat on at an evening party where everybody else was bareheaded and wearing low-cut gowns? My temperature jumped seven points at the news. I cannot imagine even Scarlett showing such poor taste. I foresee that I will get at least one good belly laugh out of this picture, and it will be during this scene.

Miss Marcella Rabwin   Atlanta, Georgia
Assistant to Mr. Selznick   February 15, 1939
Culver City, California

My dear Miss Rabwin:

The seven pictures arrived yesterday afternoon. I thank you for sending them and I thank Mr. Selznick for his courtesy in wanting me to see them. A number of the cast have been merely names to me and, of course, I was curious to see what they looked like. I had never seen Barbara O'Neil, Ann Rutherford, Fred Crane, George Besselo or any of the Negro characters except Hattie McDaniel. Of course the pictures interested me very much. There is one thing I find expecially touching—perhaps that's because I am the author—Carreen looks so much her mother's child, in expression and gesture and dependence. I do not know how such things are managed in the moving pictures, but this seems beautifully subtle to me.

You wrote that these pictures were for my private use and not for publication and you requested that I keep them from "the prying eyes of the news hawks." Of course I will do this, and any other pictures or communications which may come to me from you or Mr. Selznick will be held equally confidential. I write you this so that you will not think

I betrayed your confidence and gave to the newspapers the pictures which appeared yesterday and which I am enclosing. They are from our morning paper.[1] One of our afternoon papers[2] carried an entire page of stills. They were different from the morning paper, with the exception of the one of the O'Hara family. I would send you these but I do not have an extra copy of the afternoon paper. I do not know where the papers got the pictures, but they did not come from me.

I will be so happy to have any other photographs you wish to send me in the future. With thanks and best wishes to you and Mr. Selznick.

Mr. Jere Moore   Atlanta, Georgia
Union-Recorder   February 16, 1939
Milledgeville, Georgia

Dear Jere:

In yesterday's Constitution I read the story about the replica of "Tara" that would house the Georgia exhibits at the World's Fair. To say that I was pleased, flattered and excited is putting it mildly. I can't thank you and the other members of the World's Fair Commission enough for this wonderful compliment. As I think I told you at one of the Press Institutes, the kindness and the enthusiasm of Georgia folks has meant more to me than anything that has happened to me since "Gone With the Wind" came out.

I had thought of waiting to talk to you personally at Athens at the Institute about a matter in connection with this, but something might prevent us from coming to Athens. So, I will sketch my idea now and hope that I do see you in Athens where I can amplify it.

Of course, I have no notion what kind of "Tara" the Commission intends to build. I have no way of knowing, but, Jere, I implore you if they wish to put up a Southern Colonial house of the Greek revival type, such as the beautiful ones in Milledgeville, please use your influence to prevent it. Or if they insist on building that type of house, please don't let them call it "Tara."

It is not that I do not think your Milledgeville houses are beautiful. To me they are the most beautiful in all the world—nothing can ever compare with them. But they are not North Georgia houses, and they are not the kind of houses "Tara" was.

I described it as a typical Clayton County house, "ugly and sprawling"

[1] The Atlanta *Constitution*.
[2] The Atlanta *Georgian*.

but comfortable looking. This section of Georgia was so much newer than Middle Georgia and it was cruder, architecturally speaking. I wrote about hardy, hearty *country* people, whose civilization was only a few years away from the Indians.

Maybe I can give you some idea of what "Tara" looked like by saying it was more or less of the same general type as Alex Stephens's Liberty Hall, with a dash of Crawford Long's birthplace thrown in, except that it was not as attractive as those houses are.[1] Gerald's house was far from being the best looking one in "the County," for he was a rough, bluff man and he built the house according to his own ideas, without the help of architects. "Tara" was very definitely not a white-columned mansion.

I am mortally afraid the movies will depict it as a combination of the Grand Central Station, the old Capitol at Milledgeville[2] and the Natchez houses of "So Red the Rose." I fear they will have columns not only on the front of "Tara" but on the sides and back as well, and probably on the smokehouse too. But I can't do anything about that, as I have no connection with the picture. I do hope, however, that the "Tara" that goes to the World's Fair will be a North Georgia house in keeping with its times and not a Middle Georgia or Coast Georgia house. . . .

Col. Telamon Cuyler
Wayside, Georgia

Atlanta, Georgia
February 17, 1939

My dear Colonel Cuyler:

This is just for your confidential ear. I was greatly distressed by the story the Constitution ran at the time the pictures of the film were published. The headline was completely at variance with the story, for the headline read "Margaret Mitchell Puts Okay on First Screen Stills of Novel." A careful reading of the story will show that I put no okay on anything. But who reads carefully? Doubtless you know of my long struggle to keep from either endorsing or criticizing anything about this film. I have felt that either course would be presumptuous on my part, as I had nothing to do with the picture. Yet, I am continually misquoted, and in the future I intend to say "No comment."

Far from "okaying" the pictures, I cried "Godlmighty" in horror before I caught myself. My eye had lighted on Scarlett's widow's bonnet and long veil in the midst of the decollete gowns of the Atlanta belles. I

---

[1] Liberty Hall is at Crawfordville, Ga. Dr. Long's birthplace is at Danielsville, Ga.
[2] The Old Capitol at Milledgeville is not in the Greek revival style of architecture. Miss Mitchell was doubtless thinking of the Governor's Mansion there. It is a very handsome example of Greek revival architecture.

cannot imagine even Scarlett having such bad taste as to wear a hat at
an evening party, and my heart sank at the sight of it. Probably the reporter mistook my exclamation for one of pleasure. A quick view of the
uniforms showed not a one that looked as if it had seen active service.
Nor was there a wounded man to be found even with a microscope.
The Armory looked vaguely like Versailles and not like the rough room
in which drills were held.[1] However, it was not my place to remark on
these things as the Constitution had only requested that I identify the
chapters from which the scenes were taken. Should I be asked at some
later date if these scenes were correct in detail, I will be in an embarrassing position for I will have to tell the truth. I have an idea that Mr. Kurtz
and Susan were overridden on these points. After all, they can only
suggest and can do nothing if their suggestions are not followed....

My cold is about over, thank you, and I expect to be out again tomorrow. I am anxious to see Miss Blair and hear the plans for buying the
old Inman house across the street from the Biltmore for a permanent
home for the Historical Society.

<table>
<tr><td>Mr. Stark Young</td><td>Atlanta, Georgia</td></tr>
<tr><td>Austin, Texas</td><td>February 28, 1939</td></tr>
</table>

My dear Stark:

You were right, I found the Lunts delightful.[1] I had only two regrets
about the whole affair—that I could not take them to dinner or cocktails
and see more of them and that I was just up from influenza and looked
like a hant. A condemned woman on her way to the chair never possessed
shakier knees than I possessed that afternoon, but I was determined to
meet them and I was long past the infectious stage, so I somehow managed to. I noticed as I went into their dressing rooms that quite a crowd
of young students—autograph hunters, admirers and the stage struck—
were waiting for a glimpse of the Lunts. They were all so excited at the
prospect that they were white as hants, too, and their hands and voices
shaking, so perhaps my condition was not conspicuous!

---

[1] These complaints are echoed in Selznick's memorandum of March 11 to Victor
Fleming and others: "I feel that our sets always look exactly what they are—sets that
have been put up hours before, instead of seeming in their aging and in their dressing to be rooms that have existed for some time and that have been lived in. The
same is true of the costumes. They always look exactly what they are—fresh out of
the Costume Department, instead of looking like clothes that have been worn."
Selznick, p. 197.

---

[1] Alfred Lunt and Lynn Fontanne appeared at Atlanta's Erlanger Theatre in
Robert E. Sherwood's *Idiot's Delight* on the evening of February 23 and in matinee
and evening performances of Jean Giraudoux's *Amphitryon 38* on February 24.

Mr. Lunt came into Miss Fontanne's room to talk and smoke. He was still in his last act costume, silver wig and beard and metallic eyebrows and lids. He was as impressively Jovian offstage as on and, still being under the spell of the play, I felt very much a mere mortal until he pushed a cigarette through that classic beard. I am sure they would laugh if they knew that I liked them because they seemed so simple. Perhaps "simplicity" is not the word I'm hunting for, but it will have to do. It is a quality I've found very rarely except in people who really amounted to something or in country folks living in the back of beyond. Thank you for making it possible for me to have the pleasure of knowing them. I was sorry John could not meet them. He had gone to the University of Georgia for the annual editors' convention. We have been going every year for fifteen years, but this time I felt too weak to manage the trip. Now I'm glad I did not go, for I would have missed the Lunts.

I'm buying "The Sea Gull" today and I look forward to reading it next week-end. This is a tiresome kind of life when I must plan time to read! I know I'll enjoy it and I am looking forward to your introduction.[2]

Miss Katharine Brown   Atlanta, Georgia
New York, New York   February 28, 1939

My dear Katharine:

You have probably received—or will receive shortly—a letter from Medora Field Perkerson, assistant editor of the Magazine Section of the Atlanta Journal. You met her during your stay in Atlanta but I do not know if you remember her, as you met a great many people in a short space of time. . . .

Medora is the newly elected president of the Atlanta Women's Press Club. She is an old friend of mine and we worked together on the Magazine Section for a number of years. I promised her and the other members of the Press Club that I would write to you about the letter she is sending so you would not think it another one of those idiotic requests with which you must have been pestered during the last two years.

Medora is writing you about the premiere of "Gone With the Wind." The ladies of the press hope it will be held here in Atlanta. When I told them that any premiere was a long way off and that there was every probability it would not be held here, they replied that the first showing of the film in Atlanta would be a premiere for Atlanta whether it was a world premiere or not, and they cared little about whether it was actually

[2] Young translated and wrote the introduction for an edition of Anton Chekhov's *The Sea Gull* (New York, London, 1939).

the first screen showing. What the ladies want to do is to give me a party—dinner, buffet supper or cocktails—before the show begins.

I have been a member of the Press Club since it was organized. I am the only member not in active newspaper work and I am proud of my membership. When I arrived at the last meeting the girls told me they had already begun making arrangements for the party, with me as honor guest. They are my good friends and the Club is one of the few organizations to which I belong, so I accepted.

Medora's letter to you is for the purpose of inviting you, Mr. Selznick and any others who may come to Atlanta for the premiere to be the guests of the Club at the party before the performance. She was planning to write to Mr. Selznick but I suggested that the letter go to you instead. With George Cukor just off the set and with Mr. Fleming just coming on,[1] I knew that Mr. Selznick would be up to his ears.

Please consider the matter entirely on its merits. I believe you and the others will enjoy this party but I know what a problem you will have deciding among the numerous invitations you will receive, and I am not urging you to accept this one on my account. My main purpose in writing is to let you know that Medora's letter is bona fide. (I have turned down so many hundreds of invitations, as you know, and I thought you might question her statement that I would be honor guest at the party.) I also wanted you to know that the party will be purely social, non-commercial and a by-invitation-only affair—a fairly large one probably but not a

---

[1] Cukor was replaced as director of *GWTW* in mid-February by Victor Fleming. A statement issued by Selznick and Cukor February 13 declared: "As a result of a series of disagreements between us over many of the individual scenes of *Gone With the Wind*, we have mutually decided that the only solution is for a new director to be selected at as early a date as is practicable." Selznick, p. 191. On the next day Fleming was taken off his finishing work on "The Wizard of Oz" and signed to direct *GWTW*. Shooting was resumed March 1. Selznick, p. 192.

In a long letter of February 14 Miss Myrick wrote unhappily of Cukor's departure. "It is really and actually true," she said. "George finally told me all about it. When there was a lull and I had a chance I said to him I was upset over what I had heard and he said come and talk to him. So, we sat down and he talked. . . . He hated it very much he said but he could not do otherwise. In effect he said he is an honest craftsman and he cannot do a job unless he knows it is a good job and he feels the present job is not right. For days, he told me, he has looked at the rushes and felt he was failing. He knew he was a good director and knew the actors were good ones: yet the thing did not click as it should. Gradually he became more and more convinced that the script was the trouble. . . .

"So George just told David he would not work any longer if the script was not better and he wanted the Howard script back. David told George he was [a] director —not an author and he (David) was the producer and the judge of what is a good script (or words to that effect) and George said he was a director and a dam good one and he would not let his name go out over a lousy picture and if they did not go back to the Howard script (he was willing to have them cut it down shorter) he, George was through.

"And bull-headed David said 'OK get out!' "

mob. I will be happy if you and the other Selznick folks can come but you are the ones to decide about that and I will not attempt to influence you. . . .

Miss Annetta I. Clark
Secretary of the Board of Trustees
Smith College
Northampton, Massachusetts

Atlanta, Georgia
March 4, 1939

My dear Miss Clark:

Your letter of February 25th, bearing the exciting news that Smith College wishes to bestow on me an honorary degree of Master of Arts, made me very happy. I feel so highly honored and I have an especial feeling of pride that it is my alma mater which plans to do this lovely thing for me. Of course, I accept with the greatest pleasure and I will be in Northampton on June 12th to receive the degree.

I have never received a degree, honorary or otherwise, and it will be a new experience to me, so I will be grateful if you will tell me what is expected of me and where and when I must present myself. Don't hesitate to include details that even a novice might be expected to know. I know literally nothing about such matters and any information you care to give me will be very helpful.

I would like to make another request of you if I may. Since my book was published, several individuals and organizations have invited me to make speeches at Smith College functions. When the news gets around that I am coming to Northampton to receive the degree, these same organizations or others may, perhaps, wish me to appear on their programs. If you should hear of any such discussions on the campus or in the town, you could do me a great favor by discouraging them as much as you can. I have never been a speechmaker, I have made no speeches at all since July, 1936, and I do not accept invitations even to "say a few words." So, if you should hear of any plans to invite me to talk, please let it be known that I do not make any speeches at all. This would save me a great deal of embarrassment.

I hope you will give my sincere thanks to the Board of Trustees of Smith College for their kindness and their generosity to me.

Mr. David O. Selznick   Atlanta, Georgia
Culver City, California   March 13, 1939

My dear Mr. Selznick:

I have just received a clipping of a UP story, published in the New York Telegraph on February 28th, about a letter Selznick International wrote to Congressman Hugh Peterson, who had objected to the choice of Vivien Leigh for Scarlett. Here follows a portion of the story:

> "The film company, in a three-page, single-spaced letter, attempted to set him right on the matter. It said Margaret Mitchell, author of 'Gone With the Wind,' had approved Miss Leigh in the following elegant manner:
>
> " 'She looks like she has plenty of spirit and fire, not at all like a languid Hollywood girl.' "

When the selection of Miss Leigh was announced, I neither "approved" nor disapproved her, and I have not done either since then. On the night of your announcement, when the newspaper reporters asked me my opinion of Miss Leigh, I told them I knew nothing about her. They then showed me a photograph of her, the first one I had ever seen, and I remarked, in effect, that she appeared to be a young woman of spirit and fire, with a very decided Irish look in her eyes.

That politely noncommittal comment is the only statement I have ever made about Miss Leigh. Certainly no one could construe it as an "approval." However, hundreds of newspaper items were published the following several days stating that I had "put my ok" on Miss Leigh or otherwise approved her. It was very embarrassing to me to find myself in this false position, but I did not write you about it, as I was reluctant to believe your Publicity Department was responsible for this distortion of my meaning. I was willing to believe that it was a product of the carelessness in language that sometimes gets into newspaper stories.

The item of February 28th, however, seems definitely to place responsibility on someone in your organization for circulating the false statement that I have "approved Miss Leigh." Again, the newspaper writer, rather than your organization, may have been responsible for this language, but the same item (as published in some other papers) stated that Mrs. Lamar, president general of the United Daughters of the Confederacy, had also "approved Miss Leigh's selection."[1] With these two

---

[1] Mrs. Lamar's approval was reported in the Atlanta *Constitution* January 23: "I think Miss Leigh is an excellent solution of the problem, in which all the country has been keenly interested." Miss Mitchell wrote to Katharine Brown concerning this

misstatements in the same article, I am forced to believe that the Selznick organization must have been at least partly at fault. I know what Mrs. Lamar said and it could not be construed as an "approval," any more than my comment was. Neither of us is the kind of person who would approve any actress for the difficult role of Scarlett without knowing much more about her than we know about Miss Leigh. Both of us might make polite comments about an actress whom *you* had selected but we would naturally feel resentful if our politeness was abused and our comments twisted into something we did not say.

I am writing to ask you to caution your Publicity Department and the rest of your organization (including MGM) against the misuse of my name in connection with Miss Leigh or any other matter involved in the filming of "Gone With the Wind."

I am confident you understand what my position is, and I know Katharine Brown does, but if the rest of your organization (and MGM) does not cooperate, I will be forced to do something that will be embarrassing to all of us. If publicity is put out or statements circulated saying or even hinting that I am responsible for your cast, your script or any part of the film (other than my book), I will be forced to go into the newspapers or on the radio and tell what the true situation is. I would regret to do that very much. It would lead the public to believe that you and I are on bad terms and perhaps create the impression that I disapprove of everything you have done. But unless you can control your publicity and prevent it from misrepresenting my position, I will have no choice but to tell the public myself what my position really is.

In issuing instructions to your organization, it ought not to be difficult to make clear what my position is. It is simply that I wrote the book, *and that is all.* I am responsible for my book but I am not responsible for the motion picture. My connection with the motion picture ended on July 30, 1936, when I signed the contract selling you [the] film rights. I sold them to you lock, stock and barrel and from that day forward they have been yours, to do with as you please.

You have done with them as you pleased, according to your own judgment and without interference from me. That is entirely proper, for you are the owner and producer. I am not. You are risking your money and reputation on the film. I am not. I am the author and that is all

---

"approval" on January 31, noting Mrs. Lamar's remark "that it was well that an English woman and not an American was to play 'so thoroughly objectionable' a character as Scarlett is scarcely complimentary." In response to an editorial concerning the selection of Vivien Leigh in the Boston *Herald* of January 16, Mrs. Lamar wrote the editor of the *Herald* on January 21: "I have not been able to visualize any known American actress for portrayal of the part assigned to Miss Leigh. The character of Scarlett is interesting and thoroughly objectionable throughout. I do not consider her in any way whatever typical of Southern girls of the 60's."

and I have stubbornly stayed in my position as author and stayed out of your business as producer.

What I am asking is that your publicity leave me in my position as author and not attempt to drag me into the position of co-producer. I do not intend to have my name used to back up your decisions, when I have had nothing to do with the making of the decisions. I have carefully remained on the sidelines. I have repeatedly insisted that you should have a free hand in making the film, without interference from me or anybody else, and I believe this has been an asset to you. At least, I have not added to your troubles by permitting my name to be used by various groups who were trying to force you to make decisions that might have been embarrassing. For all of these reasons, I am entitled to ask that your Publicity Department show me the consideration of not misrepresenting my connection with the film.

Perhaps I may seem to be writing a long and very serious-minded letter about a small thing, the newspaper item of February 28th. It is not a small thing to me, for it involves a question of publicity policy that is a large and important one. During the coming months, as work on the picture progresses, you and MGM will be putting out more and more publicity and it will be to your advantage as well as mine if we have a clear understanding now as to how the publicity will be handled.

Nothing in this letter means that I feel any ill will toward Miss Leigh or you. My purpose is simply to set things straight about a matter of considerable seriousness to me. Ever since the summer of 1936, your film has been a subject of public controversy and, for no good reason at all, I have been caught in the storm center of the controversy. A large part of the public apparently believes that I have complete control over you and everything you do in making the film. This has created a problem for me many times greater than any of my other problems as the author of "Gone With the Wind." If I did have control over the film and you, I would take the situation philosophically and make the best of it. But having no control over any detail of the film and no connection with it of any kind, I cannot permit my life to be made more burdensome by publicity items linking me up with the film more closely than the facts justify.

It may be that your Publicity Department has been encouraged to do this by the friendly attitude I have taken all along toward you and the film. In fighting my own fight against the popular misconception of my connection with the film, I have also fought for you. I have assured thousands of people of my confidence in you, and I have also made friendly comments, when I could sincerely do so, such as I made about Miss Leigh. But if my friendly attitude is taken advantage of and my polite comments are twisted into something very different from what I said, I will be forced to abandon both friendliness and politeness. If I am to be rewarded for my courtesy by being placed in a false position and having my name misused, I will be forced to take steps of my own to make my position perfectly clear to the public.

With best regards to you and best wishes for the success of "Gone With the Wind" in the films.

Mr. Stanley F. Horn   Atlanta, Georgia
Southern Lumberman   March 20, 1939
Nashville, Tennessee

My dear Mr. Horn:

If the experiences of my publishers, The Macmillan Company, and myself will be of any assistance to you in your present trouble with Miss Susan Lawrence Davis,[1] I will be glad to tell you about them. I have a very sincere sympathy for you in your present predicament. Miss Davis's outrageous charges of plagiarism against "Gone With the Wind" have caused and are still causing me a great deal of trouble and annoyance. I hope that you and your publishers will not be subjected to the same bother, but I fear that you will. However, I found something encouraging for you in your description of her letters as "vaguely whining-threatening" and your statement that she had not directly announced her intention to sue. Usually she is more militant. Perhaps her lack of success in her attack on my book may have taken some of the fire out of her.

At the risk of inflicting a long letter on you, I am going to give you a detailed account of my experiences. I had never read Miss Davis's book nor had I ever heard of it prior to the time, late in 1936, when her attorneys made their claim against The Macmillan Company in New York and later filed suit in April, 1937. (*The suit was against my publishers, as owners of the copyright, and not against me.*) As I had not written anything about the Klan which is not common knowledge to every Southerner, I had done no research upon it. After she filed her claim, I went to the trouble of asking the Atlanta Carnegie Library, where I did the majority of my research, if they had ever had a copy of her book. The Reference Department said that it had never been in the Library. Atlanta book stores did not recall ever having had a copy, and I was unable to obtain a copy in Southern second-hand book stores. After great trouble, The Macmillan Company unearthed one in New York. I learned

[1] Concerning Horn's *Invisible Empire: the Story of the Ku Klux Klan, 1866–1871* (Boston, 1939).

subsequently that Miss Davis's book was brought out by some small printing house in 1924 and that this house went out of business shortly afterwards. I was told also that only a few hundred copies of the book had been put on the market, but I cannot vouch for this.

Among her other statements was this one—that she had sent me a copy to review in the Atlanta Journal when I was "book review editor of the Journal." I was never book review editor, and I probably reviewed less than a dozen books in my several years of service with that paper. I went through the files of the Journal from 1924 to 1927 and could find no review of her book.

Her suit against The Macmillan Company demanded $5,000 per infringement. The attorneys said that this could mean $5,000 for each edition of my book or $5,000 on each copy of "Gone With the Wind" that had been sold. On the latter basis she was asking for approximately $6,500,000,000. Even on the basis of editions published at that time the amount was not trifling, about $175,000. In the discussions prior to filing of the suit, her attorneys offered to settle the matter for a paltry $300,000 or some such figure. I believe Miss Davis thought that as I was in the public eye at that time I would shrink from the publicity and from the accusation of theft. She probably believed that my publishers would pay off rather than subject me to this embarrassment. She did not realize that in tackling my publisher, Mr. Brett, and me she was up against people who believe in fighting for their rights. Mr. Brett refused to settle for any amount and I made instant denial of all her charges. I am confident the case could have been settled for much less than she demanded but I am convinced that if any settlement had been made Miss Davis would have broadcast it throughout the nation as an open admission of my guilt.

The charges she brought against me were so absurd that I and my family found them very amusing, even though we realized the seriousness of the situation. Among other things she prepared a "comparison abstract" which contained more than a hundred pages of excerpts from her book and mine written in parallel columns. To show you the type of evidence on which she based her accusation of plagiarism, she said that she had mentioned the Athens (Ala.) Female Academy and that I had mentioned the Fayetteville (Ga.) Female Academy. The inference was that I could not have had knowledge of female academies except from reading her book. I mentioned General Forrest, General Gordon and Father Ryan and so had she. In the matter of Father Ryan she was especially heated, because she implied that no one knew anything about him until she had done research and written him up in her book. Any Southerner who was brought up to recite in childhood Father Ryan's poems and who saw his picture displayed everywhere on the walls of schools and homes would know how foolish this was. I mentioned "Military District No. 3" during Reconstruction, and she implied that this was a direct steal as no one had known anything about "Military District No. 3" until she went to the State Capitol at Montgomery and found the information in documents there. She listed all the pages in my book where I had used the words "taxes," "Freedmen's Bureau" et cetera, and then showed that she had used these same words a certain number of times in her book.

The rest of the document was equally absurd, but I realized the dangerous position I was in. I was so much younger than Miss Davis and had had great good fortune with my book; she was an elderly woman who had had no luck at all with hers. Public opinion is a strange thing and so are the reactions of juries. I set out to compile not one but four references to back up each historical item in my book, drawing these references from books published prior to 1924 when her book appeared. I wanted to show that all the historical facts I used were matters of public record long before her book was published. You can, perhaps, imagine what a burden this was. Fortunately, before I completed the job, I was notified by Mr. Walbridge Taft, attorney for The Macmillan Company, that he was planning to use different tactics. While the suit was not against me, it was my reputation for integrity that was involved and I was anxious to help in any way possible. I would have made the compilation if it had been necessary but was saved part of this job.

Mr. Taft filed a demurrer and motion to dismiss, on the grounds that Miss Davis had no "cause of action," and this was granted by Judge Goddard[2] of the United States District Court, Southern District of New York. The two books themselves were about the only evidence submitted and the judge was asked to base his decision on his own comparison of them. The judgment was handed down July 30, 1937, and a decree was issued on November 4, 1937 assessing the court costs against Miss Davis and ordering her to pay $2,000 attorneys' fees. The following quotations from the judgment may be of interest to you:

"Such similarities as appear are in the historical facts and events referred to and in the use of some common English words in describing them. . . . The historical facts referred to in the books are matters of history. They are not new or original; they belong to all. The exclusive right of an author is to her or his original manner or expression or art in describing or relating an historical fact. Many books have been written, and in the years to come many more will be, about the Civil War and the Reconstruction Period, and each author is protected by the copyright acts from others copying the author's own narrative or original expression of ideas, but no author has the exclusive right to refer to historical facts. . . . Miss Davis' work is a

[2] Judge Henry Warren Goddard.

history of the Ku Klux Klan and it is reasonable to assume that it was intended for the information of those interested in the subject, and that such information as they gained from it could be used by them."

This decision gave the victory to our side but it was not the end of our troubles with Miss Davis. She did not pay the money the court ordered her to pay and as she did not live in New York where the decision was given, Mr. Taft took steps to have the judgment entered up in the court where she lived, in Washington. Miss Davis then made one of her strangest maneuvers. Through a new attorney, she filed an answer saying she had not authorized the suit in New York and therefore she was not obligated to pay the $2,000 judgment. This gave her about a year's delay and she moved away from Washington. At least, she has been spending most of her time in her former home, Athens, Alabama, for the past several months. The action against her in Washington for collection of the attorneys' fees will probably be taken up by the court in April.

Miss Davis has not yet sued me personally but I understand she has a legal right to do this. Even though the plagiarism accusation has already been decided against her, that case was against my publishers, not me, and I am told she can file a separate suit against me directly. She came to Atlanta last September and talked to several different attorneys about this. After three or four of them had investigated and refused to take the case, she found one who agreed to represent her to the extent of coming around and having a talk with my husband. He told the attorney promptly that we would be glad to have Miss Davis go ahead and sue me and get it over with, that it would be troublesome for us but we were completely confident of the result. We have heard nothing further from him. Of course, I do not intend to settle with her on any basis. That would merely encourage her to make preposterous claims against other people.

While she was in Atlanta Miss Davis told a newspaper reporter here, very frankly, that she wanted to sue me so she could get some money to use in republishing her History of the Klan.[3] (It was originally published wholly or partly at her expense.) Getting out another edition seems to be one of her dominant passions these days, as she seems to think that she would sell a million copies of it, judging by her remarks to the reporter and others while she was here.

If Miss Davis should sue you, Judge Goddard's decision in the Macmillan case ought to be helpful to you. Also if the legal action in Washing-

---

[3] "Plans for republication of the book 'The Authentic History of the Ku Klux Klan' . . . were announced here Wednesday by Susan Lawrence Davis, Alabama writer." Atlanta *Journal*, September 1, 1938. Miss Davis's book was not republished.

ton to collect the $2,000 attorneys' fees is successful, it probably will supply some good material for your lawyers. (I should add that there is no hope of collecting any money from Miss Davis, as she appears to have none, but we all wanted the Macmillan case carried to a conclusion.) If you or your publishers want the additional legal details of the Macmillan case I suggest that you get in touch with Mr. Walbridge Taft, Cadwalader, Wickersham and Taft, 14 Wall Street, New York. I don't know what he would charge you, if anything, but I can say that he has the authority to make the information available to you....

Mr. David O. Selznick   Atlanta, Georgia
Culver City, California   March 24, 1939

My dear Mr. Selznick:

Your letter of March 16th made me very happy, and I would have answered it immediately except that I have been ill with a mild but very persistent case of influenza. When I wrote my letter of March 13th, I did not *want* to believe you were responsible for the unpleasant things I mentioned, and your explanation that no one in the Selznick organization was to blame for them was more than welcome. You and the members of your staff whom I have met have been so uniformly courteous it would have depressed me greatly if others in the organization had actually done the things about which I was complaining—without justification, as I now understand. Please accept my very sincere regrets.

Probably my letter would not have been written if it had not been preceded by a series of incidents which had gotten my nerves on edge. Even though I knew you were not responsible for them, they got me into the right state of mind to send you the kind of letter I wrote when the Peterson incident occurred. They began with the hundreds of newspaper items saying that I had "okeyed," "endorsed" or "approved" the selection of Miss Leigh. As I hope you noticed in my previous letter, I recognized that these misstatements—and the Peterson item, too—could easily have resulted from reportorial carelessness, rather than from any other cause, but they were irritating nevertheless. Then there was a very nasty item in the Hollywood Reporter saying you had whipped me into line about endorsing Miss Leigh, or some such remark. Also I received a number of letters from theatres over the country asking me to make personal appearances when "Gone With the Wind" was shown or to do other things in connection with their commercial promotion of the film. To top everything off, there was the MGM advertising man who wanted to make a movie of me for use in the advance publicity for the picture.

These and several similar things occurred in the past two or three months and they seemed to point to a change in publicity policy on the part of someone from what it had been before then, when your people had always shown me great consideration. I thought that MGM might be responsible but I did not write direct to them, as all of my dealings have been and will continue to be with you. What was happening had the appearance that someone was trying to use me personally in the film promotion, which would be very distasteful to me, so I cannot tell you how pleased I was to receive your assurances that your own policy is unchanged and that you have again cautioned MGM not to misuse me or my name.

As to the particular matter of the Peterson letter and similar matters, the policy you have outlined is all that I could ask. Using exact quotations of my comments on Miss Leigh, in the form I sent them to you, is just the way they should be handled. I stand back of what I actually said and I would not have made my comments in the first place if I had not intended to keep on standing back of them. You have my permission to use these quotations in any proper way, and as long as you follow this policy, I will not hold you to blame if other people misquote them or misrepresent them. I suppose some of that is unavoidable as long as human beings are human.

I am, of course, glad to tell you again of my friendly attitude toward you and the motion picture of "Gone With the Wind." I am sorry that my letter put doubts in your mind on that score and I am especially sorry that my misunderstanding of things added to your worries, for I realize, probably better than anyone else, how many worries and problems you have had. I know what difficulties and problems have surrounded you from the beginning, and I have admired the way you have overcome one obstacle after another.

If anything was said to Miss Leigh about my previous letter, please tell her that I have never blamed her for getting entangled in my public problems. Far from feeling any resentment toward her personally, because the controversy about her has caused me some annoyances, I have the highest admiration for the way she has conducted herself. Her dignity and sweetness in her very difficult situation have won friends for her everywhere.

For your private ear and not for repetition, I am impressed by the remarkable number of different faces she has. In the stills you have been good enough to send me, she looks like a different person every time she is shown in a different mood. In the last batch of stills sent me by Miss Rabwin, the one of Ashley and Melanie on the stairs was beautiful, and I was amused by one of the bazaar scenes showing Maybelle and her little Zouave. He looked exactly like the "out-of-town" boy who would have caused Southern matrons to flutter if he had paid his attentions to a girl as sweet and innocent as your Maybelle.

The Hon. Richard B. Russell   Atlanta, Georgia
Washington, D.C.   March 27, 1939

My dear Senator Russell:

I know you will not recall meeting me some years ago when the newspaper editors were gathered in the mountains at "Press Haven." John Paschall, my former managing editor, introduced you to me, and I enjoyed the short, informal talk you made to us that night.

I am writing to ask your assistance on a matter which seriously concerns all authors and publishers in the United States—the ratification of the Treaty which will give international copyright protection to American authors. I have heard that this will be taken up by the Senate in the near future and I hope that you can give it your support. I do not know exactly what form the legislation will take, but I do hope that I can arouse your interest in the general need for action by our government to prevent the pirating of American books which is now a common practice in some foreign countries.

My interest in this arises out of the fact that "Gone With the Wind" was pirated in Holland nearly two years ago. Since that day I have fought, without success so far, in the Dutch courts for the protection of my copyright. I have spent thousands of dollars on attorneys' fees and other expenses, and my brother Stephens, my husband, John Marsh, and I have given endless, weary hours working on my case, but I have not yet been able to get justice.

My misfortunes are of no consequence to the Senate, except as an example of the difficulties with which all American authors are faced, as a result of our country's failure to join the Berne Convention, which provides almost worldwide copyright protection for authors of other countries. The great majority of people in this country think that American books already have international protection. I used to think that myself, but now I have learned that publishers in some foreign countries brazenly appropriate American books, and almost nothing can be done about it. "Gone With the Wind" led the best-seller list for over two years and I am a citizen of one of the strongest nations in the world, but my rights were boldly disregarded in Holland and my only hope of redress is my single-handed fight in the courts of that country. My government can do nothing to help me because we have remained outside of the Berne Convention.

In spite of the foregoing statements, I have no personal axe to grind in this matter. Even if we were to join the Convention tomorrow, it would not help my situation in Holland, for the damage has already been done. Nevertheless, I feel very deeply about the need of copyright protection for our authors and I know that putting our country into the Convention would help all authors coming after me and all American publishers.

I am sure that you must have noted with pride, even as I have, the literary renaissance in the South in recent years. Scarcely a day passes but the newspapers announce another fine book by a Southern author. Georgia seems especially prolific and it appears that this State is developing a new cash crop—writers. I think that we deserve as much protection as other home industries! So, I beg you to give careful consideration to this matter and do what you can to provide some protection for American authors abroad.

Miss Susan Myrick   Atlanta, Georgia
Los Angeles, California   April 17, 1939

Dear Sue:

I know you'll have a crown in Heaven for the great joy your letters have given us. Your last one, which announced that Sidney Howard was back on the script, kept us laughing all day. Every time we thought of the history of the script and the full circle which has been made we laughed again. It is all too incredible. I suppose Mr. Howard discovered that there was practically nothing left of his original script. I would not be at all surprised to learn that the script of the sixteen other writers had been junked and Mr. Howard's original script put into production.[1]

For months I have had to restrain myself from writing Mr. Howard and telling him about the goings-on over the script. Something told me he'd be the type who would appreciate the information. But, as usual, I kept quiet, for I never discuss anything about the picture with anyone. I have never met Mr. Howard but his letters have led me to believe that

---

[1] Besides Fitzgerald, Howard's script had been worked on—in varying measure—by John Balderston, Michael Foster, Oliver H. P. Garrett, Ben Hecht, Barbara Keon, Charles MacArthur, John Lee Makin, Edwin Justus Mayer, Winston Miller, Donald Ogden Stewart, Jo Swerling, John Van Druten, and, of course, Selznick himself. In the film's credits Howard alone is listed as the author of the screenplay. Howard Dietz's souvenir program for the film quotes Selznick: "Having had the pleasure and privilege of being associated in close daily collaboration for over a year with that great craftsman, the late Sidney Howard, on the screenplay, it is my deepest regret, as it is that of my associates who worked with Mr. Howard, that he did not live to see the realization of his work."

he is a grand person and one who has a sardonic appreciation of the strange ways of Hollywood.

My congratulations for your success in the matter of the dresses which were to defy the laws of gravity and stand up by themselves.[2] I consider this victory in the same category as the Miracle of the Marne. I wish Mr. Selznick could be put into a corset and laced down to sixteen inches and be laid upon a bed with the request that he get some beauty sleep. I think he might then understand the reason for loosened stays.[3]

The picture of you and Miss Crews[4] was so good and she looks too cute to be true. She sounds as if she'd be so much fun. Confidentially, we have been expecting to see upon the screen Miss Pittypat with the face and form of Miss Crews and the voice of Annie Laurie. I knew Annie Laurie was so fond of Miss Crews and had been with her so much and I did not see how Miss Crews could resist annexing for her own use a Clayton County voice.

John begs me to ask you not to lose the memorandum about not coaching the Yankee officer for Southern accent.[5] He says that he and I will believe such a thing but no one else will without documentary proof. We laughed about that all day too.

Of course I was very interested in what you wrote about Hall Johnson and the musical background. I also got a laugh out of Mr. S.'s memorandum that he understood I objected very strenuously to having Negroes

[2] In an interoffice memorandum of March 2 Walter Plunkett wrote Miss Myrick: "In the script, the dressing room sequence at Twelve Oaks calls for 'The camera starts on a shot of about six of the young ladies afternoon frocks which stand stiffly in a prim row like so many headless bodies, on their crinoline petticoats.'

As you know, neither hoops or crinolines could stand by themselves. If they were rigid vertically it would be impossible to sit in them. I have called Mr. Selznick's attention to this but find myself ignored. I am told they are so described in the book. Have reread this part but cannot find the said reference.

"Will you see what you can do to preserve the dignity of the Old South and the integrity of our friend, Peggy, as a costume authority??"

In her letter to Miss Mitchell on April 9 Miss Myrick noted: "I finally got that out."

[3] Miss Myrick wrote on April 9: "The scene they shot of the gals taking their afternoon naps at the barbecue is going to put you in bed when (or IF) you see it. I told David the gals would have their hair loosened, their corset strings unlaxed and there would be two to the bed or maybe three if he wanted them lying cross wise. He wanted their hair to look pretty and vowed that loosening the corsets would let their busts sag and I tried to argue him into my way of doing but he had his way. That was the day before we shot the scene. The day we did shoot it, AFTER it was finished in walked D O S, known as Pappy, and said to me 'Sue, was it all right for those girls to be lying down with their hair all done up and with their corsets on?' I was so dam mad I almost busted. I think maybe the scene is to be shot over again. I don't know."

[4] Laura Hope Crews.

[5] Miss Myrick wrote in her April 9 letter that Selznick had written her: "It is probably superfluous for me to remind you that the Yankee officer in the jail scene is not to be coached on Southern accent."

singing as a background. He is utterly wrong about this and I am so glad that you set him right by stating that I did not want the field hands to suddenly burst into song on the front lawn of Tara. John, not I, was the one who made this objection, but he spoke my ideas. He told George Cukor that everyone here was sick to nausea at seeing the combined Tuskegee and Fisk Jubilee Choirs bounce out at the most inopportune times and in the most inopportune places and sing loud enough to split the eardrums. And even more wearying than the choral effects are the inevitable wavings in the air of several hundred pairs of hands with Rouben Mamoulian shadows leaping on walls. This was fine and fitting in "Porgy" but pretty awful in other shows where it had no place. I feared greatly that three hundred massed Negro singers might be standing on Miss Pittypat's lawn waving their arms and singing

> "Swing low, sweet chariot,
> Comin' for to carry me home"

when Rhett drives up with the wagon.[6] By the way, speaking of musical scores—I hope they keep the music soft. Sam Tupper went with us to "Wuthering Heights"[7] last night. Every time the action became tense and the voices dropped to a low key the music blared out loud as a symphony orchestra and drowned out every word. We followed the picture by the pantomime, which, fortunately, was excellent. But we hardly heard a word of dialogue.

Going back to Hall Johnson—thank you for telling me that he thought GWTW was good and that it made him "unhappy that some of his race failed so miserably to understand it and criticized the black and white

---

[6] "As for Tara's white columns, Susan Myrick proved her worth early on by pointing out to Selznick that at least they should not be rounded; and the design was corrected to make them squared, in the authentic style of the Old South rather than of the studio facade. Shortly afterwards, she made another objection; Selznick planned to insert a descriptive scene of cotton being chopped on the O'Hara plantation, immediately before the Twelve Oaks barbecue. However, news of Lincoln's declaration of war arrived during the barbecue and established the date as mid-April. 'Planting time,' Miss Myrick said. 'He just couldn't chop cotton then.' In his curious obsessive way, the producer argued with her through a score of memos, from February until late May. 'He had hired the Hall Johnson Choir to sing as they chopped, and he HAD to go ahead with the scene.' Finally he gave up." Lambert, pp. 69–70.

Miss Myrick wrote January 15: "I really think the exterior of Tara is lovely and I am sure the credit belongs to Wilbur [Kurtz] who insisted on square columns and a rambling look. . . . They wanted cotton chopped while dogwoods were blooming and Wilbur and I had a time stopping it. They will plough instead. I nearly died when they asked me if they couldn't show cotton right at the front yard. . . . Did succeed in making them take livery off Pork and they have promised to make Gerald's clothes look like he has worn them a year or two and I made them take riding britches of English design off Gerald and put his plain pants in his boot tops."

[7] A 1939 film released by Samuel Goldwyn and United Artists Corporation.

angle" of it. Coming from a person like him and a person of his background, I appreciated it very much, for I have been in a rather odd spot. I do not need to tell you how I and all my folks feel about Negroes. We've always fought for colored education and, even when John and I were at our worst financially, we were helping keep colored children in schools, furnishing clothes and carfare and, oh, the terrible hours when I had to help with home work which dealt in fractions. I have paid for medical care and done the nursing myself on many occasions; all of us have fought in the law courts and paid fines. Well, you know what I mean, you and your people have done the same thing. The colored people I know here in Atlanta had nothing but nice things to say, especially the older ones. Shortly after the book came out the Radical and Communistic publications, both black and white, began to hammer, but all they could say was that the book was "an insult to the Race." For two years they could not think up any reason why. I asked a number of Negroes and they replied that they did not know either but guessed it was some Yankee notion. The Radical press tried to use "Gone With the Wind" as a whip to drive the Southern Negroes into the Communist Party somewhat in the same manner that "Uncle Tom's Cabin" was used to recruit Abolitionists. Of course you know how happy it made me to have the Radical publications dislike "Gone With the Wind." I couldn't have held up my head if they had liked it, but the Negro angle bothered me, for Heaven knows I had and have no intention of "insulting the Race." Recently the Negro press has discovered the way in which they have been insulted. It is because I had various characters use the term "Nigger" and "darkey." I am enclosing a couple of clippings on this subject for your interest, and I'd like to have them back when you have finished reading them. Regardless of the fact that they call each other "Nigger" today and regardless of the fact that nice people in ante bellum days called them "darkies," these papers are in a fine frenzy.[8] I am wondering if they think I should have been inaccurate and had 1860 characters refer to them as "The Race" or "Race Members." I have had enough twisted and erroneous and insulting things written about me and "Gone With the Wind" to make me sore on the whole Negro race if I

---

[8] The Atlanta *World* of February 12 headed an Associated Negro Press story from Hollywood by Ruby Berkeley Goodwin: "Cut objectionable Words From 'Gone With the Wind!'" Mrs. Goodwin wrote: "It is with decided relief that I can report, from no higher authority than George Cukor, director for the opus, that the objectionable term 'n———' which was used thousands of times (to put it at a moderate figure) by Miss Mitchell, has been cut entirely from the script of 'Gone With the Wind.' Only in a very few instances will the term 'darkey' be allowed. Not only will all objectionable terms be omitted but the picture will present Negro characters in lovable, intelligent, brave roles. They will speak dialect, of course. It must be remembered that prior to the Civil War very few Negroes spoke anything else."

were sensitive or a fool. But I do not intend to let any number of trouble-making Professional Negroes change my feelings toward the race with whom my relations have always been those of affection and mutual respect. There are Professional Negroes just as there are Professional Southerners and, from what I can learn from Negroes I have talked to, they are no more loved by their race than Professional Southerners are by us. If you see Hall Johnson again please give him my very sincere thanks for his words.

As soon as I could get up from the flu we went on a trip to the Gulf Coast, hoping for warm weather. We got rain and bitter cold and came home after a week, but it was a nice rest and I am getting fat again.

I can't help feeling curious about an item which has been appearing in various movie magazines. This item states that Vivien Leigh's Southern accent is growing by leaps and bounds because she has living in her home "a family friend of Margaret Mitchell." Well, dearie, neither you nor the Kurtzes are living with her. I have heard that an Atlanta girl named Patricia Stewart is her secretary, but I do not know her and never heard of her until I read these articles.

The last stills which Miss Rabwin sent me showed the exteriors of Tara and, so help me God! there were white-painted, barred fences. Not a split-rail fence was to be seen. Everyone who saw the pictures spotted that immediately and yelled bloody murder. Couldn't Mr. Selznick have rented the elegant split-rail fences from the "Jesse James"[9] company? A number of people remarked that there never were fences like that in Georgia until the Bar-B-Q stands sprung up in recent years. John said they began appearing in Kentucky when he was in college and rich Northerners took up horse breeding.

Mr. George Brett, Jr.   Atlanta, Georgia
New York, New York   May 12, 1939

My dear George:

I am so very sorry that I have delayed this long in answering your letter of April 27th, about the party which you wish to give me when—and if—the GWTW premiere is held in Atlanta. I wanted to write you immediately but it seems as if the letters I am most anxious to write are always delayed. The annual summer deluge of visitors began earlier this year and until today I've hardly had time to draw a comfortable breath.

First of all, I want to tell you how genuinely pleased and grateful I

[9] A 1939 film released by Twentieth Century–Fox Film Corporation.

was when Lucien Harris and Norman Berg told me of your desire to give me a grand party. It was very thoughtful of you and kind too, and I do appreciate the invitation, even if I am not able to accept it. I do not know whether Lucien went into any details about my "previous committment" to the ladies' Press Club. On the chance that he did not, I will give you the details, for there is a great deal of background to this whole premiere situation.

The ink was hardly dry on my movie contract before various Atlanta organizations, civic and social, began angling with Hollywood for an Atlanta premiere. All of them wanted me to "use my influence" with Mr. Selznick to get the premiere here. In line with my policy of standing clear of all things pertaining to the film, I refused to do anything about it. Mr. Selznick has never yet said that the premiere will be in Atlanta, but many people have gone ahead with plans for premiere parties and I have received invitations to a great number of them. They came from civic organizations, social organizations and individuals, some were for benefits for very worthy charities, and still others were of a thinly veiled commercial nature. These invitations came in by the dozen and I have refused them all. That was also in line with my "policy" since "Gone With the Wind" was published. With the exception of the banquet when the Bohnenberger medal was given me, I have made no "public appearances" in the past two and a half years, nor have I been guest of honor at any function, social, civic or otherwise. I realized in 1936 that if I accepted one invitation I would have to accept all, and the invitations were—and still are—too numerous for one human being to handle. Atlanta people have been very good to me and I have always regretted having to decline their invitations but I do not know what else to do.

After the filming of "Gone With the Wind" got under way in January, Atlanta's interest in the premiere increased to the point where the event, as far as I was concerned, assumed the proportions of a major problem. In addition to the invitations to parties, literally hundreds of people begged me for introductions to the movie stars (if any should come) or asked me to get them passes to the premiere. Even more were willing to pay for their seats but demanded that John, Stephens, Father and I guarantee that they would be able to get seats. If only the people who have spoken to us personally were to attend, there isn't an auditorium in Atlanta big enough to hold them all. And of course the demand for seats will get heavier as the event approaches.

Altogether, it looked like an intolerable situation for me, and still does. My impulse was to get as far away from Atlanta as possible, if the premiere should be held here. But I couldn't do that. So I decided on the next best thing—to leave Atlanta two weeks before the premiere, return just in time to dress for the performance, and leave immediately after the last reel. I have made only one alteration in that plan, and that brings me to my "previous engagement."

The only organization I have joined in the last three years is the Atlanta Women's Press Club. The members are all active newspaper women. I am the only non-working member, and I am very proud of my membership, for most of the girls are old friends of mine and I am happy that they are still willing to accept me as one of them—as Peggy Mitchell, newspaper woman, rather than Margaret Mitchell, author. In addition, I am under great obligations to them, for they have played an important part in making life endurable for me these past three years. Their consideration for me in their newspaper work has eased my burden in a way that would be hard to describe. Instead of making my life more difficult, as some newspaper people might have done, they have done everything possible to shield me from unpleasantness, and I am under obligations to them that I can never repay.

Some time ago at a meeting the president arose and, after warning me to keep quiet and not interrupt, announced that the ladies of the press were going to give me a buffet supper and cocktail party directly before the premiere. They said that I had not ever permitted anyone in Atlanta to entertain for me and that, whether I liked it or not, they were going to give me a party. The fact that they were my close friends of many years' standing not only gave them a prior right over other people to entertain me, but, she said, my acceptance of their invitation, from a group of old friends, would give me a reason for declining other invitations. Moreover, their party would be small, informal and friendly—not a gawdy Hollywood affair with spotlights, champagne and ballyhoo (as some of the others to which I was invited are to be). She said that Club members knew I wouldn't go to a party of that kind—and she was right.

She said further that their plans were already complete: each member could invite her husband or beau; I could invite my family; the managing editors of the three papers, the Mayor and the Governor were to be invited; an invitation had been sent to Mr. Selznick, Katharine Brown and any members of the cast who might be here. They told Mr. Selznick that this would be the only affair I would attend, and Miss Brown has accepted for the Selznick organization—tentatively, of course, for there is no certainty that the premiere will be held here.

Although taken aback by the unexpectedness of the invitation, I accepted it. I did it partly because of old friendships, partly because of my obligations to the members of the club, but chiefly because of the *nature* of the party they were planning—one that would be simple, unpretentious and in good taste, not only because the ladies know my preferences for parties of that kind, but also because their own ideas about such matters are the same as mine. If they had been planning a Hollywoodish kind of party I would not have accepted, even for my oldest and dearest friends.

As a result, my personal arrangements in connection with the premiere have been altered in one respect but only one. I still plan to be away from Atlanta during the two weeks before the premiere and to leave immediately after the performance, but I will arrive here an hour or two before the evening program in order to attend the party the Press Club is giving.

I realize that this one deviation from my original plan is going to make trouble for me, for it will make it harder for me to decline other invitations. People will want me to add one more hour, and still another hour, to my time in Atlanta that day, in order to attend their parties. That means I will be forced to hold rigidly to my plan to attend only the one party. If I should attempt to make any more changes, I would soon find myself in a hopeless tangle.

So I am sure you understand why I cannot accept the invitation to your party. If I had known about it earlier, I might have made your party the one I would attend, for there is no one whose hospitality I would rather accept than yours. But it is too late to talk about that now. I have already accepted the other invitation, there is no way I can get out of it and, to be very frank, I do not wish to do so. I do not think you will misunderstand that last statement, for I believe you can realize how much the girls' action means to me. I can only wish that things were different.

Now, as to your suggestion that The Macmillan Company and Selznick combine with the ladies of the press in one large party—I hardly know what to say about this because, you see, I am merely the guest of the occasion. I do not believe that I could make such a suggestion to the Club, for it might give the girls the impression that I thought their party not grand enough for my high-toned taste. And that is just the opposite of the truth, for a small, quiet party is exactly what I like best.

I do not even know whether to advise you and Mr. Selznick to approach the Club with your offer. They might accept and again they might resent it as a suggestion that they were not capable of giving the right sort of party and needed the help of outsiders in order to give it properly. The girls think that *their* party is going to be the nicest one of all, even though some of the other premiere parties will be much more pretentious, and they might not wish to combine it with a Selznick and Macmillan party.

This is not entirely because Southerners are touchy about such matters; it is largely because of the peculiar attitude Atlanta people have toward my book. Even though you have been very close to "Gone With the Wind" these past three years, I do not believe that you or anyone outside of Georgia can realize how strongly Atlanta feels about this whole situation. In your letter, you referred to the premiere as "Selznick's show." I don't believe Atlanta people feel that way about it at all. Mr. Selznick will put on the show, of course, but the premiere will be *Atlanta's* night, not Selznick's. Long ago, I gave up thinking of "Gone With the Wind" as my book; it's Atlanta's, in the view of Atlantians; the movie is Atlanta's film; and the premiere will be an Atlanta event, not merely the showing of a motion picture. From the way things are shaping up, my guess is that it will be one of the biggest events in Atlanta's modern history.

If I have succeeded in giving you even a faint conception of Atlanta's strongly possessive feeling toward the book and everything connected with it, perhaps you now understand why I have some doubts that the ladies of the press would wish to have you and Mr. Selznick as joint hosts at *their* party. I believe they would feel that, on this *Atlanta* occasion, they should be the hostesses and you and Mr. Selznick the guests.

That brings me to the one suggestion I can make confidently and with assurance. Cannot you and any others of the Macmillan folks who come to Atlanta be the guests of the Press Club at their party? The president, Medora Perkerson, of the Journal, knows Lois and Harold very well and, I am sure, will be only too happy to issue an invitation to the Macmillan group. And if you accept, it would certainly please me, for it would be the only way in which I could entertain any of you. I couldn't give you a party myself at that time, much as I should like it, because I would have to hire our new City Auditorium and invite five thousand people. If you were the guests of the Press Club you'd be my guests too, and yet I would be able to say to enraged friends who had not been invited, "It wasn't my party, I was only the guest of honor and had nothing to do with the invitations."

I know this sounds very involved, but life is very complicated these days.

Mr. Alexander L. May   Atlanta, Georgia
Berlin, Germany   June 1, 1939

Dear Mr. May:
    . . . I am glad to answer the two questions you asked. Your first question was about the origin of the word "Dixie." There are several schools of thought about this word and each school has strong adherents. Many students claim that the name "Dixie" comes from the name "Dixon."

Mason and Dixon were the two surveyors who ran the Line from east to west in the early days. This Line roughly divides the Northern states from the Southern ones.

Other people say that in the early plantation days a man named "Dixie" owned one of the largest plantations in the South and this plantation was known as "Dixie's Land." The people who believed in this origin of the word declare that when Dan Emmet, the minstrel man and song writer, wrote his immortal song "Dixie" he was referring to this plantation when he sang, "In Dixie's land I'll take my stand."

The third explanation is supported by people in the deep South around New Orleans where the French population predominated. Before the United States purchased that part of the country the currency was naturally printed in French, and the ten dollar bills were stamped in large letters upon the back "DIX," meaning "ten." These bills were known to the non-French inhabitants as "dixies." It is alleged that this name spread throughout the South and that is how our section received its title.

You asked about the meaning of the sentence you had frequently seen in American books, "the memorable interview between the governors of the Carolinas."[1] This statement refers to a humorous and somewhat meaningless sentence which has passed into the consciousness of all the people of the United States, and the origin of it is somewhat blurred. Here is the best explanation I can give. At some indefinite period in the early history of the Southern states the governors of North Carolina and South Carolina met for an important conference. There were weighty matters to be discussed between them and the inhabitants of both states were waiting breathlessly to hear what the governors would say to each other. It is reported that as soon as the governors had shaken hands the Governor of North Carolina said to the Governor of South Carolina, "It's a long time between drinks." That is all anyone knows about this "memorable interview." Nowadays it is used either as an invitation to have a drink of whiskey or to express a polite desire for a drink. For instance, if a guest should come to your house and you felt sure that he wished liquid refreshment, you would say to him, "You remember what the Governor of North Carolina said to the Governor of South Carolina." If the guest wanted a drink he would reply, "Indeed, I do remember. What fine statesmen we had in those days," or, "Yes, the Governor took the words right out of my mouth." I have also heard this expression used at cocktail parties when one round of cocktails has been served early in the party and the host wants to know if the guests desire another cocktail.

[1] It is generally conceded that this whole business is twentieth-century invention, unfounded in fact. The best discussion of it appears in Burton Stevenson, *The Home Book of Quotations*, 10th ed. (New York, 1967), p. 494.

The phrase has now become a humorous piece of foolishness and one which never fails to bring a smile.

I am so glad that you and your friends liked "The Story of the Confederacy" and I have written to the author to tell him of your words. I am sure he will be very pleased. I am mailing you "The Story of Reconstruction" and I do not want you to worry about how you will pay me for it. I understand the difficulties in transferring money. I will have my payment in the knowledge that your family and your friends are reading about the history of the old South and enjoying it. . . .

Miss Annetta I. Clark   Atlanta, Georgia
Northampton, Massachusetts   June 17, 1939

Dear Miss Clark:

I reached Atlanta yesterday after a pleasant visit in New York with Lois Cole and other members of The Macmillan Company. I found your two notes waiting for me. Thank you so much for sending me the copy of the citation. Thank you, too, for forwarding to me the hood. I did not realize that I had left it in the closet with the gown until my husband asked to see it. I thought I had packed it but in the rush of getting away I obviously overlooked it. I am sorry to have inconvenienced you.

Needless to say, my visit to Northampton was such a very happy one, and I am so grateful to you for all you did for my convenience and pleasure. I want to thank you, for Lois, as well as myself, for arranging the ticket to the Commencement Exercises and the invitation to the President's luncheon. She enjoyed them both so much.

Mr. Clifford Dowdey   Atlanta, Georgia
Tucson, Arizona   June 28, 1939

Dear Clifford:

Do not expect me to say that "Gamble's Hundred" is better than "Bugles" or that I like "Bugles" better than "Gamble's." I do not "like better" one book over another any more than I like one person better than another. I like a person for his own peculiar qualities and the same applies to books. I can never understand critics who take a running jump into a review, using as a springboard a comparison between the present novel and the author's other works.

With this preamble over, let me say sincerely that I not only liked

"Gamble's Hundred" but it was a life saver to me. My stay in Quitman was not pleasant; it was made heartrending by the courage my friend displayed in the face of a tragic loss.[1] She had not slept, except in snatches, for ten days and whenever she lay down she awoke suddenly every fifteen minutes. I lay in the bedroom next to her, reading "Gamble's Hundred" by a small concealed light, and every time I heard her turn over I went in with a bottle of alcohol and rubbed her down until she dropped off again. It was wonderful having the book to come back to, and it must be a good book or I could not have come back to it and been absorbed by it.

Here are the two things that impressed me most: a paragraph on page 274—

"... He had shared in their life too, but had belonged to it no more than to Evelyn's. It seemed to him now that he had always shared in others' lives, and never belonged anywhere. He had always given of himself to those other lives, brought them what they needed, because he did not know what that was."

and another on page 300—

"He had not been free even in the wilderness, with its illimitable space and freedom of movement. He had known that when he returned to tidewater, when he met Evelyn Frane. With her he would have had a home wherever he went, because he had learned that a man's home was the way he lived when no unnamed urgencies drove him and no unvoiced hungers gnawed at him, and there was no seeking beyond the horizons of his living. It was not a place, not tidewater or the land rolling from The Falls to the Blue Ridge, not the green valley. He had believed his was to be with Evelyn, . . ."

Here spoke not only Christopher Ballard but Clifford Dowdey too. This last quotation appealed especially, even though I am a person with extremely strong and tenacious roots and I know where I belong.

You perhaps recall that at Silvermine when you had goaded me beyond endurance, I remarked that you needed to get some of the restless vitality of Clifford Dowdey into your writing. I think you've done this in "Gamble's Hundred." I think it has a great deal of oomph and, as you know, I am partial to oomph, whether it be in books or people.

I have seen only local reviews, one of which I forwarded to you. How has it fared? Have the reviews come in from the provincial press yet? They were the ones which interested me the most in my own case, and

---

[1] The death of Royal Daniel, husband of Edna Cain Daniel. Mr. and Mrs. Daniel published the Quitman *Free Press*.

I think they had a great deal to do with my sale. If the critics do not like your book there ain't no justice—but then, I have never heard for certain that there was any justice. Please let me know how the book is doing. John has not read it yet, for he has been holding the fort for me during my absence. I am impatient for him to get to it for I want to discuss it with him. . . .

This letter is for Helen, too, but I would not know how to talk about "your book" if I were writing to both of you. But this is Helen's book in part, ain't it. I wish I were with you to talk about it. I can't discuss writing on paper.

Mr. Garnett Laidlaw Eskew   Atlanta, Georgia
Chicago, Illinois   July 17, 1939

Dear Mr. Eskew:

You paid me just about the highest compliment one author can pay another when you wrote that you had read "Gone With the Wind" six times. I am sincerely grateful to you for that and also for the interest which prompted you to write me about the Georgia Negro dialect.

You asked why I had my Negro characters address white men as "Mister" instead of "Marster." I do not believe I let any Negro character use the word "Mister." If I did, it was an oversight in proof reading. I intended them to say "Mist'." I gave a great deal of thought and trouble to the dialect my Negroes spoke and over a period of years I amassed a glossary of words and pronunciations. I was very anxious for my dialect to be not only phonetically accurate but easy to read. Although I am a Southerner, I am frequently turned against books in which Negro dialect is difficult to read because of tortured spelling and too many apostrophes. I tried to simplify the spelling of words and still keep the sound correct.

Here in Georgia there are about five different dialects (if I may call them that) spoken by white people. Our mountain folk, such as my character Archie, speak differently from our Wiregrass Crackers, such as Will Benteen. Coastal Georgia, Middle Georgia and the North Georgia section where my story was laid each has its own dialect. There are just as many dialects among our Negroes. After listening to the speech of a great many old Negroes who were born and brought up in this section, I decided I would use "Mist'," for it was the closest I could approach to the word they used. Actually, it was something like "Misser," with the "er" half-swallowed.

I discovered that if a Negro was asked the question "Who was your

master?" he would reply, "My mawser (or mossah) was Mist' So-and-so."
I never heard a Georgia Negro pronounce it "Marse" or "Marster" except
in rendering one old plantation song which begins—

"My ole marster promise me
Dat w'en he die he mek me free."

Of course I may be wrong about this, but I wrote out of my own experience and my own research. Perhaps in the Middle Georgia section
"Marster" was used, but my experience has been here in our Northern
section.

As you doubtless know, white Virginians speak differently from white
Georgians. Probably Virginia Negroes speak a dialect of their own too.
My own observation is that there is no one "Southern dialect," among
either white or colored people. And among the Negroes there is a different speech among those of different social levels. As you may have
noticed in my book, the house servants speak differently from the field
hands, and there are variations even among those of the same group.
Briefly, I make no claims that the dialect in my book is "official" for the
South as a whole. I only tried to make the Negroes in my book talk as
they individually would naturally have talked, in view of their personal
origins and upbringing.

You mentioned the dialect of the Uncle Remus Negroes. Here I must
be permitted to brag a little about something that made me very happy.
Among the very first people who came to me after my book was published
and spoke with kindness and enthusiasm were the sons and the grandchildren of Joel Chandler Harris. I can't tell you how pleased I was.
(Incidentally, in connection with your study of this interesting subject
of dialect, Mr. Harris was a native of Middle Georgia and not of Atlanta,
although most of his writing was done here.) . . .

Mrs. Allan Taylor   Atlanta, Georgia
Upper Montclair, New Jersey   July 18, 1939

Dear Lois:
. . . I have been hoping to get away for a week to visit the Edwin
Granberrys on a Florida key in the Gulf, but I have had a persistent summer cold which settled in one ear and has to be treated every day. While
it is doing very well now, I don't want to put myself at the back of
beyond where I can't get to an ear specialist if I need one.

Lois, the many ramifications of GWTW become increasingly incredible and amusing. Yesterday Jimmy Pope called from the *Journal* and
said that a rumor had hit town that Ole Marse Selznick was not going
to let the premiere of his picture take place here. . . .

Jimmy said the ladies . . . descended on Mayor Hartsfield's office like a pack of well dressed Eumenides. His Honor, a passionate Confederate and a stout defender of Atlanta's civic rights and honors, leapt eight feet into the air when the ladies told him the rumor. Jimmy said the reporter at City Hall phoned in excitedly that it sounded like a WPA riot and he, for one, wanted a police reserve called out. Mayor Hartsfield announced to the press that this was the worst outrage since Sherman burned the town. Of course Atlanta was going to have the premiere. "Why," said the Mayor, "in a large way the book belongs to all of us." Various members of City Council were assembled and, for all I know, the Governor, too, and they all began bombarding poor Mr. Selznick, who is now in the last stages of the picture (and of nervous prostration, no doubt) with telegrams telling him he must quiet the unrest in Atlanta occasioned by this rumor. Jimmy wearily asked me if I had had any official confirmation that the premiere would be here and I said "no." No one else bothered with me at all because, after all, I am only the author, and upon such occasions a highly alarmed author. This morning Mr. Selznick came through handsomely and said the premiere *would* be held here but he reserved the right to have a press premiere in Hollywood first, as there were hundreds of film columnists who had to see it.[1] This is all to the good because I had been wondering if any of the local citizens would be able to get into the premiere here if the out-of-town correspondents swarmed in. . . .

John said your book was done,[2] and what a relief that must be to you both. Now you can take your vacations with lighter hearts. Heaven knows how you ever finished it with all the company you had.

Dr. Wallace McClure   Atlanta, Georgia
Department of State   July 28, 1939
Washington, D.C.

Dear Doctor McClure:

The three-volume, board-bound Japanese translation of "Gone With the Wind" has arrived and John and I thank you so much for it. We appreciate your continued courtesies so very much.

[1] Selznick wrote Mayor Hartsfield July 17: "The rumors which you heard have no foundation. Neither we, nor Loew's, Incorporated (the distributors of the picture), have ever given any thought to opening in any place but Atlanta." Selznick, p. 209.

[2] Lois Dwight Cole Taylor and her husband Allan Taylor wrote juvenile books jointly under the pseudonym Allan Dwight. This probably refers to their *Kentucky Cargo* (New York, 1939).

Recently there has been an interesting development in connection with the Japanese translation and I will tell you about it for your information. Some weeks ago I received from Japan a paperbound set of "Gone With the Wind" and a letter written in excellent English from the translator. He did not state the date of publication nor did he make any references to such delicate matters as the book having been published without my knowledge. He spoke of the popularity of the book, estimating the sale to be in the neighborhood of 150,000 copies. It had outsold Pearl Buck's "The Good Earth,"[1] he stated, and had been surpassed by only one book, "Wheat and Soldiers."[2] He asked me for an autographed copy and, as he had been good enough to supply me with a Japanese set, I sent him an American edition and wrote a pleasant letter which made no mention of the translation having been unauthorized by me. I passed his letter on to my foreign agent, Miss Marion Saunders, in New York, and she immediately wrote to the Japanese publisher. She pointed out politely that it was customary in the Occident for publishers to enter into contracts with authors and suggested that the Japanese publisher should do likewise. Yesterday we received a copy of the publisher's letter in reply. It was a very nice letter indeed. The publisher pointed out with exquisite Oriental courtesy that the translator had written me and sent the books at his (the publisher's) instigation. By the rules of polite Japanese etiquette a publisher remains in the background and puts forward the author or the translator. Really, I felt that I had committed an act of boorish ignorance in having written the translator instead of the publisher! The publisher evidenced all willingness to enter into a contract with me and suggested that Miss Saunders draw up the proper forms with financial arrangements. He begged that I take into consideration the fact that Japan was engaged in a war and that the export of money from his country was difficult. Miss Saunders replied immediately, giving the rising scale of royalties which is customary for foreign translations.

Of course, we do not know what will come of this, for the letter may have been simply Oriental courtesy with nothing else behind it. But we hope to obtain a legal contract at least, even if I never receive any money. Miss Saunders has made inquiries and discovered that Pearl Buck, whose "The Good Earth" was issued by several Japanese publishers, has received letters as pleasant as mine but has never been able to collect a penny from these publishers. Miss Saunders also discovered that, while the Japanese embargo on foreign exchange was very tight, some money does come through. We will keep you informed about this.

People who have heard of the large sale in Japan congratulate me

---

[1] Pearl Sydenstricker Buck, *The Good Earth* (New York, c. 1931).
[2] [Katsunori Tamai] *Wheat and Soldiers*, by Corporal Ashihei Hino [pseudonym] (New York, c. 1939).

upon it. Then they are bewildered when I tell them that I receive no money from this sale. I have a difficult problem on my hands whenever I try to explain that this publication is not a piracy such as the one in Holland is but that it is strictly legal under the United States–Japan agreement. To tell the truth, I find this somewhat bewildering myself. It seems hard to believe that the United States would deliberately agree to surrender the rights of its authors.

In your last letter you mentioned that the Senate debate on the Treaty might occur any day this week. I sincerely hope that this will happen and that you will have good news for us—and yourself.

I was sorry to learn that Senator McNary[3] had raised objections. I was sorry, too, that I was unable to follow your suggestion about asking some good Republican friend to present my case in Holland to him in its proper light. To tell the truth, I do not know any Republicans here who could be of assistance and Mr. George Brett, who is one of the few Northern Republicans I know, is taking a month's vacation in the wilds of the Adirondacks, far out of reach of telegrams and telephones.

Mr. and Mrs. Clifford Dowdey   Atlanta, Georgia
Tucson, Arizona   August 3, 1939

Dear Helen and Clifford:

I have wanted to write you a nice long letter but it appears that leisure will never come. We've had a bad two months—two hurried business trips to the North; the news about the movie premiere being held in Atlanta broke upon us; I had a fine and flourishing ear infection; we are trying to find a slightly larger apartment; I may possibly have to go to court again and am working up a case; I have been unusually plagued by people who met me casually at large teas and determined to write articles entitled "My Old Pal Peggy," "The Real Margaret Mitchell as I Know Her," "Does Margaret Mitchell Love Money," for sale to national magazines. On top of it all, our cook, Bessie, was out for ten days just at the time when an international convention was held here and it appeared to me that half the convention tried to come to see me. You may wonder what the premiere has to do with me and the answer is "nothing at all." Nothing except that thousands of people believe I am managing the whole affair and few people believe me when I tell them that even I will not get a pass, as I intend to pay for my own ticket.

From week to week I thought I would be wiring you to expect me,

---

[3] Senator Charles L. McNary, Republican, of Oregon.

but with things as busy as they are I do not know when I can get away. It appears that we'll be held here until after the premiere, which is to come off between Thanksgiving and Christmas. Perhaps when it's over things will quiet down. I cannot tell you of my disappointment. I grasp at a statement in your last letter that perhaps you will come East this fall. You must come to see us if you do. Remember our offer of the Biltmore is open just as it was when you visited here before.

In the light of what has been happening to us recently, I hope you appreciate my latest adage, "Whom the gods would destroy they grind exceeding fine."

Dr. Wallace McClure   Atlanta, Georgia
Washington, D.C.   October 9, 1939

My dear Doctor McClure:

Thank you for your letter of October 7th with the information about the Chinese piracy and the photostat of the Chinese publisher's pamphlet. Several weeks ago I had noticed in a New York book review section an item which stated that "Gone With the Wind," "Inside Asia"[1] and several other American books were being published in English in China. I intended to write you about this at the time but I was in the midst of moving and when that wearying job was half done my father became ill, so I have had no time until now to mention the matter to you. I did not know if anything could be done about this unfortunate situation. Your statement about the Department feeling that it is not in a position to take any immediate action at this time because of the chaotic political conditions in the Far East answers my question about this. I recall that when Mr. Brett and I met with you in Washington Mr. Brett told sad tales of Chinese piracies. This is a maddening state of affairs, to say the least.

I do not know if I have told you of the Japanese situation. It has its amusing side. I believe I wrote you that the translator had sent me a set of the Japanese edition and he requested that I send him a United States edition. I did this and wrote him a polite and formal letter, in which I made no mention of such crude matters as unauthorized editions and royalties. But Miss Marion Saunders did descend to such depths and she wrote the publishers that, in view of their success with "Gone With the Wind," I should have some money. Then I received a very pretty silk kimona from the publishers and, shortly afterwards, a Japanese doll nearly three feet high in a red lacquer and glass case about four feet

[1] John Gunther, *Inside Asia* (New York and London, 1939).

high. If ever there was a white elephant this doll and its case is the elephant. There is no place in our apartment where it can be conveniently put.[2] Again I wrote formally, thanking the publishers, and again Miss Saunders wrote them suggesting cash. I was somewhat puzzled as to why I had received these gifts. Saturday I received a letter from the translator, writing in behalf of the publisher, and this letter explained everything. They wanted a picture of me standing by the Japanese doll so that they could use it for publicity purposes. A nation with so much gall certainly should go far. Needless to say, they will not get the picture.

John and I have so often discussed the probable effect of the war on the treaty in which all of us are so interested. We've also discussed the possibility that the threat of war may make the Dutch courts a little more kindly toward American citizens. Of course, such an idea is a long shot, but if the Dutch fear the Germans and want the assistance of America perhaps they may show a little justice to an American caught in their courts.

Miss Louisa K. Smith   Atlanta, Georgia
Augusta, Georgia   November 19, 1939

Dear Miss Smith:

I read with much interest your interesting column[1] about illumination in Confederate days. Had I known I was going to be quoted, I'd have added to my statement! I, like you, was interested in just what type of light our grandmothers used in those days. I found that while the sheep and the cows were soon eaten or carried off by the commissary, the folks back home never seemed to quite run out of hogs. So they always had some lard and bacon drippings. I read some where about how they soaked pine cones with lard and set them afire. They had a small pickaninny with a basket of cones sitting by the china bowl to replenish the cones. I imagine most of the white children would gladly have changed places with him, so eager are children to play with fire!

In "Mrs. Ward's Testimony Before the Committee of the Senate on the Relations between Labor and Capital" from the Congressional Record (That sounds dreadfully dull but it's the most delightful reading. Mr. George Ward of Birmingham has published his mother's testimony in a little volume.) Mrs. Ward said, "We had no lamps or candles except those we made ourselves. A great many poured melted lard into a saucer and

[2] It was eventually put up for sale at an auction to benefit the American Red Cross. Atlanta *Constitution*, August 2, 1942.
[1] In the Augusta *Herald*.

took the sycamore balls that grow on the tree and stuck them into the lard and set them on fire and they would give some light, about as much light as a taper gives." (Mrs. Ward was living at Rome, Ga. at the time.)

I ran across many references in my researches to candles of beeswax and bayberry. Also to lighted pine knots, set in long legged "spiders" on the center of the tables.

I read your column so often and always like it. There's always something interesting in it. It has a flavor of its own, if you don't mind me being personal, and doesn't try to copy smart aleck New York columns. Our own Georgia flavor is so nice!

Dr. Douglas Southall Freeman   Atlanta, Georgia
Richmond, Virginia   November 27, 1939

My dear Doctor Freeman:

When I returned home I found your book[1] waiting for me and, of course, I was delighted to have it. You were very kind to send it to me and the inscription makes it even more valuable. Only the enormous mail keeps me from reading it immediately. By exercise of self-control I have restrained myself from doing more than peeping at the pages you had indicated. My husband and I intend to go away on our annual vacation to a quiet spot the morning after the premiere of "Gone With the Wind" in Atlanta, and I will carry your book with me and read it with gratitude and with interest when I have unbroken leisure to enjoy it.

I was so pleased that you had included Margaret Ketcham Ward's testimony. It is a delight to read. I was so charmed with it that I begged of Mr. Ward several additional copies and put them in our Library and in the Atlanta Historical Society's library. Mrs. Ward was a high-spirited and charming person and her personality shines through the testimony. Do you have a copy of it? I believe I have an extra copy tucked away somewhere and if you do not have one it would give me great pleasure to send it to you.

As my secretary wrote you, our town has been in "a state" for the last month—a very pleasant and exciting and frenzied state—over the initial showing of "Gone With the Wind" on December 15th. The stars of the film will be here and a great many visitors from over the State and there will be a three-day celebration. The frenzies arise from the fact that the theatre in which the film will be shown seats approximately two thousand; everyone wishes to be there on the first night and the scramble for tickets

[1] *The South to Posterity* (New York, 1939).

is something that has to be seen to be believed. Some of them will go on sale on December 4th. Our Community Fund will receive all the proceeds and the Fund committee is allotting tickets to all civic and social organizations. Despite the fact that this has been announced many times in the papers, a great many people are firmly convinced that I have two thousand tickets in my pocketbook and will be happy to dispose of them. So it seemed better for John and me to go away for a little trip until things quieted down a little bit.[2]

I must confess that I have flipped the pages of your book very hurriedly. I am wondering if I will find my old friend Sam Watkins, author of "Co. Aitch." Perhaps Mr. Watkins did not contribute enormously to our store of information about military strategy and campaigns, but he certainly left a record to show what the dryly humorous foot soldier thought about it all. When I came to his simple but heart-rending description of how the field at Franklin looked after the battle, I found it difficult not to weep.[3]

Now, I must ask a favor of you, not for myself but for a friend, and if you can give me this information I and my friend will be so very grateful. Miss Kate Edwards, our best known portrait painter here, is painting a picture of Brigadier General Benning, which will be hung at Fort Benning. Yesterday she sought my opinion on a matter which was troubling her greatly. It was the color of the General's trousers. Miss Edwards is the most painstakingly accurate person I know; she has read a great many books on uniforms and has examined the plates in the *Atlas* in the Rebellion Records. She said that these plates showed officers with gray coats and blue trousers. She said, furthermore, that a portrait of General Benning, which now hangs at the University of Georgia, shows blue trousers. She wonders if this can be right and she asked me if gray coats and blue trousers were regulation for brigadier generals, especially early in the War, for her picture shows General Benning in late 1861 or early 1862. I was embarrassed that I could not give her the correct information. I knew that late in the War soldiers thought themselves fortunate to possess trousers of any color, but this information was, of course, of no assistance to her. When she heard that I was writing to you to thank you for your book she asked me to ask you for this information. I myself would be interested in your answer, for I have seen many

[2] In his letter of November 30 Dr. Freeman noted this paragraph by saying: "My warmest sympathy to you and Mr. Marsh in the ordeal you now face. I hope the picture will be in every way a stunning success, and some of these times I would like to know how nearly the figures in the movie conform to your own mental picture of your characters."

[3] Samuel R. Watkins, *"Co. Aytch"* (Chattanooga, Tenn., 1900). Dr. Freeman does not mention Watkins's narrative in *The South to Posterity.*

pictures of many Confederate generals but I do not recall any which showed blue trousers.[4]

Mr. and Mrs. Clifford Dowdey Atlanta, Georgia
Tucson, Arizona November 30, 1939

Dear Helen and Clifford:

Before the final tidal wave of the GWTW premiere submerges us I want to answer your letters. Ever since the day you left Atlanta, Clifford, the waves have been coming in steadily, harder and higher, and we have been so inundated and battered that we have hardly been able to keep our ears above the water line. The reason I did not urge you to stay for the Saturday football game was that I had an advance tip that the date of the premiere would be announced on Saturday and also the plans for the ticket sale and a three-day civic celebration which would accompany the picture. We have had three and a half years' experience with these sudden tides of public interest and we knew this one would be the worst we would ever know. So that was why we did not urge you to stay. We knew there would be no chance to see you.

I know all of this is incredible but I can only ask you to believe me. Since the announcement the whole of Atlanta—and apparently the South —have been engaged in a grim and desperate struggle to get tickets for the opening night, and the theatre seats only two thousand. . . .

There is to be a civic festival with every kind of whoop-te-do you can imagine, including a parade with a brass band stationed at every corner for a mile. The papers have been full of it and of course, everybody in Christendom has been on our necks demanding tickets for the premiere. . . . It gets worse as the great day approaches. I haven't been very well and my father's condition has steadily worsened, so the excitement catches me at a bad time.

I think I'd better tell you two something now so that if you should read in the paper that I am in the hospital you will not think I am at death's door or that the premiere has cracked the Mitchell stamina. I have been needing an operation for abdominal adhesions for six months. I put it off until after the premiere, which was originally to take place in August. The date was moved up, week by week, until mid-December,

---

[4] Dr. Freeman answered: "Your friend is quite right in saying that the uniform trousers of the Confederate Army were a navy blue. Of course the Confederate officers used what they could get, but when they conformed to the regulations, they had trousers of the color indicated."

and so I moved my operation date up with it. It may be that I will have
the operation immediately after the premiere. If I do, it will probably
get into the papers and you will see it and I do not want you to be
alarmed by the news. I hope that the release of these adhesions will give
me better health than I have had for several years past and enable me
to lead a more active life. I have only told a few friends about this
impending event, and I do not want it to get into the papers beforehand. . . .

Doctor Douglas Freeman has sent me a copy of his new book, "The
South to Posterity, An Introduction to the Writing of Confederate History." I have not had the opportunity of reading it but I note with interest
that in the Introduction he refers to my "Gone" and your "Bugles."

Mr. Joseph P. Crockett   Atlanta, Georgia
U.S. Board of Tax Appeals   December 4, 1939
Washington, D.C.

My dear Mr. Crockett:
    Thank you so much for your fine and friendly letter. I have not yet
received the French review which you mentioned but I am looking forward to it with interest.[1] I hope you will thank Mr. Fleury for his kindness
in thinking of me in this matter. I have a copy of the French edition of
my book but I have been too rushed recently to do more than skim
through it. I found that a number of our good Southern idioms had
suffered delightful sea changes. I was especially amused when Gerald
O'Hara ejaculated "oo, la la."
    I am acknowledging your letter before the receipt of the review be-
cause the premiere of the motion picture of "Gone With the Wind" will
take place in Atlanta on December 15th and already the town is in a
pleasant frenzy of anticipation, with many civic and social affairs planned.
I know that during this coming week I will be too busy to write any
letters, so I am snatching this occasion to thank you not only for your
letter but for the interest which prompted you to send my book to Mr.
Fleury.

    [1] Mr. Crockett had written November 28: "Neither the passage of time nor the
horrors of war can abate interest in 'Gone With the Wind.' Some months ago I sent a
copy to M. Pierre Fleury, librarian of the municipal library of Saint-Nazaire, France.
He promptly took a vacation so that work would not interfere with his reading, and
has recently sent to me copies of the French 'Axes,' in which a friend of his has reviewed your book, with the request that I transmit them to you. I take pleasure in
doing so under separate cover."

Chief M. A. Hornsby   Atlanta, Georgia
Atlanta Police Department   December 16, 1939
Atlanta, Georgia

Dear Chief Hornsby:

It is with great pride in you and Atlanta's police force, that I add my congratulations to those of hundreds of others you must have received. You and your men did a wonderful job during our "Gone With the Wind" festival. Confronted with unprecedented crowds, with traffic tangles, with rerouted automobiles, street cars and buses, your problems must have seemed insurmountable. But everything went off as smoothly as if you and the force handled such affairs every day. The officers were so efficient and so courteous that they contributed much to the success of the whole celebration. It made me feel proud when I heard Atlanta's famous guests comment so enthusiastically on the manner in which you handled things.

My husband told me of your assurance to him that you and your men would take good care of me. As you know, everything went perfectly, and I am most grateful to you and to the men who escorted me to and from the theatre. I was unable to get their names and I hope you will thank them for me.

1940

Col. Telamon Cuyler
Wayside, Georgia

Atlanta, Georgia
January 9, 1940

My dear Colonel Cuyler:

As you know, John and I went away immediately after the premiere and were away during the holidays. When I returned and opened the Christmas package you sent me I could scarcely believe my eyes. "Battles and Leaders," and for my very own and from you![1] The beautiful and poetic page you wrote and pasted in the front of the first volume touched me and made me feel very humble. How kind and generous you are to me and how I wish I had a dozen different ways to say "thank you." I sat up most of the night looking them over, examining first the pages in which you had inserted red paper markers. I have never seen "Battles and Leaders" in this original dress. (I take it that the paper covers *are* the original dress.) The volumes I read as a child and which I consulted in later years were unwieldy and bound in dark cloth—four volumes, I believe. Were they originally brought out in paper and then bound, or were some issued in paper covers and others in stiff backs?

Didn't Atlanta do itself proud at the premiere? I can realize the real magnitude of the affair now that I have a little perspective. While it was going on, and for three months beforehand, I was so beset by people who thought I could get tickets for them, by influenza and by a thousand harassments that I hardly had time to think about what was actually going on. Now I am so proud of the town! I have one very happy memory of the premiere itself—you standing in the theatre foyer. You looked so distinguished and so appropriately a part of the occasion.

---

[1] *Battles and Leaders of the Civil War*, ed. by R. U. Johnson and C. C. Buel (New York, [c. 1884–87]; 4 vols.). The set Colonel Cuyler gave Miss Mitchell was in twenty paperbound parts, as the four volumes were first issued.

Mr. and Mrs. Alfred Lunt   Atlanta, Georgia
Biltmore Hotel   January 9, 1940
Atlanta, Georgia

Dear Mr. and Mrs. Lunt:

Welcome back to Atlanta! It was kind of you to offer, through Stark Young, to get tickets for us but of course, we had already bought tickets as soon as we heard you were coming.[1] We will be there tomorrow night.

I asked Stark to tell you how much we would enjoy having you out for supper between shows tomorrow or for an after-the-show supper. He said the latter would be more convenient for you. I recall that you told me last year that you did not dine out between shows. This letter is to back up the invitation, issued through Stark and also to ask frank, house-wifely questions. Tell me what you like to eat. It's just as easy to have what you want as something repellent to you. For instance, do you like hot biscuits? Do you like fried chicken or do you find it too greasy for you? Or would you rather have an old fashioned chicken pie? Or is it your custom to have cold meat late at night? Do such Southern dishes as turnip greens make you scream with anguish or is it snap beans which make you scream? Or do you prefer the more conservative English pea?

I ask these questions frankly and hope you will answer them with equal frankness. Whenever anyone tries to order a meal for me, they usually end up with a lovely array of dishes which makes me break out in what is known in these parts as "Whelps." I wouldn't like to do that to you.

A supper will be no trouble, for our Bessie, on hearing my conversation with Stark, was very delighted and wants to stay and have a peep at you and cook you a meal. My stock has gone up enormously recently, in the kitchen, what with the "Gone With the Winders" and with the Lunts.

Please phone me at your convenience tomorrow. I won't be here from twelve thirty till one thirty for I have an engagement at the dentist. But any other time. I'm so glad you are here and I'm looking forward to the show.

---

[1] The Lunts played in *The Taming of the Shrew* at the Erlanger Theatre, January 9 and 10.

Mr. Herschel Brickell   Atlanta, Georgia
Natchez, Mississippi   January 11, 1940

Dear Herschel:

We took our time about coming home and stopped over to spend a few days with Edna Daniel in Quitman, Georgia. I've sent you several columns from her paper in the past. We hit the most bitterly cold weather I have ever known and froze in Quitman. And all the while the camellias and flowering quince were blooming outside the house. When we came home we found an enormous accumulation of mail and business matters waiting us. We have been working night and day to get the mess cleared up so that I could go to the hospital without leaving too much undone.

My present plan is to go to the hospital Friday night and be operated on the next day. I hope nothing occurs to disarrange these plans, for both Louie and Doctor Upshaw[1] say I am in marvelous condition and that this fact should contribute to a swift recovery.

Day before yesterday Stark Young appeared in Atlanta with the Alfred Lunts, who gave two nights of "The Taming of the Shrew." Stark came to see us yesterday afternoon and stayed for supper and after the show the Lunts came over for a late supper.... I understand he is on his way back North and will travel with the Lunts a while longer.

Coming home to Atlanta right after the demise of the Georgian was like coming home after a funeral.[2] A few of the Georgian people have been taken on by the Journal and a few on the Constitution, but not many. The Journal people are feeling nervous and insecure, for rumors fly fast that Governor Cox intends to shake up the Journal soon and let out a number in every department. As far as we know, Tarleton[3] has not landed a job and third-hand reports say that he is making no attempt in this direction at present. He got a good bonus for long service and intends to do some writing. He's luckier than many of the others, like Dudley Glass. It distresses us to see friends like Medora so worried.

We did have a good Christmas, didn't we? Just now it seems like a pleasant but improbable dream that we all managed to get together in a far place. I'll always think the first batch of eggnog we made was the best I ever drank, and I wish I had the energy to make some right now. But I have decided that the best flavor eggnog can have is when it is made by

[1] Dr. Louis C. Rouglin and Dr. Charles B. Upshaw.

[2] James M. Cox, former governor of Ohio and publisher of newspapers in Florida and Ohio, purchased the Atlanta *Journal*, its radio station WSB, and the Atlanta *Georgian* in December 1939. The *Georgian* ceased publication, leaving the afternoon newspaper field to the *Journal*. New York *Times*, December 12, 13, 14, 19, and 24, 1939.

[3] Tarleton Collier, *Georgian* columnist.

the combined efforts of a very few people and these people good friends. May we all have other Christmases together, and other eggnogs. . . .

Yes, I read Marjorie Rawlings' New Yorker story[4]—without knowing it was hers—and when I came to her signature I was astonished. She is the most versatile creature alive to be able to write "The Yearling" and then turn her hand to this kind of penetrating sketch. . . .

Miss Nell Battle Lewis   Atlanta, Georgia
Raleigh News and Observer   March 15, 1940
Raleigh, North Carolina

Dear Miss Lewis:

At this late date I want to tell you how much I enjoyed your column which appeared last month after you had witnessed the film, "Gone With the Wind."[1] The column was headed "Scarlett Materializes." Mrs. John Huske Anderson, of Raleigh, sent it to me and I enjoyed it so very much. I would have written you sooner to tell you what a fine column I thought it was, but at the time it arrived I was recovering from a trip to the hospital.

I was especially interested in your paragraph about the lack of applause when the Confederate battle flag was shown fluttering over the acres of wounded Confederate soldiers at the car-shed. Here in Atlanta at the premiere there was a great deal of applause early in the picture, and later on where Scarlett shot the Yankee deserter on the stair the tense audience practically yelled. But during the scene you mentioned there was a deathly stillness, just as you noted in the Raleigh theatre. Afterwards a number of us were talking it over, each giving reasons why the audience had been so still. One man summed it up this way—"Have you ever felt like applauding in a Confederate cemetery on Memorial Day? No, you haven't; you feel something too deep for applause." I think he was on the right track. Had the Confederate flag been shown for the same length of time over a crowd of charging soldiers or even going down a dusty road in retreat, I think audiences would have yelled themselves hoarse. During that scene they probably felt as they do in a Confederate cemetery.[2]

[4] "The Pelican's Shadow," *The New Yorker*, XV, No. 47 (January 6, 1940), pp. 17–19.

[1] In the Raleigh *News and Observer*, February 18.

[2] Miss Lewis wrote: "I noted one odd phenomenon at the Raleigh showing which I am at a loss to explain. Over the big open square in Atlanta which during the siege was filled with the prostrate bodies of wounded Confederate soldiers—one of the

I'm so glad you mentioned the work Miss Susan Myrick, of Macon, did on Southern speech. The best compliment I heard about the so-called "Southern dialect" was that no one was aware of it! And all of us would have been dreadfully aware had the actors spoken as if they had their mouths full of hot okra.

I'd like to pass on to you a compliment from my husband. He liked especially your summation of Scarlett in the second paragraph and at the end of the column,[3] and he said, "I always like Miss Lewis's stuff. She writes with so much understanding, and with force, and common sense, too." I hope you don't mind the "common sense." From a man, that's a high compliment.

Mrs. Hugh Harding   Atlanta, Georgia
Pasadena, California   March 26, 1940

Dear Lillian:

I know you will understand my long delay in answering your letter of February 11th when I tell you that I was in the hospital at the time it arrived. I am just now getting back to the office and picking up the threads. You remember Doctor Upshaw, don't you? Wasn't he your doctor? He operated on me. With my adhesions a thing of the past, I hope to be in better health in time to come, but I have been warned that I must take things easy for six months to achieve this desired state.

I had delayed the operation from month to month, waiting to get the premiere of "Gone With the Wind" behind me, and the movie producers kept moving the date up and up. Finally, the date was set for mid-December, but unfortunately I had a case of flu, so by the time Atlanta was in a furore over our three-day celebration I was not up to much. . . .

---

most striking scenes in the picture—there floated the Confederate battle flag. For a good minute it fluttered before the audience in a close-up, covering about half of the scene. Expectantly I awaited the reaction. Not a sound from the Raleigh audience greeted it, not a single hand-clap, not even one faint cheer."

[3] "If the book is Scarlett's, even more so is the picture. That tumultuous, driving, wayward, daring, unconventional, egocentric heroic personality which in spite of war and desolation and poverty, 'in spite of hell and high water,' flatly refused to fail its rendezvous with life, dominated the picture. . . . My primary reaction was not 'what a fine movie!' but, 'what a gal!' " And: "The highbrow critics make me laugh. It is not comme il faut, you know, to consider 'Gone With the Wind' a very good piece of literary work. It's really not so much of a book, it seems—except in the minds of several million readers with whose low-brow opinion no real critic could agree. But, regardless of such an estimate, Scarlett is not going down in literature any more than in life. Hear me turn prophet: Scarlett is going to survive the high-brow critics. For as long as life is a challenge which men must have courage to meet, the fighting O'Hara who wouldn't say die is going to live."

But I did get to attend the rather small party the Women's Press Club gave for me and the movie people in the late afternoon of the premiere day and, of course, to the picture that night. The movie people were all charming and the Atlanta people who met them fell in love with them. I wish you, as an old Atlantan, could have been here, for we will never see the town so excited again. The crowds on the streets were larger than those which greeted Lindbergh and President Roosevelt, yet everything was so orderly and well-bred and people did not mob the stars or try to snatch off their buttons for souvenirs. I was so proud of the town I nearly burst. . . .

Mr. Herschel Brickell   Atlanta, Georgia
Natchez, Mississippi   March 28, 1940

Dear Herschel:

Thanks for the long, nice letter of March 21st. Don't bother about answering this one until you have plenty of time. I know how much the writing of personal letters interrupts the writing of books.

There was something in your letter which struck a very sympathetic chord in me; you said, "the curiosity of the natives has just about ruined me. I couldn't go anywhere without being asked about 'the book' . . . the question finally became a nightmare." I had thought that situation one peculiar to me until I met Stark Young and jokingly spoke to him of how he wrote lovingly of the Southern scene but steadfastly lived in the North. He said, "But, of course, you know you can't live in the South and write a book." I managed to write a book but one of the reasons why it took ten years was the interruptions of friends. When the book was sold and I knew I had nearly a year's work checking et cetera, I begged The Macmillan Company not to breathe a word to anyone about the book. I knew the South, I knew Southern people and, above all, I knew my friends. I realized that if the news got out I would be desperately hampered in my work, and I was, for someone in The Macmillan Company mentioned the manuscript to someone (unknown to me) who had once lived in Virginia. You know the grapevine telegraph that exists in the South. In no time at all the Virginian had told a North Carolinian in New York and the North Carolinian had told some ex-Atlanta newspaper reporters in New York and in about four days the news was all over Atlanta and I was swamped with friends, acquaintances and strangers. Many of the strangers wished to sit on our sofa and "just watch me work." It was all very kind and neighborly and loving and well-meaning, and those eight months were a perfect nightmare. I don't yet know how I got to press, and I think I would have delivered a far better manuscript had I not been so harassed. After that experience I understood in part why more Southerners who write successful books fly to the anonymity of the large cities of the North. Unfortunately, when they suddenly pull up their roots they have nothing to draw any sustenance from and their second books are not so good. Well, I was determined no one was going to drive me from the place I belonged in.

The foregoing means that I know your situation very well. Would it be possible for you to collect your books and data and go to, say, Birmingham or Memphis or some other town in the South where you do not know anyone and do your actual writing? You could be close enough to get back to Natchez if you had to. I am bothered about this phase of your present situation, for I know how maddening it can be and what a handicap it is. . . .

Mr. Hervey Allen   Atlanta, Georgia
Coconut Grove, Florida   April 1, 1940

Dear Mr. Allen:

Some days ago your publishers sent me a copy of "It Was Like This,"[1] with a note saying that you had requested this, so I am addressing my thanks to you. I have been delayed in writing because I was convalescing from an operation when the book arrived and I am only now getting back to my office.

It was a grand book for a convalescent who was fed to the teeth on murder mysteries and light love stories which friends think will not tax the mind! Of course I had read "Blood Lust" when it appeared in the magazine. It brought up in me the same shocked feeling I had many years ago when a newly returned soldier spoke of seeing prisoners shot because it was too much trouble to take them to the rear. When I re-read it this time I liked it even better. However, of the two stories, "Report to Major Roberts" is my favorite. I am passing the book on to my brother, who was in the 326 Infantry, 82nd Division, and I know it will bring back many memories to him.

Bill Howland told me he had been to see you when he was in Miami and enjoyed his visit so much. This morning when I telephoned him for your address he reiterated his statement that you are "a grand guy," and he said he had asked you to come to see him and Mary in Atlanta some day. If you do, Bill wants John and me to meet you, so we'd like to add

---

[1] *It Was Like This: Two Stories of the Great War* (New York, Toronto, [c. 1940]).

our invitation to his. We would like very much to know you and we hope we will have the opportunity some day.

I want to thank you for writing "Action at Aquila,"[2] not only because it was a grand story but because it kept me from having a nervous break-down on a bus. I had to go by bus from Blowing Rock, North Carolina, to the train at Hickory just after your book was published. The road was narrow and twisting, the fog was so thick that the road could not be seen, and the bus driver was an embittered individualist who apparently believed he had the right-of-way to both sides of the road. He also informed me that the brakes "warn't none too good." Expecting violent death at any moment, I opened your book, braced myself against my baggage and began reading. The mere physical act of reading was a triumph, for my neck was being snapped like a bull-whip. But the book held me and took my mind from my strong belief that I would never survive to see my family again. So, I arrived in Hickory with at least an appearance of calm, whereas the most of the passengers were frankly hysterical. For a long time I've wanted to thank you for this.

This letter requires no answer. I know what your mail must be.

Mr. Webster B. Otis   Atlanta, Georgia
Pasadena, California   April 20, 1940

My dear Mr. Otis:

Thank you so much for your letter and the interest in "Gone With the Wind" which prompted you and your mother to write to me. Yes, I knew that the Reverend H. D. L. Webster wrote the words of "Lorena" but I did not know the history of the song and the circumstances under which it was written.[1] Of course I found the information you sent me very interesting.

You asked if I would let you know "how a copy of this song happend to come to my attention." To tell the truth, I never saw a *copy* of "Lorena" until last year. At that time a reader of "Gone With the Wind" sent me a copy of it, published by the Oliver Ditson Company, Boston, Massachusetts. In my childhood I heard "Lorena" sung by many elderly people. It was as familiar as "Rock-a-bye Baby," "Dixie" and "The Bonnie Blue Flag." It was as great a favorite with the Confederate soldiers as

---

[2] *Action at Aquila* (New York, 1938).

[1] *GWTW*, p. 168. The words of "Lorena" are by the Rev. H. D. L. Webster, the music by J. P. Webster. The song was first published in Chicago in 1857. It was printed in several Confederate editions. Words and music may be found in Richard Bardsdale Harwell, *Songs of the Confederacy* (New York, [c. 1951]), pp. 52–54.

"Over There" was with the A.E.F. All the people I knew who had lived through the war and Reconstruction period were familiar with it and loved it. I included it in "Gone With the Wind" for this reason.

Should you and your mother order a copy of "Lorena," you will discover only six verses. Perhaps your grandfather wrote only six verses but I have heard at least twenty verses sung. Perhaps poetically inclined young ladies of the sixties added other verses to his.

Mr. Archibald MacLeish   Atlanta, Georgia
The Librarian of Congress   May 2, 1940
The Library of Congress
Washington, D.C.

My dear Mr. MacLeish:

Thank you very much for your letters of April 24th and 25th about the proposal to make a talking book for the blind from "Gone With the Wind." Thanks especially for your clearcut answers to my questions and for your recognition that such questions need to be asked and answered in a situation of this kind.

After I had written you my previous letter, I learned for the first time that you were formerly an attorney. Now that your reply has come in, with its direct and simple explanation of the copyright matters I asked about, I say—Thank God for attorneys! I come from a legal family; my father, brother and uncle are attorneys, and I grew up taking it for granted that intelligent people do not make business deals without at least trying to find out what they are doing. But my experiences as an author have been very disillusioning. Life in the literary world seems to proceed on a happy-go-lucky basis, and probably I am considered a freak, not because of my book's extraordinary sale, but because I insist on examining contracts before I sign them. Often I have encountered active resentment merely because I asked questions, instead of approving things blindly. So, it is really refreshing to deal with someone like you. You seem to consider it nothing extraordinary that I wish to know what the talking book plan *is* before I agree to it, and you have told me in such simple, understandable language! As a novelist to a poet, I say again, Thank God for attorneys, with their ability to think clearly and then to say what they think, simply and directly.

As you say, the fact that phonograph recordings of books are not subject to copyright creates a very unsatisfactory situation from the author's standpoint, but information was what I wanted and I am glad to get it, whether it is unpleasant or not. In past months, when I could get no information about such points, I could not take even the first steps toward a decision as to whether I could give my permission. But now, with the information you gave and the court decisions you listed, my attorney is re-studying the matter and I hope to have his recommendations in the near future.

There is one point which is still hazy to me. Is the talking book plan a project of federal government, with which private agencies, such as the American Foundation for the Blind, are cooperating? Or is it an activity of the Foundation and similar private agencies, with which the government, through you and the Library of Congress, is cooperating? If I agree to permit the talking book to be made from my novel, will my agreement be with a private agency, the Foundation, or with the government?

Until you first wrote me, I had been given no intimation that the government was interested in this plan to any greater extent than our city or county government might be interested in the local Red Cross chapter, that is, by encouraging and aiding a worth-while agency which remained under private control. But your letters seem to indicate that the situation is just the reverse, that the talking book plan is directly an activity of the federal government, conducted through the Library of Congress. If so, what is the status of the Foundation with reference to the plan?

Could I ask you to give me a brief explanation of this? It will help me in seeing the whole matter in its true perspective. Perhaps this and the other questions I have asked seem very foolish to you, because you are so accustomed to dealing with matters of this kind. But please try to remember that this is my first experience with the talking book plan. Since the matter was presented to me several months ago, I have been in the dark about so many things and that has caused delay, but now, thanks to your help, we are making progress.

As I told you in my previous letter, the interests of those to whom I have sold rights in my novel, as well as my own interests, must be considered in this situation. The Foundation has already asked the permission of my publishers, The Macmillan Company, and my attorney is studying whether any of the other licensees should be consulted also. Working out these details may take a little time but I will give you an answer just as soon as I can. And I hope that it will be a favorable one.[1]

[1] *GWTW* was made available as a Talking Book for the Blind by the American Printing House for the Blind, Louisville, Ky. John R. Marsh to John R. Parbs, December 15, 1949.

Mr. Hervey Allen   Atlanta, Georgia
Oxford, Maryland   June 10, 1940

Dear Mr. Allen:

When I wrote you that my letter needed no acknowledgement, it was because I knew what an unending burden your correspondence must have been through a period of many years. For that reason I appreciated all the more your interesting and frank and friendly reply. You put into words the ideas I have had about *you* for nearly four years, when you wrote, "somehow or other, although I had never met you nor corresponded, it seemed to me in a good many ways you and I were the only two authors in America who really understood from the inside what many, various, and sometimes flooring things can happen when the public en masse insists on loving your books on a planetary scale. I sort of imagined you would understand, and you did."

Since 1936, when "Gone With the Wind" was published, I have given a great deal more thought to you than one ordinarily gives to a stranger—even if that stranger has written books that are fascinating. My husband and I have talked about you and your situation many times, because you are one of the few people whose own experiences would give you an understanding of mine. You know the impossibility of giving even your closest friends a real understanding of what happened to your life when your book[1] made its big success. It seems impossible for them to grasp the strange problems that arise from such a situation. As my husband expressed it—people who haven't lived through a war can never really understand what war is. You and I are veterans of the same war and we have shared many strange experiences and, often, my husband and I have wished we could talk things over with you. We know that you would understand so many things which it seemed impossible to explain to other people who had not been through this particular "war."

We still hope that we will have the pleasure of meeting you some day. It was good of you to invite us to drop in sometime and see you at your home in Maryland. I know that such invitations are not issued lightly by someone who has been through several years of standing off hordes of people who wished to see him. So I am complimented as well as pleased by the invitation, and I hope that some day I can accept.

I have heard that you said very fine things about my book and I felt both humble and proud that the author of "Anthony Adverse" should be so generous.[2] I am one of the millions who read and liked "Anthony

[1] *Anthony Adverse.*
[2] In answering Miss Mitchell's letter of April 1, Allen wrote her on May 22: "Of course I devoured 'Gone With the Wind,' thought it a grand book and invariably said

Adverse." I obstinately postponed reading it until I should have the time to read it without interruption. That opportunity came when I was convalescing from influenza and I shall always be grateful to you, not only for the fine book and the living characters but for making that the pleasantest and shortest convalescence I ever had! I could go on for pages about it and never say all I want to say about it or "Aquila" either, so I'll postpone them till I meet you.

Mr. Stark Young   Atlanta, Georgia
New York, New York   June 13, 1940

Dear Stark:

John and I have just returned from a trip and I found your letter of June 5th waiting for me. I read the clipping, dated May 29th, about President Conant advocating that the United States send material aid to the Allies. Events have moved with such incredible rapidity since you sent me this letter and Mrs. Lunt's request that I wire the President and my Congressmen. Now aid to the Allies is going forward and public opinion seems to be very solidly behind the President's stand on the matter, so there is no need for me to lend what small weight my name would have.

These are sickening days. John and I started on our trip the day the Germans went into Holland. For our peace of mind, it was fortunate that we could not and did not listen to the radios. Reading the papers was bad enough. It's no fun having a ringside seat for that fine spectacle, the collapse of Europe.

From all I hear, the Lunts' new play[1] is a stirring and heart-breaking affair. I wish that they would take it on the road when the New York run is over. I suppose some people might call it propaganda but, if ever there was a time when the right sort of propaganda was needed, that time is now. When you see them give them our cordial regards and tell them again how much we enjoyed their visit with us. . . .

---

so. One of the saddest things that can overtake an author, and it seems to overtake an enormous number, is an inability to enjoy or admire anything by any other author. The only complaint I have about my fellow writers is that they don't keep me furnished with enough good reading, and when somebody writes something that just can't be laid down I really feel profoundly grateful for it."

[1] Robert E. Sherwood's *There Shall Be No Night.*

Mrs. Louise Withey   Atlanta, Georgia
Hollis, Long Island, New York   June 18, 1940

My dear Mrs. Withey:

Under any circumstances I would have found your letter about your father's song, "When This Cruel War Is Over,"[1] very interesting. In light of a recent occurrence I find it even more interesting. While I was away on a vacation a letter, dated March 12, 1940, came from a French soldier, a Captain Gilbert Carpentier, of 34 rue Guynemer, Paris (6[e]), France. He had read "Gone With the Wind" in the French translation and the verse from "When This Cruel War Is Over" had had "a peculiar charm" for him. He wrote, "I would like to set this little piece to music and this is to ask your permission to do so." The young man was "trained at the National Conservatory of Music in Paris" and expected to go to the front very soon. For all I know, the young man may be dead now.

In my absence my secretary attended to the matter and wrote him the following letter:

> "When Mrs. Marsh sees your letter I am sure she will appreciate the in-terest in 'Gone With the Wind' which prompted it. But Mrs. Marsh does not have the right to grant you permission to set the old song, 'When this Cruel War Is Over' to music. As she did not write the verse herself but only quoted an old song which actually was popular during the War Be-tween the States, of course she is not the person to give the permission. Nor can I help you, I am afraid, to find the proper person. I have learned today from our local public library that the words of the song were written by one Charles Carroll Sawyer and the music by Henry Tucker. As it is seventy-five years or more since the song had its first popularity, I suspect (though I do not know) that the composers of both lyrics and music are now long dead. In any case, I am sure Mrs. Marsh would not have the right to grant the permission you request."

I have never been able to find a copy of the music to this song, although I heard it sung many times when I was a child.

I am sorry you were disappointed that I did not mention your father's name as the author of this song. The reason I did not do so is that it is not the practice of novelists to do this in works of fiction. You will note that I mentioned and quoted from other songs and poems in "Gone With the Wind," such as "My Old Kentucky Home,"[2] "Somebody's

---

[1] *GWTW*, p. 194. "When This Cruel War Is Over" was issued during the Civil War in both the North and the South and was immensely popular. Harwell, *Con-federate Music* (Chapel Hill, [c. 1950]), p. 87.

[2] *GWTW*, p. 298.

Darling,"[3] "The Bonny Blue Flag"[4] et cetera, without giving the authors' names. This is not because novelists wish to deny credit to poets. It is that novelists wish to approximate reality and real actions as nearly as possible in their fiction. In real life if people are singing a song, such as "Flat Foot Floogie"[5] or "The Music Goes 'Round and 'Round,"[6] they seldom insert the author's name.

I thank you very much for writing to me and telling me that you enjoyed "Gone With the Wind." I thank you, too, for the information you gave me about your father. I get so many appeals for information from students of the sixties and I am always happy to have information to give them. Many people are interested in the old war songs. Could you tell me if "When This Cruel War Is Over" is still in print and where I could secure a copy of it?

Mr. Arthur H. Morse   Atlanta, Georgia
Boston, Massachusetts   June 24, 1940

My dear Mr. Morse:

I have received your letter of June 12th with its enclosures about the burning of Atlanta by General Sherman.

You force me to doubt that you read "Gone With the Wind" very carefully; otherwise you would have noticed that the book itself contradicts the statement in your letter that "Sherman burned every building in Atlanta, including the residences and the churches."

It appears that you have taken one or two sentences on pages 478 and 479 and, without regard for the context, you have drawn certain "inferences" from them. But is it right or fair to draw such "inferences" when they are directly denied by the book itself? Even on page 479, within a few lines after one of the statements that are objectionable to you, the book says that "Frank amended hastily" his remark that the Yankees had "burned everything." And at the top of the following page, he says:

Page 480—"There's some houses still standing, houses that set on big lots away from other houses and didn't catch fire. And the churches and the

[3] *GWTW*, p. 297. Miss Mitchell quoted the words of "Somebody's Darling" as written in 1864 by Marie LaCoste of Savannah. Rutherford, p. 284. Miss LaCoste's poem was set to music by John Hill Hewitt with the words slightly altered and a chorus added. Words and music appear in Harwell, *Songs of the Confederacy*, pp. 44–45.
[4] *GWTW*, p. 170. Words and music appear in Harwell, *Songs of the Confederacy*, pp. 11–13.
[5] By Slim Gaillard, Slam Stewart, and Bud Green, 1938.
[6] By Edward Forley and Michael Riley, 1935.

Masonic hall are left. And a few stores too. But the business section and all along the railroad tracks and at Five Points—well, ladies, that part of town is flat on the ground."

And there are a number of similar statements, such as the following:

Page 480—"Cheer up, ladies! Your Aunt Pitty's house is still standing. . . . It's about the last house on the north end of town and the fire wasn't so bad over that way."

Page 557—"The brick house of the Elsings still stood, with a new roof and a new second floor. The Bonnell home . . . managed to look livable for all its battered appearance."

Page 567—"The two-story red-brick city hall had survived the burning of the city."

In these and various other references in my book to the burning of Atlanta, I believe I have presented a picture which is historically accurate. It was one of *general* destruction, in which some churches, residences and other buildings survived. I readily agree with your statement that it was not *total* destruction, in which "every building" was burned, and my book states specifically that it was not, but if your impression is that the burning of Atlanta was a neatly and precisely controlled conflagration in which no churches and no residences were burned, I can only say that the facts of history disagree with you.

Among my authorities are many eyewitnesses who told of their return to Atlanta and how they found their own houses burned. Some of these I have talked to personally and others have set down their descriptions of the ruined town in memoirs and letters which I have read. A number of Union officers and soldiers also have described the burning of Atlanta as a general conflagration. Citing two of them, page 257 of a book called "Marching Through Georgia," by F. Y. Hedley, Adjutant of the 32nd Illinois Infantry (published 1890, Donohue, Henneberry & Co., Chicago), reads as follows:

"On the night of November 15th, the torch was applied to the railroad shops, foundries, and every one of the main buildings that had been used in fitting out the armies of the enemy in this vast 'workshop of the confederacy,' as Atlanta was called. The flames spread rapidly, and when morning came, it is doubtful whether there were a score of buildings remaining in the city, except in the very outskirts. Sherman had determined to render the place utterly incapable of any more service to the enemy."

The second description from a Federal viewpoint can be found in "Sherman's campaigns in Georgia and the Carolinas," by Captain George

W. Pepper (published 1866 by Hugh Dunne, Zanesville, Ohio), pages 239–240. It reads as follows:

> "Clouds of smoke, as we passed through, were bursting from several princely mansions. Every house of importance was burned on Whitehall street. Railroad depots, rebel factories, foundries and mills were destroyed. . . . In the solemn starlight we could see the billows of smoke, and vast sheets of flame mortal eye has seldom seen. The whole region for miles was lighted up with a strange and indescribable glare."

In my novel, I intentionally omitted any reference to the burning of the church where the funeral of General Leonidas Polk, Confederate bishop and soldier, had been held; I thought it might shock people too much. The other churches were saved by the intervention of Father O'Reilly,[1] the Catholic priest at the Immaculate Conception Church. Concerning this, the "History of Atlanta and Its Pioneers" (published 1902, Byrd Printing Company, Atlanta) states:

> ". . . and upon the evacuation it was owing to his personal efforts that that portion of the city in which his church was located was saved from the general destruction by the army; thus, likewise, saving the Presbyterian (Second), Baptist (Second), and Episcopal (St. Philip's) churches, and the City Hall."

The hospitals were spared at the moment when they were about to be burned, by a clever ruse devised by Doctor Noel D'Alvigny.

If you care to investigate the matter further, one of the most interesting items is the report of General W. P. Howard, of the Georgia State Troops, who entered Atlanta immediately after its evacuation by the Federals. He made a full military report to Governor Joseph E. Brown of the ruin left by Sherman. In this report he states, pages 632 and 633 of "Atlanta and Its Builders," by Thomas H. Martin (published 1902 by the Century Memorial Publishing Company):

> "In the angle of Hunter street commencing at the city hall, and running east, and on McDonough street, running south, all houses were destroyed. The jail and calaboose were burned. All business houses, except those on Alabama street, commencing with the City Hotel, running east to Loyd street, were burned. All the hotels except the Gate City Hotel were burned. The estimate was that out of 3,800 houses only 400 were left standing within the city limits, and when those outside the corporate limits of the city were taken into account it was estimated that the Federal army destroyed in and about Atlanta about 4,500 houses.

[1] Father Thomas O'Reilly.

"... The Protestant Methodist, the African, and the Christian Churches were all destroyed.... All the institutions of learning were destroyed.... Peachtree street was burned from the center of the city to Wesley Chapel. ... Wesley Chapel remained, but it was horribly desecrated."

General Howard thereafter reported in some detail on the locations of city blocks which were burned and houses which remained standing. Another interesting source of information is a newspaper article published soon after the burning of the city and giving a block-by-block listing of the Atlanta houses which were burned and those which remained. It was published in the Augusta (Georgia) Chronicle, December 15, 1864,[2] and has been reprinted in the Atlanta Historical Bulletin for May, 1930. The Reference Department of the Atlanta Carnegie Library has collected a variety of material relating to this subject and will be glad to supply information if you wish to query them on some point.

Your feeling that there is no virtue in perpetuating the bitterness of the War days is one with which I heartily agree. My book was not written in a bitter spirit and it has not created bitterness, if I may judge by the very friendly tone of the letters I am constantly receiving from Northern readers of the book. So I am anxious that you shall not be left with a wrong opinion of my book because of a misapprehension.

As to the inference you drew, I think you must agree that it was, at least, not "inescapable," in view of the fact that the book directly denies it. As to the historical facts, I can only say that my statements were the result of my interviewing many eyewitnesses, reading many memoirs, letters and diaries and studying many books and official documents. I made every effort to be accurate and I believe that my book is accurate, as no historical statement in it has yet been proved to be wrong.

Mr. Erskine Caldwell   Atlanta, Georgia
Darien, Connecticut   August 5, 1940

Dear Mr. Caldwell:

It was good of you to ask your publishers to send me a copy of "Jack-pot."[1] I know I will enjoy it. However, I feel that I am obtaining this book from you under false pretenses because I will not be able to make any comment upon it, as you requested.

---

[2] An earlier printing of this account appeared on December 10, 1864, in the *Atlanta Daily Intelligencer*, a broadside extra that was the first newspaper published in Atlanta after the departure of Sherman's army.

[1] *Jackpot, the Short Stories of Erskine Caldwell* (New York, [c. 1940]).

Mine has been a very strange situation. Within the year after "Gone With the Wind" was published, it seemed that everyone I knew wrote a book, and some of them were very fine books. I did not get to read them for three years, for after the publication of my novel I had such heavy going with mail, business matters, lawsuits et cetera that I had no time to read books, much less comment on them. So I was forced to deny myself the pleasure of saying that I liked certain books. Now, having refused the requests of so many writers who are friends and an equal number who were strangers, I am in the unpleasant position of not being able to make any statement about any book without appearing to slight a number of my writing friends. This is not a situation of my own choosing and I do not like it, for it makes me appear, in the face of my own good fortune, both ungenerous and ungracious. But it happens to be my situation and I have tried to adjust to it as best I can. So, I will not be able to make any comment about "Jackpot." . . .

Dr. Wallace McClure   Atlanta, Georgia
Washington, D.C.   August 8, 1940

Dear Doctor McClure:

I would be very glad to have the pirated Chinese edition of "Gone With the Wind" which you so kindly offered to me. Thank you so very much. It will round out my collection of foreign editions and it is all I will ever get out of China, I suppose. No, I have never seen this Chinese edition. My only information about it came from letters and from brief references in the newspapers some time ago.

You wrote that you would be much interested to learn what effect the German occupation has had upon my interests in The Netherlands. All I can say is that we have no news at all. My case was to have come up before the highest Dutch court just a day or two after the German invasion took place. Neither Miss Marion Saunders, my agent in New York, nor Mr. Taft nor I have heard anything from Doctor Fruin,[1] our Dutch lawyer. We have hoped to hear from him, at least to know that he is still alive, but we haven't pressed the matter because we feel that he will communicate with us if he can. At this stage of events, probably nobody could say whether a decision by the Dutch courts means anything or not, so there is nothing to do but wait until affairs settle down.

I have thought of you so often since the war situation became grave and one country after another became involved. I know how hard you

---

[1] J. A. Fruin.

have worked to solve the international copyright problems of American authors and what a disappointment it must be for you that the war came before the United States had joined the international convention. My sincere wishes that your efforts may bring results at some future date.

Because of the kind assistance you have given me in my copyright troubles and because of your interest in such things, I am taking for granted that you will be interested in further news of "Gone With the Wind's" troubles in far-off places. Not in my wildest imaginings did I think the Bulgarians would be interested in my book, especially when the threat of war hangs over their heads. But some months ago I heard that a publisher was bringing out an unauthorized edition. I believe it was translated into Bulgarian from the French translation, and I am appalled to think what a sea change my book has suffered! Miss Marion Saunders went after this publisher very vigorously, demanding that he sign a contract, publish Macmillan's United States copyright notice, and pay me a royalty. The publisher came to terms and signed a contract—and then immediately wrote me a private letter asking to be let off the royalties! It appeared from his letter that it was not the custom of "great authors" to charge Bulgarian publishers money for translations. Miss Saunders is now arguing that matter with him. At any rate, the edition is an authorized one and my rights are acknowledged in the contract.

At about the same time, I learned that I had a piracy in Cuba. A newspaper, Diario de la Marina, had been serializing it and had published a number of installments before I heard about it. I protested that this was done without my authority and without paying me anything. They replied with a letter which can best be described as "saucy." In fact, they practically told me to go to hell and that they would not pay me or acknowledge my rights. Then, abruptly and for no apparent reason, they made a right-about-face and paid the money.[2] Our private opinion about their sudden change of front is that the situation in Europe had suddenly become very grave and that fear of Germany had something to do with making this newspaper come to terms.

You will recall perhaps the piracy in Chile, for you were of great assistance to us in that matter. The original unauthorized edition, which was finally authorized by contract, was a poorly translated, badly cut affair. It did not satisfy me and we have had considerable correspondence about it. Finally, the publishers put out a new revised two-volume edition which we have just received. You were so helpful to me in this matter and I am very grateful, so I am sending you as a souvenir this two-volume Chilean edition.

---

[2] *Diario de la Marina*, Havana, paid Macmillan $100. John R. Marsh to George P. Brett, Jr., June 24, 1940.

I heard that there was a threatened radio dramatization in Argentina. As Selznick International Pictures own the radio rights, this was the problem of Selznick and MGM, not mine, thank goodness. I have heard, but am not certain, that this radio piracy was stopped.

Selznick and Metro-Goldwyn-Mayer had reports from Japan that a pirated movie of "Gone With the Wind" was being produced there. Later information, which came to me through several people, shows that MGM probably has the situation in hand. While I wish MGM all the luck in the world in this matter—still, I would like to see a Japanese movie of my novel. If they placed it back in the sixties, the Japanese Confederates would doubtless be marching forth to defend Atlanta in Samurai armor and Scarlett would be dashing about in a 'ricksha instead of a buggy.

Dr. Wallace McClure   Atlanta, Georgia
Washington, D.C.   August 16, 1940

Dear Doctor McClure:

The Chinese edition arrived and I thank you so much for it. They certainly cut corners on it, both literally and figuratively, for the paper is newsprint and the margins are cut so deeply that it is difficult to open it. I am grateful to you for making it possible for me to have this edition to round out my collection. . . .

In my last letter I forgot to include two other foreign incidents. Because of the interest expressed in your last letter to me, I will relate them. Some time ago we learned, in some manner which escapes my mind at present, that a Greek newspaper, Estia, which is published in Athens, I believe, had already begun serializing "Gone With the Wind." We and Miss Marion Saunders went into action at once. Through Miss Saunders, the aid of the Greek Consul in New York and (I think) the United States Consul in Athens were enlisted, and they both were very helpful. Letters were written and cables sent to Estia, asking by whose authority the serialization was printed and demanding a contract and a payment for publication. Some weeks went by, with no answers to cables or letters. Finally, in the last two weeks, an answer arrived. The publishers protested any piracy intent and said that they had gotten permission to publish from the Athens representative of the Societe des Gens de Lettres. We had never heard of this organization but our information is that it is a French society which looks out for the interest of French authors in the Balkans. This Greek serial had been translated from the French.

We have been in correspondence with the publisher and, while he is willing to make payment, he disagrees about the amount I am asking for serial rights. He is, however, willing to make a smaller payment. We are now in negotiation with him and will doubtless get a compromise price if he will recognize my rights and publish the United States copyright notice.

Shortly before Russia took over Esthonia, we had information that an Esthonian publisher was to bring out a translation of "Gone With the Wind" in that country. Miss Saunders has been trying to get information about this matter through someone she knows in Europe. As yet our information is scant. We do not even know if the edition *was* published. Moreover, the matter is complicated by the Russians, for we do not know what, if any, rights we have or can enforce in the face of Russian domination.

I certainly never thought when I finished the last galley proof of my book and sent it off to the press that I would be skirmishing in many foreign countries.

Miss Patricia Fraser   Atlanta, Georgia
Freeport, New York   October 11, 1940

My dear Patricia:

I have heard of publishers who kept manuscripts six months and then returned them to the authors with a rejection slip. I have heard of other publishers who kept manuscripts an equally long time and accepted them. There is no cut-and-dried length of time in such matters. If a publishing house has an enormous number of manuscripts on hand at a certain time, then it takes an enormous amount of time to read them all. The mere reading of a manuscript is only the first step. If the first reader reports favorably on it the story is sent to another reader and that second reader makes a report. Sometimes a third and fourth reader are called in. If all of them agree as to the worth of the manuscript it is then taken up in editorial conference and must be passed on by a number of people. The publishing business is the biggest gamble in the world and publishers must be sure they have something salable before they put money behind it.

So, you see, I cannot give you much advice about how you should act at this time. I believe if I were you I would wait another six weeks and if you do not hear anything by that time then write a courteous letter stating the length of time your manuscript has been in The Macmillan Company's hands and asking if they would return it.

No, I haven't forgotten about you, and to prove that I haven't forgotten I talked about you and your manuscript to a publisher's representative a couple of months ago. He is Roger Williams, of the Houghton Mifflin publishing company in Boston. He is in the selling end of the business, not the editorial end, but he is interested in manuscripts for his firm. I told him your age and he said that at one time they had published a manuscript by a boy aged twelve. He said if your story came back from The Macmillan Company to send it to him and he would look it over and give it to the readers of his company.

Should you wish to do this, write Mr. Williams a letter saying that you are the fourteen-year-old girl I told him about when he was in Atlanta on his last trip and that I have suggested that you send the manuscript to him. I can understand your impatience at not hearing from The Macmillan Company. I have several friends here in Atlanta who are far older than you, and they are on tenterhooks because their manuscripts have been so long in publishers' hands and they have heard nothing from them.

I hope, of course, that you hear good news from The Macmillan Company, but if the news is bad don't be discouraged; send the book to Roger Williams. In the meantime, why not keep on writing? Writing is a trade that must be learned the hard way, like any other trade, and constant practice is the only way to learn.

Mrs. Alfred Lunt   Atlanta, Georgia
Alvin Theatre   October 14, 1940
New York, New York

Dear Mrs. Lunt:

John and I are so grateful to you for giving us advance notice of your broadcast last night.[1] We are not radio addicts and we might have missed it but for your letter. And we would not have missed it for anything. We went straight from our radio to a cocktail party, and I was not at the cocktail party at all—I was still in England with your voice.

The poem was strong and beautiful. I wish the word "moving" was not so trite, for it is the only word I can lay hands on now. However, the poem could have been butchered and made sentimental or maudlin by someone less gifted than you. It sounded so simple to read, but, oh, how tricky it was in reality!

It was interesting to listen to your voice divorced from your face and

[1] On October 13 Mrs. Lunt read on the NBC Blue Network Mrs. Alice Duer Miller's *The White Cliffs* (New York, [c. 1940]). Atlanta *Constitution*, October 13.

figure and personality. It was so pliable and flexible, as if it were a tangible thing you took into your hands and shaped to suit your mood. All during the broadcast I thought of what lay behind so perfect a voice, not just genius, for that isn't enough. I thought of the years of unending work, and of savage work, I am sure, at times, that went to perfect this instrument.

In other words, we liked the whole broadcast immensely.

And now, I will write you the letter that has been on my mind for some time, a letter about "There Shall Be No Night." I have been burdened with a feeling of ungenerousness in not telling you and Mr. Lunt how much John and I enjoyed your play, which we saw some while ago. To explain why I have not written you or did not send a note backstage takes some explaining. I know you and Mr. Lunt are two people who will understand and will hold this confidential. It is impossible for John and me to go to New York for a week-end to see a show or two and a few friends. Going to New York is like a miniature Battle of the Beaches of Dunkirk—we have so many friends there, relatives, business associates, newspaper people et cetera whom we must see. The last time I was in New York (before we saw your play) I had to see seventy-five people in one day, and that did not count a cocktail party I attended. I do not enjoy this bedlam and it takes me weeks to recover, so we stay out of New York unless some urgent business matter makes our presence imperative. This isn't a pleasant situation, for we have a few friends there with whom we would like to spend enormous amounts of time.

We were visiting John's family in Delaware and the desire to see "There Shall Be No Night" was so strong upon us that we took the chance and came to New York for the night without letting anyone know we were there. I am sure we should get into difficulties with many people if, even at this late date, it was known that we were in town.

We forgot that you and Mr. Lunt were the people who had sat at our table and upbraided Stark Young for eating most of the turnip greens before you arrived on the scene. We forgot that you were Lunt and Fontanne, for you became two brave and decent people in a nightmare world. It was a great play and you two were truly great in it. Even now I can't tell why I felt like weeping at the simple remark about the doctor not having prescribed even so much as an aspirin tablet in fifteen years. For Mr. Lunt, we liked best the scene in the schoolroom. Those long speeches could have been difficult in any other hands; they were heartbreaking in his. As for you, the last scene was our favorite. It was keyed so low against the high pitch of outside events. Thank you both for giving us that fine experience. In our hard-working lives such an experience does not come often.

We wanted to send you some flowers afterwards or a note or something to say thank you. Instead, we took the train for Atlanta.

We were so pleased to hear that you are taking the show on the road. We hope it will play in Atlanta. I know this town has the reputation of being the worst show town in the United States, but you two have proved this is not true. Should you play Atlanta and have the time, please come to dinner with us. I promise you there will be plenty of turnip greens this time. Our cook, Bessie, declared herself outdone at the way Stark Young ate all of them and hopes that you will return and give her another chance with greens and also fried chicken.

I hope "There Shall Be No Night" will come out in book form.[2] We'd like to own it.

Mr. and Mrs. Clifford Dowdey   Atlanta, Georgia
Richmond, Virginia   October 21, 1940

Dear Helen and Clifford:

I have no idea where you two are at present and the purpose of this letter is to find out that information. John and I are trying to flee Atlanta on the morning of the 25th of October (the day after Medora Field Perkerson's movie premiere, of which more later). We do not know exactly where we are going, as a great deal will depend on the weather at that time. There is half a chance that we will come to Virginia. We especially want to see the Valley, although we realize this is a bad season for our first view. I do not know if we will get to Richmond. We mouht— and then we mouhtn't. There would be a number of complications if we did come to Richmond, and if we are as weary after this premiere as we confidently expect to be complications will not appeal to us. But we do want to see you two and we hope that if you are in Richmond the affair can be managed somehow. Perhaps you could meet us somewhere in the Valley. (I think that would be a nice song title—"Meet Us Somewhere In the Valley," words by Stonewall Jackson, music by Phil Sheridan.) For the time being please keep our plans quiet and don't even tell your family because this might come to nothing. Don't wait to write me a long letter in reply but please get me off a note stating where you are. You can't imagine how we look forward to even the possibility of a get-together.

Medora Perkerson, who worked on the Journal with me, has had great

[2] It soon appeared as a book (New York, 1940).

success with her murder mystery, "Who Killed Aunt Maggie." The movie version is to be world-premiered in Atlanta October 24th.[1] Today the preliminary horn-blowing, brawl-throwing and tea-drinking begins. It is alleged that three or four of the movie stars in the cast will be here for the event. I do not know exactly how it happened but I find myself on numerous committees for parties and, as the movie representatives here do not seem to know which end is up, I, like all others connected with the affair, am in a state of frenzy. My scientific investigation convinces me that anyone who comes within the orbit of Hollywood, even in the most distant manner, is liable to frenzy. The movie people change dates blandly, throw carefully made plans out of kilter, tear up seating arrangements, and do not even know where and when the tickets go on sale. To pile Pelion on Charybdis, we had a deluge of authors last week, among others Andre Maurois and Marion Sims. She was here for the publication of her book, "The City on the Hill." . . .[2]

Dr. and Mrs. Douglas Southall Freeman   Atlanta, Georgia
Richmond, Virginia   November 8, 1940

My dear Doctor and Mrs. Freeman:

To our regret, we did not get to Williamsburg. When we telephoned Atlanta on our last night in Richmond we discovered that some business matters were needing attention here at home and we decided to return by the most direct route. Of course our regret was keen, but we are looking forward to seeing Williamsburg and Jamestown and the rest of that section of Virginia on our next visit to your state.

Now that we look back on it, it seems hardly possible that we have actually been to Virginia. It is something we have talked about many, many times during the last four packed and hurried years, but we never thought it would come to pass. Seeing Virginia for the first time was a beautiful adventure, and your kindness and hospitality were the nicest part of the experience. We know that you are busy people and that everyone who arrives in Richmond must clamor to see you, so we appreciate all the more our pleasant dinner and unhurried visit with you.

How kind you were to arrange for us to meet Mr. and Mrs. Cabell[1] and Doctor and Mrs. Williams![2] Not having made their acquaintance

---

[1] The Atlanta Debutante Club sponsored the premiere of *Who Killed Aunt Maggie?* at the Rialto Theater.
[2] (Philadelphia, New York, [c. 1940]).

---

[1] Mr. and Mrs. James Branch Cabell.
[2] Dr. and Mrs. John Bell Williams. Dr. Freeman wrote the introduction to Mrs. Rebecca Yancey Williams's *The Vanishing Virginian* (New York, 1940).

by letter before we came to Richmond, and remembering our own experiences with complete strangers who came to town and asked to call, we were hesitant about asking them to see us. But you knew how much we wanted to meet them, and we are very grateful to you for giving us this added pleasure.

Doctor and Mrs. Williams arrived in town this morning. I have just talked to Mrs. Williams over the telephone and will see her at lunches today and tomorrow and at the other festivities which are being given in her honor. To my indignation, I discovered on my return that other Atlantans had gotten the jump on me and had planned for practically all Mrs. Williams's time while here. Therefore, I will have no opportunity to entertain for her myself. So I suppose my best service to her will be in seeing that she gets a few minutes' breathing spell between parties. I want her Atlanta visit to be a pleasant one and perhaps I can help by seeing that she is not killed with kindness.

You were so very nice to us and we hope that on your next trip to Atlanta we will have the opportunity to show you our appreciation.

Miss Ellen Glasgow   Atlanta, Georgia
Richmond, Virginia   November 11, 1940

Dear Miss Glasgow:

I did not realize until I had left your house that I had stayed over an hour. Then I was filled with remorse and anxiety that I had worn you out. The time went by so swiftly because I had the feeling that I was with someone I had known a great many years. Perhaps I had the feeling because I had read and loved your books and your personality which shone through the books. And perhaps it was because you yourself have that charm of manner which delights the stranger and makes the stranger feel at home.

At any rate, I thank you for your generosity with your time and I apologize if I wearied you.

My husband hopes that if we make another visit to Richmond he may have the pleasure of meeting you. Everything I told him about you tied in so perfectly with the things Herschel Brickell and other mutual friends had told us about you. John has long admired you, not only for your books but for the way you have carried success and public acclaim —not just a brief grassfire flare of notoriety but solid success that grew from year to year, which was based on true worth of character and back-breaking work. It is no small feat to carry success with dignity that has no stuffiness and with graciousness that has no condescension.

He'd like to have the opportunity to tell you these things personally, and I hope some day you will let him do this.

I hope your doctor is kind to you and lets you get on with your book,[1] but I hope he is firm enough to put you back in bed when you need it. We need people like you and books like yours, so please take things easily and don't try to go too fast.

I shall never forget my lovely visit in that pretty room.[2] Thank you for making it possible. My best regards to Miss Bennett.[3]

Mr. and Mrs. Herschel Brickell   Atlanta, Georgia
Ridgefield, Connecticut   November 11, 1940

Dear Herschel and Norma:

John and I have just returned from a two-weeks' trip to Virginia. We had a marvelous time in the Valley and then went to Richmond, where we saw the Dowdeys and Doctor Freeman and met Mr. Cabell and Mrs. Rebecca Yancey Williams, author of "The Vanishing Virginian."

But Ellen Glasgow is the person I want to write you about. Perhaps you already know of her illness. However, I have learned that frequently one never hears the news about friends one would like to hear because mutual friends take it for granted that all is known.

As you know, I had never met Miss Glasgow, but through Stark Young and others and her own kindness, I have known her through letters.... Not knowing Miss Glasgow had been ill, I phoned her house and spoke with a Miss Bennett. When I asked for an engagement I was told that Miss Glasgow would be glad to see me but of course I knew she had been ill in bed for some time. I did not know and I was embarrassed that I had intruded. I said that I would stay only fifteen minutes. Thereafter, everyone in Richmond told me how ill she had been following several heart attacks. The first one took place in New York some six or seven months ago. Wishing to finish her book, she disregarded doctors' orders and did not go to bed. Thereafter she had another severe attack and has been in and out of bed ever since. Miss Bennett told me that the doctors let her up a few minutes every day and that she works a little then. But she is so full of energy and so anxious to finish the book that she does

---

[1] *In This Our Life* (New York, 1941).

[2] When *In This Our Life* was awarded a Pulitzer Prize in 1942 Miss Glasgow remarked in her response of May 17, 1942, to a congratulatory telegram from Miss Mitchell: "I have a charming recollection of your flitting in and spending an hour by my bedside." *Letters of Ellen Glasgow* (New York, [c. 1958]), p. 297.

[3] Anne Virginia Bennett, a trained nurse who had become Miss Glasgow's secretary and companion. Glasgow, *Letters*, p. 64.

not relax and lies there with her motor going full tilt just waiting until she can get up and work another fifteen minutes. Her friends in Richmond seemed seriously alarmed about her and they all promised to flay and disembowel me if I tired her out. I went to see her and, to my horror, discovered that I had stayed over an hour. But I was having a wonderful time and she was talking away as if she were enjoying the visit and I just forgot to go home.

She looked so well and was so pretty and full of pep that you would never have known she was ill except for the fact that she was in bed and the pillows were quite flat. She had a slight cough which worried me because coughing isn't very good for people with bad hearts.

I thought you two might not have heard and I knew you would want to know. But should you write her, please do not say that I gave any alarmist picture. If I had not been told that she was ill, I would have thought her a very pretty and witty Southern lady who was taking her afternoon beauty rest.

She was all the nice things you have told me she was, and I cannot tell you how much the visit meant to me.

Thank Heaven, things have quieted enormously for us during the last few months. Otherwise, we could not have taken this trip. I think the war, of course, had something to do with the cessation of public interest in me, and the election naturally diverted attention. However, Atlanta has become such an enthusiastic literary center that I have spent most of my time during the past six months (when I wasn't making bandages at the Red Cross) galloping about meeting authors. I have been so busy meeting authors and buying autographed books that I have not had the time to read any of the books. Our latest visitors, Lella Warren of "Foundation Stone,"[1] and Mrs. Williams of "The Vanishing Virginian," have taken their departure after a week-end similar to the one you, Herschel, and Clifford spent here. And before then there was Marion Sims, and before her Andre Maurois, and back of him Helen Norris, and my memory refuses to go any further. We will probably have a breathing space until Harry Lee and Minnie Hite Moody burst upon us. Minnie is with Macmillan now and her new book is to be called "Long Meadow."[2] It is about her Hite ancestors in the Valley of Virginia before the Revolution. Macmillan thinks well of it and intends to put some money behind it. All of us hope Minnie has got a big thing this time, for she deserves it.

Oh yes, I finally met Julia Peterkin when she visited here several months ago. I thought she was grand and we managed, by going into the ladies' room at the Driving Club, to have a brief private conversation. I wish she'd come back oftener.

[1] (New York, London, 1940).
[2] (New York, 1941).

It's been fun getting back into circulation again after so long. I had not realized how much I missed normal life and parties and seeing friends and meeting attractive strangers. It must be good for both of us, for John has gained fifteen pounds and I am bursting the seams of all my clothes. I never felt better in my life and do not care how fat I get.

1941

Mr. Harold Latham   Atlanta, Georgia
Tannersville, New York   January 18, 1941

Dear Harold:

I feel a long letter coming over me and, as I shall not deal with any urgent business matters, you can tuck it away to be read at your leisure....

We just returned from Florida yesterday.... We had a fine and interesting trip, visiting Marjorie Kinnan Rawlings and seeing the scrub country of "The Yearling," crossing paths with the Clifford Dowdeys, who are just recuperating from his latest book which will appear in the Post soon,[1] and having a delightful time with the Edwin Granberrys. I want to tell you something about Edwin which may assist you should you visit Orlando and Winter Park, as you wrote you might. Edwin teaches English and creative writing at Rollins College. He is an exceptionally fine person, and so is Mabel, his wife. He is the author of three books written some years ago, "Strangers and Lovers," "The Ancient Hunger" and "The Erl King," published by Macaulay.[2] He also won the O. Henry Award for "A Trip to Czardis."[3] He reviewed "Gone With the Wind" for the Sun and it was just about the best review I ever got. He also wrote an article for Collier's in 1937, about "Gone With the Wind." For some time he has not written anything but has just finished what appears to be a very fine play, which is getting at least consideration in very high theatrical quarters in New York. Sam Byrd, who was in "Tobacco Road" and who produced "John Henry,"[4] is enthusiastic about it and is pushing the play in New York.

... I told him that you might come to Winter Park, as you had never covered Florida on a personal trip. I said that your time would necessarily be short and it would be too bad if you were so overwhelmed with people who really had nothing to show that you had no time for

---

[1] *Sing for a Penny* (Boston, 1941) appeared first in *The Saturday Evening Post,* March 1, 8, 15, and 22.

[2] *Strangers and Lovers* (New York, [c. 1928]); *The Ancient Hunger* (New York, [c. 1927]); *The Erl King* (New York, 1930).

[3] Included in the O'Henry Memorial Award *Prize Stories of 1932* (New York, 1932).

[4] The play after Roark Bradford's book.

the people who might have something. A stranger in a strange section is naturally at a loss and I knew if certain people down there got hold of you they would take up all your time trotting you about to meet their little nieces who wrote such spiritual poetry. Edwin said he would be very happy to assist you in any way possible, should you wish him to do so. He could and would be able to give you confidential reports on various people. Everybody in Winter Park has not one but eight manuscripts, and poor Edwin, because of his good nature and his professorial position, has had to read most of them. I think he would be very helpful to you should you go there. And please feel no hesitation about writing him that you are coming. His address is 1620 Hillcrest Avenue, Winter Park.

He said that he knew of a few manuscripts which had merit and a few people who might write good books. He mentioned one man whom he had never met but whose stuff he had seen without the man knowing it. The man's name was Standing. He has been a soldier of fortune and lived all over the world. He had a story or article in the September issue of the Atlantic Monthly.[5] Edwin said his writing had the Joseph Conrad touch.

I was interviewed by a former Atlanta reporter now writing on the Orlando paper—Mike Thomas. I was asking him about *his* book, because it's always safe to ask a reporter how he is getting along with his novel. (By the way, his novel is about Maximilian and Carlotta and the Confederate officers who took service in Mexico after the surrender and would have been executed but for the intervention of the United States Government.) Of course I asked him to send his manuscript to you or, better still, to wait until he heard whether you were coming to Florida and have a personal interview. Naturally, I spoke highly of you and of my desire to turn up manuscripts for you. The result was a very fine newspaper story which gave the impression that I was your manuscript scout. And, great God, did the phone get busy! And did the letters arrive! I don't believe anybody grows oranges down there; they all write books, and everyone wanted to know when you would arrive. One lady, a trifle on the cracked side, I am sure, for her letter made it appear that she had a persecution mania, really had a good idea and one which I recommend to you. Her book was an expose which would shake the United States. She was going to expose Communists, saboteurs and antique dealers. I told all applicants to write to you and send you their manuscripts. I am sure you must have been deluged and by this time must wish I would stay at home or else keep my mouth shut when I go traveling. After this experience, I wish I'd keep my mouth shut, too. . . .

---

[5] There was no contribution by anyone by the name of "Standing" in *The Atlantic Monthly*.

Now, to something in your letter of December 17th. You spoke of Lucien Harris's desire for me to do a school book for use in the Southeastern States. Yes, Lucien mentioned this to me, unfortunately under circumstances where we could do little discussing. The dreadful fiasco known as the "second premiere of 'Gone With the Wind'" was at is height when he mentioned it. Nothing went right at this affair, which bothered me not at all, as I had no connection with it officially. Lucien spoke of the matter at a big luncheon for the British Relief and at the minute a wire had come in that Vivien Leigh and Lawrence Olivier, who were to appear at the luncheon, would not be able to appear as their plane was grounded. There was great outcry and lamentation among the Relief ladies and MGM representatives. Lucien was talking textbook in one ear while the other ear was being bombarded by Relief ladies wanting me to pinch-hit for Miss Leigh. I could only tell him that I couldn't do the book and could give no explanation at that time. Here are my reasons.

The main one is that, even if I ardently wished to do it, I would be restrained by the fact that I am not a historian, and no one knows it better than I. There are too many real historians in this section for me to get above myself in this manner. The second reason steps out of the first. Because there are so many good historians, my task would be trebly difficult. I'd have to be microscopically careful because, no matter how accurate I was, I'd be open to criticism all the way round. It would mean that such a book would take three or four years' research and an equal time for the writing. And the last reason—I simply have no interest in writing such a book because I am only a story-teller. To use a mixed metaphor, "yarn spinners should stick to their lasts."

Mr. Kenneth Roberts   Atlanta, Georgia
Kennebunkport, Maine   January 30, 1941

Dear Mr. Roberts:

Thank you for the nice note you sent me at New Year's. I feel guilty at knowing my Christmas card had made a busy man take time from his work to write me. But, just the same, I did like hearing from you!

There was a "thank you" behind my card. As I was frenziedly trying to get away to Florida, I did not have the time to write my thanks and the reason for them. I was going away on a vacation and taking "Oliver Wiswell"[1] with me and I knew I would enjoy it, so I was grateful to you beforehand.

And I did enjoy it. Even if I did not possess Tory ancestors, I would

[1] (New York, 1940).

have found the book most interesting. But possessing these Tory ancestors and being as proud of them as I am of my Revolutionary forebears, I found the book fascinating.

Some of my ancestors were refugees from the Western Isles of Scotland. They settled in Cumberland County, North Carolina. They came with a considerable number of their friends and relatives and the remnants of broken clans. They were hard-working and thrifty, and, by the time the trouble in England was ready to break, they had accumulated a good stake in their new home. They considered themselves a number of cuts above their frontier neighbors who were running about the countryside yelling for liberty or death. A number of their neighbors had no overweening love of hard labor and were highly critical of these Highland Scots because they amounted to something. In 1775 (I think that was the date) the whole kit and boiling of the folk from the Western Isles went out to fight for the king in a royal regiment commanded by General Donald McDonald. Family legend has it that there were 1100 of them, but that sounds like an awful lot to me. My ancestor held a captain's commission in this outfit. They very speedily got into a battle at Moore's Creek bridge, were captured, sent to prison in Philadelphia in 1776, and were pardoned sometime during the next year. While their fates thereafter were far from pleasant, there were enough of them in that settlement to keep them from being persecuted like the Loyalists in your book. They stayed where they were and did not have to go to hell or Halifax.

When I was a child I heard as much about them as I did of my other ancestors who were with General Marion. However, none of my little playmates appeared to have Tories in their background and they looked on me with horror when I spoke of mine.

I am glad you wrote "Oliver Wiswell." It cast a very penetrating light upon a completely neglected part of our history and, incidentally, made my vacation an even more pleasant affair than I expected. Please don't ever stop writing books.

Miss Patricia Fraser   Atlanta, Georgia
Freeport, New York   February 1, 1941

My dear Patricia:

Here I am answering your letter a month after you wrote me. I am sorry I have delayed so long but I have only recently returned home and read it.

It was good of you to write me such a long and interesting letter and

I thank you for it. I could not help noticing your typing, for it was very good and clean, with an excellent lefthand margin. I believe you do not use the touch system, as some of your letters are darker than others. But, in spite of that, it presents a very good appearance. As you have already made a good start in typing, it seems to me that it would be a fine thing for you to take a course in typing and shorthand. If you intend to keep on with your writing, it will be very valuable to you; if you decide otherwise—well, there are not enough *good* secretaries in the world, in spite of all you may hear about girls being out of jobs. It will do no harm for you to have this profession to fall back on if writing or some other job fails you.

Your punctuation and spelling are good, too. Forgive me for remarking on that, but I get so many almost illiterate letters from people who, I know, must have had the advantages of education it gives me pleasure to read a letter from someone who is aware of the value of these things.

My secretary, Miss Baugh, wrote you why I would not be able to read your manuscript, but I must enlarge on that subject a little, for I would not have you think I am not interested in you and your work. I have been deluged with similar requests during the past few years. If I had read only a fraction of the manuscripts people wished me to read, I would have had no time to handle my business affairs, or even to eat or sleep. As I could not do this for everyone, it did not seem proper to do it for a few, so I have never read any.

A more important reason is this. I am not the proper person to read manuscripts. The only people who should read them and criticize them are the people who make their living in this way and who know what will sell and what will not sell. They are teachers, literary agents, writers' advisers, editors of magazines and book publishers. The opinions of non-professionals are not worth anything and are frequently harmful to the young writer.

Now, Patricia, I want to tell you that my blood went cold when I read that you had even thought of setting out to Atlanta with only fifteen dollars in your pocket. I thought how dreadful it would have been had you landed here penniless and without friends during my absence from town. It is not a pleasant experience for anyone of any age to be far from home and "broke" and friendless, and I should not wish that experience for you. As a reporter, I saw too many young runaways and I remember them too vividly. At best, you would have fallen into the hands of the Traveler's Aid or Judge Watkins[1] of the Juvenile Court and sent home. At worst,—well, I do not like to think of that. I hope before you set out to conquer the world, as all of us must do at some time in our

---

[1] Judge Garland M. Watkins.

lives, you will be well armed for the fight with more years than you now have, a good education and the ability to do some one job exceptionally well. You had a correct and adult viewpoint when you wrote that you knew "success comes only from hard work and many sacrifices." Just hold hard to that idea whenever you have the impulse to take the bit in your teeth.

Your lovely handkerchief was greatly admired by my friends on my visit to Florida, and I thank you for it all over again.

Mr. Erskine Caldwell   Atlanta, Georgia
Darien, Connecticut   February 13, 1941

My dear Mr. Caldwell:

I am enclosing a copy of a letter my attorney has sent to Twentieth Century–Fox Film Company. I believe it will be self explanatory.

I am sending you this because I suppose you will hear from the West Coast about the matter, and I would rather you learn of it from me and see a full statement of my position, instead of receiving third-hand, garbled reports.

The situation the movie people have created, and the necessity of writing a letter of this kind, embarrass me, and I fear it will be equally embarrassing to you. I sold a book to Hollywood, so I know that authors have little or nothing to do with the movie adaptations of their books and, unfortunately, very little control over the cheap type of publicity the movie companies delight in. The fame of your book and the record-breaking run of your play have given "Tobacco Road" such renown that there was certainly no need for the movie company to try to link up your work with my novel. "Tobacco Road" was going strong before "Gone With the Wind" was ever published, and will probably be going strong long after "Gone With the Wind" is one with Nineveh and Tyre. In spite of your great success with "Tobacco Road," the movie company is acting as if your play had to be tied up with my novel in order to get stories into the newspapers. And many people will think that you personally were responsible. The public knows so little of how such matters are handled the author frequently gets the blame for the tricks played by movie publicity departments. I know because I spent five years battling to keep my name from being misused in connection with the movie of my book.

From the "Tobacco Road" publicity I have read which has been linked up with "Gone With the Wind," it appears to me that the movie people are intending to change the basic meaning of your play completely. If they proceed as it appears they will proceed, I will not be surprised to learn that Sister Bessie is being addressed as "Little Missy" and Jeeter himself as "Ol' Mars'r."

I hope we have better luck in getting together the next time you come South. We have met, you know. I worked on the Magazine Section of the Journal when you used to come downstairs to get books to review.

Mrs. Helen Dortch Longstreet   Atlanta, Georgia
Longstreet Memorial Association   February 25, 1941
Savannah Beach, Georgia

Dear Mrs. Longstreet:

... I am sorry that you believe I "knowingly ... did irreparable wrong to the military renown of one of the greatest commanders of all time." Such was not my intent. It is true that "Gone With the Wind" contains the line you quoted, "If Longstreet had obeyed orders at Gettysburg"[1] et cetera. In writing "Gone With the Wind" I tried to write it from the viewpoint of people living at the time of the War, and not as an author looking backward over seventy years. I included in my book the thoughts and sayings and viewpoints of the people who lived in the troublous Sixties. I read hundreds of letters and documents and memoirs and I recalled innumerable conversations I had heard as a little girl when my elders spoke of those days. As you well know, there were many controversies arising out of many happenings during the War. General Longstreet's conduct at Gettysburg had both criticism and defense just as the actions of General Johnston and General Hood always brought out fiery argument. The record of nearly every great Confederate leader was the subject of pro and con argument—but you know of these historic things far better than I do. In including the "if" about General Longstreet, I was quoting from the general conversation of the day of which I wrote. This is shown clearly by the context of my book where the quotation occurs, so clearly there could be no justification for giving any different interpretation to the statement.

In my own family the memory of General Longstreet has always been revered and his high qualities as a soldier have always been appreciated. In fact, one of the family stories which is most popular centers about my grandfather on that great day in Atlanta when Jefferson Davis came to unveil the Ben Hill monument. My grandfather was riding home hastily to gather his family for the parade. He was late and the crowds were

[1] *GWTW*, p. 739.

already banking the streets. A number of Confederate veterans mistook him for General Longstreet. They raised cheers and, rushing forward, stopped his horse. The crowds took up the cheering and it was some while before my proud but embarrassed grandfather could convince them that he was not their old commander. That incident made a great day even greater for him.

You were kind enough to write that you would like to send me your story of Gettysburg.[2] I would be most happy to have it should you still wish to send it to me.

Mr. Edison Marshall   Atlanta, Georgia
Augusta, Georgia   February 26, 1941

Dear Mr. Marshall:

Your book,[1] with its wonderful inscription, has just arrived and I am so pleased and proud to have it. There is something very nice about going through a stack of business mail et cetera and finding a lovely surprise package. My curiosity about your new book had been whetted during my recent trip to Athens, Georgia, when Mr. Flythe[2] told me about it. I know I will enjoy it.

To tell the truth, I think you *owed* me this book or something else nice because you were to blame for some of my gray hairs. Back before "Gone With the Wind" was published, I got a frenzied phone call from Macon, Georgia. You were to speak before the Macon Writers' Club and something had happened (an illness or a death in your family, I believe) and you were unable to come. They wanted me to pinch hit for you and at first I laughed merrily, for I had never made a speech in my life before then, and, having learned my lesson on that occasion, have never made another one. The Macon people used threats to get me there. They threatened never to invite me to another barbecue, so I went. I have no memory whatever of what I said, as my fright and anguish were extreme. I recall only two things—a very stout lady who fell on the floor with laughter and my intense indignation at you for getting me into such a fix.[3] I have thought at times of going to Augusta and assassinating you

---

[2] *Lee and Longstreet at High Tide, Gettysburg in the Light of the Official Records* (Gainesville, Ga., 1904).

[1] *Benjamin Blake* (New York, Toronto [c. 1941]).

[2] Starkey Sharp Flythe of Augusta.

[3] Miss Mitchell's long and amusing letter to Lois Dwight Cole about her speech to the Macon Writers Club appears in Farr, pp. 116–19. The speech is also the subject of an excellent article by Marian Elder Jones, "Me and My Book," in *The Georgia Review*, XVI (1962), 180–187.

but time has mellowed me, and the gift of "Benjamin Blake" squares the matter completely.

Mr. Danton Walker   Atlanta, Georgia
New York, New York   March 28, 1941

. . . I know you are a very busy person, so I was flattered that you took the time to write me about your Atlanta and Southern connections. I know Marietta, Georgia, so well and my husband and I frequently go there. It is a beautiful old town and full of interesting houses. I must admit that I envy you your birthplace. Why couldn't I have been born in General Johnston's headquarters? Or even in one of the million houses General Sherman used for his headquarters! I wish I could claim some historic house for my birthplace.

You spoke of the remains of the Atlanta breastworks in the yard of your cousin, Doctor Herbert Reynolds. I have never trespassed in *his* back yard, but I know a section of this same entrenchment which lies a quarter of a mile west in a patch of woods almost on Peachtree Street, near one of our busiest suburban intersections. This bit of woodland has been in the possession of the same Atlanta family since the Indians left this section and it has never been built up. It is strange to find the old earthworks so close to the busy traffic of Peachtree Street. Very few people know about it. Most of the earthworks which defended Atlanta were leveled off many years ago when the town was rapidly expanding.

I thought that Robert Henry (author of "The Story of the Confederacy" and "The Story of Reconstruction") and I were the only people who liked Kurz and Allison prints.[1] Bob picked up two for me in Chicago some years ago and I treasure them. I have the "Battle of Kennesaw Mountain" which you own, and the "Battle of Atlanta." I hope you have the "Battle of Atlanta," too. Like "Kennesaw," it is a wondrous and fearsome creation and reminds me of that series of sketches Gluyas Williams made many years ago about Santa Fe (or Atlanta or Charleston), "by one who has never been there." The artists even threw in a few palm trees to make Atlanta look tropical, and I have never understood why they overlooked Spanish moss. As for Kennesaw Mountain, it looks like one of the peaks of the Andes instead of its softly curved self.

Yes, do come to see me if you ever get down to Atlanta. And if you care for entrenchments, we will trespass in Collier Woods. But please

[1] Kurz and Allison was a firm of Chicago printmakers who published a series of Civil War battle prints.

come as a friend and not as a reporter looking for copy. That's not a hospitable thing to say to one who has been as nice as you, and I do not mean it the way it sounds. It's just that I am trying to get back to a normal life. After nearly five years in the public eye, I am frankly weary of the burdens and my meetings with people are pleasanter if there is no interview lurking in the background. As a Southerner, you will understand. . . .

Mrs. Walter F. George   Atlanta, Georgia
Washington, D.C.   April 14, 1941

My dear Mrs. George:

My husband and I have just returned from our visit with his people and discovered, to our disappointment, that we had missed the recent exciting meeting in Atlanta.[1] I called the Henry Grady Hotel but discovered that you and Senator George had returned to Washington. I regret more than I can tell you that I missed the opportunity to take advantage of your invitation to call on you while you were here.

I feel that I owe you a further explanation of my inability to attend the luncheon of the Georgia delegation, to which you invited me while I was in Washington. I would not have you think that I was unappreciative or disinterested. I was really so very pleased and flattered and wanted to come very much. It happened that before leaving Atlanta I had made an engagement to see one of the officials at the Department of State on business and I did not know how long the engagement would last. The "business" had to do with the foreign copyright troubles that I have had and am having with "Gone With the Wind." I wanted to tell you the whole situation when I spoke with you over the telephone but I could not. I had a number of young and charming visitors in my room at the time and, while they were delightful young girls, I did not feel that I could trust to their discretion, and the Department of State expects me to be discreet in such matters.

Several years ago, when "Gone With the Wind" ran into its first difficulties abroad and I did not know where to turn for assistance, Senator George was most kind and helpful to me. He took the entire morning of a very busy day to accompany me to the Department of State and see that I met the proper person to handle my difficulties. I have always been so grateful to him for his consideration and assistance, for my foreign

---

[1] Senator George spoke at a regional Defense Rally in Atlanta on April 11 and at an Institute on Federal Taxation on April 12. Atlanta *Constitution*, April 11, 12.

copyright problems grew as time went on, and the people at the Department of State have been of great aid and comfort to me. So, on the occasion of my recent visit to Washington I had made an engagement without limiting the time and, as you can understand, it was an engagement I could not break, even though I wished so much to be with you and the other Georgians at the luncheon.

I hope if I am ever in Washington again you will give me two "rainchecks"—first, to call upon you, and the second to attend one of those Georgia luncheons. The kindness of the people of my State to me and my book has meant more to me than I can ever express, but I'd like to have the chance to try to demonstrate my appreciation to some of them!

I cannot close without telling you how wonderfully proud all of us are of Senator George. We not only feel honored in having such a man represent us as Senator but we feel safe in having him speak for us. In these unhappy days when there is far too little sense of safety in the world, it is good to know that we have a man of Senator George's judgment and courage as head of the Committee on Foreign Relations.

Mr. Edison Marshall   Atlanta, Georgia
Augusta, Georgia   April 23, 1941

My dear Edison:
    You wrote that I could keep your letter or throw it away, remember it or forget it—and answer it or not as I pleased. If it's just the same to you, I will keep your letter and answer it, and I am not likely to forget it because letters like this do not often come my way, or any writer's way, I imagine. Thank you very much for it. You are a kind and generous person and there is not an oversupply of these two qualities in the world. It is an exciting and humbling experience to run across them. I thank you for what you said about my book, and of course I thank you even more for that line "you are greater than the book."[1]

[1] Marshall met Miss Mitchell when he was in Atlanta in the spring of 1941 for a meeting of the Ten Club. After returning to his home in Augusta he wrote on April 19: "I have discovered who wrote GWTW. It wasn't the blind beggar, or any bed-ridden screwy uncle or aunt, and it wasn't even S. Lewis. It was written by a woman named Margaret Mitchell, and you can't believe how this simplifies matters.
    "Mind you, it was a remarkable book. I am proud to say that never once did I blame the typhoon on interest in the Civil War, or the right moment of publication, or any other of the familiar alibis of people who can't look another's fame in the face. When at the Ten Club I asked an old boy what his opinion was. (The discussion was How Come?) He answered very simply and quietly, 'Why, it was a work of art.' You don't make two million people come across with three hard bucks for mere printed matter. You don't excite the whole world so that the English say of scooting Americans

As to your closing remarks about any other work I may turn out in the future and the psychological handicap I *might* suffer because of the success of "Gone With the Wind"—I wish I could talk to you personally about this, for such things are difficult to put on paper. Fortunately, this psychological handicap of fearing that another book would not measure up to "Gone With the Wind" does not exist at all. That is, it does not exist in me, although it flourishes in the minds of many other people who have called me a "one book writer" or said that the reason I had never written anything else was because I was afraid of critical reactions. I have been writing all my life and I never wrote for a public or for publication, with the exception of my newspaper stuff. I wrote for myself and will continue to do so as long as I live. If I had written with the public in mind I would have tried to sell my stuff years before "Gone With the Wind" was published. And if I had had critics in mind I would never have written "Gone With the Wind" at all, for the Civil War was deader than Hector and long Victorian novels completely out of style. When and if I ever get the time to do any more writing, I will write what I want to write, without any worry as to comparisons with "Gone With the Wind." Of course I will never have another sale like "Gone With the Wind," even if my future books are a hundred times better. That's only to be expected. And no matter how superior another book might be to "Gone With the Wind," the reactions of critics and readers would not be as enthusiastic. That's only natural, too, and it would not bother me. I might write a good book, and I might write a very sorry one, but it would be the very best book I could write at that particular time. And I would not be worried if other people thought it inferior to "Gone With the Wind." After all, a writer is responsible only to himself, not to the critics or to the world, and I would think the only thing that could hurt would be the knowledge that a book was *not* the very best a writer had in him at that particular time.

'Gone with the wind up,' over a common book. You don't enliven the existence of millions with fiction characters on account of an accident. So what?

"I had been looking for the explanation—not the explanation of its success, which is all between the covers of the book, but the explanation for its appearance. I soon found that no bed-ridden genius would work, still nothing that I had heard about you explained it. Subconscious mind sort of twaddle? You just a loud speaker for the stream of consciousness or some other kind of hocus-pokus? It was the best I could do until the last month.

"Now I know the answer. The book, for all its magnitude, was not greater than you. You are greater than the book. Don't let anyone kid you about this, or don't kid yourself. Of course there won't be another full-reef typhoon; on second thought, I'm not even sure of that. There might be, damned possibly. But if ever, contemplating that havoc, you let your imagination run wild and whisper that you'd better not write any more books, that you can't write such a book again, address it in coarse language and tell it where to get off. You can write books till the cows come home."

I say again that you were generous to tell me that I should clout on the ear any wild imaginings that I could not write another book. You know as well as I do that many people of our profession are not extraordinarily generous to each other, so I value your letter and thank you for it. . . .

Mr. Robert Sherwood   Atlanta, Georgia
New York, New York   June 3, 1941

Dear Mr. Sherwood:

When I read the news of your recent Pulitzer Award,[1] I felt the same pleasure and satisfaction I would have had if the honor had gone to one of my close personal friends. Perhaps it is another evidence of the power of your play, when someone wholly unknown to you feels such warm pride in this new recognition of your work. So, please permit me to offer my sincere congratulations.

My husband and I saw "There Shall Be No Night" shortly after it opened, and I cannot tell you how much it impressed us. When I told Mr. and Mrs. Lunt about its powerful effect on me, they sent me "There Shall Be No Night" in book form. I have re-read it several times, and it reads as well as it acts. The play is a sobering and horrifying and simple recital of what can happen to brave and decent and gentle people in this strange world. At first glance it would seem that gentleness and decency and courage are of no value these days, but when I left the theater (and each time when I closed the book) I realized anew that these qualities are really the only valuable things, the only weapons that will not break. My husband and I were sorry to learn from the Lunts some while ago that your play would not show in Atlanta. I have seen newspaper statements that it will reopen in New York this fall and I sincerely hope so.[2] I do not get North often—once in two years seems to be my average— but I hope I have the opportunity to see it again.

While I am thanking you for your last play, I would like to include

[1] For *There Shall Be No Night*.
[2] Sherwood wrote in a letter to Miss Mitchell on June 23: "We had planned to reopen 'There Shall Be No Night' in New York about October 1st and play a few return engagements in the North and then take it on a tour of the South, from Texas to the Atlantic Coast. In view of the latest startling events, I don't know whether we shall be able to do the play again. Poor little Finland is now a part of the Axis— which provides practically the last word in chaos. However, I believe that people will realize that this new development of homicidal mania is another extension of the tragedy of Finland as a symbol of 'gentleness and decency and courage' (to quote your own words)."

thanks for your first one. I recall "The Road to Rome"[3] as the high spot of a long-ago trip to New York. I have the book and it keeps memory fresh. I wish I could see it once more!

LCDR E. John Long   Atlanta, Georgia
Washington, D.C.   June 23, 1941

My dear Lieutenant Commander Long:

Thank you for your letter, the publicity release and the picture of the old U.S.S. Atlanta.

I am enclosing some biographical material which I hope will be of assistance to you. When you boil it all down it really amounts to little more than the information you had in the second paragraph of your press release. As you probably understood, my reason for offering to send you authentic information was to avoid further circulation of untrue rumors. The facts concerning my life and the writing and publication of "Gone With the Wind" are very unexciting, and it is for this very reason that the many strange "legends" I referred to in my previous letter have sprung up about me. I suppose people who did not know me were driven to frenzies by the paucity of color surrounding me and my book, and so they invented remarkable and absurd and embarrassing stories. Ever since "Gone With the Wind" was published, I have had to fight rumors that I was blind or a hopeless invalid or had written "Gone With the Wind" while in a plaster cast with a broken back. I have no children but children have been given me by enterprising writers; I have my same husband but I have been credited with a divorce from him any number of times. Because of the public pressure upon me since my book was published and the enormous amount of business details I have had to handle, I have had no opportunity to do any writing since "Gone With the Wind." Yet, there is a firmly fixed legend, which appears in newspapers about once a week, that I have written a sequel to "Gone With the Wind," or some other book. But I have written nothing. I have also been credited with the statement that I never intended to write another line, and of course I never said that either. There is another rumor that I have made from a million to fifty million dollars out of "Gone With the Wind," but, alas, neither of these figures comes anywhere near the truth. . . .

The truth about me is quite dull and normal and it could be the story

---

[3] (New York, London, 1928). Sherwood commented: "Thank you also for remembering my first attempt at playwriting—'The Road to Rome.' "

of a thousand other Atlanta women. I was born in Atlanta of people who had lived here or in this neighborhood since the Indians left the section. I went to school here, had a year at Smith College, made my debut, worked on the Atlanta Journal as a feature writer, married John Marsh, wrote and sold "Gone With the Wind," and since that time have been trying to outride the deluge which has descended on me, somewhat disrupting my quiet life.

I cannot think of any specially new angle which you could use except this one—I know of few other Atlanta people who can claim that their families have been associated as long and intimately, and sometimes as prominently, with the birth and growth and history of this city as my family has been. On both paternal and maternal lines my people lived in the neighborhood of Atlanta before the city was founded. Atlanta is a young town, as Southern towns go, and there are not many people here who can say that six generations of their families have lived in the town. This reason, I think, qualifies me as the sponsor of the U.S.S. Atlanta far more than the authorship of "Gone With the Wind"!

Now I am going to put a heavy burden on you. I would not do it if I knew where else to turn. Besides, I feel that I know you and can speak frankly with you. I have been notified that at some later date I will be informed about the details of the launching. As yet I have heard nothing and when I do hear I am afraid the "details" may consist only of a brief note telling me the time of day and the place of the launching. I am afraid that those in charge of the matter may take it for granted that I know all about such ceremonies. The truth is that I know less than nothing. You are in a position to give me information and advise me, and that is why I am asking you for assistance.

I will be most grateful if you will write me anything you can think of which a person ought to know when she is approaching an experience such as is ahead of me but is completely ignorant of everything involved in such events. All of my life has been spent in an inland city. I have never attended a ship launching of any kind and I know no one who has. I have never been in or near a shipyard. Literally my only information is from a few pictures of launchings which I have seen in news reels but they were brief and I did not observe them carefully. I now wish that I had! So I must ask someone for information and advice and I am turning to you. Some of my questions may seem ingenuous, so I hope you will keep this part of my letter confidential.

First, I would like to know, as soon as possible, the time of day when the launching will occur. I must buy clothes for the affair and cannot do so until I know whether it is to be in the morning or the afternoon. As it takes me approximately three weeks to find and fit a dress and a hat, I really need this information as far ahead as possible. Also, my stay in the

North may be very brief, perhaps just a few hours, because my father is quite ill. As I may need to return home hurriedly, I'd like to know the time so that I can arrange my railroad schedule. I would be very grateful to you, too, if you would find out for me if anything is expected of me before or after the launching. Knowing nothing about such affairs, I do not know if a luncheon precedes or follows a christening or if there are any other formalities or festivities. If there are, again I must think of clothes and railroad schedules.

I am expecting to stay at some New York hotel, but how do I get to and from the shipyard? Would it be in accord with Navy customs for them to send a car to the hotel for me, or should I arrange my own transportation? If I am not escorted, where should I present myself in Kearny, New Jersey, and to whom? How long before the official hour of the ceremonies? How far is Kearny from New York and about how much time should I allow myself in getting there by taxicab from midtown New York? If the trip is too far to go by taxicab, what other transportation arrangements should I make?

What is the usual program at launching ceremonies and about how long do they last? Of course, if the program for August 9th has already been decided upon, I would like to know what it is. But even without that specific information, you can help me by telling me what is the traditional program on such occasions. If there is no traditional program, you might tell me what was the program at the battleship launching which you said you attended recently.

I hope it is not customary for sponsors to make speeches or even utter what is known as "a few brief words." But if such is the custom, please break it to me gently.

Here is another point, which may seem amusing to you but is serious to me. I am small, not quite five feet tall. On several dreadful occasions in the past I have found myself presented with arm bouquets made of flowers with stems a yard long. It took both my arms to hold such bouquets and I was considerably hampered in performing the duties expected of me. If the Navy has any intention of presenting me with flowers, could you please see to it that they are small? Otherwise, I wouldn't get a good enough view of the ship to swing the bottle!

I mention the flowers because I seem to remember having seen launching photographs showing the sponsor holding a bouquet in one arm and swinging the bottle with the other. If the Navy does not present the flowers, who does? I would like to know, so I can warn one and all not to make the bouquet too large. Furthermore, would I be violating one of the Navy's sacred traditions if I had no flowers at all? Or laid the flowers down some place when it came time for the launching? On account of my smallness, I would really prefer to have both arms free, so I could take a good two-handed swing with the bottle.

Along that line, have you any suggestions about the technique of smashing bottles on battleships? It would be terrible if I missed or failed to break the bottle. Is there any kind of covering on the bottle to prevent the glass from flying? Does the champagne usually spray on the sponsor as well as the battleship, so that I can expect to christen a dress as well as the U.S.S. Atlanta? And will you please ask the proper person to see that the platform is constructed with consideration for my size, so that my smallness will not prevent me from getting a proper swing.

Answering all of these questions will be burden enough on you, but I am inviting you also to offer any suggestions that occur to you about details which I have overlooked. Especially would I welcome your advice on any taboos which I should avoid and any customs which a sponsor should observe.

I would especially like to know whether it is customary for the sponsor to make a gift to the ship she christens. If not customary, would such a gift be contrary to Navy traditions or, for any other reason, in bad taste? If it is proper for me to make a gift to the U.S.S. Atlanta, I would naturally want it to be something that is truly of the City of Atlanta. After considerable thinking and searching, I have come to the conclusion that the only thing which fills the bill is some after-dinner coffee cups which our Atlanta Historical Society had made by Wedgwood in England. On each cup there is a small scene from old Atlanta—the beautiful home that was General Sherman's headquarters, the old "car-shed" which appeared so vividly in the film of "Gone With the Wind," the City Hall around which the Federal troops camped after the capture of the city, the old Kimball House which was the center of social and political activities in Reconstruction days, and a number of other scenes. If such a gift would be all right, have you any ideas as to how many of the cups I should give?

As I wrote above, these are after-dinner cups and saucers, which means that they are small and delicate. I am sure Navy officers like cups which hold a quart and if I could get large size cups I would do so. Please tell me if you think the gift of the after-dinner cups would be inappropriate to such a highly masculine set of people as Naval officers. I would not wish to put anyone in an embarrassing situation by offering a gift which they might think inappropriate.

If you think the cups would not be appropriate—and please do not hesitate to speak frankly—could you give me any suggestions about a gift that would be suitable? If you could tell me what kind of gifts have been made by some other sponsors, that might be the best way of answering this question. Also, if I do make a gift of some kind, when and to whom should it be presented?

I have written you as frankly as I know how and I hope you will reply in the same manner. No doubt, the formal notification of the arrangements, which the Navy has promised to send me, will answer some of my questions but an informal discussion of the subject by you will give me a wider and deeper understanding of what is ahead of me. Probably you have photographs in your files of previous launchings. If you could send me a few of them, I would like to study them and I will be glad to return them to you.

For all of these favors I am asking, my very sincere thanks now and always.

My photographs turned out well. I am sending under separate cover one of incredible flatteringness.

Mr. John Marquand　　　　　　　　　　　Atlanta, Georgia
Chairman, Writers' Committee　　　　　　June 25, 1941
United China Relief, Inc.
New York, New York

Dear Mr. Marquand:

I am so glad your United China Relief letter came because it gives me that small added push I needed for writing this letter to you. I have had it on my mind for several years, ever since George Apley became a dear family friend.[1] I put off writing you of my admiration for your books and my gratitude to you for them, because at the end of each business day I was too weary to collect my mind. Then a year or two ago Herschel Brickell was visiting us and he said it was highly possible that you would be in Atlanta on your way to Natchez. I thought, with pleasure, that perhaps my husband and I might have the opportunity of meeting you and then we could tell you of our great admiration for your writing. I find talking much easier than writing and there are so many fine things in your books that I knew I could never cram them all into a letter. I am sorry you didn't come. I hope if you are ever in this section you will let us know.

I have read "George Apley" and "Wickford Point"[2] a number of times, and there is something in them which always delights me and yet puzzles me. You are, I believe, a New Englander by birth. If not, you certainly

[1] John Phillips Marquand, *The Late George Apley* (Boston, 1937).
[2] (Boston, 1939).

know the New England character. And yet, how truly you know some of the sides of the old fashioned Southern character. In many ways Mr. Apley and his family and friends could have come out of an old Southern city instead of Boston. That part about the slight unpleasantness concerning the Apley burial lot is so typically Southern that I laugh whenever I re-read it. I have heard such quarrels rehashed all my life. In fact, after every funeral in some old Southern families, there are polite but somewhat embittered words about people being buried in the wrong places.

And, as for Bella and Clothilde (oh, especially Clothilde!), they are so beautifully Southern. Sectional pride and local patriotism should force me to keep silent about this, even if I believed it, but I am unable to restrain myself. Perhaps what I am trying to say is that your characters are universal. I have just finished "H. M. Pulham, Esq."[3] and I feel very sad. I want to re-read him several times before I even discuss him with my husband.

This is a very poor substitute for the letter I would like to write you. Perhaps my difficulty is in the fact that I consider you a very great writer and I don't quite know how to tell you so without seeming effusive. Perhaps I can best express my admiration by saying that I hope there will be many more books from you.

Dr. Henry C. Link   Atlanta, Georgia
New York, New York   July 28, 1941

My dear Doctor Link:

Several years ago I read, in the Saturday Evening Post, your essay on The Rediscovery of Man.[1] I found it truly exciting, for in these days it is rare to find in print anyone who says uncompromisingly that the individual is responsible for himself and that the potentialities of the individual are limitless. I had found your article vastly interesting long before I came to the close of it and discovered that you had mentioned Scarlett O'Hara and her "personal triumph over social insecurity."[2] I was

---

[3] (Boston, 1941).

[1] "The Rediscovery of Man" was printed in *Reader's Digest*, XXXIV (1939), June, pp. 42–45, as a condensation from the book *The Rediscovery of Man* (New York, 1938).

[2] Dr. Link wrote: "Aside from religion and the discoveries of psychology, the true concept of man, strange to say, has survived in the literature of fiction. At this writing the novel, *Gone With the Wind*, has been purchased by a million and a half people and read, probably, by ten million. Why? Many have asked this question. The explanation may be this: Scarlett, though in many ways not an admirable person, was

very pleased and flattered at this mention and it was my intention to write and tell you so at the time. Unfortunately, at that period of my life I was not doing many things I wished to do, as I was so beset by things I had to do. You, as a psychologist and as an author, can understand without explanation from me what happens to people who are suddenly rocketed into the limelight. The public has a way of occupying twenty-five hours a day of such people's time.

Since reading your article, I have turned it over in my mind often, and recently when life began to settle down again for me and I had time to do things of my choice, I got your book, "The Rediscovery of Man," and re-read the article. It made an even deeper impression on me at this reading than before.

I cannot tell if you are correct in your opinion that the success of "Gone With the Wind" is due to the fact that "Scarlett, though in many ways not an admirable person, was a woman who remained forever the master of her world rather than its victim." Even after this long period I am just as bewildered about the success of my book as I was during the first week of its life and have just as little explanation for its popularity. But you might be interested in this. I have had a great many letters and conversations with people who told me that Scarlett had affected them in the way you diagnosed. Some said, wonderingly, "I realized that, while I was having a bad time, my problems were not as difficult as hers and that a little bit of gumption on my part would solve them" or "I thought if she could do what she did when she had nothing to fight with but courage, then I should be ashamed to fail and whine when I had more real capacity than she had." I have heard countless variations on this theme and always there was the faintly surprised note of people discovering a use in their own lives for the spirit of Southerners "who were defeated and would not know defeat." When I wrote my novel, I had no purpose but to tell a story but the comments of many readers show that your remarks about Scarlett were very true and very penetrating.

This is a strange world when an article such as yours can be almost revolutionary. I am old enough to recall the time when little children were taught to recite "Invictus" and to believe in it. But when I grew

---

a woman who remained forever the master of her world rather than its victim. Neither war, nor disappointment in love, nor scandal, nor starvation, nor the burning of her home, nor the pain of childbirth, nor bloodshed, none of these catastrophes could daunt her spirit. Here was a woman who experienced in a short lifetime more tragedies than most people ever dream, who rushed to meet disaster, and emerged with courage unimpaired. Here was a woman who, to many suffering the comparative luxuries of a depression today, exemplified a personal triumph over social insecurity. Ten million readers! Ten million nostalgic gasps from the victims of a machine concept of social security, a people still faintly protesting against the loss of personal responsibility and power." Pp. 23–24.

up it was fashionable for the intellectuals and the sophisticates to cry down this poem and its implications and to point the finger of laughing scorn at Kipling's "If." We are in a period now when no man is expected to be the master of his fate and the captain of his soul but, as you expressed it, a mere helpless pawn of circumstance. I hope I live long enough to see us come out on the other side of this strange country in which we have been wandering. The more articles such as yours the shorter our journey will be.

I found the rest of your book every bit as interesting as the part which mentioned Miss O'Hara. Your ideas on habits and the building of personality should be as much a part of our belief as folklore. But then again, they are highly revolutionary because of the teachings of the last thirty years which have laid deficiencies in character and personality not at the door of the individual but on his genes and chromosomes or his ductless glands or that mysterious something called "the system."

Mr. Fontaine Fox   Atlanta, Georgia
Greenwich, Connecticut   August 5, 1941

Dear Mr. Fox:

I don't know anything more exciting than to receive a gift that I hadn't expected or worked for or even deserved. When I opened the package Jessie[1] left at our apartment I had no idea what it contained, and I cannot tell you of my excitement and pleasure when I saw Grandma, the Demon Chaperone, practically in the flesh. It was so very generous of you to send me this original drawing, and the inscription on it added greatly to my pleasure.

Jessie and I are graduates of the same first aid class, and it was while we were recuperating from artificial respiration that we fell to talking about Grandma. I told how, many years ago when I was a very young bride, I found myself chaperoning a house party composed of people somewhat older than I was. I took my chaperoning very seriously and felt my duty to their parents in a large way. As I look back on that house party, I recall that my charges did nothing which I had not done before I reached the exalted position of matronhood. But I thought they were conducting themselves in too loud and sprightly a manner and I made many carping remarks. As they were a high-spirited bunch, they paid no attention to my admonitions beyond screaming, "Grandma, the Demon Chaperone," to me. This was very disconcerting to my new dignity and, alas, the term hung on for several years. That I could still

[1] Mrs. Dan MacDougald.

love Grandma after this ignominious experience is a true test of Grandma's real worth.

I am so fond of all the Toonerville folks. They are so truly American, like the people of Mark Twain and Bill Nye. My husband, who is advertising manager of the Georgia Power Company and who knows transportation problems, is naturally very fond of the Toonerville Trolly. . . .

The Hon. Eugene Talmadge   Atlanta, Georgia
Atlanta, Georgia   August 30, 1941

My dear Governor Talmadge:

When you telephoned me the other night, I promised you that I would give serious thought to your request that I write a History of Georgia to be used in the Georgia public schools. I am greatly honored by your request and I have given it serious thought, but my ideas about the matter are still the same that I expressed to you on the telephone. I am a novelist and a newspaper reporter, not a scholar or historian, and I do not consider myself qualified to write a history. It is not mock modesty that makes me say this; it is only a very thorough knowledge of my limitations.

If I did undertake this task, the research alone would take me a long time, perhaps several years. It is not in me to do a slap-dash, hurried, inaccurate job which would bring embarrassment upon me and upon Georgia as well. A great deal of research for a History of Georgia would have to be done outside of this State. Unfortunately, many of the original documents, diaries, letters and other papers having to do with the history of our State are lost to Georgia forever. In years gone by, there was little official interest in securing these papers for Georgia and they were sold to institutions all over the country—to Duke University, the University of Texas, the University of Michigan and others. Because of the scattering of the research material, the work involved in assembling the necessary factual and background information would be many times more difficult.

Even after I had done the research and acquired the necessary data, if I were able to do that at all, it would still be a long time before I could complete a history, for I write very slowly. If I attempted to write a history I would need a long period of free and uninterrupted time—and free and uninterrupted time is something of which I have had less than nothing at all since my novel was published.

These are some of the difficulties that would arise if I tried to write a history. But the most important thing is that the writing of histories requires very special abilities and I do not possess them. Fiction writing is my field, and if I should ever again have the time for writing, fiction is what I shall probably try to write.

I thank you most sincerely for asking me to write a history of our State. I am thoroughly appreciative of the fact that you paid me a great compliment in saying that you thought I could do that kind of job. I wish I could oblige, for I would be proud to know that a history written by me was used in the Georgia schools. But I am not the proper person to write such a history.

Lieut. Kenneth Kalmbach, USNR   Atlanta, Georgia
Washington, D.C.   September 16, 1941

Dear Kenneth:

I have almost finished "Tory Oath"[1] and cannot tell you how much I enjoyed it. As you know, my Scottish Highland ancestors settled in the same places about which the book concerns itself and they, too, were loyal to the king, so the book was doubly interesting to me.

It was good of you to take the trouble of procuring the book and bringing it to me so that I would have something to read on the train. But then, that's like you because you always have been nice. I was sorry I had to cut short your visit but Mr. Adams, who reviewed "Gone With the Wind" in the New York Times when the book first came out, has been trying to get an interview with me since 1936. I had promised him faithfully that I'd give him some time to tell him about the book's sale and some of the history of "Gone With the Wind."

You don't know what a surprise, and what a pleasant surprise it was to have you walk up to me in uniform on that high, hot platform and say hello. If it hadn't been for three strong admirals behind me I'd probably have fallen overboard, so surprised was I. It was good to see a faithful old friend on so exciting an occasion.

Mr. J. Donald Adams   Atlanta, Georgia
New York Times   September 22, 1941
New York, New York

Dear Mr. Adams:

Now that the last bread-and-butter letter has been written and the business which had accumulated on my desk has been cleaned up, I can

[1] Tim Pridgen, *Tory Oath* (New York, 1941).

look back on my hurried trip to New York and recall in leisure the many pleasant things that happened to me. And how pleasant your call was! You doubtless did not know that you came at precisely the right moment, just after one of the most exciting yet tiring days of my life. It was good to sit and talk quietly with you about books and people we knew, and the sturdy Celtic strain in people which gives them many desirable qualities but carries its own price. I had looked forward to meeting you ever since 1936, but I certainly never dreamed it would be under such circumstances, or so much fun. I thought I'd have to be a Southern lady author on that occasion and you a gimlet-eyed critic with, for all I knew, a bowie knife in one hand and a large bag of salt in the other (the salt to be poured into the author's wounds).

I am enclosing something for your book.[1] I wish I could do it differently but I know you understand my situation and will overlook this technicality.

You will come to see us if you are in this section, I hope. My husband, who listened with great interest to the details of our conversation, adds his invitation to mine, and both our invitations are not conventional formalities but sincere.

Mr. Wesley W. Stout   Atlanta, Georgia
Saturday Evening Post   September 26, 1941
Philadelphia, Pennsylvania

Dear Mr. Stout:

I had never heard the remark you attributed to Percy Hammond about his hobby being "not writing," and I can't tell you how much I enjoyed it.

Thank you for giving me the dates of your vacation. I will try to arrange my next trip North so as not to come at a time when you are away from Philadelphia. The reason for my trip will be a visit to Wilmington, Delaware, to see my husband's family, and the time will depend largely on when John can leave his work here.

In the past I have been grateful to you on several occasions for querying me about various matters involving me, and now, after reading your item about Katharine Hepburn's biography, I am more grateful than I can tell you that you asked me about this before printing it. When I read that sentence in your letter, it actually made me weak because of the

---

[1] *The Shape of Books to Come* (New York, 1948). In this Adams discusses reasons for the popularity of *GWTW* and quotes what Dr. Link had written about it in *The Rediscovery of Man.*

sudden picture it flashed into my mind of those years when practically everybody in the United States was trying to trap me into stating my preference for Scarlett—and also in the knowledge, from bitter experience, of the enormous amount of trouble it would have caused if the item had been published by the Post.

Let me say now, flatfootedly, I never endorsed Katharine Hepburn for the part of Scarlett. From first to last, I never endorsed anybody or expressed the vaguest preference for anybody. And, to answer your question more directly, Katharine Hepburn was *not* my choice for Scarlett. Nobody was my choice; that is the literal truth, even though nobody apparently believed me then and perhaps nobody believes me now.

It is hard for me to understand why Miss Hepburn should make such a statement. The only basis she could have for it is that she knows my inner thoughts better than I do, and that my inner thoughts are just the opposite of my public denials. For I did make a public denial that she was my choice and I do not know how she could have failed to see it, for it was published in all the New York papers, in Life magazine (November 4 (?), 1938),[1] and in newspapers generally over the country.

The "Hepburn incident" in the fall of 1938 was the climax of those unbelievable events between the publication of my novel and the announcement in December 1938[2] that Vivien Leigh had been given the role of Scarlett. You have probably forgotten the details but you may remember that commentators remarked that the controversy, over who should play Scarlett, was equalled by nothing except a Presidential election. It was a strange phenomenon, especially to me, and I wanted no part of it, but never was a person so pulled and hauled about as I was. And never did a person have to fight harder to prevent her name from being misused to promote the candidacy of one actress or another.

When I sold the screen rights to David Selznick, it was with the understanding that I would have nothing to do with the picture in any way and must never be called upon to express an opinion or do any work on it. I knew nothing about the production of moving pictures, whereas Mr. Selznick has made name and fame in that field. Even if I had had strong preferences for the cast, which I did not, I would have kept silent. I would no more have presumed to tell him how to make his movie than I would permit him to tell me how to write a book. So, I had thought when I unloaded the movie rights that my problems were over, but they had just begun, and the years thereafter until the film was released were a nightmare.

It is not possible for me to give you any understanding of the many

[1] The correct date is November 7, 1938.
[2] January 1939.

and varied and incredible kinds of pressure that were brought to bear on me to make me come out in favor of one or another actress. People went to any lengths to try to entrap me into some statement they could twist in favor of their candidate. But, so help me, I never opened my mouth. I tried to be polite under this bombardment and to remain courteous in the face of frenzied people. As you can imagine, this was somewhat difficult.

And then something happened that is really incredible. Mrs. ———, of the New York Herald Tribune, announced that Katharine Hepburn was my choice for Scarlett! On October 11, 1938, Mrs. ——— telephoned me from New York to urge me to attend some sort of women's forum dinner in New York. I thanked her and declined. Thereafter Mrs. ——— spoke at length of Miss Hepburn, who was to make a talk at the dinner. Over and over she spoke words of praise for Miss Hepburn's acting, each time asking if I did not think Miss Hepburn the perfect type for Scarlett. I thought, "Oh, good God, here we go again," and told her that I had a strict rule of never discussing who should play Scarlett, that I never made any statements about it, one way or the other, that it was a matter for Mr. Selznick to decide, not me, and that I truly did not care who got the role. I also said, with considerable restraint, that here in the South we had quick ears for voices and that Miss Hepburn's perfect New England accent would scarcely be acceptable to people of this section.

The next thing I knew the news services and the press were on my neck, saying that the New York newspapers were stating that Mrs. ——— had "disclosed that she had visited Margaret Mitchell, author of 'Gone With the Wind,' at Atlanta, Georgia, and that Miss Mitchell had expressed a strong preference for Miss Hepburn for the screen role of the heroine of her famous novel." Of course they wanted a statement from me.

As you can imagine, I was on the spot—a spot I had occupied, wearily and far too often, during those years. It would have pleased the papers very much had I said flatly that Mrs. ——— had lied; and you can imagine what fine reverberations that would have had in gossip columns all over the country. At the risk of having you think me stuffy and old fashioned, I want to say that I think "brawling and feuding" in the public press is in very poor taste and, short of direct attacks upon my moral character or my private life, I do not make controversial statements. I told the press the whole situation and implored them to state my position without writing anything which might embarrass the innocent Miss Hepburn or the not-so-innocent Mrs. ———. The papers were very kind about it. Life for November 4(?), 1938, for instance, said, "In introducing her, Mrs. ———, vice-president of the Tribune, nominated Miss

Hepburn for Scarlett O'Hara in the movie of 'Gone With the Wind,' intimated the suggestion was Author Margaret Mitchell's choice. Politely, Miss Mitchell denied this, said she had no preferences." I am enclosing a copy of a story the Atlanta Journal printed. When these stories came out Mrs. ——— wired, saying she was "terribly sorry if I have caused you any annoyance," and then wrote. Her letter said, "I feel that I owe you an apology for not having asked if you minded my saying what I did." (What she had said was that Miss Hepburn was my choice "first, last and always," according to a copy of her remarks which she enclosed.) She could give little explanation for her conduct except that she thought I was merely being coy and "over-retiring" and that any movie producer ought to welcome my opinion.

Well, the "Who will play Scarlett?" controversy was ended a few months later when Miss Leigh's selection was announced and that phase of my life was over. Or is it over? If you should publish Miss Hepburn's statement that she was my secret choice, I am afraid the controversy would break out again, not as widespread and excited as before, but enough to put on me the burden of writing many letters and issuing fresh denials—and the time when I can do some more writing will be still further postponed, for the Scarlett controversy is one of the principal things that have used up my time and prevented me from attempting any writing since 1936.

Possibly, Miss Hepburn is quite innocent in her statement. It may be that Mrs. ——— led her to believe that I did secretly favor her. But it is not true and I hope you will not publish the falsehood.

I have been very frank with you in this letter, franker than I generally am, and perhaps far more frank than is wise. But I know enough of you by now to believe that you will keep this confidential.

I wish more editors of my acquaintance had been like you in the past and had asked me questions before hurrying into print. My life would certainly have been far less eventful.

Mr. and Mrs. Clifford Dowdey   Atlanta, Georgia
New York, New York   October 11, 1941

Dear Helen and Clifford:

I had a note this morning from Bob Henry. I'd written him how we three had spoken of him and John Thomason in New York and how you might at some time be in Richmond or Washington doing research. His note said, "Tell Clifford Dowdey that I shall think hard of him if he doesn't call me up when he comes to Washington. I'd tell him myself if

I knew where to write to him in New York." I had also remarked in my letter on the propensities of Southern writers of our ilk to "re-fight the War in which Our Glorious Cause was lost," like old veterans. Bob sent me a clipping which came on the same mail with my letter. It had notations on it from all his office staff. The headline read, "Robert S. Henry, Civil War Veteran, Age 93, Is Dead at Quincy." The clipping announced that he had served in Company D of the 120th Illinois Infantry. Bob said he really did feel like a veteran after reading this. I imagine it went hard with a Middle Tennessean to find himself dying, willy-nilly, in an Illinois regiment.

John and I have recently been plunged into the vortex of Atlanta social life and it has practically exterminated us. There are war weddings and attendant parties and Confederate Veterans Reunions and visitors in hordes and authors getting published. If this keeps up I'll be driven to writing another book so I can get some peace and quiet.

Mr. and Mrs. Alfred Lunt   Atlanta, Georgia
C/o Lanier Auditorium   November 11, 1941
Montgomery, Alabama

My dear Lynn and Alfred:
    I feel that the Victorian proprieties have been observed long enough between us and that we might call each other by first names without mutual loss of respect. Moreover, I cannot thank the donors of such beautiful birthday roses by their last names.

The roses were gorgeous and the red color of them was just my birthday rose shade. I suppose every couple has traditions, and red birthday roses are one of the Marsh family traditions. It was sweet and thoughtful of you both to add to my birthday happiness with your flowers as well as your presence at supper.

I am sending you the book I mentioned, "The Golden Isles of Georgia."[1] It is no formal history of our Coast section. In a way, it is almost a family history. The author is of the Couper family who were great planters in the sea island country before the Civil War. I think that the family touch in this book is what gives it charm.

You won our hearts completely when you spoke glowingly of Savannah, for the stretch of Coast from Savannah southward to Brunswick is, to us, the most beautiful place in the world. On the off chance that you may decide to take your vacation in this section, I'll tell you more

[1] Caroline Couper Lovell, *The Golden Isles of Georgia* (Boston, 1932).

about Sea Island Beach and The Cloister hotel. Sea Island has been lately developed, that is, within the last fifteen years, and is a small island lying across the marsh from the larger and more historic St. Simon's Island. Howard Coffin, the millionaire manufacturer, developed it and built the lovely but unpretentious Cloister hotel. My only objection to the hotel is that it does not look on either the sea or the marshes. Quite close to the hotel are the Cloister apartments, which are right on the edge of a lovely tidal river which meanders through the Marshes of Glynn. We like the apartments better than the hotel because they are quieter, the view is better and the rooms much larger. Should you decide to spend your vacation here, it would be well to write for reservations as far in advance as possible. Sea Island is not only popular with our Georgia people, but many Northerners patronize it during the colder months. Some of them even go swimming in the ocean in December and January, but that is beyond the desires of more thin-blooded Southerners. There are a pool to swim in, horses to ride, skeet shooting, hunting and golfing, but the nicest thing is to motor the long sandy roads under the huge trees covered with moss. Up at the end of St. Simon's Island where Fannie Kemble lived, there is a stillness of marsh water and trees like the day after creation, and this stillness never fails to have a very soothing effect on this weary and harassed pair.

I cannot begin to tell you how much Atlanta enjoyed you and the play. Yesterday when I went to town to shop, I did no shopping at all but spent the day standing on street corners discussing "There Shall Be No Night" and how marvelous you were.[2] There was in everyone I saw a deep sense of gratitude to you for going on the road, with all its inconveniences, to bring the real theatre to the hinterland. John and I share this gratitude. . . .

Captain and Mrs. S. P. Jenkins   Atlanta, Georgia
The USS Atlanta   December 26, 1941
Brooklyn Navy Yard
Brooklyn, New York

Dear Captain and Mrs. Jenkins:

Now that I am home again, my brief visit to the Navy Yard seems like the pleasantest sort of dream. It does not seem possible that I could have been to New York and returned and packed so many

---

[2] *There Shall Be No Night* played in Atlanta at the Erlanger Theatre November 6, 7, and 8. Atlanta *Constitution*, November 2.

pleasant and exciting happenings into so brief a space of time. The ceremonies of the commissioning were so impressive that I will never forget them, and the luncheon aboard the "Atlanta" was so pleasant that I must thank you both again.

Even in peace times, I would have felt a natural sense of pride at being sponsor of so fine a ship. Now, in time of war, that pride is increased a hundredfold, and with it is mingled a sense of faith in the ships and men of our Navy, and the "Atlanta" especially.

Captain Jenkins, I did not have the opportunity to discuss a certain matter with you while I was in Brooklyn, and so I will do it now. Does not each ship have a seamen's fund of some type, and has the "Atlanta" such a fund? If so, I should like to contribute something to it. If you will let me know how such a check should be made out I will send it immediately.

Thank you again for lining up the Atlanta and Georgia men for me to meet. It meant a great deal to me.

1942

Col. John William Thomason, Jr., U.S.M.C.   Atlanta, Georgia
Navy Department   January 3, 1942
Washington, D.C.

My dear Colonel Thomason:

I was overjoyed to have your note of December 31st bearing the sketch of the Confederate rifleman. I am sure you must have realized how much this picture would mean to me, and that is why you sent it. He is a fine, sturdy fellow and looks as if he could, and would, give a good account of himself. I am framing him for my office wall.

Perhaps you sent this sketch to me because I have had you on my mind recently. Like everyone else, the stand of the Marines in the Pacific has been something to make the hair on the back of my neck curl with pride. I thought of you because I had a notion that you'd like to be there, too, instead of in Washington. I know you must be full of grim pride yourself at the conduct of your corps and, from this far behind the lines, I send you my humble congratulations.

When I talked with you in Washington I told you that I had started many letters to you and never sent them. I could not put into words what I felt, no matter how hard I tried. I went through my files and found part of one of the letters I had written you and I am sending it to you. It is somewhat dirty and dogeared and I do not know when it was written. I only hope it is possible that some day you and your wife will be in Atlanta and we can sit under the rose arbor in my Aunt Aline's garden and talk about an old war which was, by comparison with the present one, a very gentlemanly affair.

My dear Col. Thomason:

This is a long letter to inflict upon a stranger but as it has been in the writing since 1926, when "Fix Bayonets!" was published,[1] I hope you will over look its length. As each new book or story by you appeared, the urge to write you and say "thank you—don't ever stop writing" has become stronger. And now, as I wait with little patience,

---

[1] John William Thomason, *Fix Bayonets!* (New York, 1926).

353

for each succeeding episode in the life of that remarkable creation, Praxiteles Swan, of Hood's Division, I can no longer deny myself the pleasure of telling you how much I have enjoyed all your stories.

I am sure that everyone who writes to you about the Elder Swan series must begin their letters with "my grandfather (or father) was one of Hood's Texans." The reason I am sure of that is that, since GWTW was published, nearly half of the letters I have received have begun that way or "one of old Joe's men." (I have found this a little baffling because if *all* the grandpas I've heard about were actually in old Joe's outfit, he'd have out numbered Sherman five to one and wiped him out at Resaca.)

So I am no different from your other readers and will not try to be different. My Mitchell grandfather, though Georgia born, was one of Hood's Texans, First Regiment of Infantry Volunteers, Company I; he enlisted at Alto, Texas, July 20, 1861, fought in eleven battles and was severely wounded at Sharpsburg—so severely wounded that when the litter bearers dumped him behind the church with the other wounded, his cousin by marriage, Surgeon General Roach,[2] declared there wasn't any use wasting time on him when he would live only a few hours. This incensed my grandfather for he felt that this was a reflection on his stamina. To be sure, a minie ball had gone through the back of his head, fracturing the skull in two places and he had minor abrasions, here and there, but he felt that Dr. Roach was speaking through ignorance. He said as much, rose up, and picking up another cousin, who was shot through the lungs, set out for Richmond. He walked, hitched hiked or was carried all the way, swimming a river or two on the road and arrived in Richmond eventually, still carrying his cousin who was somewhat the worse for wear by that time. The Richmond hospitals were full of erysipelas at that time and Grandpa thought they might be unhealthy for a man with a head wound so he swung on a flat car and went south to Atlanta. And very hot weather it was, too. He lived till 1905, acquired twelve children and a considerable amount of this world's goods. He devoted a great deal of his leisure time to telling Dr. Roach what a poor diagnostician he was, till I'm tolerably certain, the doctor wished that he *had* died at Sharpsburg.

From the foregoing, you will understand why the Elder Swan's stories hold such an appeal for me—and for the whole Mitchell clan. I hardly remember my grandfather but have heard so many stories about him that I feel that I knew him intimately. And your stories make me feel that I am marching those old roads with him, fighting those old battles and rejoicing when God in His wisdom and goodness, sends a fine

[2] Surgeon E. J. Roach.

shoat for a burnt offering. It is not only your stories and characters which are so fine and life like—it is the telling of them, the mental attitude of the people, the turns of speech. They are so familiar and so dear, like the faces and voices of those "we loved and lost awhile."

Back in April, I took my father, aged 74, to call on his younger sister, at her country place. We sat under the long rose arbor, a gathering of the type which has passed every where except in the South— and is passing here—the grandparents and the grandchildren, the great uncles and the debutante nieces, the young matrons, the small fry and the assortment of men and women called "cousin" whose family connections are too vague to be run down even by a Mitchell. And we were indulging in that pleasant summer Sunday afternoon diversion, fighting the war over. My Aunt Aline said, "I've read a story about one of Hood's Texans and a pig that sounded so much like Papa's stories that I just wondered if the man who wrote it couldn't be kin to us. Now, that part about the veteran who called it the battle of Antietam when every body knows it's Sharpsburg."

I said, "I was fifteen before I knew Sharpsburg and Antietam were the same. And Manassas and Bull Run, too. I thought they were four different battles and none of our folks happened to be in Bull Run or Antietam."

Father said, "Col. Thomason is probably distantly related. One of his relatives wrote Cousin Aurelia[3] some years ago for information about our Thomason branch—the Elbert County, Ga. ones. His branch went to Alabama, I believe." Then there followed the second most interesting Southern Sunday afternoon diversion, climbing up and down the family tree and venturing out on to limbs and twigs which will hardly bear any weight. . . .

Lt. K. H. Kalmbach, USNR   Atlanta, Georgia
Washington, D.C.   March 7, 1942

Dear Kenneth:

It was good to hear from you again and I am glad to answer your question about just how I managed to get to the Brooklyn Navy Yard for the commissioning of the "Atlanta." At this late date I wonder how I did manage it, for I certainly had to hurry to get there on the short notice I was given.

As I recall, I had been notified that the commissioning would take

[3] Aurelia Roach, daughter of Dr. Roach.

place late in December or early in January and it was my understanding
that because of wartime conditions there would be no ceremonies open
to the public. This was perfectly comprehensible to me, so I did not
expect to be present. Then, on the 22nd of December (I think that was
the date), when I was out of the house, Captain Jenkins, of the
"Atlanta," long distanced John and told him that the date of the commissioning had been moved up to eleven a.m. on Christmas Eve.
Captain Jenkins issued me an invitation to attend and also wished other
interested Atlanta people to come....

I felt that on such short notice and just at Christmas no one else
from here would be able to attend and, at the risk of being considered
sentimental, I felt that the "Atlanta" should not put out to sea without
someone from this town present to say "good luck." You never saw
such scrambling. All my clothes (both dresses) were at the dry cleaner's.
I told Captain Jenkins I had nothing except my Red Cross uniform and
he said it would be most appropriate. I managed to get a berth on a
train which put me in New York on the night before. This was fortunate,
for had I gone by the train which arrives at nine in the morning I
might have missed the commissioning. The train I did take was four
hours late. This was embarrassing as the Marquarts[1] were having a
small dinner for me.

The ceremonies were solemn and impressive to me and I was very
happy that I managed to be there. You must know by now how little
I know of Navy procedures, so I doubtless did an unprecedented thing
when I asked Captain Jenkins to let me meet the Atlanta and Georgia
boys in the crew. He was kind enough to arrange this and after the
buffet luncheon the boys lined up on deck and I was given the opportunity of shaking hands with all of them.

Admiral and Mrs. Marquart and The Admiral's aides were as kind
to me as if I had been their kin. The Admiral gave me the run of the
Navy Yard before I left and if there was anything I missed seeing I
don't know what it was. They got me a reservation South which put me
back home at four o'clock on Christmas Day.

So that's how it happened. I was so sorry, of course, that you were
not there and Jesse Draper and the Coca-Cola people who had been so
wonderfully fine on that day of the launching, and I wished, of course,
that some official Atlanta party could have come. But in wartime things
cannot proceed with leisured dignity and I was happy that I managed
to be there myself. By the way, my uniform seemed to fox everybody,
especially the New York reporters. It was referred to as that of an
ambulance driver, a Red Cross nurse, canteeneer, home defense, AWVS,

---

[1] Rear Admiral Edward J. Marquart was commandant of the Brooklyn Navy Yard.

et cetera. As I stood on the deck quite close to the still lines of sailors, I could see them very cautiously twisting their necks to try to read the words on the brassard on my sleeve. That helped them not at all, for all they could see was "American Red Cross Service."

Thank you for offering to send me some action pictures of the "Atlanta." I have a number and I am especially proud of one very large one which Captain Jenkins autographed and sent me. I believe it is the one you refer to as "showing the starboard quarter while under weigh." It is as spirited as a greyhound and as full of action. I had it framed and hung on my office wall. . . .

Mr. Virginius Dabney   Atlanta, Georgia
Richmond, Virginia   July 23, 1942

Dear Mr. Dabney:

I know I should wait until I have finished your book, "Below the Potomac,"[1] before writing to you, but war work and my father's serious illness leave me little time for reading these days and I do not know when I will have the pleasure of completing your book. So, after reading only one chapter, "The South That Never Was," I am writing to thank you for the fine things you said about Susan Myrick and me, and for the accuracy of your observations about my reactions to the film, "Gone With the Wind."[2]

I was so very pleased at the credit you gave Susan for the Southern accent (or rather, for the lack of Southern accent) in the film.[3] I've

---

[1] *Below the Potomac* (New York, London, 1942).

[2] "Miss Mitchell, who had no part in the adaptation of her book for the screen, expressed a high degree of pleasure at the way in which the job was accomplished. She said she was agreeably surprised at not finding the film full of pseudo-Southern talk. . . . She was annoyed, on the other hand, at the profusion of white columns on the Georgia plantation homes, put there by Hollywood as a concession to traditional notions about the South, despite the explicit statement in the book that Tara was a rambling old farmhouse, and the further fact that it was situated in a section of Georgia where columns were almost non-existent. Miss Mitchell must have offered up orisons to the Deity for the fact that nobody in the motion picture perpetrated that abominable slander against the fair name of Southern civilization, the use of 'you all' to denote only one person." Dabney, p. 16.

[3] "Producers should remember that there is seldom anything more obviously synthetic than synthetic Southern argot. The film version of *Gone With the Wind* was a miraculous exception, but such miracles are extremely rare. The fact that this one was [,] achieved largely because Miss Susan Myrick of Macon, Georgia, was retained by the producer as special consultant on accent, ought to be taken to heart by all those who, in the future wish to portray typically Southern characters on the boards or in the films." Dabney, pp. 15–16.

always felt that she did not get enough credit outside of her own section for the truly miraculous job she did. For nearly three years the South rared and pitched and muttered threats about seceding from the Union again if "you all" was used when addressing one person or if any actor spoke as if he had a mouth full of hot buttered okra. Unfortunately for me, who had nothing to do with the film, a great deal of this raring and pitching took place on our doorstep, in our parlor and over our telephone, as embittered Southerners demanded that I "do something" to keep travesties of our accent from the film. Susan was the one who "did something"—and far better than I could have done. I thought the finest praise she received was this—after the premiere here in Atlanta, I went to a large party and encountered some of our dowagers who had been most belligerent about the Southern accent. I questioned, "And what did you think of the accent in the picture?" They looked at me and said, rather blankly, "What accent?"

I am glad you made the statement about the prologue of the motion picture and its reference to cavaliers in the South.[4] Some people gave me the credit for writing it and thought it was "just beautiful"; others, who knew the section about which I wrote, belabored me for dislocating one of the central ideas of the book. It was useless for me to protest that I had nothing to do with the matter.[5] I certainly had no intention of writing about cavaliers. Practically all my characters, except the Virginia Wilkeses, were of sturdy yeoman stock.

Thank you for your statement about the profusion of white columns on the Georgia plantation homes. Many of us were hard put not to burst into laughter at the sight of "Twelve Oaks." We agreed afterwards that the only comparison we could bring to mind was with the State Capitol at Montgomery, Alabama. In the pages of unwritten history, no fiercer fight was ever fought than the one centering around columns on the motion picture "Tara." The Georgians present at the making of the film, Susan Myrick and Mr. and Mrs. Wilbur Kurtz, of Atlanta, weren't able to keep columns off of "Tara" entirely, but they managed a compromise by having the pillars square, as were those of our Upcountry houses in that day, if they had columns at all.

[4] "Many of the misconceptions concerning the New South stem from earlier misconceptions concerning the Old South. . . . As one example among many which may be cited, let us take the opening words of the prologue to the motion picture, *Gone With the Wind*: 'There was a land of Cavaliers and cotton!' What could be more grotesque? As a consequence of this single sentence, the milieu of Miss Mitchell's fine novel became badly distorted from the moment it was transmuted into celluloid." Dabney, p. 2.

[5] The "titles" for *GWTW* (the prologue and six additional narrative sequences used to introduce sections of the film) were written by Ben Hecht. Lambert, p. 88; Selznick, p. 214.

I think this chapter, "The South That Never Was," is fine and thoughtful writing. However, I believe that we Southerners could write the truth about the ante-bellum South, its few slaveholders, its yeomen farmers, its rambling, comfortable houses just fifty years away from log cabins, until Gabriel blows his trump—and everyone would go on believing in the Hollywood version. The sad part is that many Southerners believe this myth even more ardently than Northerners. A number of years ago some of us organized a club, The Association of Southerners Whose Grandpappies Did Not Live in Houses With White Columns. May I extend you an invitation to join? Its membership would be enormous if all of the eligibles came in.

Since my novel was published, I have been embarrassed on many occasions by finding myself included among writers who pictured the South as a land of white-columned mansions whose wealthy owners had thousands of slaves and drank thousands of juleps. I have been surprised, too, for North Georgia certainly was no such country—if it ever existed anywhere—and I took great pains to describe North Georgia as it was. But people believe what they like to believe and the mythical Old South has too strong a hold on their imaginations to be altered by the mere reading of a 1,037-page book. So I have made no effort to defend myself against the accusation but it was a great satisfaction to me that a man of your perceptiveness knew that my South was not "The South That Never Was." I thank you for your understanding and for what you wrote.

My husband and I remember with pleasure meeting you several years ago at the Biltmore in the company of Julian Harris, Mark Ethridge, et cetera. We will be happy to renew this acquaintance should you ever be in Atlanta again.

Mr. James S. Pope   Atlanta, Georgia
The Courier-Journal-Louisville Times   September 22, 1942
Louisville, Kentucky

Dear Jimmie:

I accept with dignity but becoming modesty the article in defense of mystery story addicts which you dedicated to me.[1] In justice to myself, I must say that you could not have chosen a better person as a dedicatee. I believe I was one of the first Carnegie Library haunters

[1] Pope's "Literature and the Mystery Novel" appeared in the Louisville *Courier-Journal* September 10.

who openly took murder stories from the shelves at high noon, shameless, in front of seekers after Marcel Proust and Dale Carnegie. I was
shortly joined by you and Dudley Glass and with our three shields over-
lapping we did much to shelter and encourage the more timorous. I am
happy to tell you that at present the librarians are addicts, too—at
least, some of them are. Martha Anne Kendrick shouts across the room
to me to ask if I have read "Murder In the Privy" which is fair but not
as good as "The Corpse In the Commode." Miss Fanny Hinton, who is
now head librarian, bears down on me occasionally when she has had a
hard day and asks the name of that murder mystery she heard me discussing with Grace Peeples last week.

I enjoyed your article so very much and it made me realize all over
again how much I have missed your stuff in the Journal. I am grateful
to you for sending the column to me.

The Journal is having its problems these days, like all other papers.
Boys are going off to war every day. When I was down there last week,
Frank Daniel told me he was hoping for a berth in the navy, if they
overlooked his eyes. While I was talking to him, Fred Moon came over
and asked me how I would like a job in the City Room. "Hell, Peggy,"
he said, reassuringly, "I know you are rusty but, my God, you don't
know how patient we'd be." I almost collapsed at this approach. There
are three girls already in the City Room and one of them is covering the
Federal Building. Times have certainly changed.

Almost everyone has gone to the wars and the ones who have not
gone are not fit for man or beast because they expect to be called or because they want to get into the army and can't. Even if you wanted to
get up an old-time party, you couldn't because of the absentees and the
gas shortage. We did manage to give Marguerite Steedman's book[2] a
pre-war send-off last month but it took some managing. Medora and I
and the others concerned wanted to have some celebration for Marguerite, even if she was unfortunate enough to be a wartime author. Her
book, by the way, went into the second edition before publication.
Speaking of books, have you noticed how Medora's mystery[3] keeps
popping up on the bestseller list? Everyone is as pleased as can be about
this.

John and I are wardens and whenever we attend zone or precinct
meetings we are surprised and pleased to see the faces of relatives and
friends doing the same job we are doing. During our last practice black-
out, I discovered that Angus Perkerson was a warden. Headquarters
gave his block about eighteen problems—everything from demolition

[2] *But You'll Be Back* (Boston, 1942).
[3] Medora Field Perkerson, *Blood on Her Shoe* (New York, 1942).

bombs to fourteen people bleeding to death. Frank Daniel, who is warden in the next block, remarked that Angus certainly had his hands full. . . .

Mr. Berry Fleming   Atlanta, Georgia
Augusta, Georgia   December 18, 1942

Dear Berry:

I've just had a note from Hervey,[1] telling me the exciting news about your book being a Book-of-the-Month Club choice.[2] I say "exciting," and probably I am more excited than you, for I am expressing not only my pleasure that your work has been appreciated but the memory of the goose bumps I had when "Gone With the Wind" was chosen. I am so pleased about this that I would like to run outdoors and gallop about in circles, screaming like a peanut whistle. However, such conduct would be extremely unbecoming to one of my age, so I'll have to take it out in congratulating you.

I hope so sincerely that you have the critical and financial success and that you somehow escape the lawsuits, the infringements and the far too personal questions from strangers which follow after a successful book.

You know how shameless John and I have been in our outspoken remarks about how well you write. Well, now maybe you'll believe us when them slick Nawthum gempmum agree with us.

---

[1] Dr. Hervey Cleckley.
[2] *Colonel Effingham's Raid* (New York, 1943).

1943

Cpl. Joe Aftel   Atlanta, Georgia
Camp Perry, Ohio   January 20, 1943

Dear Corporal Aftel:

Your letter enclosing the picture taken of me at the War Show camp has arrived. Thank you so much for it. I thought the picture very good and it revived my feminine vanity, which has taken a bad beating recently. I have had photographs in the Atlanta papers during the last week in connection with the campaign to raise thirty-five million dollars in bonds to replace the cruiser "Atlanta," which was sunk off Guadalcanal in November. I was sponsor of the ship when it was launched and of course I felt very distressed about its loss. I was photographed buying some bonds and the pictures were so terrible that I felt they'd have to tie me hand and foot before a camera was ever trained on me again. This snapshot makes me feel that there is some hope for me.

I am so glad that you appeared in the picture too, along with your friend and the tent and the crossed pistols. It is a fine memento of the War Show and I am tacking it on the wall of my office.

I was sorry I did not get to tell you goodby. On those last two rainy days of the War Show's stay here, a number of us in the Red Cross were scouting around trying to find dry quarters for the boys to occupy at night, and I was not at the canteen. I looked for you and asked for you but was told you had gone. I enjoyed meeting you and was so grateful to you for taking me over to inspect the camp that day.

All the people in this section of Atlanta who came in contact with the soldiers from the War Show were loud in their praises of all of you. We enjoyed having you with us and our only regret was that the Atlanta weather was so rainy then....

Mr. Berry Fleming   Atlanta, Georgia
Augusta, Georgia   February 26, 1943

My dear Easter Rabbit:

Can you have forgotten that I was the little girl who always got up early on Easter morning and spied upon you when you were hiding eggs? Do you not recall the stern letter you wrote me about this obnoxious practice? It was written in a copperplate hand so similar to that of my mother's that I felt sure you both had attended Miss Ballard's Academy for Young Ladies. Can you have forgotten that I was also the little girl who on Christmas Eve kept an eye peeled from over the upstairs bannisters and saw—but that is another story. In other words, I saw you acting very surreptitiously when you were here last Saturday night. The furtiveness of your conduct in the corner of the room near the table aroused joyful suspicions. After all of you had left, I leaped for the table and, sure enough, you had hidden a very fine egg. I should have spent Saturday night writing the Governor about my regret at not being able to accept appointment to the State Board of Education. Instead, I sat up till dawn making forays with that gallant and honest warrior, Colonel Effingham, and ever so often I laughed so loudly that John would wake up and I would read him snatches. The part about the mayor's understandable reactions of horror at the conduct of the Colonel, "like finding a rattlesnake in your bureau drawer," gave me more joy than you could know.

Berry, the book is a honey. The fact that I laughed does not mean that your deadpan irony did not impress me, for it did. The shrewd and accurate observation of some facets of Southern small town life are so fine—there are sad and bitter and hilarious truths in your book. What a seemingly simple situation—an honest man, believing in government of the people and by the people, coming in conflict with entrenched city government. And how complicated and far-reaching the results were. I think your book gained great force from the way it was presented, through the single viewpoint of the eyewitness narrator. I think the book had added power because your own personal sense of moral indignation was apparent nowhere. It takes a mature person to realize that moral indignation per se, no matter how just and honest, frequently becomes dull sound and fury on paper. You let the events and characters speak for themselves, and they rouse moral indignation in the minds of readers. . . .

I wish you were here, as there are so very many things about the book I'd like to talk about. They'll have to wait until I can get over to Augusta, although I hate to postpone them.

Thanks a million for the book and for the inscription. Dear Easter Rabbit, you can hide eggs around our apartment any time you take a notion.

Ensign S. A. Martin   Atlanta, Georgia
Philadelphia, Pennsylvania   March 18, 1943

Dear Sam:

There must be something in thought transference, for I had the enclosed clipping laid out to send you when your letter arrived. I was so swollen with pride about the success of the "Atlanta" cruiser campaign that I wanted to brag about it to you, for I knew that you, being a Navy man, would lend a receptive ear. Now I find that your Navy friends have beat me to the news. It was an exciting two months and a highly satisfying two months. It was the only time in my memory that I saw all types of people getting solidly behind one movement. For the most part I stayed in a corner of the lobby of the Citizens and Southern Bank, on Marietta Street, making out certificates for purchasers of bonds, so I had a front row seat for two months. There were newsboys who came in every day to buy ten-cent stamps and men in overalls and girls from behind the counters buying a bond a week. There were stout matrons in mink and heads of enormous businesses who bought a million dollars at a time, and housewives in bungalow aprons with money from their sons in the Army in Africa. I knew we'd get thirty-five million but I never dreamed we'd manage nearly sixty-five million. So now we'll have two destroyers to run interference for the new cruiser.

There was a big party to celebrate the victory and to honor the visiting notables. Secretary Knox[1] was there and he was as hearty and informal and full of fun as you would imagine any ex-newspaperman. Admiral Glassford,[2] from Charleston, is very popular here and he attended, as well as Admiral Murray,[3] from Pensacola. There were so many high ranking Navy people present and so much gold braid that I gave up trying to figure out their rank and just called everybody Admiral, which seemed to please everybody.

At the mass meeting at the Auditorium after this party, Secretary Knox handed Mayor Hartsfield a letter which the Mayor read. It confirmed my appointment as sponsor of the new "Atlanta." The Mayor

[1] Secretary of the Navy Frank Knox.
[2] Vice Admiral William Alexander Glassford, Jr.
[3] Rear Admiral George Dominic Murray.

had nominated me some while back but I wasn't sure until that night that I really would be the sponsor, so you can imagine how happy I was. Of course no one really knows when the cruiser will be launched but it will be some months away. It will be at Camden, New Jersey.

The enclosed picture was taken at Five Points at one of our outdoor bond sales. It was the coldest day I ever saw and the wind screamed down all five of the streets to explode in a hurricane around our table. We had a Navy and Marine guard present and their main job was holding bonds and certificates down on the table. Every time a thousand-dollar bond was purchased the Navy boys fired a cannon and before the day was over I was so deaf that when I got home I yelled things like "Please pass the biscuits" at the top of my voice. . . .

I, too, was so distressed to read of Stephen Benet's death.[4] A sense of loss as if I had buried a dear friend has hung over me. I never met him but I had letters from him and his wife and I always expected to go to see him in New York when things had quieted down enough for me to make a long visit there. He reviewed "Gone With the Wind" when it was published and was so generous that I never forgot his review. "John Brown's Body" is my favorite poem, especially those parts about Georgia. He was one short story writer who kept right on writing short stories and never succumbed to the temptation to write formless and boneless tripe, as so many short story writers. He was a story-teller, and there are few of them. . . .

Mr. and Mrs. Clifford Dowdey   Atlanta, Georgia
New York, New York   April 21, 1943

Dear Helen and Clifford:

I am sending you a pamphlet put out by Emory University, containing the 1861 letters of General Stuart to his wife.[1] There is nothing in them to go in a history book but I found them charming and sad as I thought ahead to the inevitable ending of their love story. Also I can't help wondering what was the truth of the business about the General's beard and was the "mischievous cousin" John Esten Cooke?

I got home day before yesterday and stood the trip very well. I've been able to sit up half the day, strapped up in a brace which improves my figure below the waist but does nothing for me above, as thirty

---

[4] March 14.
[1] James Ewell Brown Stuart, *Letters of General J. E. B. Stuart to His Wife, 1861* (Atlanta, 1943).

pounds below the waist have been displaced to the north. John says with the addition of a few medals I'd be a dead ringer for General Goering. . . .

I hope I haven't missed your story, Clifford, in the Post.[2] I had a rather bad three weeks in the hospital and didn't see any magazines. If it has already appeared, please let me know the date and I will get it at our library. Also let me know the publication date of your book[3] and the title you finally chose. Bob Henry (General N. B. Forrest) came over from Washington several times to see me. He has been having hard going through the first five chapters of "Forrest"[4] and had just gotten to Shiloh. He somehow managed to come on my worst days and I would get a hypodermic and we would go to work on Shiloh. I was the perfect audience for him, for I have to admit that I never have been able to remember who won Shiloh. I know the people who won the battle lost the objective (Corinth) and the people who got the objective lost the battle. So anybody can tell me about Shiloh and it is always news to me. Colonel John Thomason, who was to illustrate the book, has been suddenly removed from Washington to California and is on active duty. He and Bob are in a sweat for fear he'll be sent to the Pacific before he does the illustrations. The idea was twenty full-page pictures and about fifty little sketches.[5] Bob asked at length about both of you, telling again of his pleasure in his visit and reiterating again that he wanted to see you. How he manages to do any writing I do not know, as his job is the biggest headache of the war—keeping the railroads moving, keeping people fed et cetera.

I am also sending you a page from the Saturday Review with an article by Herschel. I thought you might have missed it. You will note that he is attached to the U.S. Embassy.[6] . . .

---

[2] This probably refers to Dowdey's "Weep Not for Them." This story was published in *The Saturday Evening Post* for October 16, 1943.

[3] *Tidewater* (Boston, 1943).

[4] *"First With the Most"* Forrest (Indianapolis, New York, 1943).

[5] Only one illustration by Colonel Thomason appears in *"First With the Most" Forrest*. It is a highly romanticized drawing of Forrest used as the frontispiece.

[6] Brickell's article is "W. H. Hudson, Bridge-Builder Between the Americas," *The Saturday Review of Literature*, XXVL, No. 5 (April 10, 1943), pp. 11–12. In the byline for the article Brickell is identified as "Cultural relations officer, U.S. Embassy, Bogota, Colombia, S.A."

Mr. Fred A. Cornell   Atlanta, Georgia
Public Relations Officer   April 26, 1943
New York Shipbuilding Corporation
Camden, New Jersey

Dear Mr. Cornell:

The reason for my delay in writing you personally was a trip to the hospital. I am now home and recovering nicely but I am sincerely glad that the launching of the new "Atlanta" will not take place immediately, for I am not yet up to launchings.

I thank you so much for your last letter to Miss Baugh (April 21st) and for the information you sent about launching procedures. Fortunately, thanks to my experience in christening the other "Atlanta," I have some knowledge of what to do, but your additional information was most helpful. I think letters such as yours are very fine, for I recall my efforts during August, 1941, to learn the exact duties of a sponsor. Being an inlander, I had never attended a launching and I wished to behave in a correct manner. But I received little information in answer to the letters I wrote, as everyone said vaguely that "oh, you just hit it." Having seen news reels of sponsors who swung and missed and sponsors who drenched themselves and the official party, I had no desire to do likewise.

After the launching of the "Atlanta," Admiral Marquart said that bottle was the most thoroughly broken bottle he had ever seen, and I did not get a drop of champagne on me. Having played baseball as a child, I swung low from the hip. . . .

May I make two requests of you? I am small, barely five feet tall. If the bunting-covered structure which surrounds the ship is too high, I won't be able to swing over it. If in war time it is still the habit of shipbuilding companies to send flowers to sponsors, would you please ask them not to send me a very large armload of flowers? Arm sprays which appear lovely and graceful for the ordinary sized woman occupy both my arms and hide my face. . . .

In the matter of guests who make up what was known in peace time as the "official party," I am sure the Mayor of Atlanta, Mr. William Hartsfield, would be happy to hear from you. Mr. Hartsfield is a very fine man and has always been solidly behind anything which was to the credit of our City. He, like many of our fellow-townsmen, worked diligently in selling the requisite amount of bonds to pay for this new cruiser. He has spoken several times to me about wishing to attend this launching and to see that Atlanta made a representative showing there. Of course we know the difficulties of war time travel and by the date of the launching the difficulties may have been so multiplied that anything like an "official party" will be out of the question. But I know Mr. Hartsfield would appreciate a letter from you informing him as to whether civilian guests representing the City of Atlanta are permitted under war time rules.

Again let me say how grateful to you I am for your full and helpful letter. It makes me feel easier to know that I have a "Sponsor's Aide."

Mr. and Mrs. Clifford Dowdey   Atlanta, Georgia
New York, New York   May 13, 1943

Dear Helen and Clifford:

...I was very interested in what you wrote me of your new Confederate aficionado, Tim Costello.[1] I know you are going to do your best in the matter of supplying him with information about the Lost Cause but I wouldn't put it past a Texan and a Virginian to let Mr. Costello think that no action other than a skirmish occurred outside of the sacred borders of Virginia. And that no officer higher than a low-ranking lieutenant ever came from anywhere but Virginia (not even from Texas). I feel perfectly certain you have never told Mr. Costello about General Pat Cleburne, who was Irish born and a good Catholic, God rest his soul, and an officer who would have gone higher had he not been born in another country. I feel certain Mr. Costello would like to know that after a long and gallant career General Cleburne fought in the retreat from Dalton and then swung back to Tennessee with General Hood's ill-fated expedition. When he was going into battle in the sleet at Franklin, Tennessee, he saw a friend who was barefooted and he took off his own good boots and gave them to him. He died with his horse's four feet on top of the Yankees' works and there were forty-nine bullets in the General and he was barefooted. I've never run across a full length biography of Pat Cleburne[2] but he keeps cropping up in biographies of other generals. Sam Watkins, who wrote "Co. Aytch—The First Tennessee Regiment" (and a better book there never was, as Stanley Horn's History can bear witness), mentions Cleburne a number of times. I think there's something about him in Ella Lonn's book, "Foreigners in the Con-

---

[1] Costello operated a New York bar which catered to authors and to the Irish.
[2] Three biographies of General Cleburne had been published as books before 1945 —by Irving Ashby Buck, Thomas Robson Hay, and Charles Edward Nash. A fourth, by Maj. Calhoun Benham, appeared in nine installments in the *Kennesaw Gazette*, January–May, 1889. None is a satisfactory account of the Irish Confederate.

federacy."[3] I doubt that you'll find the first named in the New York Public Library but Miss Lonn's book will probably be there.

I am happy to know that you are still recruiting for the Army. I discovered, too late to do me any good, that the surgeon who operated on me,[4] and who did not think I was too good a patient because I couldn't get up and do the rhumba after two weeks, had been recruited by Douglas Freeman. The doctor wrote me after I reached home that he hoped I'd write a Life of Bedford Forrest. I think he is still more the neuro-surgeon than the Confederate, and I present this evidence: I turned to read Sharpsburg first in Freeman's book because that was where Grandpa Mitchell got his. And when the surgeon arrived I told him at some length about Grandpa's gallantry, courage and the plain stupidity that made him stick his head up above the corn to lay his rifle across a splitrail fence. A minie ball went through the back of his head, fracturing it in two places. Thereafter I gave my best creative and reportorial efforts toward the inspiriting saga of Grandpa's hitch-hike to a Richmond hospital and his further travels on a flatcar to Atlanta, still without any medical attention. To show how tough Grandpa was, I spoke of his two marriages after the war, the begetting of twelve or more children and the amassing of a whacking amount of Atlanta real estate and cash. I then lay back limply on my pillows, ready for kind words about Grandpa's stamina. The great man considered my story in silence for five minutes, and then said, "How often did he have convulsions?" "What do you mean, convulsions?" said I. "Grandpa never had a convulsion in his life." "No convulsions? But he must have had convulsions with a brain injury at such a place." "He never had airy convulsion," I said, but, trying to be helpful, I went on to relate that Grandpa had the worst disposition and the shortest temper of any good looking man between the Potomac and the Rio Grande. "However," I said candidly, "Grandpa always had had a hairtrigger temper, which was awfully fortunate. Else he would have been shot by various other gentlemen whose tempers were as fast but whose draw was slower." This did not appease the great surgeon, for he rose ponderously, shaking his head and gathering the trembling entourage of white-coated internes. "No convulsions," he said, shaking his head indignantly. "I never heard the like." And took himself off, convinced that I was several kinds of a liar. If he had only waited I would have told him about my brother's wife's grandfather who suffered a similar wound and performed even greater prodigies. And I would have brought in my own Great-Grandpa Sweet,[5] who was over age and managed to do quite well after a slug as big as your hand went

---

[3] *Foreigners in the Confederacy* (Chapel Hill, N.C., 1940).
[4] Dr. Walter E. Dandy.
[5] William Charles Sweet.

through his lung. (He had twelve children, too. I bring this fact in for genealogical background and not to prove anything about fertility.)

If you have not read "Johnny Reb,"[6] I entreat you to do so. As you have doubtless learned from reviews, it is composed of letters home from Confederate soldiers. Praise God, the writers are mainly privates, stout yeomen, good Crackers and outspoken po' white trash. No one had ever taught them the proper form of a letter (a disadvantage from which officers suffered) and their letters are the real McCoy. Bob Henry knows the author and says he's very nice and has an exceptionally pretty and attractive wife. I hope I meet them some day. It was letters such as these which made me decide to write a more realistic war story than I had ever read—and, by the way, I've always been slightly amused by the New York critics who referred to GWTW as a "moonlight and magnolia romance." My God, they never read the gentle Confederate novel of the Nineties, or they'd know better. . . .

Mr. Eddy Gilmore   Atlanta, Georgia
Care of The Associated Press   June 3, 1943
Washington, D. C.

Dear Eddy:

This is a fan letter. I think you are wonderful! The stuff you've been sending out of Russia has made the war on that front more vivid to me than anything else could have done. I've picked up the paper day after day and there you were batting it out, rain or shine or snow, always good reporting. Sometimes after reading between the lines of your stories and trying to see you far off in the snows of Russia, my mind would go back to that joint in the Journal building known as the Roachery and I'd think of you and me and Journal and AP men sitting there drinking that gray beverage which passed for coffee, and I'd think "why, that's the same Eddy." I think it always comes as a shock to any normal human being that one of their friends can do fine and wonderful things. The very fact that you know somebody almost automatically keeps him from high performances. If I ever had any such feeling about you, I lost it long ago. I just have a fine sense of pride that I knew you when—and I will bet you aren't any different now.

John joins with me in congratulating you on the fine job you've done in Russia and we both say "welcome home again."

[6] Bell Irvin Wiley, *The Life of Johnny Reb* (Indianapolis, New York, [c. 1943]).

Mr. Stanley F. Horn   Atlanta, Georgia
Nashville, Tennessee   July 6, 1943

Dear Mr. Horn:

... No, I won't sue you for plagiarism if you use Miss O'Hara's ex-cursion in the lumber business in the lumber book you are writing—provided you don't scandalize her name or mine![1] Of course, if you quote verbatim you will have to get permission from The Macmillan Company and me and I suggest if you wish to quote verbatim you send The Mac-millan Company the lines you want to use and page numbers and enough of the material to show the context.

I do not know about the lumber business in other parts of the South immediately after the surrender and during reconstruction, but I do know that here in Atlanta and the surrounding countryside the bases of many present day fortunes were laid in lumber. Practically everyone who wasn't building and contracting was out lumbering. That was why I put Scarlett in that profession—it was a normal profession for an Atlantan and there was quick money in it. The reasons the lumber business zoomed around Atlanta were (1) practically all the city was burned and returning inhabitants had to rebuild, (2) the city was experiencing a boom town regrowth as new settlers poured in, not only the carpet-baggers but Union soldiers who liked the place and settled here, nice Northerners who had capital to invest in a new frontier, poverty-stricken planters from all over the country districts, and those fine people from East Tennessee who were Democrats and who were not permitted to return to Tennessee by the Unionists after the surrender. Somebody had to cut a heap of lumber to put roofs over the heads of the old in-habitants and the new settlers. I know of few Atlanta families whose grandfathers and great-grandfathers did not engage in the lumber busi-ness for a short or long time—sometimes it was chips and kindling and stove wood, also wood chunks for the railroad, as well as lumber for building.

---

[1] Horn wrote in his *This Fascinating Lumber Business* (Indianapolis, New York, [c. 1951]), p. 101: "Miss Scarlett O'Hara, readers of *Gone With the Wind* will recall, started a sawmill near Atlanta when the war was over, and what she did and why she did it were fairly typical of numbers of the more enterprising and resourceful South-erners."

Dr. Douglas Southall Freeman   Atlanta, Georgia
Richmond, Virginia   July 21, 1943

Dear Doctor Freeman:

I have just finished "Lee's Lieutenants, Volume II"[1] which I read as
I think it should be read, very slowly and with many leafings backwards
to pages already read and many re-readings of certain pages. Now, as I
reluctantly leave Virginia and these great men who move back and
forth across her, I am confronted with a very difficult problem—how to
tell you how wonderful I think both Volume I and II are.

I am not an historian, military or otherwise, and I couldn't be one
if I tried, but I wish so much that I had a better grasp of such subjects,
the better to express my admiration and appreciation. I am only a story-
teller, so, for the moment, let me tell you how engrossing these volumes
are as stories. If Lee and his lieutenants had never walked this earth and
were only characters you had imagined and put on paper, your presentation of them and of the world in which they lived would be masterly. The
humanness, the amusing sidelights on character, the inevitable tragedy
toward which they moved are all depicted in a manner intensely interesting. I have read too many military histories and military memoirs of incredible dullness not to appreciate your work for the sweep of its narrative, the characterization of the actors and the "feel" of a long gone day.
In particular, the part dealing with General Jackson, from the moment he
received his wound until his death and funeral, is great writing as well
as great history.

As a person who has done some research into Confederate matters, I
know what your research must have been—your endless reading, your
tireless ferreting, your sifting of false from true, your evaluating of well
meant but inaccurate hearsay. The truly monumental amount of spade-
work you have done is enough to take one's breath away.[2]

---

[1] Douglas Southall Freeman, *Lee's Lieutenants* (New York, 1942–1944; 3 vols.).
[2] In his reply to this letter Dr. Freeman wrote on July 23: "Of course I would
rather have your judgment of 'Lee's Lieutenants' than that of anyone else. You know
as much about the history as anyone does and you know more than anyone else about
the literary and psychological hurdles that have to be passed.

"You please me greatly by what you say, in particular, regarding the death of
Jackson. I do not believe I ever had quite so difficult a problem where literature and
history came together. It would have been so easy to slush and, on the other hand,
so easy to underwrite the scene. I had to rein myself in at the same time that I
applied the spur. The toughest part of it all, perhaps, was the little scene of Jackson's
leave-taking the morning the campaign began. The facts were well authenticated but
the treatment of them was a problem. How could I get the dramatic effect without
anticipating the tragedy? As your discerning eye quickly saw, I tried to do it by a
simple statement of the facts and by the mere addition of the words, 'good-bye,

All of us have battles which interest us most, generally for personal reasons, so, of course, I turned to Sharpsburg before even reading your Introduction. My Grandpa Mitchell, who was one of Hood's Texans, was so ill advised that day as to stick a shaggy head up out of a cornfield and, for his curiosity, got a Minie ball through his skull. It didn't kill him— he was still living when I was a child. So it is only natural that I heard more about Sharpsburg than other battles. Several years ago, immediately before I met you in Richmond, John and I visited the field of Sharpsburg. But the terrain confused me even more than the many verbal accounts of the battle. But now, having read your account, it all becomes clear, and I thank you.

I was in Johns Hopkins in November going through many clinics. I had Volume I then, and as I was pushed at a gallop in a wheel chair through those long corridors for X-rays and proddings I read this book. For some reason, it was a matter of merriment for staff and technicians— except Doctor Dandy, who was my doctor. He told me of the interesting trip he had had over the field of the Seven Days with you. When I went back to Johns Hopkins in March for a spinal operation, Doctor Dandy gave me Volume II. I did not have a very easy time in the hospital and the sight of me, flat on my back with the heavy volume balanced prac- tically on my chin, brought forth more merriment from the staff. I told them that they could not properly appreciate what General Jackson had gone through after he was wounded unless they read your book under circumstances similar to mine. Fortunately, Robert S. Henry came over from Washington to see me and, as he is a Confederate writer and now deep in the life of General Forrest, he saw nothing remarkable about "Lee's Lieutenants" as bed reading. I was grateful for the reinforcement of Forrest's Cavalry to put young internes and nurses in their places.

Your books are so good and so great that, like thousands of other Southerners, I can only say "thank you for writing this—this was our country, these were our people."

Mr. Thomas Chadwick   Atlanta, Georgia
Atlanta, Georgia   July 22, 1943

Dear Mr. Chadwick:

I am enclosing a copy of the letter I sent to your young friend Sergeant Crosland.[1] I am sorry that you did not let me know he wanted

---

good-bye.' You were the first person, I think, who has seen what I was trying to do in that exceedingly difficult passage."
[1] Sgt. Peter Crosland of Scotland.

to meet me while he was visiting you. That would have been a small favor to do for a boy in a foreign country. I had one hilarious experience with two young British flying cadets whom I picked up on the street one day. I observed them endeavoring futilely to stop a Buckhead express and I offered to give them a lift to town. I was returning from a hard day at the Red Cross, with my uniform incredibly crumpled and soiled, my hair tied back with a string and, I am afraid, my face very dirty. The boys had an hour to kill, so I took them to the Driving Club for refreshments. In the course of the conversation they remarked that they had wanted to meet Margaret Mitchell. I had, of course, introduced myself as Mrs. Marsh. I could tell that they had seen some very glamorous press photographs of me and confidently thought I was a combination of Lana Turner and Ann Sheridan. Not wishing to shatter illusions, I intended to say nothing about my identity, for I thought it might embarrass the boys, but one of the waiters at the Club called me by my maiden name. And the truth was out. When I deposited the boys at Five Points an hour later they still had bewildered and incredulous expressions on their faces and I am certain they did not believe I could possibly be an author and look so different from my photographs.

I am returning Sergeant Crosland's letter to you.

Mr. and Mrs. Charles W. Bryan, Jr.   Atlanta, Georgia
New York, New York   August 26, 1943

Dear Mr. and Mrs. Bryan:

Thank you for the July copy of "The Halyard" with the pictures and story about the U.S.S. "Atlanta." It arrives at a good time, for I am just now pasting up my scrapbook about the sinking of the "Atlanta" and the successful bond campaign we had last spring to build a new "Atlanta." The item you sent will be put on the very last page and I am grateful to you for sending it.

During the campaign to build a new "Atlanta" enough money was raised for the new cruiser and two destroyers as well. Everybody in this section was proud enough to burst. The two destroyers, the "Thomason" and the "Jordan," were launched this week at Charleston and I was very regretful that I could not be present. The new "Atlanta" will be launched sometime during cold weather, I believe. You can understand that I really did burst, publicly, when Secretary Knox, who was here at the conclusion of our bond campaign, formally made me sponsor of the new cruiser. I felt a little guilty about this honor because I honestly knew that I had had as much pleasure and pride in sponsoring the other "Atlanta" as any human being deserved....

Mr. and Mrs. Clifford Dowdey   Atlanta, Georgia
New York, New York   September 7, 1943

Dear Helen and Clifford:

I was laying off to write you about "Tidewater" after I had read it, but as I have read only one chapter I won't go into it except to say it's a swell first chapter. Father has been worse recently and I am less able to do my stint at the hospital. Trying to figure out this new income tax, which is especially baffling and difficult for people in my position—and yours— has also taken up time. So I put off reading "Tidewater" until I can read it all in one piece, for I want to get it all together rather than in hurried gulps. I think the jacket is very colorful, but I do wonder how he got into those pants. I'll bet by the time the book ends he's wearing sensible britches. Pants like those wouldn't last long on that frontier.

Our hats were in the air about the Book League of America choosing "Tidewater." One hundred and seventy-four thousand copies ain't hay in any author's life. I hope the broadcasting of "Tidewater" to the member- ship of this League will stir interest in your other books. I do not know any other writer who has covered periods of American history as you have done and as well as you have done. Generally writers pick them- selves out one brief period and spend the rest of their lives there....

P.S.

My comment about your dust jacket is just the kind of literary criti- cism I decry. After it was written I realized it was on a par with a recent experience of Berry Fleming, of Augusta, author of "Colonel Effingham's Raid." This book was so true to Augusta life and politics that when we read an advance copy we shook hands with Berry and promised to visit him in prison shortly after publication date. However, Augusta is a strange place. They are interested only in petty Augusta politics (which was the subject of the book) and, as far as we can learn, few people in the town read the book and those few saw no connection with the local scene. Few people in Augusta read books anyway, I am afraid. They certainly do not show pleasurable excitement and pride in local authors, as crude upcountry towns like Atlanta do. Anyone who does anything unlike what everyone else is doing is "peculiar, and it's too bad because they come of such good people."

Later I asked Berry what literary criticism had been made of his book in Augusta. He said that his wife had asked an opinion of a close female friend and the friend spoke as follows: "You know, until I saw Berry's new picture on the back of 'Colonel Effingham' I never realized that he had gotten so bald."

By the way, Berry and Anne are fine people and I hope you get to meet them some day. They are best friends with Doctor Cleckley and his wife Louise.

The Honorable Frank Knox   Atlanta, Georgia
Department of the Navy   November 10, 1943
Office of the Secretary
Washington, D.C.

My dear Mr. Knox:

I am sorry to worry you with small requests when you are busy running the Navy, but I do not know to whom else I can apply. Also the request I am about to make may not be a proper one. If it is not, I am sure you will tell me so. I don't know the etiquette of such matters and have no way of finding out. So, it seems sensible to write directly to you. I know you will treat the matter understandingly even if you cannot grant my request.

Last March when you were in Atlanta for the celebration of our successful bond campaign to build another cruiser "Atlanta" to replace the lost one, you honored me by designating me sponsor of the new "Atlanta." Nearly a year has gone by and I imagine that the date of the launching may be approaching. Is it proper for me, as sponsor, to request that a certain naval officer be designated as my Naval Aide for this ceremony? If this is a proper request, then I would be very happy if you would appoint Lieutenant Commander DeSales Harrison, U.S.N.R., NTS (I), NAS, Quonset Point, Rhode Island, as my Naval Aide on the occasion of the launching of the new cruiser.

The choice of Lieutenant Commander Harrison is not merely a personal one, although he is a friend. He is also the choice of our Mayor, Mr. William Hartsfield, and it would please a great many Atlanta people to have him present at the christening.

Before going further, I want to say that this letter is not being written at Lieutenant Commander Harrison's suggestion. He does not know that I am making my request or that I am writing to you at all. I am doing so, after a conversation with Mayor Hartsfield, for the following reasons:

Lieutenant Commander Harrison is a representative citizen of Atlanta, widely known and widely respected. He was an early volunteer for the

Navy and he sought active service at a considerable sacrifice financially. But the particular reasons why I believe it would be fitting to designate him are related to special services he rendered on the occasion of the launching of the lost "Atlanta."

When I went North to christen the "Atlanta" in September, 1941, there had been very unpleasant labor troubles in the shipyard in which the launching was to take place. I believe the Navy had taken over the yard. In this situation, the officials of the shipbuilding company did not feel that they could entertain upon the occasion of the launching, and naval officials also felt that it did not lie in their province. Lieutenant Commander Harrison was at that time an official of the Coca-Cola Company and was in New York. Pride in the ship which bore the name of his home town made him feel that the occasion should not pass without some social ceremony. On short notice, he arranged to have the Coca-Cola Company, at its plant just across the street from the ship-yards, entertain several hundred people after the launching, to celebrate the new ship.

As you may know, the Coca-Cola Company down here is not just a business. It is an Atlanta institution of which we are all proud. There was no suggestion of commercialism; it was an Atlanta business as a matter of civic pride stepping in to provide an appropriate celebration of an Atlanta event, when that celebration would otherwise have been lacking.

Due to certain unfortunate circumstances, no gift to be presented to the ship from the city had been provided. When Lieutenant Commander Harrison learned of this, after my arrival in New York, he again stepped into the breach. Not wishing to have his city or me put in a poor light, he and the Coca-Cola Company bought a beautiful punch bowl and tray which were presented to Captain Jenkins, of the "Atlanta," in the name of the City of Atlanta.

Atlanta people who learned of these circumstances were very grateful to Lieutenant Commander Harrison. I can think of no better way to show the appreciation of this city and my own appreciation than by requesting him as my Naval Aide.

The Honorable Frank Knox   Atlanta, Georgia
Washington, D.C.   December 3, 1943

Dear Mr. Knox:

Thank you so much for your gracious reply to my letter about Lieutenant Commander Harrison being designated my Naval Aide at the time of the launching of the new cruiser "Atlanta." After hearing from you I wrote to him and he has replied that he will be proud and honored to serve in this capacity if he has not been transferred to more active duty by the time the launching takes place.

You wrote that you had never heard of a sponsor being provided with a Naval Aide. At the time of the launching of the lost "Atlanta," I had never heard of one either. I knew nothing of Navy etiquette, so I was wholly unprepared when I was presented with several Military Aides and one very dashing Naval Aide at the launching. Being a landlubber, I did not wish to betray my ignorance and I accepted them as part of the traditions of the Navy. But normal feminine curiosity made me wonder just what a Naval Aide to a sponsor was good for. In confidence, I asked a very kind looking Admiral what were the duties of a Naval Aide under such circumstances. He assured me, solemnly, that the prime duties of an Aide were to see that the seams in the back of the sponsor's stockings were straight. The Admiral said nothing upset the Navy like crooked seams in a sponsor's stockings. Emboldened, I asked him what the Military Aides were for and he replied he did not know, being only an Admiral.

1944

Mr. *Thomas Coleman*
Columbia, South Carolina

Atlanta, Georgia
March 29, 1944

Dear Mr. Coleman:

Thank you so much for your kind letter about "Gone With the Wind." You say you have seen the film of it seven times. I did not think anyone had beaten my record, which is five-and-a-half times. The last time, I had the rare good fortune of seeing it in comfortable surroundings, sitting on a low sofa buttressed with cushions, at a private showing for Ambassador Grew[1] who had just returned from internment in Tokyo. I must say that a comfortable seat improved "Gone With the Wind"![2]

I am so glad you liked my book, and gladder still you wrote and told me so.

Miss Betty Smith
New York, New York

Atlanta, Georgia
June 9, 1944

Dear Miss Smith:

When I saw your wonderful book[1] sticking at the top of the bestseller list, I wondered how long it would be before you were sued for plagiarism, libel et cetera. It is axiomatic among writers that no one ever sues the writer of an unsuccessful book. Just let a book go over twenty-five

---

[1] Joseph C. Grew.

[2] This viewing of the film was reported, somewhat tardily, in Bennett Cerf's "Trade Winds" column of *The Saturday Review of Literature*, XXVIII, No. 24 (June 16, 1945), p. 22: "When Joseph C. Grew was visiting in Atlanta recently, he found himself seated next to Margaret Mitchell at dinner. 'I mentally determined not to mention "Gone With the Wind,"' he told John William Rogers. 'But somehow we both found ourselves talking about it within two minutes. She discussed it as something with which she had no personal connection, but which she enjoyed talking about. And when she found I had never seen the film, she remarked she thought there was a print of it in town at the moment and she would try to run it down for me. She arranged things and the next day I went to her home. The two of us sat watching it for four and a half hours—she for the eleventh and a half time—laughing and crying, taking as fresh delight in it as if it were her first time and she had nothing to do with it but enjoy it!'"

---

[1] *A Tree Grows in Brooklyn* (New York and London, 1944).

thousand copies and it is surprising how many people's feelings are hurt, how many screwballs think their brain children have been stolen, and how many people feel that they have been portrayed in a manner calculated to bring infamy upon them.

I was truly grieved when I read that you were being sued, even though I confidently expected to read this news eventually. Such suits are embarrassing and troublesome, and dangerous as there is no telling which way a jury will jump. In the years since "Gone With the Wind" was published, I have had to deal with such problems, including forays with chiselers and racketeers, and I have considerable sympathy for you. I recall my embarrassment when my first suit arose—an old lady decided that I had swiped her book, because her book was bound in Confederate gray and so was mine, and I had mentioned General Lee and General Gordon and so had she. My motto was "millions for defense but not one cent for tribute." This policy has cost me money and used up time which I might have spent in writing, but I am glad I have established a reputation for being a person who will fight rather than buy off people whose claims are unjust. I recall how comforting it was to me, amid the embarrassment of my first suit, when the late Sidney Howard wrote me of his experiences. He was working on the screen version of "Gone With the Wind" at the time, and he told me of the problems that arose whenever one of his plays was successful. He wrote, "Apart from the expense, it is not pleasant to be called a thief. But there you are, and I can't think of any startling success which has enjoyed immunity." Marjorie Kinnan Rawlings has been undergoing experiences something like yours, for she is being sued by someone who claimed she had been portrayed unfavorably in one of Marjorie's books—"Cross Creek," I think. I hope you have good fortune with your suit. I hope the world is not too much with you so that you will have time to write more books which will give me the genuine pleasure your books gave me.

Please don't bother to acknowledge this letter. I know how busy you must be. I just wanted you to know that I loved "A Tree Grows in Brooklyn"—and to know that I have a fellow feeling for you in this particular situation.

Mr. Daniel Whitehead Hicky   Atlanta, Georgia
Marietta, Georgia   September 11, 1944

Dear Jack:

I have just received a letter from a friend in the Marine Corps[1] who

[1] Leodel Coleman of Statesboro, Georgia, a Combat Correspondent in the U.S. Marine Corps.

has been in a great many hot places and is now in Guam—unless he has moved on to a hotter place. He is a South Georgia man, a newspaper editor, who was really too old for the Marine Corps but made up his mind he was going to be a Marine Corps correspondent if he busted a trace doing it. He did not know I knew you or knew your poetry, so he quoted in full your poem that he had clipped somewhere—"There is so much to say, . . . But tell me, . . . If summer's on the Georgia fields again."[2]

The poem evidently meant so much to him, brought back to him the crepe myrtle and the watermelons and the cotton fields of home. I thought you'd like to know that one of your poems is traveling about in a Marine Corps combat pack, carrying with it the sights and smells of home to one who sometimes wonders if he will ever know them again.

I have told you several times that this is my favorite of all your poems. Now I'm glad to have my judgment backed up by a man who is in better position than I am to pass judgment.

Doctor Charles A. Thomson, Chief Atlanta, Georgia
Division of Science, Education and Art October 14, 1944
Department of State
Washington, D.C.

Dear Doctor Thomson:
  . . . I am enclosing a copy of an article from the October 7th issue of Publishers' Weekly. This indicates that the French publisher, Gaston Gallimard, was a collaborationist.[1] While the article is none too clear, it says that Mr. Gallimard is in hiding and it directly states that some of the other officials of his firm, Nouvelle Revue Française, were collaborationists. Mr. Gallimard was the publisher of the French edition of "Gone With the Wind." Naturally, I have heard nothing from him since the wall of silence closed down around France after the Germans invaded it. I want to take steps immediately to protect my copyright and my financial interests in France, but I want my actions to conform with the wishes of the State Department in such matters.

  I do not know how far it is proper for you to go in advising me about a matter of this nature. So, I am going to state the questions on my mind and, if you can answer any of them, I will be grateful. However, if you

[2] Hicky's poem, "Letter from the Front," was first published in *The Saturday Evening Post*, July 17, 1943. It may be found also in his *Never the Nightingale* (Atlanta, [c. 1951]), p. 31.
  [1] This was reported in "What Has Happened to French Writers and Publishers?" by PFC Chandler B. Grannis, *Publisher's Weekly*, CXLVI, No. 15 (October 7, 1944), p. 14.

write me that my questions are improper ones, I will be equally grateful, as that will guide me in future correspondence.

What is the status of my book in France under the circumstances described? I understand that contracts between citizens of warring nations are not abrogated by a state of war, but merely suspended. Mr. Gallimard is not a citizen of a country hostile to the United States, but he is a collaborationist. Would I be in the position of "trading with the enemy" if I conducted any business with Mr. Gallimard or an agent whom he might designate?

If Mr. Gallimard is a collaborationist, then perhaps I am not legally bound to him by my contract. Am I now in a position to serve notice on him that our contract is at an end because he has been allied with the enemy? And could I then make a business agreement for the handling of the French edition of "Gone With the Wind" with another publisher?

I want to do what is right and fair, for I have always been a person who stuck to the letter of any contract I signed, regardless of how disagreeable some of the features might be. But, needless to say, I would be very happy to be completely disassociated from such a person as Mr. Gallimard, if he actually was a collaborationist. I would be glad to have a new French publisher with a good reputation. But, at present, I do not know which way to turn, because I do not know either the status of my book, if my publisher was a collaborationist, or what steps it would be proper for me to take.

Has a policy or procedure been established by the provisional French government or the Allied nations for the handling of the property and assets of collaborationists? If such assets have been taken over by some governmental agency, what is that agency and what would be my line of action in protecting my rights? Would I be expected to deal directly with that agency in France or through some agency of the United States government in this country?

One angle to the situation that causes me apprehension is a newspaper item published a few days ago. It stated that my novel would be one of the first books published in France when paper became available and it quoted as authority for this statement a publisher in France which I have never heard of. If some "collaborationist property custodian" has been established in France, would he have the authority to transfer the right to publish my book to some publisher without my knowledge or approval?

Those are the problems. If there is any information or advice you can give me, it will be very welcome.

Mr. Douglas Gilbert   Atlanta, Georgia
New York World-Telegram   October 23, 1944
New York, New York

Dear Mr. Gilbert:

I have just received two clippings from the New York World-Telegram which made mention of "Gone With the Wind." The first was in an article by Jay Nelson Tuck and was the last of a series entitled "Movie Magnettes." The other clipping was from the October 11th issue of the World-Telegram and the story, which was by you, was concerned with "Forever Amber," by Kathleen Winsor.

In both of these stories the statement was made that "Gone With the Wind" was sold to the movies in galley proof, for $50,000. In Mr. Tuck's article the statement was made that "Gone With the Wind" would have brought several times that sum a few months later.

"Gone With the Wind" was not sold in galley proof and I have never made any statement as to the amount I received for the moving picture rights. This error has more lives than twenty cats and it appears that it is useless to make another correction when I have been correcting this misstatement ever since 1936. But here we go again!

I finished reading galley proofs on "Gone With the Wind" in March, 1936. It is highly doubtful that anyone in Hollywood read it in galley proof. If they did, no offer was made to me at that time. The book was published at the end of June, 1936, and I had not disposed of the movie rights and would not dispose of them at that time. I sold the moving picture rights on July 30, 1936, as the date on my contract will show. As the pre-publication sale was something between 50,000 and 90,000 copies, I knew my book would be fairly successful. "Gone With the Wind" had sold several hundred thousand copies by the time I disposed of the moving picture rights.

I don't suppose the truth of this matter is of any great importance to anyone but me, but I do get tired of seeing this error crop up about once a month, in spite of my denials. I have no idea how this error got into circulation. If ever you or Mr. Tuck are writing on the subject of the sale of moving picture rights, I hope you omit mention of "Gone With the Wind" or else state that it was not sold in galley proof and that, far from being hornswaggled by Hollywood, the rights to "Gone With the Wind" brought the highest price ever paid for a first novel by an unknown author up to that time.

Mrs. Charles Killette   Atlanta, Georgia
Hogansville, Georgia   December 9, 1944

Dear Mrs. Killette:

I have just returned from my trip North and I want to tell you that I met your son on the day of the commissioning of the "Atlanta," and he is every bit as nice as you said he was. The commissioning ceremonies were most impressive and when they were over and we were in the captain's cabin, I asked him if it would be possible for me to meet the Georgia boys in the crew. Captain Colyear[1] is a very understanding officer and, as he comes from Arkansas, he understood about Southerners and said he would be happy to have the Georgia boys piped up to the crew's recreation room. There were about twenty from Georgia and, as the guests from Atlanta moved around speaking to them, I asked each boy to tell us what town he came from. When one nice looking young man said "Hogansville," I replied, "Then you must be Charles Killette Junior." You never saw anyone look quite as surprised as he did. I was so glad to meet him and to tell him I had heard from you on the day before I left town.

I put your contribution to the Welfare Fund in an envelope and attached your name and your son's name to it. After the commissioning ceremonies, when the colors had been broken for the first time and the captain had taken command and the first watch set, Mayor Hartsfield, General Uhl[2] and I were called to the little platform to speak briefly over the intercommunication system. The Mayor and the General gave checks from the City of Atlanta and the Fourth Service Command and then I gave my contribution and yours. Captain Colyear said he would write you and thank you.

You have a fine son. I know you must miss him. I know, too, you must be proud of him.

Mrs. William L. Plummer   Atlanta, Georgia
Atlanta, Georgia   December 11, 1944

Dear Honey:

You are more than generous to let me have the original invitation for the Paris premiere of "Gone With the Wind." Of course I love having it and will cherish it, but if you or your husband ever regret giving it to

---

[1] Captain Bayard H. Colyear.
[2] Major General Frederick Uhl.

me I will part with it. The story in the paper, which you sent, was most interesting. I wonder how I would have felt seeing that picture so far away from Georgia and under such circumstances. I think the scenes of 1864 Atlanta would have made me so homesick I would have wept.

I was interested to know that the film was privately shown and will not be released to the general public for some time. I hope the French people will like it.

Please write and tell your husband how much I enjoyed his remarks about the picture and how nice I think he is to let me have the invitation on the paper of the Embassy.[1] Please tell him, too, the following which may interest him. My book was banned in Germany and occupied countries some time before Pearl Harbor. Of course the moving picture would have been banned, too, but the producers had refused to have it exhibited in any Fascist country. There was one copy of the film in the vaults of MGM in Paris and this film was captured when the Germans took the city. Rumors came out through the Underground that the film, closely guarded, was sent to Berlin where it had a private showing before a group of five—Hitler and his four closest boy friends. I've wondered since what they thought of it. They did not think a story or a movie which had to do with a conquered people who became free again would be a good thing to show in Germany or occupied countries.

---

[1] Colonel Plummer had attended a private screening of *GWTW*, to which he had been invited by the American Ambassador, Jeffery Caffery.

1945

Lt. (j.g.) *Richard B. Harwell*
USS YMS 89
FPO, San Francisco, California

Atlanta, Georgia
March 23, 1945

Dear Mr. Harwell:

How much I enjoyed your letter of February 21st about your experiences in New Zealand. It is always difficult for me to imagine our Atlanta boys half way across the world, and I find it even more difficult to imagine an Atlanta boy being asked questions about me in New Zealand. So "Gone With the Wind" was playing at the theatres in Auckland at Christmas time! I hear it is still running in London and in its fifth year. I wouldn't be surprised if its popularity is due to the attendance by homesick Southerners anxious to see a bit of the South, even if it is synthetic.

You were such an ardent collector and protector of Confederate war materials that I know you'll be interested to know that Emory and other libraries and societies are collecting material from this war. Just the other day I was preparing to give to the paper salvage a number of circulars and mimeographed letters having to do with various war activities, and my secretary told me reproachfully that Emory wanted such material. So now I am saving all sorts of junk, which is junk now but will be valuable 80 years from now if someone wants to write a hot novel about Atlanta in 1945. The pep sheets for the Red Cross rally, reports of the USO for the year, tickets to this and that war benefit—it seems funny that they are part of history even now.

Those of us at home have happier hearts these days, as the war news seems better. I'm glad to say there is none of the false optimism current now as there was six months ago. People do not feel that the war in the Pacific will be over immediately. They are just supremely grateful to the people fighting that war that it *is* being shortened by their efforts. Atlanta is in the midst of its annual Red Cross money-raising campaign, and this time it's nearly a million dollars to be raised. This town has never yet fallen down on a big job and I don't think it will fall down on this one, as nearly $200,000 were collected in three days. People who work downtown have the excitement of getting large sums of money. As I ring door bells here in a residential section, the pickings are small and a ten dollar bill enormous. It never fails to rain whenever I go out for any patriotic purpose, and after this war I believe I will rent myself out to the Farm Bureau for use in dust bowls.

I hope you are well and as happy as one can be far away from home. I hope it won't be too long before we meet again and talk leisurely about Confederate medicine instead of the medicine of this war.

Lt. Hunt Clement, Jr., USNR   Atlanta, Georgia
Coronado, California   May 2, 1945

Dear Hunt:

When we were in Sea Island we read in an Atlanta paper that you were home. John and I regretted not being in Atlanta to see you after you had been away so long a time. The last definite news we had of you was at least a year ago when some correspondent landing (I believe) under fire on some unnamed beach, wrote that "Hunt Clement, of Atlanta, Georgia, was the beach master." I know less than nothing about what a beach master is, and I would like to know. I'd also like to know a great many things about the places you have been, and I know you are some-one who is articulate enough to make me really see what they are like. Perhaps when the war is over we can get together for a long, long evening.

Today the rumor is abroad that the Germans in North Italy have surrendered. Perhaps the war in Europe will be over before the week is out. Then twice as much force can be applied in the Pacific and perhaps victory will be won there twice as fast. I hope so. I am not one of those people who think resistance in the Pacific is going to end as soon as Hitler has surrendered.

I suppose you have heard that Wright Bryan will be home from France soon and that his leg will be all right. Allan Taylor, who's been in New York for the last ten years or so, is on the New York Times in the Sunday Magazine Section where the news of the world is broken down. Lois wrote me that he had fractured his leg in several places nearly six months ago and is just now able to get about on crutches. Bill Howland is still head of the Time-Life bureau here and has practically a war cor-respondent's status, as he has done nothing except cover training, manoeuvers, the building of the Alcan Highway et cetera. Most of the people we know are scattered to the ends of the earth. It will be good to have them home again.

Sgt. William Mauldin   Atlanta, Georgia
United Features Syndicate   May 14, 1945
New York, New York

Dear Sergeant Mauldin:

The Atlanta Constitution, which publishes your cartoons, came out yesterday with your Soldier Somewhere in Italy, writing a letter to "Dear, Dear Miss Mitchell." And now, "Dear, Dear Sergeant Mauldin, you will probably think this an awful funny letter to get from an author," but I am so flattered by the drawing that I must write and thank you. It has done me a great deal of good here in Atlanta, for it has raised my stock with the small fry to extravagant heights. I have been out ringing door bells for the Seventh Bond Drive and have met any number of children. I cannot tell you how respectful they are to me because my name appeared in your cartoon, and they believe that I really did get such a letter. To crown my joy, my young nephew, who is of grammar school age, has invited me to be present at the graduation drill of his cadet corps, and I am sure that I would never have gotten such an invitation without your cartoon. For, after all, aunts are just two-for-a-penny in any boy's pocket, while Sergeant Mauldin is something else.

Your cartoons are so wonderful and so astringent. They have made many people safe at home realize what war is like. Your soldiers are so real that we feel cold with them and hungry and wet feet-itchy, too, and unillusioned. Thanks for mentioning me in the same breath with them.

Captain Bayard H. Colyear, USN   Atlanta, Georgia
The USS "Atlanta"   July 18, 1945
FPO, San Francisco, California

Dear Captain Colyear:

Recently the news dispatches named the "Atlanta" as one of the ships immediately off Tokyo. I do not recall a time before during this war when the name of a ship was given before or during an engagement. Perhaps this *is* the first time. The exact knowledge of the "Atlanta's" whereabouts has brought mingled emotions to those of us who have friends and relatives aboard. We cannot help feeling tremendously proud that the "Atlanta" is there in the fight—in what we all pray will be the final phase of the fight—but we cannot help worrying too. If I had not stood on the decks of your good ship and seen the faces of you and your men, I would not worry so much—but then I would not be so proud. This letter is just to let you know that the thoughts and prayers and good wishes of the people who bought the ship with which you fight go with you into the fight. Some day when all this is triumphantly finished, I hope we can hear what has happened to you and to your men.

Seamen J. Ed Manget and Mackie McCrorey   Atlanta, Georgia
USS "Atlanta"   July 21, 1945
FPO, San Francisco, California

My dear Ed Manget and Mackie McCrorey:
    Several days ago when I was not feeling at all well, something happened which made me feel a hundred per cent better and I have been feeling better ever since. That something was the most beautiful vase of flowers I ever saw—a green vase in which were big fat pink roses, small lovely lilac asters, heavy-headed rose dahlias and long shoots of sweet smelling tube roses. Flowers like these would make any woman feel better, but the nicest thing about them was the card on which was printed "Best wishes for a speedy recovery" and under that "Your boys on the U.S.S. Atlanta, Ed Manget and Mackie McCrorey." This is one of the nicest things that ever happened to me and it came at just the right time, and I do not mean just because I was not feeling well. The main reason it made me feel so happy was that I had had the "Atlanta" and her crew on my mind very heavily for some time. I had been waking up at night and wondering where the ship was and how all of you boys were doing. I've often worried about you in the past, but I have a stronger reason now. Some days ago the newspapers carried a story about a part of our fleet being off Tokyo. To the surprise of everyone, the newspapers named the ships in this force. The "Atlanta" was one of them. The Journal waked me up early in the morning when I was so sleepy I hardly knew what I was saying. They told me the "Atlanta" was off the shores of Tokyo and they asked me what I thought about that. I told them I wasn't surprised because that was where you boys had told me you were going. The newspaper reporter laughed and hung up, and I felt like a fool when I read my remark in the Journal. But that is what you and the three boys standing near you told me the day of the Commissioning —that you and the "Atlanta" would be among the first ships to reach Japan. So, knowing where all of you were, I've thought so much about you. And that is why the flowers seemed like an answer to my thoughts.
    All of us who have friends or relatives on the "Atlanta" hope that the

Navy continues to print the names of ships taking part in certain engagements. There is nothing worse than not knowing where your friends are. Even if you know they are in danger, it is not as worrying as not knowing and imagining that things are worse than they are.

I hope so much that before long you boys will have the most sought after shore leave American sailors ever had, and that is shore leave in Tokyo. No, that doesn't mean the war is over. I know the hardest part of the Navy's fight may be going on right now. But I hope that special shore leave is granted before too long a time has passed.

My husband talked to your father, Ed, over the phone a few days ago, and I talked to your mother. They told us how hot it is in your part of the world and how all of you were suffering from skin rashes and heat irritations. A while back this section had a drought and the longest, hottest spell any of us can recall. The gardens were drying up and the farmers were desperate and all of us realized that food was going to be short next year and were worried. Everyone was perspirey and irritable, but we aren't ever going to complain of the heat any more—for this reason. The farming people down around Millen, Georgia, were losing all their crops for want of rain and were desperate, and they all got together and prayed for rain. There was a little item on the back page of the paper about it, and I was talking to one of my friends about it as we were going to the Red Cross. She said she wished people wouldn't do things like that or else wished the newspapers wouldn't print such stories. "Just think how silly such conduct makes us appear to Northern people," she said. "I feel right mortified that Southern people should act that way." I replied that I did not care what Northern people thought. And I had barely said these words when, with no warning, the heaviest rain I ever saw fell upon us. By the time the bus got to the Red Cross the water in the streets was above our ankles. It rained all day all over the state and in South Georgia most of the chicken coops were carried away and they do say that the rabbits were climbing trees to keep from being drowned. It slacked up around six o'clock, and the night issue of the Constitution carried a story that the Millen people were going to church the next morning in a body to thank the Lord for the rain. About a half hour after the Millen folks thanked the Lord, it began to hail and the hailstones were bigger than lemons. I was trying to get to the Red Cross again and fearing that my skull would be fractured at any minute, and it rained and hailed all day. As our old colored janitor said, "It don't do no good to trifle with the Lord, 'cause if akse him for somethin' He likely to sen' mo' than you can handle." As you know, shoes are not too plentiful and no one likes to ruin their shoes by getting them wet. And all over town I heard people saying that somebody ought to take steps about the Millen people and make them stop praying, or else we'd all be stomp barefooted. I was wet and cold so much those two days that I don't think I'll ever complain about the heat again.

Please give my regards to the Georgia boys I met. Tell the Venable boy I haven't been out to Marietta since before the Commissioning and haven't seen his people, as we haven't the gas to go that far. And tell Charles Killette I hear from his mother occasionally and read the nice articles she writes in the paper with great interest. I want all of you to know how much Atlanta and Georgia people think of you and about you and your ship. The "U.S.S. Atlanta" isn't like just any ship. She is something very special, and built to order for the people hereabouts and by the people hereabouts. All of us who bought bonds feel that we own some small fraction of your ship. Ever so often children stop me on the street and say, "What do you suppose our ship is doing now?" They are children who saved up their stamps and acquired an $18.75—"U.S.S. Atlanta"—bond. The people who bought thousands of dollars worth feel the same way. We are proud to know the ship is in what we hope is the last phase of the fight. You boys take good care of the ship and of yourselves, and when you have the time write and tell me what has happened—if the censor will let you.

And now, my dears, thanks again for the flowers. They are still beautiful.

Mr. Malcolm Cowley   Atlanta, Georgia
Gaylordsville, Connecticut   September 6, 1945

Dear Mr. Cowley:

Again I must tell you how sorry I am to have been so long in sending you the information you requested for "The Literary History of the United States."[1] My husband has been and still is quite ill, my cook has been injured, I have a damaged wrist, and have been trying to do the house work, the nursing and my own business under considerable handicap. Getting up the "Gone With the Wind" sales in foreign countries was still more hampered by the fact that I did not have my books at the time you requested the information and have just gotten them from my auditors. I hope to have reports from countries such as Denmark and Czechoslovakia soon. I have not heard from them since 1939, as you will note from the list which follows.

You asked in how many countries "Gone With the Wind" had been published. The British edition and the British "Colonial" edition and the Canadian edition appeared in the British Isles, Canada, Australia, New

---

[1] Cowley has published no book with this title.

Zealand, India and South Africa. The other countries in which "Gone With the Wind" has been published are:

Brazil	Published	January 1940 (in Portuguese)
Bulgaria	"	April 1940
Chile	"	October 1937 (in Spanish)
Czechoslovakia	"	(in Czech language)
Volume I	"	December 1937
Volume II	"	March 1938
Denmark	"	September 1937
Finland	"	Volume I November 1937
		Volume II prior to July 1938
France	"	February 1939
Germany	"	October 1937
*Holland	"	November 1937—Pirated
Hungary	"	November 1937
Italy	"	December 1937
Latvia	"	Prior to autumn 1938
Norway	"	August 1937
Poland	"	Volume I October 1938
		Volume II December 1938
Roumania	"	Late 1939, or 1940
Spain	"	July 1943
Sweden	"	August 1937
*China	"	Prior to 1941—Pirated
*Japan	"	Between 1937 and 1939—Unauthorized
Argentina	Newspaper serialization	
Cuba	"	"
Greece	"	"
Mexico	"	"
Uruguay	"	"

* The pirated edition which appeared in Holland was evidently very popular. The invasion of Holland by Hitler interfered with a lawsuit I had been conducting for four years against piratical publishers. I do not know the number of copies sold.

* The Chinese edition (in the English language) was pirated at an unknown date before 1941. I am unable to give you sales figures but I have been told by newspaper correspondents, missionaries and returning soldiers that it has sold "perhaps in the hundreds of thousands."

* At least five or six Japanese publishers brought out editions of "Gone With the Wind" probably between 1937 and 1939. I will have to call these editions "unauthorized" but not "pirated," as the United States Government very kindly gave to the Japanese, by formal treaty some years ago, the right to publish books by citizens of the United States and pay nothing for the privilege. I have been told by government people, newspaper people and returning travelers that several hundred thousand copies were sold in Japan.

As to your question number 2, "In how many foreign languages has it been translated?"—please see information above.

As to your question number 3 about approximate sales in various countries—I am giving you a list of sales figures up to the last reported dates in all countries in which "Gone With the Wind" has been published. You will doubtless note that while I have listed Poland as one of the countries in which "Gone With the Wind" was published, I have no sales figures from that country. The German machine rolled over Poland before the first sales report from that country was due. It is my understanding that my unfortunate publishers were Jewish, and what has happened to them I do not like to think. It is doubtful that I will ever know much about "Gone With the Wind" in that country except for the few Polish newspaper reviews I received and reports from Polish refugees. It was only natural that they would like a book such as "Gone With the Wind" because (as one Pole wrote me) "ours has been a country which has known too often defeat and the trampling of liberty and the bitterness of reconstruction." I understand the book sold fairly well in those tense days before the war.

Brazil	Copies sold to	June 1945	23,787
Bulgaria	" " "	April 1945	8,000
Chile	" " "	July 1944	58,415
Czechoslovakia	" " "	July 1939	6,000
Denmark	" " "	January 1940	18,811
Finland	" " "	November 1941	17,200
France	" " "	February 1945	164,391
Germany	" " "	July 1941	360,693
Hungary	" " "	April 1940	14,070
Italy	" " "	May 1941	23,466
Latvia	" " "	January 1940	2,453
Norway	" " "	January 1940	20,345
Poland	No report on account of war		
Roumania	Presumably to January '41		5,000
Spain	Copies sold to July 1944		14,205
Sweden	Presumably to January 1944		40,000

You asked for the approximate sales figures from Great Britain. I am unable to give you these figures as my English language sales are lumped together. Perhaps The Macmillan Company in New York can disentangle the British sales figures from those in this country. It would probably take me and my auditors a couple of weeks longer to dig this information out, and I have delayed so long already that I do not wish to hold up my reply to you any longer.

As to your fourth question, "When was it published..."—I have placed the publication date after the name of each country in the first list above.

In your question number 3 you asked about the date of publication and the approximate number of sales in Argentina. I cannot tell you this as "Gone With the Wind" was not published in book form in that country. It was published in Chile in Spanish and sold in Spanish-speaking South America, Central America and Mexico. I cannot say what part of the sales listed under Chile should be apportioned to Argentina.

You asked about the critical reception of "Gone With the Wind" in three or four countries. I subscribed to a foreign clipping service, and so I had reviews from most of the world. They are now in my dead files in our basement. Under my present circumstances it is just impossible for me to get to them. If your deadline is not too close and another three weeks or month do not matter, I can probably get them for you. Some of the translations are not in the smoothest idiomatic English, as, for instance, a Swede translated the Dutch reviews, a Norwegian the Finnish and a Dane the Latvian et cetera. However, quaint though some of the translations were, they made sense and I found them highly interesting. I found the critical reception in foreign countries an exciting and an humbling business. It never occurred to me "Gone With the Wind" would be translated into any foreign language. When it appeared in so many languages and had such astoundingly good reviews, I was breathless, and still am. I found it very interesting, too, that while many critics in the United States based their criticism upon the love story or the narrative, European critics evaluated it on a different basis. In practically every European country critics wrote at length of the "universal historical significance." Each nation applied to its own past history the story of the Confederate rise and fall and reconstruction. French critics spoke of 1870, Poles of the partitioning of their country, Germans of 1918 and the bitterness which followed, Czechs wrote not only of their troubled past but of their fears of the future, and I had letters from that country just before it went under, saying that if the people of the South had risen again to freedom the people of Czechoslovakia could do likewise. The same type of letters and reviews came from Norway, Finland, Denmark. The Brazilian reviews and letters were especially interesting, as the Brazilians discovered for almost the first time that they had something in common with North America. Brazil has its "North and South," one agricultural and the other industrial. They also had slavery and emancipation with economic chaos following the freeing of the slaves. During the Spanish Civil War, Americans fighting on *both* sides wrote that English editions had been read aloud at night in the camps, and each side, feeling their cause was just, identified themselves with the Confederates.

Madame Renee Rousselle Atlanta, Georgia
Paris, France September 27, 1945

Dear Madame Rousselle:

I have heard through Doctor Bateman of the wartime career of "Gone With the Wind" in France. He wrote that it was forbidden by the Germans but distributed by the Underground. It made me proud and happy to know that something I wrote could give pleasure and comfort to French people during the occupation.[1]

Doctor Bateman writes that he is bringing me a worn French volume of "Gone With the Wind" which you gave him for me. I thank you and I will treasure it. How kind of you to do this! I wish I could send you an American copy in exchange, but the book is temporarily out of print and I cannot find a copy in Atlanta. I send you as a souvenir a billet confedere such as is mentioned on page 411 of "Autant en emporte le vent."

---

[1] Dr. Needham B. Bateman wrote Mrs. Florence S. Bateman of Atlanta on August 25: "I have found that the French people read 'Gone With the Wind' during the German occupation, and liked it above all other books. They all ask me about the book and the author, Margaret Mitchell. It seems that it was a forbidden book (by the Germans) but still they published it secretly, distributed it through the underground, and passed it on to one another—many people reading a single copy. The curfew began at 6 or 7 p.m. so they had a world of time to read. I have been promised a worn and tattered volume which I hope to present to Miss Mitchell when I get back."

Bob Considine wrote in the New York *Journal American* March 25, 1944: "The massive adventures of Scarlett and Rhett are now bootlegging for $60 a copy in France, and for almost that figure in Holland, Norway and Belgium. Persons have been shot for possessing it. Orders have gone out from Germany to seize all copies."

1946

Miss *Josephine Pinckney*
Charleston, South Carolina

Atlanta, Georgia
August 2, 1946

Dear Miss Pinckney:

This morning when I was preparing to wrap and mail "Three O'Clock Dinner"[1] to a French translator-critic who has been starved for American books, a guilty feeling came over me, for I realized I had never said "thank you" to you. It must have been nearly a year ago that I first read your book with delight, sometimes waking my husband at night to read him long passages. I never thanked you for Lucian, who is one of my favorite characters and I can almost say one of my favorite Southern friends. I read a number of reviews of your book in which a great many points of story, style, character, background were discussed, but I never found anyone who gave Lucian the credit he (and you) deserve. Lucian and his mother and their relationship are wonderful. They both unashamedly love gossip and delight in other people's business. Ordinarily this can be an odious trait and indicative of bad breeding, but not with Lucian and his mother. I have known a few Lucians and have enjoyed the news of the world they brought to me, with their faintly malicious, sharply acute observations.

I liked all the rest of the book, too, of course, and could smell again the way Charleston gardens smell early in the morning in summer before the sun is up, and I thank you for the pleasure and interest your good book brought me. I did not see how you could miss getting the Pulitzer Prize and, while I am sure you have not felt the lack of the Pulitzer Prize or bothered about it, I was taken with such a fit of indignation that it took me some while to quiet down.

I had just begun reading "Three O'Clock Dinner" aloud to my husband last Christmas season when he was stricken with a serious heart attack. He has been ill all these months and is still in bed but now we hope that the doctor will let him get up soon. "Three O'Clock Dinner" is the book we are looking forward to reading together when that anticipated period of his convalescence arrives.

How well you know Southern people. So often when a writer knows

---

[1] (New York, 1945).

his section so well he is not able to communicate it, but you have done it. And how grateful I am to you for all the interest I have had from your book.

Mr. Eddy Gilmore　　　　　　　　　　　　　　Atlanta, Georgia
Belmar, New Jersey　　　　　　　　　　　　　August 6, 1946

Dear Eddy:

I have been wanting to write you a long letter but have waited for an opportunity. I don't think the opportunity will ever come. At least, not until I get John up, and I don't know when that will be. He is able to sit up in bed now but is still a long way from being well.

I was so interested to learn from your letter this morning that you have really started your book.[1] I'm glad to hear you went to The Macmillan Company—among others. When I took up the matter of a manuscript from you, Harold Latham was editor in charge of fiction and Lois Cole (who married Allan Taylor, formerly of the Journal) was assistant editor. Harold Latham has been out of the office since last Christmas and has been very ill. Lois Cole has gone to Whittlesey House and is full editor there. In case you don't know it, Whittlesey House is a publishing part of McGraw-Hill. If you don't have luck at the publishing houses you mentioned, you might try Lois. I should tell you though—and I hope you'll keep this quiet—that I heard after your previous visit to the United States that The Macmillan Company and some other publishing houses discovered that you had talked to more than one house. Now, to normal people on the outside of publishing this seems like a very sensible way of doing business. To publishers, however, the showing of a manuscript to more than one publisher at the same time ranks above the well known sin against the Holy Ghost. John and I were informed that this was unethical conduct on your part. "And who-the-hell makes up these ethics?" questioned John. "The Publishers, I am quite certain. Wolves always make up the ethics for sheep, I'm sure." However, a great deal of water has flowed under publishing bridges since then, and a war has come and gone, and people have moved around to different publishing houses, and all the above may have been forgotten. I simply pass this information on to you in case the matter should come up at some future date. . . .

If you get the time, I wish you'd write me the answer to this question—what language is spoken in the Ukraine. I've gotten a request for publishing rights "in Ukrainian translation." I've got to know, first, what

[1] *Me and My Russian Wife* (Garden City, N.Y., 1954).

language that is so I can incorporate it in a contract, and, second, whether it's a language in which the translation rights of "Gone With the Wind" are already sold. Of course it's just possible that Ukraines speak the Ukrainian language, but that would be far, far too easy.

And if you get the time, I wish you'd answer me this too. Did you ever see a Russian "Gone With the Wind"? Of course it would be a piracy if there was, for I've never been approached. I have enormous doubts that there was a piracy, for the Communists and the Left Wingers and even the Pinkoes in this country have carried on an unrelenting warfare against "Gone With the Wind" for ten years. I often wonder what the gentleman named Mr. Platt in the Daily Worker would write about if he did not have me, for I or my opus appear at least once a week. So, if the Communists are agin' "Gone With the Wind," can you figure out how somebody in the Ukraine is going to publish it without getting liquidated? . . .

I won't go into your war dispatches and will just say they were wonderful. I look forward to the Saturday Evening Post[2] and to your book. I'm glad it's going easy.

Mrs. Isabel Paterson   Atlanta, Georgia
New York, New York   October 21, 1946

Dear Miss Paterson:
    Do you have Miss Angela Thirkell's home address? And do you feel that you could trust it to me? My husband and I want to send Miss Thirkell a Christmas box of fancy food and we would rather not send it to her publishers, as we do not know what complications might arise with the English customs authorities. I do not know Miss Thirkell but I am sure she has no more ardent admirer unless it is my husband. He has been very seriously ill for a year now (of which more later) and for many months I read him a chapter from one of Miss Thirkell's books every night. He says they saved his life. We still have "Miss Bunting" to go. My husband keeps prodding me about why I haven't sent her a nice Christmas box. As I have been doing most of the nursing and some-times the cooking for about a year, I just haven't gotten around to this pleasant task. I did write Mrs. May Lamberton Becker to discover if English people have to surrender ration points for food parcels, and on learning that they do not I now take this step toward finding out Miss Thirkell's home address from you.

---

[2] His Post article is "I Get Along with Russians," *The Saturday Evening Post*, September 14.

You wrote that you doted upon Mrs. Moreland and were addicted to the Earl of Pomfret and thought considerable of Sam Adams. While we tried to be broadminded about your taste and admitted that the characters named are fine indeed, we really like Ed Pollitt better than any other character, with Mrs. Brandon and old Miss Brandon running second and third. You evidenced a curiosity about events at Gatherum Castle with more illumination upon the Duke of Omnium. Yes, I would like that, too, but more than anything else I would like to have a clear explanation of what is wrong with the Bishop of Barchester. Even the kindest curate lacks a good word for him, and a common hatred of the Bishop is enough to draw people of diverse characters to each other in bonds of eternal friendship. I believe Miss Pettinger is the only person who ever spoke a good word for the Bishop. I would like to know what is wrong with the Bishop and how he maintains his position in the face of such universal dislike. My husband says he does not wish to know this and prefers that the Bishop continue as an off-stage voice—presumably the voice of the Anti-Christ.

You were nice enough to ask if I was at work upon another book. No, I am not working on another book. I hear frequently that I am and even had a letter recently from a Polish publisher who wished to buy it. He knew all about it as it had already been published, according to him, and a number of Poles had already read it here in the United States. In spite of this, I have written nothing since "Gone With the Wind." There has been little or no time for writing. For nearly five years, my father was a helpless invalid and what time I did not spend fighting off the onslaughts of people who thought I could get them into the film of "Gone With the Wind" was spent taking care of him. I also did five years at the Red Cross in the less glamorous outfits. I did about three-and-a-half years with Civilian Defense, with its attendant paper and scrap and salvage drives, first aid classes and bond-selling. About a year ago my husband suffered a very severe heart attack and has been bedridden since then. As it has been almost impossible to get nurses or orderlies unless someone is actually dying, I've done most of the nursing. Since the German surrender the European translations of "Gone With the Wind" have been keeping me busy. Some of my old publishers, many of whom were refugees or in hiding or working with the underground of their countries, have reappeared and reestablished their publishing houses; other publishers have simply disappeared, and I am trying to find them or their heirs. New countries have requested contracts for translations and publication. It's very difficult to do business overseas these days and it takes a great deal of time. So, all in all, I haven't had time to write any books and hardly time to write letters.

My husband is better now and I hope he is out of danger, so I take this occasion to try to send something to Miss Thirkell as a token of both genuine and serious appreciation of her books and what they have meant to me and my husband during a very worrying year.

Mr. Elliott White Springs   Atlanta, Georgia
Lancaster, South Carolina   November 4, 1946

Dear Elliott:

Thank you for your letter about Carl Sandburg and thank you, too, for saying such nice things to him about me. To meet Mr. Lincoln's good friend would be as great an honor as meeting General Lee's good friend, Doctor Freeman—a pleasure which has long stayed with me. Under ordinary circumstances I would be even now putting the big pot in the little one in the hope that Mr. Sandburg would be pleased with the results. Unfortunately, my circumstances are not ordinary at present, and so I will not be able to see Mr. Sandburg when and if he comes to Atlanta, and perhaps not be able to talk with him on the phone. I would appreciate it if you would let him know the circumstances I am going to relate, for I would not want so great a person to think me rude and ungracious.

My husband has been desperately—and then seriously—ill since last Christmas Eve. He had a coronary occlusion at that time. Due to bad doctors his condition was made much worse, and before we secured a conservative doctor who knew how to treat him he had suffered greater heart damage. Until very recently he has been in bed; now he can move about in the apartment a little. During these months when it was almost impossible to secure nurses, I've done most of the nursing. I have had to let everything else slide—friends, business, letters, parties, meeting people and even answering telephone calls. It never failed that when someone got me on the phone John's bell rang. So until he is well—as well as he will ever be—and out again, I am not seeing anyone. It disappoints me greatly that I won't see Mr. Sandburg or hear his lecture, but that's the situation I am in at present.

Many nights during these last months when I could not sleep, I thought of you, because there lay upon my desk for a long time the clipping about the death of your boy. At the time it happened, I could not write you. John was so ill then and even if I had found the time to write —well, that was not the right time to write you. This is not the right time either, and I sadly realize there is never the right time, nor the right words, for someone who's had a tragedy like yours. But I've thought of you so much and I wanted you to know how truly sorry I was about it.

1947

Dr. Wallace McClure
Washington, D.C.

Atlanta, Georgia
March 31, 1947

Dear Doctor McClure:

I am now arriving at your doorstep with another of my "Gone With the Wind" foreign problems. I have had it on a number of doorsteps in this section and I would not be bothering you with it if I could get the complete information I need here in Atlanta. Government people here have been very kind and helpful to me during the last ten years, but, as I seem to have such a variety of foreign problems and am the only person in this section doing business in so many foreign countries, it is not to be wondered at that I can't get all the assistance I need here.

My present problem concerns my German edition of "Gone With the Wind" and my German publisher, Dr. Henry Goverts, of the (former—?) firm H. Goverts Verlag, G.m.b.H., Moorweidenstrasse 14, Hamburg 13. I want to know if it is legal at present for me to correspond with Dr. Goverts on matters of business. Shortly after the war was over, I was told that I could ask for and receive sales reports and accountings of royalties from him but that I could not write him about business matters. This is, of course, a little contradictory. I received a very straightforward letter from Dr. Goverts shortly after the end of the war in Europe. He wrote me from Liechtenstein, where his mother, an Englishwoman, lives. I have always understood, in a roundabout way, that Dr. Goverts, being half English, was anti-Nazi. In his letter he acknowledged the debt he owed me, which consisted of royalties he had been unable to pay to me because of Hitler's blocked marks and later because of the war. He closed his letter by saying, "As soon as book selling is open again we shall begin again in selling the German edition of your book."

I replied to his letter and addressed it to Liechtenstein. My letter was little more than a formal acknowledgement of his. However, as at that time the Government was requiring information from American citizens who had holdings in foreign countries, I asked for a report on the number of copies of "Gone With the Wind" sold in Germany and my credits; I took note of his plans for the future sale of my book.

That was in 1945. I have had no answer to my letter, nor have I

401

written to Dr. Goverts. It was my understanding that I must not hold
business correspondence with a German until the peace treaty was signed.

I have no desire to do business with a German now nor to write
letters to one, but a situation has arisen in my European affairs which is
forcing me to take some action about the German translation of "Gone
With the Wind." Since the war I have had a number of requests from
publishers in Switzerland, Sweden and lately Austria, for the German
language publication rights. I have refused all offers, stating that Dr.
Goverts had the publication rights in the German language. Day-before-
yesterday I had a letter from another publisher in Austria, making me
an offer for the translation rights. Among other matters, he stated flatly
that "his firm (Goverts) no more exists and the German rights are free."

After eleven years' experience with publishing problems in foreign
countries, I have developed a sixth sense about affairs like this, and I can
feel it in the wind when foreign publishers are getting ready to bring out
unauthorized editions of "Gone With the Wind." It has been my experience that the interest of a number of publishers in a certain country will
be aroused, I will refuse them all for one reason or another, but each
publisher will be certain that another publisher is going to pirate my
book. Therefore each publisher will begin pirating it himself. Then I
have a bad problem on my hands, and I am so worn out with such problems that I like to head them off whenever it is possible. I fear that if I
cannot say definitely to all these publishers that Goverts is my publisher,
that his firm is in existence, that he intends to bring out a new edition
as soon as he has paper, and that he will fight for his translation rights—
then I am afraid I am going to have several unauthorized German editions in a number of countries.

If Dr. Goverts indeed no longer has a publishing business and does
not intend to publish "Gone With the Wind" again, then I wish to take
my rights back in a legal and orderly fashion and enter into a German
language contract with some publisher in Switzerland. If, however, Dr.
Goverts intends to continue his business but is hampered by a demolished
building, destroyed presses, melted plates or paper shortage et cetera,
then I consider him still my authorized publisher and I do not want his
translation pirated all over Europe.

Now, having set forth this tangled mess, I come to you for the following information. Although we have not signed a peace treaty with
Germany, is it legal for me to write Dr. Goverts (probably through
Liechtenstein, as I do not know his Hamburg address) and ask him about
his present economic status, his future publishing plans and what he
intends to do about "Gone With the Wind"? I want to know if he con-
siders it out of print. If the plates were destroyed during the war, he
may consider it too long and expensive a book to re-make. In other words,

I would like to write frankly to Dr. Goverts about the danger of a piracy of the German translation. Under ordinary circumstances I could count on my authorized publisher to assist me in a piracy fight, but with my German publisher an enemy and doubtless in a dreadful state financially, I can count on no assistance from him. It is not so much that I am worried about Dr. Goverts's rights; it is that I am just exhausted at the prospect of perhaps having to fight pirated editions in Europe under the present chaotic conditions which exist there.

The "Gone With the Wind" rights in Europe have turned out to be more valuable, potentially, since the war than before, for every country has had its recent experience with war and occupation and defeat, and people in each country apply the experiences of the characters of "Gone With the Wind" to themselves. As German is the second language of all Middle Europe, there is a large market for a German language edition. So if you could tell me whether I may correspond freely with my German publisher on these matters, and may discuss such subjects as the number of copies sold in the past and the amount of money owed me, I'd be grateful to you. I do not want to break the law, and yet I cannot exactly find out what is the law. I've waited since 1945 about taking steps on these matters and they are reaching a point where I feel I must do something. I'll certainly be grateful for any advice and assistance you can give me.

Dr. W. B. Burke
Macon, Georgia

Altanta, Georgia
May 14, 1947

Dear Doctor Burke:

Many, many thanks to you for your wonderful translation of the Introduction to the Chinese edition of "Gone With the Wind." My husband and I were both amused and touched by some of the remarks in it and before I reached the end I was beginning to blush. My husband says the page was certainly torn off at exactly the wrong point, just when the writer had announced that I was "modest, pure and benevolent." I am interested to see that the Chinese have presented me with those traits which the Chinese consider attractive in a woman, and also that they have credited me with another highly thought of Chinese characteristic—that I am a perfect housekeeper!

I am waiting to hear from the young man who sent me this page. I wanted to make sure he was still at the same address before I sent him the clothing he requested. When I hear from him again, I will write and ask him for copies of his father's translation, and if I get them I will be happy to send you a copy if you would like it.

As the Chinese are not in any copyright agreement with any other country, they feel free to pirate any and all books, and so I have no say-so about my book in China. I can only hope it is a good translation. I would not be surprised if it was a very painstaking one—this "Introduction" which you translated for me shows the desire of the writer to get things correct, even if some of his statements are far from being correct. No doubt he exercised equal care in the translation. I wonder where he picked up all this information. For your interest, I am sending you a pamphlet printed by my publishers some years ago, which contains background material about my book. You can see how many things this Chinese professor had right.

You have been so kind and I am so grateful.

Mr. Boyd Fry   Atlanta, Georgia
Loew's Grand Theater   June 27, 1947
Atlanta, Georgia

Dear Mr. Fry:

Thank you so much for the passes to "Gone With the Wind" and the cordial note which accompanied them. I hope I will have the opportunity to use them and I know they will give me and my family great pleasure. Unfortunately, my husband has been ill for eighteen months and of course he will be unable to attend. Most of my time is occupied with him, and that is why I do not know when I can go to see the picture.

When I saw the photograph of the crowds in front of your theatre, my reaction was very different from yours, I am sure. My heart sank at the thought of having to stand in line for so long a time when I could spare so little time from duties at home. Then came your passes, and that problem was settled. I am very appreciative. I hope the picture has a long run, and I believe it will, for during the past few years the day never passed that people did not telephone and inquire when the film would be reissued.

Dr. Wallace McClure   Atlanta, Georgia
Washington, D.C.   July 1, 1947

Dear Doctor McClure:

Your letter of June 9th, about my German "Gone With the Wind" problems, came safely to me some time ago. I would have answered it sooner but that I began to hear from Doctor Claassen (one of my German publishers) and from various people in O.M.G. and was finding it necessary to make contact with someone in the Publications Control Branch of the British Zone. I thought I would wait until I had this complex matter in hand before writing and thanking you for your perfectly wonderful letter of June 9th. It was so full of information about my German publishers and the publication situation in Germany, Switzerland and Austria that it contained everything I needed to know. I thank you so very much for the many details you included, but when I say "thank you" it seems an inadequate expression of my appreciation. I know very well how confused matters are abroad today and the difficulties which confront anyone attempting to gather up information on a complicated matter. And I am even more grateful to you than if I were the ordinary uninformed person.

The information you sent that Doctor Goverts had been in Zurich but had returned to Liechtenstein tied in with a letter I had from his partner, Doctor Eugen Claassen. As the firm name is now Claassen & Goverts, instead of H. Goverts Verlag, I suppose that is why I received a letter signed by Doctor Claassen instead of Doctor Goverts, who used to do the writing for the firm. Evidently Doctor Claassen is in charge of the business, although Doctor Goverts is still a partner. Doctor Claassen's letter informed me that "a new edition of your book has been edited." He wrote that he had been hindered before this by a lack of paper but that this new edition had been made possible by collaboration with the Deutsche Buch-Gemeinschaft, which I understand is something like our Book-of-the-Month Club. They held an under-license from H. Goverts Verlag before the war. This new edition mentioned in Doctor Claassen's recent letter was to be brought out in the British Zone, and he announced that he hoped to bring out another edition in his "branch office in the American Zone of Germany."

I was very relieved to hear about this new edition, as I had received two or three other Swiss and Austrian offers for the German language rights and each one stated that the book was out of print. The news in your letter that Doctor Goverts considered himself my publisher still, and the news from Doctor Claassen that he was bringing out a new edition made me realize that the danger of piracy was over—I hope! Doctor Claassen had heard from Miss Saunders that she was no longer my agent but for some reason he assumed that all accounts would have to pass through her hands still. This is not the true state of affairs, for I am now dealing directly with all of my foreign publishers. I wished to make a change in my contract with Claassen & Goverts, stating that the publishers should deal directly with me and not with Miss Saunders. Of course, however, this involved a change in the contract, which is, of course, illegal, and so I had to take up the matter through our Publications Control Branch, who, in turn, would consult with Doctor Claassen about this minor change in our contract. I have not heard yet from the British Publications Control Branch, but I suppose that matters are satisfactorily arranged. As I can receive no money from Germany and very likely will never receive any from Germany, there is no hurry about hearing whether the change in my contract has been effective. . . .

As the Russians moved into Hungary, I felt that another one of my problems was settled—alas, not in the fashion I would have preferred. Whenever the Russians move into a country where "Gone With the Wind" is published, I am so fearful for the lives of my publishers that I am generally afraid to write them lest I get them in trouble. The Communists in this country and abroad have fought "Gone With the Wind" ever since its publication, and I never know whether something I might write in the friendliest manner might make a Soviet censor decide to liquidate my publishers. I feel that I have been highly privileged in the past ten years to know things about European countries which are generally not known to people unless they are foreign correspondents or State Department officials et cetera, but sometimes I wish I did not know so much and that, like many of my friends, I had no awareness of the direction in which European affairs are moving. I believe I would sleep more at night. I know I need not go into such matters with a person in your situation, for you know a million times more than I do. . . .

Mr. James C. Bonner   Atlanta, Georgia
Milledgeville, Georgia   November 6, 1947

Dear Dr. Bonner:

I am sure there was no one in the United States who would appreciate your article on "Plantation Architecture"[1] more than I. I will admit, however that two other people might possibly be runners-up in interest, and for the same reason. Those two people are Miss Susan Myrick of Macon, Georgia, and Mr. Wilbur Kurtz, of Atlanta, both of whom did time in Hollywood as technical advisers on the film of "Gone With the Wind." Their herculean efforts to keep Corinthian columns from the smokehouses and other more humble outhouses of Mr. Selznick's Clayton County have never been properly appreciated by Southerners—and if their efforts were properly known, I am quite sure most Southerners

---

[1] "Plantation Architecture of the Lower South on the Eve of the Civil War," *The Journal of Southern History*, IX (1945), 370–388.

would heartily resent all these two honest people did to keep down the size and number of white columns which appeared in "Gone With the Wind." It has been my experience that most Southerners are firmly convinced, because of the many moving pictures they have seen, that everyone in the South lived in houses of the size and general architecture of the State Capitol at Montgomery, Alabama.

I enjoyed your article so very much and read it aloud to my husband. In spots we both laughed till tears came to our eyes, remembering the moving picture people's startled horror when told of the somewhat crude and frontier-like dwellings which mainly graced our upcountry red hills. I had gone to a lot of trouble in my research about the architecture of the 1850's and 1860's and had made sure that there were indeed a few white columned country homes in the County but I very definitely described "Tara" as an ugly and sprawling habitation built with no architectural plan and growing as need for growth arose. I didn't have anything to do with the filming of "Gone With the Wind" and so am not responsible for the architecture. I did, however, hear echoes from the West Coast of the brisk fight that went on to keep "Tara" from looking like a Natchez house complete with Corinthian columns, Spanish moss and lacy iron grill work. . . .

Mr. Clifford Dowdey　　　　　　　　　　　　　Atlanta, Georgia
Richmond, Virginia　　　　　　　　　　　　　December 3, 1947

Dear Clifford:

I've been wanting to write you ever since "Experiment"[1] arrived, to thank you for the present, to tell you of my happiness that you had written this sort of book. But my secretary has been on her vacation, I've been badly smitten across the neck and shoulders with neuritis which has prevented me from using my hands, and, while John is a little better, he still is unable to do any writing.

Well, Sugar, I'd better admit right now that I have read only two chapters—the last ones first, as is my hideous custom. Needless to say, I was enchanted. I ordered a couple for Christmas presents. Then Mrs. Clifford Cabell Early called me to say that her husband had been very ill and as he is a voracious reader had run out of interesting literature and what could I suggest? I said I was reading a book about Richmond during our war, and Mrs. Early's sweet, gentle voice became most animated. Could it be Mr. Dowdey's book? She had read "Bugles" while

---

[1] *Experiment in Rebellion* (Garden City, N.Y., 1946).

they were stationed in Richmond and had walked all the places the characters had walked. She loved the way you wrote and her husband, being a Valley Virginian on one side and a Tidewater on the other, loved your stuff too. Well anyway, the Colonel got the book and I thought I could get another immediately but it wasn't published. The store told me today they are sending my Christmas gift copies. When I've read it I'll write you. You are a dear to send it to us and I'm looking forward to reading parts of it to John.

He is some better. He can sit up in a chair, he is trying a few of the steps each day, he is still very weak. I do not know when he will get stronger but I think his strength will return gradually as he becomes more active. . . .

1948

The Honorable Jesse M. Donaldson
Postmaster General of the United States
Washington, D.C.

Atlanta, Georgia
January 9, 1948

Dear Sir:

I have learned of the proposal to issue a special postage stamp commemorating the 100th anniversary of Joel Chandler Harris and I am writing to say that I hope this will be done.

The "Uncle Remus" stories are as well known in foreign countries as in the United States. They have been translated into almost every language and dialect. These stories have been told and retold in all the tongues of the world and have brought fame and honor not only to the place of Mr. Harris's birth but to our whole nation. To a remarkable extent the stories have the universal appeal that places them among the classics.

Not only Southern children but children throughout the United States have happy memories of "Uncle Remus." The Old Negro had kindliness and shrewdness and he could tell a story. The children loved to hear his stories and they ended up smarter because he gave them a better understanding of life. It seems to me that the creator of "Uncle Remus" deserves the official recognition that would be given through issuance of the special postage stamp, and I urge that it be done.

Dr. Wallace McClure
Washington, D.C.

Atlanta, Georgia
March 2, 1948

Dear Doctor McClure:

. . . I hope that, when and if the United States goes into an agreement with the other nations of the world concerning copyright of literary property, some thought will be given to the securing of all of an author's rights in his literary creation. By that I mean such things as "commercial tie-ups," so that in Ruritania it would be forbidden to make a "Forever Amber" doll without Miss Winsor's permission and in Graustark one could not sell ladies' underpants called Scarlett O'Hara panties without paying me. There is also another type of protection which I think we need. Perhaps what I am now going to discuss is not something which would affect many authors but it is a problem with me—the right of an author of a book to forbid another person to use his characters and setting for a "sequel." I have put in ten years in this country politely or sternly forbidding people to write sequels to "Gone With the Wind," or "last chapters." In wearying numbers well-meaning people decide to write another volume for me, and equally well-meaning people write a "last chapter" and try to get it published publicly or privately. For the most part such people abandon these schemes when it is put up to them that it is just as dishonest to steal characters which are the work of another's brain as to steal money. In this country I can fall back on the fair trade practice if I must and, while there is little precedent, I could make a pretty good fight if I had to. But in European countries, where there is not English "common law" and no unfair trade practice law, I am up against it and must depend on moral suasion.

I am going through this at present in France, where it has just come to my attention that a magazine, as a publicity stunt, has opened a competition with prizes for the four or five "best last chapters to 'Gone With the Wind'." The point involved is that if I do not protest and fight when someone writes a "last chapter" to "Gone With the Wind" the next thing I knew would be that people all over Europe were writing and marketing sequels to "Gone With the Wind." What these would do to my copyright I hate to think, because it seems to me I always get into the most involved copyright problems, and just now I would rather not think about what it would mean! There are a great many authors' rights which should be protected—pantomime and ballet, radio and musical, commercial tie-ups of all kinds, use of titles (not patentable in this country) for songs, pictures et cetera. When television really comes of age, there is a whole body of law to be made.

Sometimes John and I are forced to laugh, though with little mirth, at how the same reaction to "Gone With the Wind" appears in widely separated countries, showing that people are not too different after all. Each person who turns up with the bright idea of writing a "last chapter" to bring two loving hearts together thinks he or she is the only person in the world who ever thought of a "last chapter."

The events of the last week are so very disheartening and depressing to those of us who have any knowledge of and interest in European affairs. My Czech publisher has become a good friend to me although at long distance, and my agent in that country has been most diligent. I do not know how they managed it but very abruptly some eight months ago back royalties on "Gone With the Wind" began coming to me in large lumps. I wondered if they felt that trouble was coming and they, being honest people, were making every effort to get me money before they were encircled. I have been sending food, cigarettes and clothing to Czechoslovakia, as I have been doing to most of my other publishers. Now I am afraid to even send a CARE package, for fear it will get these good people into trouble. The same holds true of Finland, where, in spite of poverty and the problems they have been facing with the Russians, my publishers have managed to send me a little on the old royalty account. Now I know people all over the world, and newspaper headlines of Russia on the march mean more to me than just headlines. . . .

Miss Hedda Hopper   Atlanta, Georgia
Hollywood, California   March 23, 1948

Dear Miss Hopper:

I am grateful to you for your letter of March 5th, and its enclosures—the letter from Mr. Morrie Mink of Portland, Oregon, and the photograph of Mr. Mink, his friends and the fake Margaret Mitchell—interested my husband and me very much. I would have thanked you long before this but Atlanta has been through the same virus epidemic Los Angeles had a couple of months ago, and I have been laid up with a mild case of it.

The snapshot of the fake Margaret Mitchell shows her to be the same woman who was photographed and interviewed as me in Mexico City last summer and whose picture and interview also appeared in a San Antonio, Texas, paper around the same date. She seems to have had a very good time in Mexico City and was entertained as me. One nice newspaperwoman columnist in Mexico City wrote me about the number of Martinis the woman could down, and the astonishment of the Mexican guests who had not thought "Southern ladies able to hold so much." She also talked a great deal about her "new book," which was a sequel to "Gone With the Wind" and would soon be on the screen with Clark Gable in it. From newspapers all over the Southwest I have been able to reconstruct the woman's portrait and personality very well, but by the time I learn she has been in some town and posed as me she has disappeared into thin air and reappears somewhere else while I am trying to nab her in the former place.

For some years I have been plagued by the rumor that I was writing a sequel and that the entire cast of "Gone With the Wind" would appear in it. It has taken so much time denying this sequel business that I have had very little time to do anything else. Most of these rumors came out of Hollywood and for some time I was completely bewildered as to how they started. Now I am perfectly certain this woman is at the bottom of them. She goes to earth for a certain number of weeks or months and then apparently she cannot stand it any longer and she bursts forth as me, giving interviews about the book she is writing, the prominent moving picture personalities she knows and intimate gossip about motion picture stars. Eventually her statements find their way into gossip columns, and then I begin to get telegrams and letters about the whole affair.

The woman has been quiet for several months, but I think she must be loose again in Hollywood, for this morning I received a letter from a schoolgirl in California expressing pleasure that the sequel to "Gone With the Wind" would soon appear on the screen, with Clark Gable in it but not Vivien Leigh "because Vivien Leigh refuses to act opposite Gable any more." The young lady had read this in a Los Angeles paper. The last chummy little item about Miss Leigh sounds very much like the fake Margaret Mitchell's statements.

Some day perhaps I'll manage to catch the woman while she is giving interviews or autographing copies of "Gone With the Wind," and it will certainly be a relief to me.

You have been so kind about this whole troublesome affair. I did see the piece you ran in your column and I was so grateful to you for it. It did a lot of good in this section and I know it did more good in the West, as is evidenced by Mr. Mink's letter. I am returning the snapshot to Mr. Mink and writing to him, in the hope that I can get a lead on "Margaret Mitchell" and perhaps find out where she holes up between the times of posing as the author of "Gone With the Wind."

Mr. Louis Harris   Atlanta, Georgia
Augusta Chronicle   June 17, 1948
Augusta, Georgia

Dear Mr. Harris:

Thank you for your telegram, which I will keep "strictly confidential." I suppose I am still an ardent supporter of lost causes, for I still think we wuz robbed, and I have been asked questions here and there and looking up Old Joe Hooker in the few reference books available in the house.

I have not heard the program,[1] for we never listen to radio, and so I cannot pass on the melody. But I do find evidence that the word in question in the song about Old Joe Hooker and the Wilderness was "come" and not "get." In the book "The Story of the Confederacy," by

---

[1] *Stop the Music.*

the prominent historian Robert Henry, he quotes the song as "Old Joe Hooker, won't you *come* out of the Wilderness," page 249. In "A Virginia Girl in the Civil War," edited by Myrta Lockett Avary, she mentions this song twice, pages 228 and 234, and it appears the same as in Mr. Henry's volume. While "Virginia Girl" was published in 1903, it is written by and about women who lived through the war and who knew what they were writing about. Mrs. Avary, who put down on paper the Virginia Girl's story, was seven years old when Sheridan went past their house in the Valley, and so was old enough to remember songs. The Virginia Girl was a young matron during the Sixties and it is not likely she would have permitted a popular song of her youth to be misquoted in a book about her.

After talking to you, I called the Emory University Library. They have an excellent Confederate collection and Mr. Richard Harwell, who is in charge of it, is also an authority on Confederate songs printed in the Confederacy between Fort Sumter and Appomattox. He has just finished a book on the subject,[2] with a long list of Confederate songs. He said he did not have "Old Joe Hooker" and he doubted that it was ever printed. At any rate he had never seen a copy in all his research. "Everybody knew it, so why waste paper in printing it?" It was he who quoted from Walter Herbert's "Fighting Joe Hooker,"[3] the book in which "come" appears. He said he had never heard it sung any other way himself.

Mr. Harwell also gave this lead—the check list of recorded folk songs in the Library of Congress Music Division. Mr. John Lomax collected American folk songs and recorded them for half his lifetime. The Library of Congress has a list of them. The check list Mr. Harwell has lists two titles "Won't You Come Out of the Wilderness." Mr. Harwell was unable to say whether these two titles had to do with Joe Hooker or not.

Now, Mr. Harris, I want to tell you that if you wish to make the Confederacy spring to arms again, all you have to do is begin making inquiries on this subject of research librarians in libraries throughout the South. However, such a course of action is not to be entered into hastily or ill advisedly but after prayer and fasting, because once reference librarians get mobilized and start rolling they are in irresistible force and can't be stopped. I recall one time when Time Magazine, with its usual anti-Southern bias, was so ill advised as to query me on an item in "Gone With the Wind" about the looting of Atlanta cemeteries by Federal soldiers, the stealing of wedding rings from dead fingers and the wrenching of silver name plates from coffins. I had four or five references myself, but thought when dealing with people like Time it was better to

---

[2] *Confederate Music.*
[3] *Fighting Joe Hooker* (Indianapolis, New York, [c. 1944]).

have more, and so I spoke to some of my reference librarian friends. They are a combination of bloodhound, ferret and angel, and they aroused sister librarians all over the South, and for nearly six months eyewitness accounts of the depredations of Union soldiers in Southern cemeteries were coming in. Of course Time was very careful not to print any of it except in something which they called a supplement of Letters, which no one ever saw. But if you really want to start something, ask our librarians here at the Carnegie and those in the Washington Memorial at Macon, and try Montgomery and Charleston and don't forget Richmond, Virginia, including Doctor Douglas Southall Freeman.

By the way, who is the show producer? And what authority does he use for his statement about "get" instead of "come"?

Now you see I am almost as bad as a research librarian.

General Council of the City of Atlanta   Atlanta, Georgia
Atlanta, Georgia   July 7, 1948

Gentlemen:

On Sunday, July 25th, from five to seven p.m., the Atlanta Historical Society will keep Open House in the Society's home at 1753 Peachtree Road. This Open House is to commemorate the three battles fought in the defense of Atlanta in July 1864 (the Battle of Peachtree Creek on July 20th, the Battle of Atlanta on July 22nd and the Battle of Ezra Church on July 28th). The Society wishes to commemorate not only these engagements but the courage of the defenders of our City, both Confederate soldiers and civilian families who remained in Atlanta. John and I have been designated host and hostess for the Historical Society on that occasion, and to us has been given the privilege of inviting the members of the General Council of Atlanta and their wives to be with us that afternoon and to help us do honor to those people who defended the City in that hot summer eighty-four years ago.

A number of ladies will assist us in entertaining and serving punch and refreshments on the lawn. Confederate music will be played during the party. A collection of photographs and paintings of Atlanta during the 1860's, and especially the siege, will be on display. Colonel Allen Julian, U.S.A., an authority on the Atlanta campaign, will exhibit a number of large maps of the fighting around Atlanta and will explain the campaign to those who are interested.

The Atlanta Historical Society will be honored if members of Council and their wives can attend the party and inspect the Society's building, grounds and historical collection.

Mrs. P. Thornton Marye   Atlanta, Georgia
Loaves and Fishes Department   July 28, 1948
Atlanta Historical Society
Atlanta, Georgia

Dear Mrs. Marye:
Now that I have had more time to think over the logistics of the Historical Society's party last Sunday, I am even more impressed by the efficient manner in which the party moved. Jammed as I was into a box-wood plant in the front yard from 4:45 until 8:15 p.m., I could not get into the house, but I heard many lively exclamations of pleasure at the refreshments and the temperature thereof. When, at last, I took my tired feet onto the porch, Constance Draper still had a cup or two of the ice cream and coffee left. It didn't seem possible it could have held out when we had had several hundred more than were expected. Again, my admiration and thanks for all you did to make the party a success, especially when I know you were not feeling well.

Dr. Edward M. West   Atlanta, Georgia
Augusta, Georgia   September 13, 1948

Dear Mac:
Thank you so much for the list of old pistols you sent me. I am ordering the LeFaucheux model, mainly because you said that it would be impossible to obtain cartridges for it. I do not want my little cousin[1] to shoot himself or his brother or any other members of the family, including myself. I have not yet consulted his parents about this gift and it may be that the pistol will end up on our wall. I have been intending to make an arrangement of pistol-saber-battle flag-and-General Lee, with my relatives' Confederate service records beneath, but have put off doing so until I could have the walls re-done. For some time I have lacked what one of my mountaineer friends called impeetus, and so the walls are still as dirty as ever.
I am glad you are finding Joe Brown's letters interesting.[2] Next time you are in town I want you to read another pamphlet "Reports of the Operations of the Militia, from October 13, 1864, to February 11, 1865"

---

[1] Sims Maddox.
[2] This probably refers to Gov. Joseph E. Brown's *Correspondence Between Governor Brown and the Secretary of War, upon the Right of the Georgia Volunteers in Confederate Service, To Elect Their Own Officers* (Milledgeville, Ga., 1863).

by Maj.-Generals G. W. Smith and Wayne, "Together with Memoranda by Gen Smith, for the Improvement of the State Military Organization."[3] It is about the last real fighting in Georgia after Sherman burned Atlanta and started to Savannah—the fighting at Oconee Bridge near Ball's Ferry and Buffalo Creek, when the Confederates could muster only 500 men "with 460, aggregate, actually fit for effective service." It must have been a rag-tag and bob-tail crew. There were the little cadets from Georgia Military Institute and the Roberts Guards, which was a nice name for the convicts turned loose from the prison at Milledgeville; there were the Factory and Penitentiary Guards, a little artillery battery, a few cavalry, to stand off a large part of Sherman's army, which was reported to be 60,000 strong. I think a great story could be written about this fight. I know very few people who have ever even heard of it. . . .

Dr. Edward M. West   Atlanta, Georgia
Augusta, Georgia   November 5, 1948

Dear Mac:

   Thank you for steering me to Mr. Carr. I purchased the $12 Cooper Navy type revolver and several days ago my small cousin Sims called in the company of his Aunt Wesley (my cousin, Mrs. Thomas Beauchamp). Sims is a poker-faced little boy of perhaps ten and he is almost four feet tall. He had just purchased (through Bannerman, I think) a Confederate musket with money he had saved himself. He and his Aunt Wesley had walked from Westminster Drive through Ansley Park so that less fortunate people along the way could have the pleasure of seeing a Confederate gun. We had a formal visit in which he inspected my Confederate possessions, asked if General Lee was alive when he gave me his autographed photograph (I am still a little dizzy in the haid trying to figure the boy's exact mental processes in this question), was stern with me in my possession of the Allison & Kurz lithograph of the Battle of Nashville, and accepted the revolver with no apparent emotion. However he did not let it out of his clutches one minute, and when he and his Aunt Wesley left they refused the ride home I offered, because Sims wished to walk through Ansley Park again giving the neighbors the opportunity to observe him with a revolver while his Aunt Wesley labored under the six-foot rifle. All-in-all I think it was a great success and I thank you for your assistance. Mrs. Beauchamp told me that when the boy spent the night with her last week he insisted on sleeping with

³ (Macon, Ga. [1865]).

the rifle in the bed with them both, and she expects that she will now have to sleep with rifle and revolver.

Thank you for the list of other guns you sent me. John is meditating buying me one for Christmas. We've just returned from a visit to his mother in Wilmington, Delaware, so we haven't attended to such matters as Christmas gifts yet. He stood the trip very well, although he was very tired when he returned.

Mr. Joe Mitchell Chapple   Atlanta, Georgia
Miami, Florida   December 16, 1948

Dear Mr. Chapple:

My secretary, Miss Baugh, who wrote to you about your "Heart Songs,"[1] and I as well, feel guilty about putting you to so much trouble. But we are so glad to know that the copy of the Songs can be procured that we do not feel as guilty as we should. You wrote that the book sold at $3.50 but you did not tell me how much it cost to run this copy down for me, or the amount of postage et cetera, so I am going to make this check for $4 and if the cost is more I hope you'll let me know, and if it is less just put the change into a Salvation Army pot for Christmas.

Perhaps you'd like to know why I wanted a copy. This summer the Atlanta Historical Society was giving its annual summer party and my husband and I were to be host and hostess. As that was the week of July 20th, I thought it would be a good time to commemorate the defense of Atlanta and its defenders, soldier and civilian, in the summer of 1864. For music at the garden party I thought of our popular Negro accordionist, Graham Jackson, who can play almost anything in the world. I told him I wanted only Confederate songs or songs written before 1860, such as "Lorena," "Bonnie Blue Flag," "Maryland, My Maryland," "When This Cruel War Is Over," "Do They Miss Me At Home?" and "Dixie." He was very obliging and willing to do his best, but he did not know any of these selections except "Dixie." The time was short when I set out to find either music or recordings of these old songs, and to my surprise I could not find "Bonnie Blue Flag" anywhere or "Cruel War," and I had to buy eight or ten different collections of songs to assemble "Maryland," "Do They Miss Me," "Tenting Tonight"[2] et cetera. Mr. Richard Harwell, of the special collections of the Library-Museum of Emory University,

---

[1] *Heart Songs Dear to the American People* (Boston [c. 1937]).

[2] Walter Kittredge's "Tenting on the Old Camp Ground" was published in the North in 1864. It became especially popular with both Union and Confederate veterans.

who collects and writes about old music, came to my assistance with photostats of several valuable old pieces of music. We had the party, and a very successful one it was. However, my newspaper friends, in covering the party, told of how I had run up and down Peachtree Street for two weeks trying to find a collection of old songs which would contain the Confederate ones as well as the Union favorites. Then my phone began to ring and people told me that the collection I needed was "Heart Songs."

I could not find a copy in Atlanta. Miss Baugh, feeling certain that next year we would be celebrating the defense of Atlanta again and needing such songs just as much (for she, too, had been running up and down in the sun in July), suggested that we ask your help. I am so glad she did and, whether or not Atlanta's defenders are ever again commemorated, I would like to own "Heart Songs."

It was good of you to write that you were waiting to read more books written by me. I, too, would like to read some more written by me, and perhaps some day the opportunity will be given me to do more writing. However, since 1936 I've been a business woman and a nurse rather than a writer, for handling business matters concerning "Gone With the Wind" in this country and almost every civilized European country is a full time job. My father was ill for five years before his death and bedridden most of that time. These were the war years and the nurse shortage was great, and much of his care fell on me. My husband has been ill for three years following a heart attack, and, while he is recovering nicely, they have been hard years and I was the only nurse. . . .

1949

Mr. Granville Hicks
New York, New York

Atlanta, Georgia
February 7, 1949

Dear Mr. Hicks:

Some time ago there appeared in the Framingham, Massachusetts, News a story of a speech you made in which you were quoted as having said, "Macmillan gambled on 'Gone With the Wind' after reading only one chapter and the sales of this book have been phenomenal." This statement was picked up here and there, as is usual in literary gossip columns. The statement is an error of fact, but it has gone too far now to be corrected. I hope that if you make any mention of this subject in the future you will not repeat this statement, because such errors cause me much trouble. Coming from someone like you who is connected with The Macmillan Company, puts the seal of accuracy on it.

The story of how Mr. Latham secured the manuscript of "Gone With the Wind" has been printed and reprinted until I would think everyone in the United States had heard it until they were sick of hearing it. Far from accepting "Gone With the Wind" on the strength of one chapter, they accepted it on a far longer novel than finally got into print, for I cut it considerably myself, although The Macmillan Company did not wish me to cut it. I am enclosing a copy of a pamphlet published by The Macmillan Company, which they have sent out in thousands. In it appears the story of Mr. Latham's "discovery" of "Gone With the Wind," which appeared in the Book-of-the-Month Club News for June 1936. It was published in thousands. And the story of Mr. Latham getting a manuscript so big he had to buy a new suitcase has passed into folklore.

Apart from my desire to have things accurate is the very troublesome effect such statements have on young writers. They read that I sold "Gone With the Wind" on the strength of one chapter, and they wish to do likewise. It is rare that a publisher buys a novel on one chapter and rarer still that a publisher will even consent to look at one chapter unless the author is an established writer. Such statements make young writers think that writing is a very easy type of work. They refuse to give ear to the truth, that it is the hardest work in the world and one serves a longer apprenticeship than at any other trade. I have so many writers and would be writers on my neck, and practically none of them want to do any work because they believe erroneous statements that I wrote a bestseller with no previous experience and sold it on the strength of one chapter.

Dean Carl W. Ackerman   Atlanta, Georgia
Graduate School of Journalism   May 3, 1949
Columbia University
New York, New York

Dear Dean Ackerman:

I have received your letter of April 19th, in which you discussed the plans of the Trustees of Columbia University concerning a series of Pulitzer Prize radio and television programs. I am very sorry that I cannot cooperate in this. I cannot appear personally on such a program and I cannot permit the use of "Gone With the Wind" as material for a radio or television program.

During the years since 1936, when "Gone With the Wind" was first published, I have been forced to adopt the policy of not appearing on radio or making other public appearances, because the number of requests has been such that I would not have time for anything else. Here in this section of the country, many of the people in radio stations are good friends of mine and have been very kind to me. I could not appear on one program and not on another without seeming to slight some friend. Moreover, I am not a radio personality and have no interest at all in radio, and I thought best to let my book speak for me. As regards a radio presentation or televising of "Gone With the Wind," I have never sold my dramatic or radio or television rights and I do not wish to do so. Furthermore, I have promised a number of people that if I ever decide to release dramatic rights I will give them a chance to bid on them. So, even if I wished to deal with Columbia University and the William Morris Agency, I would have to put the rights in the open market and let the Morris Agency bid on them. All of this would just stir up one phase of the hullaballoo which I hope is behind me. Every time a rumor of dramatic or radio or television sale arises, I receive many letters, phone calls and telegrams about the matter, and it sometimes takes a couple of months to crawl from under. It's this sort of hullaballoo, arising from various causes, which has kept me from ever having time to do more writing, and I am not anxious to start it up again.

I have gone into all these details because I would not have you think that my refusal arises from a mere whim. It is a very serious matter and one most disturbing in my life. So I must ask you to eliminate me and "Gone With the Wind" from consideration in your arrangements for the radio and television series.

My Pulitzer Prize certificate hangs on the wall of my office and I see it every day. The award is one of my real treasures and I will always remember my excitement and pride when I first learned that my novel had won it. If I could, I would gladly join with you in the radio plan, but it is something I cannot do. The matters mentioned previously are only a few of the many complications that would arise. Please accept my regrets. . . .

Mr. Harold E. George, Manager   Atlanta, Georgia
10th Street Theatre   May 6, 1949
Atlanta, Georgia

Dear Mr. George:
    My husband and I thank you so much for the passes you sent us for the return engagement of "Gone With the Wind" at your theatre. We used them last night and enjoyed the picture so much. We would have told you so personally before leaving the theatre but it was so late that we decided not to bother you. I was interested to see that the theatre was packed and even the very front rows in use. A great many people seemed to be repeaters, for they knew beforehand what was going to happen and started laughing or crying before the cause for laughter or tears appeared on the screen.

    We appreciate your courtesy very much and we thank you for it.

Mr. William Faulkner   Atlanta, Georgia
Oxford, Mississippi   May 17, 1949

Dear Mr. Faulkner:
    When I was cleaning out my files recently, I came upon an old catalogue sent me by the Italian publisher of "Gone With the Wind." Going through it, I observed with interest that Arnoldo Mondadori was also your publisher. On the chance that you never saw this catalogue with the reproduction of the "Sanctuary" jacket, I am sending it to you.

    I showed it to a friend who is a great admirer of your books—"Dear me—how *explicit* the Italians are!"

Dr. Wallace McClure   Atlanta, Georgia
Washington, D.C.   July 15, 1949

Dear Dr. McClure:

This time I am coming to you with a problem which is not copyright and I know you will be surprised. It's something I think only the State Department can answer and if you can give me some help I will be very grateful. My brother has already looked up the matter in the Federal Code but we would like to have your ruling on it, too.

I have recently been notified that I have been elected an honorary citizen of the French town Vimoutiers. I am not sure whether I was "elected" or how the matter came about except that the Municipal Council of the city and the Mayor met and decided to bestow this citizenship on me. I know that an American citizen in government service, or in the armed services, may not accept decorations from a foreign government, or gifts, et cetera, except under special rulings. My brother can find nothing in the Code concerning private citizens accepting honorary citizenship in foreign countries. Is there any reason why I should not accept? I am very anxious to accept the honor for, of course, I am terribly pleased and touched but the most important reason is that if I do not I know it will be an insult to the kind French people who have offered it. In tendering me this honorary citizenship they have not only given me the highest gift in their power to bestow but also the only gift they can give.

Vimoutiers is a very old village in Normandy, in the center of the Camembert cheese industry. It was bombed almost out of existence by our air corps during the invasion. The tragic part was this bombing was an error. Under ordinary circumstances our forces would have had no reason for leveling a quiet little village which had no military importance. However, due to some misinformation furnished them, they believed Vimoutiers was an important German communications point. So our Ninth Air Force gave Vimoutiers all it had, killing a great many of the citizens, maiming others, leveling their schools, municipal buildings, hospitals and many homes. The people of Vimoutiers did not complain, and still have not complained, for they knew that liberation came with the air force. Through a French refugee air corps boy, who is the son of the Mayor of Vimoutiers, I came to know about the little town and eventually they appealed to me to get them "adopted" by a city in America or some organization. I tried and tried and had no luck until finally the Pilot Club International at their recent convention voted to "affiliate with" Vimoutiers. So the result was the City Council and Mayor have made me an honorary citizen.

It seems to me I am always face to face with situations which have no precedent. The only thing which I can think of, which even vaguely approaches this one, is that the descendants of LaFayette are always citizens of the United States as well as of France. However, I am not LaFayette and that is why I am asking your advice and assistance. . . .

Miss Alma Jamison   Atlanta, Georgia
Atlanta Carnegie Library   July 20th, 1949
Atlanta, Georgia

Dear Alma:
When I looked over the list of books purchased for the Mitchell Collection I was astounded at the number and variety and more pleased and proud than I can tell you. I was glad to note the "Miscellaneous Material," too. Thank you for getting up this list for me. I wish I had had it to show to Father. You know how his interest in the Library persisted up until the day of his death and he was always glad to have news of it. I think your selections have been excellent. I hope in the future I will be able to continue donations for Georgia material for the Library and that *you* will be the person to make the selections.
We enjoyed that dinner with you and your Mother so much.

Dr. Wallace McClure   Atlanta, Georgia
Washington, D.C.   July 26, 1949

Dear Dr. McClure:
I am so grateful to you for the trouble you took about the honorary citizenship in France. I am so glad the decision of the Legal Adviser's Office was that I could accept this honor. Naturally, I have been very pleased about it and very anxious to accept it. I know it was a lot of trouble and I thank you for taking it. You have been such a good friend to me over these years. I have often wished there was something I knew that you did not know so I could repay you. However, I am convinced by now that you know everything! It's just possible that sometime you might want to know something about the publishing or copyright situation in some foreign country where I am doing business, or have done business. Or perhaps you might some day want to know something about a foreign publisher or agent—their honesty and reliability, their methods of doing business, et cetera. I hope you know I will be happy to furnish

you any information and will be proud of being of some small help to you.

As I look back over the long years since the day Senator George introduced my brother and me to you, I realize I have had a box seat at the world's biggest show from 1936 until now. I do not know anyone in government service, or not a war correspondent, who has had the privilege of knowing about as many foreign countries and having as many kind and appreciative letters from those countries as I have. I realize now that my book has taken me to many countries and made many friends for me. I realize it all the more now when I lie awake at night wondering about the publishers, agents, newspaper critics, and just plain letter-writing friends who have suddenly become silent and disappeared as Russia rolled over their countries—Bulgaria, Roumania, Hungary, Poland, Yugoslavia, and now Czechoslovakia. The Communists have attacked "Gone With the Wind" in this country and in every other country.... My Czech publisher has just had his publishing house "Nationalized." He is still alive and still at liberty but I do not know for how long.

At night I pack food and vitamins and clothing boxes, always wondering if they will ever reach the people to whom they are sent. Sometimes when I am out in crowds I find I do not have too much conversation about what is going on in Georgia because I have been wrestling with international financial regulations and wondering about people who cannot possibly escape from the encirclement of Russia.

Sometimes I discover I know things about some foreign countries which are not public property. I tell you all this so that if ever my experience can be of help to you I hope you will call on me....

John and I both thank you for the invitation to have lunch or dinner with you. We had expected to come North to see John's Mother at the end of this month and had thought we would wire you that we would be in Washington on some particular day. However, reports of the heat wave in the North have made me decide to wait a while before taking such a trip. Wilmington, Delaware can be very damp and muggy, as well as hot, and I do not want to risk John in such weather. Perhaps we will be North in the cool weather and, if so, we would love to see you.

Governor James M. Cox   Atlanta, Georgia
Miami, Florida   July 28, 1949

Dear Governor Cox:

I hope you will forgive my unpardonably long delay in replying to your request (which I received through Medora) for an autographed copy of "Gone With the Wind" to be placed in the Library of the Atlanta Journal. . . .

Medora said that she or Angus would write you that I could not autograph the copy for The Journal and that they would explain why. But I did not want you to think me unappreciative of your request, nor uninterested in my old paper. So I thought I'd explain to you in this letter that I have not autographed a copy of "Gone With the Wind" since some time early in 1937, not even for close relatives and good friends. At that time the sales of "Gone With the Wind" were considerably over the million mark and the requests for autographs of the book and for albums, et cetera, were in proportion. It reached the point where neither John nor I were having time to eat or sleep or attend to business matters as there were always several hundred people a day at the front door. So I was forced to adopt a "no autographing" policy and since that time I have not altered it. I discovered I could not pick and choose for if I gave an autograph to one person and refused another I always hurt somebody's feelings. Everyone has been so kind to me and to my book that I would not for worlds seem to slight anybody.

I am especially sorry when it is you and The Journal who want the autograph. I am enclosing a card and a note and, if you like the idea, I wish you would paste it in a copy. I am also sending you, for your entertainment, a copy of the Yugoslavian translation of "Gone With the Wind." It appeared around the time Tito really got his grip on that country. In Yugoslavia, as in all Communist countries, the press denounced "Gone With the Wind" at the top of its lungs, stating, to my great pleasure and pride, that the book was a glorification of individual courage and individual enterprise (both qualities being highly obnoxious to Communists) and revealing in a hideous, bourgeois fashion the love of a person for their land and their home. The Communist critics observed virtuously that any school boy knew how vicious such ideas were because the STATE is everything, the individual nothing. To love one's home and fight for one's land is the act of a traitor, et cetera. . . .

John continues to improve—slowly, it is true, but steadily, and you can imagine what a relief this is to me after the last few years. He joins me in sending his regards. We hope that if you are here this summer you will let us know and we can go to supper on the porch of the Driving Club. It's very cool overlooking the pool and we would enjoy seeing you.

INDEX

Abdullah, Capt. Achmed, letter to, 139–40

Absalom, Absalom! 88–89

Accuracy, historical, *GWTW*, 25–26, 55–57, 39, 53, 77, 140, 165–66, 186–91, 209–10, 307–10

Ackerman, Dean Carl W., letter to, 420–21

Action at Aquila, 301

Adams, J. Donald, letters to, 30–34, 345–46

Advance and Retreat, 8

Africa, 174

Aftel, Cpl. Joe, 362

Alabama, 43

Allen, Hervey, letters to, 300–301, 304–5

Allies, aid to, 305

America, 126

American Foundation for the Blind, 303

American Language, The, 64

Anachronism, *GWTW*, 25–26, 86, 95–96; *and see* Accuracy, historical; "Commandeer"; "Gotterdammerung"; "Iodine"; "Grippe, la"; "Sissy"

Ancient Hunger, The, 323

Anderson, Mrs. John Huske, 297

Anderson, W. T., 119–20

Andrews, Eliza Francis, 36

Anthony Adverse, 1, 304–5

Appointment in Samara, 191–92

"Are We Still Fighting the War?" 221, 238

Argentina, *GWTW* pirated in, 313

Arthritis, MM, 3, 5

Arundel, 193

Asasno, George, 1

Associated Negro Press, 273

Atlanta (book), 140

Atlanta (cruiser), *see* U.S.S. *Atlanta*

Atlanta, Ga., xxii, xxiv, 133, 234; Battle of, 71, 414; burning of, 307–10, 416; *GWTW* movie première in, xxxi, 257–58, 274–78, 283–84, 286, 289–90, 291–92, 293, 294, 297; Reconstruction in, 31; and Scarlett O'Hara, xxvii–xxviii, xxxi, 20, 31

Atlanta Carnegie Library, 5, 101–2, 113, 263, 359–60, 423

Atlanta City Cemetery, Yankee desecration of, 55–57

Atlanta City Council, 56

Atlanta *Constitution*, xxi, 89, 90, 195, 239, 255–56, 388

Atlanta General Council, letter to, 414

Atlanta *Georgian*, 90, 195, 296

Atlanta Historical Society, 10, 16, 233, 414, 415, 417

Atlanta and Its Builders, 309–10

Atlanta *Journal*, xxiii, xxiv, xxv, xxviii, xxxi, 1, 4–5, 90, 187, 195, 239, 257, 360–61, 370, 424–25

Atlanta librarians, MM speech to, 10–11

Atlanta Women's Press Club, 257, 258, 275, 276, 277, 299

Atlanta *World*, 273

Austen, Jane, 32

Authentic History of the Ku Klux Klan, 1865–1877, 130, 144–45, 168, 263–67; *and see* Plagiarism

Autobiography with Letters (William L. Phelps), xxi

Autographs, MM and, 116–17, 127–29, 193, 198